P9-EMG-966

EMILE

Jean-Jacques Rousseau

EMILE

or On Education

Introduction, Translation,
and Notes

BY

ALLAN BLOOM

Basic Books, Inc., Publishers

NEW YORK

TO THE MEMORY OF

VICTOR BARAS

MY STUDENT AND FRIEND

Library of Congress Cataloging in Publication Data

Rousseau, Jean-Jacques, 1712–1778.
  Emile: or On education.

  Includes bibliographical references and index.
   1. Education—Early works to 1800.   I.   Title.
LB512.E5   1979   370   78-73765
ISBN: 0-465-01930-7 cloth
ISBN: 0-465-01931-5 pbk.

Foreword, Introduction, English translation, and Notes
copyright © 1979 by Basic Books, Inc.
Printed in the United States of America
DESIGNED BY VINCENT TORRE
10 9 8

Contents

EMILE *or* On Education

Foreword

WHEN I WROTE the preface to my translation of the *Republic*, I did not have to argue the importance of the book; I had to justify only the need for a new translation when there were so many famous existing versions. With *Emile* the situation is the reverse: there is general agreement that the only available translation is inadequate in all important respects, while the book itself is not held to be of great significance and has little appeal to contemporary taste. However, this is not the place to make a case for *Emile*. I can only hope that this translation will contribute to a reconsideration of this most fundamental and necessary book.

The translation aims, above all, at accuracy. Of course, no intelligible translation could be strictly literal, and simply bad English would misrepresent Rousseau's very good French. Style cannot be separated from substance. But unless the translator himself were a genius of Rousseau's magnitude, the attempt to imitate the felicity of his language would fail and would distort and narrow his meaning. One would have to look at what one can say well in English rather than at Rousseau's thought. He is a precise and careful writer. He speaks of a real world of which we all have experience, no matter what our language. He, above all writers, thought he spoke to all men. The translator must concentrate on making his English point to the same things Rousseau's French points to. And this is best done by finding the closest equivalents to his words and sticking to them, even when that causes inconvenience.

Every translation is, of course, in some sense an interpretation; and thus there can be no mechanical rules for translation. The question, then, is what disposition guides the translator: whether the impossibility of simple literalness is a fact against which he struggles and a source of dissatisfaction with himself, or whether he uses it as an excuse to display his virtuosity. As with most choices, the right one is least likely to afford opportunities for flattering one's vanity. The translator of a great work should revere his text and recognize that there is much in it he cannot understand. His translation should try to make others able to understand what he cannot understand, which means he often must prefer a dull ambiguity to a brilliant resolution. He is a messenger, not a plenipotentiary, and proves his fidelity to his great masters by reproducing what seems in them to the contemporary eye wrong, outrageous, or incomprehensible, for therein may lie what is most important for us. He resists the temptation to make the book attractive or relevant, for its relevance may lie in its appearing irrelevant to current thought. If books are to be liberating, they must seem implausible in the half-light of our plausibilities which we no longer know how to question. An old book must appear to be old-fashioned, and a translator cannot lessen the effort required of the reader; he can only make it possible for the reader to make that effort. Therefore the translator will try to imitate the text, insofar as possible following sentence structure; he will never vary terms Rousseau does not vary, but where Rousseau repeats a particular French word, the translator will also repeat its English equivalent; he will never choose English words whose origins are in later thought, even though Rousseau may have been the inspiration of that thought. This is what I have tried to do, but I have often failed. A verb of capital significance for Rousseau like *sentir* and its various derivatives—such as *sentiment, sensible, sensibilité*—simply defied reduction to Rousseau's unity of usage. Sometimes I have had to use "feel" and its derivatives and sometimes "sense" and its derivatives; and a very few times I have had to use an English word with an entirely different root (always trying to link it with "sense" or "feel"). On the other hand, I have been fortunate with other important words like *nature* and its derivatives; and the reader can be sure that if they occur in the translation, they are in the original French and vice versa. This translation is meant to give the reader a certain confidence that he is thinking about Rousseau and not about me, as well as to inspire in him a disconcerting awareness that, to be sure, he must learn French.

The notes have been kept to a minimum in order not to distract from the text; and the intention behind them was to permit the reader to confront the text without feeling hopelessly dependent on expert middlemen. Interpretation will be available in the volume of commentary to follow. The notes are limited to translations of citations from other languages and identification of their sources, to mention of a few important textual variants, and to explanations of some difficult words and references whose meanings Rousseau took for granted but are now obscure. And in order to avoid a morass of questionable scholarly conjecture about the influences on Rousseau, the notes attempt to locate only those passages in the works of other writers to which Rousseau explicitly refers. It is similarly treacherous to try to interpret one of Rousseau's books in light of another, for every phrase is conditioned by his specific intention in each work. An understanding of the whole can be attained only by a firm grasp on each of the parts; to interpret a passage in one book by a passage in another is to risk misunderstanding both and to deny their independent intelligibility. There are, therefore, such cross-references only where Rousseau himself indicates that they are appropriate. All this is done in the conviction that the profound reader need not be the scholarly reader—and vice versa.

The French editions of *Emile* used for the translation were those of François and Pierre Richard, published by Garnier, Paris, 1939, and of Charles Wirz and Pierre Burgelin, pages 239–868 in Volume IV of Rousseau's *Oeuvres Complètes*, edited by Bernard Gagnebin and Marcel Raymond, Bibliothèque de la Pléiade, Gallimard, Paris, 1969. I generally followed the text of the first edition of *Emile* and refer in the notes to significant variations provided by the various manuscripts and a copy of the first edition in which Rousseau made changes for a complete edition of his works that was to be published in 1764.

FOREWORD

I undertook this translation with a selfish motive: I thought it the best way to familiarize myself with a book which was very alien to me but which seemed to contain hidden treasures. One of the results of this project has been a new sense of what it means to be a teacher and of the peculiar beauty of the relationship between teacher and student. Only Socrates rivals Rousseau in the depth and detail of his understanding of that most generous of associations. And learning from Rousseau has given me the occasion to learn from my students while teaching them. Over the past eight years I have given several classes on *Emile*, and the interest it provoked gave evidence of its usefulness. By students' questions and suggestions I have been led toward the heart of the text. It provided a ground for community among us in the quest for understanding of ourselves. As this translation progressed, I have used it in my classes, and my first thanks go to all those students who read it and corrected it, testing it in the situation for which it was intended. They are too numerous to mention, but I should like to single out Joel Schwartz, Janet Ajzenstat, Sidney Keith, John Harper, and Marc Plattner who went over it with particular care. My old friends Irene Berns, Werner Dannhauser, and Midge Decter also helped me greatly.

I also want to thank the Canada Council, the John Simon Guggenheim Foundation, and the Earhart Foundation for their generous assistance which made it possible for me to do this work.

The Introduction is a revised version of "The Education of Democratic Man" which appeared in *Daedalus*, Summer 1978, and is reprinted with the permission of the American Academy of Arts and Sciences.

ALLAN BLOOM

Toronto, June 1978

EMILE

Introduction

IN the *Discourse on the Origins of Inequality* Rousseau summons men to hear for the first time the true history of their species.[1] Man was born free, equal, self-sufficient, unprejudiced, and whole; now, at the end of history, he is in chains (ruled by other men or by laws he did not make), defined by relations of inequality (rich or poor, noble or commoner, master or slave), dependent, full of false opinions or superstitions, and divided between his inclinations and his duties. Nature made man a brute, but happy and good. History—and man is the only animal with a history—by the development of his faculties and the progress of his mind has made man civilized, but unhappy and immoral. History is not a theodicy but a tale of misery and corruption.

Emile, on the other hand, has a happy ending, and Rousseau says he cares little if men take it to be only a novel, for it ought, he says, to be the history of his species.[2] And therewith he provides the key to *Emile*. It is, as Kant says,[3] the work which attempts to reconcile nature with history, man's selfish nature with the demands of civil society, hence, inclination with duty. Man requires a healing education which returns him to himself. Rousseau's paradoxes—his attack on the arts and the sciences while he practices them, his praise of the savage and natural freedom over against his advocacy of the ancient city, the general will, and virtue, his perplexing presentations of himself as citizen, lover, and solitary—are not expressions of a troubled soul but accurate reflections of an incoherence in the structure of the world we all face, or rather, in general, do not face; and *Emile* is an experiment in restoring harmony to that world by reordering the emergence of man's acquisitions in such a way as to avoid the imbalances created by them while allowing the full actualization of man's potential. Rousseau believed that his was a privileged moment, a moment when all of man's faculties had revealed themselves and when man had, furthermore, attained for the first time knowledge of the principles of human nature. *Emile* is the canvas on which Rousseau tried to paint all of the soul's acquired passions and learning in such a way as to cohere with man's natural wholeness. It is a *Phenomenology of the Mind* posing as Dr. Spock.

Thus *Emile* is one of those rare total or synoptic books, a book with which one can live and which becomes deeper as one becomes deeper,

1. In *Oeuvres complètes de Jean-Jacques Rousseau*, ed. Bernard Gagnebin and Marcel Raymond, 4 vols. (Paris: Gallimard, 1959–1969, Bibliothèque de la Pléiade), vol. 3, p. 133; *The First and Second Discourses*, ed. R. Masters (New York: St. Martin's, 1964), pp. 103–104.
2. P. 416 below.
3. "Conjectural Beginning of Human History," in *On History*, ed. Lewis Beck (Indianapolis, Ind.: Bobbs-Merrill, 1963), pp. 60–61.

a book comparable to Plato's *Republic,* which it is meant to rival or supersede.[4] But it is not recognized as such in spite of Rousseau's own judgment that it was his best book and Kant's view that its publication was an event comparable to the French Revolution. Of Rousseau's major works it is the one least studied or commented on. It is as though the book's force had been entirely spent on impact with men like Kant and Schiller, leaving only the somewhat cranky residue for which the book retains its fame in teacher training schools: the harangues against swaddling and in favor of breast feeding and the learning of a trade. Whatever the reasons for its loss of favor (and this would make an interesting study) *Emile* is a truly great book, one that lays out for the first time and with the greatest clarity and vitality the modern way of posing the problems of psychology.

By this I mean that Rousseau is at the source of the tradition which replaces virtue and vice as the causes of a man's being good or bad, happy or miserable, with such pairs of opposites as sincere/insincere, authentic/inauthentic, inner-directed/other-directed, real self/alienated self. All these have their source in Rousseau's analysis of *amour de soi* and *amour-propre,* a division within man's soul resulting from man's bodily and spiritual dependence on other men which ruptures his original unity or wholeness. The distinction between *amour de soi* and *amour-propre* is meant to provide the true explanation for that tension within man which had in the past been understood to be a result of the opposed and irreconcilable demands of the body and the soul. *Emile* gives the comprehensive account of the genesis of *amour-propre,* displays its rich and multifarious aspects (spreads the peacock's tail, as it were), and maps man's road back to himself from his spiritual exile (his history) during which he wandered through nature and society, a return to himself which incorporates into his substance all the cumbersome treasures he gathered en route. This analysis supersedes that based on the distinction between body and soul, which in its turn had activated the quest for virtue, seen as the taming and controlling of the body's desires under the guidance of the soul's reason. It initiates the great longing to be one's self and the hatred of alienation which characterizes all modern thought. The wholeness, unity, or singleness of man—a project ironically outlined in the *Republic*—is the serious intention of *Emile* and almost all that came afterward.

Emile is written to defend man against a great threat which bids fair to cause a permanent debasement of the species, namely, the almost inevitable universal dominance of a certain low human type which Rousseau was the first to isolate and name: the *bourgeois.* Rousseau's enemy was not the ancien régime, its throne, its altar, or its nobility. He was certain that all these were finished, that revolution would shortly sweep them away to make room for a new world based on the egalitarian principles of the new philosophy. The real struggle would then concern the kind of man who was going to inhabit that world, for the striking element of the situation was and is that a true theoretical

4. P. 40 below.

insight seems to have given rise to a low human consequence. What I mean by this is that the bourgeois, that debased form of the species, is the incarnation of the political science of Hobbes and Locke, the first principles of which Rousseau accepted. We can see this with particular clarity in Tocqueville's *Democracy in America*, the scheme of which is adopted from Rousseau. Equality, Tocqueville tells us, is now almost a providential fact; no one believes any longer in the justice of the principles on which the old distinctions between ranks or classes were made and which were the basis of the old regime. The only question remaining is whether freedom can accompany equality or universal tyranny will result from it. It is to the formation of free men and free communities founded on egalitarian principles to which both Rousseau and Tocqueville are dedicated.

Now, who, according to Rousseau, is the bourgeois? Most simply, following Hegel's formula, he is the man motivated by fear of violent death, the man whose primary concern is self-preservation or, according to Locke's correction of Hobbes, comfortable self-preservation. Or, to describe the inner workings of his soul, he is the man who, when dealing with others, thinks only of himself, and on the other hand, in his understanding of himself, thinks only of others. He is a role-player. The bourgeois is contrasted by Rousseau, on the one side, with the natural man, who is whole and simply concerned with himself, and on the other, with the citizen, whose very being consists in his relation to his city, who understands his good to be identical with the common good. The bourgeois distinguishes his own good from the common good. His good requires society, and hence he exploits others while depending on them. He must define himself in relation to them. The bourgeois comes into being when men no longer believe that there is a common good, when the notion of the fatherland decays. Rousseau hints that he follows Machiavelli in attributing this decay to Christianity, which promised the heavenly fatherland and thereby took away the supports from the earthly fatherland, leaving social men who have no reason to sacrifice private desire to public duty.

What Christianity revealed, modern philosophy gave an account of: man is not naturally a political being; he has no inclination toward justice. By nature he cares only for his own preservation, and all of his faculties are directed to that end. Men are naturally free and equal in the decisive respects: they have no known authority over them, and they all pursue the same independent end. Men have a natural right to do what conduces to their preservation. All of this Rousseau holds to be true. He differs only in that he does not believe that the duty to obey the laws of civil society can be derived from self-interest. Hobbes and Locke burdened self-interest with more than it can bear; in every decisive instance the sacrifice of the public to the private follows from nature. They produced hypocrites who make promises they cannot intend to keep and who feign concern for others out of concern for themselves, thus using others as means to their ends and alienating themselves. Civil society becomes merely the combat zone for the pursuit of power—control over things and especially over men. With enlightenment the illusions are dispelled, and men learn that they care about their own lives more than about country, family, friendship, or honor. Fanaticism, although dangerous and distorting, could at least produce selfless and extraordinary deeds. But now fanaticism gives way to calculation. And pride, although it is the spur to domination, is also allied with that noble indifference to life which seems to be a precondition of freedom and the resistance to tyranny. But quenched by fear, pride gives way to vanity, the concern for petty advantages over others. This diminution of man is the apparent result of his enlightenment about his true nature.

In response to this challenge of the new philosophy Rousseau undertakes to rethink man's nature in its relation to the need for society engendered by history. What he attempts is to present an egalitarian politics that rivals Plato's politics in moral appeal rather than an egalitarian politics that debases man for the sake of the will-of-the-wisp, security. In imagination he takes an ordinary boy and experiments with the possibility of making him into an autonomous man—morally and intellectually independent, as was Plato's philosopher-king, an admittedly rare, and hence aristocratic, human type. The success of such a venture would prove the inherent dignity of man as man, each and every ordinary man, and thus it would provide a high-level ground for the choice of democracy. Since Rousseau, overcoming of the bourgeois has been regarded as almost identical with the problem of the realization of true democracy and the achievement of "genuine personality."

The foregoing reflections give a clue to the literary character of *Emile*. The two great moral-political traditions that were ultimately displaced by the modern natural right teachings—that is, the Biblical and the classical—were accompanied by great works of what may be called poetry. This poetry depicts great human types who embody visions of the right way of life, who make that way of life plausible, who excite admiration and emulation. The Bible, on the highest level, gives us prophets and saints; and in the realm of ordinary possibility it gives us the pious man. Homer and Plutarch give us, at the peak, heroes; and, for everyday fare, gentlemen. Modern philosophy, on the other hand, could not inspire a great poetry corresponding to itself. The exemplary man whom it produces is too contemptible for the noble Muse; he can never be a model for those who love the beautiful. The fact that he cannot is symptomatic of how the prosaic new philosophy truncates the human possibility. With *Emile* Rousseau confronts this challenge and dares to enter into competition with the greatest of the old poets. He sets out to create a human type whose charms can rival those of the saint or the tragic hero—the natural man—and thereby shows that his thought too can comprehend the beautiful in man.

Emile consists of a series of stories, and its teaching comes to light only when one has grasped each of these stories in its complex detail and artistic unity. Interpretation of this "novel," the first *Bildungsroman*, requires a union of *l'esprit de géométrie* and *l'esprit de finesse*, a union which it both typifies and teaches. It is impossible here to do more than indicate the plan of the work and tentatively describe its general intention in the hope of indicating the nature of this work whose study is so imperative for an understanding of the human possibility.

I

Emile is divided into two large segments. Books I–III are devoted to the rearing of a civilized savage, a man who cares only about himself, who is independent and self-sufficient and on whom no duties that run counter to his inclinations and so divide him are imposed, whose knowledge of the crafts and the sciences does not involve his incorporation into the system of public opinion and division of labor. Books IV–V attempt to bring this atomic individual into human society and into a condition of moral responsibility on the basis of his inclinations and his generosity.

Rousseau's intention in the first segment comes most clearly to light in its culmination, when Jean-Jacques, the tutor, gives his pupil the first and only book he is to read prior to early adulthood. Before presenting his gift, Jean-Jacques expresses to the reader the general sentiment that he hates all books—including, implicitly but especially, the book of books, the guide of belief and conduct, the Bible. Books act as intermediaries between men and things; they attach men to the opinions of others rather than forcing them to understand on their own or leaving them in ignorance. They excite the imagination, increasing thereby the desires, the hopes, and the fears beyond the realm of the necessary. All of Emile's early rearing is an elaborate attempt to avoid the emergence of the imagination which, according to the *Discourse on the Origins of Inequality*, is the faculty that turns man's intellectual progress into the source of his misery. But, in spite of this general injunction against books and in direct contradiction of what he has just said, Rousseau does introduce a book, one which presents a new teaching and a new *mode* of teaching. The book is *Robinson Crusoe,* and it is not meant to be merely a harmless amusement for Emile but to provide him with a vision of the whole and a standard for the judgment of both things and men.[5]

Robinson Crusoe is a solitary man in the state of nature, outside of civil society and unaffected by the deeds or opinions of men. His sole concern is his preservation and comfort. All his strength and reason are dedicated to these ends, and utility is his guiding principle, the principle that organizes all his knowledge. The world he sees contains neither gods nor heroes; there are no conventions. Neither the memory of Eden nor the hope of salvation affects his judgment. Nature and natural needs are all that is of concern to him. *Robinson Crusoe* is a kind of Bible of the new science of nature and reveals man's true original condition.

5. Pp. 184 ff. below.

This novel, moreover, provides a new kind of play for the first activity of the imagination. In the first place, the boy does not imagine beings or places which do not exist. He imagines himself in situations and subject to necessities which are part of his experience. Actually his imagination divests itself of the imaginary beings that seem so real in ordinary society and are of human making. He sees himself outside of the differences of nation and religion which cover over nature and are the themes of ordinary poetry. Second, he does not meet with heroes to whom he must subject himself or whom he is tempted to rival. Every man can be Crusoe and actually is Crusoe to the extent that he tries to be simply man. Crusoe's example does not alienate Emile from himself as do the other fictions of poetry; it helps him to be himself. He understands his hero's motives perfectly and does not ape deeds the reasons for which he cannot imagine.

A boy, who imagining himself alone on an island uses all of his energy in thinking about what he needs to survive and how to procure it, will have a reason for all his learning; its relevance to what counts is assured; and the fear, reward, or vanity that motivate ordinary education are not needed. Nothing will be accepted on authority; the evidence of his senses and the call of his desires will be his authorities. Emile, lost in the woods and hungry, finds his way home to lunch by his knowledge of astronomy. For him astronomy is not a discipline forced on him by his teachers, or made attractive by the opportunity to show off, or an expression of his superstition. In this way Rousseau shows how the sciences, which have served historically to make men more dependent on one another, can serve men's independence. In this way the Emile who moves in civil society will put different values on things and activities than do other men. The division of labor which produces superfluity and makes men partial—pieces of a great machine —will seem like a prison, and an unnecessary prison, to him. He will treasure his wholeness. He will know real value, which is the inverse of the value given things by the vanity of social men. And he will respect the producers of real value and despise the producers of value founded on vanity. Nature will be always present to him, not as doctrine but as a part of his very senses. Thus *Robinson Crusoe,* properly prepared for and used, teaches him the utility of the sciences and makes him inwardly free in spite of society's constraints.

Here then we have Rousseau's response to Plato. Plato said that all men always begin by being prisoners in the cave. The cave is civil society considered in its effect on the mind of those who belong to it. Their needs, fears, hopes, and indignations produce a network of opinions and myths which make communal life possible and give it meaning. Men never experience nature directly but always mix their beliefs into what they see. Liberation from the cave requires the discovery of nature under the many layers of convention, the separating out of what is natural from what is man-made. Only a genius is capable of attaining a standpoint from which he can see the cave as a cave. That is why the philosopher, the rarest human type, can alone be autonomous and free of prejudice. Now, Rousseau agrees that once in the cave, genius is required to emerge from it. He also agrees that enlightenment is spurious and merely the substitution of one prejudice for another. He himself was born in a cave and had to be a genius to attain his insight into the human condition. His life is a testimony to the heroic character of the quest for nature. But he denies that the cave is natural. The right kind of education, one independent of society, can put a child into direct contact with nature without the intermixture of opinion. Plato purified poetry so as to make its view of the world less hostile to reason, and he replaced the ordinary lies by a noble lie. Rousseau banishes poetry altogether and suppresses all lies. At most he gives Emile Robinson Crusoe, who is not an "other" but only himself. Above all, no gods. At the age of fifteen, Emile has a standpoint outside of civil society, one fixed by his inclinations and his reason, from which he sees that his fellow men are prisoners in a cave and by which he is freed from any temptation to fear the punishments or seek the honors which are part of it. Rousseau, the genius, has made it possible for ordinary men to be free, and in this way he proves in principle the justice of democracy.

Thus Rousseau's education of the young Emile confines itself to fostering the development of the faculties immediately connected with his preservation. His desire for the pleasant and avoidance of the painful are given by nature. His senses are the natural means to those ends. And the physical sciences, like mathematics, physics, and astronomy, are human contrivances which, if solidly grounded on the pure experience of the senses, extend the range of the senses and protect them from the errors of imagination. The tutor's responsibility is, in the first place, to let the senses develop in relation to their proper objects; and, secondly, to encourage the learning of the sciences as the almost natural outcome of the use of the senses. Rousseau calls this tutelage, particularly with reference to the part that has to do with the senses, negative education. All animals go through a similar apprenticeship to life. But with man something intervenes that impedes or distorts nature's progress, and therefore a specifically negative education, a human effort, is required. This new factor is the growth of the passions, particularly fear of death and *amour-propre*. Fed by imagination and intermingling with the desires and the senses, they transform judgment and lead to a special kind of merely human, or mythical, interpretation of the world. Negative education means specifically the tutor's artifices invented for the purpose of preventing the emergence of these two passions which attach men to one another and to opinions.

With respect to fear of death, Rousseau flatly denies that man does naturally fear death, and hence denies the premise of Hobbes's political philosophy (as well as what appears to be the common opinion of all political thinkers). Now Rousseau does not disagree with the modern natural right thinkers that man's only natural vocation is self-preservation or that man seeks to avoid pain, but Rousseau insists that man is not at first aware of the meaning of death, nor does man change his beliefs or ways of life to avoid it. He argues that death, as Hobbes's man sees it, is really a product of the imagination; and only on the basis of that imagination will he give up his natural idle and pleasure-loving life in order to pursue power after power so as to forestall death's assaults. The conception that life can be extinguished turns life, which is the condition of living, into an end in itself. No animal is capable of such a conception, and, therefore, no animal thus transforms his life. Rousseau suggests that a man can be kept at the animal's unconscious level in regard to death long enough for him to have established a fixed and unchanging positive way of life, a way of life in which he will be accustomed to pain as well as knowledgeable enough not to be overwhelmed by the fact of death when he becomes fully aware of it. Ordinarily fear of death leads to one of two possible responses: superstition or the attempt to conquer the inevitability of dying. The first gives hope that gods will protect one in this life or provide one with another life. The second response, that of the Enlightenment, uses science to prolong life and establish solid political regimes, putting off the inevitable and absorbing men in the holding action. Neither faces the fact of death, and both pervert consciousness.

This leads us to what Socrates meant by the dictum that philosophy is "learning how to die." All men die, and many die boldly or resolutely; but practically none does so, however, without illusion. Such illusion constitutes the horizon of the cave whose conventions are designed to support human hopes and fears. Thus to know how to die is equivalent to being liberated from the cave. And Rousseau, who argues that there is no natural cave, therefore also concludes that men naturally know how to die. "Priests, doctors and philosophers unlearn us how to die." [6] He does not suggest that every savage or every baby has meditated on death as did Socrates. He means that, naturally, every man is without the illusions about death that pervert life and require the Socratic effort. The tutor's function is to forestall the ministrations of priests, doctors, and philosophers which engender and nourish the fear of death. The simple lesson is that man must rely on himself and recognize and accept necessity; Rousseau shows how this can be achieved without requiring the exercise of the rarest virtues.

Although fear of death makes it difficult to accept necessity, *amour-propre* is what makes it difficult to recognize necessity. This is the murky passion that accounts for the "interesting" relationships men have with one another, and it is the keystone of Rousseau's psychological teaching. The primary intention of the negative education is to prevent *amour de soi* from turning into *amour-propre*, for this is the true source of man's dividedness. Rousseau's treatment of this all-important theme is best introduced by his discussion of the meaning of a baby's tears.[7]

Tears, he tells us, are a baby's language and naturally express physical discomfort and are pleas for help. The parent or nurse responds by satisfying a real need, feeding the baby, for example, or removing the source of pain. But at some point the child is likely to recognize that his tears have the effect of making things serve him through the intermediary of adults. The world responds to his wishes. His will can make things move to satisfy his desires. At this point the baby loses interest in providing himself with things; his inner motive to become strong enough to get for himself the things that others now provide for him is transformed into a desire to control the instrument which provides

6. P. 55 below.
7. Pp. 64–69 below.

him with those things. His concern with his physical needs is transformed into a passion to control the will of adults. His tears become commands and frequently no longer are related to his real needs but only to testing his power. He cannot stop it from raining by crying, but he can make an adult change his mind. He becomes aware of will; and he knows that wills, as opposed to necessity, are subject to command, that they are changing. He quickly learns that, for his life, control over men is more useful than adaptation to things. Therefore the disposition of adults towards him replaces his bodily needs as his primary concern. Every wish that is not fulfilled could, in his imagination, be fulfilled if the adult only willed it that way. His experience of his own will teaches him that others' wills are selfish and plastic. He therefore seeks for power over men rather than for the use of things. He becomes a skillful psychologist, able to manipulate others.

With the possibility of change of wills emerges the justification for blame and hence for anger. Nature does not have intentions; men do. Anger is caused by intentional wrong, and the child learns to see intention to do wrong in that which opposes him. He becomes an avenger. A squalling brat is most often testing his power. If he gets what he wants, he is a master. If he fails, he is angry, resentful, and likely to become slavish. In either event he has entered into a dialectic of mastery and slavery which will occupy him for his whole life. His natural and healthy self-love and self-esteem (*amour de soi*) gives way to a self-love relative to other men's opinions of him; henceforth he can esteem himself only if others esteem him. Ultimately he makes the impossible demand that others care for him more than they care for themselves. The most interesting of psychological phenomena is this doubling or dividing of self-love; it is one of the few distinctively human phenomena (no animal can be insulted); and from it flow anger, pride, vanity, resentment, revenge, jealousy, indignation, competition, slavishness, humility, capriciousness, rebelliousness, and almost all the other passions that give poets their themes. In these first seeds of *amour-propre* as seen in tears, one can recognize the source of the human problem.

Rousseau's solution to *amour-propre*, which would seem inevitably to lead to conflict among men—their using one another as means to their own ends and the need for government and law—is, as with the fear of death, to prevent its emergence at least for a long time. No self-overcomings are required. The child must be dependent on things and not on wills. The tutor and his helpers must disappear, as it were, and everything that happens to the child must seem to be an inevitable effect of nature. Against necessity he will not rebel; it is only the possibility of overcoming necessity or the notion that there is a will lurking behind it which disturbs his unclouded relation to things as they are. It is the mediation of human beings in the satisfaction of need that causes the problem.

Now all of this has even more significance than is immediately apparent, for Rousseau suggests that superstition, all attribution of intention to inanimate things or to the world as a whole, is a result of the early experience of will. In moving things at the child's command the parent gives the child the impression that all things are moved by intention and that command or prayer can put them at man's disposal. Moreover, anger itself animates. The child who is angry at what does not bend to his will attributes a will to it. This is the case with all anger, as a moment's reflection will show. Anger is allied with and has its origin in *amour-propre*. Once it is activated, it finds intention and responsibility everywhere. Finally it animates rivers, storms, the heavens, and all sorts of benevolent and malevolent beings. It moralizes the universe in the service of *amour-propre*.

In early childhood, there is a choice: the child can see everything or nothing as possessing a will like his own. Either whim or necessity governs the world for him. Neither case is true, but for the child the notion that necessity governs his world is the more salutary because nature is necessity and the primary things are necessary. The passions must submit to necessity, whereas necessity cannot be changed by the passions.[8] Before he comes to terms with will, a man must have understood and accepted necessity. Otherwise he is likely to spend his life obeying and fearing gods or trying to become one. Unlike more recent proponents of freedom, Rousseau recognized that without necessity the realm of freedom can have no meaning.

Rousseau's teaching about *amour-propre* goes to the heart of his disagreement with Plato. Plato had argued that something akin to what Rousseau calls *amour-propre* is an independent part of the soul. This is *thymos,* spiritedness, or simply anger. It is the motive of his warriors in the *Republic* and is best embodied in Achilles, who is almost entirely *thymos*. Plato was aware of all the dangers of *thymos,* but he insisted that it must be given its due because it is part of human nature, because it can be the instrument for restraining desire, and because it is connected with a noble and useful human type. Simply, it is *thymos* that makes men overcome their natural fear of death. Rather than excise it, Plato sought to tame this lion in the soul. The education in Books II–III of the *Republic* suggests the means to make it gentle and submissive to reason. However, these warriors do require myths and noble lies. They are cave dwellers. Man naturally animates the universe and tries to make it responsive to his demands and blames it for resisting. Plato focuses on Achilles, who struggles with a river that he takes to be a god, just as Rousseau is fascinated by the madness of Xerxes, who beats a recalcitrant sea.[9] These are the extreme but most revealing instances of the passion to rule. The difference between Plato and Rousseau on this crucial point comes down to whether anger is natural or derivative. Rousseau says that a child who is not corrupted and wants a cookie will never rebel against the phrase, "There are no more," but only against, "You cannot have one." Plato insists that this is not so. Men naturally see intention where there is none and must become wise in order to separate will from necessity in nature. They do, however, both agree that *thymos* is an important part of the spiritual economy, and that, once present, it must be treated with the greatest respect. Herein they differ from Hobbes, who simply doused this great

8. P. 219 below.
9. Plato *Republic* 391a–b; pp. 87–88, 213–214 below.

INTRODUCTION

cause of war with buckets of fear, in the process extinguishing the soul's fire. Rousseau gives a complete account of pride and its uses and abuses, whereas other modern psychologists have either lost sight of it or tried to explain it away. Our education does not take it seriously, and we risk producing timid souls or ones whose untrained spiritedness is wildly erratic and seeks dangerous outlets.

Given that the child must never confront other wills, Jean-Jacques tells us that he cannot be given commandments. He would not understand even the most reasonable restriction on his will as anything other than the expression of the selfishness of the one giving the commandments. The child must always do what he wants to do. This, we recognize, is the dictum of modern-day progressive education, and Rousseau is rightly seen as its source. What is forgotten is that Rousseau's full formula is that while the child must always do what he wants to do, he should want to do only what the tutor wants him to do.[10] Since an uncorrupt will does not rebel against necessity, and the tutor can manipulate the appearance of necessity, he can determine the will without sowing the seeds of resentment. He presents natural necessity in palpable form to the child so that the child lives according to nature prior to understanding it.

Rousseau demonstrates this method in a story that shows how he improves on earlier moral teachings.[11] He puts his Emile in a garden where there are no *nos*, no forbidden fruit, and no Fall, and tries to show that in the end his pupil will be healthy, whole, and of a purer morality than the old Adam. He gets Emile to respect the fruit of another without tempting him.

The boy is induced to plant some beans as a kind of game. His curiosity, imitativeness, and childish energy are used to put him to the task. He watches the beans grow while Jean-Jacques orates to him, supporting him in the pleasure he feels at seeing the result of his work and encouraging him in the sense that the beans are his by supplying a proper rationale for that sense. The speech does not bore him as a sermon would because it supports his inclination instead of opposing it. Jean-Jacques gives him what is in essence Locke's teaching on property. The beans belong to Emile because he has mixed his labor with them. Jean-Jacques begins by teaching him his right to his beans rather than by commanding him to respect the fruits of others.

Once the child has a clear notion of what belongs to him, he is given his first experience of injustice. One day he finds that his beans have been plowed under. And therewith he also has his first experience of anger, in the form of righteous indignation. He seeks the guilty party with the intention of punishing him. His selfish concern is identical with his concern for justice. But much to his surprise, Emile finds that the criminal considers himself to be the injured party and is equally angry with him. It is the gardener, and he had planted seeds for melons —melons that were to be eaten by Emile—and Emile had plowed under those seeds to plant his beans. Here we have will against will, anger against anger. Although Emile's wrath loses some of its force—inas-

10. P. 120 below.
11. Pp. 97–100 below.

much as the gardener has an even better claim to have right on his side (he was the first occupant), and this according to the very notion of right which Emile uses and which he so eagerly imbibed from Jean-Jacques—the situation could lead to war. But Jean-Jacques avoids that outcome by means of two stratagems. First, Emile's attention is diverted from his beans by the thought of the rare melons he would have enjoyed. Second, a kind of social contract is arranged: in the future Emile will stay away from the gardener's lands if he is granted a small plot for his beans. In this way the boy is brought to understand and respect the property of others without losing anything of his own. If there were a conflict of interest, Emile would naturally prefer his own. But Jean-Jacques does not put him in that position. If Emile were commanded to keep away from what he desires, the one who commanded him to do so would be responsible for setting him against himself and encouraging him to deceive. A luscious fruit in the garden which was forbidden would only set the selfish will of the owner against Emile's nature. Jean-Jacques at least gives Emile grounds for respecting property and brings him as close to an obligation as can be grounded on mere nature. Greater demands at this stage would be both ineffective and corrupting. The tempter is the giver of commandments. Rousseau here follows Hobbes in deriving duties, or approximations to them, from rights. In this way Emile will rarely infringe the rights of others, and he will have no intention to harm them.

It is this latter that constitutes the morality of the natural man and also that of the wise man (according to Rousseau).[12] It takes the place of the Christian's Golden Rule. When Rousseau says that man is by nature good, he means that man, concerned only with his own well-being, does not naturally have to compete with other men (scarcity is primarily a result of extended desire), nor does he care for their opinions (and, hence, he does not need to try to force them to respect him). Man's goodness is identical to his natural freedom (of body and soul) and equality. And here he agrees, contrary to the conventional wisdom, with Machiavelli, who said men are all bad. For Machiavelli meant that men are bad when judged from the standpoint of the common good, or of how men ought to live, or of the imaginary cities of the old writers. These make demands on men contrary to their natural inclinations and are therefore both unfounded and ineffective. If these standards are removed and men's inclinations are accepted rather than blamed, it turns out that with the cooperation of these inclinations sound regimes can be attained. From the standpoint of imaginary perfection man's passions are bad; from that of the natural desire for self-preservation they are good. Machiavelli preaches the adoption of the latter standpoint and the abandonment of all transcendence and with it the traditional dualism. And it is this project of reconciliation with what is that Rousseau completes in justifying the wholeness of self-concern, in proving that the principles of the old morality are not only ineffective but the cause of corruption (since they cause men to deny themselves and thus to become hypocrites), and in learning how

---

12. Pp. 104–105 below; Plato *Republic* 335 a–e.

to control that imagination which gives birth to the imaginary cities (which, in their opposition to the real cities, are the signs of man's dividedness).

The moral education of the young Emile is, then, limited to the effective establishment of the rule that he should harm no one. And this moral rule cooperates with the intellectual rule that he should know how to be ignorant. This latter means that only clear and distinct evidence should ever command belief. Neither passions nor dependencies should make him need to believe. All his knowledge should be relevant to his real needs, which are small and easily satisfied. In a sense, Rousseau makes his young Emile an embodiment of the Enlightenment's new scientific method. His will to affirm never exceeds his capacity to prove. For others that method is only a tool, liable to the abuses of the passions and counterpoised by many powerful needs. All this is described in the *Discourse on the Arts and Sciences*. But to Emile, whose only desire is to know and live according to the necessary, the new science of the laws of nature is a perfect complement. With a solid floor constituted by healthy senses in which he trusts and a ceiling provided by astronomy, Emile is now prepared to admit his fellows into a structure which their tempestuous passions cannot shake. This fifteen-year-old, who has not unlearned how to die, harms no one, and knows how to be ignorant, possesses a large share of the Socratic wisdom.

II

Emile at fifteen cares no more for his father than his dog. A child who did would be motivated by fear or desire for gain induced by dependency. Rousseau has made Emile free of those passions by keeping him self-sufficient, and he has thus undermined the economic foundations of civil society laid by Hobbes and Locke. Since Rousseau agrees with the latter that man has no natural inclination to civil society and the fulfillment of obligation, he must find some other selfish natural passion that can somehow be used as the basis for a genuine—as opposed to a spurious, competitive—concern for others. Such a passion is necessary in order to provide the link between the individual and disinterested respect for law or the rights of others, which is what is meant by real morality.

Rousseau finds such a solution in the sexual passion. It necessarily involves other individuals and results in relations very different from those following from fear or love of gain. Moreover, Rousseau discovers that sexual desire, if its development is properly managed, has singular effects on the soul. Books IV–V are a treatise on sex education, notwithstanding the fact that they give a coherent account of God, love, and politics. "Civilization" can become "culture" when it is motivated and organized by sublimated sex.

Sublimation as the source of the soul's higher expressions—as the explanation of that uniquely human turning away from mere bodily gratification to the pursuit of noble deeds, arts, and thoughts—was introduced to the world by Rousseau. The history of the notion can be traced from him through Kant, Schopenhauer, and Nietzsche (who first introduced the actual term) and to Freud (who popularized it). Rousseau's attempt to comprehend the richness of man's soul within the context of modern scientific reductionism led him to an interpretation which is still our way of looking at things although we have lost clarity about its intention and meaning. Rousseau knew that there are sublime things; he had inner experience of them. He also knew that there is no place for the sublime in the modern scientific explanation of man. Therefore, the sublime had to be made out of the nonsublime; this is sublimation. It is a raising of the lower to the higher. Characteristically, those who speak about sublimation since Freud are merely lowering the higher, reducing the sublime things to their elements and losing a hold on the separate dignity of the sublime. We no longer know what is higher about the higher.

These last two books of *Emile* then undertake in a detailed way the highly problematic task of showing how the higher might be derived from the lower without being reduced to it, while at the same time giving us some sense of what Rousseau means by the sublime or noble. It has not in the past been sufficiently emphasized that everything in Books IV–V is related to sex. Yet without making that connection the parts cannot be interpreted nor the whole understood.

Rousseau takes it for granted that sex is naturally only a thing of the body. There is no teleology contained in the sexual act other than generation—no concern for the partner, no affection for the children on the part of the male, no directedness to the family. As a simply natural phenomenon, it is not more significant or interesting than eating. In fact, since natural man is primarily concerned with his survival, sex is of secondary importance inasmuch as it contributes nothing to the survival of the individual. But because it is related to another human being, sex easily mingles with and contributes to nascent *amour-propre*. Being liked and preferred to others becomes important in the sexual act. The conquest, mastery, and possession of another will thus also become central to it, and what was originally bodily becomes almost entirely imaginary. This semifolly leads to the extremes of alienation and exploitation. But precisely because the sexual life of civilized man exists primarily in the imagination, it can be manipulated in a way that the desire for food or sleep cannot be. Sexual desire, mixed with imagination and *amour-propre*, if it remains unsatisfied produces a tremendous psychic energy that can be used for the greatest deeds and thoughts. Imaginary objects can set new goals, and the desire to be well thought of can turn into love of virtue. But everything depends on purifying and elevating this desire and making it inseparable from its new objects. Thus Rousseau, although Burke could accuse him of pedantic lewdness, would be appalled by contemporary sex education, which separates out the bodily from the spiritual in sex, does not understand the problem involved in treating the bloated passions of social man as though they were natural, is oblivious to the difficulty of attaching the indeterminate drive to useful and noble objects, and fails to appreciate the salutary effect of prolonged ignorance while the bodily humors ferment. Delayed satisfaction is, according to him, the condition of idealism and love, and early satisfaction causes the whole structure to collapse and flatten.

Rousseau's meaning is admirably expressed by Kant, who, following Rousseau, indicated that there is a distinction between what might be called natural puberty and civil puberty.[13] Natural puberty is reached when a male is capable of reproduction. Civil puberty is attained only when a man is able to love a woman faithfully, rear and provide for children, and participate knowledgeably and loyally in the political order which protects the family. But the advent of civilization has not changed the course of nature; natural puberty occurs around fifteen; civil puberty, if it ever comes to pass, can hardly occur before the middle twenties. This means that there is a profound tension between natural desire and civil duty. In fact, this is one of the best examples of the dividedness caused in man by his history. Natural desire almost always lurks untamed amidst the responsibilities of marriage. What Rousseau attempts to do is to make the two puberties coincide, to turn the desire for sexual intercourse into a desire for marriage and a willing submission to the law without suppressing or blaming that original desire. Such a union of desire and duty Kant called true culture.

Rousseau effects this union by establishing successively two passions in Emile which are sublimations of sexual desire and which are, hence, not quite natural but, one might say, according to nature: compassion and love.

COMPASSION

In this first stage the young man is kept ignorant of the meaning of what he is experiencing. He is full of restless energy and becomes sensitive. He needs other human beings, but he knows not why. In becoming sensitive to the feelings of others and in needing them, his imagination is aroused and he becomes aware that they are like him. He *feels* for the first time that he is a member of a species. (Until now he was simply indifferent to other human beings, although he *knew* he was a human being.) At this moment the birth of *amour-propre* is inevitable. He compares his situation with those of other men. If the comparison is unfavorable to him, he will be dissatisfied with himself and envious of them; he will wish to take their place. If the comparison is unfavorable to them, he will be content with himself and not competitive with others. Thus *amour-propre* is alienating only if a man sees others whom he can consider happier than himself. It follows that, if one wishes to keep a man from developing the mean passions which excite the desire to harm, he must always see men whom he thinks to be unhappier than he is. If, in addition, he thinks such misfortunes could happen to him, he will feel pity for the sufferer.

This is the ground of Rousseau's entirely new teaching about compassion.[14] Judiciously chosen comparisons presented at the right stage

13. "Conjectural Beginning of Human History," p. 61, note.
14. Pp. 221 ff. below.

of life will cause Emile to be satisfied with himself and be concerned with others, making him a gentle and beneficent man on the basis of his natural selfishness. Thus compassion would be good for him and good for others. Rousseau introduces a hardheaded softness to moral and political thought.

He asserts that the good fortune of others puts a chill on our hearts, no matter what we say. It separates us from them; we would like to be in their place. But their suffering warms us and gives us a common sense of humanity. The psychic mechanism of compassion is as follows. (1) Once a man's imaginative sensibility is awakened, he winces at the wounds others receive. In an attenuated form he experiences them too, prior to any reflection; he sympathizes; somehow these wounds are inflicted on him. (2) He has a moment of reflection; he realizes that it is the other fellow, not he, who is really suffering. This is a source of satisfaction. (3) He can show his own strength and superiority by assisting the man in distress. (4) He is pleased that he has the spiritual freedom to experience compassion; he senses his own goodness. Active human compassion (as opposed to the animal compassion described in the *Discourse on the Origins of Inequality*) requires imagination and *amour-propre* in addition to the instinct for self-preservation. Moreover, it cannot withstand the demands of one's own self-preservation. It is a tender plant, but one which will bear sweet fruit if properly cultivated.

Emile's first observations of men are directed to the poor, the sick, the oppressed, and the unfortunate. This is flattering to him, and his first sentiments toward others are gentle. He becomes a kind of social worker. And, as this analysis should make clear, the motive and intention of Rousseauan compassion give it little in common with Christian compassion. Rousseau was perfectly aware that compassion such as he taught is not a virtue and that it can lead to abuse and hypocrisy. But he used this selfish passion to replace or temper other, more dangerous passions. This is part of his correction of Hobbes. Rousseau finds a selfish passion which contains fellow feeling and makes it the ground of sociality to replace those passions which set men at odds. He can even claim he goes farther down the path first broken by Hobbes, who argued that the passions, and not reason, are the only effective motives of human action. Hobbes's duties towards others are rational deductions from the passion for self-preservation. Rousseau anchors concern for others in a passion. He makes that concern a pleasure rather than a disagreeable, and hence questionably effective, conclusion.

Rousseau's teaching on compassion fostered a revolution in democratic politics, one with which we live today. Compassion is on the lips of every statesman, and all boast that their primary qualification for office is their compassion. Rousseau singlehandedly invented the category of the disadvantaged. Prior to Rousseau, men believed that their claim on civil society has to be based on an accounting of what they contribute to it. After Rousseau, a claim based not on a positive quality but on a lack became legitimate for the first time. This he introduced as a counterpoise to a society based on Locke's teaching, which has no category for the miserable other than that of the idle and the quarrelsome. The recognition of our sameness and our common vulnerability dampens the harsh competitiveness and egotism of egalitarian political orders. Rousseau takes advantage of the tendency to compassion resulting from equality, and uses it, rather than self-interest, as the glue binding men together. Our equality, then, is based less on our fear of death than on our sufferings; suffering produces a shared sentiment with others, which fear of death does not. For Hobbes, frightened men make an artificial man to protect them; for Rousseau, suffering men seek other men who feel for them.

Of course Emile will not always be able to confine his vision to poor men without station. There are rich and titled men who seem to be much better off than he is. If he were brought to their castles and had a chance to see their privileges and their entertainments, he would likely be dazzled, and the worm of envy would begin to gnaw away at his heart. Jean-Jacques finds a solution to this difficulty by making Emile read history and bringing back what had been banished in Book II.[15] This is the beginning of Emile's education in the arts, as opposed to the sciences. The former can only be studied when his sentiments are sufficiently developed for him to understand the inner movements of the heart and when he experiences a real need to know. Otherwise, learning is idle, undigested, excess baggage at best. Emile's curiosity to find out about all of Plutarch's heroes and set his own life over against their lives fuels his study. Rousseau expects that this study will reveal the vanity of the heroes' aspirations and cause revulsion at their tragic failures. Emile's solid, natural pleasures, his cheaply purchased Stoicism and self-sufficiency, his lack of the passion to rule, will cause him to despise their love of glory and pity their tragic ends. The second level of the education in compassion produces contempt for the great of this world, not a slave's contempt founded in envy, indignation, and resentment, but the contempt stemming from a conviction of superiority which admits of honest fellow feeling and is the precondition of compassion. This disposition provides a standpoint from which to judge the social and political distinctions among men, just as Robinson Crusoe's island provided one for judging the distinctions based on the division of labor. The joining of these two standards enables Emile to judge the life of tyrants. Socrates enabled Glaucon and Adeimantus to judge it by comparing it to the life of philosophers; Emile can use his own life as the basis for judgment, for his own soul contains no germ of the tyrannical temptation. The old way of using heroes in education was to make the pupil dissatisfied with himself and rivalrous with the model. Rousseau uses them to make his pupil satisfied with himself and compassionate toward the heroes. The old way alienated the child and made him prey to authorities whose titles he could not judge. Self-satisfaction of egalitarian man is what Rousseau promotes. But he is careful to insure that this satisfaction is only with a good or natural self.

Reading is again the means of accomplishing the third and final part of the education in compassion.[16] This time the texts are fables

15. Pp. 236–244; cf. 110–112 below.
16. Pp. 244–249; cf. 112–116 below; and Tocqueville, *Democracy in America*, vol. 2, part 3, chap. 1.

which contain a moral teaching. They, too, had been banished in Book II, because a child would always identify himself with, e.g., the fox who cheats the crow rather than with the crow who loses the cheese, for a child understands nothing about vanity and a great deal about cheese. At this later stage Rousseau has arranged for Emile to have been deceived by confidence men who play upon his vanity, so that when he reads the fable he will immediately identify with the crow and attain self-consciousness. Satire becomes the mirror in which he sees himself. All this is intended to remind him that he, too, is human and could easily fall victim to the errors made by others. It is as though Rousseau had used Aristotle's discourse on the passions as a text and followed Aristotle's warning that those who do not imagine that the misfortunes befalling others can befall them are insolent rather than compassionate.[17] The first stage of Emile's introduction to the human condition shows him that most men are sufferers; the second, that the great, too, are sufferers and hence equal to the small; and the third, that he is potentially a sufferer, saved only by his education. Equality, which was a rational deduction in Hobbes, thus becomes self-evident to the sentiments. Emile's first principle of action was pleasure and pain; his second, after the birth of reason and his learning the sciences, was utility; now compassion is added to the other two, and concern for others becomes part of his sense of his own interest. Rousseau studies the passions and finds a way of balancing them one against the other rather than trying to develop the virtues which govern them. He does for the soul what Montesquieu did for the government: invent the separation and balance of powers.

But for all its important consequences in its own right, compassion within the context of Emile's education is only a step on the way to his fulfillment as husband and father. Its primary function is to make Emile social while remaining whole.

LOVE

Finally Rousseau must tell Emile the meaning of his longings. He reveals sex to the young Emile as the Savoyard Vicar revealed God to the young Jean-Jacques.[18] Although it is impossible to discuss the Profession of Faith of the Savoyard Vicar here, it is essential to the understanding of Rousseau's intention to underline the profound differences between the two revelations. The Vicar's teaching is presented to the corrupt young Rousseau and never to Emile. Moreover, the Vicar teaches the dualism of body and soul, which is alien and contradictory to the unity which Emile incarnates. In keeping with this, the Vicar is otherworldly and guilt-ridden about his sexual desires, which he deprecates, whereas Emile is very much of this world and exalts his sexual desires, which are blessed by God and lead to blessing God. Emile's rewards are on earth, the Vicar's in Heaven. The Vicar is the best of the traditional, and he is only an oasis in the desert which Rousseau crossed before reaching his new Sinai.

17. Aristotle *Rhetoric* II 8 and 2.
18. Pp. 260–313, 316–334 below.

INTRODUCTION

Thus at the dawn of a new day, Emile learns that the peak of sexual longing is the love of God mediated by the love of a woman.[19] Sublimation finally operates a transition from the physical to the metaphysical. But before speaking to Emile, Rousseau explains to his readers how difficult it is to be a good rhetorician in modern times. Speech has lost its power because it cannot refer to a world with deep human significance. In Greek and Biblical antiquity the world was full of meaning put there by the great and terrible deeds of gods and heroes. Men were awe-struck by the ceremonies performed to solemnize public and private occasions. The whole earth spoke out to make oaths sacred. But now the world has been deprived of its meaning by Enlightenment. The land is no longer peopled by spirits, and nothing supports human aspiration anymore. Thus men can only affect one another by the use of force or the profit motive. The language of human relations has lost its foundations. This is, as we would say, a demythologized world. And these remarks show what Rousseau is about. He wants to use imagination to read meaning back into nature. The old meanings were also the results of imaginings the reality of which men believed. They were monuments of fear and anger given cosmic significance. But they did produce a human world, however cruel and unreasonable. Rousseau suggests a new poetic imagination motivated by love rather than the harsher passions, and here one sees with clarity Rousseau's link with romanticism.

With this preface, he proceeds to inform Emile what the greatest pleasure in life is. He explains to him that what he desires is sexual intercourse with a woman, but he makes him believe that his object contains ideas of virtue and beauty without which she would not be attractive, nay, without which she would be repulsive. His bodily satisfaction depends upon his beloved's spiritual qualities; therefore Emile longs for the beautiful. Jean-Jacques by his descriptive power incorporates an ideal into Emile's bodily lust. This is how sex becomes love, and the two must be made to appear inseparable. This is the reason for the delay in sexual awareness. Emile must learn much before he can comprehend such notions, and his sexual energy must be raised to a high pitch. Early indulgence would separate the intensity of lust from the objects of admiration. Rousseau admits that love depends upon illusions, but the deeds which those illusions produce are real. This is the source of nobility of mind and deed, and apart from fanaticism, nothing else can produce such dedication.

Rousseau develops all this with precision and in the greatest detail. Only Plato has meditated on love with comparable profundity.[20] And it is Plato who inspired Rousseau's attempt to create love. The modern philosophers with whom Rousseau began have notably unerotic teachings. Their calculating, fear-motivated men are individuals, not directed towards others, towards couplings and the self-forgetting implied in them. Such men have flat souls. They see nature as it is; and, since they are unerotic, they are unpoetic. Rousseau, a philosopher-poet like Plato, tried to recapture the poetry in the world. He knew that Plato's *Symposium* taught that *eros* is the longing for eternity, ultimately the

19. P. 426 below.
20. *La Nouvelle Heloise* II, xi, second note.

longing for oneness with the unchanging, intelligible *ideas*. Now, Rousseau held that nature is the nature of modern science—matter in motion—that there are no *ideas*; there is no *eros*, only sex. But such a soul, which has no beautiful objects to contemplate and contains no divine madness, Rousseau regarded as ignoble. He set about reconstructing Plato's soul, turning sex into *eros*, by the creation of ideals to take the place of the *ideas*. The philosopher is even more poetic for Rousseau than for Plato, for the very objects of contemplation and longing are the products of poetry rather than nature. The world of concern to man is made by the poet who has understood nature and its limits. So, imagination, once banished, returns to ascend the royal throne.

From imagination thus purified and exalted comes the possibility of Emile's first real relationship with another human being, i.e., a freely chosen enduring union between equals based upon reciprocal affection and respect, each treating the other as an end in himself. This completes Emile's movement from nature to society, a movement unbroken by alien motives such as fear, vanity, or coercion. He has neither been denatured after the fashion of Sparta nor has moral obligation been reduced to a mere product of his selfishness as is the way of the *bourgeois*. He has an overwhelming need for another, but that other must be the embodiment of the ideal of beauty, and his interest in her partakes of the disinterestedness of the love of the beautiful. Moreover it is not quite precise to say that he loves an "other," for he will not be making himself hostage to an alien will and thus engaging in a struggle for mastery. This woman will, to use Platonic language, participate in the *idea* he has of her. He will recognize in her his own highest aspirations. She will complete him without alienating him. If Emile and Sophie can be constituted as a unit and individualism thereby surmounted, then Rousseau will have shown how the building blocks of a society are formed. Individuals cannot be the basis of a real community but families can be.

Now that Emile's dominant motive is longing for an object which exists only in his imagination, the rest of his education becomes a love story within a story. This little prototype of the romantic novel has three stages: the quest for his beloved; his discovery of her and their courtship; their separation, his travels, and their marriage.

The quest. Rousseau uses this time of intense passion to lead Emile into society and instruct him about its ways without fear that he will be corrupted by it.[21] Emile knows what he wants, and Rousseau knows that he will not find it in Paris. Emile's very passion provides him the standard by which he can judge men and women and their relations while being protected from the ordinary charms and temptations. A man in love sees things differently from those who are not so possessed, and he sees their concerns as petty and dull; he is, as well, proof against the attractions of all women other than his beloved. Emile is already in love, but he does not know with whom. He is, therefore, unlike most

21. Pp. 327–355 below.

lovers, an attentive observer, seeking to recognize the one for whom he is looking. In this way Rousseau provides him with the third of four standards for the evaluation of men in society which taken together serve as a substitute for the philosopher's vantage point outside the cave. The first was Crusoe's island, which enabled Emile to understand men's purely material relations in the division of labor and exchange and to maintain his independence while profiting from the progress of civilization in the sciences and productive industries. The second was compassion, which made him aware of mankind in its natural unity and its conventional division into classes. This awareness involved him with his fellows but maintained him in his self-sufficiency. Rousseau separates out into layers what the philosopher grasps together as a whole, and Emile is given an experience, founded in sentiment and imagination, of each of these layers or aspects of man and society. These experiences take the place of the savage's instinct that the civilized man has lost and of the philosopher's rational insight that the ordinary man cannot attain. Thus Emile has principles to guide him in life. They are founded on his deep and strong feelings, and they are his own, not dependent on any authority other than himself.

The third standard or standpoint, that of the lover, puts him in intimate contact with men and their passions. And he is, for the first time, needy. But it does make him both see and despise the vanities of society and the involvements with others that are not directly related to love. Moreover, in the society of the rich and noble in a great aristocracy Emile associates for the first time with men and women of high refinement and subtlety of manners. And here he has his first experience of the fine arts which are developed to please such people and constitute their principle entertainment. These arts are always the companions of idleness and luxury and most often are products of vice and instruments of deception as manners are the substitute for virtue. But from them Emile gains an exquisite sensibility and a delicacy of taste in the passions which matches the soundness of his reasoning about things. He has learned the sciences to satisfy his bodily needs; he learns the arts to enrich the transports of love. Poetry for him is not a pastime but the very element in which his sublime longings move. The depth of his feeling is given voice by these great products of civilization and not corrupted by it. He is now a cultivated man, and the motives of his learning have kept him healthy and whole. Rousseau has answered his own objections to the arts and sciences propounded in the *Discourse on the Arts and Sciences*.

Discovery and courtship. Emile's discovery of his Sophie in the country is the occasion for Rousseau's discourse on the differences between the sexes and their proper relations.[22] No segment of *Emile* is more "relevant" than is this one nor is any likely to arouse more indignation, for Rousseau is a "sexist." The particular force of Rousseau's argument for us comes from the fact that he begins from thoroughly modern premises—not deriving from Biblical or Greek thought—and arrives

22. Pp. 357–341 below.

at conclusions diametrically opposed to those of feminism. Further-more, his analysis is unrivaled in its breadth and precision. So per-suasive was he to Tocqueville that the latter asserted that the principle cause of America's "singular prosperity and growing strength" was its women, whom he describes as though they had been educated by Rousseau.[23] This analysis will not seem nearly so persuasive today because of the political force of a movement which Rousseau pre-dicted as an almost inevitable result of the bourgeoisification of the world, a tide which he was trying to stem. He saw that rationalism and egalitarianism would tend to destroy the sexual differences just as they were leveling class and national distinctions. Man and woman, hus-band and wife, and parent and child would become roles, not natural qualities; and as in all play-acting, roles can be changed. The only un-altered fragment of nature remaining, and thus dominating, would be the selfish Hobbesian individual, striving for self-preservation, comfort, and power after power. Marriage and the family would decay and the sexes be assimilated. Children would be burdens and not fulfillments.

It is impossible in this place to comment fully on Rousseau's inten-tions and arguments in this crucial passage. I must limit myself to a few general remarks. In the first place Rousseau insisted that the fam-ily is the only basis for a healthy society, given the impossibility and undesirability in modernity of Spartan dedication to the community. Without caring for others, without the willingness to sacrifice one's private interest to them, society is but a collection of individuals, each of whom will disobey the law as soon as it goes counter to his interest. The family tempers the selfish individualism which has been released by the new regimes founded on modern natural right teachings. And Rousseau further insists that there will be no family if women are not primarily wives and mothers. Second, he argues that there can be no natural, i.e., whole, social man if women are essentially the same as men. Two similar beings, as it were atoms, who united out of mutual need would exploit one another, each using his partner as a means to his own ends, putting himself ahead of him or her. There would be a clash of wills and a struggle for mastery, unless they simply copulated like beasts and separated immediately after (leaving the woman, of course, with the care of the unintended progeny). Human beings would be divided between their attachment to themselves and their duty to others. The project undertaken by Rousseau was to overcome or avoid this tension.

Thus the relations between man and woman is the crucial point, the place where the demands of Emile's wholeness and those of civil so-ciety meet. If Rousseau can overcome the difficulties in that relation, difficulties which were always present in the past but which have be-come critically explicit in modern theory and practice, he will have re-solved the tension between inclination and duty, nature and society. What he proposes is that the two sexes are different and complementary, each imperfect and requiring the other in order to be a whole being, or rather, together forming a single whole being. Rousseau does not

23. *Democracy in America*, vol. 2, part 3, chap. 12.

seriously treat a state as an organism, but he does so treat a couple. He tries to show that male and female bodies and souls fit together like pieces in a puzzle, and he does so in such a way as to make his conclusions compatible with natural science, on the one hand, and freedom and equality on the other. In particular, Rousseau argues that woman rules man by submitting to his will and knowing how to make him will what she needs to submit to. In this way Emile's freedom of will is preserved without Sophie's will being denied. Further, Rousseau argues, a woman naturally cares for her children; thus a man, loving her exclusively, will also care for the children. So it is that the family is constituted. None of this is found in the state of nature, but it is in accord with natural potentialities and reconciles the results of civilization with them. Whatever the success of Rousseau's attempt in this matter, the comprehensiveness and power of his reasoning as well as the subtlety of his psychological observation makes this one of the very few fundamental texts for the understanding of man and woman, and a touchstone for serious discussion of the matter.

The courtship of Emile and Sophie is merely their discovery of the many facets of the essential man and the essential woman and how well suited they are to one another. They reveal to one another each of the aspects of their respective natures and educations. If these had been the same, they would not really need each other or know of love, which is the recognition of an absence in oneself. Each would be a separate machine whose only function is to preserve itself, making use of everything around it to that end. The primary aim of the education of civilized man and woman is to prepare them for one another. Such education is Rousseau's unique educational innovation and where he takes most specific exception to Locke and Plato.[24]

Travel. Emile is ready to marry and enjoy the long-awaited consummation of his desires.[25] But Jean-Jacques orders him to leave Sophie, thus reenacting both Agamemnon's taking Briseis from Achilles and God's forbidding Adam from eating of the fruit of the tree of knowledge. This is the only example of a commandment in *Emile*, and the only time Emile's inclinations are thwarted by another will. But Emile, although sorely tried, submits and becomes neither the wrathful Achilles nor the disobedient Adam. There is no Fall. For the first time Emile becomes subject to a law and has an inner experience of the tension between inclination and duty. Jean-Jacques's authority goes back to a promise he extracted from Emile at the time of the revelation of sex. This is the first and only promise Emile makes to Jean-Jacques. If his tutor will give him guidance in matters of love, he will agree to accept his advice. He joins in what might be called a sexual contract which is the original of all other contracts he will make in his life; or, to put it more accurately, this first contract contains all the others. The obligation to Sophie which Emile learns to fulfill leads to the obligations to the family and these in turn to those to civil society.

Thus the scene where Jean-Jacques finally asks Emile to keep his promise encapsulates the whole problem of morality as he envisions it:

24. Pp. 357, 362–363, 415–416 below.
25. Pp. 441–450 below.

why keep a promise? A man makes a promise because he expects some good to result to him from doing so. But when he finds that it is more advantageous to break his promise, why should he keep it? What is good in itself about keeping faith? If there is no adequate basis for obligation, there is no basis for human society. Throughout *Emile* Rousseau has shown that all previous thinkers had added some kind of reward or punishment—wealth, honor, heaven or prison, disgrace, hell —to faith, thereby reducing it to the calculation of the other palpable goods which have been allied with it. Duty seems always to stem from the will of another, as epitomized in God's prohibition or Agamemnon's command, and society has therefore always demanded an abandonment of natural freedom and an unnatural bending to the needs of community. Spartan denaturing, Christian piety, and *bourgeois* calculation are, according to Rousseau, the three powerful alternative modes of making this accommodation. The first is the only one which does not divide and hence corrupt; but the undesirability of the Spartan example is fully expressed in the word "denaturing." This is why Emile has been subjected to no law but only to necessity and has always been left free to follow his inclinations. His education up to this point has shown just how far one can go in making a man sociable without imposing a law on him. But when it comes to his relation to women, something other than inclination must be involved. Emile must contract with Sophie, and sexual desire will not suffice as a guarantee of his future fidelity. It is instructive to note that the dramatic conflict between Jean-Jacques and Emile concerns the identical problem as do the conflicts between God and Adam and Agamemnon and Achilles. And it would appear that Rousseau resolves the conflict just as his ancient predecessors did, by an act of authority, the imposition of an alien will on his pupil's desires. It seems that Rousseau remains within the tradition which holds that morality is, to use Kantian language, heteronomous. Emile's reluctance to obey Jean-Jacques's command would seem to confirm this.

But the difference in Emile's conflict with Jean-Jacques becomes apparent when we see that Emile does not rebel but acquiesces, and his obedience is not the result of fear. First of all, Jean-Jacques's authority to command is based neither on force, tradition, or age, nor on purported superior wisdom or divine right. Following modern political philosophy, it is based solely on consent. Jean-Jacques commands only because he was once begged by Emile to command. The legitimacy of the contract is supported by the fact that Emile believes that Jean-Jacques is benevolent and interested only in his happiness, in his happiness as he himself conceives of it, not as Jean-Jacques or society might wish it. The promise to obey was intimately connected with the revelation of the greatest imaginable happiness and was intended to secure the only good he did not yet possess—love—and to avoid the dangers surrounding it. Sophie is to be returned to him, and there will be no curse of original sin on sexual desire. Everything speaks in favor of Jean-Jacques's authority.

But still it is authority. If Emile had by himself seen the good in what was commanded him, it would not have had to be commanded.

INTRODUCTION

The decisive step for Rousseau is to transform the external authority—however intimate—into an internal one. Jean-Jacques reminds Emile of his ideal Sophie and tries to show him that his love of the real Sophie could well undermine it, and with it, love itself. For example, if Sophie were not faithful, his attachment would remain and drag him down. Only if he were able to give up Sophie for what Sophie ought to be could he endure the vagaries of fortune and the human will. The separation from Sophie is the precondition of accepting life and of the foundation of the family. Emile's desire for immediate possession of Sophie rebels against his own will. For the first time he is forced to make a distinction between inclination and will. The problem of morality is no longer the conflict between inclination and duty but between inclination and ideal, which is a kind of equivalent of the conflict between particular and general will. The dedication to the ideal, completing the whole education, has been a generalizing of Emile's soul and his principles of action. The first command occurs at the moment when he is ready to see that it is not Jean-Jacques who is commanding but Emile—that he is obeying a law he has in fact set for himself. Jean-Jacques appears on the scene as an authority just this once in the course of his twenty-five years with Emile—only in order to annihilate the influence of authority on him. In this way Emile can be both free and moral. *Emile* is the outline of a possible bridge between the particular will and the general will.

The separation from Sophie is used for learning politics.[26] Now he has a good motive for such learning. When he was unattached, he was cosmopolitan, staying or leaving as he pleased, able to fend for himself anywhere, always an inhabitant of Crusoe's island and hence indifferent to the laws of men. But now, with a wife and children, he must settle down and become subject to a political regime. He must know which are most just and most secure, and he must adjust his hopes to the possible. It is well that he has learned what subjection to a law is, for politics means laws. But these political laws rarely if ever conform to the standard of justice, and Emile must reflect on how he is to come to terms with unjust regimes and their commands. He knows what perfect duties are, and they will help to guide him in the less than perfect duties imposed on him by civil society. His passion for his future wife and concern for their unborn children, combined with his mature learning, make an abstract presentation of the principles of right accessible to him. He is, in effect, taught the *Social Contract*. (Rousseau thus indicates the kind of reader for whom he intended it.) This provides Emile with his fourth standard, the one which permits him to evaluate the most comprehensive human order, civil society. And his travels enable him, given this focus, to recognize the various alternative "caves" and their advantages and disadvantages.

Finally he is complete and can claim his bride and his happiness. Rousseau has made him intellectually and morally self-sufficient.[27]

26. Pp. 450–471 below.
27. Pp. 471–480 below.

Conclusion

Emile might seem to some ridiculous because it proposes a system of education which is manifestly impossible for most men and virtually impossible for any man. But this is to misunderstand the book. It is not an educational manual, any more than Plato's *Republic* is advice to rulers. Each adopts a convention—the founding of a city or the rearing of a boy—in order to survey the entire human condition. They are books for philosophers [28] and are meant to influence practice only in the sense that those who read them well cannot help but change their general perspectives.

Rousseau intends to show that only his understanding of nature and history can adequately describe what man really is and to caution his contemporaries against simplifying and impoverishing the human phenomena. The very unity of man he appears to believe he has demonstrated reveals the problematic character of any solution to man's dividedness. Emile stands somewhere between the citizen of the *Social Contract* and the solitary of the *Reveries*, lacking something of each. And this book was the inspiration for both Kant's idealism and Schiller's romanticism, each of which is somehow an elaboration of one aspect of Rousseau's complex teaching. Whatever else Rousseau may have accomplished, he presented the alternatives available to man most comprehensively and profoundly and articulated them in the form which has dominated discussion since his time. We must study him to know ourselves and to discover possibilities his great rhetoric may have overwhelmed.

28. ". . . it is a new system of education the plan of which I present for the study of the wise and not a method for fathers and mothers. . . ." (*Letters Written from the Mountain* V [*Oeuvres Complètes*, vol. 3, p. 783]). This does not mean that Rousseau's teaching is ultimately one of political moderation as is Plato's.

Note

Emile was published in 1762, almost simultaneously with the *Social Contract* and two years after the *Nouvelle Heloise*. Together these three works constitute an exploration of the consequences for modern man of the tensions between nature and civilization, freedom and society, and hence happiness and progress which Rousseau propounded in the *Discourse on the Arts and Sciences* (1750) and the *Discourse on the Origins of Inequality* (1754). They each experiment with resolutions of the fundamental human problem, the *Social Contract* dealing with civil society and the citizen, the *Nouvelle Heloise* with love, marriage, and the family, and *Emile* with the education of a naturally whole man who is to live in society. They provide Rousseau's positive statement about the highest possibilities of society and the way to live a good life within it. The major works to which he devoted the rest of his life (*Confessions, Dialogues, Dreams of a Solitary Walker*) were dedicated to meditation on and presentation to mankind of the profoundest kind of soul, his own, the soul capable of revealing the human situation as he did in his earlier writings.

EMILE [1]

or

On Education

---

*Sanabilibus aegrotamus malis; ipsaque nos
in rectum genitos natura, si emendari
velimus, iuvat.*

Seneca: *de irā* B II, c. 13 [2]

PREFACE

THIS COLLECTION of reflections and observations, disordered and almost incoherent, was begun to gratify a good mother who knows how to think. I had at first planned only a monograph of a few pages. My subject drew me on in spite of myself, and this monograph imperceptibly became a sort of opus, too big, doubtless, for what it contains, but too small for the matter it treats. For a long time I hesitated to publish it; and often, in working at it, it has made me aware that it is not sufficient to have written a few pamphlets to know how to compose a book. After vain efforts to do better, I believe I ought to present it as it is, judging that it is important to turn public attention in this direction; and that although my ideas may be bad, if I cause others to give birth to good ones, I shall not entirely have wasted my time. A man, who from his retirement casts his pages out among the public, without boosters, without a party that defends them, without even knowing what is thought or said about them, need not fear that, if he is mistaken, his errors will be accepted without examination.[3]

I will say little of the importance of a good education; nor will I stop to prove that the current one is bad. Countless others have done so before me, and I do not like to fill a book with things everybody knows. I will only note that for the longest time there has been nothing but a cry against the established practice without anyone taking it upon himself to propose a better one. The literature and the learning of our age tend much more to destruction than to edification. A magisterial tone fits censure; but another kind of tone—one less agreeable to philosophic haughtiness—must be adopted in order to make proposals. In spite of so many writings having as their end, it is said, only what is useful for the public, the first of all useful things, the art of forming men, is still forgotten. After Locke's book [4] my subject was still entirely fresh, and I am very much afraid that the same will be the case after mine.

Childhood is unknown. Starting from the false idea one has of it, the farther one goes, the more one loses one's way. The wisest men concentrate on what it is important for men to know without considering what children are in a condition to learn. They are always seeking the man in the child without thinking of what he is before being a man. This is the study to which I have most applied myself, so that even though my entire method were chimerical and false, my observations could still be of profit. My vision of what must be done may have been very poor, but I believe I have seen clearly the subject on which one must work. Begin, then, by studying your pupils better. For most assuredly you do not know them at all. Now if you read this book with this in view, I believe it will not be without utility for you.

As to what will be called the systematic part, which is here nothing but the march of nature, it is the point that will most put the reader off, and doubtless it is here that I will be attacked. And perhaps it will not be wrong to do so. It will be believed that what is being read is less an educational treatise than a visionary's dreams about education. What is to be done about it? It is on the basis not of others' ideas that I write but on that of my own. I do not see as do other men. I have long been reproached for that. But is it up to me to provide myself with other eyes or to affect other ideas? No. It is up to me not to go overboard, not to believe that I alone am wiser than everybody. It is up to me not to change sentiments but to distrust mine. That is all I can do; and that is what I do. If I sometimes adopt an assertive tone, it is not for the sake of making an impression on the reader but for the sake of speaking to him as I think. Why should I propose as doubtful what, so far as I am concerned, I do not doubt at all? I say exactly what goes on in my mind.

In expounding freely my sentiment, I so little expect that it be taken as authoritative that I always join to it my reasons, so that they may be weighed and I be judged. But although I do not wish to be obstinate in defending my ideas, I nonetheless believe that it is my obligation to propose them; for the maxims ⁵ concerning which I am of an opinion different from that of others are not matters of indifference. They are among those whose truth or falsehood is important to know and which make the happiness or the unhappiness of mankind.

"Propose what can be done," they never stop repeating to me. It is as if I were told, "Propose doing what is done," or at least, "Propose some good which can be allied with the existing evil." Such a project, in certain matters, is much more chimerical than mine. For in this alliance the good is spoiled, and the evil is not cured. I would prefer to follow the established practice in everything than to follow a good one halfway. There would be less contradiction in man. He cannot pursue two opposite goals at the same time. Fathers and mothers, what can be done is what you want to do. Ought I to be responsible for your will?

In every sort of project there are two things to consider: first, the absolute goodness of the project; in the second place, the facility of execution.

In the first respect it suffices that the project be acceptable and practicable in itself, that what is good in it be in the nature of the thing; here, for example, that the proposed education be suitable for man and well adapted to the human heart.

PREFACE

The second consideration depends on relations given in certain situations—relations accidental to the thing, which consequently are not necessary and admit of infinite variety. Thus, one education may be practicable in Switzerland and not in France; one may be for the bourgeois, and another for the noble. The greater or lesser facility of execution depends on countless circumstances that are impossible to determine otherwise than in a particular application of the method to this or that country, to this or that station. Now all these particular applications, not being essential to my subject, do not enter into my plan. Other men will be able to concern themselves with them, if they wish, each for the country or estate he may have in view. It is enough for me that wherever men are born, what I propose can be done with them; and that, having done with them what I propose, what is best both for themselves and for others will have been done. If I do not fulfill this engagement, I am doubtless wrong. But if I do fulfill it, it would also be wrong to exact more from me. For that is all I promise.

Explanation of the Illustrations [6]

I.   The illustration, which relates to the first book and serves as frontispiece to the work, represents Thetis plunging her son in the Styx to make him invulnerable. (See Frontispiece.)

II.   The illustration at the beginning of the second book represents Chiron training the little Achilles in running. (See p. 76.)

III.   The illustration at the beginning of the third book and the second volume [7] represents Hermes engraving the elements of the sciences on columns. (See p. 164.)

IV.   The illustration which belongs to the fourth book and is at the beginning of the third volume represents Orpheus teaching men the worship of the gods. (See p. 261.)

V.   The illustration at the beginning of the fifth book and the fourth volume represents Circe giving herself to Ulysses, whom she was not able to transform. (See p. 356.)

BOOK
I

EVERYTHING is good as it leaves the hands of the Author of things; everything degenerates in the hands of man. He forces one soil to nourish the products of another, one tree to bear the fruit of another. He mixes and confuses the climates, the elements, the seasons. He mutilates his dog, his horse, his slave. He turns everything upside down; he disfigures everything; he loves deformity, monsters. He wants nothing as nature made it, not even man; for him, man must be trained like a school horse; man must be fashioned in keeping with his fancy like a tree in his garden.

Were he not to do this, however, everything would go even worse, and our species does not admit of being formed halfway. In the present state of things a man abandoned to himself in the midst of other men from birth would be the most disfigured of all. Prejudices, authority, necessity, example, all the social institutions in which we find ourselves submerged would stifle nature in him and put nothing in its place. Nature there would be like a shrub that chance had caused to be born in the middle of a path and that the passers-by soon cause to perish by bumping into it from all sides and bending it in every direction.

It is to you that I address myself, tender and foresighted mother,* [1]

---

* The first education is the most important, and this first education belongs incontestably to women; if the Author of nature had wanted it to belong to men, He would have given them milk with which to nurse the children. Always speak, then, preferably to women in your treatises on education; for, beyond the fact that they are in a position to watch over it more closely than are men and always have greater influence on it, they also have much more interest in its success, since most widows find themselves almost at the mercy of their children; then their children make mothers keenly aware, for good or ill, of the effect of the way they raised their children. The laws—always so occupied with property and so little with persons, because their object is peace not virtue—do not give enough authority to mothers. However, their status is more certain than that of fathers; their duties are more painful; their cares are more important for the good order of the family; generally they are more attached to the children. There are occasions on which a son who lacks respect for his father can in some way be excused. But if on any occasion whatsoever a child were unnatural enough to lack respect for his mother—for her who carried him in her womb, who nursed him with her milk, who for years forgot herself in favor

who are capable of keeping the nascent shrub away from the highway and securing it from the impact of human opinions! Cultivate and water the young plant before it dies. Its fruits will one day be your delights. Form an enclosure around your child's soul at an early date. Someone else can draw its circumference, but you alone must build the fence.

Plants are shaped by cultivation, and men by education. If man were born big and strong, his size and strength would be useless to him until he had learned to make use of them. They would be detrimental to him in that they would keep others from thinking of aiding him.* And, abandoned to himself, he would die of want before knowing his needs. And childhood is taken to be a pitiable state! It is not seen that the human race would have perished if man had not begun as a child.

We are born weak, we need strength; we are born totally unprovided, we need aid; we are born stupid, we need judgment. Everything we do not have at our birth and which we need when we are grown is given us by education.

This education comes to us from nature or from men or from things. The internal development of our faculties and our organs is the education of nature. The use that we are taught to make of this development is the education of men. And what we acquire from our own experience about the objects which affect us is the education of things.

Each of us is thus formed by three kinds of masters. The disciple in whom their various lessons are at odds with one another is badly raised and will never be in agreement with himself. He alone in whom they all coincide at the same points and tend to the same ends reaches his goal and lives consistently. He alone is well raised.

Now, of these three different educations, the one coming from nature is in no way in our control; that coming from things is in our control only in certain respects; that coming from men is the only one of which we are truly the masters. Even of it we are the masters only by hypothesis. For who can hope entirely to direct the speeches and the deeds of all those surrounding a child?

Therefore, when education becomes an art, it is almost impossible for it to succeed, since the conjunction of the elements necessary to its success is in no one's control. All that one can do by dint of care is to come more or less close to the goal, but to reach it requires luck.

What is that goal? It is the very same as that of nature. This has just been proved. Since the conjunction of the three educations is necessary

---

of caring for him alone—one should hasten to strangle this wretch as a monster unworthy of seeing the light of day. Mothers, it is said, spoil their children. In that they are doubtless wrong—but less wrong than you perhaps who deprave them. The mother wants her child to be happy, happy now. In that she is right. When she is mistaken about the means, she must be enlightened. Fathers' ambition, avarice, tyranny, and false foresight, their negligence, their harsh insensitivity are a hundred times more disastrous for children than is the blind tenderness of mothers. Moreover, the sense I give to the name *mother* must be explained; and that is what will be done hereafter.

* Similar to them on the outside and deprived of speech as well as of the ideas it expresses, he would not be in a condition to make them understand the need he had of their help, and nothing in him would manifest this need to them.

to their perfection, the two others must be directed toward the one over which we have no power. But perhaps this word *nature* has too vague a sense. An attempt must be made here to settle on its meaning.

Nature, we are told, is only habit. What does that mean? Are there not habits contracted only by force which never do stifle nature? Such, for example, is the habit of the plants whose vertical direction is interfered with. The plant, set free, keeps the inclination it was forced to take. But the sap has not as a result changed its original direction; and if the plant continues to grow, its new growth resumes the vertical direction. The case is the same for men's inclinations. So long as one remains in the same condition, the inclinations which result from habit and are the least natural to us can be kept; but as soon as the situation changes, habit ceases and the natural returns. Education is certainly only habit. Now are there not people who forget and lose their education? Others who keep it? Where does this difference come from? If the name *nature* were limited to habits conformable to nature, we would spare ourselves this garble.

We are born with the use of our senses, and from our birth we are affected in various ways by the objects surrounding us. As soon as we have, so to speak, consciousness of our sensations, we are disposed to seek or avoid the objects which produce them, at first according to whether they are pleasant or unpleasant to us, then according to the conformity or lack of it that we find between us and these objects, and finally according to the judgments we make about them on the basis of the idea of happiness or of perfection given us by reason. These dispositions are extended and strengthened as we become more capable of using our senses and more enlightened; but constrained by our habits, they are more or less corrupted by our opinions. Before this corruption they are what I call in us *nature*.

It is, then, to these original dispositions that everything must be related; and that could be done if our three educations were only different from one another. But what is to be done when they are opposed? When, instead of raising a man for himself, one wants to raise him for others? Then their harmony is impossible. Forced to combat nature or the social institutions, one must choose between making a man or a citizen, for one cannot make both at the same time.

Every particular society, when it is narrow and unified, is estranged from the all-encompassing society. Every patriot is harsh to foreigners. They are only men. They are nothing in his eyes.[2] This is a drawback, inevitable but not compelling. The essential thing is to be good to the people with whom one lives. Abroad, the Spartan was ambitious, avaricious, iniquitous. But disinterestedness, equity, and concord reigned within his walls. Distrust those cosmopolitans who go to great length in their books to discover duties they do not deign to fulfill around them. A philosopher loves the Tartars so as to be spared having to love his neighbors.

Natural man is entirely for himself. He is numerical unity, the absolute whole which is relative only to itself or its kind. Civil man is only a fractional unity dependent on the denominator; his value is determined by his relation to the whole, which is the social body. Good social institutions are those that best know how to denature man, to take his absolute existence from him in order to give him a relative one and transport the *I* into the common unity, with the result that each individual believes himself no longer one but a part of the unity and no longer feels except within the whole. A citizen of Rome was neither Caius nor Lucius; he was a Roman. He even loved the country exclusive of himself. Regulus claimed he was Carthaginian on the grounds that he had become the property of his masters. In his status of foreigner he refused to sit in the Roman senate; a Carthaginian had to order him to do so. He was indignant that they wanted to save his life. He conquered and returned triumphant to die by torture. This has little relation, it seems to me, to the men we know.[3]

The Lacedaemonian Pedaretus runs for the council of three hundred. He is defeated. He goes home delighted that there were three hundred men worthier than he to be found in Sparta. I take this display to be sincere, and there is reason to believe that it was. This is the citizen.[4]

A Spartan woman had five sons in the army and was awaiting news of the battle. A Helot arrives; trembling, she asks him for news. "Your five sons were killed." "Base slave, did I ask you that?" "We won the victory." The mother runs to the temple and gives thanks to the gods. This is the female citizen.[5]

He who in the civil order wants to preserve the primacy of the sentiments of nature does not know what he wants. Always in contradiction with himself, always floating between his inclinations and his duties, he will never be either man or citizen. He will be good neither for himself nor for others. He will be one of these men of our days: a Frenchman, an Englishman, a bourgeois.[6] He will be nothing.

To be something, to be oneself and always one, a man must act as he speaks; he must always be decisive in making his choice, make it in a lofty style, and always stick to it. I am waiting to be shown this marvel so as to know whether he is a man or a citizen, or how he goes about being both at the same time.

From these necessarily opposed objects come two contrary forms of instruction—the one, public and common; the other, individual and domestic.

Do you want to get an idea of public education? Read Plato's *Republic*. It is not at all a political work, as think those who judge books only by their titles. It is the most beautiful educational treatise ever written.

When one wishes to refer to the land of chimeras, mention is made of Plato's institutions. If Lycurgus had set his down only in writing, I would find them far more chimerical. Plato only purified the heart of man; Lycurgus denatured it.[7]

Public instruction no longer exists and can no longer exist, because where there is no longer fatherland, there can no longer be citizens. These two words, *fatherland* and *citizen*, should be effaced from modern languages. I know well the reason why this is so, but I do not want to tell it. It has nothing to do with my subject.[8]

I do not envisage as a public education those laughable establish-

ments called *colleges*.* ⁹ Nor do I count the education of society, because this education, tending to two contrary ends, fails to attain either.
It is fit only for making double men, always appearing to relate everything to others and never relating anything except to themselves alone.
Now since these displays are common to everyone, no one is taken in
by them. They are so much wasted effort.

From these contradictions is born the one we constantly experience
within ourselves. Swept along in contrary routes by nature and by men,
forced to divide ourselves between these different impulses, we follow
a composite impulse which leads us to neither one goal nor the other.
Thus, in conflict and floating during the whole course of our life, we
end it without having been able to put ourselves in harmony with ourselves and without having been good either for ourselves or for others.

There remains, finally, domestic education or the education of nature.
But what will a man raised uniquely for himself become for others? If
perchance the double object we set for ourselves could be joined in a
single one by removing the contradictions of man, a great obstacle to
his happiness would be removed. In order to judge of this, he would
have to be seen wholly formed: his inclinations would have to have
been observed, his progress seen, his development followed. In a word,
the natural man would have to be known. I believe that one will have
made a few steps in these researches when one has read this writing.

To form this rare man, what do we have to do? Very much, doubtless.
What must be done is to prevent anything from being done. When it is
only a question of going against the wind, one tacks. But if the sea
is heavy and one wants to stand still, one must cast anchor. Take care,
young pilot, for fear that your cable run or your anchor drag and that
the vessel drift without your noticing.

In the social order where all positions are determined, each man
ought to be raised for his. If an individual formed for his position
leaves it, he is no longer fit for anything. Education is useful only insofar as fortune is in agreement with the parents' vocation. In any other
case it is harmful to the student, if only by virtue of the prejudices it
gives him. In Egypt where the son was obliged to embrace the station
of his father, education at least had a sure goal. But among us where
only the ranks remain and the men who compose them change constantly, no one knows whether in raising his son for his rank he is not
working against him.

In the natural order, since men are all equal, their common calling
is man's estate and whoever is well raised for that calling cannot
fail to fulfill those callings related to it. Let my student be destined for
the sword, the church, the bar. I do not care. Prior to the calling of his
parents is nature's call to human life. Living is the job I want to teach
him. On leaving my hands, he will, I admit, be neither magistrate nor

* There are in the academy of Geneva and the University of Paris professors
whom I like very much and believe to be very capable of instructing the young well,
if they were not forced to follow the established practice. I exhort one among them
to publish the project of reform which he has conceived. Perhaps, when it is seen
that the ill is not without remedy, there will be a temptation to cure it.

soldier nor priest. He will, in the first place, be a man. All that a man should be, he will in case of need know how to be as well as anyone; and fortune may try as it may to make him change place, he will always be in his own place. *Occupavi te fortuna atque cepi omnesque aditus tuos interclusi, ut ad me aspirare non posses.* *

Our true study is that of the human condition. He among us who best knows how to bear the goods and the ills of this life is to my taste the best raised: from which it follows that the true education consists less in precept than in practice. We begin to instruct ourselves when we begin to live. Our education begins with us. Our first preceptor is our nurse. Thus this word *education* had another meaning for the ancients which we no longer give to it. *Educit obstetrix*, says Varro, *educat nutrix, instituit pedagogus, docet magister.*†

Thus education, instruction, and teaching are three things as different in their object as are the governess, the preceptor, and the master. But these distinctions are ill drawn; and, to be well led, the child should follow only a single guide.

We must, then, generalize our views and consider in our pupil abstract man, man exposed to all the accidents of human life. If men were born attached to a country's soil, if the same season lasted the whole year, if each man were fixed in his fortune in such a way as never to be able to change it—the established practice would be good in certain respects. The child raised for his station, never leaving it, could not be exposed to the disadvantages of another. But given the mobility of human things, given the unsettled and restless spirit of this age which upsets everything in each generation, can one conceive of a method more senseless than raising a child as though he never had to leave his room, as though he were going to be constantly surrounded by his servants? If the unfortunate makes a single step on the earth, if he goes down a single degree, he is lost. This is not teaching him to bear suffering; it is training him to feel it.

One thinks only of preserving one's child. That is not enough. One ought to teach him to preserve himself as a man, to bear the blows of fate, to brave opulence and poverty, to live, if he has to, in freezing Iceland or on Malta's burning rocks. You may very well take precautions against his dying. He will nevertheless have to die. And though his death were not the product of your efforts, still these efforts would be ill conceived. It is less a question of keeping him from dying than of making him live. To live is not to breathe; it is to act; it is to make use of our organs, our senses, our faculties, of all the parts of ourselves which give us the sentiment of our existence.[12] The man who has lived the most is not he who has counted the most years but he who has most felt life. Men have been buried at one hundred who died at their birth. They would have gained from dying young; at least they would have lived up to that time.

All our wisdom consists in servile prejudices. All our practices are only subjection, impediment, and constraint. Civil man is born, lives, and dies in slavery. At his birth he is sewed in swaddling clothes; at his

* *Tuscul.* V.[10]
† Non. Marcell.[11]

death he is nailed in a coffin. So long as he keeps his human shape, he is enchained by our institutions.

It is said that many midwives claim that by kneading newborn babies' heads, they give them a more suitable shape. And this is tolerated! Our heads are ill fashioned by the Author of our being! We need to have them fashioned on the outside by midwives and on the inside by philosophers. The Caribs are twice as lucky as we are.

Hardly has the baby emerged from the mother's womb, and hardly has he enjoyed the freedom to move and stretch his limbs before he is given new bonds. He is swaddled, laid out with the head secured and the legs stretched out, the arms hanging beside the body. He is surrounded with linens and trusses of every kind which do not permit him to change position, and he is lucky if he has not been squeezed to the point of being prevented from breathing and if care was taken to lay him on his side in order that the waters that should come out of his mouth can fall by themselves, for he would not have the freedom of turning his head to the side to facilitate the flow.*

The newborn baby needs to stretch and move its limbs in order to arouse them from the torpor in which, drawn up in a little ball, they have for so long remained. They are stretched out, it is true, but they are prevented from moving. Even the head is subjected to caps. It seems that we are afraid lest he appear to be alive.

Thus, the impulse of the internal parts of a body which tends to growth finds an insurmountable obstacle to the movements that impulse asks of the body. The baby constantly makes useless efforts which exhaust its forces or retard their progress. He was less cramped, less constrained, less compressed in the amnion than he is in his diapers. I do not see what he gained by being born.

The inaction, the constraint in which a baby's limbs are kept can only hinder the circulation of the blood, of the humors, prevent the baby from fortifying himself, from growing, and cause his constitution to degenerate. In the places where these extravagant precautions are not taken, men are all tall, strong, and well proportioned.† The countries where children are swaddled teem with hunchbacks, cripples, men with stunted or withered limbs, men suffering from rickets, men misshapen in every way. For fear that bodies be deformed by free movements, we hurry to deform the children by putting them into a press. We would gladly cripple them to keep them from laming themselves.

Could not so cruel a constraint have an influence on their disposition as well as on their constitution? Their first sentiment is a sentiment of pain and suffering. They find only obstacles to all the movements which they need. Unhappier than a criminal in irons, they make vain efforts, they get irritable, they cry. Their first voices, you say, are tears. I can well believe it. You thwart them from their birth. The first gifts they receive from you are chains. The first treatment they experience is

---

* Buffon, *Histoire Naturelle*, vol. IV, p. 190.[13]
† See note ‡ on page 60.

torment. Having nothing free but the voice, how would they not make use of it to complain? They cry because you are hurting them. Thus garroted, you would cry harder than they do.

Where does this unreasonable practice come from? From a denatured practice. Since mothers, despising their first duty, have no longer wanted to feed their children, it has been necessary to confide them to mercenary women who, thus finding themselves mothers of alien children on whose behalf nature tells them nothing, have sought only to save themselves effort. It would be necessary to be constantly watchful over a child in freedom. But when it is well bound, one throws it in a corner without being troubled by its cries. Provided that there be no proofs of negligence on the part of the nurse, provided that her charge does not break an arm or a leg, beyond that what difference does it make that he wastes away or remains infirm for the rest of his days? His limbs are preserved at the expense of his body, and, whatever happens, the nurse is exonerated.

Do they know, these gentle mothers who, delivered from their children, devote themselves gaily to the entertainments of the city, what kind of treatment the swaddled child is getting in the meantime in the village? At the slightest trouble that arises he is hung from a nail like a sack of clothes, and while the nurse looks after her business without hurrying, the unfortunate stays thus crucified. All those found in this position had violet faces. The chest was powerfully compressed, blocking circulation, and the blood rose to the head. The sufferer was believed to be quite tranquil, because he did not have the strength to cry. I do not know how many hours a child can remain in this condition without losing its life, but I doubt that this can go on very long. This is, I think, one of the great advantages of swaddling.

It is claimed that children in freedom could assume bad positions and make movements capable of hurting the good conformation of their limbs. This is one of those vain reasonings of our false wisdom that has never been confirmed by any experience. Of that multitude of children who, among peoples more sensible than us, are reared with complete freedom of their limbs, not a single one is seen who wounds or cripples himself. They could not give their movements sufficient force to make them dangerous; and, when they take a strained position, the pain soon warns them to change it.

We have not yet taken it into our heads to swaddle little dogs or cats. Do we see that they have any problems as a result of this negligence? Children are heavier. Agreed. But they are also proportionately weaker. They can hardly move. How would they cripple themselves? If they were stretched out on their backs, they would die in this position, like the tortoise, without ever being able to turn themselves over.

Not satisfied with having given up nursing their children, women give up wanting to have them. The result is natural. As soon as the condition of motherhood becomes burdensome, the means to deliver oneself from it completely is soon found. They want to perform a useless act so as always to be able to start over again, and they turn to the prejudice of the species the attraction given for the sake of multiplying it. This practice, added to the other causes of depopulation, presages the impending fate of Europe. The sciences, the arts, the philosophy, and the morals that this practice engenders will not be long in making a desert of it. It will be peopled with ferocious beasts. The change of inhabitants will not be great.

I have sometimes seen the little trick of young women who feign to want to nurse their children. They know how to have pressure put on them to give up this whim. Husbands, doctors, especially mothers, are adroitly made to intervene. A husband who dared to consent to his wife's nursing her child would be a man lost. He would be made into a murderer who wants to get rid of her. Prudent husbands, paternal love must be immolated for the sake of peace; you are fortunate that women more continent than yours can be found in the country, more fortunate yet if the time your wives save is not destined for others than you!

There is no question about the duty of women. But there is dispute as to whether, given the contempt they have for it, it makes any difference for the children to be nursed with the mother's milk or that of another. Let me take this question, of which the doctors are the judges, to be decided just as the women would like. For my part I, too, certainly think that it is preferable for a child to suck the milk of a healthy nurse than of a spoiled mother, if he had some new ill to fear from the same blood out of which he was formed.

But should the question be envisaged only from the physical side, and does the child have less need of a mother's care than of her breast? Other women, even beasts, will be able to give him the milk that she refuses him. There is no substitute for maternal solicitude. She who nurses another's child in place of her own is a bad mother. How will she be a good nurse? She could become one, but slowly; habit would have to change nature; and the child, ill cared for, will have the time to perish a hundred times before his nurse has gained a mother's tenderness for him.

From this very advantage results a drawback which alone should take from every sensitive woman the courage to have her child nursed by another. The drawback is that of sharing a mother's right, or rather of alienating it, of seeing her child love another woman as much as and more than her, of feeling that the tenderness that he preserves for his own mother is a favor and that the tenderness he has for his adoptive mother is a duty. Where I found a mother's care do not I owe a son's attachment?

Their way of remedying this drawback is to inspire contempt in the children for their nurses by treating them as veritable servants. When their service is completed, the child is taken back or the nurse dismissed. By dint of giving her a poor reception, she is discouraged from coming to see her charge. At the end of a few years he no longer sees her, no longer knows her. The mother who believes she replaces the nurse and makes up for her neglect by her cruelty is mistaken. Instead of making a tender son out of a denatured nursling, she trains him in ingratitude, she teaches him one day to despise her who gave him life as well as her who nursed him with her milk.

How I would insist on this point were it not so discouraging to keep raising useful subjects in vain! More depends on this one than is thought. Do you wish to bring everyone back to his first duties? Begin with mothers. You will be surprised by the changes you will produce. Everything follows successively from this first depravity. The whole moral order degenerates; naturalness is extinguished in all hearts; home life takes on a less lively aspect; the touching spectacle of a family aborning no longer attaches husbands, no longer imposes respect on outsiders; the mother whose children one does not see is less respected. One does not reside in one's family; habit does not strengthen the blood ties. There are no longer fathers, mothers, children, brothers, or sisters. They all hardly know each other. How could they love each other? Each thinks only of himself. When home is only a sad solitude, one must surely go elsewhere for gaiety.

But let mothers deign to nurse their children, morals will reform themselves, nature's sentiments will be awakened in every heart, the state will be repeopled. This first point, this point alone, will bring everything back together. The attraction of domestic life is the best counterpoison for bad morals. The bother of children, which is believed to be an importunity, becomes pleasant. It makes the father and mother more necessary, dearer to one another; it tightens the conjugal bond between them. When the family is lively and animated, the domestic cares constitute the dearest occupation of the wife and the sweetest enjoyment of the husband. Thus, from the correction of this single abuse would soon result a general reform; nature would soon have reclaimed all its rights. Let women once again become mothers, men will soon become fathers and husbands again.

Superfluous speeches! The very boredom of worldly pleasures never leads back to these. Women have stopped being mothers; they will no longer be; they no longer want to be. If they should want to be, they hardly could be. Today the contrary practice is established. Each one would have to combat the opposition of every woman who comes near her, all in league against an example that some did not give and the rest do not want to follow.

There are, nevertheless, still sometimes young persons of a good nature who on this point, daring to brave the empire of fashion and the clamors of their sex, fulfill with a virtuous intrepidity this duty so sweet imposed on them by nature. May their number increase as a result of the attraction of the goods destined for those who devote themselves to it! Founded on conclusions given by the simplest reasoning and on observations that I have never seen belied, I dare to promise these worthy mothers a solid and constant attachment on the part of their husbands, a truly filial tenderness on the part of their children, the esteem and respect of the public, easy deliveries without mishap and without aftermath, a firm and vigorous health; finally the pleasure of seeing themselves one day imitated by their own daughters and cited as examples to others' daughters.

No mother, no child. Between them the duties are reciprocal, and if they are ill fulfilled on one side, they will be neglected on the other. The child ought to love his mother before knowing that he ought to. If the voice of blood is not strengthened by habit and care, it is extinguished in the first years, and the heart dies, so to speak, before being born. Here we are, from the first steps, outside of nature.

One leaves it by an opposite route as well when, instead of neglecting a mother's care, a woman carries it to excess; when she makes an idol of her child; when she increases and nurses his weakness in order to prevent him from feeling it; and when, hoping to exempt him from the laws of nature, she keeps hard blows away from him. She preserves him for a moment from a few discomforts without thinking about how many mishaps and perils she is thereby accumulating for him to bear later, and how barbarous a precaution it is which adds childhood's weakness to mature men's toils. Thetis, to make her son invulnerable, plunged him, according to the fable, in the water of the Styx.[14] This allegory is a lovely one, and it is clear. The cruel mothers of whom I speak do otherwise: by dint of plunging their children in softness, they prepare them for suffering; they open their pores to ills of every sort to which they will not fail to be prey when grown.

Observe nature and follow the path it maps out for you. It exercises children constantly; it hardens their temperament by tests of all sorts; it teaches them early what effort and pain are. Teething puts them in a fever; sharp colics give them convulsions; long coughs suffocate them; worms torment them; plethora corrupts their blood; various leavens ferment in it and cause perilous eruptions. Almost all the first age is sickness and danger. Half the children born perish before the eighth year. The tests passed, the child has gained strength; and as soon as he can make use of life, its principle becomes sounder.

That is nature's rule. Why do you oppose it? Do you not see that in thinking you correct it, you destroy its product, you impede the effect of its care? To do on the outside what nature does on the inside redoubles the danger, according to you; and, on the contrary, this diverts the danger and weakens it. Experience teaches that even more children raised delicately die than do others. Provided the limit of their strength is not exceeded, less is risked in employing that strength than in sparing it. Exercise them, then, against the attacks they will one day have to bear. Harden their bodies against the intemperance of season, climates, elements; against hunger, thirst, fatigue. Steep them in the water of the Styx. Before the body's habit is acquired, one can give it the habit one wants to give it without danger. But when it has once gained its consistency, every alteration becomes perilous for it. A child will bear changes that a man would not bear; the fibers of the former, soft and flexible, take without effort the turn that they are given; those of the man, more hardened, change only with violence the turn they have received. A child, then, can be made robust without exposing its life and its health; and if there were some risk, still one must not hesitate. Since these are risks inseparable from human life, can one do better than shift them to that part of its span when they are least disadvantageous?

A child becomes more precious as he advances in age. To the value of his person is joined that of the effort he has cost; to the loss of his life is joined in him the sentiment of death. It is, then, especially of the future that one must think in looking after his preservation. It is against the ills of youth that he must be armed before he reaches them; for if the value of life increases up to the age of making use of it, what folly is it not to spare childhood some ills while multiplying them for the age of reason? Are those the lessons of the master?

The fate of man is to suffer at all times. The very care of his preservation is connected with pain. Lucky to know only physical ills in his childhood—ills far less cruel, far less painful than are the other kinds of ills and which far more rarely make us renounce life than do the others! One does not kill oneself for the pains of gout. There are hardly any but those of the soul which produce despair. We pity the lot of childhood, and it is our own that should be pitied. Our greatest ills come to us from ourselves.

A child cries at birth; the first part of his childhood is spent crying. At one time we bustle about, we caress him in order to pacify him; at another, we threaten him, we strike him in order to make him keep quiet. Either we do what pleases him, or we exact from him what pleases us. Either we submit to his whims, or we submit him to ours. No middle ground; he must give orders or receive them. Thus his first ideas are those of domination and servitude. Before knowing how to speak, he commands; before being able to act, he obeys. And sometimes he is chastised before he is able to know his offenses or, rather, to commit any. It is thus that we fill up his young heart at the outset with the passions which later we impute to nature and that, after having taken efforts to make him wicked, we complain about finding him so.

A child spends six or seven years thus in the hands of women, victim of their caprice and of his own. And after having made him learn this and that—that is, after having burdened his memory either with words he cannot understand or with things that are good for nothing to him; after having stifled his nature by passions that one has caused to be born in him—this factitious being is put in the hands of a preceptor who completes the development of the artificial seeds that he finds already all formed and teaches him everything, except to know himself, except to take advantage of himself, except to know how to live and to make himself happy. Finally when this child, slave and tyrant, full of science and bereft of sense, frail in body and soul alike, is cast out into the world, showing there his ineptitude, his pride, and all his vices, he becomes the basis for our deploring human misery and perversity. This is a mistake. He is the man of our whims; the man of nature is differently constituted.

Do you, then, want him to keep his original form? Preserve it from the instant he comes into the world. As soon as he is born, take hold of him and leave him no more before he is a man. You will never succeed without that. As the true nurse is the mother, the true preceptor is the father. Let them be in agreement both about the order of their functions and about their system; let the child pass from the hands of the one into those of the other. He will be better raised by a judicious and limited father than the cleverest master in the world; for zeal will make up for talent better than talent for zeal.

But business, offices, duties . . . Ah, duties! Doubtless the least is that of father? * Let us not be surprised that a man whose wife did not deign to nurse the fruit of their union does not deign to raise him. There is no picture more charming than that of the family, but a single missing feature disfigures all the others. If the mother has too little health to be nurse, the father will have too much business to be preceptor. The children, sent away, dispersed in boarding schools, convents, colleges, will take the love belonging to the paternal home elsewhere, or to put it better, they will bring back to the paternal home the habit of having no attachments. Brothers and sisters will hardly know one another. When all are gathered together for ceremonial occasions, they will be able to be quite polite with one another. They will treat one another as strangers. As soon as there is no more intimacy between the parents, as soon as the society of the family no longer constitutes the sweetness of life, it is of course necessary to turn to bad morals to find a substitute. Where is the man stupid enough not to see the chain formed by all these links?

A father, when he engenders and feeds children, does with that only a third of his task. He owes to his species men; he owes to society sociable men; he owes to the state citizens. Every man who can pay this triple debt and does not do so is culpable, and more culpable perhaps when he pays it halfway. He who cannot fulfill the duties of a father has no right to become one. Neither poverty nor labors nor concern for public opinion exempts him from feeding his children and from raising them himself. Readers, you can believe me. I predict to whoever has vitals and neglects such holy duties that he will long shed bitter tears for his offense and will never find consolation for it.[16]

But what does this rich man—this father of a family, so busy, and forced, according to him, to leave his children uncared for—do? He pays another man to take responsibility for these cares which are a burden to him. Venal soul! Do you believe that you are with money giving your son another father? Make no mistake about it; what you are giving him is not even a master but a valet. This first valet will soon make a second one out of your son.

We spend a lot of time trying to figure out the qualities of a good governor. The first quality I would exact of him, and this one alone presupposes many others, is that he not be a man for sale. There are callings so noble that one cannot follow them for money without proving oneself unworthy of following them. Such is that of the man of war; such is that of the teacher. "Who then will raise my child?" I already told you: you, yourself. "I cannot." You cannot! . . . Find yourself a friend then. I see no other solution.

A governor! O what a sublime soul . . . in truth, to make a man,

* When one reads in Plutarch that Cato the Censor, who governed Rome so gloriously, himself raised his son from the cradle and with such care that he left everything to be present when the nurse—that is to say, the mother—changed and bathed him; when one reads in Suetonius that Augustus, master of the world that he had conquered and that he himself ruled, himself taught his grandsons to write, to swim, the elements of the sciences, and that he had them constantly around him—one cannot keep from laughing at the good little people of those times who enjoyed themselves in the like foolishness, doubtless too limited to know how to mind the great business of the great men of our days.[15]

one must be either a father or more than a man oneself.[17] That is the function you calmly confide to mercenaries.

The more one thinks about it, the more one perceives new difficulties. It would be necessary that the governor had been raised for his pupil, that the pupil's domestics had been raised for their master, that all those who have contact with him had received the impressions that they ought to communicate to him. It would be necessary to go from education to education back to I know not where. How is it possible that a child be well raised by one who was not well raised himself?

Is this rare mortal not to be found? I do not know. In these degraded times who knows to what point of virtue a human soul can still attain? But let us suppose this marvel found. It is in considering what he ought to do that we shall see what he ought to be. What I believe I see in advance is that a father who sensed all the value of a good governor would decide to do without one, for he would expend more effort in acquiring him than in becoming one himself. Does he then want to find a friend? Let him raise his son to be one. Thus, he is spared seeking for him elsewhere, and nature has already done half the work.

Someone of whom I know only the rank had the proposal to raise his son conveyed to me. He doubtless did me a great deal of honor; but far from complaining about my refusal, he ought to congratulate himself on my discretion. If I had accepted his offer and my method were mistaken, the education would have been a failure. If I had succeeded, it would have been far worse. His son would have repudiated his title; he would no longer have wished to be a prince.

I am too impressed by the greatness of a preceptor's duties, I feel my incapacity too much ever to accept such employment from whatever quarter it might be offered to me, and the interest of friendship itself would be but a further motive for refusal. I believe that after having read this book, few people will be tempted to make me this offer, and I beg those who might be, not to make this useless effort any more. In the past I made a sufficient trial of this calling to be certain that I am not proper for it,[18] and my condition would excuse me from it if my talents made me capable of it. I believed I owed this public declaration to those who appear not to accord me enough esteem to believe me sincere and well founded in my resolutions.

Not in a condition to fulfill the most useful task, I will dare at least to attempt the easier one; following the example of so many others, I shall put my hand not to the work but to the pen; and instead of doing what is necessary, I shall endeavor to say it.

I know that in undertakings like this one, an author—always comfortable with systems that he is not responsible for putting into practice—may insouciantly offer many fine precepts which are impossible to follow. And in the absence of details and examples, even the feasible things he says, if he has not shown their application, remain ineffectual.

I have hence chosen to give myself an imaginary pupil, to hypothesize that I have the age, health, kinds of knowledge, and all the talent suitable for working at his education, for conducting him from the moment of his birth up to the one when, become a grown man, he will no longer have need of any guide other than himself. This method appears to me useful to prevent an author who distrusts himself from getting lost in visions; for when he deviates from ordinary practice, he has only to make a test of his own practice on his pupil. He will soon sense, or the reader will sense for him, whether he follows the progress of childhood and the movement natural to the human heart.

This is what I have tried to do in all the difficulties which have arisen. In order not to fatten the book uselessly, I have been content with setting down the principles whose truth everyone should sense. But as for the rules which might need proofs, I have applied them all to my Emile or to other examples; and I have shown in very extensive detail how what I have established could be put into practice. Such at least is the plan that I have proposed to follow. It is up to the reader to judge if I have succeeded.

The result of this procedure is that at first I have spoken little of my Emile, because my first educational maxims,[19] although contrary to those which are established, are so evident that it is difficult for any reasonable man to refuse his consent to them. But in the measure I advance, my pupil, differently conducted than yours, is no longer an ordinary child. He requires a way of life special to him. Then he appears more frequently on the scene, and toward the last times I no longer let him out of sight for a moment until, whatever he may say, he has no longer the least need of me.

I do not speak at all here of a good governor's qualities; I take them for granted, and I take for granted that I myself am endowed with all these qualities. In reading this work, one will see with what liberality I treat myself.

I shall only remark that, contrary to common opinion, a child's governor ought to be young and even as young as a wise man can be. I would want him to be a child himself if it were possible, to be able to become his pupil's companion and attract his confidence by sharing his enjoyments. There are not enough things in common between childhood and maturity for a really solid attachment ever to be formed at this distance. Children sometimes flatter old men, but they never love them.

One would wish that the governor had already educated someone. That is too much to wish for; the same man can only give one education. If two were required in order to succeed, by what right would one undertake the first?

With more experience one would know how to do better, but one would no longer be able to. Whoever has once fulfilled this function well enough to sense all its difficulties does not attempt to engage himself in it again; and if he has fulfilled it poorly the first time, that is an unfavorable augury for the second.

It is quite different, I agree, to follow a young man for four years than to lead him for twenty-five. You give a governor to your son after he is already all formed; as for me, I want him to have one before he is born. Your short-term man can change pupils; mine will have only one. You distinguish the preceptor from the governor: another folly! Do you distinguish the student from the pupil? There is only one science to teach to children. It is that of man's duties. This science is one, and whatever Xenophon says about the education of the Persians,[20] it is not divisible. Moreover, I call the master of this science *governor* rather than *preceptor* because his task is less to instruct than to lead. He ought to give no precepts at all; he ought to make them be discovered.

If the governor must be chosen with so much care, it is certainly permissible for him to choose his pupil as well, especially when what we are about is propounding a model. This choice cannot be made on the basis of the child's genius or character, which can be known only at the end of the work, whereas I am adopting the child before his birth. If I could choose, I would take only a common mind, such as I assume my pupil to be. Only ordinary men need to be raised; their education ought to serve as an example only for that of their kind. The others raise themselves in spite of what one does.[21]

Locale is not unimportant in the culture of men. They are all that they can be only in temperate climates. The disadvantage of extreme climates is obvious. A man is not planted like a tree in a country to remain there forever; and he who leaves one extreme to get to the other is forced to travel a road double the length of that traveled by him who leaves from the middle point for the same destination.

Let the inhabitant of a temperate country visit the two extremes one after the other. His advantage is still evident, for although he is affected as much as the one who goes from one extreme to the other, he is nevertheless only half as far from his natural constitution. A Frenchman can live in Guinea and in Lapland; but a Negro will not live likewise in Torne, nor a Samoyed in Benin. It appears, moreover, that the organization of the brain is less perfect in the two extremes. Neither the Negroes nor the Laplanders have the sense of the Europeans. If, then, I want my pupil to be able to be an inhabitant of the earth, I will get him in a temperate zone—in France, for example—rather than elsewhere.

In the north, men consume a lot on barren soil; in the south, they consume little on fertile soil. From this a new difference is born which makes the ones industrious and the others contemplative. Society presents us in a single place the image of these differences between the poor and the rich. The former inhabit the barren soil, and the latter the fertile country.

The poor man does not need to be educated. His station gives him a compulsory education. He could have no other. On the contrary, the education the rich man receives from his station is that which suits him least, from both his own point of view and that of society. Besides, the natural education ought to make a man fit for all human conditions. Now, it is less reasonable to raise a poor man to be rich than a rich man to be poor, for, in proportion to the number of those in the two stations, there are more men who fall than ones who rise. Let us, then, choose a rich man. We will at least be sure we have made one more man, while a poor person can become a man by himself.

For the same reason I will not be distressed if Emile is of noble birth. He will, in any event, be one victim snatched from prejudice.

Emile is an orphan. It makes no difference whether he has his father and mother. Charged with their duties, I inherit all their rights. He ought to honor his parents, but he ought to obey only me. That is my first or, rather, my sole condition.

I ought to add the following one, which is only a consequence of the other, that we never be taken from one another without our consent. This clause is essential, and I would even want the pupil and the governor to regard themselves as so inseparable that the lot of each in life is always a common object for them. As soon as they envisage from afar their separation, as soon as they foresee the moment which is going to make them strangers to one another, they are already strangers. Each sets up his own little separate system; and both, engrossed by the time when they will no longer be together, stay only reluctantly. The disciple regards the master only as the insignia and the plague of childhood; the master regards the disciple only as a heavy burden of which he is burning to be relieved. They agree in their longing for the moment when they will see themselves delivered from one another; and since there is never a true attachment between them, the one is not going to be very vigilant, the other not very docile.

But when they regard themselves as people who are going to spend their lives together, it is important for each to make himself loved by the other; and by that very fact they become dear to one another. The pupil does not blush at following in his childhood the friend he is going to have when he is grown. The governor takes an interest in concerns whose fruit he is going to harvest, and whatever merit he imparts to his pupil is an investment he makes for his old age.

This agreement made in advance assumes a satisfactory delivery, a child well formed, vigorous, and healthy. A father has no choice and ought to have no preferences in the family God gives him. All his children are equally his children; he owes to them all the same care and the same tenderness. Whether they are crippled or not, whether they are sickly or robust, each of them is a deposit of which he owes an account to the hand from which he receives it; and marriage is a contract made with nature as well as between the spouses.

But whoever imposes on himself a duty that nature has in no way imposed on him ought to be sure beforehand that he has the means of fulfilling it. Otherwise he makes himself accountable even for what he will have been unable to accomplish. He who takes charge of an infirm and valetudinary pupil changes his function from governor to male nurse. In caring for a useless life, he loses the time which he had intended to use for increasing its value. He exposes himself to facing an afflicted mother reproaching him one day for the death of a son whom he has preserved for her for a long time.

I would not take on a sickly and ill-constituted child, were he to live until eighty. I want no pupil always useless to himself and others, involved uniquely with preserving himself, whose body does damage to the education of his soul. What would I be doing in vainly lavishing my cares on him other than doubling society's loss and taking two men from it instead of one? Let another in my stead take charge of this invalid. I consent to it and approve his charity. But that is not my talent. I am not able to teach living to one who thinks of nothing but how to keep himself from dying.

The body must be vigorous in order to obey the soul. A good servant ought to be robust. I know that intemperance excites the passions; in the long run it also wears out the body. Mortifications and fasts often produce the same effect by a contrary cause. The weaker the body, the more it commands; the stronger it is, the more it obeys. All the sensual passions lodge in effeminated bodies. They become more inflamed to the extent that the body can satisfy them less.

A frail body weakens the soul. This is the origin of the empire of medicine, an art more pernicious to men than all the ills it claims to cure. As for me, I do not know of what illness the doctors cure us; but I do know that they give us quite fatal ones: cowardice, pusillanimity, credulousness, terror of death. If they cure the body, they kill courage. What difference does it make to us that they make cadavers walk? It is men we need, and none is seen leaving their hands.

Medicine is the fashion among us. It ought to be. It is the entertainment of idle people without occupation who, not knowing what to do with their time, pass it in preserving themselves. If they had had the bad luck to be born immortal, they would be the most miserable of beings. A life they would never fear losing would be worthless for them. These people need doctors who threaten them in order to cater to them and who give them every day the only pleasure of which they are susceptible—that of not being dead.

I have no intention of enlarging on the vanity of medicine here. My object is only to consider it from the moral point of view. I can, nevertheless, not prevent myself from remarking that men make, concerning its use, the same sophisms as they make concerning the quest for truth. They always assume that, in treating a sick person, one cures him and that, in seeking a truth, one finds it. They do not see that it is necessary to balance the advantage of a cure effected by the doctor against the death of a hundred sick persons killed by him, and the usefulness of a truth discovered against the harm done by the errors which become current at the same time. Science which instructs and medicine which cures are doubtless very good. But science which deceives and medicine which kills are bad. Learn, therefore, to distinguish them. That is the crux of the question. If we knew how to be ignorant of the truth, we would never be the dupes of lies; if we knew how not to want to be cured in spite of nature, we would never die at the doctor's hand. These two abstinences would be wise; one would clearly gain by submitting to them. I do not, therefore, dispute that medicine is useful to some men, but I say that it is fatal to humankind.

I will be told, as I am incessantly, that the mistakes are the doctor's, while medicine in itself is infallible. That is all very well. But then let it come without the doctor, for so long as they come together, there will be a hundred times more to fear from the errors of the artist than to hope from the help of the art.

This lying art, made more for the ills of the mind than for those of the body, is no more useful for the former than for the latter. It less cures us of our maladies than impresses us with terror of them. It less puts off death than makes it felt ahead of time. It wears out life more than prolongs it. And even if it did prolong life, this would still be at the expense of the species, since it takes us from society by the care it imposes on us and from our duties by the terror it inspires in us. It is the knowledge of dangers that makes us fear them; he who believed himself invulnerable would fear nothing. By dint of arming Achilles against peril, the poet takes from him the merit of valor; every other man in his place would have been an Achilles at the same price.

Do you want to find men of a true courage? Look for them in the places where there are no doctors, where they are ignorant of the consequences of illnesses, where they hardly think of death. Naturally man knows how to suffer with constancy and dies in peace. It is doctors with their prescriptions, philosophers with their precepts, priests with their exhortations, who debase his heart and make him unlearn how to die.[22]

Let me be given, then, a pupil who does not need all those people, or I shall refuse him. I do not want others to ruin my work. I want to raise him alone or not get involved. The wise Locke, who spent a part of his life in the study of medicine, strongly recommends never using drugs on children either as a precaution or for slight discomforts.[23] I shall go farther, and I declare that, never calling a doctor for myself, I shall never call one for my Emile, unless his life is in evident danger, for then the doctor can do him no worse than kill him.

I know quite well that the doctor will not fail to take advantage of this delay. If the child dies, the doctor will have been called too late; if the child recovers, it will be the doctor who saved him. So be it. Let the doctor triumph, but, above all, let him be called only *in extremis*.

For want of knowing how to cure himself, let the child know how to be sick. This art takes the place of the other and is often much more successful. It is nature's art. When an animal is sick, it suffers in silence and keeps quiet. Now one does not see more sickly animals than men. How many people whose disease would have spared them and whom time by itself would have cured have been killed by impatience, fear, anxiety, and, above all, remedies? I will be told that animals, living in a way that conforms more to nature, ought to be subject to fewer ills than we are. Well, their way of life is precisely the one I want to give to my pupil. He ought, therefore, to get the same advantage from it.

The only useful part of medicine is hygiene. And hygiene is itself less a science than a virtue. Temperance and work are the two true doctors of man. Work sharpens his appetite, and temperance prevents him from abusing it.

In order to know what regimen is the most useful for life and health, one need only know the way of life followed by the peoples who are healthiest, most robust, and longest-lived. If on the basis of general observations one does not find that the use of medicine gives men sounder health or a longer life, by the very fact that this art is not useful, it is harmful, since it employs time, men, and things at a total loss. It is not only that the time spent in preserving life, lost for use, must be subtracted from it, but that when this time is employed in tormenting ourselves, it is worse than nothing. It is a negative quantity, and, to calculate equitably, we must subtract an equal amount from the remainder of our time. A man who lives ten years without doctors lives more for himself and for others than he who lives thirty years as their victim. Having had the experience of both alternatives, I believe I have more right than anyone to draw this conclusion.

These are my reasons for wanting only a robust and healthy pupil and my principles for keeping him that way. I will not stop to prove at length the utility of manual labor and bodily exercise for reinforcing constitution and health. That is disputed by no one; the examples of the longest lives are almost all drawn from men who exercised most, who endured the most fatigue and work.* Neither shall I enter into lengthy detail about the efforts I shall take to achieve this single objective. It will be seen that they enter so necessarily into my practice that it suffices to grasp their spirit not to need further explanation.

With life there begin needs. For the newly born a nurse is required. If the mother consents to perform her duty, very well. She will be given written instructions, for this advantage has its counterpoise and keeps the governor at something more of a distance from his pupil. But it is to be believed that the child's interest and esteem for the one to whom she is willing to confide so dear a deposit will make the mother attentive to the master's opinion. And whatever she is willing to do, one can be sure will be done better by her than anyone else. If we have to have a stranger for a nurse, let us begin by choosing her well.

One of the miseries of rich people is to be deceived in everything. If they judge men poorly, need one be surprised? It is riches which corrupt them, and by a just return they are the first to feel the defect of the only instrument known to them. Everything is done badly in their houses, except what they do themselves; and they almost never do anything there. Is it a question of looking for a nurse? They let the obstetrician choose her. What is the result of that? That the best nurse is always the one who paid him best. I shall not, hence, go consult an obstetrician about Emile's nurse. I shall take care to choose her myself. I will not perhaps reason so fluently about the issue as a surgeon, but I will certainly be in better faith, and my zeal will deceive me less than his avarice.

This choice is not such a great mystery. The rules for it are known. But I do not know whether one ought not to pay a bit more attention to the age of the milk as well as to its quality. New milk is completely serous. It must be almost a laxative in order to purge the remains of the meconium, thickened in the intestines of the child who has just been

---

* Here is an example drawn from English papers which provides so many reflections concerning my subject that I cannot refrain from reporting it:

> An individual named Patrick O'Neil, born in 1647, has just remarried for the seventh time in 1760. He served in the Dragoons in the seventeenth year of the reign of Charles II and in different regiments until his discharge in 1740. He took part in all the campaigns of King William and the Duke of Marlborough. This man has never drunk anything but ordinary beer. He has always fed on vegetables and never eaten meat except at some meals he gave for his family. His practice has always been to rise and go to bed with the sun unless his duties prevented him from doing so. He is at present in his one hundred and thirteenth year, of good understanding, in good health, and walking without a cane. In spite of his great age, he does not remain idle for a single minute, and every Sunday he goes to his parish accompanied by his children, grandchildren, and great-grandchildren.

born. Little by little the milk gains consistency and provides a solider food for the child who has become stronger to digest it. It is surely not for nothing that in the females of every species nature changes the milk's consistency according to the age of the nursling.

Therefore, a nurse who has newly given birth would be required for a newly born child. This has its complications, I know. But as soon as one leaves the natural order, to do anything well has its complications. The only easy expedient is to do it badly; that is, thus, the expedient men choose.

What is needed is a nurse as healthy of heart as of body. Imbalance of the passions, like that of the humors, can cause the milk to deteriorate. Moreover, to restrict the question to the physical alone is to see only half of the object. The milk can be good, and the nurse bad. A good character is as essential as a good constitution. If one takes a vicious woman, I do not say that one's nursling will contract her vices, but I do say he will suffer as a result of them. Does she not, along with her milk, owe him care which requires zeal, patience, gentleness, cleanliness? If she is a glutton, an intemperate, she will soon have spoiled her milk. If she is negligent or easily angered, what will become of a poor unfortunate who is at her mercy and who can neither defend himself nor complain? Never in anything whatsoever are the wicked good for anything good.

The choice of the nurse is all the more important because her nursling is going to have no other governess than her, just as he is going to have no other preceptor than his governor. This was the practice of the ancients, less reasoners and wiser than we are. After having nursed female children, nurses never left them. That is why in their theater plays most of the confidants are nurses. It is impossible that a child who passes successively through so many different hands ever be well raised. At every change he makes secret comparisons which always tend to diminish his esteem for those who govern him and consequently their authority over him. If he once comes to the thought that there are adults who are no more possessed of reason than are children, all the authority of age is lost, and the education is a failure. A child ought to know no other superiors than his father and his mother or, in default of them, his nurse and his governor; even one of the two is already too many. But this division is inevitable, and all that one can do to remedy it is to make sure that the persons of the two sexes who govern him are in such perfect agreement concerning him that the two are only one as far as he is concerned.

The nurse must live a bit more comfortably, eat a little more substantial food, but not change her manner of living entirely, for a sudden and total change, even from bad to better, is always dangerous for the health. And since her ordinary diet left or rendered her healthy and well constituted, what is the good of making her change it?

Peasant women eat less meat and more vegetables than do city women. This vegetable diet appears to be more beneficial than injurious to them and their children. When they have bourgeois nurslings, they are given boiled beef in the conviction that soup and meat both produce better chyle in them and result in more milk. I by no means share this sentiment, and I am supported by experience which teaches that children thus nursed are more subject to colic and worms than are others.

This is hardly surprising, since animal substance in a state of putrefaction is crawling with worms, which does not happen in like manner with vegetable substance. Milk, although developed in the body of the animal, is a vegetable substance.* Its analysis demonstrates it. It easily turns into acid; and, far from giving any vestige of volatile alkali, as do animal substances, it gives, as do plants, a neutral essence of salt.

The milk of herbivorous females is sweeter and healthier than that of carnivores. Formed from a substance homogeneous with its own, it preserves its nature better and becomes less subject to putrefaction. If one looks to quantity, everyone knows that the farinaceous foods produce more blood than does meat; they ought, therefore, to make more milk, too. I cannot believe that a child who was not weaned too soon, or who was weaned only on vegetable foods and whose nurse also lived only on vegetables, would ever be subject to worms.

It is possible that vegetable foods produce milk that sours more quickly. But I am far from regarding sour milk as an unhealthy food. Whole peoples who have no other kind are quite well off, and all these devices for absorbing acids appear to me to be pure charlatanry. There are constitutions for which milk is just not suitable, and then no absorbent can make it bearable for them; the others bear it without absorbents. Separated or curdled milk is feared; that is foolish, since it is known that milk always curdles in the stomach. It is thus that it becomes a food solid enough to nourish children and animal babies. If it did not curdle at all, it would just go through; it would not nourish them.† One can very well cut milk in countless ways, use countless absorbents, but whoever eats milk digests cheese. This is without exception. The stomach is so well made for curdling milk that it is with a calf's stomach that rennet is made.

I think, then, that instead of changing the ordinary food of nurses, it suffices to give them the same kind of food but in more abundant quantity and better quality. It is not due to the nature of the foods that the vegetarian diet constipates. It is only their seasoning that makes them unhealthy. Reform the rules of your kitchen. Have neither brown sauce nor grease. Put neither butter nor salt nor dairy products on the fire. Let your vegetables, cooked in water, be seasoned only on coming hot to the table. Vegetarian food, far from constipating the nurse, will provide her with milk in abundance and of better quality.‡ Is it possible

---

* Women eat bread, vegetables, dairy produce. The females of dogs and cats eat them, too. Even she-wolves graze. These are the sources of vegetable juices for their milk. There remains to be examined the milk of species which can eat absolutely only flesh, if there are any such, which I doubt.

† Although the juices which nourish us are in liquid form, they have to be pressed out of solid foods. A man at work who lived only on broth would very quickly waste away. He would sustain himself much better with milk because it curdles.

‡ Those who want to discuss at greater length the advantages and the disadvantages of the Pythagorean diet can consult the treatises which Dr. Cocchi and his adversary, Dr. Bianchi, wrote on this important subject.[21]

that the vegetable diet being recognized as best for the child, the animal diet is the best for the nurse? There is something contradictory in that.

It is especially in the first years of life that the air acts on the constitution of children. It penetrates a delicate and soft skin by all the pores. It has a powerful effect on these newborn bodies; it makes on them impressions which are never effaced. I would not, hence, be of the opinion that one should take a peasant woman from her village to close her up in a room in the city and make her nurse the child at home. I prefer his going to breathe the good air of the country to her breathing the bad air of the city. He will assume the station of his new mother; he will live in her rustic house, and his governor will follow him there. The reader will well remember that this governor is not a hired man; he is the father's friend. "But if this friend is not to be found, if this move is not easy, if nothing of what you advise is feasible, what is to be done instead?" I will be asked. . . . I have already told you: what you are doing. One needs no advice for that.

Men are made not to be crowded into anthills but to be dispersed over the earth which they should cultivate. The more they come together, the more they are corrupted. The infirmities of the body, as well as the vices of the soul, are the unfailing effect of this overcrowding. Man is, of all the animals, the one who can least live in herds. Men crammed together like sheep would all perish in a very short time. Man's breath is deadly to his kind. This is no less true in the literal sense than the figurative.

Cities are the abyss of the human species. At the end of a few generations the races perish or degenerate. They must be renewed, and it is always the country which provides for this renewal. Send your children, then, to renew themselves, as it were, and to regain in the midst of the fields the vigor that is lost in the unhealthy air of overpopulated places. Pregnant women who are in the country rush to return to the city for their confinement. They ought to do exactly the opposite, particularly those who want to nurse their children. They would have less to regret than they think; and in an abode more natural to the species, the pleasures connected with the duties of nature would soon efface the taste for the pleasures not related to those duties.

At first, after the confinement, the child is washed with some warm water in which wine is ordinarily mixed. This addition of wine hardly appears to me to be necessary. Since nature produces nothing fermented, it is not to be believed that the use of an artificial liquor is important for the life of its creatures.

For the same reason this precaution of warming the water is not indispensable either; and, in fact, multitudes of peoples wash newborn children in rivers or the sea without further ado. But ours, softened before birth by the softness of the fathers and the mothers, bring with them, on coming into the world, an already spoiled constitution that must not be exposed at the beginning to all the trials which would restore it. It is only by degrees that our children can be led back to their primitive vigor. Begin, then, at first by following the established practice, and deviate from it only little by little. Wash the children often; their dirtiness proves the need for it; when one only wipes them, one lacerates them. But to the extent that they regain strength, diminish by degrees the warmth of the water, until at the end you wash them summer and winter in cold and even chilly water. Since in order not to expose them it is important that this diminution be slow, successive, and imperceptible, a thermometer can be used to measure it exactly.

This practice of bathing, once established, ought never again be interrupted, and it is important to keep to it for the whole of life. I am considering it not only from the point of view of cleanliness and present health; but I also see it as a salutary precaution for making the texture of the fibers more flexible and able to adapt to various degrees of heat and cold without effort and without risk. For that purpose I would want him in growing up to become accustomed little by little to bathing sometimes in hot water at all bearable degrees and often in cold water at all possible degrees. Thus, after being habituated to bear the various temperatures of water which, being a denser fluid, touches us at more points and affects us more, one would become almost insensitive to the various temperatures of the air.

From the moment that the child breathes on leaving its envelope, do not suffer his being given other envelopes which keep him more restricted: no caps, no belts, no swaddling; loose and large diapers which leave all his limbs free and are neither so heavy as to impede his movements nor so hot as to prevent him from feeling the impressions of the air.* Put him in a large, well-padded cradle,† where he can move at ease and without danger. When he begins to grow stronger, let him crawl around the room. Let him spread out, stretch his little limbs. You will see them gaining strength day by day. Compare him with a well-swaddled child of the same age; you will be surprised at the difference in their progress.‡

---

* Children in cities are suffocated by dint of being kept closed up and dressed. Those who govern them have yet to learn that cold air, far from doing children harm, strengthens them and that hot air weakens them and that hot air weakens them, gives them fever, and kills them.

† I say a "cradle" to use a current word, for want of another; for I am, moreover, persuaded that it is never necessary to rock children, and that this practice is often pernicious for them.

‡ The ancient Peruvians left the arms of the children free in a very large swaddling band. When they took the children out, they set them free in a hole made in the ground and lined with linen; into it they lowered the children up to the waist. In this way the children had their arms free, and they could move their heads and bend their bodies at will without falling and without getting hurt. As soon as they could take a step, the breast was offered to them from a little farther away, as a lure to oblige them to walk. Little Negroes are sometimes in a far more fatiguing position for sucking. They embrace one of their mother's hips with their knees and their feet, and they hold on so tightly that they can support themselves there without aid of the mother's arms. They attach themselves to the breast with their hands, and they suck continuously without moving from their place and without falling, in spite of the different movements of the mother, who during this time works as usual. These children begin to walk from the second month or, rather, to drag themselves on their hands and knees. This exercise gives them a facility for later running in this position almost as fast as if they were on their feet. [Buffon, *Histoire Naturelle,* Vol. IV, in-12, p. 192.]

To these examples M. de Buffon could have added that of England, where the extravagant and barbarous practice of swaddling is being done away with day by day. See also la Loubère, *Voyage de Siam,* Mr. le Beau, *Voyage du Canada,* etc. I could fill twenty pages with citations, if I needed to confirm this by facts.[25]

BOOK I

One must expect strong opposition on the part of the nurses, who are less bothered by a well-garroted child than by one who has to be constantly watched. Moreover, his dirtiness becomes more easily sensed in an open garment; he must be cleaned more often. Finally, in certain countries custom is an argument that one will never refute to the satisfaction of the people no matter what their station.

Do not reason with nurses. Give orders, see that they are followed, and spare no effort to make things easy for the nurses in carrying out the care that you have prescribed. Why would you not share that care? In ordinary nursing where one only looks to the physical side, provided that the child lives and does not waste away the rest has little importance. But here, where the education begins with life, the child is at birth already a disciple, not of the governor, but of nature. The governor only studies under this first master and prevents its care from being opposed. He watches over the nursling, observes him, follows him. He vigilantly spies out the first glimmer of his weak understanding as the Muslims at the approach of the new moon spy out the instant of its rise.

We are born capable of learning but able to do nothing, knowing nothing. The soul, enchained in imperfect and half-formed organs, does not even have the sentiment of its own existence. The movements and the cries of the child who has just been born are purely mechanical effects, devoid of knowledge and of will.

Let us suppose that a child had at his birth the stature and the strength of a grown man, that he emerged, so to speak, fully armed from his mother's womb as did Pallas from the brain of Jupiter. This man-child would be a perfect imbecile, an automaton, an immobile and almost insensible statue. He would see nothing, hear nothing, know no one, would not be able to turn his eyes toward what he needed to see. Not only would he perceive no object outside of himself, he would not even relate any object to the sense organ which made him perceive it: the colors would not be in his eyes; the sounds would not be in his ears; the bodies he touched would not be on his body; he would not even know that he had one. The contact of his hands would be in his brain; all his sensations would come together in a single point; he would exist only in the common *sensorium*; he would have only a single idea, that is, of the *I* to which he would relate all his sensations; and this idea or, rather, this sentiment would be the only thing that he would have beyond what an ordinary baby has.

Nor would this man formed all of a sudden be able to stand on his feet; he would need a good deal of time to learn to maintain himself in equilibrium on them. Perhaps he would not even make the attempt, and you would see this big body, strong and robust, staying in place like a stone, or crawling and dragging himself along like a newborn puppy.

He would feel the discomfort of the needs without knowing them and without imagining any means of providing for them. There is no immediate communication between the muscles of the stomach and those of the arms and legs which, even if he were surrounded by food, would cause him to make a step to approach it or stretch out his hand to grasp it. And since his body would have had its growth, his limbs would be entirely developed, and consequently he would not have the restlessness and constant movement of children. He could die of hunger before stirring to seek subsistence. However little one may have reflected on the order and the progress of our knowledge, it cannot be denied that such was pretty nearly the primitive state of ignorance and stupidity natural to man before he learned anything from experience or his fellows.

Hence we know, or can know, the first point from which each of us starts in order to get to the common level of understanding. But who knows the other limit? Each advances more or less according to his genius, his taste, his needs, his talents, his zeal, and the occasions he has to devote himself to them. I know of no philosopher who has yet been so bold as to say: this is the limit of what man can attain and beyond which he cannot go. We do not know what our nature permits us to be. None of us has measured the distance which can exist between one man and another. What soul is so base that he has never been warmed by this idea and does not sometimes in his pride say to himself: "How many men I have already surpassed! How many I can still reach! Why should my equal go farther than I?"

I repeat: the education of man begins at his birth; before speaking, before understanding, he is already learning. Experience anticipates lessons. The moment he knows his nurse, he has already acquired a great deal. One would be surprised at the knowledge of the coarsest man if one followed his progress from the moment of his birth to where he is now. If one divided all of human science into two parts—the one common to all men, the other particular to the learned—the latter would be quite small in comparison with the former. But we are hardly aware of what is generally attained, because it is attained without thought and even before the age of reason; because, moreover, learning is noticed only by its differences, and as in algebraic equations, common quantities count for nothing.

Even animals acquire much. They have senses; they have to learn to make use of them. They have needs; they have to learn to provide for them. They have to learn how to eat, to walk, to fly. The quadrupeds who stand on their legs from birth do not on that account know how to walk. One sees from their first steps that these are unsure attempts. Canaries escaped from their cages do not know how to fly because they have never flown. Everything is learning for animate and sensitive beings. If plants had progressive movement, they would have to have senses and to acquire knowledge. Otherwise, the species would soon perish.

Children's first sensations are purely affective; they perceive only pleasure and pain. Able neither to walk nor to grasp, they need a great deal of time to come little by little into possession of the representative sensations which show them objects outside of themselves. But, while waiting for these objects to gain extension, to move, so to speak, farther away from their eyes, to take on dimensions and shapes for them, the recurrence of the affective sensations begins to submit them to the empire of habit. One sees their eyes constantly turning toward the light and, if it comes to them from the side, imperceptibly taking that direction, so that we ought to take care to set them facing the light, lest they become cross-eyed or accustomed to looking askance. They must also early get habituated to darkness. Otherwise, they cry and scream as soon as they are in obscurity. Food and sleep too exactly measured become necessary for them at the end of the same spans of time, and soon desire no longer comes from need but from habit, or, rather, habit adds a new need to that of nature. That is what must be prevented.

The only habit that a child should be allowed is to contract none. Do not carry him on one arm more than the other; do not accustom him to give one hand rather than the other, to use one more than the other, to want to eat, sleep, or be active at the same hours, to be unable to remain alone night or day. Prepare from afar the reign of his freedom and the use of his forces by leaving natural habit to his body, by putting him in the condition always to be master of himself and in all things to do his will, as soon as he has one.

From the moment that the child begins to distinguish objects, it is important that there be selectivity in those one shows him. Naturally all new objects interest man. He feels so weak that he fears everything he does not know. The habit of seeing new objects without being affected by them destroys this fear. Children raised in clean houses where no spiders are tolerated are afraid of spiders, and this fear often stays with them when grown. I have never seen a peasant, man, woman, or child, afraid of spiders.

Why, then, should a child's education not begin before he speaks and understands, since the very choice of objects presented to him is fit to make him timid or courageous? I want him habituated to seeing new objects, ugly, disgusting, peculiar animals, but little by little, from afar, until he is accustomed to them, and, by dint of seeing them handled by others, he finally handles them himself. If during his childhood he has without fright seen toads, snakes, crayfish, he will, when grown, without disgust see any animal whatsoever. There are no longer frightful objects for whoever sees such things every day.

All children are afraid of masks. I begin by showing Emile a mask with a pleasant face. Next someone in his presence puts this mask over his face. I start to laugh; everybody laughs; and the child laughs like the others. Little by little I accustom him to less pleasant masks and finally to hideous faces. If I have arranged my gradation well, far from being frightened by the last mask, he will laugh at it as at the first. After that I no longer fear that he can be frightened by masks.

When, during the farewell of Andromache and Hector, the little Astyanax, frightened by the plume waving on his father's helmet, fails to recognize him, flings himself crying on his nurse's bosom, and extracts from his mother a smile mingled with tears, what must be done to cure this fright? Precisely what Hector does: put the helmet on the ground, and then caress the child. In a more tranquil moment one would not stop at that. One would approach the helmet, play with the feathers, make the child handle them. Finally, the nurse would take the helmet and, laughing, put it on her own head—if, that is, a woman's hand dare touch the arms of Hector.[26]

Is one trying to train Emile to the sound of a firearm? At first I set off a cap in a pistol. The sudden and momentary flash, that sort of lightning, delights him. I repeat the same thing with more powder. Little by little I put a small charge without a wad into the pistol; then a bigger one. Finally I accustom him to rifle shots, to grapeshot explosions, to canons, to the most terrible detonations.

I have noticed that children are rarely afraid of thunder, unless the claps are terrible and really wound the organ of hearing. Otherwise, this fear comes to them only when they have learned that thunder sometimes wounds or kills. When reason begins to frighten them, make habit reassure them. With a slow and carefully arranged gradation man and child are made intrepid in everything.

At the beginning of life when memory and imagination are still inactive, the child is attentive only to what affects his senses at the moment. Since his sensations are the first materials of his knowledge, to present them to him in an appropriate order is to prepare his memory to provide them one day to his understanding in the same order. But inasmuch as he is attentive only to his sensations, it suffices at first to show him quite distinctly the connection of these same sensations with the objects which cause them. He wants to touch everything, handle everything. Do not oppose yourself to this restlessness. It is suggestive to him of a very necessary apprenticeship; it is thus that he learns to feel the hotness, the coldness, the hardness, the softness, the heaviness, the lightness, of bodies, and to judge their size, their shape, and all their sensible qualities by looking, feeling,* listening, particularly by comparing sight to touch, by estimating with the eye the sensation that they would make on his finger.

It is only by movement that we learn that there are things which are not us, and it is only by our own movement that we acquire the idea of extension. It is because the child does not have this idea that, without making any distinction, he reaches out his hand to grasp the object which touches him or the object which is at a hundred paces from him. This effort he makes appears to you a sign of the desire to dominate, an order he gives to the object to approach or to you to bring it to him; but that is not at all so. It is only that the same objects which he sees at first in his brain, then in his eyes, he now sees at the end of his arms and can imagine no extension other than that which he can reach. Take care then to walk him often, to transport him from one place to another, to make him feel change of place, in order to teach him to judge distances. When he begins to know them, then the method must be changed, and he must be carried as you please and not as he pleases; for as soon as he is no longer abused by sense, the cause of his effort changes. This change is remarkable and requires explanation.

The discomfort of the needs is expressed by signs when another's help is necessary to provide for them. This is the source of children's screams. They cry a lot; such ought to be the case. Since all their

---

* Smell is of all the senses the one that develops the latest in children. Up to the age of two or three years it does not appear that they are sensitive to either good or bad smells. They have in this respect the indifference or, rather, the insensibility that is observed in many animals.

sensations are affective, when they are pleasant, children enjoy them in silence. When they are painful, children say so in their language and ask for relief. Now so long as they are awake, they are almost unable to remain in an indifferent state. They sleep or are affected.

All our languages are works of art. Whether there was a language natural and common to all men has long been a subject of research. Doubtless there is such a language, and it is the one children speak before knowing how to speak. This language is not articulate, but it is accented, sonorous, intelligible. The habit of our languages has made us neglect that language to the point of forgetting it completely. Let us study children, and we shall soon relearn it with them. Nurses are our masters in this language. They understand everything their nurslings say; they respond to them; they have quite consistent dialogues with them; and, although they pronounce words, these words are perfectly useless; it is not the sense of the word that children understand but the accent which accompanies it.

To the language of the voice is joined that of gesture, no less energetic. This gesture is not in children's weak hands; it is on their visages. It is surprising how much expression these ill-formed faces already have. Their features change from one instant to the next with an inconceivable rapidity. You see a smile, desire, fright come into being and pass away like so many flashes of lightning. Each time you believe you are seeing a different visage. Their facial muscles are certainly more mobile than ours. On the other hand, their dull eyes say almost nothing. Such should be the character of the signs they give at an age when one has only bodily needs. The expression of the sensations is in grimaces; the expression of sentiments is in glances.

Since the first condition of man is want and weakness, his first voices are complaint and tears. The child feels his needs and cannot satisfy them. He implores another's help by screams. If he is hungry or thirsty, he cries; if he is too cold or too hot, he cries; if he needs to move and is kept at rest, he cries; if he wants to sleep and is stirred, he cries. The less his mode of being is in his control, the more frequently he asks for it to be changed. He has only one language because he has, so to speak, only one kind of discomfort. In the imperfection of his organs he does not distinguish their diverse impressions; all ills form for him only one sensation of pain.

From these tears that we might think so little worthy of attention is born man's first relation to all that surrounds him; here is formed the first link in that long chain of which the social order is formed.

When the child cries, he is uncomfortable; he has some need which he does not know how to satisfy. One examines, one seeks this need, one finds it, one provides for it. When one does not find it or when one cannot provide for it, the tears continue. One is bothered by them; one caresses the child to make him keep quiet, one rocks him, one sings to him to make him go to sleep. If he persists, one gets impatient, one threatens him; brutal nurses sometimes strike him. These are strange lessons for his entrance in life.

I shall never forget having seen one of these difficult cryers thus struck by his nurse. He immediately kept quiet. I believed he was intimidated. I said to myself, "This will be a servile soul from which one will get nothing except by severity." I was mistaken. The unfortunate was suffocating with anger; he had lost his breath; I saw him become violet. A moment after came sharp screams; all the signs of the resentment, fury, and despair of this age were in his accents. I feared he would expire in this agitation. If I had doubted that the sentiment of the just and the unjust were innate in the heart of man, this example alone would have convinced me. I am sure that a live ember fallen by chance on this child's hand would have made less of an impression than this blow, rather light but given in the manifest intention of offending him.

This disposition of children to fury, spite, and anger requires extreme attentiveness. Boerhaave [27] thinks that their illnesses belong for the most part to the convulsive class; since their heads are proportionally larger and their nerves more extended than in adults, the nervous system is more susceptible to irritation. Keep away from them with the greatest care domestics who provoke, irritate, or annoy them; they are a hundred times more dangerous, more deadly for children than the injuries of the air and the seasons. As long as children find resistance only in things and never in wills, they will become neither rebellious nor irascible and will preserve their health better. Here is one of the reasons why the children of the people, freer, more independent, are generally less infirm, less delicate, more robust than those who are allegedly better brought up by being endlessly thwarted. But it must always be borne in mind that there is quite a difference between obeying children and not thwarting them.

The first tears of children are prayers. If one is not careful, they soon become orders. Children begin by getting themselves assisted; they end by getting themselves served. Thus, from their own weakness, which is in the first place the source of the feeling of their dependence, is subsequently born the idea of empire and domination. But since this idea is excited less by their needs than by our services, at this point moral effects whose immediate cause is not in nature begin to make their appearance; and one sees already why it is important from the earliest age to disentangle the secret intention which dictates the gesture or the scream.

When the child stretches out his hand without saying anything, he believes he will reach the object because he does not estimate the distance. He is mistaken. But when he complains and screams in reaching out his hand, he is no longer deceived as to the distance; he is ordering the object to approach or you to bring it to him. In the first case carry him to the object slowly and with small steps. In the second act as though you do not even hear him. The more he screams, the less you should listen to him. It is important to accustom him early not to give orders either to men, for he is not their master, or to things, for they do not hear him. Thus, when a child desires something that he sees and one wants to give it to him, it is better to carry the child to the object than to bring the object to the child. He draws from this practice a conclusion appropriate to his age, and there is no other means to suggest it to him.

BOOK I

The Abbé de Saint-Pierre [28] called men big children. One could, reciprocally, call children little men. These propositions have their truth as sententious phrases; as principles they need clarification. But when Hobbes called the wicked man a robust child,[29] he said something absolutely contradictory. All wickedness comes from weakness. The child is wicked only because he is weak. Make him strong; he will be good. He who could do everything would never do harm. Of all the attributes of the all-powerful divinity, goodness is the one without which one can least conceive it. All peoples who have recognized two principles have always regarded the bad as inferior to the good; if they had done otherwise, they would have been supposing something absurd. See hereafter the Profession of Faith of the Savoyard Vicar.[30]

Reason alone teaches us to know good and bad. Conscience, which makes us love the former and hate the latter, although independent of reason, cannot therefore be developed without it. Before the age of reason we do good and bad without knowing it, and there is no morality in our actions, although there sometimes is in the sentiment of other's actions which have a relation to us. A child wants to upset everything he sees; he smashes, breaks everything he can reach. He grabs a bird as he would grab a stone, and he strangles it without knowing what he does.

Why is that? In the first place, philosophy will explain it as being a result of natural vices: pride, the spirit of domination, amour-propre, the wickedness of man; and the feeling of his weakness, philosophy could add, makes the child avid to perform acts of strength and to prove his own power to himself. But see this old man, infirm and broken, led back by the circle of human life to the weakness of childhood. Not only does he remain immobile and peaceful, he also wants everything around him to remain that way. The least change troubles and disturbs him. He would want to see a universal calm reign. How would the same impotence joined to the same passions produce such different effects in the two ages if their primary cause were not changed? And where can one look for this diversity of causes if not in the respective physical condition of the two individuals? The active principle common to both is developing in the one and being extinguished in the other; the one is being formed, the other destroyed; the one is tending toward life, the other toward death. The failing activity is concentrated in the old man's heart; in that of the child it is superabundant and extends outward; he senses within himself, so to speak, enough life to animate everything surrounding him. That he do or undo is a matter of no importance; it suffices that he change the condition of things, and every change is an action. If he seems to have more of an inclination to destroy, it is not from wickedness but because the action which gives shape is always slow and the action which destroys, being more rapid, fits his vivacity better.

At the same time that the Author of nature gives children this active principle, by allowing them little strength to indulge it, He takes care that it do little harm. But as soon as they can consider the people who surround them as instruments depending on them to be set in motion, they make use of those people to follow their inclination and to supplement their own weakness. That is how they become difficult, tyrannical, imperious, wicked, unmanageable—a development which does not come from a natural spirit of domination but which rather gives one to them, for it does not require long experience to sense how pleasant it is to act with the hands of others and to need only to stir one's tongue to make the universe move.

In growing, one gains strength, becomes less restless, less fidgety, withdraws more into oneself. Soul and body find, so to speak, an equilibrium, and nature asks no more of us than the movement necessary to our preservation. But the desire to command is not extinguished with the need that gave birth to it. Dominion awakens and flatters *amour-propre*, and habit strengthens it. Thus, whim [31] succeeds need; thus, prejudices and opinion take their first roots.

Once we know the principle, we see clearly the point where one leaves the path of nature. Let us see what must be done to stay on it.

Far from having superfluous strength, children do not even have enough for everything nature asks of them. One must, therefore, let them have the use of all the strength nature gives them—a strength they could not know how to abuse. First maxim.

One must aid them and supplement what is lacking to them, whether in intelligence or strength, in all that is connected with physical need. Second maxim.

One must, in the help one gives them, limit oneself solely to the really useful, without granting anything to whim or to desire without reason; for whim, inasmuch as it does not come from nature, will not torment them if it has not been induced in them. Third maxim.

One must study their language and their signs with care in order that, at an age at which they do not know how to dissimulate, one can distinguish in their desires what comes immediately from nature and what comes from opinion. Fourth maxim.

The spirit of these rules is to accord children more true freedom and less dominion, to let them do more by themselves and to exact less from others. Thus, accustomed early to limiting their desires to their strength, they will feel little the privation of what is not going to be in their power.

So we have another very important reason for leaving children's bodies and limbs absolutely free, with the sole precaution of keeping them away from the danger of falls and putting all that can wound them out of their reach.

Unfailingly, a child whose body and arms are free will cry less than a child bound in swaddling. The one who knows only the physical needs cries only when he suffers. And that is a very great advantage, for then one knows exactly when he needs help and should not delay a moment to give it to him if it is possible. But if you cannot relieve him, keep quiet without humoring him in order to pacify him. Your caresses will not cure his colic; however, he will remember what must be done to be humored, and if he once knows how to make you take care of him at his will, he has become your master. All is lost.

Less hindered in their movements, children will cry less; less importuned by their tears, one will torment oneself less to make them keep quiet; threatened or humored less often, they will be less fearful or less stubborn and will stay better in their natural state. It is less in letting children cry than in rushing to pacify them that they get hernias, and my proof is that the most neglected children are a great deal less subject to hernias than are others. I am very far from wanting them to be neglected on that account. On the contrary, it is important to be beforehand with them and not let oneself be informed of their needs by their cries. But no more do I want that the care given them be misunderstood. Why would they stint tears once they see that their tears are good for so many things? Schooled in the value put on their silence, they are quite careful not to be prodigal with it. They finally put such a price on it that it can no longer be paid, and it is then that, by dint of crying unsuccessfully, they exert themselves, get exhausted, and die.

The lengthy tears of a child who is neither bound nor sick, who is allowed to want for nothing, are only tears of habit and obstinacy. They are the work not of nature but of the nurse who, not knowing how to endure the importunity, multiplies it without dreaming that in making the child keep quiet today one is encouraging him to cry more tomorrow.

The only means to cure or prevent this habit is not to pay any attention to it. No one likes to make a useless effort, not even children. They are obstinate in their attempts; but if you are more constant than they are stubborn, they get weary and never return to crying again. It is thus that they are spared tears and are accustomed to shed them only when pain forces them to do so.

Besides, when they cry from whim or obstinacy, a sure means of preventing them from continuing is to distract them by some pleasant and striking object which makes them forget that they wanted to cry. Most nurses excel in this art; and, well controlled, it is very useful. But it is of the most extreme importance that the child not perceive the intention to distract him, and that he enjoy himself without believing that one is thinking of him. Now this is where all nurses are maladroit.[32]

All children are weaned too soon. The time when they should be weaned is indicated by teething, and teething is commonly difficult and painful. With a machine-like instinct the child then regularly brings to his mouth whatever he has in his hand in order to chew on it. It is thought that one facilitates the operation by giving him some hard bodies, such as ivory or a bolt, as a teething ring. I believe this is a mistake. These hard bodies applied to the gums, far from softening them, make them callous, harden them, and prepare a more difficult and more painful cutting. Let us always take instinct as our example. Puppies are seen to exercise their growing teeth not on pebbles, iron, bones, but on wood, leather, rags, soft matter which give and in which the tooth leaves an imprint.

One no longer knows how to be simple in anything, not even with children: rattles of silver and gold, and coral, cut crystal glasses, teething rings of every price and kind. What useless and pernicious affectations! Nothing of all that. No rattles, no teething rings; little branches of trees with their fruit and their leaves, a poppy flower in which one can hear the seeds striking one another, a licorice stick that he can suck and chew, will give him as much enjoyment as these magnificent gewgaws and will not have the disadvantage of accustoming him to luxury from his birth.

It has been recognized that pap is not very healthy food. Cooked milk and raw meal produce a lot of indigestible matter and ill suit our stomachs. In pap the meal is cooked less than in bread, and what is more it has not fermented. Bread soup and cream of rice appear preferable to me. If one absolutely wants to make pap, it is proper to roast the meal a bit beforehand. In my country they make a quite agreeable and healthy porridge from meal thus toasted. Meat broth and soup are also mediocre nutriments which ought to be used only as little as possible. It is important for children to get accustomed to chew in the first place. This is the true means of facilitating teething, and when they begin to swallow, the salivary juices mixed with the food facilitate its digestion.

I would, then, first make them chew on dry fruits and on crusts. I would give them little sticks of hard bread or crackers similar to the bread in Piedmont, which they call there *grisse,* to play with. By dint of softening this bread in their mouths, they would finally swallow a bit of it, their teeth would be cut, and they would be weaned almost before one noticed it. Peasants ordinarily have quite good stomachs, and they are weaned with no more ado than that.

Children hear speech from their birth. They are spoken to not only before they understand what is said to them, but before they can reproduce the voices they hear. Their still dull organs lend themselves only little by little to imitation of the sounds dictated to them, and it is not even sure that these sounds at first carry to their ear as distinctly as to ours. I do not disapprove of the nurse's entertaining the child with songs and very gay and varied accents. But I do disapprove of her making him constantly giddy with a multitude of useless words of which he understands nothing other than the tone she gives them. I would want the first articulations which he is made to hear to be rare, easy, distinct, often repeated, and that the words they express relate only to objects of the senses which can in the first place be shown to the child. The unfortunate facility we have for dazzling people with words we do not understand begins earlier than is thought. The schoolboy listens in class to the verbiage of his teacher as he listened in swaddling clothes to the prattle of his nurse. It seems to me that if he were raised to understand none of it, this instruction would be most useful.

When one wants to take up the question of the formation of language and of children's first speech, reflections crowd upon one. Whatever one does, children will always learn to talk in the same way, and all the philosophic speculations are of the greatest uselessness here.

In the first place, they have, so to speak, a grammar of their age, whose syntax has rules more general than ours; and if careful attention were paid, one would be surprised by the exactness with which they follow certain analogies, very faulty ones, if you please, but very regular and shocking only by their harshness or because usage does not admit them. I just heard a poor child well scolded by his father for having said to him: "Mon pere, irai-je-t-y?" Now, one sees that this child followed the analogy better than do our grammarians. For since one said "Vas-y" to him, why should he not say "Irai-je-t-y?" Note, moreover, with what address he avoided the hiatus of "Irai-je-y?" or "Y irai-je?" Is it the poor child's fault if we have inopportunely removed the determining adverb *y* from the sentence because we did not know what to do with it? It is insupportable pedantry and a most superfluous care to concentrate on correcting children for all these little mistakes in usage which they never with time fail to correct by themselves. Always speak correctly before them, arrange that they enjoy themselves with no one as much as with you, and be sure that imperceptibly their language will be purified on the model of yours without your ever having chided them.

But an abuse of an entirely different importance and one no less easy to prevent is when one is in too much of a hurry to make them talk, as if one were afraid that they will not learn to talk by themselves. This indiscriminate fussing produces an effect directly contrary to the one sought. As a result, they talk later, more confusedly; the extreme attention given to everything they say spares them having to articulate well; and since they hardly deign to open their mouths, many of them preserve as a consequence for their whole lives faulty pronunciation and indistinct speech which makes them almost unintelligible.

I have lived a great deal among peasants and have never heard one— either man or woman, girl or boy—with a burr.[33] How does that come to pass? Are the organs of peasants differently constructed from ours? No, but they are differently exercised. Facing my window is a hillock on which the local children gather to play. Although they are rather distant from me, I distinguish perfectly all they say, and I often draw from it good material for this writing. Every day my ear misleads me as to their ages. I hear the voices of ten-year-olds; I look, I see the stature and the features of three- or four-year-olds. I do not limit this experiment to myself alone. City folk who come to see me and whom I consult about it all fall into the same error.

What produces it is that, up to five or six, city children, raised indoors and under the wing of a governess, need only to mutter to make themselves understood. As soon as they stir their lips, effort is made to hear them. Words are dictated to them which they repeat poorly; and since the same people are constantly with them, these people, by dint of paying attention to them, guess what they want to say rather than what they say.

In the country it is an entirely different thing. A peasant woman is not constantly with her child; he is forced to learn to say very clearly and loudly what he needs to make her understand. In the fields the children, scattered, removed from the father, from the mother, and from the other children, get practice in making themselves understood at a distance and in measuring the strength of their voices according to the space which separates them from those by whom they want to be understood. That is how one truly learns to pronounce, and not by stuttering some vowels in the ear of an attentive governess. Thus, when a peasant's child is questioned, shame can prevent him from answering, but what he says he says clearly; while the maid must serve as an interpreter for the city child, without which one understands nothing of what he mutters between his teeth.*

As they grow up boys should correct themselves of this defect in the colleges, and girls in the convents. In fact, both do speak in general more distinctly than those who have always been raised in the paternal household. But what prevents them from ever acquiring a pronunciation as clear as that of peasants is the necessity of learning many things by heart and of reciting aloud what they have learned: their study habituates them to mumbling, to pronouncing negligently and badly; the effect of the recitations is even worse; they look for their words with effort; they drag out and elongate their syllables. It is impossible when memory falters that the tongue should not stammer as well. Thus are contracted or preserved the vices of pronunciation. It will be seen hereafter that my Emile will not have these, or at least that he will not have contracted them from the same causes.

I agree that the people and the villagers fall into another extreme: that they almost always talk louder than they should; that, in pronouncing too exactly, they articulate harshly and coarsely; that they overemphasize; that they choose their terms poorly; etc.

But to begin with, this extreme appears much less defective to me than the other: granted that the first law of speech is to make oneself understood, the greatest mistake one can make is to speak without being understood. To pride oneself on not accentuating is to pride oneself on depriving sentences of their grace and their energy. Accentuation is the soul of speech. It gives speech sentiment and truth. Accentuation lies less than the word does. This is perhaps why well-brought-up people fear it so much. From the practice of saying everything in the same tone came the practice of mocking people without their being aware of it. The proscribed accentuation is succeeded by ways of pronunciation which are ridiculous, affected, and subject to fashion, such as one notices particularly in the young people of the court. This affectation of speech and bearing is what generally makes the aspect of the Frenchman repulsive and disagreeable to other nations. Instead of accentuating his speech, his affected language insinuates his meaning. This is no way to predispose others in his favor.

All the little defects of language that one is so afraid of letting children contract are nothing. They can be prevented or corrected with the greatest ease. But those that one causes children to contract by making their speech dull, obscure, and timid, by incessantly criticizing their tone, by picking all their words to pieces, are never corrected. A man who learns to speak only in his bedroom will fail to make himself understood at the head of a battalion and will hardly impress the

* This is not without exception; often the children who at first make themselves understood least, later become the most deafening when they have begun to raise their voices. But if I had to enter into all these minutiae, I would not finish. Every sensible reader should see that the excess and the defect derived from the same abuse are equally corrected by my method. I regard these two maxims as inseparable: "Always enough," and "Never too much." When the first is well established, the other follows necessarily.

people in a riot. First teach children to speak to men; they will know how to speak to women when they have to.

Nursed in the country amidst all the pastoral rusticity, your children will get more sonorous voices, they will not contract the obscure stuttering of city children. Nor will they contract there either the expressions or the tone of the village; or at least they will easily lose them when the master, living with them from their birth, and doing so more exclusively every day, will, by the correctness of his language, obviate or efface the impression of the peasants' language. Emile will speak a French just as pure as I can know it, but he will speak it more distinctly and will articulate it much better than I do.

The child who wants to speak should hear only words he can understand and say only those he can articulate. The efforts he makes to do so cause him to reiterate the same syllable as if to give himself practice in pronouncing it more distinctly. When he begins to stammer, do not torment yourself so much to guess what he is saying. To claim that one must always be heard is yet another kind of domination, and the child should exercise none. Let it suffice you that you provide most attentively for what is necessary. It is up to him to endeavor to make you understand what is not. Still less must one be in a hurry to insist that he talk. He will know how to talk well on his own to the extent that he comes to sense the utility of it.

One observes, it is true, that those who begin to talk very late never speak so distinctly as the others. But it is not because they talked late that their speech remains impeded; it is, on the contrary, because they are born with a speech impediment that they begin to talk late, for without that why would they talk later than the others? Have they less occasion to talk, and are they less encouraged to do so? On the contrary, the anxiety caused by this lateness, as soon as one becomes aware of it, makes one torment oneself to make these children blurt out something much more than one did with those who articulated earlier. And this ill-advised fuss can contribute a great deal to making obscure their speech, which, with less hurry, they would have had time to perfect more.

Children whom one hurries to talk have time neither to learn to pronounce well nor to conceive well what they are made to say; while, when they are allowed to proceed on their own, they practice first the easiest syllables to pronounce; and giving these syllables little by little a meaning which can be understood from their gestures, they give you their words before receiving yours. That done, they receive yours only after having understood them; not being pressed to make use of them, they begin by observing well what sense you give to them; and when they have made sure of it, they adopt them.

The greatest harm from the hurry one is in to make children talk before the proper age is not that the first speeches one makes to them and the first words they say have no meaning for them, but that they have another meaning than ours without our being able to perceive it; so that, appearing to answer us quite exactly, they speak to us without understanding us and without our understanding them. It is ordinarily due to such equivocations that we are sometimes surprised by their remarks, to which we lend ideas that they did not attach to them. This lack of attention on our part to the true meaning which words have for children appears to me to be the cause of their first errors; and these errors, even after they are cured of them, have an influence on their turn of mind for the rest of their lives. I shall have more than one occasion to clarify this by examples in what follows.

Restrict, therefore, the child's vocabulary as much as possible. It is a very great disadvantage for him to have more words than ideas, for him to know how to say more things than he can think. I believe one of the reasons why peasants generally have clearer minds than city people is that their lexicon is less extensive. They have few ideas, but they are very good at the comparison of ideas.

The first developments of childhood occur almost all at once. The child learns to talk, to feed himself, to walk, at about the same time. This is, strictly speaking, the first period of his life. Before it he is nothing more than he was in his mother's womb. He has no sentiment, no idea; hardly does he have sensations. He does not even sense his own existence.

*Vivit, et est vitae nescius ipse suae.** [34]

End of the First Book

* Ovid *Tristia* I. 3.

BOOK
II

2-3 years old

THIS is the second period of life, and now infancy, strictly speaking, has ended. For the words *infans* and *puer* are not synonymous. The former is contained in the latter and signifies "one who cannot speak"; this is why *puerum infantem* is found in Valerius Maximus.[1] But I shall continue to use this word according to the usage of our language until I reach an age for which it has another name.

When children begin to speak, they cry less. This is a natural progress. One language is substituted for the other. As soon as they can say with words that they are in pain, why would they say it with cries, except when the pain is too intense for speech to express it? If they continue to cry then, it is the fault of the people around them. As soon as Emile has once said, "It hurts," very intense pains indeed will be needed to force him to cry.

If the child is delicate, sensitive, if naturally he starts crying for nothing, by making his cries useless and ineffective, I will soon dry up their source. So long as he cries, I do not go to him. I run as soon as he has stopped. Soon his way of calling me will be to keep quiet or, at the most, to let out a single cry. It is by the effect they sense their cries make that children judge their own senses. There is no other convention for them. Whatever injury a child may do to himself, it is very rare that he cries when he is alone, unless he hopes to be heard.

If he falls, if he bumps his head, if his nose bleeds, if he cuts his fingers, instead of fussing around him as though I were alarmed, I will remain calm, at least for a short time. The harm is done; it is a necessity that he endure it; all my fussing would only serve to frighten him more and increase his sensitivity. At bottom, it is less the blow than the fear which torments when one has been hurt. I will at least spare him this latter anxiety, for quite certainly he will judge of his injury as he sees me judge of it. If he sees me run in agitation to console and pity him, he will consider himself lost. If he sees me keep my composure, he will soon regain his and will believe the injury cured when he no longer feels it. It is at this age that one gets the first lessons in courage, and that, bearing slight pains without terror, one gradually learns to bear great pains.

Far from being attentive to protecting Emile from injury, I would be most distressed if he were never hurt and grew up without knowing pain. To suffer is the first thing he ought to learn and the thing he will most need to know. It seems that children are little and weak only in order that they may get these important lessons without danger. If the child falls down, he will not break his leg; if he hits himself with a stick, he will not break his arm; if he grabs a knife, he will hardly tighten his grip and will not cut himself very deeply. I do not know of a child at liberty who was ever seen to kill, cripple, or do himself any considerable harm, unless he was carelessly exposed on high places or alone near fire, or dangerous instruments were left in his reach. What is to be said about these arsenals of machines set up around a child to arm him at all points against pain, so that when he is grown, he is at its mercy without courage and without experience, believes he is dead at the first prick, and faints on seeing the first drop of his blood?

Our didactic and pedantic craze is always to teach children what they would learn much better by themselves and to forget what we alone could teach them. Is there anything more foolish than the effort made to teach them to walk, as if anyone were ever seen who, due to his nurse's negligence, did not when grown know how to walk? How many people, on the contrary, does one see walk badly for their whole lives because they were badly taught how to walk?

Emile will not have padded bonnets, strollers, buggies, or leading strings; or, at least, as soon as he begins to know how to put one foot before the other, he will be supported only in paved places, and we shall hastily pass them by.* Instead of letting him stagnate in the stale air of a room, let him be taken daily to the middle of a field. There let him run and frisk about; let him fall a hundred times a day. So much the better. That way he will learn how to get up sooner. The well-being of freedom makes up for many wounds. My pupil will often have bruises. But, in compensation, he will always be gay. If your pupils have fewer bruises, they are always hindered, always enchained, always sad. I doubt whether the advantage is theirs.

Another progress makes complaint less necessary to children; this is the progress of their strength. Able to do more by themselves, they need to have recourse to others less frequently. With their strength develops the knowledge which puts them in a condition to direct it. It is at this second stage that, strictly speaking, the life of the individual begins. It is then that he gains consciousness of himself. Memory extends the sentiment of identity to all the moments of his existence; he becomes truly one, the same, and consequently already capable of happiness or unhappiness. It is important, therefore, to begin to consider him here as a moral being.

Although the furthest limit of human life can be pretty nearly de-

* There is nothing more ridiculous and more lacking in assurance than the step of people who were led too much by leading strings when they were little. This is another of those observations that are trivial by dint of being accurate and that are accurate in more than one sense.

[78]

[margin note: we should consider them as objects of moral action — they are owed moral consideration, but they are not doing anything moral]

termined, as well as one's probabilities at each age of approaching that limit, nothing is more uncertain than the duration of each man's life in particular. Very few attain this furthest limit. Life's greatest risks are in its beginnings; the less one has lived, the less one ought to hope to live. Of the children born, half, at the most, reach adolescence; and it is probable that your pupil will not reach the age of manhood.[2]

What, then, must be thought of that barbarous education which sacrifices the present to an uncertain future, which burdens a child with chains of every sort and begins by making him miserable in order to prepare him from afar for I know not what pretended happiness which it is to be believed he will never enjoy? Even if I were to suppose this education reasonable in its object, how can one without indignation see poor unfortunates submitted to an unbearable yoke and condemned to continual labor like galley slaves, without any assurance that so many efforts will ever be useful to them? The age of gaiety passes amidst tears, punishments, threats, and slavery. The unlucky fellow is tormented for his own good; and the death that is being summoned is unseen, the death which is going to seize him in the midst of this gloomy setup. Who knows how many children perish victims of a father's or a master's extravagant wisdom? Happy to escape his cruelty, the only advantage they get from the ills he has made them suffer is to die without regretting life, of which they knew only the torments.

Men, be humane. This is your first duty. Be humane with every station, every age, everything which is not alien to man. What wisdom is there for you save humanity? Love childhood; promote its games, its pleasures, its amiable instinct. Who among you has not sometimes regretted that age when a laugh is always on the lips and the soul is always at peace? Why do you want to deprive these little innocents of the enjoyment of a time so short which escapes them and of a good so precious which they do not know how to abuse? Why do you want to fill with bitterness and pains these first years which go by so rapidly and can return no more for them than they can for you? Fathers, do you know the moment when death awaits your children? Do not prepare regrets for yourself in depriving them of the few instants nature gives them. As soon as they can sense the pleasure of being, arrange it so that they can enjoy it, arrange it so that at whatever hour God summons them they do not die without having tasted life.

How many voices are going to be raised against me! I hear from afar the clamors of that false wisdom which incessantly projects us outside of ourselves, which always counts the present for nothing, and which, pursuing without respite a future that retreats in proportion as we advance, by dint of transporting us where we are not, transports us where we shall never be.

This is, you answer me, the time to correct man's bad inclinations; it is during the age of childhood, when we are least sensitive to pains, that they must be multiplied so as to spare them in the age of reason. But who tells you that this whole arrangement is at your disposition, and that all this fair instruction with which you overwhelm the child's feeble mind will not one day be more pernicious to him than useful? Who assures you that you are sparing him something by the sorrows you lavish on him? Why do you give him more ills than his condition entails without being sure that these present ills are for the relief of the future? And how will you prove to me that these bad inclinations, of which you claim you are curing him, do not come to him from your ill-considered care far more than from nature? Unhappy foresight which makes a being unhappy now in the hope, well or ill founded, of making him happy one day! In case these vulgar reasoners confuse license with liberty and the child one makes happy with the child one spoils, let us teach them to distinguish the two.

In order not to pursue chimeras let us not forget what is appropriate to our situation. Humanity has its place in the order of things; childhood has its in the order of human life. The man must be considered in the man, and the child in the child. To assign each his place and settle him in it, to order the human passions according to man's constitution is all that we can do for his well-being. The rest depends on alien causes which are in no way in our power.

We do not know what absolute happiness or unhappiness is. Everything is mixed in this life; in it one tastes no pure sentiment; in it one does not stay two moments in the same state. The affections of our souls, as well as the states of our bodies, are in a continual flux. The good and the bad are common to us all, but in different measures. The happiest is he who suffers the least pain; the unhappiest is he who feels the least pleasure. Always more suffering than enjoyment; this relation between the two is common to all men. Man's felicity on earth is, hence, only a negative condition; the smallest number of ills he can suffer ought to constitute its measure.

Every feeling of pain is inseparable from the desire to be delivered from it; every idea of pleasure is inseparable from the desire to enjoy it; every desire supposes privation, and all sensed privations are painful. Our unhappiness consists, therefore, in the disproportion between our desires and our faculties. A being endowed with senses whose faculties equaled his desires would be an absolutely happy being.

In what, then, consists human wisdom or the road of true happiness? It is not precisely in diminishing our desires, for if they were beneath our power, a part of our faculties would remain idle, and we would not enjoy our whole being. Neither is it in extending our faculties, for if, proportionate to them, our desires were more extended, we would as a result only become unhappier. But it is in diminishing the excess of the desires over the faculties and putting power and will in perfect equality. It is only then that, with all the powers in action, the soul will nevertheless remain peaceful and that man will be well ordered.

It is thus that nature, which does everything for the best, constituted him in the beginning. It gives him with immediacy only the desires necessary to his preservation and the faculties sufficient to satisfy them. It put all the others, as it were, in reserve in the depth of his soul, to be developed there when needed. Only in this original state are power and desire in equilibrium and man is not unhappy. As soon as his potential faculties are put in action, imagination, the most active of all, is awakened and outstrips them. It is imagination which extends for us the measure of the possible, whether for good or bad, and which consequently excites and nourishes the desires by the hope of satisfying them. But the object which at first appeared to be at hand flees more quickly than it can be pursued. When one believes that one has reached it, it transforms and reveals itself in the distance ahead of us. No longer seeing the country we have already crossed, we count it for nothing; what remains to cross ceaselessly grows and extends. Thus one exhausts oneself without getting to the end, and the more one gains on enjoyment, the further happiness gets from us.

On the contrary, the closer to his natural condition man has stayed, the smaller is the difference between his faculties and his desires, and consequently the less removed he is from being happy. He is never less unhappy than when he appears entirely destitute, for unhappiness consists not in the privation of things but in the need that is felt for them.

The real world has its limits; the imaginary world is infinite. Unable to enlarge the one, let us restrict the other, for it is from the difference between the two alone that are born all the pains which make us truly unhappy. Take away strength, health, and good witness of oneself, all the goods of this life are in opinion; take away the pains of the body and the remorse of conscience, all our ills are imaginary. This principle is common, it will be said. I agree. But its practical application is not common, and we are dealing solely with practice here.

When it is said that man is weak, what is meant? This word *weak* indicates a relation, a relation obtaining within the being to which one applies it. He whose strength surpasses his needs, be he an insect or a worm, is a strong being. He whose needs surpass his strength, be he an elephant or a lion, be he a conqueror or a hero, be he a god, is a weak being. The rebellious angel who misapprehended his nature was weaker than the happy mortal who lives in peace according to his nature. Man is very strong when he is contented with being what he is; he is very weak when he wants to raise himself above humanity. Therefore, do not fancy that in extending your faculties you extend your strength. On the contrary, you diminish your strength if your pride is extended farther than it. Let us measure the radius of our sphere and stay in the center like the insect in the middle of his web; we shall always be sufficient unto ourselves; and we shall not have to complain of our weakness, for we shall never feel it.

All the animals have exactly the faculties necessary to preserve themselves. Man alone has superfluous faculties. Is it not very strange that this superfluity should be the instrument of his unhappiness? In every country the arms of a man are worth more than his subsistence. If he were wise enough to count this superfluity for nothing, he would always have what is necessary because he would never have anything too much. The great needs, said Favorinus,* are born of great possessions; and often the best way to provide oneself with the things one lacks is to give up those that one has. It is by dint of agitating ourselves to increase our happiness that we convert it into unhappiness. Any man

---

* Noct. attic. B. IX. c.8.³

who only wanted to live would live happily. Consequently he would live as a good man, for what advantage would there be for him in being wicked?

If we were immortal, we would be most unhappy beings. It is hard to die doubtless; but it is sweet to hope that one will not live forever, and that a better life will end the pains of this one. If we were to be offered immortality on the earth, who would want to accept this dreary present? [4] What resource, what hope, what consolation would remain to us against the rigors of fate and the injustices of men? The ignorant man, who foresees nothing, little senses the value of life and little fears the loss of it; the enlightened man sees goods of a greater value which he prefers to this good. It is only half knowledge and false wisdom which, prolonging our views up to the point of death and not beyond, make it the worst of evils for us. The necessity of dying is for the wise man only a reason for bearing the pains of life. If one were not certain of losing life sometime, it would cost too much to preserve.

Our moral ills are all matters of opinion, except for a single one—crime; and this ill depends on us. Our physical ills are themselves destroyed or destroy us. Time or death is our remedy. But we suffer more the less we know how to suffer; and we give ourselves more torment in curing our maladies than we would have in enduring them. Live according to nature, be patient, and drive away the doctors. You will not avoid death, but you will feel it only once, while they bring it every day into your troubled imagination; and their lying art, instead of prolonging your days, deprives you of the enjoyment of them. I shall always ask what true good this art has done for men. Some of those it cures would die, it is true, but the millions it kills would remain alive. Man of sense, do not wager in this lottery where too many chances are against you. Suffer, die, or get well; but, above all, live until your last hour.

Everything is only folly and contradiction in human institutions. We worry about our life more in proportion to its losing its value. Old men regret it more than young people; they do not want to lose the preparations they have made for enjoying it. At the age of sixty it is most cruel to die before having begun to live. It is believed that man has an intense love for his own preservation, and that is true. But it is not seen that this love, in the way in which we feel it, is in large part the work of men. Naturally man worries about his preservation only insofar as the means to it are in his power. As soon as these means escape him, he becomes calm and dies without tormenting himself uselessly. The first law of resignation comes to us from nature. Savages as well as beasts struggle very little against death and endure it almost without complaint. When this law is destroyed, another one which comes from reason takes shape; but few know how to derive it, and this artificial resignation is never so full and complete as the primary one.

Foresight! Foresight, which takes us ceaselessly beyond ourselves and often places us where we shall never arrive. This is the true source of all our miseries. What madness for a fleeting being like man always to look far into a future which comes so rarely and to neglect the present of which he is sure. It is a madness all the more destructive since it increases continuously with age; and old men, always distrustful, full of foresight, and miserly, prefer to deny themselves what is necessary today so as not to lack it a hundred years from now. Thus, we are attached to everything, we cling to everything—times, places, men, things; everything which is, everything which will be, is important to each of us. Our individual persons are now only the least part of ourselves. Each one extends himself, so to speak, over the whole earth and becomes sensitive over this entire large surface. Is it surprising that our ills are multiplied by all the points where we can be wounded? How many princes grieve over the loss of a country they have never seen? How many merchants are there whom it suffices to touch in India in order to make them scream in Paris?

Is it nature which thus carries men so far from themselves? Is it nature which wants each to learn of his destiny from others and sometimes to be the last to learn it? Thus, a man dies happy or miserable without ever knowing it. I see a man, fresh, gay, vigorous, healthy, his presence inspires joy, his eyes proclaim contentment, well-being; he brings with him the image of happiness. A letter comes in the post; the happy man looks at it; it is addressed to him; he opens it, reads it. Instantly his aspect changes. He becomes pale and faints. Coming to, he weeps, writhes, moans, tears his hair, makes the air resound with his cries, seems to have a frightful fit of convulsions. Senseless man, what ill has this piece of paper done to you then? Of what limb has it deprived you? What crime has it made you commit? Altogether, what has it changed in you yourself to put you in the state in which I see you? [5]

If the letter had gone astray, if a charitable hand had thrown it into the fire, the fate of this mortal, happy and unhappy at once, would have been, it seems to me, a strange problem. His unhappiness, you will say, was real. Very well, but he did not feel it; where was it then? His happiness was imaginary. I understand. Health, gaiety, well-being, contentment of mind are no longer anything but visions. We no longer exist where we are; we only exist where we are not. Is it worth the effort to have so great a fear of death if what we live off of remains?

O man, draw your existence up within yourself, and you will no longer be miserable. Remain in the place which nature assigns to you in the chain of being. Nothing will be able to make you leave it. Do not rebel against the hard law of necessity; and do not exhaust your strength by your will to resist that law—strength which heaven gave you not for extending or prolonging your existence but only for preserving it as heaven pleases and for as long as heaven pleases. Your freedom and your power extend only as far as your natural strength, and not beyond. All the rest is only slavery, illusion, and deception. Even domination is servile when it is connected with opinion, for you depend on the prejudices of those you govern by prejudices. To lead them as you please, you must conduct yourself as they please. They have only to change their way of thinking, and you must perforce change your way of acting. Those who come near you have only to know how to govern the opinions of the people whom you believe you govern, or of the favorites who govern you, or those of your family, or your own. These viziers, courtiers, priests, soldiers, valets, babblers, and even babies—were you a Themistocles in genius *—are going to lead you like a baby yourself in the very midst of your legions. You can do what you like: never will your real authority go farther than your real faculties. As soon as one must see with the eyes of others, one must will with their wills. "My peoples are my subjects," you say proudly. So be it. But you, what are you? The subject of your ministers; and your ministers, in turn, what are they? The subjects of their clerks, their mistresses, the valets of their valets. Take everything, usurp everything; and then pour out handfuls of money, set up batteries of cannon, erect gallows and wheels, give laws and edicts, multiply spies, soldiers, hangmen, prisons, chains. Poor little men, what does all that do for you? You will be neither better served, nor less robbed, nor less deceived, nor more absolute. You will always say, "We want," and you will always do what others want.

The only one who does his own will is he who, in order to do it, has no need to put another's arms at the end of his own; from which it follows that the first of all goods is not authority but freedom. The truly free man wants only what he can do and does what he pleases. That is my fundamental maxim. It need only be applied to childhood for all the rules of education to flow from it.

Society has made man weaker not only in taking from him the right he had over his own strength but, above all, in making his strength insufficient for him. That is why his desires are multiplied along with his weakness, and that is what constitutes the weakness of childhood compared to manhood. If the man is a strong being and the child is a weak being, this is not because the former has more strength absolutely than the latter, but it is because the former can naturally be sufficient unto himself and the latter cannot. The man should, hence, have more will and the child more whim, a word by which I mean all desires which are not true needs and which can only be satisfied with another's help.[7]

I have given the reason for this state of weakness. Nature provides for it by the attachment of fathers and mothers; but this attachment can have its excess, its defect, its abuses. Parents who live in the civil state transport their child into it before the proper age. In giving him more needs than he has, they do not relieve his weakness; they increase it. They increase it still more by exacting from him what nature did not exact. They do so by subjecting to their will the bit of strength which he has for serving his own, by changing into slavery on one side or the other the reciprocal dependence in which his weakness keeps him and their attachment keeps them.

The wise man knows how to stay in his place; but the child, who does not know his place, would not be able to keep to it. Among us he is given a thousand exits by which to leave it. It is for those who

---

* "This little boy that you see there," said Themistocles to his friends, "is the master of Greece, for he governs his mother, his mother governs me, I govern the Athenians, and the Athenians govern Greece." [6] O what little leaders would often be found in the greatest empires, if from the prince one descended by degrees to the first hand which secretly sets things in motion!

govern him to keep him in his place, and this is not an easy task. He ought to be neither beast nor man, but child. It is necessary that he feel his weakness and not that he suffer from it. It is necessary that he be dependent and not that he obey. It is necessary that he ask and not that he command. He is only subject to others by virtue of his needs, and because they see better than he does what is useful to him, what can contribute to, or be harmful to, his preservation. No one, not even the father, has a right to command the child what is not for his good.

Before prejudices and human institutions have corrupted our natural inclinations, the happiness of children, like that of men, consists in the use of their freedom. But in the case of children this freedom is limited by their weakness. Whoever does what he wants is happy if he is self-sufficient; this is the case of the man living in the state of nature. Whoever does what he wants is not happy if his needs surpass his strength; this is the case of the child in the same state. Children, even in the state of nature, enjoy only an imperfect freedom, similar to that enjoyed by men in the civil state.[8] No longer able to do without others, each of us becomes in this respect weak and miserable again. We were made to be men; laws and society have plunged us once more into childhood. The rich, the nobles, the kings are all children who, seeing that men are eager to relieve their misery, derive a puerile vanity from that very fact and are very proud of care that one would not give to them if they were grown men.

These considerations are important and serve to resolve all the contradictions of the social system. There are two sorts of dependence: dependence on things, which is from nature; dependence on men, which is from society. Dependence on things, since it has no morality, is in no way detrimental to freedom and engenders no vices. Dependence on men, since it is without order,* engenders all the vices, and by it, master and slave are mutually corrupted. If there is any means of remedying this ill in society, it is to substitute law for man and to arm the general wills with a real strength superior to the action of every particular will. If the laws of nations could, like those of nature, have an inflexibility that no human force could ever conquer, dependence on men would then become dependence on things again; in the republic all of the advantages of the natural state would be united with those of the civil state, and freedom which keeps man exempt from vices would be joined to morality which raises him to virtue.[10]

Keep the child in dependence only on things. You will have followed the order of nature in the progress of his education. Never present to his undiscriminating will anything but physical obstacles or punishments which stem from the actions themselves and which he will recall on the proper occasion. Without forbidding him to do harm, it suffices to prevent him from doing it. Experience or impotence alone ought to take the place of law for him. Grant nothing to his desires because he asks for it but because he needs it. Let him not know what obedience is when he acts nor what dominion is when one acts for him. Let him sense his liberty equally in his actions and yours. Add to the

* In my *Principles of Political Right*[9] it is demonstrated that no particular will can be ordered in the social system.

strength he lacks exactly as much as he needs in order to be free but not imperious; do so in such a way that he receives your services as a sort of humiliation and longs for the moment when he can do without them and have the honor of serving himself.

Nature has, for strengthening the body and making it grow, means that ought never be opposed. A child must not be constrained to stay when he wants to go nor to go when he wants to stay. When children's wills are not spoiled by our fault, children want nothing uselessly. They have to jump, run, and shout when they wish. All their movements are needs of their constitution seeking to strengthen itself. But one should distrust what they desire but are unable to do for themselves and others have to do for them. Then true need, natural need, must be carefully distinguished from the need which stems from nascent whim or from the need which comes only from the superabundance of life of which I have spoken.[11]

I have already said what must be done when a child cries to have this or that. I shall only add that as soon as he can ask by saying what he desires, and, to get it more quickly or overcome a refusal, he supports his request with tears, it ought to be irrevocably refused him. If need has made him speak, you ought to know it and do immediately what he asks. But to cede anything to his tears is to incite him to shed them, is to teach him to doubt your good will and to believe that importunity can have more effect on you than benevolence. If he does not believe you are good, soon he will be wicked; if he believes you are weak, soon he will be stubborn. It is important always to grant at the first sign what one does not want to refuse. Do not be prodigal with refusal, but revoke it never.

Guard, above all, against giving the child vain formulas of politeness which serve at need as magic words for him to submit to his will everything which surrounds him and to obtain instantly what he pleases. The fancy education of the rich never fails to leave them politely imperious, by prescribing to them the terms they are to use in order that no one dare resist them. Their children have neither the tones nor the wiles of supplication; they are as arrogant when they beg as when they command—indeed, even more so—since they are all the more sure of being obeyed. One sees from the first that in their mouths "If you please" signifies "I please" and that "I beg you" signifies "I order you." Admirable politeness which results only in their changing the sense of words and never being able to speak other than in the accents of dominion! As for me who am less afraid that Emile be coarse than that he be arrogant, I much prefer him to beg by saying, "Do this!" than to command by saying, "I beg you." It is not the term he uses which is important to me but rather the meaning he gives to it.

There is an excess of rigor and an excess of indulgence, both equally to be avoided. If you let children suffer, you expose their health, their life. You make them miserable in the present. If by too much care you spare them every kind of discomfort, you are preparing great miseries for them; you make them delicate, sensitive; you cause them to leave man's estate to which they will return one day in spite of you. So as not to expose them to some ills of nature, you are the artisan of those nature did not give them. You will tell me that I fall into the class of those bad fathers whom I reproached with sacrificing children's happiness to the consideration of a distant time which may never be.

Not at all, for the freedom I give my pupil amply compensates him for the slight discomforts to which I leave him exposed. I see little rascals playing in the snow, blue and numb with cold, hardly able to move their fingers. Nothing prevents them from going to get warm; they will have none of it. If they were forced to do so, they would feel the rigors of constraint a hundred times more than they feel those of the cold. What then do you complain about? Shall I make your child miserable by not exposing him to discomforts he wants to suffer? I act for his good in the present moment by leaving him free; I act for his good in the future by arming him against the ills he must bear. If he had the choice of being my pupil or yours, do you think he would hesitate for an instant?

Can you conceive of some true happiness possible for any being outside of its constitution? And is not wanting to exempt man from all the ills of his species equally to make him quit his constitution? Yes, I maintain that to feel the great goods he must know the little ills. Such is his nature. If the physical prospers, the moral is corrupted. The man who did not know pain would know neither the tenderness of humanity nor the sweetness of commiseration. His heart would be moved by nothing. He would not be sociable; he would be a monster among his kind.

Do you know the surest means of making your child miserable? It is to accustom him to getting everything; since his desires grow constantly due to the ease of satisfying them, sooner or later powerlessness will force you, in spite of yourself, to end up with a refusal. And this unaccustomed refusal will give him more torment than being deprived of what he desires. First, he will want the cane you are holding; soon he will want your watch; after that he will want the bird flying by; he will want the star he sees shining; he will want everything he sees. Without being God, how will you content him?

It is a disposition natural to man to regard everything in his power as his. In this sense Hobbes's principle is true up to a certain point. Multiply not only our desires but the means of satisfying them, and each will make himself the master of everything.[12] Hence, the child who has only to want in order to get believes himself to be the owner of the universe; he regards all men as his slaves. When one is finally forced to refuse him something, he, believing that at his command everything is possible, takes this refusal for an act of rebellion. All reasons given him at an age when he is incapable of reasoning are to his mind only pretexts. He sees ill will everywhere. The feeling of an alleged injustice souring his nature, he develops hatred toward everyone; and, without ever being grateful for helpfulness, he is indignant at every opposition.

How could I conceive that a child thus dominated by anger and devoured by the most irascible passions might ever be happy? Happy, he! He is a despot. He is at once the most vile of slaves and the most miserable of creatures. I have seen children raised in this way who wanted that the house be turned over by a bump of the shoulder, that they be given the weathercock they see on a steeple, that a marching regiment be stopped so that the drums could be heard longer; who pierced the air with their cries, unwilling to listen to anyone, as soon as there was a delay in their being obeyed. All hastened vainly to oblige them. With their desires exacerbated by the ease of getting, they were obstinate about impossible things and found everywhere only contradiction, obstacles, efforts, pains. Always grumbling, always rebellious, always furious, they spent their days in screaming, in complaining. Were those very fortunate beings? Weakness and domination joined engender only folly and misery. Of two spoiled children, one beats the table and the other has the sea whipped. They will have to do a lot of whipping and beating before they will live contentedly.[13]

If these ideas of dominion and tyranny make them miserable already in their childhood, what will it be when they grow up and their relations with other men begin to extend and multiply? Accustomed to seeing everything give way before them, what a surprise on entering into the world to feel that everything resists them and to find themselves crushed by the weight of this universe they thought they moved at their pleasure! Their insolent airs, their puerile vanity, attract to them only mortification, disdain, and mockery. They drink affronts like water; cruel experiences soon teach them that they know neither their situation nor their strength. Not omnipotent, they believe they are impotent. So many unaccustomed obstacles dishearten them; so much contempt debases them. They become cowardly, fearful, and fawning and fall as far below themselves as they had previously been raised above themselves.

Let us return to the primary rule. Nature has made children to be loved and helped, but has it made them to be obeyed and feared? Has it given them an imposing air, a severe eye, a rough and threatening voice to make them dreaded? I understand that a lion's roar scares animals and that they tremble on seeing his terrible head. But if an indecent, odious, laughable spectacle has ever been seen, it is a body of magistrates, in ceremonial robes and headed by its chief, prostrate before a child in swaddling whom they harangue in stately terms and who screams and drools as his only response.[14]

To consider childhood in itself, is there in the world a weaker being, a more miserable one, one more at the mercy of everything surrounding him, who has a greater need of pity, care, and protection, than a child? Does it not seem that he presents so sweet a face and so touching a manner only so that all who come near him will take an interest in his weakness and hasten to help him? What is there, then, more shocking, more contrary to order than to see an imperious and rebellious child command all that surrounds him and impudently take on the tone of a master with those who have only to abandon him to make him perish?

On the other hand, who does not see that the weakness of the first age enchains children in so many ways that it is barbarous to add to this subjection a further subjection—that of our caprices—by taking from them a freedom so limited, which they are so litle capable of abusing

BOOK II

and the deprivation of which is of so little utility to them and to us? If there is no object so worthy of ridicule as a haughty child, there is no object so worthy of pity as a fearful child. Since with the age of reason civil servitude begins, why anticipate it with private servitude? Let us suffer that a moment of life be exempt from this yoke which nature did not impose on us, and leave to childhood the exercise of natural freedom that keeps at a distance, for a time at least, vices contracted in slavery. Let these severe teachers and these fathers subjugated by their children both come, then, with their frivolous objections and, before vaunting their methods, learn for once the method of nature.

I return to practice. I have already said that your child ought to get a thing not because he asks for it but because he needs it,* and do a thing not out of obedience but only out of necessity. Thus the words *obey* and *command* will be proscribed from his lexicon, and even more so *duty* and *obligation*. But *strength, necessity, impotence,* and *constraint* should play a great role in it. Before the age of reason one cannot have any idea of moral beings or of social relations. Hence so far as possible words which express them must be avoided, for fear that the child in the beginning attach to these words false ideas which you will not know about or will no longer be able to destroy. The first false idea which enters his head is the germ in him of error and vice. It is to this first step above all that attention must be paid. Arrange it so that as long as he is struck only by objects of sense, all his ideas stop at sensations; arrange it so that on all sides he perceive around him only the physical world. Without that, you may be sure that he will not listen to you at all, or that he will get fantastic notions of the moral world of which you speak to him, notions that you will never in your life be able to blot out.

To reason with children was Locke's great maxim.[15] It is the one most in vogue today. Its success, however, does not appear to me such as to establish its reputation; and, as for me, I see nothing more stupid than these children who have been reasoned with so much. Of all the faculties of man, reason, which is, so to speak, only a composite of all the others, is the one that develops with the most difficulty and latest. And it is this one which they want to use in order to develop the first faculties! The masterpiece of a good education is to make a reasonable man, and they claim they raise a child by reason! This is to begin with the end, to want to make the product the instrument. If children understood reason, they would not need to be raised. But by speaking to them from an early age a language which they do not understand, one accustoms them to show off with words, to control all that is said to them, to believe themselves as wise as their masters, to become disputatious and rebellious; and everything that is thought to be gotten from them out of reasonable motives is never obtained other than out of

---

* It ought to be sensed that just as pain is often a necessity, pleasure is sometimes a need. There is, therefore, only one single desire of children which ought never be satisfied: that of being obeyed. From this it follows that in everything they ask for, attention must above all be paid to the motive which leads them to ask for it. So, as far as possible, grant them everything that can give them a real pleasure; always refuse them what they ask for only due to whim or in order to assert their authority.

motives of covetousness or fear or vanity which are always perforce joined to the others.

This is the formula to which all the lessons in morality that are given, and can be given, to children can just about be reduced:

MASTER   You must not do that.
CHILD   And why must I not do it?
MASTER   Because it is bad to do.
CHILD   Bad to do! What is bad to do?
MASTER   What you are forbidden to do.
CHILD   What is bad about doing what I am forbidden to do?
MASTER   You are punished for having disobeyed.
CHILD   I shall fix it so that nothing is known about it.
MASTER   You will be spied on.
CHILD   I shall hide.
MASTER   You will be questioned.
CHILD   I shall lie.
MASTER   You must not lie.
CHILD   Why must I not lie?
MASTER   Because it is bad to do, etc.

This is the inevitable circle. Get out of it, and the child does not understand you any longer. Is this not most useful instruction? I would be quite curious to know what could be put in the place of this dialogue. Locke himself would certainly have been very much at a loss. To know good and bad, to sense the reason for man's duties, is not a child's affair.

Nature wants children to be children before being men. If we want to pervert this order, we shall produce precocious fruits which will be immature and insipid and will not be long in rotting. We shall have young doctors [16] and old children. Childhood has its ways of seeing, thinking, and feeling which are proper to it. Nothing is less sensible than to want to substitute ours for theirs, and I would like as little to insist that a ten-year-old be five feet tall as that he possess judgment. Actually, what would reason do for him at that age? It is the bridle of strength, and the child does not need this bridle.

In trying to persuade your pupils of the duty of obedience, you join to this alleged persuasion force and threats or, what is worse, flattery and promises. In this way, therefore, lured by profit or constrained by force, they pretend to be convinced by reason. They see quite well that obedience is advantageous to them and rebellion harmful when you notice either. But since everything you insist on is unpleasant and, further, it is always irksome to do another's will, they arrange to do their own will covertly. They are persuaded that what they do is right if their disobedience is unknown, but are ready on being caught—in order to avoid a worse evil—to admit that what they do is wrong. Since the reason for duty cannot be grasped at their age, there is not a man in the world who could succeed in giving duty a truly palpable sense for them. But the fear of punishment, the hope of pardon, importunity, awkwardness in answering, wrest all the confessions from them that

BOOK II

are demanded; and it is believed that they have been convinced when they have only been pestered or intimidated.

What results from this? Firstly, by imposing on them a duty they do not feel, you set them against your tyranny and turn them away from loving you. Secondly, you teach them to become dissemblers, fakers, and liars in order to extort rewards or escape punishments. Finally, by accustoming them always to cover a secret motive with an apparent motive, you yourselves give them the means of deceiving you ceaselessly, of depriving you of the knowledge of their true character, and of fobbing you and others off with vain words when the occasion serves. Laws, you will say, although they obligate conscience, nevertheless also use constraint with grown men. I admit it, but what are these men if not children spoiled by education? This is precisely what must be prevented. Use force with children, and reason with men. Such is the natural order. The wise man does not need laws.

Treat your pupil according to his age. At the outset put him in his place, and hold him there so well that he no longer tries to leave it. Then, before knowing what wisdom is, he will practice its most important lesson. Command him nothing, whatever in the world it might be, absolutely nothing. Do not even allow him to imagine that you might pretend to have any authority over him. Let him know only that he is weak and you are strong, that by his condition and yours he is necessarily at your mercy. Let him know it, learn it, feel it. Let his haughty head at an early date feel the harsh yoke which nature imposes on man, the heavy yoke of necessity under which every finite being must bend. Let him see this necessity in things, never in the caprice* of men. Let the bridle that restrains him be force and not authority. Do not forbid him to do that from which he should abstain; prevent him from doing it without explanations, without reasonings. What you grant him, grant at his first word, without solicitations, without prayers—above all, without conditions. Grant with pleasure; refuse only with repugnance. But let all your refusals be irrevocable; let no importunity shake you; let "no," once pronounced, be a wall of bronze against which the child will have to exhaust his strength at most five or six times in order to abandon any further attempts to overturn it.

It is thus that you will make him patient, steady, resigned, calm, even when he has not got what he wanted, for it is in the nature of man to endure patiently the necessity of things but not the ill will of others. The phrase "There is no more" is a response against which no child has ever rebelled unless he believed that it was a lie. Besides, there is no middle point here: nothing must be demanded from him at all, or he must be bent from the outset to the most perfect obedience. The worst education is to leave him floating between his will and yours and to dispute endlessly between you and him as to which of the two will be the master. I would a hundred times prefer that it were always he.

It is quite strange that since people first became involved with raising children, no instrument for guiding them has been imagined

---

* One should be sure that the child will treat as a caprice every will opposed to his own when he does not appreciate the reason for it. Now a child does not appreciate the reason for anything which clashes with his whims.

other than emulation, jealousy, envy, vanity, avidity, and vile fear—all the most dangerous passions, the quickest to ferment and the most appropriate to corrupt the soul, even before the body has been formed. With each lesson that one wants to put into their heads before its proper time, a vice is planted in the depth of their hearts. Senseless teachers think they work wonders when they make children wicked in order to teach them what goodness is. And then they solemnly tell us, "Such is man." Yes, such is the man you have made.

All the instruments have been tried save one, the only one precisely that can succeed: well-regulated freedom. One ought not to get involved with raising a child if one does not know how to guide him where one wants by the laws of the possible and the impossible alone. The sphere of both being equally unknown to him, they can be expanded and contracted around him as one wants. One enchains, pushes, and restrains him with the bond of necessity alone without his letting out a peep. He is made supple and docile by the force of things alone without any vice having the occasion to germinate in him, for the passions never become animated so long as they are of no effect.

Do not give your pupil any kind of verbal lessons; he ought to receive them only from experience. Inflict no kind of punishment on him, for he does not know what it is to be at fault. Never make him beg pardon, for he could not know how to offend you. Devoid of all morality in his actions, he can do nothing which is morally bad and which merits either punishment or reprimand.

I already see the startled reader judging this child by our children. He is mistaken. The perpetual constraint in which you keep your pupils exacerbates their vivacity. The more they are held in check under your eyes, the more they are turbulent the moment they get away. They have to compensate themselves when they can for the harsh constraint in which you keep them. Two schoolboys from the city will do more damage in a place than the young of an entire village. Close up a little gentleman and a little peasant in a room. The former will have turned everything upside down, broken everything, before the latter has left his place. Why is this, if it is not because the one hastens to abuse a moment of license, while the other, always sure of his freedom, is never in a hurry to make use of it? And nevertheless the children of the village people, themselves often indulged or opposed, are still quite far from the state in which I want them kept.

Let us set down as an incontestable maxim that the first movements of nature are always right. There is no original perversity in the human heart. There is not a single vice to be found in it of which it cannot be said how and whence it entered. The sole passion natural to man is amour de soi or amour-propre taken in an extended sense.[17] This amour-propre in itself or relative to us is good and useful; and since it has no necessary relation to others, it is in this respect naturally neutral. It becomes good or bad only by the application made of it and the relations given to it. Therefore, up to the time when the guide of amour-propre, which is reason, can be born, it is important for a child to do nothing because he is seen or heard—nothing, in a word, in relation to others; he must respond only to what nature asks of him, and then he will do nothing but good.

I do not mean that he will never do damage, that he will not hurt himself, that he will not perhaps break a valuable piece of furniture if he finds it in his reach. He could do a considerable amount of wrong without wrongdoing, because the bad action depends on the intention of doing harm, and he will never have this intention. If he had it one single time, all would be lost already; he would be wicked almost beyond recall.

Some things are bad in the eyes of avarice which are not so in the eyes of reason. In leaving children full freedom to exercise their giddiness, it is proper to put away from them everything that could make it costly and to leave nothing fragile and precious within their reach. Let their quarters be fitted with coarse and solid furniture, no mirrors, no china, no objects of quality. As for my Emile, whom I am raising in the country, his room will have nothing which distinguishes it from a peasant's. What is the use of decorating it so carefully, since he is going to stay in it so little? But I am mistaken. He will decorate it himself, and we shall soon see with what.

If in spite of your precautions, the child succeeds in creating some disorder, in breaking some useful piece, do not punish him for your negligence; do not chide him; let him hear not a single word of reproach; do not permit him even to glimpse that he has brought you grief; act exactly as if the thing had been broken of itself. In short, believe you have accomplished a lot if you can say nothing.

Dare I expose the greatest, the most important, the most useful rule of all education? It is not to gain time but to lose it. Common readers, pardon me my paradoxes. When one reflects, they are necessary and, whatever you may say, I prefer to be a paradoxical man than a prejudiced one.[18] The most dangerous period of human life is that from birth to the age of twelve. This is the time when errors and vices germinate without one's yet having any instrument for destroying them; and by the time the instrument comes, the roots are so deep that it is too late to rip them out. If children jumped all at once from the breast to the age of reason, the education they are given might be suitable for them. But, according to the natural progress, they need an entirely contrary one. They ought to do nothing with their soul until all of its faculties have developed, because while the soul is yet blind, it cannot perceive the torch you are presenting to it or follow the path reason maps out across the vast plain of ideas, a path which is so faint even to the best of eyes.

Thus, the first education ought to be purely negative. It consists not at all in teaching virtue or truth but in securing the heart from vice and the mind from error. If you could do nothing and let nothing be done, if you could bring your pupil healthy and robust to the age of twelve without his knowing how to distinguish his right hand from his left, at your first lessons the eyes of his understanding would open up to reason. Without prejudice, without habit, he would have nothing in him which could hinder the effect of your care. Soon he would become in your hands the wisest of men; and in beginning by doing nothing, you would have worked an educational marvel.

Take the opposite of the practiced path, and you will almost always do well. Since what is wanted is not to make a child out of a child but a doctor out of a child, fathers and masters can never soon enough scold, correct, reprimand, flatter, threaten, promise, instruct, talk reason. Do better: be reasonable, and do not reason with your pupil, especially to get his approbation for what displeases him. Bringing reason to bear on unpleasant things only makes reason tedious for him and discredits it early in a mind not yet in a condition to understand it. Exercise his body, his organs, his senses, his strength, but keep his soul idle for as long as possible. Be afraid of all sentiments anterior to the judgment which evaluates them. Restrain, arrest alien impressions; and in order to prevent the birth of evil, do not hurry to do good, for good is only truly such when reason enlightens it. Regard all delays as advantages; to advance toward the end without losing anything is to gain a lot. Let childhood ripen in children. And what if some lesson finally becomes necessary to them? Keep yourself from giving it today if you can without danger put it off until tomorrow.

Another consideration confirms the utility of this method. One must know well the particular genius of the child in order to know what moral diet suits him. Each mind has its own form, according to which it needs to be governed; the success of one's care depends on governing it by this form and not by another. Prudent man, spy out nature for a long time; observe your pupil well before saying the first word to him. To start with, let the germ of his character reveal itself freely; constrain it in no way whatsoever in order better to see the whole of it. Do you think this time of freedom is lost for him? Not at all. This is the best way to use it, for you are learning now not to lose a single moment in a more valuable time; while if you begin to act before knowing what must be done, you will act haphazardly. Subject to error, you will have to retrace your steps; you will be farther removed from the goal than if you had been in less of a rush to reach it. Do not therefore act like the miser who loses a great deal for wanting not to lose anything. In the earliest age sacrifice time that you will regain with interest at a more advanced age. The wise doctor does not at first sight giddily give prescriptions but in the first place studies the constitution of his patient before prescribing anything to him. He may begin to treat the patient late but he cures him, whereas the doctor who is in too much of a rush kills him.

But where will we put this child to raise him like a being without sensation, like an automaton? Will we keep him in the moon's orb or on a desert island? Will we keep him away from all human beings? Will he not constantly have in the world the spectacle and the example of others' passions? Will he never see other children of his age? Will he not see his parents, his neighbors, his nurse, his governess, his lackey, even his governor who, after all, will not be an angel?

This objection is strong and solid. But did I tell you that a natural education was an easy undertaking? O men, is it my fault if you have made everything good difficult? I sense these difficulties; I agree that they are difficulties. Perhaps they are insurmountable. But it is still certain that in applying oneself to overcoming them, one does overcome them up to a certain point. I show the goal that must be set; I do not say that it can be reached. But I do say that he who comes nearest to it will have succeeded best.

Remember that before daring to undertake the formation of a man, one must have made oneself a man. One must find within oneself the example the pupil ought to take for his own. While the child is still without knowledge, there is time to prepare everything that comes near him in order that only objects suitable for him to see meet his first glances. Make yourself respectable to everyone. Begin by making yourself loved so that each will seek to please you. You will not be the child's master if you are not the master of all that surrounds him; and this authority will never be sufficient if it is not founded on the esteem for virtue. It is not a question of emptying one's purse and spending money by the handful. I have never seen that money has made anyone loved. One ought not to be miserly and hard nor merely pity the poverty that one can relieve. But you can open your coffers all you want; if you do not also open your heart, others' hearts will always remain closed to you. It is your time, your care, your affection, it is you yourself that must be given. For no matter what you do, people never feel that your money is you. There are tokens of interest and benevolence which produce a greater effect and are really more useful than any gifts. How many unfortunate people, how many sick people need consolation more than alms! How many oppressed people need protection more than money! Reconcile people who have quarreled; forestall litigations; bring children to their duty, fathers to indulgence; encourage happy marriages; prevent harassment; use, lavish the influence of your pupil's parents in favor of the weak man to whom justice is denied and who is crushed by the powerful man. Loudly proclaim yourself the protector of the unfortunate. Be just, humane, and beneficent. Give not only alms; give charity. Works of mercy relieve more ills than does money. Love others, and they will love you. Serve them, and they will serve you. Be their brother, and they will be your children.

This is again one of the reasons why I want to raise Emile in the country far from the rabble of valets—who are, after their masters, the lowest of men—far from the black morals of cities which are covered with a veneer seductive and contagious for children, unlike peasants' vices which, unadorned and in all their coarseness, are more fit to repel than to seduce when there is no advantage in imitating them.

In a village a governor will be much more the master of the objects he wants to present the child. His reputation, his speeches, and his example will have an authority which they could not have in the city. Since he is useful to everyone, all will be eager to oblige him, to be esteemed by him, to show themselves to the disciple as the master would want them really to be. And if they do not actually reform, they will at least abstain from scandal; this is all we need for our project.

Stop blaming others for your own faults; the evil children see corrupts them less than that which you teach them. Always sermonizers, always moralists, always pedants, for one idea you give them, believing it to be good, you give them at the same time twenty that are worthless. Full of what is going on in your head, you do not see the effect you are producing in theirs. In this long stream of words with which you constantly exasperate them, do you think there is not one which they misapprehend? Do you think that they do not make their own commentaries on your diffuse explanations, and that they do not find in these explanations the material for setting up a system on their own level, which they will know how to use against you when the occasion demands?

Listen to a little fellow who has just been indoctrinated. Let him chatter, question, utter foolishness at his ease, and you are going to be surprised at the strange turn your reasonings have taken in his mind. He mixes up everything, turns everything upside down; he makes you lose your patience, sometimes grieves you by unforeseen objections. He reduces you to silence or to silencing him, and what can he think of this silence on the part of a man who likes to talk so much? If ever he gains this advantage and notices it, farewell to education. Everything is finished from this moment: he no longer seeks to learn; he seeks to refute you.

Zealous masters, be simple, discreet, restrained; never hasten to act except to prevent others from acting. I shall repeat it endlessly: put off, if possible, a good lesson for fear of giving a bad one. On this earth, out of which nature has made man's first paradise, dread exercising the tempter's function in wanting to give innocence the knowledge of good and evil. Unable to prevent the child's learning from examples out of doors, limit your vigilance to impressing these examples upon his mind accompanied by the images suitable for him.

Impetuous passions produce a great effect on the child who is witness to them because their manifestations are such as to strike his senses and force him to pay attention. Anger, in particular, is so noisy in its transports that one cannot fail to notice it if one is within its range. It need not be asked whether this is the occasion for a pedagogue to start out on a fine speech. Now, no fine speeches! Nothing at all; not a single word. Let the child come; surprised at the spectacle, he will not fail to question you. The response is simple; it is drawn from the very objects which strike his senses. He sees an inflamed face, glittering eyes, threatening gestures; he hears shouts—all signs that the body is out of kilter. Tell him calmly, without affectation and without mystery, "This poor man is sick; he is in a fit of fever." On this basis you can find occasions to give him, but in a few words, an idea of illnesses and their effects, for that, too, belongs to nature and is one of the bonds of necessity to which he should feel himself subjected.[19]

Is it possible that from this idea, which is not false, he will not early on contract a certain repugnance to abandoning himself to the excesses of the passions, which he will regard as diseases? And do you believe that some such notion, given apropos, will not produce an effect as salutary as the most boring moral sermon? Moreover, just consider the future ramifications of this notion! Now you are authorized, if you are ever forced to do so, to treat a rebellious child as a sick child, to shut him up in his room, in his bed if necessary, to keep him on a diet, to frighten him with his own nascent vices, to render them odious and redoubtable to him, without his ever being able to regard as a chastisement the severity you will perhaps be forced to use to cure him of them. If it should happen that you yourself, in a moment of heat, lose that coolness and moderation which you should make your study, do not seek to disguise your mistake before him, but tell him frankly with a tender reproach, "My friend, you hurt me."

Furthermore, it is important that none of a child's naïve statements— the products of the simplicity of the ideas on which he feeds—ever be picked up in his presence or quoted in such a way that he can learn of it. An indiscreet outburst of laughter can ruin the work of six months and do irreparable harm for the whole of life. I cannot repeat often enough that to be the child's master one must be one's own master. I see my little Emile, at the height of a fracas between two neighbors, approaching the more furious of the two and saying to her in a tone of commiseration, "My good woman, you are sick. I am so sorry about it." This sally will surely not remain without effect on the spectators or perhaps on the actresses. Without laughing, without scolding him, without praising him, I take him away willingly or forcibly before he can see this effect, or at least before he thinks about it, and I hasten to distract him with other objects which make him forget it right away.

It is my design not to enter into all the details but only to expound the general maxims and to give examples for difficult occasions. I hold it to be impossible to bring a child along to the age of twelve in the bosom of society without giving him some idea of the relations of man to man and of the morality of human actions. It is enough if one takes pains to ensure that these notions become necessary to him as late as possible and, when their presentation is unavoidable, to limit them to immediate utility, with the sole intention of preventing him from believing himself master of everything and from doing harm to others without scruple and without knowing it. There are gentle and quiet characters whom one can take a long way in their first innocence without danger. But there are also violent natures whose ferocity develops early and whom one must hasten to make into men so as not to be obliged to put them in chains.

Our first duties are to ourselves; our primary sentiments are centered on ourselves; all our natural movements relate in the first instance to our preservation and our well-being. Thus, the first sentiment of justice does not come to us from the justice we owe but from that which is owed us; and it is again one of the mistakes of ordinary educations that, speaking at first to children of their duties, never of their rights, one begins by telling them the opposite of what is necessary, what they cannot understand, and what cannot interest them.[20]

If, therefore, I had to guide one of those children I just mentioned, I would say to myself, "A child does not attack persons * but things; and

---

* One ought never to permit a child to play with grownups as with his inferiors or even as with his equals. If he seriously dares to strike someone, be it his lackey, be it the hangman, arrange that his blows be always returned with interest and in such a way as to destroy the desire to revert to the practice. I have seen imprudent governesses animate the unruliness of a child, incite him to strike, let themselves be

soon he learns by experience to respect whoever surpasses him in age and strength. But things do not defend themselves. The first idea which must be given him is therefore less that of liberty than that of property; and for him to be able to have this idea, he must have something that belongs to him. To mention to him his clothing, his furniture, his toys, is to say nothing to him, since, although he disposes of these things, he knows neither why nor how he came by them. To say to him that he has them because they were given to him is hardly to do better, for, in order to give, one must have. Here is, therefore, a property anterior to his, and it is the principle of property one wants to explain to him, not to mention that a gift is a convention and that the child cannot know yet what convention is." * Readers, in this example and in a hundred thousand others, I beg you to note how we stuff children's heads with words which have no meaning within their reach and then believe we have instructed them very well.

The thing to do therefore is to go back to the origin of property, for it is there that the first idea of it ought to be born. The child, living in the country, will have gotten some notion of labor in the fields. For this only eyes and leisure are necessary; he will have both. It belongs to every age, especially his, to want to create, imitate, produce, give signs of power and activity. It will not take two experiences of seeing a garden plowed, sowed, sprouting, and growing vegetables for him to want to garden in his turn.

According to the principles previously established, I in no way oppose his desire. On the contrary, I encourage it, I share his taste. I work with him, not for his pleasure, but for mine; at least he believes it to be so. I become his gardener's helper. Until he has arms I plow the earth for him. He takes possession of it by planting a bean in it. And surely this possession is more sacred and more respectable than that taken of South America when Núñez Balboa in the name of the King of Spain planted his standard on the shore of the South Sea.

We come every day to water the beans; with transports of joy we see them sprout. I increase this joy by saying to him: "This belongs to you." And then, explaining to him this term "belong," I make him feel that he has put his time, his labor, his effort, finally his person there; that there is in this earth something of himself that he can claim against anyone whomsoever, just as he could withdraw his arm from the hand of another man who wanted to hold on to it in spite of him.[21]

One fine day he arrives eagerly with the watering can in his hand. O what a sight! O pain! All the beans are rooted out, the plot is torn up, the very spot is not to be recognized. O, what has become of my labor, my product, the sweet fruit of my care and my sweat? Who has stolen my goods? Who took my beans from me? This young heart is

---

struck, and laugh at his feeble blows, without thinking that in the intention of the little enraged one these blows were so many murders and that he who wants to strike when young will want to kill when grown.

* This is why most children want to have back what they have given and cry when one does not want to return it to them. This no longer occurs when they have gotten a good conception of what a gift is, but then they are more circumspect about giving.

aroused. The first sentiment of injustice comes to shed its sad bitterness in it. Tears flow in streams. The grieving child fills the air with moans and cries. I partake of his pain, his indignation. We look; we investigate; we make searches.²² Finally we discover that the gardener did the deed. He is summoned.

But we certainly do not get what we expect. The gardener, learning what we are complaining about, begins to complain more loudly than we do. "What, sirs! Is it you who have thus ruined my work? I had sowed Maltese melons there, the seeds of which had been given me as a treasure and with which I hoped to regale you when they were ripe. But now, in order to plant your miserable beans there, you destroyed my melons for me when they were already sprouting, and they can never be replaced. You have done me an irreparable wrong, and you have deprived yourselves of the pleasure of eating exquisite melons."

JEAN-JACQUES Excuse us, my poor Robert. You had put your labor, your effort there. I see clearly that we did wrong in ruining your work. But we will have other Maltese seeds sent to you. And we will never again work the land before knowing whether someone has put his hand to it before us.

ROBERT Very well, sirs! You can then take your rest. There is hardly any fallow land left. I work what my father improved. Each in turn does the same, and all the lands you see have been occupied for a long time.

EMILE Monsieur Robert, are melon seeds often lost then?

ROBERT Pardon me, my young fellow, but little gentlemen as giddy as you do not often come our way. No one touches his neighbor's garden. Each respects the labor of others so that his own will be secure.

EMILE But I don't have a garden.

ROBERT What do I care? If you ruin mine, I won't let you go around in it any more, for, you see, I don't want to waste my effort.

JEAN-JACQUES Couldn't we propose an arrangement with the good Robert? Let him grant us, my little friend and me, a corner of his garden to cultivate on the condition that he will have half the produce.

ROBERT I grant it to you without condition. But remember that I will go and plow up your beans if you touch my melons.

In this model of the way of inculcating primary notions in children one sees how the idea of property naturally goes back to the right of the first occupant by labor. That is clear, distinct, simple, and within the child's reach. From there to the right of property and to exchange there is only a step, after which one must simply stop short.

One sees further that an explanation that I enclose here in two pages of writing will perhaps take a year to put into practice, for in the career of moral ideas one cannot advance too slowly nor consolidate oneself too well at each step. Young masters, think, I beg you, about this example, and remember that in everything your lessons ought to be more in actions than in speeches; for children easily forget what they have said and what has been said to them, but not what they have done and what has been done to them.

Instruction of the kind ought, as I have said, to be given sooner or later as the peaceful or turbulent nature of the pupil accelerates or delays the need. How it should be given is obvious; but so as to leave out nothing of importance in difficult matters, let us give yet another example.

Your ill-tempered child ruins everything he touches. Do not get angry; put what he can damage out of his reach. He breaks the furniture he uses. Do not hurry to replace it for him. Let him feel the disadvantage of being deprived of it. He breaks the windows of his room; let the wind blow on him night and day without worrying about colds, for it is better that he have a cold than that he be crazy. Never complain about the inconveniences he causes you, but make him be the one to feel those inconveniences first. Finally, you have the windows repaired, continuing to say nothing about it. He breaks them again. Then change method. Tell him curtly but without anger, "The windows are mine; they were put there by my efforts; I want to protect them." Then you will close him up in darkness in a place without windows. In response to such a new procedure he begins by crying and ranting. No one listens to him. Soon he tires and changes tone. He moans and groans. A domestic turns up; the rebel begs him for deliverance. Without seeking pretexts for not doing it, the domestic responds, "I too have windows to protect," and leaves. Finally, after the child has remained there several hours, long enough to get bored and to remember it, someone will suggest to him that he propose an agreement by means of which you will give him back his freedom if he no longer breaks windows. He will not ask for better. He will have you asked to come and see him. You will come. He will make you his proposition, and you will accept it on the instant, saying to him, "That is very well thought out; we will both be gainers by it. Why didn't you have this good idea sooner?" And then, without asking that he declare or confirm his promise, you will embrace him with joy and take him to his room right away, regarding this agreement as sacred and inviolable as if an oath had been given on it. What idea do you think he will get from this procedure about the faith of commitments and their utility? I am mistaken if there is a single child on earth, not already spoiled, who would be proof against this conduct and take it into his head after that to break a window intentionally.* Follow all the links of this chain. The naughty

* Moreover, if this duty to keep commitments were not consolidated in the child's mind by the weight of its utility, soon the inner sentiment, beginning to sprout, would impose it on him like a law of conscience, like an innate principle which awaits in order to bloom only the kinds of knowledge to which it applies. This first sketch is not drawn by the hand of man but is graven in our hearts by the Author of all justice. Take away the primary law of conventions and the obligation it imposes, and everything is illusory and vain in human society. He who keeps his promise only for profit is hardly more bound than if he had promised nothing, or, at most, he is in the position to violate it like the tennis players who put off using a *bisque* [28] only in order to wait for the moment to use it most advantageously. This principle is of the utmost importance and merits deeper study. For it is here that man begins to set himself in contradiction to himself.

the hands. All the other virtues which are taught children resemble this one, and it is to preach these solid virtues to them that one uses up their young years in gloom. Is this not an informed education!

Masters, leave off pretenses. Be virtuous and good. Let your examples be graven in your pupils' memories until they can enter their hearts. Instead of hastening to exact acts of charity from my pupil, I prefer to do them in his presence and to deprive him of even the means of imitating me in this, as an honor which is not for his age; for it is important that he not get accustomed to regarding the duties of men as only the duties of children. If, seeing me assisting the poor, he questions me about it, and it is time to answer him,* I shall say to him: "My friend, this is because, when the poor were willing to let there be rich men, the rich promised to sustain all those who do not have the means of life, either from their goods or from their labor." "Then did you, too, promise that?" he will rejoin. "Certainly, I am master of the wealth that passes through my hands only on the condition attached to its being property."

After having heard this speech (and it has been seen how a child can be put in a condition to understand it), another than Emile would be tempted to imitate me and to behave like a rich man. In such a case I would at least prevent him from doing so ostentatiously. I would prefer his robbing me of my right and covertly giving. This is a fraud appropriate to his age, and the only one I would pardon him.

I know that all these virtues by imitation are the virtues of apes, and that no good action is morally good except when it is done because it is good and not because others do it. But at an age when the heart feels nothing yet, children just have to be made to imitate the acts whose habit one wants to give them, until the time when they can do them out of discernment and love of the good. Man is an imitator. Even animals are. The taste for imitation belongs to well-ordered nature, but in society it degenerates into vice. The ape imitates man whom he fears and does not imitate the animals whom he despises. He judges to be good what is done by a being better than he. Among us, on the other hand, our Harlequins of every sort imitate the beautiful to degrade it, to make it ridiculous. They seek, in the feeling of their own baseness, to level what surpasses them in worth. Or if they make efforts to imitate what they admire, one sees in the choice of objects the false taste of the imitators. They want to make an impression on others or to get applause for their talent far more than to make themselves better or wiser. The foundation of imitation among us comes from the desire always to be transported out of ourselves. If I succeed in my enterprise, Emile surely will not have this desire. We must, therefore, give up the apparent good which imitation can produce.

Think through all the rules of your education; you will find them misconceived, especially those that concern virtues and morals. The only lesson of morality appropriate to childhood, and the most important for every age, is never to harm anyone. The very precept of

* It should be grasped that I do not answer his questions when he pleases but when I please; otherwise I would be the servant of his will and put myself in the most dangerous dependence in which a governor can be in relation to his pupil.

child hardly dreamed, while making a hole for planting his bean, that he was digging for himself a dungeon where his science would not be long in shutting him up.

Here we are in the moral world; here the door on vice opens. With conventions and duties are born deceit and lying. As soon as one can do what one ought not, one wants to hide what one ought not to have done. As soon as an interest causes a promise, a greater interest can cause the violation of the promise. The only concern now is to violate it with impunity. The means are natural; one conceals and one lies. Not having been able to forestall vice, we are now already reduced to punishing it. Here are the miseries of human life which begin with its errors.

I have said enough to make it understood that punishment as punishment must never be inflicted on children, but it should always happen to them as a natural consequence of their bad action. Thus you will not declaim against lying; you will not precisely punish them for having lied; but you will arrange it so that all the bad effects of lying—such as not being believed when one tells the truth, of being accused of the evil that one did not do although one denies it—come in league against them when they have lied. But let us explain what lying is for children.

There are two sorts of lies: the de facto lie, which is with respect to the past; the de jure, which is with respect to the future. The former takes place when one denies having done what one has done, or when one affirms having done what one has not done, and in general when one knowingly speaks contrary to the truth of things. The other takes place when one makes a promise that one does not plan to keep, and, in general, when one gives evidence of an intention contrary to the intention one has. These two lies can sometimes be joined in a single one,* but I am considering them here under the aspect of their difference.

He who is aware of the need he has of others' help, and who never fails to experience their benevolence, has no interest in deceiving them; on the contrary, he has a palpable interest in their seeing things as they are, for fear that they might make a mistake prejudicial to him. It is, therefore, clear that the de facto lie is not natural to children. But it is the law of obedience which produces the necessity of lying, because since obedience is irksome, it is secretly dispensed with as much as possible, and the present interest in avoiding punishment or reproach wins out over the distant interest of revealing the truth. In the natural and free education why would your child lie to you? What has he to hide from you? You do not reprove him; you punish him for nothing; you exact nothing from him. Why would he not tell you everything he has done as naïvely as he would his little comrade? He can see in this admission no more danger from one direction than the other.

The de jure lie is still less natural, since promises to do or to forbear are conventional acts which depart from the state of nature and impair freedom. What is more, all commitments of children are in themselves null, because, since their limited view cannot extend beyond the present,

* Such as, when accused of a bad action, the guilty party defends himself by claiming he is an honest man. His lie is then de facto and de jure.

in committing themselves they do not know what they are doing. The child hardly can lie when he commits himself; for, thinking only how to get through a situation at the present moment, every means which does not have a present effect becomes the same for him. In promising for a future time, he promises nothing, and his imagination, still dormant, does not know how to extend his being over two different times. If he could avoid the whip or get a bag of sugared almonds by promising to throw himself out of the window tomorrow, he would make the promise on the spot. This is why laws take no account of children's commitments; and when, more severe, fathers and masters exact their fulfillment, it is only in those things the child ought to do even if he had not promised.

Since the child does not know what he is doing when he commits himself, then he cannot lie in committing himself. It is not the same when he breaks his promise, which is now a kind of retroactive lie, for he remembers very well having made this promise; but what he does not see is the importance of keeping it. Not in a condition to read the future, he cannot foresee the consequences of things, and when he violates his commitments, he does nothing contrary to the reason of his age.

It follows from this that children's lies are all the work of masters, and that to want to teach them to tell the truth is nothing other than to teach them to lie. In one's eagerness to control them, to govern them, to instruct them, one finds one never has sufficient means for reaching the goal. One wants to give oneself new holds on their minds by means of maxims without foundation and precepts without reason; one prefers that they know their lessons and lie, rather than remain ignorant and true.

For us who give our pupils only lessons in practice and who prefer that they be good rather than learned—we do not exact the truth from them lest they disguise it, and we make them give no promises that they would be tempted not to keep. If in my absence something bad were to happen and I did not know the author of it, I would take care not to accuse Emile and say to him, "Was it you?" *—for what else would I be doing by this than teaching him to deny it? If his difficult natural disposition compels me to come to some agreement with him, I will arrange things so carefully that the suggestion always comes from him, never from me; that when he has committed himself, he always has a present and palpable interest in fulfilling his commitment; and that if he ever fails to do so, the lie attracts evils to him which he sees as coming from the very order of things and not from the vengeance of his governor. But, far from needing to resort to expedients so cruel, I am almost sure that Emile will learn quite late what it is to lie and that, in learning, he will be quite surprised, unable to conceive what a lie might be

---

* Nothing is more indiscreet than such a question, especially when the child is guilty: then if he believes that you know that he did it, he will see that you are setting a trap for him, and this opinion cannot fail to turn him against you. If he does not believe it, he will say to himself, "Why should I reveal my offense?" And this is the first temptation to lie, the effect of your imprudent question.

good for. It is quite clear that the more I make his well-being independent of either the will or the judgments of others, the more I reduce any interest in him to lie.

When one is not in a hurry to instruct, one is not in a hurry to demand and takes one's time so as to demand nothing except opportunely. Then, the child is formed by the very fact of not being spoiled. But when a giddy preceptor, not knowing how to go about it, makes him promise this or that at every instant, without distinction, selectivity, or moderation, the child, bored, overburdened with all these promises, neglects them, forgets them, finally despises them, and, regarding them as so many vain formulas, makes a game out of making them and breaking them. Do you want, then, that he be faithful to his word? Be discreet in exacting it.

The detail I have just gone into about lying can in many respects be applied to all the other duties, which are never prescribed to children except in such a way as to make them not only hateful but impracticable. Appearing to preach virtue to children, one makes them love all the vices. The vices are given to them by forbidding them to have them. Does one want to make them pious? They are taken to church to be bored. Constantly made to mumble prayers, they are driven to aspire to the happiness of no longer praying to God. That charity be inspired in them, they are made to give alms—as if one despised giving them oneself. Oh no, it is not the child who ought to give; it is the master. To the extent that he is attached to his pupil, he ought to dispute this honor with him; he ought to make the pupil judge that at his age one is not yet worthy of it. Alms giving is an action for a man who knows the value of what he gives and the need that his fellow man has of it. In the child, who knows nothing about that, giving cannot be a merit. He gives without charity, without beneficence. He is almost ashamed to give when, based on his example and yours, he believes that it is only children who give and that, grown up, one no longer gives alms.

Note that the child is always made to give only things of whose value he is ignorant—some pieces of metal which he has in his pocket and which he uses only for giving. A child would rather give a hundred louis than a cake. But commit this prodigal distributor to give things which are dear to him—toys, candies, his snack—and we shall soon know if you have made him truly liberal.

A remedy for this, too, is found: it is at once to return to the child what he gave, so that he gets accustomed to giving everything which he is certain of getting back. I have scarcely seen in children any but these two kinds of generosity: giving what is good for nothing for them, or giving what they are sure is going to be returned to them. Arrange it so, says Locke, that they be convinced by experience that the most liberal man always comes off best.[24] That is to make a child in appearance liberal and in fact a miser. Locke adds that children will contract in this way the habit of liberality. Yes, of a usurious liberality which gives an egg to have a cow. But when the case involves straightforward giving, farewell to the habit. When one stops returning, they will soon stop giving. One must look to the habit of the soul rather than to that of

doing good, if it is not subordinated to this one, is dangerous, false, and contradictory. Who does not do good? Everybody does it—the wicked man as well as others. He makes one man happy at the expense of making a hundred men miserable; and this is the source of all our calamities. The most sublime virtues are negative. They are also the most difficult, because they are without ostentation and above even that pleasure so sweet to the heart of man, the pleasure of sending someone away satisfied with us. O what good is necessarily done to his fellows by the one among them, if there is such a one, who never does them harm! What an intrepid soul, what a vigorous character he needs for that! It is not in reasoning about this maxim, but in trying to put it into practice, that one feels how great it is and how difficult of success.*

These are but a few feeble ideas of the precautions I would wish to see taken in giving children instruction that one sometimes cannot refuse them without exposing them to harming themselves and others—and especially to contracting bad habits which would be hard to correct in them later. But we can be sure that this necessity will rarely present itself for children raised as they ought to be. Because it is impossible for them to become intractable, wicked, lying, greedy, when one has not sowed in their hearts the vices which make them such. Thus, what I have said on this point serves more for the exception than the rule. But to the extent that children have more occasions to step out of their condition and contract the vices of men, exceptions of this kind are the more frequent. Those raised in the midst of men must of necessity have earlier instruction than those raised in an out-of-the-way place. This solitary education would, therefore, be preferable even if its only effect were to give childhood the time for ripening.

There is on the other side another kind of exception for those whom a happy nature raises above their age. As there are men who never leave childhood, there are others who, so to speak, do not go through it and who are men almost at birth. The difficulty is that this latter exception is very rare, very hard to recognize, and that every mother, imagining that a child might be a prodigy, has no doubt that hers is one. Mothers go yet farther; they take as marks of extraordinary promise the very things which point to the accustomed order: vivacity, flashes of wit, giddiness, piquant naïveté—all the most characteristic and telling signs that a child is only a child. Is it surprising that he who is made to talk a lot, who is permitted to say everything, and who is not hindered by deference or propriety, should by chance make some lucky hit? It would be far more surprising if he never did, just as it would be if along with a thousand lies an astrologer never predicted a single truth.

---

* The precept of never hurting another carries with it that of being attached to human society as little as possible, for in the social state the good of one necessarily constitutes the harm of another. This relation is in the essence of the thing, and nothing can change it. On the basis of this principle, let one investigate who is the better: the social man or the solitary man. An illustrious author says it is only the wicked man who is alone.[25] I say that it is only the good man who is alone. If this proposition is less sententious, it is truer and better reasoned than the former one. If the wicked man were alone, what harm would he do? It is in society that he sets up his devices for hurting others. If one wishes to turn this argument around to apply to the good man, I answer with the passage to which this note belongs.

They will lie so much, said Henri IV, that finally they will tell the truth.[26] Whoever wishes to come up with a certain number of *bons mots* has only to say many stupid things. God save the fashionable folk who have no other claim to fame.

The most brilliant thoughts can come into children's brains, or, rather, the best lines into their mouths, as diamonds of the greatest value might come into their hands, without either the thoughts or the diamonds thereby belonging to them. There is no true property of any kind at that age. The things a child says are not to him what they are to us; he does not attach the same ideas to them. His ideas, if indeed he has any at all, will have neither order nor connection in his head— nothing fixed, nothing certain in all that he thinks. Examine your alleged prodigy. At certain moments you will find in him an extremely taut mainspring, a clarity of mind which can pierce the clouds. Most often this same mind will seem lax to you, soggy, and, as it were, surrounded by a thick fog. At one time it gets ahead of you, the next, it remains immobile. At one moment you would say, "He's a genius," and at the next, "He's a fool." You would be mistaken in both cases: what he is is a child. He is an eaglet who for an instant cleaves the air and then falls back into his eyrie.

Treat him, then, according to his age, in spite of the appearances, and be afraid of exhausting his strength for having wanted to exercise it too much. If this young brain warms up, if you see it beginning to boil, let it ferment freely at first, but never stimulate it lest it expend itself. And when the first spirits have evaporated, retain and compress the others until, over the years, all turns into heat and true strength. Otherwise, you will waste your time and your effort. You will destroy your own work; and after having intoxicated yourself out of season on all these inflammable vapors, you will be left with only a *marc* [27] without vigor.

From giddy children come vulgar men. I know of no observation more universal and more certain than this one. Nothing is more difficult in respect of childhood than to distinguish real stupidity from that merely apparent and deceptive stupidity which is the presage of strong souls. It seems strange at first that the two extremes should have such similar signs. Nevertheless, it is properly so; for at an age when man as yet has nothing that is truly an idea, the entire difference between one who has genius and one who does not is that the latter accepts only false ideas, and the former, finding only such, accepts none. Thus the genius resembles the stupid child in that the latter is capable of nothing while nothing is suitable for the former. The only sign which permits the two to be distinguished depends on chance, which may present the genius some idea within his reach, while the stupid child is always the same everywhere. Cato the Younger during his childhood seemed an imbecile at home. He was taciturn and stubborn—this is all he was judged to be. It was only in Sulla's antechamber that his uncle learned to know him. If he had not entered that antechamber, perhaps he would have passed for a brute until the age of reason. If Caesar had not lived, perhaps they would always have treated as a visionary this very Cato who discerned Caesar's fatal genius and foresaw all his projects so far in advance.²⁸ O how those who make such hasty judgments about children are liable to mistakes! They are often more children than the children. I have seen a man who honored me with his friendship taken, at a rather advanced age, to be a limited mind by his family and his friends. This excellent head ripened in silence. Suddenly he proved to be a philosopher, and I do not doubt that posterity will give him an honorable and distinguished place among the best reasoners and the most profound metaphysicians of his age.²⁹

Respect childhood, and do not hurry to judge it, either for good or for ill. Let the exceptional children show themselves, be proved, and be confirmed for a long time before adopting special methods for them. Leave nature to act for a long time before you get involved with acting in its place, lest you impede its operations. You know, you say, the value of time and do not want to waste any of it? You do not see that using time badly wastes time far more than doing nothing with it and that a badly instructed child is farther from wisdom than the one who has not been instructed at all. You are alarmed to see him consume his early years in doing nothing. What? Is it nothing to be happy? Is it nothing to jump, play, and run all day? He will never be so busy in his life. Plato in his republic, believed to be so austere, raises the children only by festivals, games, songs, and pastimes; ³⁰ one could say that he has done everything when he has taught them well how to enjoy themselves. And Seneca, speaking of the old Roman youth, says: "They were always on their feet; they were taught nothing that had to be taught sitting." ³¹ Were they for that worth any the less on reaching manhood? Therefore, do not be overly frightened by this alleged idleness. What would you say of a man who, in order to profit from his whole life, never wanted to sleep? You would say, "That man is crazy; he does not gain time for his joy; he deprives himself of it. To flee sleep, he races toward death." Be aware, then, that we have here the same thing and that childhood is reason's sleep.

Apparent facility at learning is the cause of children's ruin. It is not seen that this very facility is the proof they learn nothing. Their brain, smooth and polished, returns, like a mirror, the objects presented to it. But nothing remains; nothing penetrates. The child retains the words; the ideas are reflected off of him. Those who hear him understand them; only he does not understand them.

Although memory and reasoning are two essentially different faculties, nevertheless the one develops truly only with the other. Before the age of reason the child receives not ideas but images; and the difference between the two is that images are only absolute depictions of sensible objects, while ideas are notions of objects determined by relations. An image can stand all alone in the mind which represents it, but every idea supposes other ideas. When one imagines, one does nothing but see; when one conceives, one is comparing. Our sensations are purely passive, while all our perceptions or ideas are born out of an active principle which judges. This will be demonstrated hereafter.

Therefore I say that children, not being capable of judgment, do not have true memory. They retain sounds, figures, sensations, ideas rarely, the connections between ideas more rarely. Those who object, saying that children learn some elements of geometry, believe this to be good proof against me; whereas on the contrary, it is proof for my case. It is demonstrable that, far from knowing how to reason by themselves, little geometers do not even know how to retain the reasonings of others. For follow them in their method, and you see immediately that they have retained only the exact impression of the figure and the terms of the demonstration. At the least new objection they can no longer follow. Turn the figure upside down, they can no longer follow. Their entire learning is in sensation; nothing has gone through to the understanding. Their memory itself is hardly more perfect than their other faculties, since they must almost always, when they are grown, relearn the things for which they learned the words in childhood.

I am, however, very far from thinking that children have no kind of reasoning.* On the contrary, I see that they reason very well in everything they know that relates to their immediate and palpable interest. But one is mistaken about their knowledge, ascribing to them knowledge they do not have and making them reason about what they could not understand. One is again mistaken in wanting to make them pay attention to considerations which do not touch them in any way, such as their future concerns, their happiness when they are men, the esteem in which they will be held as adults—speeches which, given to beings unendowed with any foresight, signify absolutely nothing to them. Now all the studies forced on these poor unfortunates are directed to these objects entirely alien to their minds. You can judge of the attention they can pay to them!

The pedagogues who present such a showy display of the instruction they give their disciples are paid for using other language than mine. However, one sees by their very conduct that they think exactly as I do, for what do they teach them after all? Words, more words, always words. Among the various sciences that they boast of teaching their pupils, they are quite careful not to include those which would be truly useful to them, because they would be sciences of things, and with these they would not succeed. Rather they choose those sciences one appears to know when one knows their terminology: heraldry, geography, chronology, languages, etc.—all studies so far from man, and especially from the child, that it would be a wonder if anything at all in them were of use to him a single time in his life.

People will be surprised that I number the study of languages among

---

* I have a hundred times in writing made the reflection that it is impossible in a long work always to give the same meanings to the same words. There is no language rich enough to furnish as many terms, turns, and phrases as our ideas can have modifications. The method of defining all the terms and constantly substituting the definition in the place of the defined is fine but impracticable, for how can a circle be avoided? Definitions could be good if words were not used to make them. In spite of that, I am persuaded that one can be clear, even in the poverty of our language, not by always giving the same meanings to the same words, but by arranging it so that as often as each word is used, the meaning given it be sufficiently determined by the ideas related to it and that each period where the word is found serves it, so to speak, as a definition. One time I say children are incapable of reasoning; another time I make them reason quite keenly. I do not believe that with that I contradict myself in my ideas; but I cannot gainsay that I often contradict myself in my expressions.

the useless parts of education. But remember that I am speaking here only of studies appropriate to the early years; and, whatever may be said, I do not believe that up to the age of twelve or fifteen any child, prodigies apart, has ever truly learned two languages.

I agree that if the study of languages were only the study of words—that is to say, of figures or the sounds which express them—it could be suitable for children. But in changing the signs, languages also modify the ideas which these signs represent. Minds are formed by languages; the thoughts take on the color of the idioms. Only reason is common; in each lanuage the mind has its particular form. This is a difference which might very well be a part of the cause or of the effect of national characters; and what appears to confirm this conjecture is that in all the nations of the world language follows the vicissitudes of morals and is preserved or degenerates as they are.

Normal usage gives but one of all these various forms to the child, and it is the only one he keeps until the age of reason. To have two, he would have to know how to compare ideas, and how could he compare them when he is hardly in a condition to conceive them? Each thing can have for him a thousand different signs. But each idea can have only one form. He can, therefore, learn to speak only one language. I am told, however, that he learns several. I deny it. I have seen these little prodigies who believed that they spoke five or six languages. I have heard them speak German in Latin terms, in French terms, in Italian terms successively. They did in truth make use of five or six lexicons. But they always spoke only German. In a word: give children as many synonyms as you please; you will change the words, not the language. They will never know any but one.

It is to hide this ineptitude of theirs that they are by preference trained in the dead languages, of which there are no more judges to whom one can have recourse. The familiar usage of these languages having long been lost, one is satisfied with imitating what is found written in books. And that is what is called speaking them. If such is the masters' Greek and Latin, you can judge the children's! Hardly have they learned by heart the rudiments, of which they understand absolutely nothing, when they are first taught to render a French discourse in Latin words; then, when they are more advanced, to stitch together in prose some phrases of Cicero and in verse some morsels of Virgil. Then they believe that they speak Latin. Who will come and contradict them?

In any study whatsoever, unless one has the ideas of the things represented, the representative signs are nothing. However, one always limits the child to these signs without ever being able to make him understand any of the things which they represent. Thinking he is being taught a description of the earth, he learns only to know some maps. He is taught the names of cities, of countries, of rivers which he does not conceive as existing anywhere else but on the paper where he is showed them. I remember having seen somewhere a geography text which began thus: "What is the world? It is a cardboard globe." Such precisely is the geography of children. I set down as a fact that after two years of globe and cosmography there is not a single child of ten who, following the rules he has been given, knows how to get from Paris to Saint-Denis. I set down as a fact that there is not one who, on the basis of a map of his father's garden, is able to follow its winding paths without getting lost. These are the doctors who know on the spur of the moment where Peking, Ispahan, Mexico, and all the countries of the earth are.

I hear it said that it is suitable to busy children with studies requiring only their eyes. That might be, if there were some study in which only eyes were required. But I know of none such.

By an error even more ridiculous they are made to study history. One imagines that history is within their reach because it is only a collection of facts. But what is meant by this word *facts*? Can anyone believe that the relations which determine historical facts are so easy to grasp that ideas are effortlessly formed from the facts in children's minds? Can anyone believe that the true knowledge of events is separable from that of their causes or of their effects and that the historical is so little connected with the moral that one can be known without the other? If you see in men's actions only the exterior and purely physical movements, what do you learn from history? Absolutely nothing. And this study, devoid of all interest, gives you no more pleasure than it does instruction. If you want your pupils to appreciate such actions in their moral relations, try to make them understand these relations, and you will see then whether history is a proper study at their age.

Readers, always remember that he who speaks to you is neither a scholar nor a philosopher, but a simple man, a friend of the truth, without party, without system; a solitary who, living little among men, has less occasion to contract their prejudices and more time to reflect on what strikes him when he has commerce with them. My reasonings are founded less on principles than on facts; and I believe that I cannot better put you in a position to judge of them than often to report to you some example of the observations which suggested them to me.

I had gone to spend a few days in the country at the home of a good mother of a family who took great care of her children and their education. One morning when I was present at the lessons of the eldest, his governor, who had instructed him very well in ancient history, was reviewing the history of Alexander. He took up the famous story about Philip, the physician, which has been a subject of painting, and which was surely well worth the effort.[32] The governor, a man of merit, made several reflections on Alexander's intrepidity, which did not please me at all, but which I avoided disputing so as not to discredit him in his pupil's mind. At table they did not fail, according to the French method, to make the little gentleman babble a great deal. The vivacity natural to his age, along with the expectation of certain applause, made him reel off countless stupidities, in the midst of which from time to time there came a few lucky words which caused the rest to be forgotten. Finally came the story of Philip, the physician. He told it quite clearly and with much grace. After the ordinary tribute of praises exacted by the mother and expected by the son, there was discussion about what he had said. The greater number blamed the temerity of Alexander; some, after the governor's example, admired his firmness and his courage—which made me understand that none of those present saw wherein lay the true beauty of this story. "As for me," I said to them, "it seems that if there is the least courage, the least firmness, in Alexander's action, it is foolhardy." [33] Then everyone joined in and agreed that it was foolhardy. I was going to respond and was getting heated when a woman sitting beside me, who had not opened her mouth, leaned toward my ear and said softly to me, "Keep quiet, Jean-Jacques, they won't understand you." I looked at her; I was struck; and I kept quiet.

After the dinner, suspecting, on the basis of several bits of evidence, that my young doctor had understood nothing at all of the story he had told so well, I took him by the hand and went for a turn in the park with him. Having questioned him at my ease, I found that more than anyone he admired Alexander's much-vaunted courage. But do you know in what he found this courage to consist? Solely in having swallowed at a single gulp a bad-tasting potion, without hesitation, without the least sign of repugnance. The poor child, who had been made to take medicine not two weeks before, and who had taken it only after a mighty effort, still had its aftertaste in his mouth. Death and poisoning stood in his mind only for disagreeable sensations; and he did not conceive, for his part, of any other poison than senna. Nevertheless, it must admitted that the hero's firmness had made a great impression on the boy's young heart, and that, at the next medicine he would have to swallow, he had resolved to be an Alexander. Without going into clarifications which were evidently out of his reach, I confirmed him in these laudable dispositions; and I went back laughing to myself at the lofty wisdom of fathers and masters who think they teach history to children.

It is easy to put into their mouths the words *kings, empires, wars, conquests, revolutions, laws*. But if it is a question of attaching distinct ideas to these words, there is a long way from the conversation with Robert the gardener to all these explanations.

Some readers, discontented with the "Keep quiet, Jean-Jacques," will, I foresee, ask what, after all, do I find so fair in Alexander's action? Unfortunate people! If you have to be told, how will you understand it? It is that Alexander believed in virtue; it is that he staked his head, his own life on that belief; it is that his great soul was made for believing in it. Oh, what a fair profession of faith was the swallowing of that medicine! No, never did a mortal make so sublime a one. If there is some modern Alexander, let him be showed to me by like deeds.

If there is no science of words, there is no study proper for children. If they have no true ideas, they have no true memory, for I do not call by that name the mere retention of sensations. What is the use of inscribing in their heads a catalogue of signs which represent nothing for them? In learning the things, will they not learn the signs? Why put them to the useless effort of learning the signs twice? And, meanwhile, what dangerous prejudices does one not begin to inspire in them by making them take for science words which have no sense for them? It is with the first word the child uses in order to show off, it is with the first thing he takes on another's word without seeing its utility himself, that his judgment is lost. He will have to shine in the eyes of fools for a long time in order to make up for such a loss.*

No, if nature gives the child's brain the suppleness that fits it to receive all sorts of impressions, it is not in order to engrave on this brain the names of kings, dates, terms of heraldry, globes and geography, and all those words without any sense for the child's age, and devoid of utility for any age whatsoever, with which his sad and sterile childhood is burdened. Rather, the suppleness is there in order that all the ideas which he can conceive and are useful to him—all those which are related to his happiness and are one day going to enlighten him about his duties—may be impressed on his brain with an indelible stamp at an early age and help him during his life to behave in a way suitable to his being and his faculties.

The kind of memory a child can have does not, without his studying books, for this reason remain idle. Everything he sees, everything he hears strikes him, and he remembers it. He keeps in himself a record of the actions and the speeches of men, and all that surrounds him is the book in which, without thinking about it, he continually enriches his memory while waiting for his judgment to be able to profit from it. It is in the choice of these objects, it is in the care with which one constantly presents him the objects he can know, and hides from him those he ought not to know, that the true art of cultivating in him this first faculty consists; and it is in this way that one must try to form in him a storehouse of knowledge which serves his education during his youth and his conduct at all times. This method, it is true, does not form little prodigies and does not make governors and preceptors shine. But it forms men who are judicious, robust, healthy of body and understanding, men who, without having made themselves admired when young, make themselves honored when grown.

Emile will never learn anything by heart, not even fables, not even those of La Fontaine,[34] as naïve, as charming as they are, for the words of fables are no more fables than the words of history are history. How can people be so blinded as to call fables the morality of children? They do not think about how the apologue,[35] in giving enjoyment to children, deceives them; about how, seduced by the lie, they let the truth escape; and about how what is done to make the instruction agreeable to them prevents them from profiting from it. Fables can instruct men, but the naked truth has to be told to children. When one

---

* Most learned men are learned in the way of children. Vast erudition results less from a multitude of ideas than from a multitude of images. Dates, proper names, places, all objects isolated or devoid of ideas are retained solely by memory of signs; and rarely does one recall some one of these things without at the same time seeing the page on the right- or the left-hand side where it was read or the form in which it was seen for the first time. Pretty nearly such was the science fashionable in the last ages. That of our age is something else. One no longer studies, one no longer observes, one dreams; and we are gravely presented with the dreams of some bad nights as philosophy. I will be told that I, too, dream. I agree; but I give my dreams as dreams, which others are not careful to do, leaving it to the reader to find out whether they contain something useful for people who are awake.

starts covering the truth with a veil, they no longer make the effort to lift it.[36]

All children are made to learn the fables of La Fontaine; and there is not a single one who understands them. If they were to understand them, that would be still worse, for the moral in them is so mixed and so disproportionate [37] to their age that it would lead them more to vice than to virtue. These again, you will say, are paradoxes. So be it; but let us see whether they are truths.

I say that a child does not understand the fables he is made to learn, because, no matter what effort is made to simplify them, the instruction that one wants to draw from them compels the introduction of ideas he cannot grasp; and because poetry's very skill at making them easier for him to retain makes them difficult for him to conceive, so that one buys delight at the expense of clarity. Without citing that multitude of fables which contain nothing intelligible or useful for children and which they are made to learn along with the others indiscriminately because they are found mixed in with them, let us limit ourselves to those the author seems to have made especially for children.

I know in the whole collection of La Fontaine only five or six fables in which childish naïveté genuinely predominates. Of these five or six I take for example the very first because it is the one whose moral is most fitting to all ages, the one children grasp best, the one they learn with the most pleasure, finally the one that for this very reason the author chose to put at the head of his book.[38] Supposing that his object were to be really understood by children, to please and instruct them, this fable is assuredly his masterpiece. Permit me then to follow it through and examine it in a few words.

The Crow and the Fox

FABLE

Master Crow, on a tree perched,

Master! What does this word signify in itself? What does it signify in front of a proper name? What meaning has it on this occasion? [39]

What is a crow?

What is *a tree perched*? One does not say: "on a tree perched"; one says: "perched on a tree." Consequently one has to talk about poetic inversions; one has to tell what prose and verse are.

Held in his beak a cheese.

What cheese? Was it a Swiss cheese. a Brie, or a Dutch? If the child has not seen crows, what do you gain by speaking to him about them? If he has seen them, how will he conceive of their holding a cheese in their beak? Let us always make images according to nature.

Master Fox by the odor atticed

Another master! But to this one the title really belongs: he is a past-master in the tricks of his trade. One has to say what a fox is and distinguish its true nature from the conventional character it has in fables.

Atticed. This word is not current. One has to explain it; one has to say that it is not used anymore except in verse. The child will ask why one speaks differently in verse than in prose. What will you respond to him?

"Atticed by the odor of a cheese!" This cheese held by a crow perched on a tree must have quite an odor to be smelled by the fox in a copse or in his hole! Is this the way you give your pupil practice in that spirit of judicious criticism which does not allow itself to be impressed except by real likelihoods and knows how to discern truth from lie in others' narrations?

Made to him a speech of this kind.

A speech! Foxes speak, then? They speak, then, the same language as crows? Wise preceptor, be careful. Weigh your response well before making it. It is more important than you think.

Well, good day, Monsieur Crow!

Monsieur! A title that the child sees used derisively even before he knows that it is a title of honor.[40] Those who say "Monsieur du Crow" will have a lot of explaining to do before they explain that *du*.[41]

How charming you are! [42] *How handsome you seem to me!*

Padding, useless redundancy. The child, seeing the same things repeated in other terms, learns slovenly speech. If you say that the redundancy is part of the author's art and belongs to the plan of the fox who wants to appear to multiply the praises with the words, this excuse will be good for me but not for my pupil.

Without lying, if your song

Without lying! One lies sometimes, then? Where will the child be if you teach him that the fox says "without lying" only because he is lying?

Corresponds to your plumage,

Corresponds! What does this word signify? Teach the child to compare qualities so different as voice and plumage. You will see how he will understand you!

You would be the Phoenix of the landlords of these woods.

The Phoenix! What is a phoenix? Here we are cast suddenly into antiquity's lies, almost into mythology.

The landlords of these woods! What figurative speech! The flatterer ennobles his language and gives it more dignity to make it more seductive. Will a child understand this finesse? Does he so much as know, can he know, what is a noble style and a low style?

At these words the Crow cannot contain his joy.

One must have already experienced very lively passions to have a feeling for this proverbial expression.

And to show his fine voice

Do not forget that to understand this verse and the whole fable, the child ought to know what the crow's fine voice is.

He opens his big beak, lets fall his prey.

This verse is admirable. The harmony alone produces an image. I see a big ugly beak opened; I hear the cheese falling through the branches. But this sort of beauty is lost on children.

BOOK II

The Fox grabs it and says: My good monsieur,
Here, then, goodness is already transformed into stupidity. Assuredly, no time is lost in instructing children.

Learn that every flatterer
General maxim. We can no longer follow.

Lives at the expense of the one who listens to him.
Never did a ten-year-old child understand that verse.

This lesson is doubtless worth a cheese.
This is understandable, and the thought is very good. However, there will still be very few children who know how to compare a lesson with a cheese and who would not prefer the cheese to the lesson. One must, therefore, make them understand that this remark is only mockery. What finesse for children!

The Crow, ashamed and embarrassed,
Another pleonasm; but this one is inexcusable.

Swore, but a little late, that he would not be caught that way again.
Swore! Who is the fool of a master who dares to explain to the child what an oath is?

A lot of detail. A lot less, however, than would be required to analyze all the ideas of this fable and to reduce them to the simple and elementary ideas from which each of them is composed. But who believes he needs this analysis to make himself understood by youth? None of us is philosophic enough to know how to put himself in a child's place. Let us now pass on to the moral.

I ask whether it is necessary to teach six-year-old children that there are men who flatter and lie for profit? One could at most teach them that there are mockers who ridicule little boys and in secret make fun of their stupid vanity. But the cheese spoils everything. They are taught less not to let it fall from their beaks than to make it fall from the beak of another. This is my second paradox; and it is not the least important.

Follow children learning their fables; and you will see that when they are in a position to apply them, they almost always do so in a way opposite to the author's intention, and that instead of looking within themselves for the shortcoming that one wants to cure or prevent, they tend to like the vice with which one takes advantage of others' shortcomings. In the preceding fable children make fun of the crow, but they all take a fancy to the fox. In the fable which follows, you believe you are giving them the cicada as an example, and it is not at all so.[43] It is the ant they will choose. One does not like being humiliated. They will always take the advantageous role. It is the choice of *amour-propre*; it is a very natural choice. Now what a horrible lesson for childhood! The most odious of all monsters would be an avaricious and hard child who knew what was asked of him and refused. The ant does yet more; it teaches him to mix mockery with his refusal.

In all the fables where the lion is one of the personages, since he is ordinarily the most brilliant, the child does not fail to make himself a lion; and when he presides over some dividing up of portions, well instructed by his model, he takes great care to take everything for himself. But when the gnat fells the lion, the situation is entirely different;

the child is then no longer a lion; he is a gnat. He learns how one day to kill with stings those he would not dare to stand and attack.[44]

In the fable of the lean wolf and the fat dog, instead of a lesson in moderation, which is what it is claimed the child is being given, he gets one in license.[45] I shall never forget having seen a little girl weeping bitterly, upset by this fable which was supposedly preaching docility to her. It was difficult to get at the cause of her tears. Finally we found out. The poor child was irritated by being chained. She felt her neck rubbed raw. She was crying at not being a wolf.

Thus, the moral of the first fable cited is for the child a lesson in the basest flattery; of the second, a lesson in inhumanity; of the third, a lesson in injustice; of the fourth, a lesson in satire; of the fifth, a lesson in independence. This last lesson, superfluous as it is for my pupil, is no more suitable for yours. When you give him contradictory precepts, what fruit do you hope for from your efforts? But, perhaps, with this exception, this whole morality which serves me as an objection to fables provides as many reasons for preserving them. In society there is needed one morality in words and one in action, and these two moralities do not resemble each other. The first is in the cathechism, where it is left. The other is in La Fontaine's fables for children and in his tales for mothers. The same author suffices for everything.[46]

Let us come to terms, Monsieur de La Fontaine. I promise, for my part, to read you discriminately, to like you, to instruct myself in your fables, for I hope not to be deceived about their object. But, as for my pupil, permit me not to let him study a single one of them until you have proved to me that it is good for him to learn things a quarter of which he will not understand; that in those he will be able to understand, he will never be led astray; and that he will not, instead of improving himself on the dupe's example, form himself after the rascal's example.

In thus taking away all duties from children, I take away the instruments of their greatest misery—that is, books. Reading is the plague of childhood and almost the only occupation we know how to give it. At twelve Emile will hardly know what a book is. But, it will be said, he certainly must at least know how to read. I agree. He must know how to read when reading is useful to him; up to then it is only good for boring him.

If one ought to demand nothing of children through obedience, it follows that they can learn nothing of which they do not feel the real and present advantage in either pleasure or utility. Otherwise, what motive would bring them to learn it? The art of speaking to and hearing from absent people, the art of communicating our feelings, our wills, our desires to them at a distance without a mediator is an art whose utility can be rendered palpable to all ages. What wonderful means were used to turn so useful and so agreeable an art into a torment for childhood? Because the young are constrained to apply themselves to it in spite of themselves, it is put to uses of which they understand nothing. A child is not very eager to perfect the instrument with which he is tormented. But arrange things so that this instrument serves his pleasures, and soon he will apply himself to it in spite of you.

BOOK II

A great business is made of seeking the best methods of teaching reading. Desks and cards are invented; a child's room is made into a printing shop. Locke wants him to learn to read with dice.[47] Now is that not a clever invention? What a pity! A means surer than all these, and the one always forgotten, is the desire to learn. Give the child this desire; then let your desks and your dice go. Any method will be good for him.

Present interest—that is the great mover, the only one which leads surely and far. Sometimes Emile receives from his father, from his mother, from his relatives, from his friends, notes of invitation for a dinner, for a walk, for an outing on the water, for watching some public festival. These notes are short, clear, distinct, well written. Someone has to be found who can read them to him. This someone either is not always to be found on the spur of the moment or is paying the child back for his unwillingness to oblige him the day before. Thus the occasion, the moment, is missed. Finally the note is read to him, but it is too late. Oh, if he had known how to read himself! Other notes are received. They are so short! Their subject is so interesting! He would like to try to decipher them. Sometimes he is given help, and sometimes he is refused it. Finally he deciphers half of a note. It has to do with going tomorrow to eat custard . . . he does not know where or with whom . . . how many efforts he makes to read the rest! I do not believe Emile will need the desk. Shall I speak now of writing? No. I am ashamed of playing with this kind of foolishness in an educational treatise.

I shall add this one word which constitutes an important maxim: it is that usually one gets very surely and quickly what one is not in a hurry to get. I am almost certain that Emile will know how to read and write perfectly before the age of ten, precisely because it makes very little difference to me that he knows how before fifteen. But I would rather that he never knew how to read if this science has to be bought at the price of all that can make it useful. Of what use will reading be to him if it has been made repulsive to him forever? *Id in primus cavere opportebit, ne studia, qui amare nondum poterit, oderit, et amaritudinem semel perceptam etiam ultra rudes annos reformidet.**

The more I insist on my inactive method, the stronger I see your objections grow. If your pupil learns nothing from you, he will learn from others. If you do not forestall error by means of truth, he will learn lies. The prejudices you are afraid of giving him, he will receive from everything around him. They will enter by all his senses: either they will corrupt his reason even before it is formed, or his mind, stupefied by long inactivity, will be engrossed in matter. The lack of the habit of thinking in childhood takes away the faculty for the rest of life.

It seems to me that I could easily answer that. But why always answers? If my method by itself answers objections, it is good. If it does not answer them, it is worthless. I shall proceed.

If, according to the plan I have begun to outline, you follow rules directly contrary to the established ones; if instead of taking your pupil's mind far away; if instead of constantly leading it astray in other

* Quintilian *Institutio Oratorio* I:20.[48]

places, other climates, other times, at the extremities of the earth and up to the heavens, you apply yourself to keeping him always within himself and attentive to what touches him immediately, then you will find him capable of perception, memory, and even reasoning. This is nature's order. To the extent the sensitive being becomes active, he acquires a discernment proportionate to his strengths; and it is only with a surplus of strength beyond what he needs to preserve himself that there develops in him the speculative faculty fit to employ this excess of strength for other uses. Do you, then, want to cultivate your pupil's intelligence? Cultivate the strengths it ought to govern. Exercise his body continually; make him robust and healthy in order to make him wise and reasonable. Let him work, be active, run, yell, always be in motion. Let him be a man in his vigor, and soon he will be one in his reason.

You will make him sodden, it is true, by this method if you go about always giving him directions, always telling him, "Go, come, stay, do this, don't do that." If your head always controls his arms, his head becomes useless to him. But remember our conventions. If you are only a pedant, it is not worth the effort to read me.

It is a most pitiable error to imagine that the exercise of the body is harmful to the operations of the mind, as if these two activities ought not to move together in harmony and that the one ought not always to direct the other!

There are two sorts of men whose bodies are in constant activity, and who both surely think equally little of cultivating their souls—that is, peasants and savages. The former are crude, heavy, maladroit; the latter, known for their good sense, are also known for their subtlety of mind. To put it generally, nothing is duller than a peasant and nothing sharper than a savage. What is the source of this difference? It is that the former, doing always what he is ordered or what he saw his father do or what he has himself done since his youth, works only by routine; and in his life, almost an automaton's, constantly busy with the same labors, habit and obedience take the place of reason for him.

For the savage it is another story. Attached to no place, without prescribed task, obeying no one, with no other law than his will, he is forced to reason in each action of his life. He does not make a movement, not a step, without having beforehand envisaged the consequences. Thus, the more his body is exercised, the more his mind is enlightened; his strength and his reason grow together, and one is extended by the other.

Learned preceptor, let us see which of our two pupils resembles the savage and which resembles the peasant. Submitted in everything to an authority which is always teaching, yours does nothing unless given the word. He dares not eat when he is hungry, nor laugh when he is gay, nor cry when he is sad, nor put out one hand instead of the other, nor move his foot except as has been prescribed to him. Soon he will dare to breathe only according to your rules. About what do you want him to think when you think about everything for him? Assured of your foresight, what need has he of any? Seeing that you take the responsibility for his preservation, for his well-being, he feels delivered from this care. His judgment rests on yours. Everything you do not forbid him, he does without reflection, knowing well that he does it without risk. What need does he have to foresee rain? He knows that you look at the sky for him. What need has he to organize his walk? He has no fear that you would let the dinner hour pass. So long as you do not forbid him to eat, he eats. When you forbid him, he eats no more. He no longer listens to the opinions of his stomach but yours. You may very well soften his body by inactivity, you do not for that make his understanding more flexible. All to the contrary, you complete the work of discrediting reason in his mind by making him use the little he possesses on the things which appear to him the most useless. Never seeing what it is good for, he finally makes the judgment that it is good for nothing. The worst that can happen to him from reasoning badly is to be admonished; and that happens to him so often that he hardly thinks about it; a danger so common no longer frightens him.

You find, however, that he is clever, and so he is when it comes to babbling with women in the manner about which I have already spoken. But when it comes to a case of personal risk, to his taking a position in some difficult situation, you will find him to be a hundred times stupider and more foolish than the son of the biggest yokel.

As for my pupil, or rather nature's, trained early to be as self-sufficient as possible, he is not accustomed to turning constantly to others; still less is he accustomed to displaying his great learning for them. On the other hand, he judges, he foresees, he reasons in everything immediately related to him. He does not chatter; he acts. He does not know a word of what is going on in society, but he knows very well how to do what suits him. Since he is constantly in motion, he is forced to observe many things, to know many effects. He acquires a large experience early. He gets his lessons from nature and not from men. He instructs himself so much the better because he sees nowhere the intention to instruct him. Thus his body and his mind are exercised together. Acting always according to his own thought and not someone else's, he continually unites two operations: the more he makes himself strong and robust, the more he becomes sensible and judicious. This is the way one day to have what are believed incompatible and what are united in almost all great men: strength of body and strength of soul; a wise man's reason and an athlete's vigor.

Young teacher, I am preaching a difficult art to you, that of governing without precepts and doing everything by doing nothing. This art, I agree, is not one that goes with your age; it is not fit to make your talents conspicuous from the outset nor to make an impression on fathers. But it is the only one fit for succeeding. You will never get to the point of producing wise men if you do not in the first place produce rascals. This was the education of the Spartans: instead of being glued to books, they began by being taught how to steal their dinner. Were the Spartans as a result crude when grown? Who does not know the force and saltiness of their rejoinders? Always made to conquer, they crushed their enemies in every kind of war; and the Athenian babblers feared their words as much as their blows.

In the most careful educations the master commands and believes he governs. It is actually the child who governs. He uses what you exact from him to obtain from you what pleases him; and he always knows how to make you pay a week of obligingness for an hour of assiduity. At every instant pacts must be made with him. These treaties, which you propose in your fashion and he executes in his, always turn to the profit of his whims, especially when you are so clumsy as to promise him something as your part of the bargain which he is quite sure of getting whether or not he fulfills his part. The child usually reads the master's mind much better than the master reads the child's heart. And that is the way it should be; for all the sagacity the child would have used to provide for the preservation of his person had he been left to himself he uses to save his natural freedom from his tyrant's chains. On the other hand, the latter, having no interest so pressing for seeing through the child, sometimes finds it to his own advantage to let the child have his laziness or vanity.

Take an opposite route with your pupil. Let him always believe he is the master, and let it always be you who are. There is no subjection so perfect as that which keeps the appearance of freedom. Thus the will itself is made captive. The poor child who knows nothing, who can do nothing, who has no learning, is he not at your mercy? Do you not dispose, with respect to him, of everything which surrounds him? Are you not the master of affecting him as you please? Are not his labors, his games, his pleasures, his pains, all in your hands without his knowing it? Doubtless he ought to do only what he wants; but he ought to want only what you want him to do. He ought not to make a step without your having foreseen it; he ought not to open his mouth without your knowing what he is going to say.

It is then that he will be able to give himself over to the exercises of the body that his age demands of him without stultifying his mind. It is then that instead of sharpening his ruses for eluding your uncomfortable grip, you will see him busy himself only with taking the greatest possible advantage of everything around him for his real well-being. It is then that you will be surprised by the subtlety of his inventions for appropriating all objects he can attain and for truly enjoying things without the help of opinion.

In leaving him thus master of his will, you will not be fomenting his caprices. By never doing anything except what suits him, he will soon do only what he ought to do; and although his body is in continuous motion, so long as he is concerned only with his immediate and palpable interest, you will witness developing all the reason of which he is capable much better and in a way much more appropriate to him than it would in purely speculative studies.

Thus, not seeing you eager to oppose him, not distrusting you, with nothing to hide from you, he will not deceive you, he will not lie to you, he will fearlessly show himself precisely as he is. You will be able to study him at your complete ease and arrange all around him the lessons you want to give him without his ever thinking he is receiving any.

He will also not be spying on your morals with a curiosity motivated by jealousy and will not find a secret pleasure in catching you misbehaving. This disadvantage which we are forestalling is a very great one. One of children's first efforts, as I have said, is to discover the weakness of those who govern them. This inclination leads to wickedness but does not come from it. It comes from the need to elude an authority which importunes them. Overburdened by the yoke inposed on them, they seek to shake it off, and the shortcomings they find in the masters furnish them with good means for that. However, the habit of scrutinizing people for their shortcomings and getting pleasure at finding them grows on children. Here clearly is yet another source of vice stopped up in Emile's heart. With no interest in finding shortcomings in me, he will not look for them and will be little tempted to look for them in others.

All these practices seem difficult because one does not really consider them, but at bottom they ought not to be. I have a right to assume that you possess the enlightenment necessary for exercising the vocation you have chosen; I have to assume that you know the natural development of the human heart, that you know how to study man and the individual, that you know beforehand what will bend your pupil's will when he confronts all the objects of interest to his age that you will cause to pass before his eyes. Now, to have the instruments and to know their use well, is that not to be the master of an operation?

You raise as an objection children's caprices, and you are wrong. The capriciousness of children is never the work of nature but is the work of bad discipline. It is that they have either obeyed or commanded, and I have said a hundred times that they must do neither. Your pupil will, therefore, have only the caprices you have given him. It is only just that you pay the penalty for your mistakes. But, you will say, how can this be remedied? It is still possible with better conduct and much patience.

For a few weeks I took care of a child accustomed not only to do his will but to make everyone else do it as well—consequently a child full of whims.[49] Right on the first day, to try out my obligingness, he wanted to get up at midnight. When I was sleeping most soundly, he jumped down from his bed, took his robe, and called me. I got up, lit the candle. He wanted nothing more. Within a quarter of an hour sleep overcame him, and he went back to bed satisfied with his test. Two days later he repeated it with the same success and without the least sign of impatience on my part. As he kissed me on going back to bed, I said to him in a deliberate tone, "My little friend, this is all very well, but do not try it again." This phrase aroused his curiosity, and the very next day, wanting to get a glimpse of how I would dare to disobey him, he did not fail to get up again at the same time and call me. I asked him what he wanted. He told me he could not sleep. "Too bad," I replied, and kept quiet. He asked me to light the candle. "What for?" and I kept quiet. This laconic tone began to distress him. He started feeling about, looking for the steel, which he made a show of striking; and I could not keep from laughing, hearing him give himself blows on the fingers. Finally, quite convinced he would not succeed at it, he brought me the lighter to my bed. I told him I had no need of it and turned on my other side. Then he started running giddily around the room, yelling, singing, making a lot of noise, purposely bumping into the table and chairs, which he took care not to do too hard while letting out great cries, hoping to worry me. None of this worked; and I saw that, counting on high exhortations or anger, he had in no way prepared himself for this coolness.

However, resolved to overcome my patience by dint of his obstinacy, he continued his racket with such success that in the end I began to flare up; and, sensing that I was going to ruin everything by an inopportune loss of temper, I decided on another course. I got up without saying a thing and went to the steel, which I could not find. I asked him for it. He gave it to me bubbling over with joy at having at last triumphed over me. I struck the steel, lit the candle, took my little gentleman by the hand, led him calmly into a nearby little room, the shutters of which were tightly closed and where there was nothing to break. I left him there without light; then, locking the door with the key, I went back to bed without having said a single word to him. You need not ask if at first there was an uproar. I was expecting it and was not moved by it. Finally the noise abated. I listened, heard him settling down. I put my mind at rest. The next day in the morning I went into the little room and found my tiny rebel lying on a couch sleeping a profound sleep, which, after so much fatigue, he must have badly needed.

The affair did not end there. His mother learned that the child had spent two-thirds of the night out of his bed. Immediately all was lost; he was a child as good as dead. Seeing that the occasion was good for getting his revenge, he played sick without foreseeing he would gain nothing from it. The doctor was called. Unhappily for the mother, this doctor was a jester and, to enjoy her terrors, made an effort to increase them. Meanwhile he whispered in my ear, "Leave it to me. I promise you that the child will be cured for some time of the whim of being sick." Indeed, diet and bed were prescribed, and the child was turned over to the apothecary. I sighed at seeing this poor mother thus the dupe of all that surrounded her, with the single exception of me, for whom she conceived hatred, precisely because I did not deceive her.

After rather harsh reproaches she told me that her son was delicate, that he was his family's sole heir, that he must be preserved at whatever cost, and that she did not want him provoked. In that I quite agreed with her. But what she understood by provoking him was not obeying him in everything. I saw that the same tone had to be taken with the mother as with the child. "Madame," I said to her rather coldly, "I do not know how one raises an heir, and, what is more, I do not want to learn how. You can take care of that for yourself." I was still needed for a time; the father quieted it all down; the mother wrote the preceptor to hasten his return; and the child, seeing he got nothing out of disturbing my sleep or in being sick, finally made the decision to sleep himself and to be in good health.

It cannot be imagined to how many similar caprices the little tyrant had subjected his unlucky governor, for the education was conducted under the eyes of the mother who did not tolerate the heir's being disobeyed in anything. At whatever hour he wanted to go out, one had to be ready to lead or, rather, follow him, and he was always very careful to choose the moment when he saw that his governor was busiest.

BOOK II

He wanted to hold the same sway over me and get revenge during the day for the rest he was forced to leave me at night. I lent myself good-heartedly to everything; and I began by establishing in his eyes the pleasure I took in obliging him. After that when the issue was to cure him of his whim, I went about it in a different way.

He had in the first place to be put in the wrong, and that was not difficult. Knowing that children think only of the present, I took the easy advantage of foresight over him. I took care of providing for him at home a game which I knew to be very much to his taste; and at the moment when I saw him most infatuated with it, I went and proposed a walk to him. He turned me down flat. I persisted. He did not listen to me. I had to give up. He took careful note in himself of this sign of subjection.

The day after, it was my turn. He was bored. I had arranged for that. I, on the contrary, appeared profoundly busy. He needed nothing more to decide him. He did not fail to come to tear me away from my work to take him for a walk immediately. I refused; he insisted. "No," I said to him, "in doing your will, you have taught me to do mine. I do not want to go out." "Very well," he responded hotly, "I shall go out all alone." "As you wish," and I returned to my work.

He got dressed, a bit uneasy at seeing me let him go ahead and not following his example. Ready to go out, he came to bid me farewell. I bade him farewell. He tried to alarm me with the account of the trips he was going to make. To hear him one would have thought he was going to the end of the world. Without any disturbance on my part, I wished him bon voyage. His embarrassment was redoubled. However, he put a good face on it; and ready to go out, he told his lackey to follow him. The lackey, already forewarned, answered that he did not have the time, and, busy at my orders, he had to obey me rather than him. Now at this the child was upset. How could it be conceived that he be allowed to go out alone, he who believed himself the being most important to everyone else, and who thought that sky and earth took an interest in his preservation? Meanwhile he began to feel his weakness. He understood that he was going to be alone among people who did not know him. He saw beforehand the risks he was going to run. Obstinacy alone still sustained him. He went down the stairs slowly and very ill at ease. He finally stepped out on the street, consoling himself somewhat for the harm that could happen to him by the hope that I would be made responsible for it.

This was just what I was waiting for. Everything was prepared in advance; and since a kind of public scene was involved, I had provided myself with the father's consent. Hardly had the child taken a few steps before he heard, right and left, remarks about him. "Neighbor, look at the pretty monsieur! Where is he going all alone? He is going to get lost. I want to ask him to come in our house." "Don't you dare, neighbor. Don't you see that this is a little libertine who has been driven out of his father's house because he did not want to be good for anything? Sanctuary must not be given libertines. Let him go where he will." "Too bad. Let God guide him. I would be sorry if misfortune were to come to him." A bit farther on he met up with some rascals of about his age who provoked him and jeered at him. The farther he went, the more confused he became. Alone and without protection, he saw himself everybody's plaything; and he experienced with much surprise that his epaulettes and gold trim did not make him more respected.

Meanwhile one of my friends, whom he did not know and to whom I had given the responsibility of watching over him, was following him step by step without his noticing it, and accosted him when the time was right. This role, which resembled Sbrigani's in *Pourceaugnac,*[50] called for a man of ready wit and was perfectly filled. Without making the child timid and fearful by striking too great a terror in him, he made him so well aware of the imprudence of his escapade that at the end of half an hour he brought him back to me, tractable, embarrassed, and not daring to lift his eyes.

To complete the disaster of his expedition, precisely at the moment that he came home, his father was coming down to go out, and met him on the stairs. The child had to say where he was coming from and why I was not with him.* The poor child would have wanted to be a hundred feet under the earth. Without wasting his time in giving him a long reprimand, the father said to him more curtly than I would have expected, "If you want to go out alone, you are the master. But since I do not want to have a bandit in my home, if it does happen that you do so, take care not to come back anymore."

As for me, I received him without reproach and without ridicule, but with a bit of gravity; and lest he suspect that all that had taken place was only a game, I did not want to take him for a walk the same day. The next day I saw with great pleasure that in my company he passed with a triumphant bearing before the same people who had jeered at him the day before because he was all alone when they met him. It can be well conceived that he did not threaten me anymore with going out without me.

It is by these means and others like them that during the short time I was with the child I got to the point of being able to make him do everything I wanted without prescribing anything to him, without forbidding him anything, without sermons, without exhortations, without boring him with useless lessons. Thus, so long as I spoke, he was satisfied; but he was afraid of my silence. He understood that something was not going well, and the lesson always came to him from the thing itself. But let us return.

These constant exercises, left in this way to the direction of nature alone, in strengthening the body not only do not stultify the mind but, on the contrary, form the only kind of reason of which the first age is susceptible and which is the most necessary to any age whatsoever. They teach us to know well the use of our strength, the relations of our bodies to surrounding bodies, and the use of the natural instruments which are within our reach and are suitable for our organs. Is there any stupidity equal to that of a child always raised indoors and under his mother's eyes who, ignorant of what weight and resistance are,

* In such a case one can without risk demand the truth from a child, for he knows well then that he could not disguise it, and that, if he dared to tell a lie, he would be convicted of it on the spot.

wants to rip up a big tree or lift a boulder? The first time I went out of Geneva, I wanted to keep up with a galloping horse; I threw stones at Mount Salève which was two leagues away from me. Plaything of all the children of the village, I was a veritable idiot to them. At eighteen one learns in philosophy what a lever is. There is not a little peasant of twelve who does not know how to use a lever better than the Academy's premier expert in mechanics. The lessons pupils get from one another in the schoolyard are a hundred times more useful to them than everything they will ever be told in class.

Look at a cat entering a room for the first time. He inspects, he looks around, he sniffs, he does not relax for a moment, he trusts nothing before he has examined everything, come to know everything. This is just what is done by a child who is beginning to walk and entering, so to speak, in the room of the world. The whole difference is that, in addition to the vision which is common to both child and cat, the former has the hands that nature gave him to aid in observation, and the latter is endowed by nature with a subtle sense of smell. Whether this disposition is well or ill cultivated is what makes children adroit or clumsy, dull or alert, giddy or prudent.

Since man's first natural movements are, therefore, to measure himself against everything surrounding him and to experience in each object he perceives all the qualities which can be sensed and relate to him, his first study is a sort of experimental physics relative to his own preservation, from which he is diverted by speculative studies before he has recognized his place here on earth. While his delicate and flexible organs can adjust themselves to the bodies on which they must act, while his still pure senses are exempt from illusions, it is the time to exercise both in their proper functions, it is the time to teach the knowledge of the sensible relations which things have with us. Since everything which enters into the human understanding comes there through the senses, man's first reason is a reason of the senses; this sensual reason serves as the basis of intellectual reason. Our first masters of philosophy are our feet, our hands, our eyes. To substitute books for all that is not to teach us to reason. It is to teach us to use the reason of others. It is to teach us to believe much and never to know anything.

To exercise an art one must begin by procuring for oneself the instruments for it; and, to be able to employ these instruments usefully, one has to make them solid enough to resist wear. To learn to think, therefore, it is necessary to exercise our limbs, our senses, our organs, which are the instruments of our intelligence. And, to get the greatest possible advantage from these instruments, the body which provides them must be robust and healthy. Thus, far from man's true reason being formed independently of the body, it is the body's good constitution which makes the mind's operations easy and sure.

In showing how the long idleness of childhood ought to be employed, I go into the kind of detail which will appear ridiculous. "Funny lessons," I will be told, "which, open to your own criticism, are limited to teaching that which no one needs to learn! Why waste time on the instruction that always comes of itself and costs neither effort nor care.

What twelve-year-old child does not know all you want to teach yours, and, in addition, what his masters have taught him?"

Messieurs, you are mistaken. I am giving my pupil instruction in an art that is very long, very hard, one that your pupils surely do not possess; it is the art of being ignorant, for the science possessed by him who believes that he knows only what he does in fact know amounts to very little. You give science—splendid. I busy myself with the instrument fit for acquiring it. It is said that one day when the Venetians with great pomp showed their treasure of Saint Mark to a Spanish ambassador, he, as his only compliment, after looking under the tables, said to them, "Quì non c' è la radice." [51] I never see a preceptor displaying the learning of his disciple without being tempted to say as much to him.

All those who have reflected on the way of life of the ancients attribute to gymnastic exercises that vigor of body and soul which distinguishes them most palpably from the moderns. The way in which Montaigne supports this sentiment shows that he was powerfully impressed by it. He returns to it endlessly and in countless ways in speaking of a child's education. To stiffen his soul, he says, his muscles must be hardened; by becoming accustomed to work, he becomes accustomed to pain; one must break him to the harshness of exercise in order to train him in the harshness of dislocations, colics, and all illness. The wise Locke, the good Rollin, the learned Fleury, the pedant Crousaz—so different among themselves in everything else—all agree on this single point that there should be much exercise for children's bodies. It is the most judicious of their precepts; it is the one which is and always will be the most neglected. I have already spoken sufficiently of its importance, and since on this point one cannot give better reasons or more sensible rules than those to be found in Locke's book, I shall content myself with referring you to it after having taken the liberty of adding some observations to his. [52]

The limbs of a growing body ought all to have room in their garments. Nothing ought to hinder either their movement or their growth; nothing too tight; nothing which clings to the body; no belts. French dress, constraining and unhealthy for men, is particularly pernicious for children. The humors, stagnant, arrested in their circulation, grow rotten in a state of rest which is increased by the inactive and sedentary life, become corrupt, and cause scurvy, an illness every day more common among us and almost unknown to the ancients whose way of dressing and living preserved them from it. The hussar's costume, [53] far from remedying this difficulty, increases it and, in order to spare children braces, puts pressure on their whole body. The best thing to do is to leave them in smocks as long as possible, then to give them a very large garment and not make a point of showing off their figure, which serves only to deform it. Their defects of body and of mind come almost all from the same cause: one wants to make them men before it is time.

There are gay colors and sad colors. The former are more to children's taste. They are also more flattering to them; and I do not see why one would not consult such natural fitness in this. But from the moment that children prefer a material because it is rich, their hearts are already abandoned to luxury, to all the whims of opinion; and this taste surely did not come to them from themselves. I cannot tell you how much the choice of clothing and the motives of this choice influence education. Not only do blind mothers promise their children adornment as a reward; one even sees foolish governors threatening their pupils with a coarser and simpler costume as a punishment. "If you do not study better, if you don't take better care of your things, you will be dressed like this little peasant." This is as if they were told, "Know that man is nothing except by his costume, that your worth is wholly in yours." Is it surprising that the young profit from such wise lessons, that they esteem only adornment, and that they judge merit by the exterior only?

If I had to straighten out the views of a child thus spoiled, I would take care that his richest costumes were his most uncomfortable, that he be always ill at ease, always constrained in them, always subjected by them in countless ways. I would make liberty and gaiety flee before his magnificence. If he wanted to join in the games of other children more simply outfitted, on the spot everything would stop, everything would disappear. Finally, I would so bore him, I would so satiate him with his splendor, I would render him so much the slave of his gold-trimmed costume that I would make it the plague of his life, make him see the darkest dungeon with less fright than the laying out of his adornment. So long as the child has not been made the servant of our prejudices, to be at his ease and free is always his first desire. The simplest garment, the most comfortable, the one which subjects him least, is always the most precious for him.

There is a habit of the body suitable to exercise and another more suitable to inaction. The latter, allowing the humors an even and uniform flow, ought to protect the body from changes in the air. The former, making the body constantly pass from agitation to rest and from heat to cold, ought to accustom it to those changes. It follows from this that stay-at-home and sedentary people ought to be warmly dressed at all times so as to keep the body at a uniform temperature, almost the same in all seasons and at all hours of the day. On the other hand, those who come and go, in the wind, in the sun, in the rain, who are very active and spend most of their time *sub dio*,[54] ought always to be lightly dressed so as to habituate themselves to all the vicissitudes of the air and all the degrees of temperature without being uncomfortable in them. I would counsel both not to change costume according to the seasons, and that will be the constant practice of my Emile. By this I do not mean that he will wear his winter clothes in the summer, as do sedentary people, but that he will wear his summer clothes in the winter, as do working people. This latter practice was that of Sir Isaac Newton during his whole life, and he lived eighty years.

Little or no headgear in any season. The ancient Egyptians were always bare-headed. The Persians covered their heads with large tiaras and still cover them with large turbans, the use of which, according to Chardin, the air of the country makes necessary. I have mentioned elsewhere * the distinction that Herodotus made on a battlefield between the skulls of the Persians and those of the Egyptians. Since it is important, then, that the bones of the head become harder, more compact, less fragile, and less porous the better to arm the brain not only against wounds but also against colds, inflammations, and all the impressions of the air, accustom your children to remain always bareheaded summer and winter, day and night. If for the sake of cleanliness and to keep their hair in order you want to give them headgear during the night, let it be a cap thin enough to see through, similar to the netting with which the Basques cover their hair. I know well that most mothers, more struck by Chardin's observation than by my reasons, will believe they find everywhere the air of Persia; but I did not choose my pupil a European to make an Asian of him.[56]

In general, children are overdressed, especially during their early age. They should be hardened to cold rather than to heat. Very cold weather never indisposes them if one lets them be exposed to it early. But their skin tissue, still too tender and too slack, leaving too free a passage for perspiration, inevitably makes them prone to exhaustion in extreme heat. Thus, it is noted that more of them die in the month of August than in any other month. Moreover, it appears to be a constant, from the comparison of the northern peoples with the southern, that one is made more robust by enduring excessive cold than excessive heat. But as the child grows and his fibers are strengthened, accustom him little by little to brave the sun's rays. In going by degrees you will harden him without danger to the ardors of the torrid zone.

Locke, in the midst of the masculine and sensible precepts that he gives us, falls back into contradictions one would not expect from so exact a reasoner. The same man who wants children bathed in icy water in summer does not want them, when they are heated up, to have cool drinks or to lie down on the ground in damp places.* But since he wants children's shoes to take in water at all times, will they take it in less when the child is warm; and can one not make for him the same inductions about the body in relation to the feet that he makes about the feet in relation to the hands and about the body in relation to the face? "If you want man to be all face," I would say to him, "why do you blame me for wanting him to be all feet?" [57]

To prevent children from drinking when they are hot, he prescribes accustoming them to eat a piece of bread as a preliminary to drinking. It is quite strange that when a child is thirsty he has to be given something to eat. I would prefer to give him drink when he is hungry. Never will I be persuaded that our first appetites are so unruly that they cannot be satisfied without exposing ourselves to destruction. If that were so, mankind would have been destroyed a hundred times before men learned what must be done to preserve it.

* *Lettre à M. d'Alembert sur les spectacles,* first edition p. 189.[55]

† As if little peasants chose very dry earth to sit or lie on, and as if it had ever been heard said that the earth's dampness had done any harm to one of them? To hear the physicians on this point, one would believe savages are completely crippled by rheumatism.

BOOK II

Every time Emile is thirsty, I want him given drink. I want him given water, pure and without any preparation, not even to take the chill off it, even if he is bathed in sweat and it is the heart of winter. The only care I recommend is to distinguish the quality of the water. If it is river water, give it to him on the spot just as it comes from the river. If it is spring water, it must be left for a time in the air before he drinks it. In hot seasons rivers are hot; it is not the same with springs which have not had contact with the air. One must wait for them to get to the temperature of the atmosphere. In the winter, on the contrary, spring water is in this respect less dangerous than river water. But it is neither natural nor frequent that one gets in a sweat in the winter, especially out of doors, for the cold air, constantly striking the skin, represses the sweat within and prevents the pores from opening enough to give it free passage. Now I intend for Emile to exercise in winter not next to a good fireplace but outside in open country in the midst of ice. So long as he gets heated up only in making and throwing snowballs, we shall allow him to drink when he is thirsty and to continue his exercise after having drunk without our fearing any accident as a result. But if in some other exercise he gets into a sweat and is thirsty, let him drink cold water even at that time. Only arrange it so that you lead him far and slowly in search of his water. In the kind of cold I mean he will cool off sufficiently in getting there to drink it without danger. Above all, take these precautions without his noticing them. I would rather that he be sick sometimes than constantly attentive to his health.

Children must sleep long because their exercise is extreme. The one serves as corrective to the other. And it is seen that they need both. The time of rest is night; it has been marked out by nature. It is an established observation that sleep is calmer and sweeter while the sun is below the horizon and that air heated by its rays does not keep our senses in so deep a repose. Thus, the most salutary habit is certainly to get up and go to bed with the sun. It follows from this that in our climates man and all the animals generally need to sleep longer in winter than in summer. But civil life is not simple enough, natural enough, exempt enough from extreme changes and accidents for man properly to get accustomed to this uniformity to the point of making it necessary to him. Doubtless one must be subjected to rules. But the first is to be able to break them without risk when necessity wills. Therefore, do not go and imprudently soften your pupil by allowing him a peaceful sleep which endures without interruption. Deliver him at first without hindrance to the law of nature, but do not forget that among us he must be above that law, that he must be able to go to bed late, get up in the morning, be abruptly awakened, and spend nights up without getting upset. By going about it soon enough, by proceeding always gently and gradually, one can form the temperament by the very things that destroy it when it is submitted to them already fully formed.

It is important in the first instance to get used to being ill bedded. This is the way never again to find an uncomfortable bed. In general, the hard life, once turned into habit, multiplies agreeable sensations; the soft life prepares for an infinity of unpleasant ones. People raised too delicately no longer find sleep elsewhere than on down; people accustomed to sleep on boards find it everywhere. There is no hard bed for him who falls asleep as soon as he lies down.

A soft bed where one sinks into feathers or eiderdown, so to speak, melts and dissolves the body. The kidneys, too warmly enveloped, heat up. The results are stones or other indispositions and, infallibly, a delicate constitution which feeds them all.

The best bed is the one which provides a better sleep. That is the bed Emile and I are preparing for ourselves during the day. We do not need to have Persian slaves brought to us to make our beds; in plowing the soil we are shaking out our mattresses.

I know from experience that when a child is healthy, one is master of making him sleep and wake up almost as one wills. When the child is in bed and his babble bores his nurse, she tells him, "Sleep." This is as though she were to tell him, "Be healthy," when he is sick. The true means of making him sleep is to bore him himself. Talk so much that he is forced to keep quiet, and soon he will sleep. Sermons are always good for something. Preaching to him is about equivalent to rocking him. But if you do use this narcotic in the evening, be careful not to use it during the day.

Sometimes I shall wake Emile up, less for fear that he get the habit of sleeping too long than to accustom him to everything, even to being awakened, even to being awakened abruptly. What is more, I would have very little talent for my job if I did not know how to force him to wake himself and get up, so to speak, at my will without my saying a single word to him.

If he does not sleep enough, I let him get a glimpse of a boring morning for the next day; and he himself will regard as so much gained all that he can give to sleep. If he sleeps too much, I give him the prospect of an entertainment to his taste on waking. Do I want him to wake himself at a certain moment? I say to him, "Tomorrow at six we are leaving to go fishing. We are going to walk to such and such a place. Do you want to join us?" He agrees and asks me to wake him. I promise or I do not promise, according to need. If he wakes up too late, he finds us gone. Woe, if he does not soon learn to wake himself up on his own.

Further, if it happens—which is rare—that some indolent child has an inclination to stagnate in laziness, he must not be abandoned to this inclination by which he would be totally benumbed but must be administered some stimulant which will wake him up. It is, of course, to be understood that this is not a question of making him act by force but of moving him by some appetite which draws him to it, and this appetite taken discriminatingly in the order of nature leads us to two ends at the same time.

I can imagine nothing the taste, even the rage, for which cannot with a bit of skill be inspired in children, without vanity, without emulation, without jealousy. Their vivacity, their imitative spirit suffice; their natural gaiety especially is an instrument which provides a sure hold, one of which no preceptor ever takes advantage. In all games, when they are quite persuaded that they are only games, children endure

without complaining and even in laughing what they would never otherwise endure without shedding torrents of tears. Long fasts, blows,
burns, fatigues of all kinds are the amusements of young savages—
proof that even pain has a seasoning that can take away bitterness. But
it does not belong to every master to know how to prepare this stew,
nor perhaps to every disciple to savor it without grimace. Here I am
once more, if I do not watch out, lost in the exceptions.

What does not admit of exceptions, however, is man's subjection to
pain, to the ills of his species, to the accidents, to the dangers of life,
finally to death. The more he is familiarized with all these ideas, the
more he will be cured of the importunate sensitivity which only adds
to the ill itself the impatience to undergo it. The more he gets used to
the sufferings which can strike him, the more, as Montaigne would say,
the sting of strangeness is taken from them, and also the more his soul
is made invulnerable and hard.[58] His body will be the shield which
will turn away all the arrows by which he might be mortally struck. The
very approach of death not being death, he will hardly feel it as such.
He will not, so to speak, die. He will be living or dead; nothing more.
It is of him that the same Montaigne could say, as he did say of a king
of Morocco, that no man has lived so far into death.[59] Constancy and
firmness, like the other virtues, are apprenticeships of childhood. But
it is not by teaching the names of these virtues that one teaches them
to children. It is by making the children taste them without knowing
what they are.

But, apropos of dying, how shall we behave with our pupil concerning the danger of smallpox? Shall we have him inoculated with it at an
early age, or wait for him to get it naturally? The first choice, more in
conformity with our practice, defends against danger at the age when
life is most precious by taking a risk at the age when life is less so—if,
indeed, the name *risk* can be given to inoculation well administered.

But the second choice is more in accord with our general principles
of letting nature alone in everything, in the care it is wont to take by itself and which it abandons as soon as man wants to interfere. The man
of nature is always prepared; let him be inoculated by the master; it
will choose the moment better than we would.

Do not conclude from this that I am against inoculation, for the reasoning on whose basis I exempt my pupil from it would ill suit your
pupils. Your education prepares them not to escape smallpox at the
time they are attacked by it. If you leave its coming to chance, they will
probably die from it. I see that in the various countries inoculation is
resisted the more as it becomes more necessary; and the reason for
this is easily grasped. So I shall hardly deign to treat this question for
my Emile. He will be inoculated, or he will not be, according to times,
places, and circumstances. It is almost a matter of indifference in his
case. If he is given smallpox, one will have the advantage of foreseeing
and knowing his illness ahead of time; that is something. But if he gets
it naturally, we will have preserved him from the doctor. That is even
more.[60]

An exclusive education—an education whose only goal is to distinguish those who receive it from the people—always gives the preference

to the more costly forms of training over the more common and, consequently, over the more useful ones. Thus all carefully raised young
people learn to ride horseback because that costs a lot. But almost none
of them learns to swim because it costs nothing, and an artisan can
know how to swim as well as anyone. However, without having gone to
the academy, a traveler rides, holds on, and makes use of the horse
adequate to the need. But in water if one does not swim, one drowns;
and one does not swim without having learned. Finally, riding horseback is never a matter of life or death, whereas nobody is sure of avoiding a danger to which one is so often exposed as drowning. Emile will
be in water as on land. Why should he not live in all the elements? If
he could be taught to fly in the air, I would make an eagle of him. I
would make a salamander of him if a man could be hardened against
fire.

It is feared that in learning to swim a child might drown. If he drowns
while he is learning or because he has not learned, in either case it will
be your fault. It is only vanity which makes us rash. A person is
never rash when he is seen by no one. Emile would not be rash even if
the whole universe were watching. Since risk is not required for practicing swimming, he could learn to cross the Hellespont in a canal in his
father's park. But one must even get used to risk, so as to learn not to be
disturbed by it. This is an essential part of the apprenticeship of which I
spoke a while ago. Moreover, being careful to balance the degree of
danger with the amount of his strength and sharing the danger with him
always, I will hardly have to fear imprudence when my own preservation is also the basis for the care I give to him. ·

A child is not as big as a man. He has neither a man's strength nor
his reason. But he sees and hears as well, or very nearly as well, as a
man. His taste is as sensitive, although less delicate; and he distinguishes smells as well, although he does not bring the same sensuality
to them. The first faculties which are formed and perfected in us are the
senses. They are, therefore, the first faculties that ought to be cultivated; they are the only ones which are completely ignored or the ones
which are most neglected.

To exercise the senses is not only to make use of them, it is to learn
to judge well with them. It is to learn, so to speak, to sense; for we know
how to touch, see, and hear only as we have learned.

There are purely natural and mechanical exercises which serve to
make the body robust without giving any occasion for the exercise of
judgment. Swimming, running, jumping, spinning a top, throwing
stones, all that is quite good. But have we only arms and legs? Have we
not also eyes and ears; and are these organs superfluous to the use of
the former? Therefore, do not exercise only strength; exercise all
the senses which direct it. Get from each of them all that they can do.
Then verify the impression of one by the other. Measure, count, weigh,
compare. Use strength only after having estimated resistance. Always
arrange it so that the estimate of the effect precedes the use of the
means. Interest the child in never making insufficient or superfluous
efforts. If you accustom him to foresee thus the effect of all his move-

ments and to set his mistakes right by experience, is it not clear that the more he acts, the more judicious he will become?

Is there a mass to lift? If he takes too long a lever, he will waste motion. If he takes too short a one, he will not have enough strength. Experience can teach him to choose precisely the stick he needs. This wisdom is, hence, not beyond his age. Is there a load to carry? If he wants to take one as heavy as he can carry and not try any he cannot lift, will he not be forced to estimate its weight by sight? Does he know how to compare masses of the same matter and of different size? Let him choose between masses of the same size and different matters. He will have to set himself to comparing their specific weights. I have seen a very well-raised young man who, only after putting it to the test, was willing to believe that a container full of big pieces of oak was less heavy than the same container filled with water.

We are not masters of the use of all our senses equally. There is one of them—that is, touch—whose activity is never suspended during waking. It has been spread over the entire surface of our body as a continual guard to warn us of all that can do it damage. It is also the one of which, willy-nilly, we acquire the earliest experience due to this continual exercise and to which, consequently, we have less need to give a special culture. However, we observe that the blind have a surer and keener touch than we do; because, not being guided by sight, they are forced to learn to draw solely from the former sense the judgments which the latter furnishes us. Why, then, are we not given practice at walking as the blind do in darkness, to know the bodies we may happen to come upon, to judge the objects which surround us—in a word, to do at night without light all that they do by day without eyes? As long as the sun shines, we have the advantage over them. In the dark they are in their turn our guides. We are blind half of our lives, with the difference that the truly blind always know how to conduct themselves, while we dare not take a step in the heart of the night. We have lights, I will be told. What? Always machines? Who promises you that they will follow you everywhere in case of need? As for me, I prefer that Emile have eyes in the tips of his fingers than in a candlemaker's shop.

Are you enclosed in a building in the middle of the night? Clap your hands. You will perceive by the resonance of the place whether the area is large or small, whether you are in the middle or in a corner. At half a foot from a wall the air, circulating less and reflecting more, brings a different sensation to your face. Stay in place, and turn successively in every direction. If there is an open door, a light draft will indicate it to you. Are you in a boat? You will know by the way the air strikes your face not only in what direction you are going but whether the river's current is carrying you along slow or fast. These observations and countless others like them can be made well only at night. However much attention we might want to give to them in daylight, we will be aided or distracted by sight; they will escape us. Here, meanwhile, we do not even use our hands or a cane. How much ocular knowledge can be acquired by touch, even without touching anything at all?

Many night games. This advice is more important than it seems. Night naturally frightens men and sometimes animals as well.* Reason, knowledge, wit, and courage deliver few men from the exaction of this tribute. I have seen reasoners, strong-minded men, philosophers, soldiers intrepid by daylight tremble like women at the sound of a leaf at night. This fright is attributed to the tales of nurses.[61] That is a mistake. It has a natural cause. What is this cause? The same one which makes deaf men distrustful and the people [62] superstitious: ignorance of the things which surround us and of what is going on about us.†
Accustomed to perceive objects from afar and to foresee their impressions in advance, how—when I no longer see anything around me— would I not suppose there to be countless beings, countless things in motion which can harm me and from which it is impossible for me to protect myself? I may very well know that I am secure in the place I am; I never know it as well as if I actually saw it. I am therefore always subject to a fear that I do not have in daylight. True, I know that a foreign body can hardly act on mine without proclaiming itself by some sound. So how alert I constantly keep my ears! At the slightest sound whose cause I cannot make out, interest in my preservation immediately brings to my mind everything that most makes me keep on my guard and consequently everything that is most likely to frighten me.

Do I hear absolutely nothing? That does not make me calm, for, after all, without noise I can still be surprised. I must assume that things are as they were before, as they still should be, that I see what I do not see. Compelled thus to set my imagination in motion, I am soon no longer its master, and what I did to reassure myself serves only to alarm me more. If I hear a noise, I hear robbers. If I hear nothing, I see phantoms. The vigilance inspired in me by concern for my preservation gives me only grounds for fear. Everything that ought to reassure me exists only in my reason. Instinct, stronger, speaks to me in a man-

---

* This fright becomes very manifest in great eclipses of the sun.

† This is again another cause well explained by a philosopher whose book I often cite and whose great views instruct me even more often.

When due to particular circumstances we cannot have an exact idea of distance, and we can judge objects only by the size of the angle or, rather, of the image they form in our eyes, then we necessarily make mistakes about the size of these objects. Everybody has the experience in traveling at night of taking a bush which is near for a big tree which is far, or of taking a big tree at a distance for a bush next to one. Similarly, if one does not know the objects by their form and one cannot in this way have any idea of the distance, one will again necessarily make mistakes. A fly which passes rapidly by a few inches away from our eyes will appear to us in this case to be a bird which is at a very great distance. A horse which is not moving in the middle of a field and is in a posture similar, for example, to that of a sheep will not appear to us to be anything other than a big sheep, so long as we do not recognize that it is a horse. But as soon as we have recognized it, it will at that instant appear to us as big as a horse, and we will rectify our first judgment on the spot.

Every time, therefore, that one is at night in unknown places where one cannot judge distance, and where one cannot recognize the form of things due to the darkness, one will at every instant be in danger of falling into error with respect to the judgments one makes about the objects which one meets. From this come the terror and kind of inner fear that the darkness of night causes almost all men to feel. On this is founded the appearance of specters and gigantic, frightful figures that so many people say they have seen. Ordinarily one responds to them that these figures were in their imagination. However, they could really have been in their eyes, and it is quite possible that they have indeed seen what they say they have seen; for it must necessarily

ner quite different. What is the good of thinking that there is nothing to fear, since then there is nothing to do?

The discovery of the cause of the ill indicates the remedy. In everything habit kills imagination. Only new objects awaken it. In those one sees every day, it is no longer imagination which acts, but memory; and that is the reason for the axiom *ab assuetis non fit passio*,[63] for only by the fire of the imagination are the passions kindled. Do not, then, reason with him whom you want to cure of loathing of the dark. Take him out in it often, and rest assured that all the arguments of philosophy are not equal in value to this practice. Tilers on roofs do not get dizzy, and one never sees a man who is accustomed to being in the dark afraid in it.

This is, therefore, an additional advantage of our night games. But for these games to succeed, I cannot recommend enough that there be gaiety in them. Nothing is so sad as darkness. Do not go and close your child up in a dungeon. Let him be laughing as he enters the dark; let laughter overtake him again before he leaves it. While he is still there, let the idea of the entertainments he is leaving and those he is going to find again forbid him fantastic imaginings which could come there to seek him out.

There is a stage of life beyond which, in progressing, one retrogresses. I sense that I have passed that stage. I am beginning again, so to speak, another career. The emptiness of ripe age, which has made itself felt in me, retraces for me the steps of the sweet time of an earlier age. In getting old, I become a child again, and I recall more gladly what I did at ten than at thirty. Readers, pardon me, therefore, for sometimes drawing my examples from myself, for to do this book well I must do it with pleasure.[64]

I was in the country boarding with a minister named M. Lambercier. I had as my comrade a cousin who was richer than I and who was

---

happen, every time one can judge an object only by the angle it forms in the eye, that this unknown object will swell and get larger as one gets nearer to it; and if it at first appeared to the spectator, who cannot know what he is seeing or judge at what distance he is seeing it from—if it appeared, I say, at first to be several feet high when he was twenty or thirty feet away, it must appear several fathoms high when he is no longer more than a few feet away. This must, indeed, surprise and frighten him up until he finally gets to touch the object or to recognize it, for at the very instant he recognizes what it is, that object which appeared gigantic will suddenly diminish and will no longer appear to be anything but its real size. But if one flees or does not dare to come close, it is certain that one will have no other idea of this object than the one of the image it formed in the eye and that one will have really seen an object gigantic and frightful by its size and form. The prejudice of specters is, therefore, founded in nature, and these appearances do not depend, as the philosophers believe, solely on the imagination. [Buffon, *Histoire Naturelle*, vol. VI., p. 22.]

I have tried to show in the text how it always depends in part on the imagination, and, as for the cause explained in this passage, one sees that the habit of walking at night ought to teach us to distinguish the appearances objects take on in our eyes in darkness owing to the resemblance of forms and the diversity of distances. When the air is still lighted enough to let us perceive the contours of objects, and since there is more air interposed in a greater distance, we ought always to see these contours less distinctly when the object is farther from us; this suffices by dint of habit to guarantee us from the error explained here by M. de Buffon. Whatever explanation one prefers my method is, therefore, always effective; and this is perfectly confirmed by experience.

treated as an heir, while I, far away from my father, was only a poor orphan. My big cousin Bernard was a poltroon to a singular degree, especially at night. I mocked him so much for his fright that M. Lambercier, bored by my boasting, wanted to put my courage to the test. One autumn evening when it was very dark, he gave me the key to the temple and told me to go and get from the pulpit the Bible that had been left there. He added, so as to involve my honor, a few words which put me in the position of not being able to hang back.

I left without light. If I had had it, things would have perhaps been still worse. I had to go by way of the cemetery. I crossed it heartily, for so long as I felt I was in the open air, I never had nocturnal fright.

On opening the door, I heard a certain echoing up in the arch, which I believed resembled voices and which began to shake my Roman firmness. With the door opened, I determined to go in, but hardly had I taken a few steps before I stopped. In perceiving the profound darkness which reigned in this vast place, I was seized by a terror which made my hair stand on end. I moved back; I went out; I took flight, trembling all over. I found in the court a little dog named Sultan whose caresses reassured me. Ashamed of my fright, I retraced my steps, this time, however, trying to bring along Sultan, who did not want to follow me. I briskly crossed the threshold and entered the church. Hardly had I gone in again when the fright came back, but so powerfully that I lost my head; and although the pulpit was to the right, and I knew it very well, having turned without being aware of it, I sought it for a long time to the left; I floundered among the pews; I no longer knew where I was; and unable to find either pulpit or door, I fell into a state of inexpressible consternation. Finally I perceived the door. I succeeded in getting out of the temple and made off as I had the first time, fully resolved never to go in there alone again except by daylight.

I went back as far as the house. About to enter, I made out M. Lambercier's voice bursting with laughter. I immediately supposed it to be directed at me; and embarrassed at seeing myself exposed, I hesitated to open the door. In this interval I heard Mademoiselle Lambercier expressing worry about me, telling the serving girl to bring the lantern, and M. Lambercier getting ready to come and look for me escorted by my intrepid cousin, to whom afterward they would without fail have given all the honor resulting from the expedition. Instantly all my frights ceased, leaving me only the fright of being encountered in my flight. I ran—I flew—to the temple without losing my way; without groping around, I got to the pulpit, mounted it, took the Bible, jumped down, in three bounds was out of the temple, whose door I even forgot to close. I entered the room, out of breath, threw the Bible on the table, flustered but palpitating with joy at having been ahead of the help intended for me.

One might ask if I tell this story as a model to follow and as an example of the gaiety which I exact in this kind of exercise? No, but I give it as proof that nothing is more reassuring to someone frightened of shadows in the night than to hear company, assembled in a neighboring room, laughing and chatting calmly. I would want that, instead of playing alone with one's pupil in this way, one brings together many good-humored children in the evening, that at first they be sent out not separately but several together, that no chance be taken with a single child all alone, unless one is quite sure beforehand that he will not be too frightened.

I can imagine nothing so pleasant and so useful as such games if one is willing to put a bit of skill into organizing them. In a large room I would make a kind of labyrinth with tables, chairs, and screens. In the tortuous and complex passages through this labyrinth, I would set, amidst eight or ten boxes which are decoys, another box, almost the same, well lined with bonbons. I would describe in clear but succinct terms the precise place where the right box is to be found. I would give enough information to make it clear for persons more attentive and less giddy than children.* Then after having made the little competitors draw lots, I would send them all out, one after the other, until the right box was found. I would take care to make finding it difficult in proportion to their skill.

Just think of a little Hercules arriving with a box in his hand, full of pride in his expedition. The box is put on the table and ceremoniously opened. I can already hear the bursts of laughter, the jeers of the joyous band when, instead of the candies that were expected, they find, very nicely set out on moss or cotton, a June bug, a snail, a piece of coal, an acorn, a turnip or some other similar foodstuff. Other times, in a room freshly whitewashed, we will hang near the wall some toy, some little decoration; the object will be to go and get it without touching the wall. Hardly will the one who brings it have returned—however minor his infraction of the rule—before his maladroitness will be betrayed by the white at the tip of his cap, at the tip of his shoes, on the edge of his jacket, or on his sleeve. This is quite enough, perhaps too much, to make the spirit of this kind of game understood. If you have to be told everything, do not read me.

What advantages will a man thus raised not have over other men at night? Accustomed to having a good footing in darkness, practiced at handling with ease all surrounding bodies, his feet and hands will lead him without difficulty in the deepest darkness. His imagination, full of the nocturnal games of his youth, will be loath to turn to frightening objects. If he believes he hears bursts of laughter, instead of belonging to sprites they will be those of his old comrades. If an assemblage appears, it will not be for him the witches' sabbath but his governor's room. The night, recalling to him only gay ideas, will never be frightening for him. Instead of fearing it, he will like it. Is there a military expedition? He will be ready at any hour, alone as well as with his company. He will enter Saul's camp, go through it without losing his way, will go up to the king's tent without awakening anyone, and will return without being noticed. Must the horses of Rhesus be abducted? Call on him without fear. Among men raised in a different way you will have difficulty finding a Ulysses.[65]

---

* To give them practice in paying attention, never tell them anything but things which they have a palpable and immediate interest in understanding well—above all, nothing drawn out, never a superfluous word. But, also, let there be neither obscurity nor ambiguity in your speech.

I have seen people who wanted to accustom children to be fearless at night by surprising them. This is a very bad method. It produces an effect exactly the opposite of the one sought and serves always to make children only more fearful. Neither reason nor habit can reassure us when we have the idea of a present danger whose extent and kind cannot be known, or when we fear surprises we have often experienced. Nevertheless, how are you to ensure that your pupil be always kept out of the way of such accidents? Here is the best advice, it seems to me, with which he can be forearmed against them: "In such a case," I would say to my Emile, "you may justly defend yourself, for the aggressor does not let you judge if he wants to do you harm or frighten you; and since he has taken the advantage, even flight is not a refuge for you. Therefore, boldly grab the one who surprises you at night, man or beast—it makes no difference. Hold on and squeeze him with all your might. If he struggles, hit him. Do not stint your blows; and whatever he may say or do, never loosen your hold on him until you know for sure what is going on. Probably his explanation will show you that there was not much to fear, and this way of treating jesters should naturally discourage them from trying again."

Although touch is, of all our senses, the one we exercise the most continually, its judgments nevertheless remain, as I have said, imperfect and more crude than those of any other sense, because we continually use along with it the sense of sight; and since the eye reaches the object sooner than the hand, the mind almost always judges without the latter. On the other hand, precisely because they are most limited, tactile judgments are surer; for, extending only so far as our hands can reach, they rectify the giddiness of the other senses which leap far ahead to objects they hardly perceive, while everything that touch perceives, it perceives well. In addition, since we join when we please the strength of muscles to the activity of nerves, we are able to unite judgment of weight and solidity with judgment of temperature, size, and shape simultaneously in a single sensation. Thus touch, being of all the senses the one which best informs us about the impression foreign bodies can make on our own, is the one whose use is the most frequent and gives us most immediately the knowledge necessary to our preservation.

Since a trained touch supplements sight, why could it not also up to a certain point supplement hearing, given the fact that sounds set off vibrations which can be sensed by touch in sonorous bodies? In placing a hand on the body of a cello, one can, without the aid of eyes or ears, distinguish solely by the way the wood vibrates and quivers whether the sound it produces is low or high, whether it comes from the A string or the C string. Let the senses be trained in these differences. I have no doubt that with time one could become sensitive enough to be able to hear an entire air with the fingers. And if this is the case, it is clear that one could easily speak to the deaf with music, for sounds and rhythms, no less susceptible of regular combinations than articulations and voices, can similarly be taken for the elements of speech.

There are practices which dull the sense of touch and make it blunter. Others, on the contrary, sharpen it and make it keener and more delicate. The former, those that join much motion and force to constant contact with hard bodies, make the skin rough and callous and take the natural feeling away from it. The latter are those which vary this same feeling by a light and frequent contact, so that the mind, attentive to impressions incessantly repeated, acquires facility at judging all their modifications. This difference is palpable in the use of musical instruments. The hard and bruising touch of the cello, the bass, even of the violin, in making the fingers more flexible, hardens their extremities. The smooth and polished touch of the harpsichold makes them as flexible and more sensitive at the same time. In this, therefore, the harpsichord is to be preferred.

It is important that the skin be hardened to the impressions of, and able to brave changes in, the air, for it defends all the rest, except that I would not want the hand to get hardened from too servile an application to the same labors nor its skin, become almost bony, to lose that exquisite sensitivity that permits it to recognize the bodies over which one passes it and which in the dark sometimes cause us to shudder—in ways that differ according to the kind of contact.

Why must my pupil be forced always to have a cow's skin under his feet? What harm would there be if in case of need his own skin were able to serve him as a sole? In this part of the body the delicacy of the skin clearly can never be useful for anything and can often do much harm. Awakened at midnight in the heart of winter by the enemy in the city, the Genevans found their muskets before their shoes. If none of them had known how to march barefoot, who knows whether Geneva might not have been taken? [66]

Let us always arm man against unexpected accidents. In the morning let Emile run barefoot in all seasons, in his room, on the stairs, in the garden. Far from reproaching him, I shall imitate him. I shall take care only that glass be removed. I shall soon speak of manual labor and games. Beyond that let him learn to do all the steps which help the body's development, to find a comfortable and stable posture in all positions. Let him know how to jump long and high, to climb a tree, to get over a wall. Let him learn to keep his balance; let all his movements and gestures be ordered according to the laws of equilibrium, long before the study of statics is introduced to explain it all to him. By the way his foot touches the ground and his body rests on his legs, he ought to be able to feel whether he is well or ill positioned. An assured bearing is always graceful, and the firmest postures are also the most elegant. If I were a dancing master, I would not perform all the monkeyshines of Marcel,* good only for that country where he engages in them. Instead of eternally busying my pupil with leaps, I would take him to the foot of a cliff. There I would show him what attitude he must take, how he must bear his body and his head, what

---

* Celebrated dancing master of Paris, who, knowing his world well, played the fool out of cunning and attributed to his art an importance which others feigned to find ridiculous, but for which, at bottom, they respected him very greatly. In another art, no less frivolous, one can also today see an actor-artist play the man of importance and the madman and succeed no less well. This is the sure method in France. True talent, simpler and with less charlatanry, does not make its fortune there. Modesty is there the virtue of fools.

movements he must make, in what way he must place now his foot, now his hand, so as to follow lightly the steep, rough, uneven paths and to bound from peak to peak in climbing up as well as down. I would make him the emulator of a goat rather than of a dancer at the Opéra.

As touch concentrates its operations in the immediate vicinity of man, so sight extends its operations beyond him. That is what makes the operations of sight deceptive. At a glance a man embraces half of his horizon. In this multitude of simultaneous sensations and the judgments they call forth, how is it possible not to be deceived by any? Thus of all our senses sight is the most defective, precisely because it is the most extended; and far in advance of all the others, its operations are too quick and too vast to be rectified by them. What is more, the very illusions of perspective are necessary for us to come to a knowledge of extension and to compare its parts. Without false appearances we would see nothing in perspective; without the gradations of size and light we could not estimate any distance, or, rather, there would be none for us. If, of two equal trees, the one a hundred paces from us appeared as large and as distinct as the one at ten, we would place them side by side. If we perceived all the dimensions of objects in their true measure, we would see no space, and everything would appear to be in our eye.

The sense of sight has only a single measure for judging the size of objects and their distance—namely, the width of the angle they make in our eye; and since that angle width is a simple effect of a complex cause, the judgment it calls forth leaves each particular cause indeterminate or becomes necessarily defective. For how is it possible to distinguish by simple sight whether the angle by which I see one object as smaller than another is so because this first object is actually smaller or because it is more distant?

Therefore, a method contrary to the former must be followed here. Instead of simplifying the sensation, double it, always verify it by another. Subject the visual organ to the tactile organ, and repress, so to speak, the impetuosity of the former sense by the heavy and regular step of the latter. If we fail to submit ourselves to this practice, our estimated measurements are very inexact. There is no precision in our glance for judging heights, lengths, depths, and distances. And the proof that it is not so much the fault of the sense as it is of its use is that engineers, surveyors, architects, masons, and painters generally have a much surer glance than we do and appraise the measurements of extension with more exactness. Because their professions give them the experience that we neglect to acquire, they remove the ambiguity of the angle by the appearances which accompany it and which determine more exactly to their eyes the relation of that angle's two causes.

Anything which gives movement to the body without constraining it is always easy to obtain from children. There are countless means of interesting them in measuring, knowing, and estimating distances. Here is a very tall cherry tree. How shall we go about picking the cherries? Will the barn ladder do for that? Here is quite a large stream. How shall we cross it? Will one of the planks from the courtyard reach both banks? We would like to fish from our windows in the mansion's

BOOK II

ponds. How many spans ought our line to have? I would like to hang a swing between these two trees: will a rope two fathoms long be enough for us? I am told that in the other house our room will be twenty-five square feet. Do you believe that it will suit us? Will it be larger than this one? We are very hungry. There are two villages. At which of the two will we arrive sooner for dinner? Et cetera.

There was an indolent and lazy child who was to be trained in running—a child not of himself drawn to this exercise or to any other, although he was intended for a military career. He had persuaded himself, I do not know how, that a man of his rank ought to do and know nothing, and that his noble birth was going to take the place of arms and legs as well as of every kind of merit. To make of such a gentleman a light-footed Achilles, the skill of Chiron himself would have hardly sufficed. The difficulty was all the greater since I wanted to prescribe to him absolutely nothing. I had banished from among my rights exhortations, promises, threats, emulation, the desire to be conspicuous. How could I give him the desire to run without saying anything to him? To run myself would have been a very uncertain means and one subject to disadvantages. Moreover, the intention was also to get for him from this exercise some object of instruction, so as to accustom the operations of the machine and those of judgment always to work harmoniously. Here is how I went about it—I, that is to say, the man who speaks in this example.

In going walking with him in the afternoon I sometimes put in my pocket two cakes of a kind he liked a lot. We each ate one of them during the walk,* and we came back quite contented. One day he noticed that I had three cakes. He could have eaten six of them comfortably. He dispatched his promptly in order to ask me for the third. "No," I said to him, "I could very well eat it myself, or we could divide it. But I prefer to see those two little boys there compete for it by running." I called them, showed them the cake, and proposed the condition to them. They asked for nothing better. The cake was set on a large stone which served as the finish. The course was marked out. We went and sat down. At a given signal the little boys started. The victor seized the cake and ate it without mercy before the eyes of the spectators and the vanquished.

This entertainment was better than the cake, but at first it did not register and produced nothing. I did not give up, nor did I hurry; the education of children is a vocation in which one must know how to lose time in order to gain it. We continued our walks. Often we took three cakes, sometimes four, and from time to time there was one, even two, for the runners. If the prize was not big, those who competed for it were not ambitious. The one who won it was praised and given a celebration; it was all done with ceremony. To provide variety and increase interest, I marked off a longer course. I allowed several contestants. Hardly

---

* Walk in the country, as will be seen immediately. The public walks of cities are pernicious for children of both sexes. It is there that they begin to become vain and to want to be looked at. It is in the Luxembourg, the Tuileries, especially the Palais-Royal, that the brilliant young of Paris go to get that impertinent and foppish air which makes them so ridiculous and causes them to be hooted and detested throughout Europe.

were they in the lanes when all the passers-by stopped to see them. Acclamations, shouts, and clapping cheered them on. I sometimes saw my little fellow tremble, get up, and shout when one was near to catching up with or passing another. These were for him the Olympic games.

However, sometimes the contestants cheated. They held onto or tripped one another or pushed pebbles in one another's way. That gave me the occasion to separate them and make them start from different points, although at equal distances from the goal. The reason for this provision will soon be seen, for I am going to treat this important affair in great detail.

Irritated by always seeing cakes, which he desired very much for himself, eaten before his eyes, the knight finally got into his head the suspicion that running well could be good for something; and, seeing that he also had two legs, he began to take a try in secret. I was careful not to see a thing. But I understood that my stratagem had worked. When he believed himself to be up to it, and I had read his thought ahead of him, he affected to importune me for the remaining cake. I refused him. He was stubborn and, in a vexed tone, said to me finally: "Very well, put it on the stone, mark out the field, and we shall see." "Good," I said to him, laughing. "Does a knight know how to run? You will get a bigger appetite and nothing to satisfy it with." Goaded by my mockery, he made an effort and carried off the prize, all the more easily since I had made the lists very short and had taken care to keep the best runner away. It can be conceived how, this first step made, it was easy for me to keep him on his toes. Soon he got such a taste for this exercise that without favor he was almost sure of vanquishing my little scamps at running, however long the course.

This accomplishment produced another of which I had not dreamed. When he had rarely carried off the prize, he almost always ate it alone, as did his competitors. But, in accustoming himself to victory, he became generous and often shared with the vanquished. That provided a moral observation for me, and I learned thereby what the true principle of generosity is.

Continuing with him to mark in different places the points from which each boy was to begin at the same time, without his noticing it I made the distances unequal. Thus one boy, having to cover more ground than another to get to the same goal, had a visible disadvantage. But although I left the choice to my disciple, he did not know how to avail himself of the opportunity. Without bothering about the distance, he always preferred the path that looked good; so that, easily foreseeing his choice, I was practically the master of making him lose or win the cake at will, and this skill also had its uses for more than one end. However, since my plan was that he notice the difference, I tried to make it evident to his senses. But though he was indolent when calm, he was so lively in his games and distrusted me so little that I had the greatest difficulty in making him notice that I was cheating. Finally I succeeded despite his giddiness. He reproached me for it. I said to him, "What are you complaining about? With a gift that is within my pleasure to give, am I not master of my conditions? Who is forcing you to run? Did I promise to make equal lanes for you? Have you not the choice? Take the shorter one. Nobody is preventing you. How do you not see that it is you I am favoring, and that the inequality you are grumbling about is entirely to your advantage if you know how to avail yourself of it?" This was clear; he understood it; and to choose he had to look more closely. At first he wanted to count the paces. But measurement by a child's pace is slow and defective. Moreover, I planned it so that the number of races on a single day was multiplied; and then, the play becoming a sort of passion, he regretted to lose, in measuring the lanes, the time intended to be used for running them. The vivacity of child-hood adjusts itself poorly to these delays. He practiced himself, there-fore, at seeing better, at estimating a distance better by sight. Then I had little difficulty in extending and nourishing this taste. Finally a few months of tests and corrected errors formed the visual compass in him to such an extent that when I told him to think of a cake on some distant object, he had a glance almost as sure as a surveyor's chain.

Since sight is, of all the senses, the one from which the mind's judg-ments can least be separated, much time is needed to learn how to see. Sight must have been compared with touch for a long time to accustom the former to give us a faithful report of shapes and distances. Without touch, without progressive movement, the most penetrating eyes in the world would not be able to give us any idea of extension. The entire universe must be only a point for an oyster. It would not appear to it as anything more even if a human soul were to inform this oyster. It is only by dint of walking, grasping, counting, of measuring dimensions that one learns to estimate them. But also if one always measured, sense, always relying on the instrument, would not acquire any exact-ness. Neither must the child go all of a sudden from measurement to estimation. At first, continuing to compare part by part what he would not know how to compare all at once, he must substitute for precise divisors estimated ones and, instead of always applying the measure with his hand, get accustomed to applying it with his eyes alone. I would, however, want his first operations to be verified by real measures in order that he correct his errors, and that if some false appearance remains in the sense, he learn to rectify it by a better judgment. There are natural measures which are almost the same in all places—a man's pace, his outstretched arms, his stature. When the child estimates the height of a story, his governor can serve him as measuring rod; if he estimates the height of a steeple, let him measure it against houses. If he wants to know the number of leagues covered by a road, let him count the hours it takes to walk it. And, above all, let nothing of all this be done for him, but let him do it himself.

One could not learn to judge the extension and the size of bodies well without also getting to know their shapes and even learning to imitate them; for, at bottom, this imitation depends absolutely only on the laws of perspective, and one can estimate extension by its appear-ances only if one has some feeling for these laws. Children, who are great imitators, all try to draw. I would want my child to cultivate this art, not precisely for the art itself but for making his eye exact and his hand flexible. And in general it is of very little importance that he know this or that exercise, provided that his senses acquire the perspicacity and his body the good habits one gains by this exercise. I will, therefore, carefully avoid giving him a drawing master who would give him only imitations to imitate and would make him draw only from drawings. I want him to have no other master than nature and no other model than objects. I want him to have before his eyes the original itself and not the paper representing it, to sketch a house from a house, a tree from a tree, a man from a man, so that he gets accustomed to observing bodies and their appearances well and not to taking false and conventional imitations for true imitations. I will even divert him from drawing from memory in the absence of the objects until their exact shapes are well imprinted on his imagination by frequent observations, for fear that, by substituting bizarre and fantastic shapes for the truth of things, he will lose the knowledge of proportions and the taste for the beauties of nature.[67]

I know that in this way he will dabble for a long time without making anything recognizable; that the artist's elegance of contour and light touch he will get late, and discernment in picturesque effects and good taste in drawing, perhaps never. On the other hand, he will certainly develop a more accurate glance, a surer hand, the knowledge of the true relations of size and shape which exist among animals, plants, and natural bodies, and a quicker capacity for experiencing the play of perspective. This is precisely what I wanted to accomplish, and my intention is that he be able not so much to imitate objects as to know them. I prefer that he show me an acanthus plant and sketch the foliage of a capital less well.

Moreover, in this exercise as in all the others, I do not want my pupil to be the only one to have fun. I want to make it even more agreeable for him by constantly sharing it with him. I do not want him to have any emulator other than me, but I will be his emulator without respite and without risk. That will put interest in his occupations without causing jealousy between us. I will take up the pencil following his example. I will use it at first as maladroitly as he. Were I an Apelles,[68] I would now be only a dabbler. I will begin by sketching a man as lackeys sketch them on walls: a line for each arm, a line for each leg, and the fingers thicker than the arm. Quite a while later one or the other of us will notice this disproportion. We will observe that a leg has thickness, that this thickness is not the same all over, that the arm has its length determined by relation to the body, etc. In this progress I will at very most advance along with him, or I will be so little ahead of him that it will always be easy for him to catch up with me and often to surpass me. We shall have colors, brushes. We shall try to imitate the coloring of objects and their whole appearance as well as their shape. We shall color, paint, dabble. But, in all our dabblings, we shall not stop spying on nature; we shall never do anything except under the master's eye.

We were in want of adornment for our room. Here it is found. I have our drawings framed. I have them covered with fine glass so that they no longer can be touched, and each of us, seeing them remain in the state in which we put them, will have an interest in not neglecting his own. I arrange them in order around the room, each drawing re-

peated twenty, thirty times, and each copy showing the author's progress, from the moment when a house is only an almost formless square
until its façade, its profile, its proportions, and its shadows are present
in the most exact truth. These gradations cannot fail constantly to
present pictures of interest to us and objects of curiosity for others and
to excite ever more our emulation. On the first, the crudest, of these
drawings I put quite brilliant, well-gilded frames which enhance them.
But when the imitation becomes more exact, and the drawing is truly
good, then I give it nothing more than a very simple black frame. It
needs no adornment other than itself, and it would be a shame for the
border to get part of the attention the object merits. Thus each of us
aspires to the honor of the plain frame, and when one wants to express
contempt for a drawing of the other, he condemns it to the gilded frame.
Someday perhaps these gilded frames will serve as proverbs for us, and
we shall wonder at how many men do themselves justice in providing
such frames for themselves.

I have said that geometry is not within the reach of children. But it is
our fault. We are not aware that their method is not ours, and that
what becomes for us the art of reasoning, for them ought to be only the
art of seeing. Instead of giving them our method, we would do better to
take theirs. For our way of learning geometry is an affair just as much
of imagination as of reasoning. When the proposition is stated, it is
necessary to imagine its demonstration—that is to say, to find of which
proposition already known this one must be a consequence and, out of
all the consequences that can be drawn from that same proposition,
to choose precisely the one required.

In this way the most exact reasoner, if he is not inventive, has to
stop short. So what is the result of this? Instead of our being made to
find the demonstrations, they are dictated to us. Instead of teaching us
to reason, the master reasons for us and exercises only our memory.

Make exact figures, combine them, place them on one another, examine their relations. You will find the whole of elementary geometry in
moving from observation to observation, without there being any question of definitions or problems or any form of demonstration other than
simple superimposition. As for me, I do not intend to teach geometry to
Emile; it is he who will teach it to me; I will seek the relations, and he
will find them, for I will seek them in such a way as to make him find
them. For example, instead of using a compass to draw a circle, I shall
draw it with a point at the end of a string turning on a pivot. After that,
when I want to compare the radii among themselves, Emile will ridicule
me and make me understand that the same string, always taut, cannot
have drawn unequal distances.

If I want to measure an angle of sixty degrees, I describe from the
vertex of this angle not an arc but an entire circle, for with children
nothing must ever be left implicit. I find that the portion of the circle
contained between the two sides of the angle is one-sixth of the circle.
After that I describe from the same vertex another larger circle, and I
find that this second arc is still one-sixth of its circle. I describe a third
concentric circle on which I make the same test, and I continue thus

on new circles—until Emile, shocked by my stupidity, informs me that each arc, big or little, contained by the same angle, will always be one-sixth of its circle, etc. Now it will soon be time to use the protractor.

To prove that adjacent angles are equal to two right angles, one describes a circle. I, on the contrary, arrange it so that Emile first notes this in the circle; and then I say to him, "If the circle were taken away and the right lines were left, would the angles' size have changed?" Et cetera.

People neglect the exactness of the figures; it is presupposed, and one concentrates on the demonstration. With us, on the contrary, the issue will never be demonstration. Our most important business will be to draw lines very straight, very exact, very equal—to make a very perfect square, to trace a very round circle. To verify the exactness of the figure, we shall examine it in all its properties which are grasped by the senses, and this will give us the opportunity to discover new ones every day. We shall get two semicircles by folding along the diameter; the halves of the square, by folding along the diagonal. We shall compare our two figures to see whose edges fit most exactly and, consequently, which is best made. We shall argue whether this equality of division ought always to be found in parallelograms, in trapezoids, etc. We shall sometimes attempt to foresee the success of the experiment before making it; we shall try to find reasons, etc.

Geometry is for my pupil only the art of using the ruler and the compass well. He ought not to confuse geometry with drawing, in which he will use neither of these instruments. The ruler and the compass will be kept under lock and key, and he will be granted the use of them only rarely and for a short time, so that he does not get accustomed to dabbling with them. But we can sometimes take our figures on our walks and chat about what we have done or want to do.

I shall never forget seeing at Turin a young man who had in his childhood been taught the relations between contours and surface areas by being given the choice every day of waffles with equal perimeters done in all the geometric figures. The little glutton had exhausted the art of Archimedes in finding out in which there was the most to eat.

When a child plays with the shuttlecock, he practices his eye and arm in accuracy; when he whips a top, he increases his strength by using it but without learning anything. I have sometimes asked why the same games of skill men have are not given to children: tennis, croquet, billiards, the bow, football, musical instruments. I was answered that some of these games are beyond a child's strength and that his limbs and his organs are not sufficiently developed for the others. I find these reasons poor: a child does not have a man's height but nonetheless is able to wear clothes made like a man's. I do not mean that he should play with our cues on a billiard table three feet high; I do not mean that he should hit the ball around in our courts, or that his little hand should be weighed down by a tennis racket; but I mean that he should play in a room where the windows are protected, that he should use only soft balls, that his first rackets should be of wood, then of sheepskin, and finally strung with catgut, commensurate with his progress. You will prefer shuttlecock because it is less tiring and without danger.

BOOK II

You are wrong in both of these reasons. Shuttlecock is a woman's game. But there is not a woman whom a moving ball does not cause to flee. Women's fair skins ought not to be hardened to bruises, and it is not contusions that their faces await. But we, made to be vigorous, do we believe we can become so painlessly? And of what defense will we be capable if we are never attacked? One is always lax in playing games in which one can be maladroit without risk. A falling shuttlecock does not harm anyone; but nothing arouses the arm like having to cover the head; nothing makes the glance so accurate as having to protect the eyes. To bound from one end of the room to the other, to judge a ball's bounce while still in the air, to return it with a hand strong and sure—such games are less suitable for a grown man than useful for forming him.

A child's fibers are, it is said, too soft. They have less spring, but they are also more pliant. His arm is weak, but, still, it is an arm; one ought to be able to do with it, proportionately, all that is done with another similar machine. Children's hands have no dexterity; that is why I want it given to them. A man as little practiced as they would have no more. We can know the use of our organs only after having employed them. It is only long experience which teaches us to turn ourselves to account, and this experience is the true study to which we cannot apply ourselves too soon.

Everything which is done can be done. Now, nothing is more common than seeing adroit and well-built children having the same agility in their limbs as a man can have. At almost every fair they are seen doing balancing acts, walking on their hands, leaping, tightrope dancing. For how many years have companies of children attracted spectators to the Comédie Italienne for their ballet? Who has not heard in Germany and in Italy of the pantomime company of the celebrated Nicolini? Has anyone ever noticed in these children less developed movements, less graceful attitudes, a less exact ear, a dance less light than in fully formed dancers? Does their having at first thick, short, hardly mobile fingers and chubby hands hardly capable of grasping anything prevent many children from knowing how to write or draw at an age when others do not yet know how to hold a pencil or pen? All of Paris still remembers the little English girl who at ten performed marvels on the harpsichord.* At the home of a magistrate I saw his son—a little fellow of eight who was put on the table at dessert like a statue amidst the plates—play a violin almost as big as he was. The quality of his execution surprised even the artists.

All these examples and a hundred thousand others prove, it seems to me, that the supposed ineptitude of children at our exercises is imaginary and that, if they are not seen to succeed at some, it is because they have never been given practice in them.

I will be told that I fall here, with respect to the body, into the mistake of premature culture of children which I criticize with respect to the mind. The difference is very great, for progress in one of these areas is only apparent, but in the other it is real. I have proved that the

---

* A little boy of seven has since that time performed even more astonishing ones.[69]

intelligence children appear to have, they do not have; but all that they appear to do, they in fact do. Moreover, it ought always to be borne in mind that all this is or ought to be only a game, an easy and voluntary direction of the movements nature asks of children, an art of varying their play to render it more pleasant to them without the least constraint ever turning it into work. Really, what will they play with that I cannot turn into an object of instruction for them? And if I cannot, provided that they play without causing any problem and the time passes, their progress in everything is not important for the present; whereas, those who feel that, no matter what, they just have to teach them this or that always find it impossible to succeed without constraint, without quarreling, and without boredom.

What I have said about the two senses whose use is the most continuous and the most important can serve to exemplify the way of exercising the others. Sight and touch are applied equally to bodies at rest and moving bodies; but since it is only disturbance of the air which can arouse the sense of hearing, it is only a body in motion which makes noise or sound, and if everything were at rest, we would never hear anything. At night, therefore, when we ourselves move only so much as we please and consequently have only moving bodies to fear, it is important for us to have an alert ear, to be able to judge by the sensation which strikes us whether the body causing it is big or little, far or near, whether its motion is violent or weak. When air is disturbed, it is subject to repercussions which reflect it and which, producing echoes, repeat the sensation and make the loud or resonant body heard in a place other than where it is. If in a plain or a valley one puts one's ear to the ground, one hears the voices of men and the hoofs of horses much farther away than when one stands up.

As we have compared sight to touch, it is similarly good to compare it to hearing and to know which of the two impressions, starting out from the same body at the same time, first reaches the organ that perceives it. When one sees a cannon's fire, one can still find cover from the shot; but so soon as one hears the noise, there is no longer time; the ball is there. The distance from which thunder is coming can be judged by the time which passes from the lightning to the clap. Arrange things so that the child has knowledge of all these experiments, that he makes all those within his reach, and that he finds the others by induction. But I prefer a hundred times over his being ignorant of them to your having to tell them to him.

We have an organ which corresponds to hearing—namely, the voice. We do not similarly have one which corresponds to sight; and we do not transmit colors as we do sounds. This is one more means to cultivate the former sense, by using the active organ and the passive organ to exercise one another reciprocally.

Man has three kinds of voice—the speaking or articulate voice, the singing or melodic voice, and the passionate or accentuated voice, which serves as language to the passions and which animates song and word. The child has these three kinds of voice as does the man, but without knowing how to join them in the same way. He has, as we do, laughter, cries, groans, exclamations, wailing; but he does not know how to blend their inflections with the two other voices. A perfect music is one which best brings together these three voices. Children are incapable of this music, and their singing never has soul. Similarly, in the spoken voice their language has no accent. They shout, but they do not accentuate; and as there is little energy in their speech, there is little accent in their voice. Our pupil will speak even more plainly and simply, because his passions, not yet awakened, will not blend their language with his. Therefore, do not go giving him roles from tragedy and comedy to recite, or wish to teach him, as they say, to declaim. He will have too much sense to know how to give a tone to things he cannot understand or to give expression to feelings he never experienced.

Teach him to speak plainly and clearly, to articulate well, to pronounce exactly and without affectation, to know and follow grammatical accent and prosody, always to employ enough voice to be heard but never to employ more than is required, a defect common in children raised in colleges. In all things, nothing superfluous.

Similarly in singing, make his voice exact, even, flexible, resonant, his ear sensitive to rhythm and harmony, but nothing more. Imitative and theatrical music is not for his age. I would not even want him to sing words. If he wanted to, I would try to write songs especially for him, interesting for his age and as simple as his ideas.

It can well be believed that as I am in so little hurry to teach him to read writing, I will not be in a hurry to teach him to read music either. Let us set aside an effort of attention too great for his brain and not rush to fix his mind on conventional signs. This, I admit, seems to involve a difficulty, for although the knowledge of notes does not at first appear more necessary for knowing how to sing than does knowledge of letters for knowing how to speak, there is, however, this difference: in speaking we transmit our own ideas, while in singing we transmit hardly anything but others' ideas. Now, to transmit them, one must read them.

But in the first place, instead of reading them, one can hear them, and a song is transmitted with even more fidelity to the ear than to the eye. Moreover, in order to know music well, it does not suffice to transmit it; it is necessary to compose it. The one ought to be learned with the other; otherwise one never knows music well. Train your little musician at first in making very regular, very well-cadenced phrases; then in connecting them together by a very simple modulation; finally, in marking their different relations by correct punctuation, which is done by the good choice of cadences and rests. Above all, never a bizarre song, never a passionate one, and never an expressive one. Always a lilting and simple melody, always deriving from the key's basic notes, and always emphasizing the bass so much that he feels it and can accompany it without difficulty; for, to form the voice and the ear, he ought to sing only with the harpsichord.

To mark the sounds better, one articulates them by pronouncing them; hence, the practice of sol-faing with certain syllables. To distinguish the degrees of the scale, one must give names both to them and to the fixed starting points of the different scales; hence the names of the intervals and also the letters of the alphabet with which the keys of the harpsichord and the notes of the scale are marked. C and A designate fixed, invariable sounds, which are always produced by the same harpsichord keys. *Do* and *la* are something else. *Do* is without exception the tonic of a major mode or the mediant of a minor mode. *La* is without exception the tonic of a minor mode or the sixth of a major mode. Thus the letters mark the immutable terms of our musical system's relations, and the syllables mark the homologous terms of the similar relations in the various keys. The letters indicate the harpsichord's keys, and the syllables, the degrees of the mode. French musicians have strangely mixed up these distinctions. They have confused the meaning of the syllables with the meaning of the letters, and by uselessly doubling the designations of the keys, they have not left any to express the degrees of the scale; so that for them *do* and C are always the same thing, which they are not and should not be, for then what would be the use of C? Thus their way of sol-faing is excessively difficult without being of any use and without presenting any distinct idea to the mind, since by this method the two syllables *do* and *mi,* for example, can equally signify a major, minor, augmented or diminished third. By what strange fatality is the country where the finest books in the world on music are written precisely the one where music is learned with most difficulty? [70]

Let us follow a simpler and clearer practice with our pupil. Let there be for him only two modes, the relations of which are always the same and always indicated by the same syllables. Whether he sings or plays an instrument, let him know how to build his mode on each of the twelve notes that can be used as its base; and, whether one is in the key of D, C, G, etc., let the last note always be *do* or *la* according to the mode. In this way he will always comprehend you, the mode's essential relations for singing and playing in tune will always be present to his mind, and his execution will be more accurate and his progress more rapid. There is nothing more bizarre than what the French call sol-faing naturally. This separates the ideas from the thing and substitutes for them ideas alien to it that are only misleading. Nothing is more natural than to transpose when one sol-fas, if the mode is transposed. But this is too much about music. Teach it as you wish, provided that it is never anything but play.

Now we are well informed about the character of foreign bodies in relation to our own, about their weight, shape, color, solidity, size, distance, temperature, rest, and motion. We are informed about those it is suitable for us to be near or to keep at a distance, about the way we have to go about overcoming their resistance or setting up a resistance against them which keeps us from being injured. But that is not enough. Our own body is constantly being used up and needs constantly to be renewed. Although we have the faculty of changing other bodies into our own substance, the choice among them is not a matter of indifference. Everything is not food for man; and, of the substances which can be, there are ones more or less suitable for him according to the constitution of his species, according to the climate he inhabits, according to his individual temperament, and according to the way of life prescribed to him by his station.

BOOK II

We would die of hunger or be poisoned if, to choose the nourishment suitable to us, we had to wait until experience had taught us to know it and choose it. But the supreme goodness, which has made the pleasure of beings capable of sensation the instrument of their preservation, informs us what suits our stomach by what pleases our palate. Naturally there is no doctor surer for man than his own appetite; and, regarding its primitive state, I do not doubt that the foods it then found most pleasant were also the healthiest.

What is more, the Author of things provides not only for the needs He gives us but also for those we give ourselves; and it is in order to place desire always at the side of need that He causes our tastes to change and be modified with our ways of life. The farther we are removed from the state of nature, the more we lose our natural tastes; or, rather, habit gives us a second nature that we substitute for the first to such an extent that none of us knows this first nature any more.

It follows from this that the most natural tastes ought also to be the simplest, for it is they which are most easily transformed; while by being sharpened and inflamed by our whims, they get a form which can no longer be changed. The man who is not yet of any country will adapt himself without difficulty to the practices of any country whatsoever, but the man of one country can no longer become the man of another.

This appears true to me in every sense, and still more so when applied to taste strictly speaking. Our first food is milk. We get accustomed to strong flavors only by degrees; at first they are repugnant to us. Fruits, vegetables, herbs, and finally some meats grilled without seasoning and without salt constituted the feasts of the first men.* The first time a savage drinks wine, he grimaces and throws it away; and even among us whoever has lived to twenty without tasting fermented liquors can no longer accustom himself to them. We would all be abstemious if we had not been given wine in our early years. In sum, the simpler our tastes, the more universal they are. The most common repugnances are to composite dishes. Has anyone ever been seen to have a disgust for water or bread? That is the trace left by nature; that is, therefore, also our rule. Let us preserve in the child his primary taste as much as is possible. Let his nourishment be common and simple; let his palate get acquainted only with bland flavors and not be formed to an exclusive taste.

I am not investigating here whether this way of life is healthier or not; that is not the way I am looking at it. For me to prefer it, it suffices to know that it conforms most to nature and is the one most easily adaptable to every other. Those who say that children must be accustomed to the foods they will use when grown do not reason well, it seems to me. Why should their nourishment be the same while their way of life is so different? A man exhausted by work, cares, and sorrows needs succulent foods which carry new spirits to the brain. A child who has just frolicked, and whose body is growing, needs abundant nourishment which will produce a lot of chyle for him. Moreover, the

---

* See the *Arcadia* of Pausanias; [71] see also the passage from Plutarch transcribed hereafter.

mature man already has his station, his work, and his domicile. But who can be sure what fortune reserves for the child? In everything let us not give him a form so determined that it costs him too much to change it in case of need. Let us not make it so that he will die of hunger in other countries if he is not everywhere attended by a French cook, or that he will say one day that only in France do they know how to eat. That is, parenthetically, amusing praise! As for me, on the contrary, I would say it is only the French who do not know how to eat, since so special an art is required to make dishes edible for them.

Of our various sensations taste provides those which generally affect us most. Thus we are interested more in having good judgment about substances which are going to be a part of our own substance than we are about those which are only around it. Countless things are indifferent to touch, to hearing, to sight. But there is almost nothing indifferent to taste. What is more, the activity of this sense is entirely physical and material; it is the only one which says nothing to the imagination, or at least it is the one into whose sensations the imagination enters least, whereas imitation and imagination often mix something moral with the impression of all the others. Thus, tender and voluptuous hearts, passionate and truly sensitive characters, easily moved by the other senses, are generally lukewarm about this one. From this very fact, which seems to put taste beneath them and to make more contemptible the inclination that delivers us to it, I would conclude, on the contrary, that the most suitable means for governing children is to lead them by their mouths. The motive of gluttony is in particular preferable to that of vanity, in that the former is an appetite of nature, immediately dependent on sense, while the latter is a work of opinion subject to the caprice of men and to all sorts of abuses. Gluttony is the passion of childhood. This passion does not hold out in the face of any other. At the least competition, it disappears. Oh, believe me! The child will only too soon stop thinking about what he eats, and when his heart is too occupied, his palate will hardly occupy him. When he is grown, countless impetuous sentiments will sidetrack gluttony and will only inflame vanity, for this latter passion alone profits from the others and in the end swallows them all up. I have sometimes examined these people who gave importance to delicacies, who thought on awaking of what they would eat during the day, and described a meal with more exactness than Polybius puts into the description of a battle. I found that all these pretended men were only forty-year-old children without vigor or solidity. *Fruges consumere nati.*[72] Gluttony is the vice of hearts that have no substance. A glutton's soul is all in his palate; it is made only for eating. In his stupid incapacity he is only at home at the table. He only knows how to judge dishes. Let us leave him this employment without regret. It is better—as much for us as for him—that he have this one than another.

To fear that gluttony will take root in a child capable of something is a small-minded concern. In childhood one thinks only about what one eats. In adolescence one thinks about it no more. Anything is good for us, and we have much other business. I would not, however, want us to go and make indiscriminate use of so low an incentive or bolster the honor of doing a fair deed with a delicacy. But since all of child-hood is or ought to be only games and frolicsome play, I do not see why there should not be for purely corporeal exercises a prize which is material and speaks only to the senses. When a little Majorcan, seeing a basket on top of a tree, knocks it down with a slingshot, is it not entirely just that he get the profit from it, and that a good lunch make up for the strength he used in getting it? * When a young Spartan, at the risk of a hundred lashes of the whip, slips skillfully into a kitchen, steals a live fox cub, and, in carrying it under his robe, is scratched by it, bitten, made bloody; when, so as not to be shamed by being found out, the child lets his entrails be torn up without frowning, without letting out a single cry, is it not just that finally he profit from his prey and eat it after having been eaten by it? A good meal ought never to be a reward, but why should it not be the result of the care taken in getting it for oneself? Emile does not regard the cake I put on the stone as the prize for having run well. He knows only that the sole means of having this cake is to get there sooner than somebody else.

This does not contradict the maxims I advanced just now on the simplicity of food; for, to gratify children's appetites, there is no need to arouse their sensuality but only a need to satisfy it. And that can be done by the most common things in the world, if one does not work at refining children's tastes. Their constant appetite, aroused by the need to grow, is a reliable seasoning which takes the place for them of many others. Fruits, dairy products, some baked thing a bit more delicate than ordinary bread, and, above all, the art of dispensing it all soberly —with these, armies of children can be led to the ends of the earth without being given the taste for vivid flavors and without their palates becoming blasé.

One of the proofs that the taste for meat is not natural to man is the indifference that children have for that kind of food and the preference they all give to vegetable foods, such as dairy products, pastry, fruits, etc. It is, above all, important not to denature this primitive taste and make children carnivorous. If this is not for their health, it is for their character; for, however one explains the experience, it is certain that great eaters of meat are in general more cruel and ferocious than other men. This is observed in all places and all times. English barbarism is known; † the Zoroastrians, on the contrary, are the gentlest of men.‡ All savages are cruel, and it is not their morals which cause them to be so. This cruelty comes from their food. They go to war as to the hunt and treat men like bears. Even in England butchers are not ac-cepted as witnesses, and neither are surgeons.[74] Great villains harden themselves to murder by drinking blood. Homer makes the Cyclopes, eaters of human flesh, horrible, while he makes the lotus-eaters a peo-

---

* The Majorcans lost this practice many years ago. It belongs to the time when their slingers were famous.

† I know that the English greatly vaunt their humanity and the good nature of their nation; they call themselves "good-natured people"; but however much they may shout that, no one repeats it after them.

‡ The Banians who abstain from all meat more strictly than the Gaures are almost as gentle as the Gaures are; but since their morality is less pure and their religion less reasonable, they are not so decent.[73]

ple so lovable that, as soon as one had any dealings with them, one even forgot one's own country to live with them.[75]

> You ask me why [said Plutarch] Pythagoras abstained from eating the flesh of animals? But I ask you, on the contrary, was it a courage appropriate to men that possessed the first one who brought his mouth to wounded flesh, who used his teeth to break the bones of an expiring animal, who had dead bodies—cadavers—served to him, and swallowed up in his stomach parts which a moment before bleated, lowed, walked, and saw? How could his hand have plunged a knife into the heart of a feeling being? How could his eyes have endured a murder? How could he see a poor, defenseless animal bled, skinned, and dismembered? How could he endure the sight of quivering flesh? How did the smell not make him sick to his stomach? How was he not disgusted, repulsed, horrified, when he went to handle the excrement from these wounds, to clean the blood, black and congealed, which covered them?

> The skins, stripped off, crawled on the earth;
> The flesh, on the spit, lowed in the fire;
> Man could not eat them without a shudder;
> And in his breast heard them moan.[76]

This is what he must have imagined and felt the first time that he overcame nature to make this horrible meal, the first time that he was hungry for a living animal, that he wanted to feed on an animal which was still grazing, and that he said how the ewe who licked his hands was to be slaughtered, cut up, and cooked. It is by those who began these cruel feasts, and not by those who gave them up, that one ought to be surprised. And yet these first men could justify their barbarism with excuses which we lack and whose absence makes us a hundred times more barbarous than they.

"Mortals, well-loved of the Gods," these first men would say to us, "compare the times. See how happy you are and how miserable we were. The earth, newly formed, and the air, laden with vapors, were not yet willing to submit to the order of the seasons. The uncertain course of rivers caused them constantly to overflow their banks; pools, lakes, and deep marshes inundated three-quarters of the earth's surface. The other quarter was covered with sterile woods and forests. The earth produced no good fruits. We had no plowing instruments; we were ignorant of the art of using them; and harvest time never came for him who had sowed nothing. Thus hunger never left us. In winter, moss and the bark of trees were our ordinary dishes. Some green roots of couch grass and heather were a banquet for us; and when men were able to find beechnuts, walnuts, or acorns, they danced for joy around a chestnut or a beech to the sound of some rustic song, calling the earth their nurse and mother. This was their only festival; these their only games. All the rest of human life was only pain, effort, and want.

"Finally when the earth, stripped and naked, had nothing more to offer us, we were forced to violate nature to preserve ourselves and ate the companions of our want rather than perish with them. But you, cruel men, who forces you to shed blood? See what an abundance of goods surrounds you! How many fruits the earth produces for you! What riches the fields and the vines give you! How many animals offer you their milk for your nourishment and their fleece for your clothing! What more do you ask of them; what rage brings you, sated with goods and overflowing with victuals, to commit so many murders? Why do you lie about our mother by accusing her of not being able to feed you? Why do you sin against Ceres, inventress of the holy laws, and against gracious Bacchus, consoler of men, as if their prodigal gifts were not sufficient for the preservation of humankind? How do you have the heart to mix bones with their sweet fruits on your tables and to drink along with milk the blood of the animals who give it to you? The panthers and the lions that you call ferocious animals follow their instinct perforce and kill other animals to live. But you, a hundred times more ferocious than they, you combat instinct without necessity in order to abandon yourselves to your cruel delights. The animals you eat are not those which eat others. You do not eat these carnivorous beasts; you imitate them. You are hungry only for innocent and gentle animals who do no harm to anyone, who become attached to you, who serve you, and whom you devour as a reward for their services.

"O murderer against nature, if you insist on maintaining that nature made you to devour your kind, beings of flesh and bone, feeling and living like you, then smother the horror of these frightful meals it inspires in you. Kill the animals yourself—I mean with your own hands, without iron tools, without knives. Tear them apart with your nails, as do lions and bears. Bite this cow and rip him to pieces; plunge your claws in its skin. Eat this lamb alive; devour its still warm flesh; drink its soul with its blood. You shudder? You do not dare to feel living flesh palpitating in your teeth? Pitiful man! You begin by killing the animal; and then you eat it, as if to make it die twice. This is not enough. The dead flesh is still repugnant to you; your entrails cannot take it. It has to be transformed by fire, to be boiled or roasted, and to be seasoned with drugs disguising it. You have to have butchers, cooks, and roasters, people to take away the horror of the murder and dress up dead bodies so that the sense of taste, fooled by these disguises, does not reject what is alien to it and savors with pleasure cadavers whose sight even the eye would have difficulty bearing!" [77]

Although this passage is foreign to my subject, I was not able to resist the temptation to transcribe it; and I believe that few readers will be annoyed with me for it.

In any event, whatever diet you give to children—provided that you accustom them only to common and simple dishes—let them eat, run, and play as much as they please, and be sure that they will never eat too much and will have no indigestion. But if you starve them half the time, and they find the means of escaping your vigilance, they will compensate themselves with all their might, they will eat to the point of overflowing, of exploding. Our appetite is immoderate only because we want to give it other rules than those of nature. Always regulating, prescribing, adding, subtracting, we do nothing without weighing it on a scale. But this scale measures our whims and not our stomachs. I always go back to my examples. In peasants' homes the bread and fruit bins are always open, and the children as well as the men there do not know what indigestion is.

If it came to pass, nevertheless, that a child ate too much (which I do not believe possible by my method), it is so easy to distract him with entertainments to his taste that one might succeed in exhausting him from starvation without his thinking about it. How do means so sure and easy escape all teachers? Herodotus tells how the Lydians, hard pressed by an extreme famine, got the idea of inventing games and other diversions with which they deceived their hunger and spent entire days without thinking of eating.* [78] Your learned teachers have perhaps read this passage a hundred times without seeing how it can be applied to children. Someone among them will perhaps tell me that a child does not willingly leave his dinner to go and study his lessons. Master, you are right. I was not thinking of that kind of entertainment.

The sense of smell is to taste what sight is to touch. It anticipates taste and informs it about how this or that substance is going to affect it and disposes one to seek it or flee it according to the impression that one has received of it in advance. I have heard that savages have a sense of smell which is affected quite otherwise than ours and judge good and bad smells quite differently. As for me, I can certainly believe it. Smells by themselves are weak sensations. They move the imagination more than the sense and affect us not so much by fulfillment as by expectation. On this assumption the tastes of some, having become so different from the tastes of others due to their ways of life, must cause them to make contrary judgments about tastes and consequently about the smells which announce them. A Tartar must catch the scent of a stinking quarter of a dead horse with as much pleasure as one of our hunters catches the scent of a half-rotten partridge.

Men who walk too much to like strolling and who do not work enough to make a voluptuous experience out of rest ought to be insensitive to our idle sensations, such as enjoying the odor of garden flowers. People who are always famished would not know how to get great pleasure from fragrances which announce nothing to eat.

Smell is the sense of imagination. Keying up the nerves, it must agitate the brain a good deal. This is why it revives the temperament for a moment and exhausts it in the long run. Its effects are known well enough in love. The sweet fragrance of a dressing room is not so weak a trap as is thought; and I know not whether one ought to congratulate

* The ancient historians are filled with views which one could use even if the facts which present them were false. But we do not know how to get any true advantage from history. Critical erudition absorbs everything, as if it were very important whether a fact is true, provided that a useful teaching can be drawn from it. Sensible men ought to regard history as a tissue of fables whose moral is very appropriate to the human heart.

or pity that prudent and insensitive man who has never been made to quiver by the smell of the flowers on his beloved's bosom.

Smell must not be very active in the first age, when imagination, as yet animated by few passions, is hardly susceptible to emotion, and when we do not have enough experience to foresee with one sense what is promised to it by another sense. Indeed, this conclusion is perfectly confirmed by observation; and it is certain that the sense of smell is still obtuse and almost numb in most children. Not that the sensation is not as sharp in them as in men—and perhaps more so—but because, not joining to it any other idea, they are not easily affected by a sentiment of pleasure or pain in connection with it and are neither charmed nor offended by it as we are. I believe that without going beyond the same method and without having recourse to the comparative anatomy of the two sexes, it would be easy to find the reason why women in general are more intensely affected by smells than men.

It is said that Canadian savages, from their youth on, make their sense of smell so subtle that, although they have dogs, they do not deign to use them in the hunt and act as their own dogs. I can indeed conceive that, if children were raised to catch wind of their dinner as a dog catches wind of game, one could perhaps succeed in perfecting their sense of smell to the same degree. But, at bottom, I do not see that it is possible to gain anything very useful for them from the exercise of this sense, unless it is by making known to them its relations with the sense of taste. Nature has taken care to force us to become well acquainted with these relations. It has made the action of the sense of taste almost inseparable from that of the sense of smell by making their organs adjacent and placing in the mouth an immediate communication between the two, so that we taste nothing without smelling it. I would only want that these natural relations not be changed—for example, that a child be deceived by covering the bitterness of a medicine with a pleasant aroma, for the discord between the two senses is then too great to be able to fool him. The more active sense absorbs the effect of the other one, and he does not take the medicine with less distaste. This distaste is extended to all the sensations which strike him at the same time. In the presence of the weaker one his imagination also recalls the other to him. A very sweet fragrance is now to him only a disgusting smell; and it is thus that our indiscriminate precautions increase the sum of unpleasant sensations at the expense of pleasant ones.

It remains for me to speak in the following books of the cultivation of a sort of sixth sense called *common sense*, less because it is common to all men than because it results from the well-regulated use of the other senses, and because it instructs us about the nature of things by the conjunction of all their appearances. This sixth sense has consequently no special organ. It resides only in the brain, and its sensations, purely internal, are called *perceptions* or *ideas*. It is by the number of these ideas that the extent of our knowledge is measured. It is their distinctness, their clarity which constitutes the accuracy of the mind. It is the art of comparing them among themselves that is called *human reason.* Thus what I would call *sensual* or *childish* reason consists in forming simple ideas by the conjunction of several sensations, and what I call *intellectual* or *human reason* consists in forming complex ideas by the conjunction of several simple ideas.

Supposing, then, that my method is that of nature, and that I did not make mistakes in its application, we have led our pupil through the land of sensations up to the boundaries of childish reason. The first step we are going to make beyond these boundaries has to be a man's step. But before entering upon this new career, let us for a moment cast our eyes back over the one we have just completed. Each age, each condition of life, has its suitable perfection, a sort of maturity proper to it. We have often heard of a mature man, but let us consider a mature child. This spectacle will be newer for us and will perhaps be no less pleasant.

The existence of finite beings is so poor and so limited that when we see only what is, we are never moved. Chimeras adorn real objects; and if imagination does not add a charm to what strikes us, the sterile pleasure one takes in it is limited to the perceiving organ and always leaves the heart cold. The earth adorned with autumn's treasures displays a richness that the eye admires; but this admiration is not touching; it comes more from reflection than from sentiment. In spring the countryside, almost naked, is not yet covered with anything, the trees provide no shade, the green is only beginning to peep out, and the heart is touched by its aspect. In seeing nature thus reborn, one feels revived oneself. The image of pleasure surrounds us. Those companions of voluptousness, those sweet tears always ready to join with every delicious sentiment, are already on the edge of our eyelids. But though the aspect of the grape harvests may very well be animated, lively, pleasant, one always sees it with a dry eye.

Why this difference? It is that imagination joins to the spectacle of spring that of the seasons which are going to follow it. To these tender buds that the eye perceives imagination adds the flowers, the fruits, the shadows, and sometimes the mysteries they can cover. It concentrates in a single moment the times which are going to follow one another, and sees objects less as they will be than as it desires them because it is free to choose them. In autumn, on the contrary, one can only see what is. If one wants to get to spring, winter stops us, and imagination, frozen, expires on the snow and frost.

Such is the source of the charm one finds in contemplating a fair childhood in preference to the perfection of a ripe age. When is it that we taste a true pleasure in seeing a man? It is when the memory of his actions causes us to go back over his life and rejuvenates him, so to speak, in our eyes. If we are reduced to considering him as he is or to supposing what he will be in his old age, the idea of nature declining effaces all our pleasure. There is none in seeing a man advance with great steps toward his grave, and the image of death makes everything ugly.

But when I represent to myself a child between ten and twelve, vigorous and well formed for his age, he does not cause the birth of a single idea in me which is not pleasant either for the present or for the future. I see him bubbling, lively, animated, without gnawing cares, without long and painful foresight, whole in his present being, and enjoying a fullness of life which seems to want to extend itself beyond him. I foresee him at another age exercising the senses, the mind, and the strength which is developing in him day by day, new signs of which he gives every moment. I contemplate the child, and he pleases me. I imagine him as a man, and he pleases me more. His ardent blood seems to reheat mine. I believe I am living his life, and his vivacity rejuvenates me.

The hour sounds. What a change! Instantly his eyes cloud over; his gaiety is effaced. Goodbye, joy! Goodbye, frolicsome games! A severe and angry man takes him by the hand, says to him gravely, "Let us go, sir," and takes him away. In the room into which they go I catch a glimpse of books. Books! What sad furnishings for his age! The poor child lets himself be pulled along, turns a regretful eye on all that surrounds him, becomes silent, and leaves, his eyes swollen with tears he does not dare to shed, and his heart great with sighs he does not dare to breathe.

O you who have nothing of the kind to fear; you for whom no time of life is a time of constraint and of boredom; you who see the day come without disquiet, the night without impatience, and count the hours only by your pleasures—come my happy, my lovable pupil, console us by your presence for the departure of that unfortunate boy, come . . . He comes, and I feel at his approach a movement of joy which I see him share. It is his friend, his comrade, it is the companion of his games whom he approaches. He is quite sure on seeing me that he will not for long remain without entertainment. We never depend on one another, but we always agree, and with no one else are we so well off as we are together.

His figure, his bearing, his countenance proclaim assurance and contentment; health shines from his face; his firm steps give him an air of vigor; his complexion, still delicate without being washed out, has no effeminate softness; the air and the sun have already put on it the honorable imprint of his sex; his muscles, still rounded, begin to show some signs of their nascent features; his eyes, which are not yet animated by the fire of sentiment, at least have all their native * serenity; long sorrows have not darkened them; unending tears have not lined his cheeks. See in his movements, quick but sure, the vivacity of his age, the firmness of independence, and the experience of much exercise. His aspect is open and free but not insolent or vain. His face, which has not been glued to books, does not fall toward his stomach; there is no need to say to him, "Lift your head." Neither shame nor fear ever caused him to lower it.

Let us make him a place in the midst of the assemblage. Gentlemen, examine him, interrogate him confidently. Do not fear his importunities, or his chatter, or his indiscreet questions. Have no fear that he take you over, that he claim all your attention for himself alone, and that you will not be able to get rid of him.

* *Natia.* I use this word in an Italian sense for want of finding a synonym for it in French. If I am wrong, it is unimportant, provided I am understood.[79]

Do not expect, either, agreeable remarks from him or that he tell you what I have dictated to him. Expect only the naïve and simple truth, unadorned, unaffected, without vanity. He will tell you the bad thing he has done or thinks just as freely as the good, without worrying in any way about the effect on you of what he has said. He will use speech with all the simplicity present in its first founding.

One likes to augur well of children; and one always regrets that stream of ineptitudes that almost always comes to overturn the hopes one would like to found on some lucky observation which falls by chance into their mouths. If my pupil rarely gives such hopes, he will never give this regret, for he never says a useless word and does not exhaust himself with a chatter to which he knows no one listens. His ideas are limited but distinct. If he knows nothing by heart, he knows much by experience. If he reads less well in our books than does another child, he reads better in the book of nature. His mind is not in his tongue but in his head. He has less memory than judgment. He knows how to speak only one language, but he understands what he says; and if what he says he does not say so well as others, to compensate for that, what he does, he does better than they do.

He does not know what routine, custom, or habit is. What he did yesterday does not influence what he does today.* He never follows a formula, does not give way before authority or example, and acts and speaks only as it suits him. So do not expect from him dictated speeches or studied manners, but always the faithful expression of his ideas and the conduct born of his inclinations.

You find in him a small number of moral notions which relate to his present condition, none concerning men's relative condition. Of what use would these latter be to him, since a child is not yet an active member of society? Speak to him of freedom, of property, even of convention: he can know something up to that point. He knows why what is his is his and why what is not his is not his. Beyond this he knows nothing. Speak to him of duty, of obedience: he does not know what you mean. Give him some command: he will not understand you. But tell him, "If you do me such and such a favor, I will return it when the occasion arises," and he will immediately be eager to gratify you, for he asks for nothing better than to extend his domain and to acquire rights over you that he knows to be inviolable. Perhaps he even finds it not disagreeable to have a position, to be a part, to count for something. But if this last is his motive, he has already left nature, and you have not closed tightly all the gates of vanity ahead of time.

On his side, if he needs some assistance, he will ask for it from the first person he meets without distinction. He would ask for it from the king as from his lackey. All men are still equal in his eyes. You see by

* The appeal of habit comes from the laziness natural to man, and that laziness increases in abandoning onself to habit. One does more easily what one has already done; the trail once blazed becomes easier to follow. Thus it is to be observed that the empire of habit is very great over the aged and the indolent, very small over the young and the lively. This way of life is good only for weak souls and weakens them more from day to day. The only habit useful to children is to subject themselves without difficulty to the necessity of things, and the only habit useful to men is to subject themselves without difficuly to reason. Every other habit is a vice.

the way in which he makes a request that he is aware that he is owed nothing. He knows that what he asks is a favor; he also knows that humanity inclines toward according it. His expressions are simple and laconic. His voice, his look, and his gesture are those of a being accustomed equally to compliance and refusal. This is neither the crawling and servile submission of a slave nor the imperious accent of a master. It is a modest confidence in his fellow man; it is the noble and touching gentleness of a free but sensitive and weak being who implores the assistance of a being who is free but strong and beneficent. If you grant him what he asks of you, he will not thank you, but he will feel that he has contracted a debt. If you refuse it to him, he will not complain; he will not insist. He knows that would be useless. He will not say to himself, "I have been refused," but he will say, "It was impossible." And as I have already said, one hardly rebels against well-recognized necessity.

Leave him alone at liberty. Watch him act without saying anything to him. Consider what he will do and how he will go about it. Having no need to prove to himself that he is free, he never does anything from giddiness and solely to perform an act of power over himself. Does he not know that he is always master of himself? He is alert, light, quick, and his movements have all the vivacity of his age, but you do not see one of them which does not have an end. Whatever he wants to do, he will never undertake anything beyond his strength, for he has tested it well and knows it. His means are always appropriate to his designs, and rarely will he act without being assured of success. He will have an attentive and judicious eye. He will not stupidly question others about everything he sees, but he will examine it himself and will tire himself out to discover what he wants to learn before asking. If he gets in unforeseen difficulties, he will be less disturbed than another; if there is risk, he will also be less frightened. Since his imagination still remains inactive, and nothing has been done to animate it, he sees only what is, estimates dangers only at what they are worth, and always keeps his composure. Necessity weighs heavy on him too often for him still to baulk at it. He bears its yoke from his birth. Now he is well accustomed to it. He is always ready for anything.

Whether he is busy or playing, it is all the same to him. His games are his business, and he is aware of no difference. He brings to whatever he does an interest which makes people laugh and a freedom which pleases them, thereby showing at once the turn of his mind and the sphere of his knowledge. Is this not the spectacle appropriate to this age, the charming and sweet spectacle of seeing a pretty child with an eye that is lively and gay, a manner contented and serene, a face open and laughing, doing the most serious things at play or profoundly busy with the most frivolous entertainments?

Do you now want to judge him by comparisons? Let him mix with other children and do as he pleases. You will soon see which is the most truly formed, which best approaches the perfection of his age. Among the city children none is more adroit than he, but he is stronger than any other. Among young peasants he is their equal in strength and surpasses them in skill. Concerning all that is within the reach of childhood he judges, reasons, and foresees better than all of them. Is there a matter involving action, running, jumping, moving bodies, lifting masses, estimating distances, inventing games, winning prizes? One would say nature is at his command, so easily does he know how to bend everything to his will. He is made for guiding, for governing his equals. Talent and experience take the place for him of right and authority. Clothe and name him as you please. It is not important. Everywhere he will be first, everywhere he will become the chief of the others. They will always sense his superiority over them. Without wanting to command, he will be the master; without believing they are obeying, they will obey.

He has come to the maturity of childhood. He has lived a child's life. He has not purchased his perfection at the expense of his happiness; on the contrary, they have cooperated with each other. In acquiring all the reason belonging to his age, he has been happy and free to the extent his constitution permits him. If the fatal scythe comes to harvest the flower of our hopes in him, we shall not have to lament his life and his death at the same time. We shall not embitter our sorrows with the memory of those we caused him. We shall say to ourselves, "At least he enjoyed his childhood. We did not make him lose anything that nature had given him."

The great difficulty with this first education is that it is perceptible only to clear-sighted men and that in a child raised with so much care, vulgar eyes see only a little rascal. A preceptor thinks of his own interest more than of his disciple's. He is devoted to proving that he is not wasting his time and that he is earning the money he is paid. He provides the child with some easily displayed attainments that can be showed off when wanted. It is not important whether what he teaches the child is useful, provided that it is easily seen. He accumulates, without distinction or discernment, a rubbish heap in the child's memory. When the child is to be examined, he is made to spread out his merchandise. He displays it; satisfaction is obtained. Then he closes up his pack again and leaves. My pupil is not so rich. He has no pack to spread out. He has nothing to show other than himself. Now, a child, no more than a man, is not to be seen in a moment. Where are the observers who know how to grasp at first glance the traits which characterize him? Such observers exist, but they are few; and in a hundred thousand fathers not one of them will be found.

Too many questions bore and repulse everyone, and children even more so. At the end of a few minutes their attention wanders; they no longer listen to what an obstinate questioner asks them and respond only at random. This way of examining them is vain and pedantic; often a word caught in midflight depicts their bent and their mind better than a long speech would. But care must be taken that this word is neither dictated nor fortuitous. One must have a great deal of judgment oneself to appreciate a child's.

I heard the late Lord Hyde tell the story of one of his friends who, returning from Italy after three-years absence, wanted to examine his nine- or ten-year-old son's progress. They went for a walk one evening with the boy and his governor in a field where schoolboys were playing at flying kites. The father asked his son, in passing, "Where is the kite whose shadow is here?" Without hesitation, without lifting his head, the child said, "Over the highway." "And, indeed," added Lord Hyde, "the highway was between us and the sun." The father at this response kissed his son and, leaving his examination at that, went away without saying anything. The next day he sent the governor the title to a lifetime pension in addition to his salary.

What a man that father was, and what a son was promised him! The question suits his age precisely; the response is quite simple. But see what it implies about the incisiveness of the child's judgment! It is thus that Aristotle's pupil tamed that famous steed which no horseman had been able to break.[80]

End of the Second Book

"What a disparity," it will perhaps be said. "A while ago we were concerned only with what touches us, with what immediately surrounds us. All of a sudden here we are traveling around the globe and leaping to the ends of the universe!" This disparity is the effect of the development of our strength and the bent of our mind. In the state of weakness and insufficiency concern for our preservation concentrates us within ourselves. In the state of power and strength the desire to extend our being takes us out of ourselves and causes us to leap as far as is possible for us. But since the intellectual world is still unknown to us, our thought does not go farther than our eyes, and our understanding is extended only along with the space it measures.

Let us transform our sensations into ideas but not leap all of a sudden from objects of sense to intellectual objects. It is by way of the former that we ought to get to the latter. In the first operations of the mind let the senses always be its guides. No book other than the world, no instruction other than the facts. The child who reads does not think, he only reads; he is not informing himself, he learns words.

Make your pupil attentive to the phenomena of nature. Soon you will make him curious. But to feed his curiosity, never hurry to satisfy it. Put the questions within his reach and leave them to him to resolve. Let him know something not because you told it to him but because he has understood it himself. Let him not learn science but discover it. If ever you substitute in his mind authority for reason, he will no longer reason. He will be nothing more than the plaything of others' opinion.

You want to teach geography to this child, and you go and get globes, cosmic spheres, and maps for him. So many devices! Why all these representations? Why do you not begin by showing him the object itself, so that he will at least know what you are talking to him about?

One fine evening we go for a walk in a suitable place where a broad, open horizon permits the setting sun to be fully seen, and we observe the objects which make recognizable the location of its setting. The next day, to get some fresh air, we return to the same place before the sun rises. We see it announcing itself from afar by the fiery arrows it launches ahead of it. The blaze grows; the east appears to be wholly in flames. By their glow one expects the star for a long time before it reveals itself. At every instant one believes that he sees it appear. Finally one sees it. A shining point shoots out like lightning and immediately fills all of space. The veil of darkness is drawn back and falls. Man recognizes his habitat and finds it embellished. The verdure has gained a new vigor during the night. The nascent day which illuminates it, the first rays which gild it, show it covered by a shining web of dew which reflects the light and the colors to the eye. The birds in chorus join together in concert to greet the father of life. At that moment not a single one keeps quiet. Their chirping, still weak, is slower and sweeter than during the rest of the day; it has the feel of the languor of a peaceful awakening. The conjunction of these objects brings to the senses an impression of freshness which seems to penetrate to the soul. There is here a half-hour of enchantment which no man can resist. So great, so fair, so delicious a spectacle leaves no one cold.

Full of the enthusiasm he feels, the master wants to communicate

BOOK III

ALTHOUGH the whole course of life up to adolescence is a time of weakness, there is a point during this first age when the growth of strength has passed that of need, and the growing animal, still weak absolutely, becomes strong relatively. His needs are not all developed, and his present strength is more than sufficient to provide for those he has. As a man he would be very weak; as a child he is very strong.

From where does man's weakness come? From the inequality between his strength and his desires. It is our passions that make us weak, because to satisfy them we would need more strength than nature gives us. Therefore, diminish desires, and you will increase strength. He who is capable of more than he desires has strength left over; he is certainly a very strong being. This is the third stage of childhood, and the one about which I now must speak. I continue to call it *childhood* for want of a term to express it, for this age approaches adolescence without yet being that of puberty.

At twelve or thirteen the child's strength develops far more rapidly than his needs. The most violent, the most terrible of these needs has not yet made itself felt in him. Its very organ remains in a state of imperfection and, in order to emerge from it, seems to wait only for his will to force it to do so. The child is hardly sensitive to injury from the air and the seasons, and his nascent heat takes the place of clothing. His appetite takes the place of seasoning; all that can nourish is good at his age. If he is tired, he stretches out on the earth and sleeps. He sees himself everywhere surrounded by all that is necessary to him. No imaginary need torments him. Opinions can have no effect on him. His desires go no farther than his arms. Not only is he self-sufficient, he has strength beyond what he needs. It is the only time in his life when this will be the case.

I anticipate the objection. It will not be said that the child has more needs than I give him, but it will be denied that he has the strength I attribute to him. It will not be remembered that I am speaking of my pupil rather than of those walking dolls who travel from one room to another, who plow in a box and bear cardboard loads. I will be told that virile strength is manifested only in virility, that the vital spirits prepared in the appropriate vessels and spread through the whole body can alone give to muscles the consistency, the activity, the tone, and the resiliency from which true strength results. This is armchair philosophy; but I appeal to experience. I see big boys in your fields plow, hoe, drive a team, load a barrel of wine, and control a cart just like their fathers. One would take them for men if the sound of their voices did not betray them. Even in our cities, young laborers, ironworkers, toolmakers, and blacksmiths are almost as robust as the masters and would be hardly less skilled if they had been trained in time. If there is a difference, and I admit that there is, it is much less, I repeat, than the difference between a man's impetuous desires and a child's limited desires. Moreover, the question here is not only one of physical strength but particularly one of the mental strength and capacity which supplements physical strength or directs it.

Although this interval during which the individual is capable of more than he desires is not the time of his greatest absolute strength, it is, as I have said, the time of his greatest relative strength. It is the most precious time of life, a time which comes only once, a very short time, one even shorter—as will be seen in what follows—because of the importance of his using it well.

What will he do, then, with this surplus of faculties and strength, of which he has too much at present and which he will lack at another age? He will try to use it in ways which can be of profit to him when needed. He will channel, so to speak, the overflow of his present being into the future. The robust child will make provisions for the weak man, but he will not store them in coffers that can be stolen from him or in barns that are alien to him. In order to appropriate truly his acquisitions, he will house them in his arms and in his head; he will house them in himself. This is, therefore, the time of labors, of instruction, of study. And note that it is not I who arbitrarily make this choice. It is nature itself that points to it.

Human intelligence has its limits; and not only is it impossible for a man to know everything, he cannot even know completely the little that other men know. Since the contradictory of each false proposition is a truth, the number of truths is as inexhaustible as that of errors. A choice must, therefore, be made of the things that ought to be taught as well as of the proper time for learning them. Of the fields of learning that are available to us, some are false, others are useless, others serve to feed the pride of the man who possesses them. The small number of those which really contribute to our well-being is alone worthy of the researches of a wise man and, consequently, of a child whom one wants to make wise. It is a question not of knowing what is but only of knowing what is useful.

From this small number it is necessary to remove the truths which demand for their comprehension an understanding already completely formed: those that presuppose a knowledge of man's relations which a child cannot acquire; those that, although true in themselves, dispose an inexperienced soul to think falsely about other subjects.

Thus we are reduced to a very small circle relative to the existence

of things. But what an immense sphere for the scope of a child's this circle still forms! Darkness of human understanding, what re hand dared to touch your veil? What abysses I see opened up a this young unfortunate by our vain sciences! O tremble, you, wh going to lead him in these perilous paths and raise nature's s curtain before his eyes. Be sure, in the first place, of his balance yours; fear lest one or the other, and perhaps both of you, get o Fear the specious attraction of lies and the intoxicating vapors of p Remember, remember constantly that ignorance never did any h that error alone is fatal, and that one is misled not by what he o not know but by what he believes he knows.

The child's progress in geometry can serve you as a test and a tain measure of the development of his intelligence. But as soon as can discern what is useful and what is not, it is important to use mu tact and art to lead him to speculative studies. Do you, for examp want him to look for a proportional mean between two lines? Begin arranging it so that he has to find a square equal to a given rectangl If the problem has to do with two proportional means, you would fir have to interest him in the problem of doubling a cube, etc. See how w gradually approach moral notions which distinguish good and bad! U to now we have known no law other than that of necessity. Now we are dealing with what is useful. We shall soon get to what is suitable and good.

The same instinct animates man's diverse faculties. To the activity of the body which seeks development succeeds the activity of the mind which seeks instruction. At first children are only restless; then they are curious; and that curiosity, well directed, is the motive of the age we have now reached. Let us always distinguish between the inclinations which come from nature and those which come from opinion. There is an ardor to know which is founded only on the desire to be esteemed as learned; there is another ardor which is born of a curiosity natural to man concerning all that might have a connection, close or distant, with his interests. The innate desire for well-being and the impossibility of fully satisfying this desire make him constantly seek for new means of contributing to it. This is the first principle of curiosity, a principle natural to the human heart, but one which develops only in proportion to our passions and our enlightenment. Picture a philosopher relegated to a desert island with instruments and books, sure of spending the rest of his days there. He will hardly trouble himself any longer about the system of the world, the laws of attraction, differential calculus. He will perhaps not open a single book in his life. But never will he refrain from visiting the last nook and cranny of his island, however large it may be. Let us, therefore, also reject in our first studies the kinds of knowledge for which man does not have a natural taste and limit ourselves to those instinct leads us to seek.

The island of humankind is the earth. The most striking object to our eyes is the sun. As soon as we begin to get a distance on ourselves, our first observations must concern them. Thus the philosophy of almost all savage peoples turns solely on imaginary divisions of the earth and on the divinity of the sun.

it to the child. He believes he moves the child by making him attentive to the sensations by which he, the master, is himself moved. Pure stupidity! It is in man's heart that the life of nature's spectacle exists. To see it, one must feel it. The child perceives the objects, but he cannot perceive the relations linking them; he cannot hear the sweet harmony of their concord. For that is needed experience he has not acquired; in order to sense the complex impression that results all at once from all these sensations, he needs sentiments he has not had. If he has not long roamed arid plains, if burning sands have not scorched his feet, if the suffocating reflections of stones struck by the sun have never oppressed him, how will he enjoy the cool air of a fine morning? How will the fragrances of the flowers, the charm of the verdure, the humid vapors of the dew, and the soft and gentle touch of the grass underfoot enchant his senses? How will the song of the birds cause a voluptuous emotion in him, if the accents of love and pleasure are still unknown to him? With what transports will he see so fair a day dawning, if his imagination does not know how to paint for him those transports with which it can be filled? Finally, how can he be touched by the beauty of nature's spectacle, if he does not know the hand responsible for adorning it?

Do not make speeches to the child which he cannot understand. No descriptions, no eloquence, no figures, no poetry. It is not now a question of sentiment or taste. Continue to be clear, simple, and cold. The time for adopting another kind of language will come only too soon.

Raised in the spirit of our maxims, accustomed to draw all his instruments out of himself and never to have recourse to another person before he has himself recognized his insufficiency, he examines each new object he sees for a long time without saying anything. He is pensive, and not a questioner. Be satisfied, therefore, with presenting him with objects opportunely. Then, when you see his curiosity sufficiently involved, put to him some laconic question which sets him on the way to answering it.

On this occasion, after having contemplated the rising sun with him, after having made him notice the mountains and the other neighboring objects in that direction, after having let him chat about it at his ease, keep quiet for a few moments like a man who dreams, and then say to him, "I was thinking that yesterday evening the sun set here and that this morning it rose there. How is that possible?" Add nothing more. If he asks you questions, do not respond to them. Talk about something else. Leave him to himself, and be sure that he will think about it.

For a child to get accustomed to being attentive and for him to be strongly impressed by some truth involving objects of sense, he has to worry over it for a few days before he discovers it. If he does not conceive of this one adequately in this way, there is a means of making it even more evident to his senses; and that means is to turn the question around. If he does not know how the sun gets from its setting to its rising, he knows at least how it gets from its rising to its setting. His eyes alone teach him that. Clarify, therefore, the former question by the latter. Either your pupil is absolutely stupid, or the analogy is too clear to be able to escape him. This is his first lesson in cosmography.[1]

Since we always proceed slowly from one idea based on the senses to another, we familiarize ourselves with one for a long time before going on to another, and, finally, we never force our pupil to be attentive; it is a long way from this first lesson to knowledge of the path of the sun and the shape of the earth. But since all the apparent movements of the celestial bodies depend on the same principle and the first observation leads to all the others, less effort, although more time, is needed to get from a diurnal revolution to the calculation of eclipses than is needed to understand day and night well.

Since the sun turns around the earth, it describes a circle, and every circle must have a center. We already know that. This center cannot be seen, for it is at the heart of the earth. But one can mark on its surface two points which correspond to it. A spike passing through the three points and lengthened up to the heavens on both sides will be the axis of the earth and of the sun's daily movement. A round top turning on its tip represents the heavens turning on their axis; the top's two tips are the two poles. The child will be delighted to know one of them. I show it to him on the tail of the Little Bear. This is our entertainment for the night. Little by little he gains familiarity with the stars, and from there is born the first taste for knowing the planets and observing the constellations.

We have seen the sun rising on Midsummer Day. We also go to see it rising on Christmas Day or some other fair winter day, for you know that we are not lazy and that we make a game of braving the cold. I am careful to make this second observation in the same place where we made the first; and, provided that some skill has been used in preparing the observation, one or the other will not fail to cry out, "Oh, oh! Here is something funny! The sun does not rise anymore in the same place. Here are our old markers, and now it is rising over there, etc. . . . there is, then, a summer east and a winter east, etc. . . . ." Young master, you are now on your way. These examples ought to suffice for you to teach the celestial sphere very clearly while taking the earth as the earth and the sun as the sun.

In general, never substitute the sign for the thing except when it is impossible for you to show the latter, for the sign absorbs the child's attention and makes him forget the thing represented.

The armillary sphere [2] appears to me an ill-conceived device and poorly proportioned in its execution. This confusion of circles and the bizarre figures with which they are labeled give it the air of a sorcerer's book which scares off a child's mind. The earth is too small; the circles are too big and too numerous; some of them, like the colures,[3] are perfectly useless. Each circle is larger than the earth; the thickness of the cardboard gives them an air of solidity which causes them to be taken for really existing circular masses; and when you tell the child these circles are imaginary, he does not know what he sees; he no longer understands.

We never know how to put ourselves in the place of children; we do not enter into their ideas; we lend them ours, and, always following our own reasonings, with chains of truths we heap up only follies and errors in their heads.

BOOK III

There is a dispute about the choice of analysis or synthesis for studying the sciences. It is not always necessary to choose. Sometimes one can use both resolution and combination in the same researches and guide the child by the method of instruction when he believes he is only analyzing. Then if both were used at the same time, they would serve as reciprocal proofs. Starting at the same time from the two opposite points, without thinking he is traveling the same road, he would be quite surprised to meet himself, and this surprise could only be very agreeable. I would, for example, want to take geography by its two extremes and join to the study of the globe's revolutions the measurement of its parts, beginning with the place where one lives. While the child studies the celestial sphere and is thus transported into the heavens, lead him back to the division of the earth and show him first his own habitat.[4]

His two first points of geography will be the city in which he dwells and his father's country house; then will come the intermediate places, then the neighboring rivers, and finally the sun's position and the way of orienting oneself by it. This is the meeting place. Let him make a map of all these things himself, a very simple map, at first formed by two objects alone, to which he adds the others little by little to the extent that he knows or estimates their distance and their position. You see already what an advantage we have procured for him in putting a compass in his eyes.

In spite of that, he will doubtless have to be guided a little—but very little, and without its becoming apparent. If he makes a mistake, let him do so; do not correct his errors. Wait in silence until he is ready to see and correct them himself; or, at most, on a favorable occasion carry out some operation which will make him aware of them. If he never made mistakes, he would not learn so well. Moreover, the goal is not that he know exactly the topography of the region, but that he know the means of learning about it. It is of little importance that he have maps in his head, provided that he is able to get a good conception of what they represent, and that he has a distinct idea of the art which serves to draw them. See the difference there already is between your pupils' knowledge and mine's ignorance! They know maps, and he makes them. Here are new ornaments for his room.

Remember always that the spirit of my education consists not in teaching the child many things, but in never letting anything but accurate and clear ideas enter his brain. Were he to know nothing, it would be of little importance to me provided he made no mistakes. I put truths into his head only to guarantee him against the errors he would learn in their place. Reason and judgment come slowly; prejudices come in crowds; it is from them that he must be preserved. But if you look at science in itself, you enter into a bottomless sea, without shores, full of reefs. You will never get away. When I see a man, enamoured of the various kinds of knowledge, let himself be seduced by their charm and run from one to the other without knowing how to stop himself, I believe I am seeing a child on the shore gathering shells and beginning by loading himself up with them; then, tempted by those he sees next, he throws some away and picks up others, until, overwhelmed by their multitude and not knowing anymore which to choose, he ends by throwing them all away and returning empty-handed.

During the first age time was long. We sought only to waste it for fear of making bad use of it. Now it is exactly the opposite, and we do not have enough time to do everything which would be useful. Reflect that the passions are approaching, and that as soon as they knock on the door, your pupil will no longer pay attention to anything but them. The peaceful age of intelligence is so short, it passes so rapidly, it has so many other necessary uses, that it is folly to wish that it suffice for making a child learned. The issue is not to teach him the sciences but to give him the taste for loving them and methods for learning them when this taste is better developed. This is very certainly a fundamental principle of every good education.

Now is also the time to accustom him little by little to paying continual attention to the same object. But this attention ought always to be produced by pleasure or desire, never by constraint. Great care must be taken that it does not become a burden to him and get to the point of boredom. Always, therefore, keep on the lookout and, whatever you do, stop everything before he gets bored, for it is never as important that he learn as that he do nothing in spite of himself.

If he questions you himself, answer enough to feed his curiosity, but not so much as to sate it. Above all, when you see that instead of questioning for the sake of instruction he is beating around the bush and overwhelming you with silly questions, stop immediately, with the certainty that now he cares no longer about the thing but about subjecting you to his interrogation. You must pay less attention to the words he pronounces than to the motive which causes him to speak. This warning, less necessary before now, becomes of the greatest importance when the child begins to reason.

There is a chain of general truths by which all the sciences are connected with common principles out of which they develop successively. This chain is the method of philosophers. We are not dealing with it here. There is another entirely different chain by which each particular object attracts another and always shows the one that follows. This order, which fosters by means of constant curiosity the attention that they all demand, is the one most men follow and, in particular, is the one required for children. In orienting ourselves to draw our maps, we had to draw meridians. Two points of intersection between the equal shadows of morning and evening provide an excellent meridian for an astronomer of thirteen.[5] But these meridians disappear. Time is needed to draw them. They subject one to working always in the same place. So much care, so much constraint would end by boring him. We foresaw it. We provide for it in advance.

Here I am once again in my lengthy and minute details. Reader, I hear your grumbling, and I brave it. I do not want to sacrifice the most useful part of this book to your impatience. Make your decision about my delays, for I have made mine about your complaints.

A long time ago my pupil and I had noticed that amber, glass, wax, and various other bodies when rubbed attracted straws and that others did not attract them. By chance we find one which has a still more singular virtue, that of attracting at some distance—without being rubbed—shavings and other bits of iron. How long this quality entertains us without our being able to see anything more in it! Finally, we find that the iron itself acquires this quality from the lodestone when drawn across it in any single direction. One day we go to the fair; [6] a magician attracts a wax duck floating in a tub of water with a piece of bread. Although we are quite surprised, we nevertheless do not say, "He is a sorcerer," for we do not know what a sorcerer is. Constantly struck by effects whose causes we do not know, we are in no hurry to make any judgments, and we remain at rest in our ignorance until we happen to find the occasion to escape it.

After returning home, by dint of talking about the duck at the fair, we get it into our heads to imitate it. We take a good, well-magnetized needle; we surround it with white wax that we do our best to shape in the form of a duck, with the needle going through the body and its point constituting the bill. We put the duck in the water, we bring the top part of a key close to the bill, and we see with a joy easy to understand that our duck follows the key exactly as the one at the fair followed the piece of bread. To observe the direction the duck faces when left at rest in the water is something we can do another time. As for now, busy with our plan, we do not want more.

The very same evening we return to the fair with bread ready in our pockets, and as soon as the magician does his trick, my little doctor, who was hardly able to contain himself, says to him that this trick is not difficult and that he himself will do as much. He is taken at his word. Immediately he pulls the bread with the piece of iron hidden in it from his pocket. On approaching the table, his heart thumps. Practically quaking, he holds out the bread. The duck comes and follows him. The child cries out and shivers with delight. At the crowd's clapping and acclamation he gets dizzy; he is beside himself. The mountebank, confounded, comes nevertheless and embraces him, congratulates him, and begs the child to honor him again by his presence the next day, adding that he will make an effort to gather a still larger crowd to applaud his skill. My proud little naturalist wants to chatter. But I immediately shut him up and take him away covered with praise.

The child counts the minutes till the next day with a ridiculous excitement. He invites everyone he meets; he would want the whole of humankind to be witness to his glory. He hardly can wait for the hour. He is ahead of time; we fly to the appointment. The hall is already full. On entering, his young heart swells. Other games are going to be first. The magician surpasses himself and does surprising things. The child sees nothing of all that. He is agitated; he sweats; he is hardly able to breathe. He spends his time handling the piece of bread in his pocket with a hand trembling with impatience. Finally his time comes. The master announces him to the public with pomp. He comes forward with a bit of shame; he takes out his bread and . . . new vicissitude of things human! The duck, so responsive the day before, has turned wild today. Instead of offering its bill, it turns tail and flees. It avoids the bread and the hand offering it with as much care as it followed them previously. After countless useless attempts and constantly being jeered at, the child complains, says that he is being deceived, that another duck has been substituted for the first one; he defies the magician to attract this one.

The magician, without responding, takes a piece of bread and offers it to the duck. Immediately the duck follows the bread and comes toward the retreating hand. The child takes the same piece of bread, but far from succeeding better than before, he sees the duck make fun of him and do pirouettes all around the tub. He finally steps back in confusion and no longer dares to expose himself to the jeers.

Then the magician takes the piece of bread the child has brought and uses it with as much success as his own. He pulls the iron out of it in front of everyone. Another laugh at our expense. Then, with the bread thus emptied, he attracts the duck as before. He does the same thing with another piece cut in front of everyone by another's hand. He does the same with his glove, the tip of his finger. Finally he moves away to the middle of the room and in the emphatic tone peculiar to such people, declaring that his duck will obey his voice no less than his gesture, he speaks to it, and the duck obeys. He tells it to go right and it goes right, to return and it returns, to turn and it turns. The movement is as prompt as the order. The redoubled applause is that much more of an affront to us. We escape unnoticed and shut ourselves up in our room without going to recount our successes to everyone as we had planned.

The next morning there is a knock at our door. I open it, and there is the magician. Modestly he complains of our conduct. What did he do to us to make us want to discredit his games and take away his livelihood? What is so wonderful about the art of attracting a wax duck to make it worth purchasing this honor at the expense of an honest man's subsistence? "My faith, messieurs, if I had some other talent by which to live, I would hardly glorify myself with this one. You should have believed that a man who has spent his life practicing this paltry trickery knows more about it than do you who have devoted only a few moments to it. If I did not show you my master strokes right off, it is because one ought not to be in a hurry to show off giddily what one knows. I am always careful to keep my best tricks for the proper occasion; and after this one I have still others to stop tactless young men. Finally, messieurs, I come out of the goodness of my heart to teach you the secret that perplexed you so. I beg you not to abuse it to my hurt and to be more restrained the next time."

Then he shows us his device, and we see with the greatest surprise that it consists only of a strong lodestone, well encased in soft iron, which a child hidden under the table moved without being noticed.

The man puts his device away, and, after giving him our thanks and apologies, we wish to make him a present. He refuses it. "No, messieurs, I am not pleased enough with you to accept your gifts. I leave you obliged to me in spite of yourselves. It is my only vengeance. Learn that there is generosity in every station. I get paid for my tricks and not my lessons."

In leaving, he addresses a reprimand to me explicitly and out loud. "I willingly excuse," he says to me, "this child. He has sinned only from ignorance. But you, monsieur, who ought to know his mistake, why did you let him make it? Since you live together, as the elder you owe him your care and your counsel; your experience is the authority which ought to guide him. In reproaching himself for the wrongs of his youth when he is grown up, he will doubtless reproach you for those against which you did not warn him."

He departs, leaving us both very embarrassed. I blame myself for my soft easygoingness. I promise the child to sacrifice it to his interest the next time and to warn him of his mistakes before he makes them; for the time is approaching when our relations are going to change, when the master's severity must succeed the comrade's compliance. This change ought to take place gradually. Everything must be foreseen, and everything must be foreseen very far ahead of time.

The next day we return to the fair to see again the trick whose secret we have learned. We approach our magician-Socrates with profound respect. Hardly do we dare to raise our eyes to him. He covers us with attentions and gives us a place of distinction, which humiliates us again. He does his tricks as usual, but he entertains and indulges himself for a long time with the duck trick while looking often at us with quite a proud air. We know everything, and we do not breathe a word. If my pupil dared so much as to open his mouth, he would deserve to be annihilated.

Each detail of this example is more important than it seems. How many lessons in one! How many mortifying consequences are attracted by the first movement of vanity! Young master, spy out this first movement with care. If you know thus how to make humiliation and disgrace arise from it, be sure that a second movement will not come for a long time. "So much preparation!" you will say. I agree—and all for the sake of making ourselves a compass to take the place of a meridian.

Having learned that the magnet acts through other bodies, we have nothing more pressing to do than to make a device like the one we have seen. A table hollowed out, a very flat tub fitted into the table and filled with a few inches of water, a duck made with a bit more care, etc. Often busy around the tub, we finally notice that the duck at rest always points in pretty nearly the same direction. We follow up this experience; we examine this direction; we find that it is from south to north. Nothing more is needed; our compass is found, or as good as found. Now we are into physics.

There are various climates on the earth and various temperatures in these climates. One feels the variation of the seasons more as one approaches the pole. All bodies contract with cold and expand with heat. This effect is more measurable in liquids and more accessible to the senses in spirituous liquids: hence the thermometer. Wind strikes the face; air is, therefore, a body, a fluid; one feels it although one has no means of seeing it. Turn a glass upside down in water; the water will not fill it unless you allow the air a way out; air is, therefore, capable of resistance. Push the glass farther down; the water will make headway in the airspace without being able to fill that space completely; air is, therefore, capable of compression up to a certain point. A ball filled with compressed air bounces better than any other matter; air is, therefore, an elastic body. When you are stretched out in the bath, lift your arm horizontally out of the water; you will feel that it is loaded with a terrible weight; air is, therefore, a heavy body. By putting air in equilibrium with other fluids, its weight can be measured; this is the source of the barometer, the siphon, the air gun, and the pneumatic pump. All the laws of statics and hydrostatics are to be found by experiments just as crude. I do not want to go into an experimental physics laboratory for any of this. This whole apparatus of instruments and machines displeases me. The scientific atmosphere kills science. Either all these machines frighten a child, or their appearance divides and steals the attention he ought to pay to their effects.

I want us to make all our machines ourselves, and I do not want to begin by making the instrument prior to the experiment. But I do want us, after having caught a glimpse, as it were by chance, of the experiment to be performed, to invent little by little the instrument for verification. I prefer that our instruments be less perfect and accurate and that we have more distinct ideas about what they ought to be and the operations which ought to result from them. For my first lesson in statics, instead of going to look for scales, I put a stick across the back of a chair, and I measure the length of the two parts of the stick in balance. I add weights to both sides, sometimes equal, sometimes unequal, and, pushing and pulling as much as is necessary, I finally find that balance is the result of a reciprocal proportion between the quantity of the weights and the length of the levers. Now my little physicist is already capable of rectifying scales before seeing one.

Without question, one gets far clearer and far surer notions of the things one learns in this way by oneself than of those one gets from another's teachings. One's reason does not get accustomed to a servile submission to authority; furthermore, we make ourselves more ingenious at finding relations, connecting ideas, and inventing instruments than we do when, accepting all of these things as they are given to us, we let our minds slump into indifference—like the body of a man who, always clothed, shod, and waited on by his servants and drawn by his horses, finally loses the strength and use of his limbs. Boileau boasted of having taught Racine to have difficulty in rhyming. Among so many admirable methods for abridging the study of the sciences we greatly need someone to provide us with a method for learning them with effort.

The most palpable advantage of these slow and laborious researches is that they keep the body active and the limbs supple during speculative studies and continuously form the hands for the work and the practices useful to man. All the instruments invented to guide us in our experiments and to take the place of accuracy of the senses cause the senses to be neglected. The graphometer frees us from having to estimate the size of angles. The eye, which used to measure distances with precision, relies on the chain which measures them for it. The balance frees me from judging by hand the weight I know by means of the balance. The more ingenious are our tools, the cruder and more maladroit our organs become. By dint of gathering machines around us, we no longer find any in ourselves.

BOOK III

But when we put the skill which used to take the place of these machines into manufacturing them, when we use the sagacity which was required to do without them for making them, we gain without losing anything, we add art to nature, and we become more ingenious without becoming less adroit. If, instead of glueing a child to books, I bury him in a workshop, his hands work for the profit of his mind; he becomes a philosopher and believes he is only a laborer. Finally, this exercise has other uses of which I shall speak hereafter, and it will be seen how from the games of philosophy one can rise to the true functions of man.

I have already said that purely speculative knowledge is hardly suitable for children, even those nearing adolescence. But without making them go very far in systematic physics, nonetheless arrange that all their experiments are connected with one another by some sort of deduction, in order that with the aid of this chain they can order them in their minds and recall them when needed; for it is quite difficult for isolated facts and even reasonings to stick in the memory if one lacks some connection by which to recall them.

In the quest for the laws of nature, always begin with the phenomena most common and most accessible to the senses, and accustom your pupil to take these phenomena not for reasons but for facts. I take a stone and feign placing it in the air. I open my hand; the stone falls. I look at Emile, who is attentive to what I am doing, and I say to him, "Why did this stone fall?"

What child will stop short at this question? None, not even Emile, if I have not made a great effort to prepare him not to know how to respond. All will say that the stone falls because it is heavy. And what is heavy? That is what falls. The stone falls, therefore, because it falls? Here my little philosopher is really stumped. This is his first lesson in systematic physics, and, whether it profits him in this study or not, it will still be a lesson in good sense.

To the extent that the child advances in intelligence, other important considerations oblige us to be more selective in his occupations. As soon as he gets to know himself sufficiently to conceive in what his well-being consists; as soon as he can grasp relations comprehensive enough to enable him to judge what suits him and what does not suit him; from then on he is in a condition to sense the difference between work and play and to regard the latter as nothing but relaxation from the former. Then objects of real utility can enter into his studies and induce him to give a more constant application than he gave to simple play. The irrepressible law of necessity always teaches man early to do what does not please him in order to prevent an evil which would displease him more. Such is the use of foresight, and from this foresight, well or ill controlled, is born all human wisdom or all human misery.

Every man wants to be happy; but to succeed in being so, one would have to begin by knowing what happiness is. The happiness of the natural man is as simple as his life. It consists in not suffering; health, freedom, and the necessities of life constitute it. The happiness of the moral man is something else. But that kind of happiness is not the question here. I cannot repeat too often that only physical objects can interest children, especially those whose vanity has not been awakened, and who have not been corrupted ahead of time by the poison of opinion.

When they foresee their needs before feeling them, their intelligence is already quite advanced, and they begin to know the value of time. It is then important to accustom them to direct its employment to useful objects—but objects whose utility they can sense at their age and is within the reach of their understanding. All that depends on the moral order and on the practice of society ought not to be presented to them yet, because they are not in a condition to understand it. It is inept to demand that they apply themselves to things one tells them vaguely are for their own good (without their knowing what that good is) and to things they are assured they will profit from when they are grown up (without their taking any interest now in that alleged profit, which they would not be able to understand).

Let the child do nothing on anybody's word. Nothing is good for him unless he feels it to be so. In always pushing him ahead of his understanding, you believe you are using foresight, and you lack it. To arm him with some vain instruments which he will perhaps never use, you take away from him man's most universal instrument, which is good sense. You accustom him to let himself always be led, never to be anything but a machine in others' hands. You want him to be docile when little: that is to want him to be credulous and a dupe when he is grown up. You constantly tell him, "All that I ask of you is for your own advantage. But you are not in a condition to know it. What difference does it make to me whether you do what I demand? It is only for you yourself that you are working." With all these fine speeches that you make to him now in order to get him to be obedient, you are preparing the success of those speeches which will be made to him one day by a visionary, an alchemist, a charlatan, a cheat, or any kind of madman in order to catch your pupil in his trap or to get him to adopt his madness.

It is important for a man to know many things whose utility a child could not understand. But must and can a child learn everything it is important for a man to know? Try to teach the child everything useful for his age, and you will see that all his time will be more than filled. Why do you, to the detriment of the studies which are suitable for him today, want to apply him to those of an age which it is so uncertain he will reach? "But," you will say, "will there be time to learn what one ought to know when the moment has come to make use of it?" I do not know. But I do know that it is impossible to learn it sooner, for our true masters are experience and sentiment, and man has a good sense of what suits man only with respect to those relations in which he himself has actually participated. A child knows that he is made to become a man; all the ideas he can have of man's estate are opportunities of instruction for him; but he must remain in absolute ignorance of ideas of that estate which are not within his reach. My whole book is only a constant proof of this principle of education.

As soon as we have succeeded in giving our pupil an idea of the word *useful*, we have another great hold for governing him, for this word is very striking to him, provided only that it has a sense relative to his

BOOK III

age and that he sees clearly its relation to his present well-being. Your children are not struck by this word because you have not been careful to give them an idea of it that is within their reach; and because others always take care of providing what is useful for your children, they never need to think about it themselves and do not know what utility is.

"What is that good for?" This is now the sacred word, the decisive word between him and me in all the actions of our life. This is the question of mine which infallibly follows all his questions and which serves as a brake to those multitudes of stupid and tedious interrogations with which children ceaselessly and fruitlessly fatigue all those around them, more to exercise some kind of dominion over them than to get some profit. He who is taught as his most important lesson to want to know nothing but what is useful interrogates like Socrates. He does not put a question without giving himself the reason for it, which he knows will be demanded of him before he is answered.

See what a powerful instrument for acting on your pupil I am putting into your hands. Not knowing the reasons for anything, he is now almost reduced to silence whenever you please. And what an advantage your knowledge and experience give you for showing him the utility of everything you suggest to him! For—do not be deceived—to put this question to him is to teach him to put it to you in turn; and afterward you must count on his following your example and asking about everything you suggest to him, "What is that good for?"

This is perhaps the most difficult trap for a governor to avoid. If at the child's question you seek only to get out of it and give him a single reason he is not in a condition to understand, he will see that you reason according to your ideas and not his and will believe that what you tell him is good for your age and not for his. He will no longer rely on you, and all is lost. But where is the master who is willing to stop short and admit his failings to his pupil? All make it a law for themselves not to admit even those failings they have, while I would make it my law to admit even those I do not have when I cannot put my reasons within his reach. Thus my conduct, always clear in his mind, would never be suspect to him, and I would preserve more credit for myself in pretending I have faults than other masters do in hiding theirs.

In the first place, you should be well aware that it is rarely up to you to suggest to him what he ought to learn. It is up to him to desire it, to seek it, to find it. It is up to you to put it within his reach, skillfully to give birth to this desire and to furnish him with the means of satisfying it. It follows, therefore, that your questions should be infrequent but well chosen; since he will put many more questions to you than you to him, you will always be less exposed and more often in the position to say to him, "In what way is what you ask me useful to know?"

Moreover, it is of little importance whether he learns this or that, provided that he get a good conception of what he learns and the use of what he learns; therefore, if you do not have any clarification of what you say which is valid for him, do not give him one at all. Tell him without scruple, "I do not have a good response to make to you. I was wrong. Let us leave it at that." If your instruction was really misplaced, there is no harm in simply abandoning it. If it was not misplaced, with a bit of effort you will soon find the occasion to make its utility palpable to him.

I do not like explanations in speeches. Young people pay little attention to them and hardly retain them. Things, things! I shall never repeat enough that we attribute too much power to words. With our babbling education we produce only babblers.

Let us suppose that while I am studying with my pupil the course of the sun and how to get one's bearings, suddenly he interrupts me to ask what is the use of all that. What a fine speech I will make to him! I shall seize the occasion to instruct him about so many things in answering his question, especially if we have witnesses to our conversation! * I shall tell him of the utility of travels, of the advantages of commerce, of the products peculiar to each climate, of the manners of different peoples, of the use of the calendar, of the calculation of the return of the seasons for agriculture, of the art of navigation, of the means to find one's way at sea and to follow one's route exactly without knowing where one is. Politics, natural history, astronomy, even morality and the right of nations will enter into my explanation in such a way as to give my pupil a great idea of all these sciences and a great desire to learn them. When I have finished, I shall have made a true pedant's display of which he will have understood not a single idea. He will have a great longing to ask me, as before, what is the use of getting one's bearings, but he does not dare for fear that I will get angry. He finds it more to his advantage to feign understanding of what he has been forced to hear. That is the way fine educations are given.

But our Emile, more rustically raised and with so much effort made a slow learner, will not listen to any of that. At the first word he does not understand, he is going to run away, frolic around the room, and let me perorate all alone. Let us seek a cruder solution. My scientific gear is worthless for him.

We were observing the position of the forest north of Montmorency when he interrupted me with his importunate question, "What's the use of that?" "You are right," I say to him, "we must think about it at our leisure, and if we find that this work is good for nothing, we won't pick it up again, for we have no lack of useful entertainments." We busy ourselves with something else, and geography is not an issue for the rest of the day.

The next morning I suggest to him a walk before lunch. He does not ask for better. Children are always ready to take a run, and this one has good legs. We go up to the forest; we roam the fields; we get lost; we no longer know where we are; and when we have to go back, we can no longer find our path again. Time passes; it gets hot; we are hungry. We hurry; we wander in vain in one direction and another. We find everywhere only woods, quarries, plains, and no sign by which to

---

* I have often noticed that in the learned instructions one gives to children one thinks less of getting a hearing from them than from the grownups who are present. I am very sure about what I am saying here, for I have observed it in myself.

BOOK III

locate ourselves. Very hot, very tired, and very hungry, we accomplish nothing by our racing around other than to get more lost. Finally we sit down to rest and deliberate. Emile, who I am supposing has been raised like any child, does not deliberate; he cries. He does not know we are at the gate of Montmorency and that a simple copse hides it from us. But this copse is a forest for him; a man of his stature is buried in bushes.

After some moments of silence I say to him with a worried air, "My dear Emile, what shall we do to get out of here?"

EMILE (all in a sweat and crying hot tears) I don't know. I'm tired, I'm hungry, I'm thirsty. I can't go on.

JEAN-JACQUES Do you believe I am in a better condition than you, and do you think I would blame myself for crying if my tears would do for my lunch? Crying isn't what has to be done. What we have to do is find ourselves. Let's see your watch. What time is it?

EMILE It's noon, and I haven't eaten.

JEAN-JACQUES That's true. It is noon, and I haven't eaten.

EMILE Oh, how hungry you must be!

JEAN-JACQUES The misfortune is that my dinner won't come and look for me here. It is noon? That is exactly the time yesterday when we were observing the position of the forest from Montmorency. If we could observe the position of Montmorency from the forest in the same way. . . ."

EMILE Yes, but yesterday we saw the forest, and from here we don't see the city.

JEAN-JACQUES That's the difficulty. . . . If we could find its position without seeing it. . . .

EMILE Oh, my good friend!

JEAN-JACQUES Did we not say that the forest was . . .

EMILE North of Montmorency. . . .

JEAN-JACQUES Consequently Montmorency ought to be . . .

EMILE South of the forest.

JEAN-JACQUES We have a means of finding the north at noon.

EMILE Yes, by the direction of the shadow.

JEAN-JACQUES But the south?

EMILE What's to be done?

JEAN-JACQUES South is the opposite of north.

EMILE That's true. We have only to look for the opposite of the shadow. Oh, there is the south! There is the south! Surely Montmorency is in that direction. Let's look in that direction.

JEAN-JACQUES You might be right. Let's take this path through the woods.

EMILE (clapping his hands and letting out a cry of joy) Oh, I see Montmorency! There it is straight ahead of us in full view. Let's have lunch! Let's dine! Let's run fast! Astronomy is good for something.

Note that if he does not say this last phrase, he will think it. What is the difference, provided that it is not I who say it? Now, you can be certain that he will not in his life forget this day's lesson; whereas if I had only made him suppose all this in his room, my speech would have been forgotten the very next day. One must speak as much as one can by deeds and say only what one does not know how to do.

The reader does not expect me to despise him so much as to give him an example for every kind of study. But whatever the question may be, I cannot exhort the governor too much to be sure that his proofs match the pupil's capacity to understand them; for, to repeat, the harm is not in what the pupil does not understand but is in what he believes he understands.

I remember that once I wanted to give a child a taste for chemistry, and after I had shown him precipitates of several metals, I explained to him how ink is made. I told him that its blackness comes only from iron very finely broken up, separated from the vitriol and precipitated by an alkaline solution. In the midst of my learned explanation the little traitor stopped me short with my question, which I had taught him. Now I was quite at a loss.

After having mused about it a bit, I made my decision. I sent for wine from the master of the house's cellar and for another wine at eight pennies from a wine merchant's. I took a fixed alkaline solution in a little flask. Then, with these two different wines in two glasses before me,* I spoke to him thus:

"Many foodstuffs are adulterated to make them appear to be better than they are. These adulterations deceive the eye and the taste, but they are harmful and make the adulterated thing, for all its fine appearance, worse than it was before.

"Drinks, particularly wines, are adulterated, because the deception is more difficult to recognize and gives more profit to the deceiver.

"The adulteration of green or bitter wines is done with litharge. Litharge is a lead preparation. Lead combined with acids makes a very mild salt which corrects the greenness of wine to the taste but is poison for those who drink it. It is, therefore, important before drinking suspect wine to know whether or not it has been treated with litharge. Now here is how I reason in order to discover this.

"The solution of wine contains not only inflammable spirits, as you have seen from the brandy drawn from it; it contains, in addition, acid, as you can know from the vinegar and the tartar also gotten from it.

"Acid has a relation to metallic substances and combines with them by dissolving them to form a compound salt, such as rust for example (which is only iron dissolved by the acid contained in air or water), and also verdegris (which is only copper dissolved in vinegar).

"But this same acid has even more relation to alkaline substances than to metallic substances, so that at the intervention of the former in the compound salts of which I just spoke to you, the acid is forced to let go of the metal with which it is combined to attach itself to the alkali.

* For each explanation one wants to give the child, a little ceremony which precedes it is very useful in making him attentive.

"Then the metallic substance, released from the acid which kept it dissolved, precipitates and makes the liquid opaque.

"If, therefore, one of these two wines is treated with litharge, its acid keeps the litharge in solution. When I pour alkaline liquid into it, it will force the acid to let go of its hold to combine with it. The lead, no longer kept in solution, will reappear, cloud the solution, and finally precipitate at the bottom of the glass.

"If there is no lead * or any other metal in the wine, the alkali will combine peacefully † with the acid, the whole will remain dissolved, and there will be no precipitate."

Then I poured my alkaline solution into each of the two glasses. The one with the house wine remained clear and diaphanous. The other was cloudy in a moment, and at the end of an hour one clearly saw the lead precipitate at the bottom of the glass.

"Here," I went on, "is natural and pure wine that can be drunk; and here is adulterated wine that poisons. This is discovered by means of the same knowledge about whose utility you asked. He who knows well how ink is made also knows how to recognize doctored wines."

I was quite satisfied by my example; nevertheless, I perceived that the child was not struck by it. I needed a bit of time to sense that I had only committed a blunder; for—not to speak of the impossibility of a twelve-year-old child's following my explanation—the usefulness of this experiment never entered his mind. Having tasted the two wines and finding them both good, the word *adulteration*, which I thought I had explained to him so well, did not correspond to any idea he had. The other words—*unhealthy, poison*—did not even have any meaning for him. He was, in this respect, in the same situation as the historian of the physician Philip.[7] That is the situation of all children.

Relations of effects to causes whose connection we do not perceive, goods and ills of which we have no idea, needs we have never experienced—these are nothing to us. It is impossible by means of them to interest us in doing anything which relates to them. At fifteen one sees the happiness of a wise man as one does the glory of paradise at thirty. If one does not have a good conception of these, one will do little to acquire them; and even if one does conceive of them, one will still do little to acquire them if one does not desire them, if one does not feel them to be suitable to oneself. It is easy to prove to a child that what one wants to teach him is useful; but to prove it is nothing if one does not know how to persuade him. In vain does tranquil reason make us approve or criticize; it is only passion which makes us act—and how can one get passionate about interests one does not yet have?

Never show the child anything he cannot see. While humanity is

* The wines sold retail by the wine merchants of Paris, although they are not always treated with litharge, are rarely free of lead, because the counters of these merchants are covered with this metal, and the wine which overflows the measuring cup comes into contact with this lead, stays on it for a time, and always dissolves some part of it. It is strange that so manifest and so dangerous an abuse is tolerated by the police. But it is true that people in easy circumstances, hardly drinking those wines, are little subject to being poisoned by them.

† Vegetable acid is very mild. If it were a mineral acid and less diluted, the combination would not take place without effervescence.

almost alien to him, and you are unable to raise him to man's estate, for his sake lower man to the child's estate. In thinking about what can be useful to him at another age, speak to him only about things whose utility he sees right now. Moreover, let there never be any comparisons with other children, no rivals, no competitors, not even in running, once he has begun to be able to reason. I prefer a hundred times over that he not learn what he would only learn out of jealousy or vanity. However, every year I shall note the progress he has made; I shall compare it to that which he will make the following year. I shall tell him, "You have grown so many inches. That is the ditch you jumped over, the load you carried, the distance you threw a pebble, the course you ran before getting winded, etc. Let us now see what you will do." Thus I arouse him without making him jealous of anyone. He will want to outdo himself. He ought to. I see no problem in his being his own competitor.

I hate books. They only teach one to talk about what one does not know. It is said that Hermes engraved the elements of the sciences on columns in order to shelter his discoveries from a flood.[8] If he had left a good imprint of them in man's head, they would have been preserved by tradition. Well-prepared minds are the surest monuments on which to engrave human knowledge.

Is there no means of bringing together so many lessons scattered in so many books, of joining them in a common object which is easy to see and interesting to follow and can serve as a stimulant even at this age? If one can invent a situation where all man's natural needs are shown in a way a child's mind can sense, and where the means of providing for these needs emerge in order with equal ease, it is by the lively and naïve depiction of this state that the first exercise must be given to his imagination.[9]

Ardent philosopher, I see your imagination kindling already. Do not put yourself out. This situation has been found; it has been described and, without prejudice to you, much better than you would describe it yourself—at least with more truth and simplicity. Since we absolutely must have books, there exists one which, to my taste, provides the most felicitous treatise on natural education. This book will be the first that my Emile will read. For a long time it will alone compose his whole library, and it will always hold a distinguished place there. It will be the text for which all our discussions on the natural sciences will serve only as a commentary. It will serve as a test of the condition of our judgment during our progress; and so long as our taste is not spoiled, its reading will always please us. What, then, is this marvelous book? Is it Aristotle? Is it Pliny? Is it Buffon? No. It is *Robinson Crusoe.*

Robinson Crusoe on his island, alone, deprived of the assistance of his kind and the instruments of all the arts, providing nevertheless for his subsistence, for his preservation, and even procuring for himself a kind of well-being—this is an object interesting for every age and one which can be made agreeable to children in countless ways. This is how we realize the desert island which served me at first as a comparison. This state, I agree, is not that of social man; very likely it is not going

BOOK III

to be that of Emile. But it is on the basis of this very state that he ought to appraise all the others. The surest means of raising oneself above prejudices and ordering one's judgments about the true relations of things is to put oneself in the place of an isolated man and to judge everything as this man himself ought to judge of it with respect to his own utility.

This novel, disencumbered of all its rigmarole, beginning with Robinson's shipwreck near his island and ending with the arrival of the ship which comes to take him from it, will be both Emile's entertainment and instruction throughout the period which is dealt with here. I want it to make him dizzy; I want him constantly to be busy with his mansion, his goats, his plantations; I want him to learn in detail, not from books but from things, all that must be known in such a situation; I want him to think he is Robinson himself, to see himself dressed in skins, wearing a large cap, carrying a large saber and all the rest of the character's grotesque equipment, with the exception of the parasol, which he will not need. I want him to worry about the measures to take if this or that were lacking to him; to examine his hero's conduct; to investigate whether he omitted anything, whether there was nothing to do better; to note Robinson's failings attentively; and to profit from them so as not to fall into them himself in such a situation. For do not doubt that he is planning to go and set up a similar establishment. This is the true "castle in Spain" of this happy age when one knows no other happiness than the necessities and freedom.

What a resource this folly would be for a skillful man who knew how to engender it solely for the sake of taking advantage of it. The child, in a hurry to set up a storehouse for his island, will be more ardent for learning than is the master for teaching. He will want to know all that is useful, and he will want to know only that. You will not need to guide him; you will have only to restrain him. Now let us hurry to establish him on this island while he still limits his felicity to it; for the day is nearing when, if he still wants to live there, he will not want any longer to live there alone, and when Friday, who now hardly concerns him, will not for long be enough for him.

The practice of the natural arts, for which a single man suffices, leads to the investigation of the arts of industry, which need the conjunction of many hands. The former can be exercised by solitaries, by savages; but the others can be born only in society and make it necessary. So long as one knows only physical need, each man suffices unto himself. The introduction of the superfluous makes division and distribution of labor indispensable; although a man working alone earns only subsistence for one man, a hundred men working in harmony will earn enough to give subsistence to two hundred. Therefore, as soon as a part of mankind rests, it is necessary that the joint efforts of those who work make up for the idleness of those who do nothing.

Your greatest care ought to be to keep away from your pupil's mind all notions of social relations which are not within his reach. But when the chain of knowledge forces you to show him the mutual dependence of men, instead of showing it to him from the moral side, turn all his attention at first toward industry and mechanical arts which make men useful to one another. In taking him from workshop to workshop, never allow him to view any work without putting his hand to the job himself or to leave without knowing perfectly the reason for all that is done there, or at least all that he has observed. To achieve this, work yourself; everywhere provide the example for him. To make him a master, be everywhere an apprentice; and reckon that an hour of work will teach him more things than he would retain from a day of explanations.

There is a public esteem attached to the different arts in inverse proportion to their real utility. This esteem is calculated directly on the basis of their very uselessness, and this is the way it ought to be. The most useful arts are those which earn the least, because the number of workers is proportioned to men's needs, and work necessary to everybody must remain at a price the poor man can pay. On the other hand, these important fellows who are called artists instead of artisans, and who work solely for the idle and the rich, set an arbitrary price on their baubles. Since the merit of these vain works exists only in opinion, their very price constitutes a part of that merit, and they are esteemed in proportion to what they cost. The importance given them by the rich does not come from their use but from the fact that the poor cannot afford them. *Nolo habere bona nisi quibus populus inviderit.**

What will your pupils become if you let them adopt this stupid prejudice, if you encourage it yourself, if, for example, they see you enter a goldsmith's shop with more respect than a locksmith's? What judgment will they make of the true merit of arts and the veritable value of things, when they see that the price is set by whim everywhere in contradiction to the price based on real utility, and that the more a thing costs the less it is worth? The first moment you let these ideas into their heads, abandon the rest of their education. In spite of you, they will be raised like everyone else. You have wasted fourteen years of effort.

Emile, planning to furnish his island, will have other ways of seeing. Robinson Crusoe would have attached much more importance to a toolmaker's shop than to all Said's [11] gewgaws. The former would have appeared to him to be a very respectable man, and the other a little charlatan.

"My son is made to live with others. He will live not with wise men but with madmen. Therefore, he must know their madnesses since they wish to be led by them. The real knowledge of things may be good, but that of men and their judgments is even more valuable, for in human society the greatest instrument of man is man, and the wisest is he who best makes use of this instrument. What is the use of giving children the idea of an imaginary order which is entirely opposed to the established one they will find and according to which they will have to govern themselves? Give them lessons in the first place for being wise, and then you can give them lessons for judging how other men are mad."

* Petronius.[10]

BOOK III

These are the specious maxims which guide the false prudence of fathers in making their children slaves of the prejudices they feed them and playthings themselves of the senseless mob which they expect to make the tool of their passions. To get to know man, how many things must be known before him! Man is the last study of the wise, and you claim to make it a child's first! Before instructing him in our sentiments, begin by teaching him to evaluate them. Does one know a folly when one takes it to be reasonable? To be wise one must discern what is not wise. How will your child know men if he does not know how to judge their judgments or detect their errors? It is bad to know what they think when one does not know whether what they think is true or false. Teach him, therefore, in the first place what things are in themselves, and you can teach him afterward what they are in our eyes. It is thus that he will know how to compare the opinion to the truth and to raise himself above the vulgar; for one does not know prejudices when one adopts them, and one does not lead the people when one resembles them. But if you begin by instructing him in public opinion before teaching him to appraise it, rest assured that, whatever you may do, it will become his, and you will no longer be able to destroy it. I draw the conclusion that to make a young man judicious, we must form his judgments well instead of dictating ours to him.

You see that up to now I have not spoken of men to my pupil. He would have had too much good sense to listen to me. He does not yet have a sufficient sense of his relations with his species to be able to judge of others by himself. He knows no human being other than himself alone, and he is even far from knowing himself. But if he makes few judgments about his person, at least he makes only exact ones. He does not know the place of others, but he feels his own and stays in it. In place of the social laws which he cannot know, we have bound him with the chains of necessity. He is still almost only a physical being. Let us continue to treat him as such.

It is by their palpable relation to his utility, his security, his preservation, and his well-being that he ought to appraise all the bodies of nature and all the works of men. Thus, iron ought to be much more valuable in his eyes than gold, and glass than diamonds. Similarly, he honors a shoemaker or a mason far more than a Lempereur, a Leblanc,[12] and all the jewelers of Europe. A pastry chef especially is a very important man in his eyes, and he would give the whole Academy of Sciences for the lowest candymaker of the rue des Lombards. The goldsmiths, the engravers, and the gilders are in his view nothing but loafers who play perfectly useless games. He does not treat even clockmaking very seriously. The happy child enjoys time without being its slave. He profits from it and does not know its value. The calm of the passions, which makes the passage of time always uniform, takes the place for him of an instrument for measuring it at need.* In assuming he has a watch as well as in making him cry, I gave myself a common

---

* Time loses its measure for us when our passions want to adjust its course according to their taste. The wise man's watch is evenness of temper and peace of soul. He is always on time for himself, and he always knows what that time is.

Emile, to be useful and to make myself understood; for, with respect to the true one, a child so different from others would not serve as an example for anything.

There is an order no less natural and still more judicious by which one considers the arts according to the relations of necessity which connect them, putting in the first rank the most independent and in the last those which depend on a greater number of others. This order, which provides important considerations about the order of society in general, is similar to the preceding one and subject to the same inversion in men's esteem. The result of this is that raw materials are used in crafts without honor and almost without profit, and that the more hands they pass through, the more labor increases in price and becomes honorable. I am not examining whether it is true that the skill is greater and merits more recompense in the detailed arts which give the final form to these materials than in the initial work which converts them to the use of men. But I do say that, with each thing, the art whose use is the most general and the most indispensable is incontestably the one which merits the most esteem; and the one to which other arts are less necessary also merits esteem ahead of the more subordinate ones, because it is freer and nearer independence. These are the true rules for appraising the arts and manufactures. Anything else is arbitrary and depends on opinion.

The first and most respectable of all the arts is agriculture; I would put ironworking in the second rank, woodworking in the third, and so on. The child who has not been seduced by vulgar prejudices will judge of them precisely thus. What important reflections on this point our Emile will draw from his *Robinson Crusoe*! What will he think on seeing that the arts are only perfected in being subdivided, in infinitely multiplying the instruments of all of them? He will say to himself, "All these people are stupidly ingenious. One would believe they are afraid that their arms and their fingers might be of some use, so many instruments do they invent to do without them. To practice a single art they are subjected to countless others. A city is needed for every worker. As for my companion and me, we put our genius in our adroitness. We make ourselves tools that we can take everywhere with us. All those people so proud of their talents in Paris would not know how to do anything on our island and would be our apprentices in their turn."

Reader, do not stop here to view the training of our pupil's body and the skill of his hands; but consider what direction we are giving to his childish curiosities; consider his sense, his inventive spirit, and his foresight; consider what a head we are putting on his shoulders. In all that he will see, in all that he will do, he will want to know everything; he will want to learn the reason for everything. From instrument to instrument he will want always to go back to the first; he will accept no assumption. He would refuse to learn whatever demands prior knowledge he does not have. If he sees a spring, he will want to know how the steel was taken from the mine. If he sees the pieces of a box being assembled, he will want to know how the tree was cut. If he works himself, with every tool he uses he will not fail to ask himself,

BOOK III

"If I did not have this tool, how would I go about making one like it or doing without it?"

An error difficult to avoid is always to assume the child has the same taste for the activities about which the master is enthusiastic. When the entertainment of work carries you away, be careful that in the meantime he is not bored without daring to indicate it to you. The child ought to be wholly involved with the thing, but you ought to be wholly involved with the child—observing him, spying on him without letup and without appearing to do so, sensing ahead of time all his sentiments and forestalling those he ought not to have—in a word, busying him in such a way that he not only feels he is of use in the work but is pleased by dint of understanding well the purpose of that work.

The society of the arts consists in exchange of skills, that of commerce in exchange of things, that of banks in exchange of signs and money. All these ideas are connected, and the elementary notions are already grasped. We laid the foundations for all this at an early age with the help of Robert, the gardener. It only remains for us now to generalize these same ideas and extend them to more examples to make him understand the workings of trade taken by itself and presented to his senses by the details of natural history regarding the products peculiar to each country, by the details of arts and sciences regarding navigation, and finally, by the greater or lesser problems of transport according to distance, the situation of lands, seas, rivers, etc.

No society can exist without exchange, no exchange without a common measure, and no common measure without equality. Thus all society has as its first law some conventional equality, whether of men or of things.

Conventional equality among men, very different from natural equality, makes positive right—that is, government and laws—necessary. The political knowledge of a child ought to be distinct and limited; he ought to know about government in general only what relates to the right of property, of which he already has some idea.

Conventional equality among things prompted the invention of money, for money is only a term of comparison for the value of things of different kinds; and in this sense money is the true bond of society. But everything can be money. Once cattle was; shells still are among many peoples; iron was money in Sparta; leather has been in Sweden; gold and silver are among us.

Metals, since they are easier to transport, have generally been chosen as mean terms for all exchanges; and these metals have been converted into money to spare measuring or weighing at each exchange. For the stamping of money is only an attestation that the piece thus stamped is of a certain weight; the prince alone has the right to strike money, given that he alone has the right to demand that his witness be authoritative among a whole people.

Thus explained, the use of this invention is made apparent to the stupidest of persons. It is difficult to compare directly things of different natures—cloth, for example, to wheat. But when one has found a common measure—money—it is easy for the manufacturer and the farmer to relate to this common measure the value of the things they want to exchange. If such a quantity of cloth is worth such a sum of money, and such a quantity of wheat should also be worth the same sum of money, it follows that the merchant, receiving this wheat for his cloth, makes an equitable exchange. Thus it is by money that goods of various kinds become commensurable and can be compared.

Do not go farther than this, and do not enter into an explanation of the moral effects of this institution. With all things it is important that the uses be well presented before the abuses are shown. If you aspire to explain to children how the signs make the things neglected, how all the chimeras of opinion are born from money, how countries rich in money must be poor in everything else, you would be treating these children not only as philosophers but as wise men, and you would be aspiring to make them understand a thing of which even few philosophers have had a good conception.

To what an abundance of interesting objects can one thus turn a pupil's curiosity without ever abandoning the real material relations which are within his reach or allowing a single idea that he cannot conceive to spring up in his mind! The art of the master consists in never letting his pupil's observations dwell on minutiae which lead nowhere but in bringing him ever closer to the great relations he must know one day in order to judge well of the good and bad order of civil society. One must know how to match the conversations with which one entertains him to the turn of mind he has been given. A question which could not even stir the attention of another is going to torment Emile for six months.

We go to dine in an opulent home. We find the preparations for a feast—many people, many lackeys, many dishes, an elegant and fine table service. All this apparatus of pleasure and festivity has something intoxicating about it which goes to the head when one is not accustomed to it. I have a presentiment of the effect of all this on my young pupil. While the meal continues, while the courses follow one another, while much boisterous conversation reigns at the table, I lean toward his ear and say, "Through how many hands would you estimate that all you see on this table has passed before getting here?" What a crowd of ideas I awaken in his brain with these few words! Instantly, all the vapors of the delirium are dispelled. He dreams, he reflects, he calculates, he worries. While the philosophers, cheered by the wine, perhaps by the ladies next to them, prate and act like children, he is all alone philosophizing for himself in his corner. He questions me; I refuse to answer; I put him off to another time. He gets impatient; he forgets to eat and drink; he burns to get away from the table to discuss with me at his ease. What an object for his curiosity! What a text for his instruction! With a healthy judgment that nothing has been able to corrupt, what will he think of this luxury when he finds that every region of the world has been made to contribute; that perhaps twenty million hands have worked for a long time; that it has cost the lives of perhaps thousands of men, and all this to present to him with pomp at noon what he is going to deposit in his toilet at night?

Spy out with care the secret conclusions he draws in his heart from all his observations. If you have guarded him less well than I assume, he may be tempted to turn his reflections in another direction and to regard himself as an important person in the world, seeing so many efforts concerted to prepare his dinner. If you get a presentiment of this reasoning, you can easily forestall it before he makes it, or at least efface its impression immediately. Not yet knowing how to appropriate things other than by material enjoyment, he can judge of their suitability or lack of it for him only by means of relations accessible to his senses. The comparison of a simple, rustic dinner, prepared by exercise, seasoned by hunger, freedom, and joy, with his magnificent formal feast will suffice to make him feel that all the apparatus of the feast did not give him any real profit, and that since his stomach left the peasant's table as satisfied as it left the financier's, there was nothing more in the one than in the other that he could truly call his own.

Let us imagine what a governor will be able to say to him in such a case: "Recall these two meals, and decide for yourself which you ate with the most pleasure. At which did you notice more joy? At which did one eat with greater appetite, drink more gaily, laugh more good-heartedly? Which went on longest without boredom and without needing to be renewed by other courses? Meanwhile, look at the difference: this wholewheat bread you find so good comes from wheat harvested by this peasant; his wine, black and coarse but refreshing and healthy, is the product of his own vine; the linen comes from his hemp, woven in the winter by his wife, his daughters, and his servant girl. No hands other than those of his family made the preparations for his table; the nearest mill and the neighboring market are the limits of the universe for him. In what way then did you really enjoy everything additional provided for that other table by distant lands and the hands of men? If all that did not give you a better meal, what have you gained from this abundance? What was in it that was made for you? If you had been the master of the house," he will be able to add, "all this would have remained even more alien to you, for the effort of displaying your enjoyment to the eyes of others would have succeeded in taking that enjoyment away from you. You would have had the discomfort, and they the pleasure."

This speech may be very fine, but it is worthless for Emile, whose reach it exceeds and whose reflections are not dictated by others. Speak to him therefore more simply. After these two tests say to him one morning, "Where shall we dine today? Next to that mountain of silver which covers three-quarters of the table and those beds of paper flowers which are served on mirrors with dessert? Amidst those women with great skirts who treat you like a puppet and insist that you have said what you do not know? Or, rather, in that village two leagues from here with those good people who receive us so joyfully and give us such good custard?" There is no doubt about Emile's choice, for he is neither a babbler nor vain. He cannot endure constraint, and all our delicate relishes do not please him. But he is always ready to run in the country, and he very much likes good fruits, good vegetables, good custard, and good people.* On our way, the reflection comes of it-self. I see that these crowds of men who work at these grand meals simply waste their efforts, or that they hardly think of our pleasures.

My examples, good perhaps for one pupil, will be bad for countless others. If one catches the spirit of these examples, one will surely know how to vary them according to need. The choice depends on the genius peculiar to each pupil, and the study of that genius depends on the occasions one offers each to reveal himself. It cannot be imagined that, in the space of the three or four years we have to fill here, we can give the most fortunately born child a sufficient idea of all the arts and all the natural sciences for him to learn them one day by himself. But in thus making all the objects it is important for him to know pass be-fore him, we put him in a position to develop his taste and his talent, to make the first steps toward the object to which his genius leads him, and to indicate to us the route which must be opened to him in order to assist nature.

Another advantage of this chain of limited but precise knowledge is to show him the different kinds of knowledge in their connections and relations, to give them all a place in his esteem, and to forestall in him the prejudices most men have in favor of the talents they cultivate and against those they have neglected. He who sees well the order of the whole sees the place where each part ought to be. He who sees a part well and knows it in depth may be a learned man; the other is a judicious man; and you remember that what we are proposing to acquire is less science than judgment.

However that may be, my method is independent of my examples. It is founded on the measure of man's faculties at his different ages and on the choice of occupations which suit these faculties. I believe that another method would easily be found which would appear to do bet-ter. But if it were less appropriate to the species, the age, the sex, I doubt that it would have the same success.

In beginning this second period we have taken advantage of the su-perabundance of our strength over our needs in order to take us out-side of ourselves. We have launched ourselves into the heavens; we have measured the earth; we have harvested the laws of nature. In a word, we have visited the whole island. Now we come back to ourselves. We are imperceptibly coming nearer to the place we dwell, only too happy on returning there to find it still not possessed by the enemy which threatens us and which is preparing to take hold of it!

What remains for us to do after having observed all that surrounds us? To convert to our use all that we can appropriate for ourselves and to profit from our curiosity for the advantage of our well-being. Up to

* The taste for the country I assume in my pupil is a natural fruit of his educa-tion. Moreover, with none of the foppish and affected air which is so pleasing to women, he is made less of by them than are other children. Consequently, he enjoys himself less with them and is less spoiled by their society, whose charms he is not yet in a condition to sense. I have been careful not to teach him to kiss their hands, to say insipidities to them, or even to show them, in preference to men, the atten-tions due them. I have set myself an inviolable law to demand nothing from him whose reason is not within his reach, and there is no good reason for a child to treat one sex differently from the other.

now we have provided for instruments of every kind without knowing which we shall need. Perhaps useless to ourselves, ours will be able to serve other men; and perhaps, in our turn, we shall need theirs. Thus we would all be advantaged by these exchanges. But to make them, our mutual needs must be known. Each must know what others have which he can use and what he can offer them in return. Let us suppose ten men, each of whom has ten sorts of needs. Each must, for what he needs, apply himself to ten sorts of work; but, given the differences of genius and talent, one man will be less successful at one sort of work, another man at another. Although fit for diverse things, all will do the same ones and will be ill served. Let us form a society of these ten men and let each apply himself, for himself and for the nine others, to the kind of occupation which suits him best. Each will profit from the talents of the others as if he alone had them all. Each will perfect his own by continuous practice, and it will turn out that all ten, perfectly well provided for, will even have a surplus for others. That is the apparent principle of all our institutions. It is not part of my subject to examine its consequences here. I have done it in another writing.[13]

According to this principle, a man who wanted to regard himself as an isolated being, not depending at all on anything and sufficient unto himself, could only be miserable. It would even be impossible for him to subsist. For, finding the whole earth covered with thine and mine and having nothing belonging to him except his body, where would he get his necessities? By leaving the state of nature, we force our fellows to leave it, too. No one can remain in it in spite of the others, and it would really be leaving it to want to remain when it is impossible to live there, for the first law of nature is the care of preserving oneself.

Thus the ideas of social relations are formed little by little in a child's mind, even before he can really be an active member of society. Emile sees that, in order to have instruments for his use, he must in addition have instruments for the use of other men with which he can obtain in exchange the things which are necessary to him and are in their power. I easily bring him to feel the need for these exchanges and to put himself in a position to profit from them.

"My lord, I have to live," said an unfortunate satiric author to the minister who reproached him for the disgracefulness of his trade. "I do not see why it is necessary," the man in office responded coldly. This response, excellent for a minister, would have been barbarous and false in any other mouth. Every man must live. This argument, which is more or less weighty for a man to the extent he is more or less humane, appears to me to be unanswerable for him who makes it relative to himself. Since the aversion to dying is the strongest of all those aversions nature gives us, it follows that it permits everything to anyone who has no other possible means of living. The principles according to which the virtuous man learns to despise his life and to sacrifice it to his duty are very far from this primitive simplicity. Happy are the peoples among whom one can be good without effort and just without virtue! If there is some miserable state in the world where a man cannot live without doing harm and where the citizens are rascals by necessity, it is not the malefactor who should be hanged, but he who forces him to become one.

So soon as Emile knows what life is, my first care will be to teach him to preserve it. Up to now I have not distinguished stations, ranks, and fortunes; and I shall hardly distinguish them in what follows. This is because man is the same in all stations; the rich man does not have a bigger stomach than the poor one and does not digest better than he; the master does not have arms longer or stronger than his slave's; a man of great family is no greater than a man of the people; and finally, as the natural needs are everywhere the same, the means of providing for them ought to be equal everywhere. Suit the education of man to man, not to what is not man. Do you not see that in working to form him exclusively for one station you are making him useless for any other, and that if fortune pleases, you will have worked only to make him unhappy? What is more ridiculous than a great lord who has become destitute and brings the prejudices of his birth with him to his distress? What is viler than an impoverished rich man who, remembering the contempt owed to poverty, feels himself to have become the lowest of men? The one has as his only recourse the trade of public rascal; the other that of crawling valet who uses this fair phrase, "I have to live."

You trust in the present order of society without thinking that this order is subject to inevitable revolutions, and it is impossible for you to foresee or prevent the one which may affect your children. The noble become commoners, the rich become poor, the monarch becomes subject. Are the blows of fate so rare that you can count on being exempted from them? We are approaching a state of crisis and the age of revolutions.* Who can answer for what will become of you then? All that men have made, men can destroy. The only ineffaceable characters are those printed by nature; and nature does not make princes, rich men, or great lords. What, then, will this satrap whom you have raised only for greatness do in lowliness? What will this publican who knows how to live only with gold do in poverty? What will this gaudy imbecile, who does not know how to make use of himself and puts his being only in what is alien to himself, do when he is deprived of everything? Happy is the man who knows how to leave the station which leaves him and to remain a man in spite of fate! That vanquished king who, full of rage, wants to be buried under the debris of his throne may be praised as much as one pleases; I despise him. I see that he exists only by his crown, and that he is nothing at all if he is not a king. But he who loses it and does without it is then above it. From the rank of king which a coward, a wicked man, or a madman can fill, he rises to the station of man, which so few men know how to fill. Then he triumphs over fortune; he braves it. He owes nothing except to himself; and when there remains nothing for him to show

---

* I hold it to be impossible that the great monarchies of Europe still have long to last. All have shined, and every state which shines is on the decline. I have reasons more particular than this maxim for my opinion, but it is unseasonable to tell them, and everyone sees them only too well.

except himself, he is not nothing, he is something. Yes, I prefer a hundred times over the king of Syracuse becoming a schoolmaster at Corinth and the king of Macedonia becoming a clerk at Rome [14] to an unfortunate Tarquin not knowing what to become if he does not reign, and to the heir and son of a king of kings,* the plaything of whoever dares to insult his distress, wandering from court to court, seeking help everywhere, and finding affronts everywhere for want of knowing how to do anything other than perform a trade which is no longer in his power.

A man and a citizen, whoever he may be, has no property to put into society other than himself. All his other property is in it in spite of him; and when a man is rich, either he does not enjoy his riches or the public enjoys them, too. In the first case, he robs from others that of which he deprives himself; and in the second, he gives them nothing. Thus the social debt remains with him in its entirety so long as he pays only with his property. "But my father, in earning it, served society . . ." So be it; he has paid his debt, but not yours. You owe others more than if you were born without property, since you were favored at birth. It is not just that what one man has done for society should relieve another from what he owes it; for each, owing himself wholly, can pay only for himself and no father can transmit to his son the right to be useless to his fellows. This is, however, what he does, according to you, in transmitting to him his riches, which are the proof and the price of work. He who eats in idleness what he did not earn himself steals it. A man whom the state pays an income for doing nothing hardly differs in my eyes from a brigand who lives at the expense of passers-by. Outside of society isolated man, owing nothing to anyone, has a right to live as he pleases. But in society, where he necessarily lives at the expense of others, he owes them the price of his keep in work. This is without exception. To work is therefore an indispensable duty for social man. Rich or poor, powerful or weak, every idle citizen is a rascal. [16]

Now, of all the occupations which can provide subsistence to man, that which brings him closest to the state of nature is manual labor. Of all conditions, the artisan's is the most independent of fortune and men. The artisan depends only on his work. He is as free as the farmer is slave. For the latter is dependent on his field, whose harvest is at another's discretion. The enemy, the prince, a powerful neighbor, or a lawsuit can take this field away from him. By means of this field he can be vexed in countless ways. But wherever they want to vex the artisan, his baggage is soon packed. He takes his hands and goes away. However, agriculture is man's first trade. It is the most decent, the most useful, and consequently the most noble he can practice. I do not say to Emile, "Learn agriculture." He knows it. He is familiar with all the kinds of rustic work. He began with them, he constantly returns to them. I say to him therefore, "Cultivate the inheritance of your fathers. But if you lose that inheritance, or if you have none, what is to be done? Learn a trade."

* Vonones, son of Phrates, king of the Parthians. [15]

"A trade for my son! My son an artisan! Sir, are you in your right mind?" I am thinking clearly, more clearly than you, madame, who want to reduce him to never being able to be anything but a lord, a marquess, a prince, and perhaps one day less than nothing. I want to give him a rank which he cannot lose, a rank which does him honor at all times; and whatever you may say about it, he will have fewer equals with this title than with all those he will get from you.

The letter kills, and the spirit enlivens. The goal is less to learn a trade in order to know a trade than to conquer the prejudices that despise a trade. You will never be reduced to working to live. Well, too bad—too bad for you! But, that is not important; do not work out of necessity; work out of glory. Lower yourself to the artisan's station in order to be above your own. In order to subject fortune and things to yourself, begin by making yourself independent of them. To reign by opinion, begin by reigning over it.

Remember that it is not a talent that I ask of you. It is a trade, a true trade, a purely mechanical art in which the hands work more than the head, one which does not lead to fortune but enables one to do without it. In homes far above the danger of lacking bread I have seen fathers carry foresight to such a point that they join to the care of instructing their children that of providing them with knowledge which in any eventuality they could draw on to live. These foresighted fathers believe that they are doing a great deal. They are doing nothing, because the resources they think they are husbanding for their children depend on that same fortune above which they want to place them. The result is that with all these fine talents, if he who has them does not find himself in circumstances favorable for making use of them, he will perish from want just as if he had no talents.

As soon as it is a question of wiles and intrigues, one might as well use them to maintain oneself in abundance as to regain, from the bosom of want, the means to climb up to one's former station again. If you cultivate arts whose success depends on the artist's reputation, if you make yourself fit for employments which are obtained only by favor, of what use will all this be to you when you, because you have become disgusted with society, will disdain the means without which one cannot succeed in it? You have studied politics and the interests of princes. That is very good. But what will you do with this knowledge if you do not know how to get to ministers, to the women of the court, to the heads of bureaus, if you do not have the secret of pleasing them, if all do not find in you the rascal who suits them? You are an architect or a painter. So be it. But you have to make your talent known. Do you think you can just start out by showing a work at the Salon? Oh, that is not the way it goes! You have to belong to the Academy. You even have to have pull in it in order to obtain some obscure place in a corner. Leave your ruler and your brush, I tell you. Take a cab and run from door to door. It is thus that celebrity is acquired. You ought to know that all these illustrious doors have Swiss [17] or doormen who understand only by gesture and whose ears are in their hands. Do you want to teach what you have learned and become a master of geography, or mathematics, or languages, or music, or drawing? In order to do even that, you have to find students, and to do that, you have to find boosters. Count on its being more important to be a charlatan than a capable man and on your never being anything but an ignoramus if the only trade you know is your own.

See, therefore, how little solid are all those brilliant resources and how many other resources are necessary for you to take advantage of them. And then what will become of you in this cowardly debasement? Reverses degrade you without instructing you. How will you—more than ever a plaything of public opinion—raise yourself above the prejudices which are the arbiters of your fate? How will you despise the baseness and the vices which you need to subsist? You depended only on riches, and now you depend on the rich. You have only worsened your slavery and added your poverty on top of it. Now you are poor without being free. It is the worst condition into which man can fall.

But if instead of having recourse, in order to live, to these high kinds of knowledge, made for feeding the soul and not the body, you have recourse in need to your hands and the use you know how to make of them, all the difficulties disappear, all the wiles become useless. The resource is always ready when it has to be used. Probity and honor are no longer an obstacle to life. You no longer need to be a coward and a liar with the nobles, pliable and groveling with rascals, basely obliging to everyone, a borrower or a thief—which are almost the same thing when one has nothing. The opinion of others does not touch you. You do not have to pay court to anyone; no fool to flatter, no Swiss to move, no courtesan to pay and, what is worse, to butter up. That rogues have the conduct of great affairs is of little importance to you. It will not prevent you, in your obscure life, from being an honest man and having bread. You enter the first shop of the trade you have learned. "Master, I need work." "Journeyman, set yourself there and work." Before the dinner hour has come, you have earned your dinner. If you are diligent and sober, before a week has passed you will have the means to live another week. You will have lived free, healthy, true, industrious, and just. It is not wasting time to earn your livelihood in this way.

I absolutely want Emile to learn a trade. A decent trade at least, will you say? What does this word mean? Is not every trade decent that is useful to the public? I do not want him to be an embroiderer, a gilder, or a varnisher, like Locke's gentleman.[18] I do not want him to be a musician, an actor, or a writer of books. With the exception of these professions and those that resemble them, let him take the one he wants. I do not presume to restrain him in anything. I prefer that he be a shoemaker to a poet, that he pave highways to making porcelain flowers. But, you will say, policemen, spies, and hangmen are useful people. They owe their usefulness entirely to the government, which could also make them useless. But let that pass. I was wrong. It does not suffice to choose a useful trade. It must, further, not demand from those practicing it qualities of soul that are odious and incompatible with humanity. Thus, returning to the first word, let us take a decent trade. But let us always remember that there is no decency without utility.

A celebrated author of this age,[19] whose books are full of great projects and small views, took the vow, like all the priests of his communion, not to have a wife of his own; but, being more scrupulous than the others about adultery, he is said to have chosen the course of having pretty servants with whom he did his best to atone for the outrage he had committed against his species by this rash commitment. He regarded it as a citizen's duty to give other citizens to his country; and, with the tribute of this kind he paid it, he peopled the class of artisans. As soon as these children were at the proper age, he made all of them learn a trade that suited their taste, excluding only professions that are idle, futile, or subject to fashion, such as that of wigmaker, which is never necessary and can become useless from one day to the next, so long as nature does not cease providing us with hair.

This is the spirit which should guide us in the choice of Emile's trade; or, rather, it is not for us to make this choice but for him. For the maxims with which he is imbued preserve in him the natural contempt for useless things, and thus he will never want to consume his time in labors of no value. He knows no value in things other than their real utility. He has to have a trade that could serve Robinson Crusoe on his island.

In making the products of nature and art pass in review before a child, in exciting his curiosity, in following him where it leads him, one has the advantage of studying his tastes, his inclinations, and his penchants and of seeing the first spark of his genius ignite, if he has one which is well defined. But a common error, from which you must be preserved, is to attribute to the ardor of talent the effect of circumstances and to take for a definite inclination to such and such an art the imitative spirit common to man and ape, which leads both mechanically to want to do everything they see done without quite knowing what it is good for. The world is full of artisans, and especially of artists, who do not possess natural talent for the art they practice but were pushed into it by others from an early age, whether prompted by other considerations or deceived by an apparent zeal which would have similarly led them to any other art if they had seen it practiced as soon. One hears a drum and believes he is a general. Another sees a building and wants to be an architect. Each is tempted by the trade he sees performed when he believes it is esteemed.

I knew a lackey who, seeing his master paint and draw, took it into his head to be a painter and drawer. From the moment he formed this resolve, he picked up the pencil and no longer put it down except to pick up the brush, which he will never put down for the rest of his life. Without lessons and without rules he set himself to drawing everything that came to hand. He spent three whole years glued to his scribblings, without anything other than his work able to tear him away from them and without ever losing heart at the small progress that his mediocre gifts permitted him to make. I saw him during six months of a hot summer—in a little antechamber facing south where one suffocated just on passing through—seated, or rather nailed, on his chair all day in front of a globe, drawing this globe and drawing it again, constantly beginning and beginning again with invincible obstinacy, until he had rendered the high relief well enough to be satisfied with his work. Finally, encouraged by his master and guided by an artist, he reached the point of leaving the livery and living from his brush. Up to a certain limit perseverance takes the place of talent. He has reached that limit and will never go beyond it. The constancy and the emulation of this decent boy are laudable. He will make himself esteemed forever for his assiduity, his fidelity, and his morals. But he will never paint anything but pictures for the panels placed above doors. Who would not have been deceived by his zeal and taken him for a true talent? There is a great difference between enjoying some kind of work and being fit for it. We need sharper observations than is thought to get assurances of the true genius and the true taste of a child who shows his desires far more than his disposition, and who is always judged by the former for want of knowing how to study the latter. I would want a judicious man to give us a treatise on the art of observing children. This art would be very important to know. Fathers and masters have not yet learned its elements.

But perhaps we are giving too much importance here to the choice of a trade. Since the issue is only one of some kind of work done with the hands, this choice is nothing for Emile, and his apprenticeship is already more than half completed by the exercises with which we have kept him busy up to now. What do you want him to do? He is ready for anything. He already knows how to handle a spade and a hoe. He knows how to use a lathe, a hammer, a plane, and a file. The tools of all the trades are already familiar to him. The issue is now nothing more than to be able to use one of these tools quickly and easily enough to equal in rapidity the good workers who employ it. And he has in this respect a great advantage over them all: he has an agile body and limbs flexible enough to enable him to get into all sorts of postures without difficulty and to prolong all sorts of movements without effort. Moreover, his organs are sound and well exercised. All the operations of the arts are already known to him. In order to be able to work as a master, he lacks only experience, and experience is gotten only with time. To which of the trades from which we may still choose, then, will he give enough time to make himself proficient at it? This is the only question left.

Give a man a trade which suits his sex and a young man a trade which suits his age. Every sedentary and indoor profession which effeminates and softens the body neither pleases nor suits him. Never did a young boy by himself aspire to be a tailor. Art is required to bring to this woman's trade the sex for which it is not made.* The needle and the sword cannot be wielded by the same hands. If I were sovereign, I would permit sewing and the needle trades only to women and to cripples reduced to occupations like theirs. Assuming eunuchs to be necessary, I find it quite mad for Orientals to make them specially. Why are they not satisfied with those made by nature, with those crowds of cowardly men whose heart it has mutilated? They would have more than enough for the need. Every weak, delicate, and fearful man is condemned by nature to a sedentary life. He is made to live with women

* There were no tailors among the ancients. Men's costumes were made at home by the women.

or in their manner. Let him practice one of those trades which are fit for them; that is all very well. And if there absolutely must be true eunuchs, let men who dishonor their sex by taking jobs which do not suit it be reduced to this condition. Their choice proclaims nature's mistake. Correct its mistake one way or another. You will have only done good.

I forbid my pupil unhealthy trades but not hard trades or even dangerous ones. They exercise strength and courage at the same time; they are fit for men alone; women do not pretend to them. How can men not be ashamed to encroach on those that women do?

> Lucatantur paucae, comedunt colliphia paucae.
> Vos lanam trahitis, calathisque peracta refertis
> Vellera . . .*

In Italy one does not see women in shops, and nothing gloomier than the sight of the streets in that country can be imagined by those who are accustomed to the streets of France and England. On seeing fashion merchants sell ribbons, tassels, net, and chenille to ladies, I found these delicate adornments quite ridiculous in big hands made for using the bellows on a forge and striking an anvil. I said to myself, "In this country the women ought to take reprisal by setting up shop as swordmakers and gunsmiths." Oh, let each make and sell the arms of his own sex! To know them, they must be used.

Young man, put the imprint of a man's hand on your labors. Learn to wield the ax and the saw with a vigorous arm, to square a beam, to climb up to the roof of a house, set the ridge on it, and prop it with struts and tie-rods. Then yell for your sister to come to help you with your work as she told you to work at her needlepoint.

I sense that I am saying too much about this for my refined contemporaries, but I sometimes let myself be carried away by the force of arguments. If any man, whoever he may be, is ashamed to work in public armed with a cooper's ax and girded with a leather apron, I see in him nothing more than a slave of opinion, ready to blush at doing good whenever decent people are ridiculed. However, let us cede to the prejudice of fathers all that can do no harm to children's judgment. It is not necessary to practice all the useful professions in order to honor them all. It suffices not to esteem any as beneath oneself. When there is a choice and nothing otherwise determines us, why should we not consult attractiveness, inclination, and suitability in professions of the same rank? Metalwork is useful, even the most useful of all. However, unless a special reason brings me to it, I will not make your son a blacksmith, a locksmith, or an ironsmith. I would not like to see him at his forge with the aspect of a Cyclops. Similarly, I will not make him a mason, still less a shoemaker. All the trades have to be done. But he who can choose ought to look to cleanliness, for this preference is not a result of opinion. On this point the senses decide for us. Finally, I would not like those stupid professions in

---

* Juvenal, *Satires* II 53–55.[20]

which the workers, without industry and almost automatons, never exercise their hand at anything but the same work—weavers, stocking makers, stonecutters. What is the use of employing men of sense in these trades? It is a case of one machine guiding another.

All things well considered, the trade I would most like to be to my pupil's taste is the carpenter's. It is clean; it is useful; it can be practiced at home. It keeps the body sufficiently in shape; it requires skill and industry from the worker; and while the form of the work is determined by utility, elegance and taste are not excluded.

If by chance your pupil's genius were definitely turned toward the speculative sciences, then I would not blame his being given a trade conformable to his inclinations—that he learn, for example, to make mathematical instruments, spyglasses, telescopes, etc.[21]

When Emile learns his trade, I want to learn it with him, for I am convinced that he will only ever learn well what we learn together. We shall, therefore, put both of ourselves in apprenticeship; and we shall not expect to be treated as gentlemen but as true apprentices who are not in it for laughs. Why should we not go the whole way? Czar Peter was a carpenter in the workyard and a drummer for his own troops. Do you think this prince is not your equal in birth or merit? You understand that it is not to Emile that I say this. It is to you, whoever you may be.

Unhappily we cannot spend all of our time at the workbench. We are not only apprentice workers, we are apprentice men; and the apprenticeship in this latter trade is harder and longer than in the former one. How will we do it then? Shall we hire a master of the plane one hour a day as one hires a dancing master? No, for then we would be not apprentices but disciples, and our ambition is not so much to learn carpentry as to raise ourselves to the station of carpenter. Therefore, I am of the opinion that we must go at least once or twice a week and spend the whole day at the master's—that we get up at his hour, be at work before him, eat at his table, work under his orders, and after having had the honor of supping with his family, return, if we wish, to sleep in our hard beds. That is how several trades are learned at once and how one gets practice in manual labor without neglecting the other apprenticeship.

Let us be simple in doing good. Let us not go and reproduce vanity by our efforts to combat it. To pride oneself on having conquered prejudices is to be subjected to them. It is said that, by an ancient practice of the Ottoman house, the great lord is obliged to work with his hands; and everyone knows that the works of a royal hand can only be masterpieces. He therefore distributes magnificently these masterpieces to the nobles of the Porte,[22] and the work is paid for according to the quality of the worker. The evil I see in this is not the alleged harassment; that, on the contrary, is a good thing. By forcing the nobles to share with him the spoils taken from the people, the prince is that much less obliged to pillage the people directly. It is a relief necessary to despotism without which this horrible government would not be able to subsist.

The true evil of such a practice is the idea of his merit which it gives to this poor man. Like King Midas he sees everything he touches turn into gold, but he does not perceive what ears grow as a result.[23] To preserve short ones for our Emile, let us protect his hands from that rich talent. Let the value of what he makes be drawn not from the worker but from the work. Let us never allow his work to be judged except by comparing it to that of good masters; let his work be valued for the work itself and not because it is his. Say of what is well made, "This is well made." But do not add, "Who made that?" If he himself says with a proud and self-satisfied air, "I made it," add coldly, "You or another, it makes no difference; in any event it is work well done."

Good mother, protect yourself above all against the lies which are prepared for you. If your son knows many things, distrust everything he knows. If he has the misfortune of being raised in Paris and of being rich, he is lost. So long as there are skillful artists there, he will have all their talents; but far away from them, he will no longer have any. In Paris the rich man knows everything; the only ignoramus is the poor man. This capital is full of amateurs, especially among the ladies, who produce their work as M. Guillaume contrived his colors.[24] I know of three honorable exceptions to this among men; there may be more. But I know of none among women, and I doubt that there are any. In general, one gets a name in the arts as in the law; one becomes an artist and judges artists as one becomes a doctor of law and a magistrate.

If, therefore, it were once established that it is a fine thing to know a trade, your children would soon know one without learning it. They would pass as masters like the Councillors of Zurich.[25] None of this ceremony for Emile—no appearance and always reality. Let it not be said that he knows, but let him learn in silence. Let him always produce his masterpiece and never pass for a master; he should prove himself a worker not by his title but by his work.

If I have made myself understood up to now, one should conceive how I imperceptibly give my pupil, with the habit of exercising his body and of manual labor, the taste for reflection and meditation. This counterbalances in him the idleness which would result from his indifference to men's judgments and from the calm of his passions. He must work like a peasant and think like a philosopher so as not to be as lazy as a savage. The great secret of education is to make the exercises of the body and those of the mind always serve as relaxations from one another.

But let us avoid beginning too soon instruction which demands a riper spirit. Emile will not be a worker for long without experiencing for himself the inequality of conditions which he had at first only glimpsed. On the basis of the maxims I give him—maxims which are within his reach—he will want to examine me in my turn. In receiving everything from me alone, in seeing himself so close to the state of the poor, he will want to know why I am so far from it. He will perhaps catch me unprepared and ask ticklish questions. "You are rich, you told me so, and I see it. A rich man also owes his work to society, since he is a man. But you, what do you then do for it?" What would a fine governor say to that? I do not know. He would perhaps be fool enough to speak to the child of the care he takes of him. As for me, the workshop gets me out of it. "That is, dear Emile, an excellent question. I promise you to answer concerning my case when you give an answer with which you are satisfied concerning your own case. In the meantime I shall take care to give to you and the poor what surplus I have and to produce a table or a bench every week so as not to be completely good for nothing."

Now we have returned to ourselves. Now our child, ready to stop being a child, has become aware of himself as an individual. Now he senses more than ever the necessity which attaches him to things. After having begun by exercising his body and his senses, we have exercised his mind and his judgment. Finally, we have joined the use of his limbs to that of his faculties. We have made an active and thinking being. It remains for us, in order to complete the man, only to make a loving and feeling being—that is to say, to perfect reason by sentiment. But before entering this new order of things, let us cast our eyes on the one we are leaving and see as exactly as possible where we have gotten.

At first our pupil had only sensations. Now he has ideas. He only felt; now he judges; for from the comparison of several successive or simultaneous sensations and the judgment made of them is born a sort of mixed or complex sensation which I call an idea.

The manner of forming ideas is what gives a character to the human mind. The mind which forms its ideas only on the basis of real relations is a solid mind. The one satisfied with apparent relations is a superficial mind. The one which sees relations such as they are is a precise mind. The one which evaluates them poorly is a defective mind. The one which makes up imaginary relations that have neither reality nor appearance is mad. The one which does not compare at all is imbecilic. The greater or lesser aptitude at comparing ideas and at finding relations is what constitutes in men greater or lesser intelligence, etc.

Simple ideas are only compared sensations. There are judgments in simple sensations as well as in the complex sensations which I call simple ideas. In sensation, judgment is purely passive. It affirms that one feels what one feels. In perception or idea, judgment is active. It brings together, compares, and determines relations which the senses do not determine. This is the entire difference, but it is great. Nature never deceives us. It is always we who deceive ourselves.

I see an eight-year-old child served ice cream. He brings the spoon to his mouth without knowing what it is, and, surprised by the cold, shouts, "Oh, it's burning me!" He experiences a very lively sensation. He knows of none livelier than the heat of fire, and he believes he feels that one. However, he is mistaken. The chill of the cold hurts him, but it does not burn him, and these two sensations are not similar, since those who have experienced both do not confound them. It is not, therefore, the sensation which deceives him but the judgment he makes about it.

It is the same for someone who sees a mirror or an optical gadget for the first time, or who goes into a deep cellar in the heart of winter or summer, or who dips a very hot or very cold hand in tepid water, or who rolls a little ball between two crossed fingers, etc. If he is satisfied with saying what he perceives, what he feels, with his judgment remaining purely passive, it is impossible that he be deceived. But when he judges a thing by its appearance, he is active, he compares, and he establishes by induction relations he does not perceive; then he is deceived or can be deceived. To correct or prevent the error, he needs experience.

Show your pupil at night clouds passing between him and the moon. He will believe that it is the moon passing in the opposite direction and that the clouds are stationary. He will believe it as a result of a hasty induction, because he ordinarily sees little objects moving instead of large ones, and the clouds seem larger to him than the moon, whose distance he cannot estimate. When he is in a drifting boat and looks at the shore from a little way off, he falls into the opposite error and believes he sees the land gliding by. Not sensing that he is in motion, he regards the boat, the sea or the river, and his whole horizon as an immobile whole, of which the shore he sees gliding by seems to him only a part.

The first time a child sees a stick dropped halfway in water, he sees a broken stick. The sensation is true, and it would not fail to be so even if we did not know the reason for this appearance. Therefore, if you ask him what he sees, he says, "A broken stick"—and what he says is true, for it is quite certain he has the sensation of a broken stick. But when, deceived by his judgment, he goes farther and, after affirming that he sees a broken stick, he affirms in addition that what he sees actually is a broken stick, then what he says is false. Why is that? Because then he becomes active and no longer judges by inspection, but rather by induction, in affirming what he does not sense—that is, that the judgment he receives from one sense would be confirmed by another.

Since all our errors come from our judgments, it is clear that if we never needed to judge, we would not need to learn. We would never be in a position to be deceived. We would be happier with our ignorance than we can be with our knowledge. Who denies that the learned know countless true things which the ignorant will never know? Are the learned thereby closer to the truth? On the contrary, they get farther from it in advancing; because the vanity of judging makes even more progress than enlightenment does, each truth that they learn comes only with a hundred false judgments. It is entirely evident that the learned companies of Europe are only public schools of lies. And there are very certainly more errors in the Academy of Sciences than in a whole nation of Hurons.

Since the more men know, the more they are deceived, the only means of avoiding error is ignorance. Do not judge, and you will never be mistaken. That is the lesson of nature as well as of reason. Beyond the immediate relations—very small in number and very easily sensed —which things have to us, we naturally have only a profound indifference toward all the rest. A savage would not take a step out of his way to go and see the working of the finest machine and all the wonders of electricity. "Of what importance is it to me?" is the phrase most familiar to the ignorant man and most suitable for the wise one.

BOOK III

But unhappily this phrase does not work for us anymore. Everything is important for us, since we are dependent on everything; and our curiosity necessarily extends with our needs. That is why I attribute very great curiosity to the philosopher and none at all to the savage. The latter needs no one; the former needs everyone and especially admirers.

I will be told that I abandon nature. I do not believe that at all. It chooses its instruments and regulates them according to need, not to opinion. Now, needs change according to the situation of men. There is a great difference between the natural man living in the state of nature and the natural man living in the state of society. Emile is not a savage to be relegated to the desert. He is a savage made to inhabit cities. He has to know how to find his necessities in them, to take advantage of their inhabitants, and to live, if not like them, at least with them.

Amidst so many new relations on which he is going to depend, he will, in spite of himself, have to judge; let us teach him, therefore, to judge well.

The best way to teach someone to judge well is the one which tends to simplify our experiences and even to make us able to omit them without falling into error. From this it follows that after having for a long time verified the relations of one sense by another, one still has to learn to verify the relations of each sense by itself without need of recourse to another sense. Then each sensation will become an idea for us, and this idea will always conform to the truth. This is the sort of accomplishment with which I have tried to fill this third age of human life.

This way of proceeding demands a patience and a circumspection of which few masters are capable, and without which the disciple will never learn to judge. If, for example, he is deceived about the appearance of the broken stick, and to show him his error you are in a hurry to pull the stick out of the water, you will perhaps undeceive him. But what will you teach him? Nothing but what he would soon have learned by himself. Oh, it is not that which has to be done! The goal is less to teach him a truth than to show him how he must always go about discovering the truth. In order to instruct him better, you must not undeceive him so soon. Let us take Emile and me as an example.

In the first place, every child raised in the ordinary way will not fail to answer affirmatively the second of the two questions posed above. "It is surely a broken stick," he will say. I doubt very much that Emile would give me the same answer. Not seeing the necessity of being learned, or of appearing to be, he is never in a hurry to judge. He judges only on the basis of evidence, and he is far removed from finding it on this occasion—he who knows how much our judgments about appearances are subject to illusion, be it only the illusion of perspective.

Moreover, since he knows by experience that my most frivolous questions always have some object that he does not perceive at first, he has not gotten the habit of answering them lightly. On the contrary, he is distrustful of them. He is attentive to them. He examines them with great care before responding to them. He never gives me a response with which he himself is not satisfied, and he is difficult to satisfy. Finally, we both pride ourselves not on knowing the truth of things but only on not falling into error. We would be far more embarrassed at contenting ourselves with a reason which is not good than at not finding one at all. "I don't know" is a phrase which goes over so well with both of us and which we repeat so often that it no longer costs either of us a thing. But whether he blurts out this lightheaded answer or avoids it with our convenient "I don't know," my reply is the same, "Let's see, let's examine it."

The stick, half dipped in water, is fixed in a perpendicular position. To know if it is broken, as it appears to be, how many things must we do before drawing it from the water or putting a hand to it?

1. First we walk all around the stick, and we see that the break turns as we do. Therefore, it is our eye alone which changes it, and glances do not move bodies.

2. We look from straight above at the end of the stick which is out of the water. Then the stick is no longer curved. The end near our eye exactly hides the other end from us.[26] Did our eye straighten out the stick?

3. We stir the water's surface. We see the stick fold up in many pieces, move in zigzags, and follow the undulations of the water. Does the movement we give to this water suffice to break, soften, and thus dissolve the stick?

4. We let the water flow out, and we see the stick straighten out little by little as the water goes down. Is this not more than enough for clarifying the fact and discovering refraction? Then it is not true that sight deceives us, since we need nothing but it alone to rectify the errors we attribute to it.

Let us suppose that the child is stupid enough not to sense the result of these experiences. It is then that touch must be called to the aid of sight. Instead of pulling the stick out of the water, leave it in its position, and let the child run his hand from one end to the other. He will not feel an angle. Therefore, the stick is not broken.[27]

You will tell me that there are not only judgments here but formal reasonings. It is true. But do you not see that as soon as the mind has gotten as far as ideas, every judgment is a reasoning? The consciousness of every sensation is a proposition, a judgment. Therefore, as soon as one compares one sensation with another, one reasons. The art of judging and the art of reasoning are exactly the same.

I would prefer that Emile never know dioptrics if he cannot learn it around this stick. He will not have dissected insects; he will not have counted the spots on the sun. He will not know what a microscope and a telescope are. Your learned pupils will make fun of his ignorance. They will not be wrong; for before he uses these instruments, I intend him to invent them. And you may well suspect that this will not come so soon.

This is the spirit of my whole method in this part. If the child rolls a little ball between two crossed fingers and believes he feels two balls, I shall not permit him to look at it before he is convinced there is only one.

These clarifications will suffice, I think, to show distinctly the progress of my pupil's mind up to now and the route by which he made this progress. But you are perhaps frightened off by the multitude of things I have caused to pass before him. You are afraid that I am overwhelming his mind with this quantity of knowledge. On the contrary, I teach him far more to be ignorant of these things than to know them. I show him the route of science—easy, it is true, but long, immense, slow to traverse. I make him take the first steps so that he recognizes the way in, but I never permit him to go far.

Forced to learn by himself, he uses his reason and not another's; for to give nothing to opinion, one must given nothing to authority, and most of our errors come to us far less from ourselves than from others. From this constant exercise there ought to result a vigor of mind similar to the vigor given to bodies by work and fatigue. Another advantage is that one advances only in proportion to one's strength. The mind, no less than the body, bears only what it can bear. When understanding appropriates things before depositing them in memory, what it draws from memory later belongs to it; whereas, by overburdening memory without the participation of understanding, one runs the risk of never withdrawing anything from memory suitable for understanding.

Emile has little knowledge, but what he has is truly his own. He knows nothing halfway. Among the small number of things he knows and knows well, the most important is that there are many things of which he is ignorant and which he can know one day; there are many more that other men know that he will never know in his life; and there are an infinite number of others that no man will ever know. Emile has a mind that is universal not by its learning but by its faculty to acquire learning; a mind that is open, intelligent, ready for everything, and, as Montaigne says, if not instructed, at least able to be instructed.[28] It is enough for me that he knows how to find the "what's it good for?" in everything he does and the "why?" in everything he believes. Once again, my object is not to give him science but to teach him to acquire science when needed, to make him estimate it for exactly what it is worth, and to make him love the truth above all. With this method one advances little, but one never takes a useless step, and one is not forced to go backward.

Emile has only natural and purely physical knowledge. He does not know even the name of history, or what metaphysics and morals are. He knows the essential relations of man to things but nothing of the moral relations of man to man. He hardly knows how to generalize ideas and hardly how to make abstractions. He sees common qualities in certain bodies without reasoning about these qualities in themselves. He knows abstract extension with the aid of the figures of geometry, and he knows abstract quantity with the aid of the signs of algebra. These figures and these signs are the supports of the abstractions on which his senses rest. He seeks to know things not by their nature but only by the relations which are connected with his interest. He estimates what is foreign to him only in relation to himself. But this estimation is exact and sure. Whim and convention count for nothing in it. What is more useful to him, he takes more seriously; never deviating from this way of evaluating, he grants nothing to opinion.

Emile is laborious, temperate, patient, firm, and full of courage. His imagination is in no way inflamed and never enlarges dangers. He is sensitive to few ills, and he knows constancy in endurance because he has not learned to quarrel with destiny. With respect to death, he does not yet know well what it is; but since he is accustomed to submitting to the law of necessity without resistance, when he has to die, he will die without moaning and without struggling. This is all that nature permits at this most abhorred of all moments. To live free and to depend little on human things is the best means of learning how to die.

In a word, of virtue Emile has all that relates to himself. To have the social virtues, too, he lacks only the knowledge of the relations which demand them; he lacks only the learning which his mind is all ready to receive.

He considers himself without regard to others and finds it good that others do not think of him. He demands nothing of anyone and believes he owes nothing to anyone. He is alone in human society; he counts on himself alone. More than anyone else, he has the right to count on himself, for he is all that one can be at his age. He has no errors, or only those that are inevitable for us. He has no vices, or only those against which no man can guarantee himself. He has a healthy body, agile limbs, a precise and unprejudiced mind, a heart that is free and without passions. *Amour-propre*, the first and most natural of all the passions, is still hardly aroused in him. Without troubling the repose of anyone, he has lived satisfied, happy, and free insofar as nature has permitted. Do you find that a child who has come in this way to his fifteenth year has wasted the preceding ones?

End of the Third Book

BOOK IV

HOW RAPID is our journey on this earth! The first quarter of life has been lived before one knows the use of it. The last quarter is lived when one has ceased to enjoy it. At first we do not know how to live; soon we can no longer live; and in the interval which separates these two useless extremities, three-quarters of the time remaining to us is consumed by sleep, work, pain, constraint, and efforts of all kinds. Life is short, not so much because it lasts a short time as because we have almost none of that short time for savoring it. The moment of death may well be distant from that of birth, but life is always too short when this space is poorly filled.

We are, so to speak, born twice: once to exist and once to live; once for our species and once for our sex. Those who regard women as an imperfect man are doubtless wrong, but the external analogy is on their side. Up to the nubile age children of the two sexes have nothing apparent to distinguish them: the same visage, the same figure, the same complexion, the same voice. Everything is equal: girls are children, boys are children; the same name suffices for beings so much alike. Males whose ulterior sexual development is prevented maintain this similarity their whole lives; they are always big children. And women, since they never lose this same similarity, seem in many respects never to be anything else.

But man in general is not made to remain always in childhood. He leaves it at the time prescribed by nature; and this moment of crisis, although rather short, has far-reaching influences.

As the roaring of the sea precedes a tempest from afar, this stormy revolution is proclaimed by the murmur of the nascent passions. A mute fermentation warns of danger's approach. A change in humor, frequent anger, a mind in constant agitation, makes the child almost unmanageable. He becomes deaf to the voice which made him docile. His feverishness turns him into a lion. He disregards his guide; he no longer wishes to be governed.

To the moral signs of a deteriorating humor are joined noticeable changes in his looks. His face develops expression and takes on character. The sparse and soft cotton growing on the lower part of his cheeks darkens and gains consistency. His voice breaks or, rather, he loses it; he is neither child nor man and can take the tone of neither. His eyes, those organs of the soul which have said nothing up to now, find a language and acquire expressiveness. A nascent fire animates them; their glances, more lively, still have a holy innocence, but they no longer have their first imbecility. He senses already that they can say too much; he begins to know how to lower them and to blush. He becomes sensitive before knowing what he is sensing. He is uneasy without reason for being so. All this can come slowly and still leave you time. But if his vivacity makes him too impatient; if his anger changes into fury; if he is irritable and then tender from one moment to the next; if he sheds tears without cause; if, when near objects which begin to become dangerous for him, his pulse rises and his eye is inflamed; if the hand of a woman placed on his makes him shiver; if he gets flustered or is intimidated near her—Ulysses, O wise Ulysses, be careful. The goatskins you closed with so much care are open. The winds are already loose. No longer leave the tiller for an instant, or all is lost.[1]

This is the second birth of which I have spoken. It is now that man is truly born to life and now that nothing human is foreign to him. Up to now our care has only been a child's game. It takes on true importance only at present. This period, when ordinary educations end, is properly the one when ours ought to begin. But to present this new plan well, let us treat more fundamentally the state of the things which relate to it.

Our passions are the principal instruments of our preservation. It is, therefore, an enterprise as vain as it is ridiculous to want to destroy them—it is to control nature, it is to reform the work of God. If God were to tell men to annihilate the passions which He gives him, God would will and not will; He would contradict Himself. Never did He give this senseless order. Nothing of the kind is written in the human heart. And what God wants a man to do, He does not have told to him by another man. He tells it to him Himself; He writes it in the depths of his heart.

I would find someone who wanted to prevent the birth of the passions almost as mad as someone who wanted to annihilate them; and those who believed that this was my project up to now would surely have understood me very badly.

But would it be reasoning well to conclude, from the fact that it is in man's nature to have passions, that all the passions that we feel in ourselves and see in others are natural? Their source is natural, it is true. But countless alien streams have swollen it. It is a great river which constantly grows and in which one could hardly find a few drops of its first waters. Our natural passions are very limited. They are the instruments of our freedom; they tend to preserve us. All those which subject us and destroy us come from elsewhere. Nature does not give them to us. We appropriate them to the detriment of nature.

The source of our passions, the origin and the principle of all the others, the only one born with man and which never leaves him so long as he lives is self-love—a primitive, innate passion, which is anterior to every other, and of which all others are in a sense only modifications. In this sense, if you wish, all passions are natural. But most of these modifications have alien causes without which they would never have come to pass; and these same modifications, far from being advantageous for us, are harmful. They alter the primary goal and are at odds with their own principle. It is then that man finds himself outside of nature and sets himself in contradiction with himself.

The love of oneself is always good and always in conformity with order. Since each man is specially entrusted with his own preservation, the first and most important of his cares is and ought to be to watch over it constantly. And how could he watch over it if he did not take the greatest interest in it?

Therefore, we have to love ourselves to preserve ourselves; and it follows immediately from the same sentiment that we love what preserves us. Every child is attached to his nurse. Romulus must have been attached to the wolf that suckled him. At first this attachment is purely mechanical. What fosters the well-being of an individual attracts him; what harms him repels him. This is merely a blind instinct. What transforms this instinct into sentiment, attachment into love, aversion into hate, is the intention manifested to harm us or to be useful to us. One is never passionate about insensible beings which merely follow the impulsion given to them. But those from whom one expects good or ill by their inner disposition, by their will—those we see acting freely for us or against us—inspire in us sentiments similar to those they manifest toward us. We seek what serves us, but we love what wants to serve us. We flee what harms us, but we hate what wants to harm us.

A child's first sentiment is to love himself; and the second, which derives from the first, is to love those who come near him, for in the state of weakness that he is in, he does not recognize anyone except by the assistance and care he receives. At first the attachment he has for his nurse and his governess is only habit. He seeks them because he needs them and is well off in having them; it is recognition rather than benevolence. He needs much time to understand that not only are they useful to him but they want to be; and it is then that he begins to love them.

A child is therefore naturally inclined to benevolence, because he sees that everything approaching him is inclined to assist him; and from this observation he gets the habit of a sentiment favorable to his species. But as he extends his relations, his needs, and his active or passive dependencies, the sentiment of his connections with others is awakened and produces the sentiment of duties and preferences. Then the child becomes imperious, jealous, deceitful, and vindictive. If he is bent to obedience, he does not see the utility of what he is ordered, and he attributes it to caprice, to the intention of tormenting him; and he revolts. If he is obeyed, as soon as something resists him, he sees in it a rebellion, an intention to resist him. He beats the chair or the table for having disobeyed him. Self-love, which regards only ourselves, is contented when our true needs are satisfied. But *amour-propre,* which makes comparisons, is never content and never could be, because this sentiment, preferring ourselves to others, also demands others to prefer us to themselves, which is impossible. This is how the gentle and affectionate passions are born of self-love, and how the hateful and irascible passions are born of *amour-propre*. Thus what makes man essentially good is to have few needs and to compare himself little to others; what makes him essentially wicked is to have many needs and to depend very much on opinion. On the basis of this principle it is easy to see how all the passions of children and men can be directed to good or bad. It is true that since they are not able always to live alone, it will be difficult for them always to be good. This same difficulty will necessarily increase with their relations; and this, above all, is why the dangers of society make art and care all the more indispensable for us to forestall in the human heart the depravity born of their new needs.

The study suitable for man is that of his relations. So long as he knows himself only in his physical being, he ought to study himself in his relations with things. This is the job of his childhood. When he begins to sense his moral being, he ought to study himself in his relations with men. This is the job of his whole life, beginning from the point we have now reached.[2]

As soon as man has need of a companion, he is no longer an isolated being. His heart is no longer alone. All his relations with his species, all the affections of his soul are born with this one. His first passion soon makes the others ferment.

The inclination of instinct is indeterminate. One sex is attracted to the other; that is the movement of nature. Choice, preferences, and personal attachments are the work of enlightenment, prejudice, and habit. Time and knowledge are required to make us capable of love. One loves only after having judged; one prefers only after having compared. These judgments are made without one's being aware of it, but they are nonetheless real. True love, whatever is said of it, will always be honored by men; for although its transports lead us astray, although it does not exclude odious qualities from the heart that feels it—and even produces them—it nevertheless always presupposes estimable qualities without which one would not be in a condition to feel it. This choosing, which is held to be the opposite of reason, comes to us from it. Love has been presented as blind because it has better eyes than we do and sees relations we are not able to perceive. For a man who had no idea of merit or beauty, every woman would be equally good, and the first comer would always be the most lovable. Far from arising from nature, love is the rule and the bridle of nature's inclinations. It is due to love that, except for the beloved object, one sex ceases to be anything for the other.

One wants to obtain the preference that one grants. Love must be reciprocal. To be loved, one has to make oneself lovable. To be preferred, one has to make oneself more lovable than another, more lovable than every other, at least in the eyes of the beloved object. This is the source of the first glances at one's fellows; this is the source of the first comparisons with them; this is the source of emulation, rivalries, and jealousy. A heart full of an overflowing sentiment likes

BOOK IV

to open itself. From the need for a mistress is soon born the need for a friend. He who senses how sweet it is to be loved would want to be loved by everyone; and all could not want preference without there being many malcontents. With love and friendship are born dissensions, enmity, and hate. From the bosom of so many diverse passions I see opinion raising an unshakable throne, and stupid mortals, subjected to its empire, basing their own existence on the judgments of others.

Extend these ideas, and you will see where our *amour-propre* gets the form we believe natural to it, and how self-love, ceasing to be an absolute sentiment, becomes pride in great souls, vanity in small ones, and feeds itself constantly in all at the expense of their neighbors. This species of passion, not having its germ in children's hearts, cannot be born in them of itself; it is we alone who put it there, and it never takes root except by our fault. But this is no longer the case with the young man's heart. Whatever we may do, these passions will be born in spite of us. It is therefore time to change method.

Let us begin with some important reflections on the critical state we are dealing with here. The transition from childhood to puberty is not so determined by nature that it does not vary in individuals according to their temperaments and in peoples according to their climates. Everyone knows the distinction observable in this regard between hot and cold countries; and each of us sees that ardent temperaments are formed sooner than others. But one can be deceived as to the causes and can often attribute to physical causes what must be imputed to moral ones. This is one of the most frequent abuses committed by the philosophy of our age. Nature's instruction is late and slow; men's is almost always premature. In the former case the senses wake the imagination; in the latter the imagination wakes the senses; it gives them a precocious activity which cannot fail to enervate and weaken individuals first and in the long run the species itself. An observation more general and more certain than that of the effect of climates is that puberty and sexual potency always arrive earlier in learned and civilized peoples than in ignorant and barbarous peoples.* Children have a singular sagacity in discerning the bad morals covered over by all the apish posturings of propriety. The purified language dictated to them, the lessons of decency given to them, the veil of mystery that is supposed to be drawn over their eyes, are only so many spurs to their curiosity. From the way this is gone about it is clear that

* "In the cities," says M. de Buffon, "and among the well-to-do, accustomed to abundant and succulent foods, children come to this state sooner. In the country and among poor people the children are slower because they are badly and too little fed. They need two or three years more." [*Histoire naturelle*, vol. IV, p. 238.] I accept the observation but not the explanation, since in countries where villagers are very well fed and eat a lot, as in the Valois, and even in certain mountainous cantons of Italy, like Friuli, the age of puberty in the two sexes is also later than in the bosom of cities where, to satisfy vanity, an extreme parsimony governs spending on food and where most people have, as the proverb says, "velvet robes and stomachs filled with bran." One is surprised in these mountains to see big boys, as strong as men, who still have high voices and beardless chins, and big girls, otherwise quite developed, who do not have the periodic sign of their sex. This difference appears to me to come solely from the fact that, due to the simplicity of their morals, their imagination, peaceful and calm for a longer time, causes their blood to ferment later and makes their temperament less precocious.

the pretense of hiding something from them serves only to teach them about it; of all the instruction given them, this is the one of which they take most advantage.

Consult experience. You will understand to what extent this senseless method accelerates nature's work and ruins the temperament. This is one of the principal causes of the degeneracy of the races in cities. The young people, exhausted early, remain small, weak, and ill-formed; they age instead of growing, as the vine that has been made to bear fruit in the spring languishes and dies before autumn.

It is necessary to have lived among coarse and simple peoples to know up to what age a happy ignorance can prolong the innocence of children there. It is a spectacle that is at the same time touching and laughable to see the two sexes, abandoned to the security of their hearts, prolong in the flower of age and beauty the naïve games of childhood and show by their very familiarity the purity of their pleasures. When finally these amiable young people come to marriage, the two spouses give each other the first fruits of their persons and are thereby dearer to one another. Multitudes of healthy and robust children become the pledges of an incorruptible union and the fruit of the prudence of their parents' early years.

If the age at which man acquires knowledge of his sex differs as much due to the effect of education as to the action of nature, it follows that this age can be accelerated or retarded according to the way in which children are raised; and if the body gains or loses consistency to the extent that this progress is retarded or accelerated, it follows again that the greater the effort made to retard it, the more a young man acquires vigor and force. I am still speaking only of purely physical effects. It will soon be seen that the effects are not limited to these.

From these reflections I draw the solution to the question so often debated—whether it is fitting to enlighten children early concerning the objects of their curiosity, or whether it is better to put them off the trail with little falsehoods? I think one ought to do neither the one nor the other. In the first place, this curiosity does not come to them without someone's having provided the occasion for it. One must therefore act in such a way that they do not have such curiosity. In the second place, questions one is not forced to answer do not require deceiving the child who asks them. It is better to impose silence on him than to answer him by lying. He will be little surprised by this law if care has been taken to subject him to it in inconsequential things. Finally, if one decides to answer, let it be with the greatest simplicity, without mystery, without embarrassment, without a smile. There is much less danger in satisfying the child's curiosity than there is in exciting it.

Let your responses always be solemn, short, and firm, without ever appearing to hesitate. I do not need to add that they ought to be true. One cannot teach children the danger of lying to men without being aware of the greater danger, on the part of men, of lying to children. A single proved lie told by the master to the child would ruin forever the whole fruit of the education.

An absolute ignorance concerning certain matters is perhaps what would best suit children. But let them learn early what is impossible to hide from them always. Either their curiosity must not be aroused in any way, or it must be satisfied before the age at which it is no longer without danger. Your conduct with your pupil in this respect depends a great deal on his particular situation, the societies which surround him, the circumstances in which it is expected that he might find himself, etc. It is important here to leave nothing to chance; and if you are not sure of keeping him ignorant of the difference between the sexes until he is sixteen, take care that he learn it before he is ten.

I do not like it when too pure a language is affected with children or when long detours, which they notice, are made to avoid giving things their true names. Good morals in these matters always contain much simplicity, but imaginations soiled by vice make the ear delicate and force a constant refinement of expression. Coarse terms are inconsequential; it is lascivious ideas which must be kept away.

Although modesty is natural to the human species, naturally children have none. Modesty is born only with the knowledge of evil, and how could children, who do not and should not have this knowledge, have the sentiment which is its effect? To give them lessons in modesty and decency is to teach them that there are shameful and indecent things. It is to give them a secret desire to know those things. Sooner or later they succeed, and the first spark which touches the imagination inevitably accelerates the inflammation of the senses. Whoever blushes is already guilty. True innocence is ashamed of nothing.

Children do not have the same desires as men; but since they are just as subject to uncleanness offensive to the senses, they can from that very subjection get the same lessons in propriety. Follow the spirit of nature which, by putting in the same place the organs of the secret pleasures and those of the disgusting needs, inspires in us the same cares at different ages, now due to one idea, then due to another; in the man due to modesty, in the child due to cleanliness.

I see only one good means of preserving children in their innocence; it is for all those who surround them to respect and to love it. Without that, all the restraint one tries to use with them is sooner or later belied. A smile, a wink, a careless gesture, tells them everything one seeks to hide from them. To learn it, they need only see that one wanted to hide it from them. The delicacy of the turns of phrase and of the expressions which polite people use with one another is completely misplaced in relation to children since it assumes an enlightenment they ought not to have; but when one truly honors their simplicity, one easily takes on, in speaking to them, the simplicity of the terms which suit them. There is a certain naïveté of language which fits and pleases innocence. This is the true tone which turns a child away from a dangerous curiosity. In speaking simply to him about everything, one does not let him suspect that anything remains to be told him. In joining to coarse words the displeasing ideas suitable to them, the first fire of imagination is smothered. He is not forbidden to pronounce these words and to have these ideas; but without his being aware of it, he is made to have a repugnance against recalling them. And how much embarrassment this naïve freedom spares those who, drawing such freedom from their own hearts, always say what should be said and always say just what they feel!

"Where do children come from?" An embarrassing question which comes naturally enough to children, and to which an indiscreet or a prudent answer is sometimes decisive for their morals and their health for their whole lives. The most expeditious way that a mother can imagine for putting it off without deceiving her son is to impose silence on him. That would be good if one had accustomed him to it for a long time in regard to unimportant questions and he did not suspect mysteries in this new tone. But rarely does she leave it at that. "That's the secret of married people," she will tell him. "Little boys shouldn't be so curious." This is very good for getting the mother out of trouble. But she should know that the little boy, stung by this contemptuous air, will not have a moment's rest before he has learned the secret of married people, and that he will not be long in learning it.

Permit me to report a very different answer which I heard given to the same question, one which was all the more striking as it came from a woman as modest in her speech as in her manners. When necessary, however, she knew how to trample on the false fear of blame and the vain remarks of mockers for the sake of virtue and her son's good. Not long before the child had passed in his urine a little stone which had torn his urethera but had been forgotten when the illness passed. "Mama," said the giddy little fellow, "where do children come from?" "My child," answered the mother without hesitation, "women piss them out with pains which sometimes cost them their lives." Let madmen laugh and fools be scandalized; but let the wise consider whether they can ever find a more judicious answer or one that better achieves its purposes.

In the first place, the idea of a need which is natural and known to the child turns aside that of a mysterious process. The accessory ideas of pain and death cover this process with a veil of sadness which deadens the imagination and represses curiosity. Everything turns the mind toward the consequences of the delivery and not toward its causes. The infirmities of human nature, distasteful objects, images of suffering—these are the clarifications to which this answer leads, if the repugnance it inspires permits the child to ask for them. How will the restlessness of the desires be awakened in conversations thus directed? And, nevertheless, you see that the truth has not been adulterated and there was no need to take advantage of one's pupil instead of instructing him.

Your children read. From their reading they get knowledge they would not have if they had not read. If they study, the imagination catches fire and intensifies in the silence of their rooms. If they live in society, they hear odd talk; they see things that strike them. They have been well persuaded that they are men; therefore, whatever men do in their presence serves as the occasion for them to investigate how it applies to them. The actions of others must surely serve as models for them when the judgments of others serve as laws for them. The domestics who are made dependent on them, and are consequently interested in pleasing them, pay their court to them at the expense of good morals. Laughing governesses make remarks to them at four which the most brazen women would not dare to make to them at fifteen. Soon the governesses forget what they said, but the children do not forget what they heard. Naughty conversations prepare the way for libertine morals. The rascally lackey debauches the child, and the latter's secret acts as a guarantee for the former's.

The child raised according to his age is alone. He knows no attachments other than those of habit. He loves his sister as he loves his watch, and his friend as his dog. He does not feel himself to be of any sex, of any species. Man and woman are equally alien to him. He does not consider anything they do or say to be related to himself. He neither sees nor hears nor pays any attention to it. Their speeches interest him no more than do the examples they set. All of that is unsuitable for him. It is not an artful untruth which is imparted to him by this method; it is nature's ignorance. The time is coming when this same nature takes care to enlighten its pupil; and it is only then that it has put him in a condition to profit without risk from the lessons it gives him. This is the principle. The detailed rules do not belong to my subject, and the means I propose with a view to other goals serve also as examples for this one.

Do you wish to put order and regularity in the nascent passions? Extend the period during which they develop in order that they have the time to be arranged as they are born. Then it is not man who orders them; it is nature itself. Your care is only to let it arrange its work. If your pupil were alone, you would have nothing to do. But everything surrounding him influences his imagination. The torrent of prejudices carries him away. To restrain him, he must be pushed in the opposite direction. Sentiment must enchain imagination, and reason silence the opinion of men. The source of all the passions is sensibility; imagination determines their bent. Every being who has a sense of his relations ought to be affected when these relations are altered, and he imagines, or believes he imagines, others more suitable to his nature. It is the errors of imagination which transform into vices the passions of all limited beings—even those of angels, if they have any,[3] for they would have to know the nature of all beings in order to know what relations best suit their nature.

This is, then, the summary of the whole of human wisdom in the use of the passions: (1) To have a sense of the true relations of man, with respect to the species as well as the individual. (2) To order all the affections of the soul according to these relations.

But is man the master of ordering his affections according to this or that relation? Without a doubt, if he is master of directing his imagination toward this or that object or of giving it this or that habit. Besides, the issue here is less what a man can do for himself than what we can do for our pupil by the choice of circumstances in which we put him. To set forth the proper means for keeping him in the order of nature is to say enough about how he can depart from it.

So long as his sensibility remains limited to his own individuality, there is nothing moral in his actions. It is only when it begins to extend outside of himself that it takes on, first, the sentiments and, then, the notions of good and evil which truly constitute him as a man and an integral part of his species. It is on this first point, then, that we must initially fix our observations.

These observations are difficult because, in order to make them, we must reject the examples which are before our eyes and seek for those in which the successive developments take place according to the order of nature.

A mannered, polite, civilized child, who only awaits the power of putting to work the premature instructions he has received, is never mistaken as to the moment when this power has come to him. Far from waiting for it, he accelerates it. He gives a precocious fermentation to his blood. He knows what the object of his desires ought to be long before he even experiences them. It is not nature which excites him; it is he who forces nature. It has nothing more to teach him in making him a man. He was one in thought a long time before being one in fact.

The true course of nature is more gradual and slower. Little by little the blood is inflamed, the spirits are produced, the temperament is formed. The wise worker who directs the manufacture takes care to perfect all his instruments before putting them to work. A long restlessness precedes the first desires; a long ignorance puts them off the track. One desires without knowing what. The blood ferments and is agitated; a superabundance of life seeks to extend itself outward. The eye becomes animated and looks over other beings. One begins to take an interest in those surrounding us; one begins to feel that one is not made to live alone. It is thus that the heart is opened to the human affections and becomes capable of attachment.

The first sentiment of which a carefully raised young man is capable is not love; it is friendship. The first act of his nascent imagination is to teach him that he has fellows; and the species affects him before the female sex. Here is another advantage of prolonged innocence— that of profiting from nascent sensibility to sow in the young adolescent's heart the first seeds of humanity. This advantage is all the more precious since now is the only time of life when the same attentions can have a true success.

I have always seen that young people who are corrupted early and given over to women and debauchery are inhuman and cruel. The heat of their temperaments made them impatient, vindictive, and wild. Their imaginations, filled by a single object, rejected all the rest. They knew neither pity nor mercy. They would have sacrificed fathers, mothers, and the whole universe to the least of their pleasures. On the contrary, a young man raised in a happy simplicity is drawn by the first movements of nature toward the tender and affectionate passions. His compassionate heart is moved by the sufferings of his fellows. He has a thrill of satisfaction at seeing his comrade again; his arms know how to find caressing embraces; his eyes know how to shed tears of tenderness. He is sensitive to the shame of displeasing, to the regret of having offended. If the ardor of his inflamed blood makes him too intense, easily carried away, and angered, a moment later all the goodness of his heart is seen in the effusion of his repentance. He cries, he moans about the wound he has inflicted. He would want to redeem the blood he has shed with his own. All of his fury is extinguished, all of his pride humiliated before the sentiment of his wrong. Is he offended himself? At the height of his fury, an excuse, a word disarms him. He pardons the injuries of others as gladly as he makes amends for his own. Adolescence is not the age of vengeance or of hate; it is that of commiseration, clemency, and generosity. Yes, I maintain, and I do not fear being contradicted by experience, that a child who is not ill born, and who has preserved his innocence until he is twenty, is at that age the most generous, the best, the most loving and lovable of men. You have never been told anything of the kind. I can well believe it. Your philosophers, raised in all the corruption of the colleges, make no effort to learn this.

It is man's weakness which makes him sociable; it is our common miseries which turn our hearts to humanity; we would owe humanity nothing if we were not men. Every attachment is a sign of insufficiency. If each of us had no need of others, he would hardly think of uniting himself with them. Thus from our very infirmity is born our frail happiness. A truly happy being is a solitary being. God alone enjoys an absolute happiness. But who among us has the idea of it? If some imperfect being could suffice unto himself, what would he enjoy according to us? He would be alone; he would be miserable. I do not conceive how someone who needs nothing can love anything. I do not conceive how someone who loves nothing can be happy.

It follows from this that we are attached to our fellows less by the sentiment of their pleasures than by the sentiment of their pains, for we see far better in the latter the identity of our natures with theirs and the guarantees of their attachment to us. If our common needs unite us by interest, our common miseries unite us by affection. The sight of a happy man inspires in others less love than envy. They would gladly accuse him of usurping a right he does not have in giving himself an exclusive happiness; and *amour-propre* suffers, too, in making us feel that this man has no need of us. But who does not pity the unhappy man whom he sees suffering? Who would not want to deliver him from his ills if it only cost a wish for that? Imagination puts us in the place of the miserable man rather than in that of the happy man. We feel that one of these conditions touches us more closely than the other. Pity is sweet because, in putting ourselves in the place of the one who suffers, we nevertheless feel the pleasure of not suffering as he does. Envy is bitter because the sight of a happy man, far from putting the envious man in his place, makes the envious man regret not being there. It seems that the one exempts us from the ills he suffers, and the other takes from us the goods he enjoys.

Do you wish, then, to excite and nourish in the heart of a young man the first movements of nascent sensibility and turn his character toward beneficence and goodness? Do not put the seeds of pride, vanity, and envy in him by the deceptive image of the happiness of men. Do not expose his eyes at the outset to the pomp of courts, the splendor of palaces, or the appeal of the theater. Do not take him to the circles of the great, to brilliant assemblies. Show him the exterior of high society only after having put him in a condition to evaluate it in itself. To show him the world before he knows men is not to form him, it is to corrupt him; it is not to instruct him, it is to deceive him.

Men are not naturally kings, or lords, or courtiers, or rich men. All are born naked and poor; all are subject to the miseries of life, to sorrows, ills, needs, and pains of every kind. Finally, all are condemned to death. This is what truly belongs to man. This is what no mortal is exempt from. Begin, therefore, by studying in human nature what is most inseparable from it, what best characterizes humanity.

At sixteen the adolescent knows what it is to suffer, for he has himself suffered. But he hardly knows that other beings suffer too. To see it without feeling it is not to know it; and as I have said a hundred times, the child, not imagining what others feel, knows only his own ills. But when the first development of his senses lights the fire of imagination, he begins to feel himself in his fellows, to be moved by their complaints and to suffer from their pains. It is then that the sad picture of suffering humanity ought to bring to his heart the first tenderness it has ever experienced.

If this moment is not easy to notice in your children, whom do you blame for it? You instruct them so early in playing at sentiment; you teach them its language so soon that, speaking always with the same accent, they turn your lessons against you and leave you no way of distinguishing when they cease to lie and begin to feel what they say. But look at my Emile. At the age to which I have brought him he has neither felt nor lied. Before knowing what it is to love, he has said, "I love you," to no one. The countenance he ought to put on when he goes into the room of his sick father, mother, or governor has not been prescribed to him. He has not been showed the art of affecting sadness he does not feel. He has not feigned tears at the death of anyone, for he does not know what dying is. The same insensibility he has in his heart is also in his manners. Indifferent to everything outside of himself like all other children, he takes an interest in no one. All that distinguishes him is his not caring to appear interested and his not being false like them.

Emile, having reflected little on sensitive beings, will know late what it is to suffer and die. He will begin to have gut reactions at the sounds of complaints and cries, the sight of blood flowing will make him avert his eyes; the convulsions of a dying animal will cause him an ineffable distress before he knows whence come these new movements within him. If he had remained stupid and barbaric, he would not have them; if he were more learned, he would know their source. He has already compared too many ideas to feel nothing and not enough to have a conception of what he feels.

Thus is born pity, the first relative sentiment which touches the human heart according to the order of nature. To become sensitive and pitying, the child must know that there are beings like him who suffer what he has suffered, who feel the pains he has felt, and that there are others whom he ought to conceive of as able to feel them too. In fact, how do we let ourselves be moved by pity if not by transporting ourselves outside of ourselves and identifying with the suffering animal, by leaving, as it were, our own being to take on its being? We suffer only so much as we judge that it suffers. It is not in ourselves, it is in him that we suffer. Thus, no one becomes sensitive until his imagination is animated and begins to transport him out of himself.

To excite and nourish this nascent sensibility, to guide it or follow it in its natural inclination, what is there to do other than to offer the young man objects on which the expansive force of his heart can act—objects which swell the heart, which extend it to other beings, which make it find itself everywhere outside of itself—and carefully to keep away those which contract and concentrate the heart and tighten the spring of the human *I*? That is, to say it in other terms, to excite in him goodness, humanity, commiseration, beneficence, and all the attractive and sweet passions naturally pleasing to men, and to prevent the birth of envy, covetousness, hate, and all the repulsive and cruel passions which make sensibility, so to speak, not only nothing but negative and torment the man who experiences them.

I believe I can summarize all the preceding reflections in two or three maxims which are precise, clear, and easy to grasp.

First Maxim

It is not in the human heart to put ourselves in the place of people who are happier than we, but only in that of those who are more pitiable.

If one finds exceptions to this maxim they are more apparent than real. Thus one does not put oneself in the place of the rich or noble man to whom one is attached. Even in attaching oneself sincerely, one is only appropriating a part of his well-being. Sometimes one loves him in his misfortunes; but so long as he prospers, he has as a true friend only that man who is not the dupe of appearances, and who pities him more than he envies him, in spite of his prosperity.[4]

We are touched by the happiness of certain conditions—for example, of the rustic and pastoral life. The charm of seeing those good people happy is not poisoned by envy; we are truly interested in them. Why is this? Because we feel that we are the masters of descending to this condition of peace and innocence and of enjoying the same felicity. It is a resource for a rainy day which causes only agreeable ideas, since in order to be able to make use of it, it suffices to want to do so. There is always pleasure in seeing our resources, in contemplating our own goods, even when we do not wish to make use of them.

It follows, therefore, that, in order to incline a young man to humanity, far from making him admire the brilliant lot of others, one must show him the sad sides of that lot, one must make him fear it. Then, by an evident inference, he ought to cut out his own road to happiness, following in no one else's tracks.

Second Maxim

One pities in others only those ills from which one does not feel oneself exempt.

Non ignora mali, miseris succurrere disco.[5]

I know nothing so beautiful, so profound, so touching, so true as this verse.

Why are kings without pity for their subjects? Because they count on never being mere men. Why are the rich so hard toward the poor? It is because they have no fear of becoming poor. Why does the nobility have so great a contempt for the people? It is because a noble will never be a commoner. Why are the Turks generally more humane and more hospitable than we are? It is because, with their totally arbitrary government, which renders the greatness and the fortune of individuals always precarious and unsteady, they do not regard abasement and poverty as a condition alien to them.* Each may be tomorrow what the one whom he helps is today. This reflection, which comes up constantly in Oriental stories, gives them a certain touching quality that all the affectation of our dry moralizing totally lacks.[6]

Do not, therefore, accustom your pupil to regard the sufferings of the unfortunate and the labors of the poor from the height of his glory; and do not hope to teach him to pity them if he considers them alien to him. Make him understand well that the fate of these unhappy men can be his, that all their ills are there in the ground beneath his feet, that countless unforeseen and inevitable events can plunge him into them from one moment to the next. Teach him to count on neither birth nor health nor riches. Show him all the vicissitudes of fortune. Seek out for him examples, always too frequent, of people who, from a station higher than his, have fallen beneath these unhappy men. Whether it is their fault is not now the question. Does he even know what fault is? Never violate the order of his knowledge, and enlighten him only with explanations within his reach. He does not need to be very knowledgeable to sense that all of human prudence is incapable of assuring him whether in an hour he will be living or dying; whether the pain of nephritis will not make him grit his teeth before nightfall; whether in a month he will be rich or poor; whether within a year perhaps he will not be rowing under the lash in the galleys of Algiers. Above all, do not go and tell him all this coldly like his catechism. Let him see, let him feel the human calamities. Unsettle and frighten his imagination with the perils by which every man is constantly surrounded. Let him see around him all these abysses and, hearing you describe them, hold on to you for fear of falling into them. We shall make him timid and cowardly, you will say. We shall see in what follows, but for now let us begin by making him humane. That, above all, is what is important for us?

* This appears to be changing a bit now. The conditions seem to become more fixed; and thus the men become harder.

BOOK IV

Third Maxim

The pity one has for another's misfortune is measured not by the quantity of that misfortune but by the sentiment which one attributes to those who suffer it.

One pities an unhappy man only to the extent one believes he is pitiable. The physical sentiment of our ills is more limited than it seems. But it is by means of memory, which makes us feel their continuity, and of imagination, which extends them into the future, that they make us truly pitiable. This, I think, is one of the causes which hardens us more to the ills of animals than to those of men, although the common sensibility ought to make us identify with them equally. One hardly pities a cart horse in his stable because one does not presume that the horse, while eating his hay, thinks of the blows he has received and of the fatigues awaiting him. Neither does one pity a sheep one sees grazing, although one knows it will soon be slaughtered, because one judges that it does not foresee its fate. By analogy one is similarly hardened against the fate of men, and the rich are consoled about the ill they do to the poor, because they assume the latter to be stupid enough to feel nothing of it. In general, I judge the value each sets on the happiness of his fellows by the importance he appears to give them. It is natural that one consider cheap the happiness of people one despises. Do not be surprised, therefore, if political men speak of the people with so much disdain, or if most of the philosophers affect to make man so wicked.

It is the people who compose humankind. What is not the people is so slight a thing as not to be worth counting. Man is the same in all stations. If that is so, the stations having the most members merit the most respect. To the man who thinks, all the civil distinctions disappear. He sees the same passions, the same sentiments in the hod-carrier and the illustrious man. He discerns there only a difference in language, only a more or less affected tone; and if some essential difference distinguishes them, it is to the disadvantage of those who dissemble more. The people show themselves such as they are, and they are not lovable. But society people have to be disguised. If they were to show themselves such as they are, they would be disgusting.

There is, our wise men also say, the same proportion of happiness and misery in every station—a maxim as deadly as it is untenable. If all are equally happy, what need have I to put myself out for anyone? Let each remain as he is. Let the slave be mistreated. Let the infirm suffer. Let the beggar perish. There is no gain for them in changing stations. These wise men enumerate the miseries of the rich and show the inanity of their vain pleasures. What a crude sophism! The miseries of the rich man come to him not from his station but from himself alone, because he abuses his station. Were he unhappier than the poor man himself, he would not be pitiable, because his ills are all his own doing, and whether he is happy depends only on himself. But the misery of the poor man comes to him from things, from the rigor of his lot, which weighs down on him. No habit can take from him the physical sentiments of fatigue, exhaustion, and hunger. Neither intelligence nor wisdom serves in any way to exempt him from the ills of his station. What does Epictetus gain in foreseeing that his master is going to break his leg? Does the master break Epictetus' leg any the less for that? He has, in addition to his misfortune, the misfortune of foresight.[7] If the people were as clever as we assume them to be stupid, what could they be other than what they are? What could they do other than what they do? Study persons of this order. You will see that although their language is different, they have as much wit and more good sense than you do. Respect your species. Be aware that it is composed essentially of a collection of peoples; that if all the kings and all the philosophers were taken away, their absence would hardly be noticeable; and that things would not be any the worse. In a word, teach your pupil to love all men, even those who despise men. Do things in such a way that he puts himself in no class but finds his bearings in all. Speak before him of humankind with tenderness, even with pity, but never with contempt. Man, do not dishonor man!

It is by these roads and other similar ones—quite contrary to those commonly taken—that it is fitting to penetrate the heart of a young adolescent in order to arouse the first emotions of nature and to develop his heart and extend it to his fellows. To this I add that it is important to mix the least possible personal interest with these emotions—above all, no vanity, no emulation, no glory, none of those sentiments that force us to compare ourselves with others, for these comparisons are never made without some impression of hatred against those who dispute with us for preference, even if only preference in our own esteem. Then one must become blind or get angry, be wicked or stupid. Let us try to avoid being faced with this choice. These dangerous passions will, I am told, be born sooner or later in spite of us. I do not deny it. Everything has its time and its place. I only say that one ought not to assist their birth.

This is the spirit of the method which must be prescribed. Here examples and details are useless because the almost infinite division of characters begins at this point, and each example I might give would perhaps not be suitable for even one in a hundred thousand. It is also at this age that the skillful master begins to take on the true function of the observer and philosopher who knows the art of sounding hearts while working to form them. As long as the young man does not think of dissembling and has not yet learned how to do it, with every object one presents to him one sees in his manner, his eyes, and his gestures the impression it makes on him. One reads in his face all the movements of his soul. By dint of spying them out, one gets to be able to foresee them and finally to direct them.

It is to be noted in general that all men are affected sooner and more generally by wounds, cries, groans, the apparatus of painful operations, and all that brings objects of suffering to the senses. The idea of destruction, since it is more complex, is not similarly striking; the image of death has a later and weaker effect because no one has within himself the experience of death. One must have seen corpses to feel the agonies of the dying. But when this image has once been well formed in our mind, there is no spectacle more horrible to our eyes—

whether because of the idea of total destruction it then gives by means of the senses, or whether because, knowing that this moment is inevitable for all men, one feels oneself more intensely affected by a situation one is sure of not being able to escape.

These diverse impressions have their modifications and their degrees which depend on the particular character of each individual and his previous habits. But they are universal, and no one is completely exempt from them. There exist later and less general impressions which are more appropriate to sensitive souls. These are the ones resulting from moral suffering, from inner pains, affliction, languor, and sadness. There are people who can be moved only by cries and tears. The long, muted groans of a heart gripped by anguish have never wrested sighs from them. Never has the sight of a downcast countenance, of a gaunt gray visage, of a dull eye no longer able to cry, made them cry themselves. The ills of the soul are nothing for them. They are judged; their souls feel nothing. Expect from them only inflexible rigor, hardness, and cruelty. They may be men of integrity and justice, but never clement, generous, and pitying. I say that they may be just—if, that is, a man can be just when he is not merciful.

But do not be in a hurry to judge young people by this rule, especially those who, having been raised as they ought to be, have no idea of moral suffering that they have never been made to experience; for, to repeat, they can pity only ills they know, and this apparent insensibility, which comes only from ignorance, is soon changed into compassion when they begin to feel that there are in human life countless pains they did not know. As for my Emile, if he has had simplicity and good sense in his childhood, I am sure that he will have soul and sensibility in his youth—for truth of sentiments depends in large measure on correctness of ideas.

But why recall it here? More than one reader will doubtless reproach me for forgetting my first resolve and the constant happiness I had promised my pupil. Unhappy men, dying ones, sights of pain and misery! What happiness! What enjoyment for a young heart being born to life! His gloomy teacher, who designed so sweet an education for him, treats him as born only to suffer. This is what will be said. What difference does it make to me? I promised to make him happy, not to appear to be. Is it my fault if you, always dupes of appearance, take it for reality?

Let us take two young men, emerging from their first education and entering into society by two directly opposite paths. One suddenly climbs up to Olympus and moves in the most brilliant world. He is brought to the court, to the nobles, to the rich, to the pretty women. I assume that he is made much of everywhere, and I do not examine the effect of this greeting on his reason—I assume that his reason resists it. Pleasures fly to him; every day new objects entertain him. He abandons himself to everything with an interest which seduces you. You see him attentive, eager, curious. His initial admiration strikes you. You take him to be satisfied; but look at the condition of his soul. You believe he is enjoying himself; I believe he is suffering.

What does he first perceive on opening his eyes? Multitudes of alleged goods which he did not know, and most of which, since they are only for a moment within his reach, seem to be revealed to him only to make him regret being deprived of them. Does he wander through a palace? You see by his worried curiosity that he is asking himself why his paternal house is not like it. All his questions tell you that he is ceaselessly comparing himself with the master of this house; and that all that he finds mortifying for himself in this parallel makes his vanity rebel and thus sharpens it. If he encounters a young man better dressed than himself, I see him secretly complain about his parents' avarice. Is he more adorned than another? He is pained to see this other outshine him by birth or wit, and to see all his gilding humiliated in the presence of a simple cloth suit. Is he the only one to shine in a gathering? Does he stand on tiptoe to be seen better? Who is not secretly disposed to put down the splendid and vain manner of a young fop? All combine as though by plan: the disturbing glances of a serious man, the scoffing words of a caustic one are not long in reaching him. And were he despised by only a single man, that man's contempt instantly poisons the others' applause.

Let us give him everything. Let us lavish charms and merit on him. Let him be handsome, very clever, and lovable. He will be sought out by women. But in seeking him out before he loves them, they will unhinge him rather than make a lover out of him. He will have successes, but he will have neither transports nor passion for enjoying them. Since his desires, always provided for in advance, never have time to be born, he feels in the bosom of pleasures only the boredom of constraint. The sex made for the happiness of his sex disgusts him and satiates him even before he knows it. If he continues to see women, he does so only out of vanity. And if he were to attach himself to them out of a true taste, he will not be the only young man, the only brilliant one, or the only attractive one and will not always find his beloveds to be prodigies of fidelity.

I say nothing of the worries, the betrayals, the black deeds, the repentings of all kinds inseparable from such a life. It is known that experience of society causes disgust with it. I am speaking only of the troubles connected with the first illusion.

What a contrast for someone who has been restricted to the bosom of his family and his friends, where he has seen himself the sole object of all their attentions, to enter suddenly into an order of things where he counts for so little, to find himself, as it were, drowned in an alien sphere—he who for so long was the center of his own sphere! How many affronts, how many humiliations must he absorb before losing, amidst strangers, the prejudices of his importance which were acquired and nourished amidst his own relatives! As a child everything gave way to him, everything around him was eager to serve him; as a young man he must give way to everyone. Or, for the little he forgets himself and keeps his old ways, how many hard lessons are going to make him come back to himself! The habit of easily getting the objects of his desires leads him to desire much and makes him sense continual privations. Everything that pleases him tempts him; everything others have, he wants to have. He covets everything; he is envious of everyone. He would want to dominate everywhere. Vanity gnaws at him. The ardor of unbridled desires inflames his young heart; jealousy and hate are born along with them. All the devouring passions take flight at the same time. He brings their agitation into the tumult of society. He brings it back with him every night. He comes home discontented with himself and others. He goes to sleep full of countless vain projects, troubled by countless whims. And even in his dreams his pride paints the chimerical goods, desire for which torments him and which he will never in his life possess. This is your pupil. Let us see mine.

If the first sight that strikes him is an object of sadness, the first return to himself is a sentiment of pleasure. In seeing how many ills he is exempt from, he feels himself to be happier than he had thought he was. He shares the sufferings of his fellows; but this sharing is voluntary and sweet. At the same time he enjoys both the pity he has for their ills and the happiness that exempts him from those ills. He feels himself to be in that condition of strength which extends us beyond ourselves and leads us to take elsewhere activity superfluous to our well-being. To pity another's misfortune one doubtless needs to know it, but one does not need to feel it. When one has suffered or fears suffering, one pities those who suffer; but when one is suffering, one pities only oneself. But if, since all are subject to the miseries of life, we accord to others only that sensibility that we do not currently need for ourselves, it follows that commiseration ought to be a very sweet sentiment, since it speaks well of us. A hard man, on the contrary, is always unhappy, for the condition of his heart leaves him no superabundant sensibility he can accord to the suffering of others.

We judge happiness too much on the basis of appearances; we suppose it to be there where it is least present. We seek it where it could not be. Gaiety is only a very equivocal sign. A gay man is often only an unfortunate one who seeks to mislead others and to forget himself. These people who are so given to laughter, so open, so serene in a group, are almost all gloomy and scolds at home, and their domestics pay the penalty for the entertainment they provide in society. True satisfaction is neither gay nor wild. One is jealous of so sweet a sentiment, and, in tasting it, one thinks about it, savors it, fears it will evaporate. A truly happy man hardly speaks and hardly laughs. He draws, so to speak, the happiness up around his heart. Boisterous games and turbulent joy veil disgust and boredom. But melancholy is the friend of delight. Tenderness and tears accompany the sweetest enjoyments, and excessive joy itself plucks tears rather than laughs.

If at first the multitude and the variety of entertainments appear to contribute to happiness, if the uniformity of a steady life at first appears boring, upon taking a better look one finds, on the contrary, that the sweetest habit of soul consists in a moderation of enjoyment which leaves little opening for desire and disgust. The restlessness of desire produces curiosity and inconstancy. The emptiness of turbulent pleasure produces boredom. One is never bored with his condition when one knows none more agreeable. Of all the men in the world savages are the least curious and the least bored. They are indifferent to everything. They enjoy not things but themselves. They pass their lives in doing nothing and are never bored.

The man of the world is whole in his mask. Almost never being in himself, he is always alien and ill at ease when forced to go back there. What he is, is nothing; what he appears to be is everything for him.

I cannot prevent myself from imagining on the face of the young man of whom I have previously spoken something impertinent, sugary, affected, which displeases and repels plain people; and on that of my young man an interesting and simple expression that reveals satisfaction and true serenity of soul, inspires esteem and confidence, and seems to await only the offering of friendship to return friendship to those who approach him. It is believed that the face is only a simple development of features already drawn by nature. I, however, think that beyond this development the features of a man's visage are imperceptibly formed and take on a typical cast as a result of the frequent and habitual impression of certain affections of the soul. These affections leave their mark on the visage; nothing is more certain. And when they turn into habits, they must leave durable impressions on it. This is my conception of how the face indicates character, and the latter can sometimes be judged by the former without looking for mysterious explanations which assume knowledge we do not have.[8]

A child has only two marked affections, joy and pain. He laughs or he cries; the intermediates are nothing for him. He ceaselessly passes from one of these movements to the other. This constant alternation prevents them from making any permanent impression on his face and giving it a characteristic expression. But at the age when he has become more sensitive and is more intensely or more constantly affected, more profound impressions leave traces that are more difficult to destroy; and from the habitual condition of the soul there results an arrangement of the features which time renders ineradicable. Nevertheless, it is not rare to see men's faces change at different ages. I have seen several men in whom this has occurred, and I have always found that those I had been able to observe well and to follow had also changed habitual passions. This observation alone, which is well confirmed, would appear to me to be decisive; and it is not misplaced in a treatise on education, in which it is important to learn to judge movements of the soul by external signs.

I do not know whether my young man, because he has not learned to imitate conventional manners and to feign sentiments he does not have, will be less lovable. That is not the object here. I only know that he will be more loving, and I have difficulty believing that someone who loves only himself can disguise himself well enough to be as pleasing as someone who draws from his attachment to others a new sentiment of happiness. But as for this sentiment itself, I believe I have said enough about it to guide a reasonable reader on this question and to show that I have not contradicted myself.

I return, therefore, to my method, and I say: when the critical age approaches, furnish young people with sights which restrain them and not with sights which arouse them. Put their nascent imaginations off the track with objects which, far from inflaming, repress the activity of their senses. Remove them from big cities where the adornment and the immodesty of women hasten and anticipate nature's lessons, where everything presents to their eyes pleasures they ought to know only when they are able to choose among them. Bring them back to their first abodes where rustic simplicity lets the passions of their age develop less rapidly. Or if their taste for the arts still attaches them to the city, keep them from a dangerous idleness by means of this very taste. Choose with care their society, their occupations, their pleasures. Show them only scenes which are touching but modest, which stir them without seducing them, and which nourish their sensibilities without moving their senses. Be aware also that everywhere there are excesses to fear and that immoderate passions always do more harm than what one wants to avoid by means of them. The object is not to make your pupil a male nurse or a brother of charity, not to afflict his sight with constant objects of pain and suffering, not to march from sick person to sick person, from hospital to hospital, and from the Grève [9] to the prisons. He must be touched and not hardened by the sight of human miseries. Long struck by the same sights, we no longer feel their impressions. Habit accustoms us to everything. What we see too much, we no longer imagine; and it is only imagination which makes us feel the ills of others. It is thus by dint of seeing death and suffering that priests and doctors become pitiless. Therefore, let your pupil know the fate of man and the miseries of his fellows, but do not let him witness them too often. A single object well chosen and shown in a suitable light will provide him emotion and reflection for a month. It is not so much what he sees as his looking back on what he has seen that determines the judgment he makes about it; and the durable impression he receives from an object comes to him less from the object itself than from the point of view which one induces him to take in recalling it. It is by thus husbanding examples, lessons, and images that you will long blunt the needle of the senses and put nature off the track by following its own directions.

To the extent he becomes enlightened, choose ideas which take account of that fact; to the extent his desires catch fire, choose scenes fit to repress them. An old soldier who had distinguished himself as much by his morals as by his courage told me that in his early youth, when his father, a sensible but very pious man, saw his son's nascent temperament delivering him to women, he spared no effort to restrain him. But finally, sensing that his son was about to get away from him in spite of all his efforts, the father took the expedient of bringing him to a hospital for syphilitics and, without giving him any warning, made him enter a room where a troop of these unfortunates expiated by a horrible treatment the dissoluteness which had exposed them to it. At this hideous sight, which revolted all the senses at once, the young man almost got sick. "Go on, miserable profligate," his father then said in a vehement tone, "follow the vile inclination which drags you along. Soon you will be only too happy to be admitted to this room where, a victim of the most infamous pains, you will force your father to thank God for your death."

These few words, joined to the emphatic scene which struck the young man, made an impression on him which was never effaced. Condemned by his station to spend his youth in garrisons, he preferred to absorb all the mockery of his comrades rather than to imitate their libertinism. "I was a man," he said to me, "I had weaknesses. But up to my present age I have never been able to see a public woman without disgust." Master, make few speeches! But learn to choose places, times, and persons. Then give all your lessons in examples, and be sure of their effect.

The way childhood is employed is not very important. The evil which slips in then is not without remedy, and the good done then can come later. But this is not the case with the first age at which man begins truly to live. This age never lasts long enough for the use that ought to be made of it, and its importance demands an unflagging attention. This is why I insist on the art of prolonging it. One of the best precepts of good culture is to slow up everything as much as is possible. Make progress by slow and sure steps. Prevent the adolescent's becoming a man until the moment when nothing remains for him to do to become one. While the body grows, the spirits designed to provide balm for the blood and strength for the fibers are formed and developed. If you cause those spirits, which are intended for the perfection of an individual, to take a different course and be used for the formation of another individual, both remain in a state of weakness, and nature's work stays imperfect. The operations of the mind feel in their turn the effect of this corruption, and the soul, as debilitated as the body, performs its functions only in a weak and languorous fashion. Large and robust limbs make neither courage nor genius; and I can conceive that strength of soul may not accompany that of the body, especially when the organs of communication between the two substances are in poor condition. But, however good the condition of those organs may be, they will always act weakly if they have as their principle only blood that is exhausted, impoverished, and bereft of the substance giving strength and activity to all the springs of the machine. Generally one notices more vigor of soul in men whose young years have been preserved from premature corruption than in those whose dissoluteness began with their power to give themselves over to that corruption. And this is doubtless one of the reasons why peoples with morals ordinarily surpass peoples without morals in good sense and courage. The latter shine solely by certain subtle qualities which they call wit, sagacity, and delicacy. But those great and noble functions of wisdom and reason which distinguish and honor man by fair actions, by virtues, and by truly useful efforts are hardly to be found except among the former.

Masters complain that the fire of this age makes youth unmanageable, and I see that this is so. But is it not their fault? So soon as they have let this fire take its course through the senses, do they not know that one can no longer give it another course? Will a pedant's long, cold sermons efface in his pupil's mind the image of the pleasures he has conceived? Will they banish from his heart the desires which torment him? Will they stifle the ardor of a temperament which he knows

how to put to use? Will he not become enflamed against the obstacles
opposed to the only happiness of which he has an idea? And in the harsh
law prescribed to him without his being enabled to understand it, what
will he see other than the caprice and hatred of a man who seeks to
torment him? Is it strange that he rebels and hates that man in turn?

I can well conceive that in making himself pliant a master can make
himself more bearable and preserve an apparent authority. But I do
not see very well the use of the authority kept over one's pupil only
by fomenting the vices it ought to repress. It is as though to calm an
impetuous horse the equerry were to make him jump over the edge of
a precipice.

This adolescent fire, far from being an obstacle to education, is the
means of consummating and completing it. It gives you a hold on a young
man's heart when he ceases to be weaker than you. His first affections
are the reins with which you direct all his movements. He was free,
and now I see him enslaved. So long as he loved nothing, he depended
only on himself and his needs. As soon as he loves, he depends on his
attachments. Thus are formed the first bonds linking him to his species.
In directing his nascent sensibility to his species, do not believe that
it will at the outset embrace all men, and that the word *mankind* will
signify anything to him. No, this sensibility will in the first place be
limited to his fellows, and for him his fellows will not be unknowns;
rather, they will be those with whom he has relations, those whom
habit has made dear or necessary to him, those whom he observes
to have ways of thinking and feeling clearly in common with him,
those whom he sees exposed to the pains he has suffered and sensitive
to the pleasures he has tasted, those, in a word, whose nature has a
more manifest identity with his own and thus make him more disposed to love himself. It will be only after having cultivated his nature
in countless ways, after many reflections on his own sentiments and on
those he observes in others, that he will be able to get to the point of
generalizing his individual notions under the abstract idea of humanity
and to join to his particular affections those which can make him
identify with his species.

In becoming capable of attachment, he becomes sensitive to that of
others * and thereby attentive to the signs of this attachment. Do you
see what a new empire you are going to acquire over him? How many
chains you have put around his heart before he notices them! What
will he feel when, opening his eyes to himself, he sees what you have
done for him, when he can compare himself to other young people of his
age and you to other governors? I say when he sees, but resist telling
him. If you tell him, he will no longer see it. If you exact obedience
from him in return for the efforts you have made on his behalf, he will
believe that you have trapped him. He will say to himself that, while
feigning to oblige him for nothing, you aspired to put him in debt and

* Attachment can exist without being returned, but friendship never can. It is an
exchange, a contract like others, but it is the most sacred of all. The word *friend*
has no correlative other than itself. Any man who is not his friend's friend is most
assuredly a cheat, for it is only in returning or feigning to return friendship that
one can obtain it.

to bind him by a contract to which he did not consent. It will be in vain that you add that what you are demanding from him is only for himself. You are demanding in any event, and you are demanding in virtue of what you have done without his consent. When an unfortunate takes the money that one feigned to give him, and finds himself enlisted in spite of himself, you protest against the injustice.[10] Are you not still more unjust in asking your pupil to pay the price for care he did not request?

Ingratitude would be rarer if usurious benefactions were less common. We like what does us good. It is so natural a sentiment! Ingratitude is not in the heart of man, but self-interest is. There are fewer obligated ingrates than self-interested benefactors. If you sell me your gifts, I shall haggle about the price. But if you feign giving in order to sell later at your price, you are practicing fraud. It is their being free that makes these gifts priceless. The heart receives laws only from itself. By wanting to enchain it, one releases it; one enchains it by leaving it free.

When the fisherman puts a lure in the water, the fish comes and stays around it without distrust. But when caught by the hook hidden under the bait, it feels the line being pulled back and tries to flee. Is the fisherman the benefactor, and is the fish ungrateful? Does one ever see that a man forgotten by his benefactor forgets him? On the contrary, he always speaks of him with pleasure; he does not think of him without tenderness. If he finds an occasion to show his benefactor that he recalls his services by some unexpected service of his own, with what inner satisfaction does he then act to demonstrate his gratitude! With what sweet joy he gains the other's gratitude! With what transport does he say to him, "My turn has come!" This is truly the voice of nature. Never did a true benefaction produce an ingrate.

If, therefore, gratitude is a natural sentiment, and you do not destroy its effect by your errors, rest assured that your pupil, as he begins to see the value of your care, will be appreciative of it—provided that you yourself have not put a price on it—and that this will give you an authority in his heart that nothing can destroy. But until you are quite sure you have gained this advantage, take care not to lose it by insisting on what you deserve from him. To vaunt your services is to make them unendurable for him. To forget them is to make him remember them. Until it is time to treat him like a man, let the issue be never what he owes you but what he owes himself. To make him docile, leave him all his freedom; hide yourself so that he may seek you. Lift his soul to the noble sentiment of gratitude by never speaking to him of anything but his interest. I did not want him to be told that what was done was for his good before he was in a condition to understand it. In this speech he would have seen only your dependence, and he would have taken you only for his valet. But now that he begins to feel what it is to love, he also feels what a sweet bond can unite a man to what he loves; and in the zeal which makes you constantly busy yourself with him, he sees a slave's attachment no longer but a friend's affection. Nothing has so much weight in the human heart as the voice of clearly recognized friendship, for we know that it never speaks to us for anything other than our interest. One can believe that a friend makes a mistake but not that he would want to deceive us. Sometimes one resists his advice, but one never despises it.

Finally we enter the moral order. We have just made a second step into manhood. If this were the place for it, I would try to show how the first voices of conscience arise out of the first movements of the heart, and how the first notions of good and bad are born of the sentiments of love and hate. I would show that *justice* and *goodness* are not merely abstract words—pure moral beings formed by the understanding—but are true affections of the soul enlightened by reason, are hence only an ordered development of our primitive affections; that by reason alone, independent of conscience, no natural law can be established; and that the entire right of nature is only a chimera if it is not founded on a natural need in the human heart.* But I am reminded that my business here is not producing treatises on metaphysics and morals or courses of study of any kind. It is sufficient for me to mark out the order and the progress of our sentiments and our knowledge relative to our constitution. Others will perhaps demonstrate what I only indicate here.

Since my Emile has until now looked only at himself, the first glance he casts on his fellows leads him to compare himself with them. And the first sentiment aroused in him by this comparison is the desire to be in the first position. This is the point where love of self turns into *amour-propre* and where begin to arise all the passions which depend on this one. But to decide whether among these passions the dominant ones in his character will be humane and gentle or cruel and malignant, whether they will be passions of beneficence and commiseration or of envy and covetousness, we must know what position he will feel he has among men, and what kinds of obstacles he may believe he has to overcome to reach the position he wants to occupy.

To guide him in this research, we must now show him men by means of their differences, having already showed him men by means of the accidents common to the species. Now comes the measurement of natural and civil inequality and the picture of the whole social order.

Society must be studied by means of men, and men by means of society. Those who want to treat politics and morals separately will never understand anything of either of the two. We see how men,

---

* Even the precept of doing unto others as we would have them do unto us has no true foundation other than conscience and sentiment; for where is the precise reason for me, being myself, to act as if I were another, especially when I am morally certain of never finding myself in the same situation? And who will guarantee me that in very faithfully following this maxim I will get others to follow it similarly with me? The wicked man gets advantage from the just man's probity and his own injustice. He is delighted that everyone, with the exception of himself, be just. This agreement, whatever may be said about it, is not very advantageous for good men. But when the strength of an expansive soul makes me identify myself with my fellow, and I feel that I am, so to speak, in him, it is in order not to suffer that I do not want him to suffer. I am interested in him for love of myself, and the reason for the precept is in nature itself, which inspires in me the desire of my well-being in whatever place I feel my existence. From this I conclude that it is not true that the precepts of natural law are founded on reason alone. They have a base more solid and sure. Love of men derived from love of self is the principle of human justice. The summation of all morality is given by the Gospel in its summation of the law.

in attaching themselves at first to the primary relations, ought to be affected by them and what passions ought to arise from them. We see that it is by the progress of the passions in turn that these relations are multiplied and become closer. It is less the strength of arms than the moderation of hearts which makes men independent and free. Whoever desires few things depends on few people. But always confusing our vain desires with our physical needs, those who have made the latter the foundations of human society have always taken the effects for the causes and have only succeeded in going astray in all their reasonings.

In the state of nature there is a de facto equality that is real and indestructible, because it is impossible in that state for the difference between man and man by itself to be great enough to make one dependent on another. In the civil state there is a de jure equality that is chimerical and vain, because the means designed to maintain it themselves serve to destroy it, and because the public power, added to that of the stronger to oppress the weak, breaks the sort of equilibrium nature had placed between them.* From this first contradiction flow all those that are observed in the civil order between appearance and reality. The multitude will always be sacrificed to the few, and the public interest to particular interest. Those specious names, justice and order, will always serve as instruments of violence and as arms of iniquity. From this it follows that the distinguished orders who claim they are useful to the others are actually useful only to themselves at the expense of their subordinates; it is on this basis that one ought to judge the consideration which is due them according to justice and reason. In order to know how each of us ought to judge his own lot, it remains to be seen whether the rank these men have grabbed is more advantageous for the happiness of those who occupy it. This is now the study which is important for us. But to do it well, we must begin by knowing the human heart.[11]

If the object were only to show young people man by means of his mask, there would be no need of showing them this; it is what they would always be seeing in any event. But since the mask is not the man and his varnish must not seduce them, portray men for them such as they are—not in order that young people hate them but that they pity them and not want to resemble them. This is, to my taste, the best-conceived sentiment that man can have about his species.

With this in view, it is important here to take a route opposed to the one we have followed until now and to instruct the young man by others' experience rather than his own. If men deceive him, he will hate them; but if, respected by them, he sees them deceive one another mutually, he will pity them. The spectacle of society, Pythagoras said, resembles that of the Olympic games. Some keep shop there and think only of their profit; others spend their persons and seek glory; others are content to see the games, and these are not the worst.[12]

I would want a young man's society to be chosen so carefully that he

---

* The universal spirit of the laws of every country is always to favor the strong against the weak and those who have against those who have not. This difficulty is inevitable, and it is without exception.

thinks well of those who live with him; and I would want him to be taught to know the world so well that he thinks ill of all that takes place in it. Let him know that man is naturally good; let him feel it; let him judge his neighbor by himself. But let him see that society depraves and perverts men; let him find in their prejudices the source of all their vices; let him be inclined to esteem each individual but despise the multitude; let him see that all men wear pretty much the same mask, but let him also know that there are faces more beautiful than the mask covering them.

This method, it must be admitted, has its difficulties and is not easy in practice; for if he becomes an observer too soon, if you give him practice at spying on others' actions too closely, you make him a scandalmonger and a satirist, peremptory and quick to judge. He will get an odious pleasure out of seeking for sinister interpretations of everything and of seeing nothing from the good side, even what is good. He will, at the least, get accustomed to the spectacle of vice and to seeing wicked men without disgust, as one gets accustomed to seeing unhappy men without pity. Soon the general perversity will serve him less as a lesson than as an example. He will say to himself that if man is thus, he himself ought not to want to be otherwise.

If you want to instruct him by principles and teach him, along with the nature of the human heart, the external causes which are brought to bear on it and turn our inclinations into vices, you employ a metaphysic he is not in a condition to understand by thus transporting him all of a sudden from sensible objects to intellectual objects. You fall back into the difficulty so carefully avoided up to now of giving him lessons resembling lessons, of substituting in his mind the master's experience and authority for his own experience and the progress of his reason.

To remove both of these obstacles at once and to put the human heart in his reach without risk of spoiling his own, I would want to show him men from afar, to show him them in other times or other places and in such a way that he can see the stage without ever being able to act on it. This is the moment for history. It is by means of history that, without the lessons of philosophy, he will read the hearts of men; it is by means of history that he will see them, a simple spectator, disinterested and without passion, as their judge and not as their accomplice or as their accuser.

To know men, one must see them act. In society one hears them speak. They show their speeches and hide their actions. But in history their actions are unveiled, and one judges them on the basis of the facts. Even their talk helps in evaluating them; for in comparing what they do with what they say, one sees both what they are and what they want to appear to be. The more they disguise themselves, the better one knows them.

Unhappily this study has its dangers, its disadvantages of more than one kind. It is difficult to find a viewpoint from which one can judge his fellows equitably. One of the great vices of history is that it paints men's bad sides much more than their good ones. Because history is interesting only by means of revolutions and catastrophes, so long as a people grows and prospers calmly with a peaceful government, history says nothing of it. History begins to speak of a people only when, no longer sufficing unto itself, it gets involved in its neighbors' affairs or lets them get involved in its affairs. History makes a people illustrious only when it is already in its decline; all our histories begin where they ought to finish. We have a very precise history of peoples who are destroying themselves; what we lack is the history of peoples who are thriving. They are fortunate enough and prudent enough for history to have nothing to say of them; in fact, we see even in our day that the best-conducted governments are those of which one speaks least. We know, therefore, only the bad; the good is hardly epoch-making. It is only the wicked who are famous; the good are forgotten or made ridiculous. And this is how history, like philosophy, ceaselessly calumniates humankind.

Moreover, the facts described by history are far from being an exact portrayal of the same facts as they happened. They change form in the historian's head; they are molded according to his interests; they take on the complexion of his prejudices. Who knows how to put the reader exactly on the spot of the action to see an event as it took place? Ignorance or partiality disguise everything. Without even altering a historical deed, but by expanding or contracting the circumstances which relate to it, how many different faces one can give to it! Put the same object in different perspectives, it will hardly appear the same; nevertheless nothing will have changed but the eye of the spectator. Is it sufficient for truth's honor to tell me a true fact while making me see it quite otherwise than the way it took place? How many times did a tree more or less, a stone to the right or to the left, a cloud of dust raised by the wind determine the result of a combat without anyone's having noticed it? Does this prevent the historian from telling you the cause of the defeat or the victory with as much assurance as if he had been everywhere? Of what importance to me are the facts in themselves when the reason for them remains unknown to me, and what lessons can I draw from an event of whose true cause I am ignorant? The historian gives me one, but he counterfeits it; and critical history itself, which is making such a sensation, is only an art of conjecture, the art of choosing among several lies the one best resembling the truth.

Have you never read *Cleopatra* or *Cassandra* [13] or other books of this kind? The author chooses a known event; then, accommodating it to his views, adorning it with details of his invention, with personages who never existed and imaginary portraits, he piles fictions on fictions to make reading him more agreeable. I see little difference between these novels and your histories, unless it be that the novelist yields more to his own imagination, while the historian enslaves himself to another's. I shall add to this, if one wishes, that the former sets himself a moral goal, good or bad, which is hardly a concern for the latter.

I will be told that the fidelity of history is of less interest than the truth of morals and characters; provided that the human heart is well depicted, it is of little importance that events be faithfully reported; for, after all, it is added, what difference do facts occurring two thousand years ago make to us? That is right if the portraits are well rendered according to nature. But if most have their model only in the historian's imagination, is this not to fall back into the difficulty one wanted to flee, and to give to the authority of the writer what one wanted to take away from that of the master? If my pupil is only going to see pictures based on fantasy, I prefer that they be drawn by my hand rather than that of another. They will at least be better suited for him.

The worst historians for a young man are those who make judgments. Facts! Facts! And let him make his own judgments. It is thus that he learns to know men. If the author's judgment guides him constantly, all he does is see with another's eye; and when that eye fails him, he no longer sees anything.

I leave modern history aside, not only because it no longer has a physiognomy and our men all resemble one another; but because our historians, mindful only of being brilliant, dream of nothing but producing highly colored portraits which often represent nothing.* Generally the ancients make fewer portraits and put less wit and more sense in their judgments. Even with them one must be very selective, and not the most judicious but the simplest must be chosen first. I would not want to put either Polybius or Sallust in the hand of a young man. Tacitus is the book of old men; young people are not ready for understanding him. One has to learn to see in human actions the primary features of man's heart before wanting to sound its depths. One has to know how to read facts well before reading maxims. Philosophy in maxims is suitable only to those who have experience. Youth ought to generalize in nothing. Its whole instruction should be in particular rules.

Thucydides is to my taste the true model of historians. He reports the facts without judging them, but he omits none of the circumstances proper to make us judge them ourselves. He puts all he recounts before the reader's eyes. Far from putting himself between the events and his readers, he hides himself. The reader no longer believes he reads; he believes he sees. Unhappily, Thucydides always speaks of war; and one sees in his narratives almost nothing but the least instructive thing in the world—that is, battles. *The Retreat of the Ten Thousand* and Caesar's *Commentaries* have pretty nearly the same wisdom and the same defect. The good Herodotus, without portraits, without maxims, but flowing, naïve, full of the details most capable of interesting and pleasing, would perhaps be the best of historians if these very details did not often degenerate into puerile simplicities more fit to spoil the taste of youth than to form it. One must already have discernment to read him. I say nothing of Livy. His turn will come. But he is political; he is rhetorical; he is everything which is unsuitable for this age.

History in general is defective in that it records only palpable and distinct facts which can be fixed by names, places, and dates, while the slow and progressive causes of these facts, which cannot be similarly assigned, always remain unknown. One often finds in a battle won or lost the reason for a revolution which even before this battle had

* See Davila, Guicciardini, Strada, Solis, Machiavelli, and sometimes de Thou himself. Vertot is almost the only one who knew how to depict without making portraits.

[239]

already become inevitable. War hardly does anything other than make manifest outcomes already determined by moral causes which historians rarely know how to see.

The philosophic spirit has turned the reflections of several writers of our age in this direction. But I doubt that the truth gains by their work. The rage for systems having taken possession of them all, each seeks to see things not as they are but as they agree with his system.

Add to all these reflections the fact that history shows actions far more than men, because it grasps the latter only in certain selected moments, in their parade clothes. It exhibits only the public man who has dressed himself to be seen. It does not follow him in his home, in his study, in his family, among his friends. It depicts him only when he plays a role. It depicts his costume far more than his person.

I would prefer to begin the study of the human heart with the reading of lives of individuals; for in them, however much the man may conceal himself, the historian pursues him everywhere. He leaves him no moment of respite, no nook where he can avoid the spectator's piercing eye; and it is when the subject believes he has hidden himself best that the biographer makes him known best. "Those who write lives," says Montaigne, "are more suited to me to the extent that they are interested in intentions more than in results, in what takes place within more than in what happens without. This is why Plutarch is my man." [14]

It is true that the genius of assembled men or of peoples is quite different from a man's character in private, and that one would know the human heart very imperfectly if he did not examine it also in the multitude. But it is no less true that one must begin by studying man in order to judge men, and that he who knew each individual's inclinations perfectly could foresee all their effects when combined in the body of the people.

We must again have recourse to the ancients here—for the reasons I have already mentioned, and also because all the intimate and low, but true and characteristic details are banished from modern style. Men are as adorned by our authors in their private lives as on the stage of the world. Propriety, no less severe in writings than in actions, now permits to be said in public only what it permits to be done in public. And since one can show men only when they are forever playing a part, they are no more known in our books than in our theaters. The lives of kings may very well be written and rewritten a hundred times; we shall have no more Suetoniuses.*

Plutarch excels in these very details into which we no longer dare to enter. He has an inimitable grace at depicting great men in small things; and he is so felicitous in the choice of his stories that often a word, a smile, or a gesture is enough for him to characterize his hero. With a joking phrase Hannibal reassures his terrified army and makes it march laughing to the battle which won Italy for him.[16] Agesilaus

---

* One of our historians who imitated Tacitus in the grand details was the only one to dare to imitate Suetonius and sometimes to copy Commines in the petty ones; and this very fact, which adds to the value of his book, has caused him to be criticized among us.[15]

BOOK IV

astride a stick makes me love the Great King's conqueror.[17] Caesar passing through a poor village and chatting with his friends betrays, unthinkingly, the deceiver who said he wanted only to be Pompey's equal.[18] Alexander swallows medicine and does not say a single word; it is the most beautiful moment of his life.[19] Aristides writes his own name on a shell and thus justifies his surname.[20] Philopoemen, with his cloak off, cuts wood in his host's kitchen.[21] This is the true art of painting. Physiognomy does not reveal itself in large features, nor character in great actions. It is in bagatelles that nature comes to light. The public things are either too uniform or too artificial; and it is almost solely on these that modern dignity permits our authors to dwell.

M. de Turenne was incontestably one of the greatest men of the last century. We have had the courage to make his life interesting by means of little details which make him known and loved. But how many details have we been forced to suppress which would have made him still better known and loved. I shall mention only one which I have from a good source and which Plutarch would have been careful not to omit, but which Ramsay [22] would have been careful not to write had he known it.

One summer day when it was very hot, Viscount de Turenne, wearing a little white jacket and a cap, was at the window in his antechamber. One of his servants happened along and, deceived by his clothing, took him for a kitchen helper with whom this domestic was familiar. He quietly approached from behind and with a hand that was not light gave him a hard slap on the buttocks. The man struck turned around immediately. The valet saw with a shudder his master's face. He fell to his knees in utter despair. "My lord, I believed it was George!" "And if it had been George," shouted Turenne, while rubbing his behind, "there was no need to hit so hard." Is this, then, what you dare not tell? Wretches! Then be forever without naturalness, without vitals. Temper and harden your iron hearts in your vile propriety. Make yourselves contemptible by dint of dignity. But you, good young man, who read this story and who sense with emotion all the sweetness of soul it reveals at the very first reaction, read also about the pettiness of this great man as soon as it was a question of his birth and his name. Think that it is the same Turenne who affected giving way to his nephew everywhere in order that it be clearly seen that this child was the head of a sovereign house.[23] Set these contrasts side by side, love nature, despise opinion, and know man.

Very few people are in a condition to conceive the effects that reading directed in this way can have on a young man's completely fresh mind. We are bent over books from our childhood and accustomed to read without thinking; what we read is all the less striking to us since we already contain within ourselves the passions and the prejudices which fill history and the lives of men, and therefore all men do appears natural to us because we are outside of nature and judge others by ourselves. But picture a young man raised according to my maxims. Think of my Emile. Eighteen years of assiduous care have had as their only object the preservation of a sound judgment and a healthy heart.

Think of him at the raising of the curtain, casting his eyes for the first time on the stage of the world; or, rather, set backstage, seeing the actors take up and put on their costumes, counting the cords and pulleys whose crude magic deceives the spectators' eyes. His initial surprise will soon be succeeded by emotions of shame and disdain for his species. He will be indignant at thus seeing the whole of humankind its own dupe, debasing itself in these children's games. He will be afflicted at seeing his brothers tear one another apart for the sake of dreams and turn into ferocious animals because they do not know how to be satisfied with being men. Certainly, given the pupil's natural dispositions, if the master brings a bit of prudence and selectivity to his readings, if the master gives him a small start on the way to the reflections he ought to draw from them, this exercise will be for him a course in practical philosophy, better, surely, and better understood than all the vain speculations by which young people's minds are scrambled in our schools. When Cyneas, after having heard out the romantic projects of Pyrrhus, asks him what real good the conquest of the world will procure for him which he cannot enjoy right now without so much torment,[24] we see only a fleeting *bon mot*; but Emile will see a very wise reflection which he would have been the first to make and which will never be effaced from his mind, because this reflection finds no contrary prejudice that can prevent it from making an impression. When he then reads the life of this madman and finds that all the latter's great designs ended in his getting killed by a woman's hand, instead of admiring this pretended heroism Emile will see nothing in all the exploits of so great a captain, in all the intrigues of so great a statesman, other than so many steps on the road to that fateful tile which would terminate his life and his projects by a dishonorable death.[25]

All conquerors have not been killed; all usurpers have not failed in their enterprises; several will appear happy to minds biased by vulgar opinions. But he who does not stop at appearances but judges the happiness of men only by the condition of their hearts will see their miseries in their very successes; he will see their desires and their gnawing cares extend and increase with their fortune; he will see them getting out of breath in advancing without ever reaching their goals. He will see them as being similar to those inexperienced travelers who, setting out for the first time in the Alps, think that at each mountain they have crossed them, and when they are at a summit are discouraged to find higher mountains ahead.

Augustus, after having subjected his fellow citizens and destroyed his rivals, ruled for forty years the greatest empire which has ever existed. But did all that immense power prevent him from beating his head against the walls and filling his vast palace with his cries asking Varus for his exterminated legions back? [26] If he had conquered all his enemies, what use would all his vain triumphs have been to him when suffering of every kind was arising constantly around him, when his dearest friends made attempts on his life, and when the shame or the death of all those closest to him reduced him to tears? This unfortunate man wanted to govern the world and did not know how to govern his own household! What was the result of this negligence? He saw his nephew, his adopted son, and his son-in-law perish in the prime of life. His grandson was reduced to eating the stuffing of his bed in order to prolong his miserable life for a few hours. His daughter and his granddaughter died after having covered him with their infamy—one of poverty and hunger on a desert island, the other in prison by an executioner's hand. Finally, he himself, the last survivor of his unhappy family, was reduced by his own wife to leaving nothing but a monster as his successor. Such was the fate of this master of the world, so famous for his glory and his happiness.[27] Can I believe that a single one of those who admire that glory and that happiness would be willing to acquire them at the same price?

I have taken ambition as an example. But the play of all the human passions offers similar lessons to whoever wants to study history in order to know himself and to make himself wise at the expense of the dead. The time is approaching when the life of Antony will provide the young man with more relevant instruction than the life of Augustus. Emile will hardly recognize himself in the strange objects which will strike his glance during these new studies. But he will know ahead of time how to dispel the illusion of the passions before they are born; and, seeing that in all times they have blinded men, he will be warned of the way in which they can blind him in turn, if ever he yields to them. These lessons, I know, are ill suited to him; perhaps in case of need they will be too late and insufficient. But remember that they are not the lessons I wanted to draw from this study. In beginning it, I set myself another goal; and certainly, if this goal is not well fulfilled, it will be the master's fault.

Remember that as soon as *amour-propre* has developed, the relative *I* is constantly in play, and the young man never observes others without returning to himself and comparing himself with them. The issue, then, is to know in what rank among his fellows he will put himself after having examined them. I see from the way young people are made to read history that they are transformed, so to speak, into all the persons they see; one endeavors to make them become now Cicero, now Trajan, now Alexander, and to make them discouraged when they return to themselves, to make each of them regret being only himself. This method has certain advantages which I do not discount; but, as for my Emile, if in these parallels he just once prefers to be someone other than himself—were this other Socrates, were it Cato—everything has failed. He who begins to become alien to himself does not take long to forget himself entirely.

It is not philosophers who know men best. They see them only through the prejudices of philosophy, and I know of no station where one has so many. A savage has a healthier judgment of us than a philosopher does. The latter senses his own vices, is indignant at ours, and says to himself, "We are all wicked." The former looks at us without emotion and says, "You are mad." He is right. No one does the bad for the sake of the bad. My pupil is that savage, with the difference that Emile, having reflected more, compared ideas more, seen our errors from closer up, is more on guard against himself and judges only what he knows.

It is our passions which arouse us against those of others. It is our interest which makes us hate the wicked. If they did us no harm, we would have more pity for them than hate. The harm the wicked do us makes us forget the harm they do themselves. We would pardon them their vices more easily if we knew how much they are punished by their own heart. We feel the offense, and we do not see the chastisement. The advantages are apparent; the pain is interior. He who believes he enjoys the fruit of his vices is no less tormented than if he had not succeeded. The object has changed; the anxiety is the same. They may very well show off their fortunes and hide their hearts, but their conduct shows their hearts in spite of themselves; but in order to see that, one must not have a heart like theirs.

The passions we share seduce us; those that conflict with our interests revolt us; and, by an inconsistency which comes to us from these passions, we blame in others what we would like to imitate. Aversion and illusion are inevitable when we are forced to suffer from another the harm we would do if we were in his place.

What would be required, then, in order to observe men well? A great interest in knowing them and a great impartiality in judging them. A heart sensitive enough to conceive all the human passions and calm enough not to experience them. If there is a favorable moment in life for this study, it is the one I have chosen for Emile. Earlier, men would have been alien to him; later, he would have been like them. Opinion, whose action he sees, has not acquired its empire over him. The passions, whose effect he feels, have not yet agitated his heart. He is a man; he is interested in his brothers; he is equitable; he judges his peers. Surely, if he judges them well, he will not want to be in the place of any of them; for since the goal of all the torments they give themselves is founded on prejudices he does not have, it appears to him to be pie in the sky. For him, all that he desires is within his reach. Sufficient unto himself and free of prejudices, on whom will he be dependent? He has arms, health,* moderation, few needs, and the means of satisfying them. Nurtured in the most absolute liberty, he conceives of no ill greater than servitude. He pities these miserable kings, slaves of all that obey them. He pities these false wise men, chained to their vain reputations. He pities these rich fools, martyrs to their display. He pities these conspicuous voluptuaries, who devote their entire lives to boredom in order to appear to have pleasure. He would pity even the enemy who would do him harm, for he would see his misery in his wickedness. He would say to himself, "In giving himself the need to hurt me, this man has made his fate dependent on mine."

One more step, and we reach the goal. *Amour-propre* is a useful but dangerous instrument. Often it wounds the hand making use of it and

---

* I believe I can confidently count health and a good constitution among the advantages acquired through his education or, rather, among the gifts of nature his education has preserved for him.

rarely does good without evil. Emile, in considering his rank in the human species and seeing himself so happily placed there, will be tempted to honor his reason for the work of yours and to attribute his happiness to his own merit. He will say to himself, "I am wise, and men are mad." In pitying them, he will despise them; in congratulating himself, he will esteem himself more, and in feeling himself to be happier than them, he will believe himself worthier to be so. This is the error most to be feared, because it is the most difficult to destroy. If he remained in this condition, he would have gained little from all our care; and if one had to choose, I do not know whether I would not prefer the illusion of the prejudices to that of pride.

Great men are not deceived about their superiority; they see it, feel it, and are no less modest because of it. The more they have, the more they know all that they lack. They are less vain about being raised above us than they are humbled by the sentiment of their poverty; and with the exclusive goods which they possess, they are too sensible to be vain about a gift they did not give themselves. The good man can be proud of his virtue because it is his. But of what is the intelligent man proud? What did Racine do not to be Pradon? What did Boileau do in order not to be Cotin?

Here the issue is entirely different. Let us always remain in the common order. I have assumed for my pupil neither a transcendent genius nor a dull understanding. I have chosen him from among the ordinary minds in order to show what education can do for man. All rare cases are outside the rules. Therefore, if as a consequence of my care Emile prefers his way of being, of seeing, and of feeling to that of other men, Emile is right. But if he thus believes himself to be of a more excellent nature and more happily born than other men, Emile is wrong. He is deceived. One must undeceive him or, rather, anticipate the error for fear that afterward it will be too late to destroy it.

The sole folly of which one cannot disabuse a man who is not mad is vanity. For this there is no cure other than experience—if, indeed, anything can cure it. At its birth, at least, one can prevent its growth. Do not get lost in fine reasonings intended to prove to the adolescent that he is a man like others and subject to the same weaknesses. Make him feel it, or he will never know it. This again is a case of an exception to my own rules; it is the case in which my pupil is to be exposed voluntarily to all the accidents that can prove to him that he is no wiser than we are. The adventure with the magician would be repeated in countless ways. I would let flatterers take every advantage of him. If giddy fellows dragged him into some folly, I would let him run the risk. If swindlers went after him at gambling, I would give him over to them so that they could make him their dupe.* I would let him be

---

* Moreover, our pupil will not often be caught in this trap—he who is surrounded by so many entertainments, who was never bored in his life, and who hardly knows what money is good for. Since the two motives by which one leads children are interest and vanity, these same two motives are used by courtesans and confidence men to get hold of them later. When you see their avidity aroused by prizes and rewards, when you see them at age ten applauded in a public document at school, you see how at twenty they will be made to leave their purses in a gaming house and their health in a house of ill fame. It is always a good bet that the most

flattered, fleeced, and robbed by them. And when, having cleaned him out, they ended by making fun of him, I would further thank them in his presence for lessons they were so good as to give him. The only traps from which I would carefully protect him are those of courtesans. The only consideration I would have for him would be to share all the dangers I let him run and all the affronts I let him receive. I would endure everything silently without complaint, without reproach, without ever saying a single word to him about it. And you can be certain that, if this discretion is well maintained, everything he has seen me suffer for him will make more of an impression on his heart than what he has suffered himself.

Here I cannot prevent myself from mentioning the false dignity of governors who, in order stupidly to play wise men, run down their pupils, affect always to treat them as children, and always distinguish themselves from their pupils in everything they make them do. Far from thus disheartening your pupils' youthful courage, spare nothing to lift up their souls; make them your equals in order that they may become your equals; and if they cannot yet raise themselves up to you, descend to their level without shame, without scruple. Remember that your honor is no longer in you but in your pupil. Share his faults in order to correct them. Take on the burden of his shame in order to efface it. Imitate that brave Roman who, seeing his army flee and not being able to rally it, turned and fled at the head of his soldiers, crying, "They do not flee. They follow their captain." [28] Was he dishonored for that? Far from it. In thus sacrificing his glory, he increased it. The force of duty and the beauty of virtue attract our approbation in spite of ourselves and overturn our insane prejudices. If I received a slap in fulfilling my functions with Emile, far from avenging myself for this slap, I would go everywhere to boast about it, and I doubt whether there is a man in the world vile enough not to respect me the more for it.

It is not that the pupil ought to suppose an understanding as limited as his own in the master and the same facility at letting himself be seduced. This opinion is good for a child who, knowing how to see nothing and compare nothing, takes everyone to be on his level and trusts only those who actually know how to get down to it. But a young man of Emile's age, and as sensible as he is, is not stupid enough to be thus taken in; and it would not be good if he were taken in. The confidence he ought to have in his governor is of another kind. It ought to rest on the authority of reason, on superiority of understanding, on advantages that the young man is in a condition to know and whose utility to himself he senses. A long experience has convinced him that he is loved by his guide, that the guide is a wise and enlightened man who, wishing for his happiness, knows what can procure it for him. He ought to know that in his own interest it is proper to listen to his guide's advice. Now, if the master were to let himself be deceived like the dis-

---

learned member of his class will be the biggest gambler and the biggest debauché. It is true that means which were not used in childhood are not subject to the same abuse in youth. But one ought to remember that here my constant maxim is always to take a thing at its worst. I seek first to prevent the vice, and then I assume it in order to remedy it.

ciple, he would lose the right to exact deference and to give his disciple lessons. Still less should the latter suppose that the master purposely lets him be ensnared and sets traps for his simplicity. What then must be done to avoid both of these difficulties at once? That which is best and most natural: be simple and true like him, warn him of the perils to which he is exposed, and show them to him clearly and sensibly, but without exaggeration, ill humor, pedantic display, and, above all, without giving him your advice as an order until it has become one and this imperious tone is absolutely necessary. Is he obstinate after that, as he will very often be? Then say nothing more to him; leave him free; follow him; imitate him, and do it gaily and frankly. Let yourself go, enjoy yourself as much as he does, if it is possible. If the consequences become too great, you are always there to put a stop to them. And meanwhile, will not the young man, witnessing your foresight and your kindness, be at once greatly struck by the one and touched by the other? All his faults are so many bonds he provides you for restraining him in case of need. What here constitutes the master's greatest art is to provide occasions and to manage exhortations in such a way that he knows in advance when the young man will yield and when he will be obstinate. Thus the master can surround him on all sides with the lessons of experience without ever exposing him to too great dangers.

Warn him about his mistakes before he falls into them. When he has fallen into them, do not reproach him for them. You would only inflame his *amour-propre* and make it rebel. A lesson that causes revolt is of no profit. I know of nothing more inept than the phrase: "I told you so!" The best means of making him remember what one has told him is to appear to have forgotten it. Instead of reproaching him when you see him ashamed of not having believed you, gently efface this humiliation with good words. He will surely be more fond of you when he sees that you forget yourself for him, and that, instead of finishing the job of crushing him, you console him. But if you add reproaches to his sorrow, he will conceive a hatred of you and will make it a law unto himself not to listen to you anymore, as though to prove to you that he does not agree with you about the importance of your advice.

The manner of your consolations can provide further instruction for him, instruction so much the more useful in that he will not be on his guard against it. In saying to him, for example, that countless others make the same mistakes, you do not exactly fill the bill for him; you correct him by appearing only to pity him; for, to him who believes he is worth more than other men, it is a most mortifying excuse to be consoled by their example. It is to suggest that the most he can pretend to is that they be not worth more than he is.

The time of mistakes is the time of fables. By censuring the guilty party under an alien mask, one instructs him without offending him; and he understands then, from the truth which he applies to himself, that the apologue is not a lie. The child who has never been deceived by praise understands nothing of the fable I examined earlier. But the giddy young man who has just been the dupe of a flatterer conceives marvelously that the crow was only a fool. Thus, from a fact he draws a maxim; and by means of the fable the experience he would soon have forgotten is imprinted on his judgment. There is no moral knowledge which cannot be acquired by another's or one's own experience. In the cases where this experience is dangerous, instead of having it oneself, one draws one's lesson from the story. When the test is inconsequential, it is good that the young man remain exposed to it. Then, by means of the apologue, one frames the particular cases known to him in the form of maxims.

I do not mean, however, that these maxims ought to be elaborated or even stated. Nothing is so vain or so ill conceived as the moral with which most fables end—as if this moral were not or should not be understood in the fable itself in such a way as to be palpable to the reader. Why, then, by adding this moral at the end, take from him the pleasure of finding it on his own? Talent at instruction consists in making the disciple enjoy the instruction. But in order for him to enjoy it, his mind must not remain so passive at everything you tell him that he has absolutely nothing to do in order to understand you. The master's *amour-propre* must always leave some hold for the disciple's; he must be able to say to himself, "I conceive, I discern, I act, I learn." One of the things that makes the Pantaloon [29] of Italian comedy a bore is the care he always takes to interpret to the pit platitudes which are only too well understood. I do not want a governor to be Pantaloon; still less do I want him to be an author. One must always make oneself understood, but one must not always say everything. He who says everything says little, for finally he is no longer listened to. What is the meaning of those four verses La Fontaine adds to the fable of the frog who puffs himself up? Is he afraid he will not be understood? [30] Does this great painter need to write names beneath the objects he paints? Far from thereby generalizing his moral, he particularizes it, he restricts it in a way to the examples cited and prevents its being applied to others. Before putting this inimitable author's fables into a young man's hands, I would want to cut out all these conclusions where La Fontaine makes an effort to explain what he has just said no less clearly than agreeably. If your pupil understands the fable only with the help of the explanation, be sure that he will not understand it even in that way.

It would also be important to give these fables an order that is more didactic and more in conformity with the progress of the young adolescent's sentiments and understanding. Can one conceive of anything less reasonable than following exactly the numerical order of the book without regard to need or occasion? First the crow, then the cicada, then the frog, then the two mules, etc. These two mules rankle me, because I remember having seen a child—who was being raised to become a financier, and whom they were making giddy with the function he was going to fulfill—read this fable, learn it, tell it, and retell it hundreds of times without ever drawing from it the least objection to the trade for which he was destined. Not only have I never seen children make any solid application of the fables they learned, but

BOOK IV

I have never seen anyone take care to get them to make this application. The pretext of this study is moral instruction, but the true object of the mother and the child is only to get a whole gathering to pay attention to him reciting his fables. So he forgets them all on growing up, when it is a question no longer of reciting them but of profiting from them. To repeat, it is only men who get instruction from fables, and now is the time for Emile to begin.

I show from afar—for I also do not want to say everything—the roads deviating from the right one in order that one may learn to avoid them. I believe that in following the one I have indicated, your pupil will purchase knowledge of men and of himself as cheaply as possible, and that you will put him in a position to contemplate the games of Fortune without envying the fate of its favorites, and to be satisfied with himself without believing himself to be wiser than others. You have also begun to make him an actor in order to make him a spectator; you must finish the job; for from the pit one sees objects as they appear, but from the stage one sees them as they are. To embrace the whole, one must move back to get perspective; one must come near to see the details. But what claim has a young man to admission into the affairs of the world? What right has he to be initiated in these shadowy mysteries? The interests of his age limit him to affairs of pleasure. He still disposes only of himself; it is as though he disposed of nothing. Man is the lowest kind of merchandise; and among our important rights of property that of the person is always the least of all.

When I see that at the age of the greatest activity young people are limited to purely speculative studies, and that then without the least experience they are all of a sudden cast into the world and business, I find that reason no less than nature is offended, and I am no longer surprised that so few people know how to take care of themselves. By what bizarre turn of mind are we taught so many useless things while the art of action is counted for nothing? They claim they form us for society, and they instruct us as if each of us were going to spend his life in thinking alone in his cell or treating airy questions with disinterested men. You believe you are teaching your children how to live by training them in certain contortions of the body and certain formulas of speech signifying nothing. I, too, have taught my Emile how to live, for I have taught him how to live with himself and, in addition, how to earn his bread. But this is not enough. To live in the world, one must know how to deal with men, one must know the instruments which give one a hold over them. One must know how to calculate the action and the reaction of particular interests in civil society and to foresee events so accurately that one is rarely mistaken in one's undertakings, or at least has chosen the best means for succeeding. The laws do not permit young people to manage their own business and dispose of their own goods. But what use to them would be these precautions if up to the prescribed age they could acquire no experience? They would have gained nothing by waiting and would be just as new at things at twenty-five as at fifteen. Doubtless a young man blinded by his ignorance or deceived by his passions must be prevented from doing harm to himself. But at any age beneficence is permitted; at any age one can, under a wise man's direction, protect the unfortunate who need only support.

Nurses and mothers are attached to children by the care they give them. The exercise of the social virtues brings the love of humanity to the depths of one's heart. It is in doing good that one becomes good; I know of no practice more certain. Busy your pupil with all the good actions within his reach. Let the interest of indigents always be his. Let him assist them not only with his purse but with his care. Let him serve them, protect them, consecrate his person and his time to them. Let him be their representative; he will never again in his life fulfill so noble a function. How many of the oppressed who would never have been heard will obtain justice when he asks for it on their behalf with that intrepid firmness given by the practice of virtue, when he forces the doors of the noble and the rich, when he goes, if necessary, to the foot of the throne to make heard the voice of the unfortunates to whom all access is closed by their poverty and who are prevented by fear of being punished for the ills done to them if they even dare to complain?

But will we make of Emile a knight errant, a redresser of wrongs, a paladin? Will he go and meddle in public affairs, play the wise man and the defender of the laws with the nobles, with the magistrates, with the prince, play the solicitor with the judges and the lawyer with the courts? I know nothing about all that. Terms of denigration and ridicule change nothing in the nature of things. He will do all that he knows to be useful and good. He will do nothing more, and he knows that nothing is useful and good for him which is not suitable to his age. He knows that his first duty is toward himself, that young people ought to distrust themselves, be circumspect in their conduct, respectful before older people, reserved and careful not to talk without purpose, modest in inconsequential things, but hardy in good deeds and courageous in speaking the truth. Such were those illustrious Romans who, before being admitted to public offices, spent their youth in prosecuting crime and defending innocence, without any other interest than that of instructing themselves in serving justice and protecting good morals.

Emile dislikes both turmoil and quarrels, not only among men *

---

* But if someone picks a quarrel with him, how will he behave? I answer that he will never have a quarrel, that he will never lend himself to it enough to have one. But finally, it will be pursued, who is safe from a slap or from being given the lie by a bully, a drunk, or a brave scoundrel who, in order to have the pleasure of killing his man, begins by dishonoring him? That is something else. Neither the honor nor the life of citizens must be at the mercy of a bully, of a drunk, or of a brave scoundrel, and one can no more secure oneself from such an accident than from the fall of a tile. To meet and put up with a slap or being given the lie has civil effects which no wisdom can anticipate, and for which no tribunal can avenge the injured party. The insufficiency of the laws, therefore, gives him back his independence in this. He is then the only magistrate, the only judge between the offender and himself. He is the only interpreter and minister of the natural law. He owes himself justice and is the only one who can render it, and there is no government on earth so mad as to punish him for having done himself justice in such a case. I do not say that he ought to fight a duel. That is a folly. I say that he owes himself justice, and that he is the only dispenser of it. If I were sovereign, I guarantee that, without so many vain edicts against duels, there would never be either slap or giving of the lie in my states, and that this would be accomplished by a very simple means in which the tribunals would not mix. However that may

but even among animals. Never did he incite two dogs to fight with one another, never did he get a dog to chase a cat. This spirit of peace is an effect of his education which, not having fomented *amour-propre* and a high opinion of himself, has diverted him from seeking his pleasures in domination and in another's unhappiness. He suffers when he sees suffering. It is a natural sentiment. A young man is hardened and takes pleasure at seeing a sensitive being tormented when a reflection of vanity makes him regard himself as exempt from the same pains as a result of his wisdom or his superiority. He who has been protected against this turn of mind could not fall into the vice which is its work. Emile therefore loves peace. The image of happiness delights him, and when he can contribute to producing happiness, this is one more means of sharing it. I have not supposed that when he sees unhappy men, he would have only that sterile and cruel pity for them which is satisfied with pitying ills it can cure. His active beneficence soon gives him understanding which with a harder heart he would not have acquired or would have acquired much later. If he sees discord reigning among his comrades, he seeks to reconcile them; if he sees men afflicted, he informs himself as to the subject of their suffering; if he sees two men who hate each other, he wants to know the cause of their enmity; if he sees an oppressed man groaning under the vexations of the powerful and the rich, he finds out what maneuvers are used to cover over those vexations; and, with the interest he takes in all men who are miserable, the means of ending their ills are never indifferent to him. What, then, do we have to do in order to take advantage of those dispositions in a way suitable to his age? We have to regulate his concern and his knowledge and employ his zeal to increase them.

I do not tire of repeating it: put all the lessons of young people in actions rather than in speeches. Let them learn nothing in books which experience can teach them. What an extravagant project it is to train them in speaking without their having a subject about which to say anything; to believe that on the benches of a college they can be made to feel the energy of the language of the passions and all the force of the art of persuasion without interest in persuading anyone of anything! All the precepts of rhetoric seem to be only pure verbiage to whoever does not sense their use for his profit. Of what import is it to a schoolboy to know how Hannibal went about convincing his soldiers to cross the Alps? If, in place of these magnificent harangues, you told him how he ought to go about getting his principal to give him a vacation, be sure that he would be more attentive to your rules.

If I wanted to teach rhetoric to a young man whose passions all were already developed, I would constantly present him with objects fit to delight those passions, and I would examine with him what language he ought to use with other men in order to engage them to favor his desires. But my Emile is not in so advantageous a situation for the oratorical art. Limited almost solely to what is physically necessary, he

---

be, Emile knows the justice he owes to himself in such a case and the example he owes to the security of men of honor. The firmest of men is not in a position to prevent someone from insulting him, but he is in a position to prevent anyone's boasting for long of having insulted him.

has less need of others than others have of him; and having nothing to ask of them for himself, what he wants to persuade them of does not touch him enough to move him excessively. It follows from this that in general he ought to have a language which is simple and hardly at all figurative. Ordinarily he speaks literally and solely to be understood. His speech is little given to sententiousness, because he has not learned to generalize his ideas; he uses few images, because he is rarely passionate.

It is not the case, however, that he is completely phlegmatic and cold. Neither his age nor his morals nor his tastes permit it. In the fire of adolescence the vivifying spirits, retained and distilled in his blood, bring to his young heart a warmth which shines forth in his glance, which is sensed in his speech, which is visible in his actions. His language has gained expression and sometimes vehemence. The noble sentiment inspiring him gives him force and elevation. Suffused with the tender love of humanity, he transmits the emotions of his soul in speaking. His generous frankness has an indefinable something about it that is more enchanting than the artificial eloquence of others; or, rather, he alone is truly eloquent since he has only to show what he feels to communicate it to those who hear him.

The more I think about it, the more I find that in thus putting beneficence in action and drawing from our greater or lesser successes reflections on their causes, there is little useful knowledge which cannot be cultivated in a young man's mind; in this way, along with all the true learning that can be acquired in colleges, he will acquire another science still more important, which is the application of these attainments to the uses of life. Since he takes so much interest in his fellows, it is impossible that he not learn early to weigh and appraise their actions, their tastes, and their pleasures and to evaluate what can contribute to or detract from men's happiness more accurately than can those who are interested in no one and never do anything for others. Those who never deal with anything other than their own affairs are too passionate to judge things soundly. Relating everything to themselves alone and regulating their ideas of good and bad according to their own interest, they fill their minds with countless ridiculous prejudices, and in everything that hampers their slightest advantage, they immediately see the overturning of the whole universe.

Let us extend *amour-propre* to other beings. We shall transform it into a virtue, and there is no man's heart in which this virtue does not have its root. The less the object of our care is immediately involved with us, the less the illusion of particular interest is to be feared. The more one generalizes this interest, the more it becomes equitable, and the love of mankind is nothing other than the love of justice. Do we, then, want Emile to love the truth; do we want him to know it? In his activities let us always keep him at a distance from himself. The more his cares are consecrated to the happiness of others, the more they will be enlightened and wise and the less he will deceived about what is good or bad. But let us never tolerate in him a blind preference founded solely on consideration of persons or on unjust bias. And why would he hurt one to serve another? It is of little importance to him who gets a greater share of happiness provided that it contributes to the greatest happiness of all. This is the wise man's first interest after his private interest, for each is part of his species and not of another individual.[31]

To prevent pity from degenerating into weakness, it must, therefore, be generalized and extended to the whole of mankind. Then one yields to it only insofar as it accords with justice, because of all the virtues justice is the one that contributes most to the common good of men. For the sake of reason, for the sake of love of ourselves, we must have pity for our species still more than for our neighbor, and pity for the wicked is a very great cruelty to men.

Moreover, it must be remembered that all these means by which I take my pupil out of himself, always have, nevertheless, a direct relation to him; for not only does he get an inner enjoyment from them, but also, in making him beneficent for the profit of others, I work for his own instruction.

I have first given the means, and now I show the effect. What great views I see settling little by little in his head! What sublime sentiments stifle the germ of the petty passions in his heart! What judicial clarity, what accuracy of reason I see forming in him, as a result of the cultivation of his inclinations, of the experience which concentrates the wishes of a great soul within the narrow limit of the possible and makes a man who is superior to others and, unable to raise them to his level, is capable of lowering himself to theirs! The true principles of the just, the true models of the beautiful, all the moral relations of beings, all the ideas of order are imprinted on his understanding. He sees the place of each thing and the cause which removes it from its place; he sees what can do good and what stands in its way. Without having experienced the human passions, he knows their illusions and their effects.

I go forward, attracted by the force of things but without gaining credibility in the judgment of my readers. For a long while they have seen me in the land of chimeras. I always see them in the land of prejudices. In separating myself so far from vulgar opinions I do not cease keeping them present in my mind. I examine them, I meditate on them, neither to follow them nor to flee them but to weigh them in the scale of reasoning. Every time that this reasoning forces me to separate myself from those opinions, I have learned from experience to take it for granted that my readers will not imitate me. I know that they persist in imagining only what they see; and therefore they will take the young man whom I evoke to be an imaginary and fantastic being because he differs from those with whom they compare him. They do not stop to think that he must certainly differ from these young men, since he is raised quite differently, affected by quite contrary sentiments, and instructed quite otherwise from them; indeed, it would be much more surprising if he were to resemble them than to be such as I suppose him. This is not the man of man; it is the man of nature. Assuredly he should be very alien to their eyes.

In beginning this work, I supposed nothing that everyone cannot observe just as I do, because there is a point—the birth of man—from which we all equally begin. But the more we go forward, I to cultivate nature and you to deprave it, the farther we get from each other. My pupil at the age of six differed little from yours, whom you had not had the time to disfigure. Now they are no longer similar in anything; and the age of maturity, which he is approaching, ought to show that he is of an absolutely different kind, if I have not wasted all my care. The extent of their attainments is perhaps fairly equal on both sides; but the things they have attained bear no resemblance. You are surprised to find in the one sublime sentiments of which the others do not have the slightest germ. But consider also that the latter are already all philosophers and theologians before Emile knows what philosophy is and has even heard of God.

If, then, someone came and said to me, "Nothing of what you suppose exists. Young people are not made that way. They have such or such a passion. They do this or that," it would be as if he were to deny that there was ever a big pear tree because one only sees dwarf pear trees in our gardens.

I beg these judges who are so quick to censure to consider that I know what they are saying here just as well as they do, that I have probably reflected on it longer, and that as I have no interest in foisting anything on them, I have the right to demand that they at least take the time to seek out where I am mistaken. Let them examine carefully the constitution of man and follow the first developments of the heart in various circumstances in order to see how much one individual can differ from another due to the force of education; next let them compare my education with the effects I attribute to it, and then say where I have badly reasoned. I shall have nothing to respond.

What makes me more assertive—and, I believe, more to be excused for being so—is that, instead of yielding to the systematic spirit, I grant as little as possible to reasoning and I trust only observation. I found myself not on what I have imagined but on what I have seen. It is true that I have not restricted my experience to the compass of a city's walls or to a single class of people. But after having compared as many ranks and peoples as I could see in a life spent observing them, I have eliminated as artificial what belonged to one people and not to another, to one station and not to another, and have regarded as incontestably belonging to man only what was common to all, at whatever age, in whatever rank, and in whatever nation.

Now if in accordance with this method you follow a young man from childhood who has not received a particular form and who depends as little as possible on the authority and opinion of others, whom do you think he will most resemble—my pupil or yours? This, it seems to me, is the question which must be resolved in order to know whether I have gone astray.

Man does not easily begin to think. But as soon as he begins, he never stops. Whoever has thought will always think, and once the understanding is practiced at reflection, it can no longer stay at rest. It might, therefore, be believed that I do too much or too little, that the human mind is not naturally so quick to open itself, and that, after having given it faculties it does not possess, I keep it inscribed for too long in a circle of ideas it should have gone beyond.

But consider, in the first place, that although I want to form the man of nature, the object is not, for all that, to make him a savage and to relegate him to the depths of the woods. It suffices that, enclosed in a social whirlpool, he not let himself get carried away by either the passions or the opinions of men, that he see with his eyes, that he feel with his heart, that no authority govern him beyond that of his own reason. In this position it is clear that the multitude of objects striking him, the frequent sentiments affecting him, and the various means of providing for his real needs are all going to give him many ideas that he would never have had or that he would have acquired more slowly. The progress natural to the mind is accelerated but not upset. The same man who ought to remain stupid in the forests ought to become reasonable and sensible in the cities when he is a simple spectator there. Nothing is more fit to make a man wise than follies that are seen without being shared; and even he who shares them is still instructed, provided he is not their dupe and does not bring to them the error of men who commit them.

Consider also that since we are limited by our faculties to things which can be sensed, we provide almost no hold for abstract notions of philosophy and purely intellectual ideas. To arrive at them we must either separate ourselves from the body—to which we are so strongly attached—or make a gradual and slow climb from object to object, or, finally, clear the gap rapidly and almost at a leap, by a giant step upward of which childhood is not capable and for which even men need many rungs especially made for them. The first abstract idea is the first of these rungs, but I have great difficulty in seeing how anyone got it into his head to construct it.

The incomprehensible Being who embraces everything, who gives motion to the world and forms the whole system of beings, is neither visible to our eyes nor palpable to our hands; He escapes all our senses. The work is revealed, but the worker is hidden. It is no small undertaking to know even that He exists; and when we have succeeded at that and ask ourselves, "What is He? Where is He?" our mind is confused and goes astray, and we no longer know what to think.

Locke wants one to begin by the study of spirits and later go on to that of bodies. This method is that of superstition, of prejudices, and of error. It is not that of reason nor even of nature in its proper order. It is to stop up our eyes in order to learn to see. One must have studied bodies for a long time in order to form for oneself a true notion of spirits and to suspect that they exist. The opposite order serves only to establish materialism.[32]

Since our senses are the first instruments of our knowledge, corporeal and sensible beings are the only ones of which we immediately have an idea. The word *spirit* has no sense for anyone who has not philosophized. To the people and to children, a spirit is only a body. Do they not imagine spirits who cry out, speak, flutter, and make noise? Now, it will be granted me that spirits which have arms and tongues bear a strong resemblance to bodies. This is why all the peoples of the world, without excepting the Jews, have made corporeal gods for themselves. We ourselves, with our terms *spirit, trinity, persons,* are for the most part veritable anthropomorphites. I admit that we are taught to say that God is everywhere, but we also believe that air is everywhere, at least in our atmosphere. And in its origin the word *spirit* itself signifies only breath and wind. As soon as people are accustomed to say words without understanding them, it is easy to make them say whatever one wants.

The sentiment of our action on other bodies must at first have made us believe that when they acted on us they did so in a manner similar to the way we acted on them. Thus man began by animating all the beings whose action he felt. Not only did he feel himself less strong than most of these beings, but for want of knowing the limits of their power, he assumed it to be unlimited, and he construed them to be gods as soon as he construed them to be bodies. During the first ages men were frightened of everything and saw nothing dead in nature. The idea of matter was formed no less slowly in them than that of spirit, since the former idea is an abstraction itself. They thus filled the universe with gods which could be sensed. Stars, winds, mountains, rivers, trees, cities, even houses, each had its soul, its god, its life. The teraphim of Laban,[33] the manitous of savages,[34] the fetishes of Negroes, all the works of nature and of men, were the first divinities of mortals. Polytheism was their first religion, and idolatry their first form of worship. They were able to recognize a single god only when, generalizing their ideas more and more, they were in a condition to ascend to a first cause, to bring together the total system of beings under a single idea, and to give a sense to the word *substance,* which is at bottom the greatest of abstractions. Every child who believes in God is, therefore, necessarily an idolator or at least an anthropomorphite. And once the imagination has seen God, it is very rare that the understanding conceives Him. This is precisely the error to which Locke's order leads.

Once the abstract idea of substance has—I know not how—been arrived at, one sees that, in order to admit of only one substance, this substance must be assumed to have incompatible qualities, such as thought and extension, which are mutually exclusive since one is essentially divisible and the other excludes all divisibility. One conceives, moreover, that thought or, if you wish, sentiment is a primary quality inseparable from the substance to which it belongs, and that the same is the case for extension in relation to its substance. From this one concludes that beings that lose one of these qualities lose the substance to which it belongs; that consequently death is only a separation of substances; and that beings in which these two qualities are joined are composed of the two substances to which these two qualities belong.[35]

Now just consider what a distance still remains between the notion of two substances and that of the divine nature, between the incomprehensible idea of the action of our soul on our body and the idea of the action of God on all beings! The ideas of creation, annihilation, ubiquity, eternity, omnipotence, the idea of the divine attributes—all these ideas that are seen to be as confused and obscure as they really are by so few men, but that are in no way obscure for the people because they do not comprehend them at all—how will these ideas be presented in all their force—that is to say, in all their obscurity—to young minds still busy with the first operations of the senses and able to conceive only what they touch? It is in vain that the abysses of the infinite are open all around us. A child does not know enough to be terrified by them; his weak eyes cannot probe their depths. Everything is infinite for children. They do not know how to set limits to anything— not because they make the measure very long, but because their understanding is short. I have even noticed that they put the infinite less beyond than below the dimensions known to them. They will estimate an immense space far more by their feet than by their eyes. It will extend for them, not farther than they can see, but farther than they can go. If one speaks to them of God's power, they will estimate Him to be almost as strong as their father. Since in everything their knowledge is the measure of the possible, they always judge everything of which they are told to be less than that which they know. Such are the judgments natural to ignorance and weakness of mind. Ajax was afraid to pit himself against Achilles and yet defied Jupiter to combat, because he knew Achilles and did not know Jupiter. A Swiss peasant who believed himself the richest of men, and to whom someone tried to explain what a king is, asked proudly whether the king could really have a hundred cows on the mountain.

I foresee how many readers will be surprised at seeing me trace the whole first age of my pupil without speaking to him of religion. At fifteen he did not know whether he had a soul. And perhaps at eighteen it is not yet time for him to learn it; for if he learns it sooner than he ought, he runs the risk of never knowing it.

If I had to depict sorry stupidity, I would depict a pedant teaching the catechism to children. If I wanted to make a child go mad, I would oblige him to explain what he says in saying his catechism. Someone will object to me that since most of the dogmas of Christianity are mysteries, to wait for the human mind to be capable of having a conception of them is not to wait for the child to be a man but to wait for the man to exist no more. To that I answer, in the first place, that there are mysteries it is impossible for man not only to conceive but to believe, and that I do not see what is gained by teaching them to children, unless it be that they learn how to lie early. I say, moreover, that, to accept the mysteries, one must at least comprehend that they are incomprehensible, and children are not even capable of this conception. At the age when everything is mystery, there are no mysteries strictly speaking.

You must believe in God to be saved. This dogma badly understood is the principle of sanguinary intolerance and the cause of all those vain instructions that strike a fatal blow to human reason in accustoming it to satisfy itself with words. Doubtless there is not a moment to lose in order to merit eternal salvation. But if in order to obtain it, it is enough to repeat certain words, I do not see what prevents us from peopling heaven with starlings and magpies just as well as with children.

The obligation to believe assumes the possibility of doing so. The philosopher who does not believe is wrong, because he uses badly the reason he has cultivated and because he is in a position to understand the truths he rejects. But what does the child who professes the Christian religion believe? What he has a conception of; and he has a conception of so little of what he is made to say that, if you say to him the opposite, he will adopt it just as gladly. The faith of children and of many men is a question of geography. Are they to be recompensed for being born in Rome rather than in Mecca? One is told that Mohammed is God's prophet, and he says that Mohammed is God's prophet. The other is told that Mohammed is a deceiver, and he says that Mohammed is a deceiver. Each of the two would have affirmed what the other affirms if they had happened to be transposed. Can one proceed from two such similar dispositions to send one to paradise and the other to hell? When a child says that he believes in God, it is not in God that he believes, it is in Peter or James who tell him that there is something called God. And he believes after the fashion of Euripides.

> Oh Jupiter! For other than the name
> I know nothing of you.*

We hold that no child who dies before the age of reason will be deprived of eternal happiness. The Catholics believe the same thing of all children who have been baptized, even if they have never heard of God. There are, therefore, cases in which one can be saved without believing in God, and these cases have their place when the human mind is incapable—as in childhood or in madness—of the operations necesry to recognize the divinity. The whole difference I see here between you and me is that you claim that children have this capacity at seven, and I do not even accord it to them at fifteen. Whether I am wrong or right, it is a question here not of an article of faith but of a simple observation of natural history.

By the same principle it is clear that a man who has come to old age without believing in God will not for that be deprived of his presence in the other life if his blindness was not voluntary; and I say that it is not always voluntary. You agree in the case of madmen whom an illness deprives of their spiritual faculties but not of their quality of being men or, consequently, of their right to the benefits of their Creator. Why, therefore, do you not also agree in the case of those who have been sequestered from all society from their childhood and have led an absolutely savage life, deprived of the enlightenment which is acquired only in commerce with men;† for it is a demonstrated impossibility that such a savage could ever raise his reflections up to the knowledge of the true God. Reason tells us that a man can be punished only for the mistakes of his will, and that an invincible ignorance could not be imputed to crime. From this it follows that before the

---

* Plutarch, *Treatise on Love*, Amyot trans. It is thus that the tragedy *Menalippe* began at first; but the clamor of the people of Athens forced Euripides to change this beginning.[36]

† On the natural state of the human mind and on the slowness of its progress, see the first part of the *Discourse on Inequality*.

bar of eternal justice every man who would believe if he had the necessary enlightenment is reputed to believe, and that the only unbelievers
who will be punished are those whose heart closes itself to the truth.

Let us refrain from proclaiming the truth to those who are not in a
condition to understand it, for to do this is to want to substitute error
for truth. It would be better to have no idea of the divinity than to have
ideas of it that are base, fantastic, insulting, or unworthy. It is a lesser
evil to be unaware of the divinity than to offend it. "I would rather,"
says the good Plutarch, "have it believed that there is no Plutarch in
the world than have it said that Plutarch is unjust, envious, jealous,
and such a tyrant that he demands more than he grants the power to
do." [37]

The great evil of the deformed images of the divinity which are drawn
in the minds of children is that they remain there all their lives; when
the children become men, they no longer conceive of any other God
than that of children. In Switzerland I have seen a good and pious
mother of a family so convinced of this maxim that she did not want
to instruct her son in religion during his first years, for fear that he
would be satisfied with this crude instruction and would neglect a
better one in the age of reason. This child never heard God spoken of
except with devotion and reverence; and when he himself wanted to
speak of Him, silence was imposed, as though the subject were too
sublime and too great for him. This reserve excited his curiosity, and
his *amour-propre* longed for the moment of knowing this mystery which
was being hidden from him with such care. The less one spoke to him
of God, the less he himself was allowed to speak of Him, the more he
was preoccupied by Him. This child saw God everywhere, and what I
would be afraid of, if this air of mystery were inopportunely affected,
is that one might influence a young man's imagination too much,
thereby troubling his brain and finally making a fanatic of him rather
than a believer.

But let us fear nothing of the kind for my Emile, who constantly
refuses his attention to everything beyond his reach and listens to
things he does not understand with the most profound indifference.
There are so many things about which he is accustomed to say, "This is
not within my competence," that one more hardly embarrasses him.
And when he begins to worry about these great questions, it is not
because he has heard them propounded; it is when the progress of his
enlightenment leads his researches in that direction.

We have seen by what path the cultivated human mind approaches
these mysteries, and I will gladly agree that even in the bosom of society it does not naturally reach them except at a more advanced age.
But since in this same society there are inevitable causes by which the
progress of the passions is accelerated, if one did not similarly accelerate the progress of the enlightenment which serves to regulate these
passions, then one would truly depart from the order of nature, and
the equilibrium would be broken. When one cannot moderate the too
rapid development of one aspect, it is necessary to manage with the
same rapidity the development of the others which ought to correspond
to it. In this way the order will not be inverted, what ought to go

together will not be separated, and man, whole at every moment of his life, will not have reached one stage of development with respect to one of his faculties while he remains at another stage with respect to the rest.

What a difficulty I see arising here, a difficulty all the greater for being less in things than in the pusillanimity of those who do not dare to resolve it! Let us begin at least by daring to propound it. A child has to be raised in his father's religion. He is always given powerful proofs that this religion, such as it is, is the only true one, that all the others are only folly and absurdity. The strength of the arguments on this point depends absolutely on the country where they are propounded. Let a Turk who finds Christianity so ridiculous at Constantinople go and see how they think of Mohammedanism at Paris! It is especially in matters of religion that opinion triumphs. But we who pretend to shake off the yoke of opinion in everything, we who want to grant nothing to authority, we who want to teach nothing to our Emile which he could not learn by himself in every country, in what religion shall we raise him? To what sect shall we join the man of nature? The answer is quite simple, it seems to me. We shall join him to neither this one nor that one, but we shall put him in a position to choose the one to which the best use of his reason ought to lead him.

Incedo per ignes
Suppositos cineri doloso.[38]

It makes no difference. Zeal and good faith have taken the place of prudence for me up to now. I hope these guarantors will not abandon me in time of need. Readers, do not fear from me precautions unworthy of a friend of the truth. I shall never forget my motto.[39] But it is only too permissible for me to distrust my judgments. Instead of telling you here on my own what I think, I shall tell you what a man more worthy than I thought. I guarantee the truth of the facts which are going to be reported. They really happened to the author of the paper I am going to transcribe. It is up to you to see if useful reflections can be drawn from it about the subject with which it deals. I am not propounding to you the sentiment of another or my own as a rule. I am offering it to you for examination.[40]

"Thirty years ago in an Italian city a young expatriate found himself reduced to utter destitution. He was born a Calvinist, but as a consequence of a giddy escapade he found himself a fugitive without resources in a foreign land, and he changed his religion in order to have bread. There was in this city an almshouse for proselytes. He was admitted to it. In instructing him there about the religious controversy, they gave him doubts he had not had and taught him evils of which he had been ignorant. He heard new dogmas; he saw morals that were still newer to him. He saw them and almost became their victim. He wanted to flee; they locked him up. He complained; he was punished for his complaints. At the mercy of his tyrants, he saw himself treated as a criminal for not wanting to give way to crime. Those who know how much the first taste of violence and injustice arouses a young

heart without experience will be able to picture the condition of his own heart. Tears of rage flowed from his eyes; indignation choked him. He implored heaven and men; he confided in everyone and was listened to by no one. He saw only vile domestics subjected to the infamous person who outraged him, or accomplices of the same crime who jeered at his resistance and urged him to imitate them. He would have been lost were it not for a decent ecclesiastic who came to the alms-house on some business and whom he found the means to consult in secret. The ecclesiastic was poor and needed everyone; but the oppressed lad had even more need of him; and the ecclesiastic did not hesitate to assist the boy's escape, at the risk of making a dangerous enemy for himself.

"Having escaped from vice only to return to indigence, the young man struggled against his destiny without success. For a moment he believed himself above it. At the first glimmer of fortune his ills and his protector were forgotten. He was soon punished for this ingratitude. All his hopes vanished. Vain was the advantage of his youth; his ideas, absorbed from novels, spoiled everything. Having neither enough talent nor enough adroitness to get ahead easily, and knowing neither how to be moderate nor how to be wicked, he aspired to so many things that he was unable to achieve anything. Fallen back into his former distress, without bread, without shelter, ready to die of hunger, he was reminded of his benefactor.

"He returns there, finds him, and is well received by him. The sight of the lad recalls to the ecclesiastic a good deed he had done; the soul always rejoices in such a memory. This man was naturally humane and compassionate. He felt the sufferings of others by his own, and well-being had not hardened his heart. Finally the lessons of wisdom and an enlightened virtue had strengthened his good nature. He greets the young man, seeks lodging for him, and gives him a recommendation. He shares with him his provisions for the necessities, hardly sufficient for two. He does more: he instructs the lad, consoles him, teaches him the difficult art of patiently bearing adversity. Prejudiced people, is it from a priest, is it in Italy, that you would have hoped for all that?

"This decent ecclesiastic was a poor Savoyard vicar whom a youthful adventure had put in disfavor with his bishop, and who had crossed the mountains to seek the resources lacking to him in his own country. He was neither unintelligent nor unlettered and, as he had an interesting face, he had found protectors who procured him a place raising the son of a prince's minister. He preferred poverty to dependence and was ignorant of how to behave with nobles. He did not stay long with this one; but in leaving him, he did not lose his esteem, and since the ecclesiastic lived wisely and made himself loved by everyone, he cherished the illusion that he would return to his bishop's good graces and obtain some little parish in the mountains where he might spend the rest of his days. Such was the furthest goal of his ambition.

"A natural inclination interested him in the young fugitive and made him examine him carefully. He saw that ill fortune had already dried up the young man's heart, that opprobrium and contempt had beaten down his courage, and that his pride, changed into bitter spite, took men's injustice and hardness only as proof of the viciousness of their nature and the chimerical character of virtue. He had seen that religion served only as the mask of interest and sacred worship only as the safeguard of hypocrisy. He had observed the subtleties of vain disputes where paradise and hell were made the prize of word games. He had seen the sublime original ideas of the divinity disfigured by the fantastic imaginations of men; and finding that in order to believe in God he had to renounce the judgment he had received from Him, he held in the same disdain our ridiculous reveries and the object to which we apply them. Without knowing anything of what is, without imagining anything about the generation of things, he wallowed in his stupid ignorance with a profound contempt for all those who thought they knew more about these things than he did.

"The forgetting of all religion leads to the forgetting of the duties of man. This progress was already more than half accomplished in the libertine's heart. Nevertheless, he was not an ill-born child. But incredulity and poverty, stifling his nature little by little, were leading him rapidly to his destruction and heading him toward the morals of a tramp and the morality of an atheist.

"The evil was almost inevitable but was not absolutely consummated. The young man had some knowledge, and his education had not been neglected. He was at that happy age when the blood is in fermentation and begins to heat up the soul without enslaving it to the furies of the senses. His soul still had all of its vigor. A native shame and a timid character took the place of constraint and prolonged for him this period in which you keep your pupil with so much care. The odious example of brutal depravity and vice without charm, far from animating his imagination, had deadened it. For a long time disgust took the place of virtue for him in preserving his innocence—an innocence that was to succumb only to gentler seductions.

"The ecclesiastic saw the danger and the resources. The difficulties did not dishearten him. He took pleasure in his work. He resolved to complete it and to render to virtue the victim he had snatched from infamy. He made long-range plans for the execution of his project. The beauty of the motive animated his courage and inspired him with means worthy of his zeal. Whatever the success, he was sure of not wasting his time. One always succeeds when one only wishes to do good.

"The first thing he did was to gain the proselyte's confidence by not selling him his benefactions, by not pestering him, by not preaching to him, by always putting himself within his reach, by making himself small in order to be his proselyte's equal. It was, it seems to me, a rather touching spectacle to see a grave man become a rascal's comrade and to see virtue lend itself to the tone of license in order to triumph over it more surely. When the giddy boy came to make his mad confidences and unbosom himself, the priest listened to him and put him at his ease. Without approving evil, the priest was interested in everything. Never did a tactless censure come to stop the boy's chatter and contract his heart. The pleasure which the boy believed the priest took in listening to him increased that which he took in saying everything.

Thus he made his general confession without thinking he was confessing anything.

"After having studied the boy's sentiments and his character well, the priest saw clearly that although he was not ignorant for his age, he had forgotten everything it was important for him to know; and that the opprobrium to which fortune had reduced the boy stifled every true sentiment of good and evil in him. There is a degree of degradation which takes away life from the soul, and the inner voice cannot make itself heard to someone who thinks only of feeding himself. To protect the unfortunate young fellow from this moral death to which he was so near, the priest began by awakening *amour-propre* and self-esteem in him. He showed him a happier future in the good employment of his talents. He reanimated a generous ardor in his heart by the account of others' noble deeds. In making the boy admire those who had performed them, the priest gave him the desire to perform like deeds. To detach him gradually from his idle and vagrant life, he had the boy make extracts from selected books; and, feigning to need these extracts, he fed the noble sentiment of gratitude in him. He instructed him indirectly by these books. He made the boy regain a good enough opinion of himself so as not to believe he was a being useless for anything good and so as not to want any longer to make himself contemptible in his own eyes.

"A bagatelle will provide a basis for judging the art this beneficent man used for gradually lifting his young disciple's heart above baseness without appearing to think of instruction. The ecclesiastic had a probity so well recognized and a discernment so sure that many persons preferred to have their alms distributed by his hand rather than by that of the rich city curés. One day, when he had been given some money to pass out to the poor, the youth, claiming his right as a poor man, was so craven as to ask him for some of it. 'No,' the priest said, 'we are brothers; you are part of me, and I ought not to touch this deposit for my use.' Then he gave the youth from his own money as much as he had asked for. Lessons of this kind are rarely lost on the hearts of young people who are not completely corrupted.

"I am tired of speaking in the third person. And the effort is quite superfluous, for you are well aware, dear fellow citizen, that this unhappy fugitive is myself. I believe myself far enough from the disorders of my youth to dare to admit them, and the hand which drew me away from these disorders merits that, at the expense of a bit of shame, I render at least some honor to his benefactions.

"What struck me the most was seeing in my worthy master's private life virtue without hypocrisy, humanity without weakness, speech that was always straight and simple, and conduct always in conformity with this speech. I did not see him worrying whether those he aided went to vespers, whether they confessed often, whether they fasted on the prescribed days, whether they kept meatless days, or imposing other similar conditions on them—conditions which must be fulfilled if one is to hope for any assistance from the devout, even if one is dying of poverty.

"Encouraged by these observations—far from displaying to him an affectation of the new convert's zeal—I did not do much to hide from him my ways of thinking and did not see him any the more scandalized by them. Sometimes I could have said to myself, 'He passes over my indifference for the worship I have embraced for the sake of the indifference he also sees in me for the worship in which I was born. He knows that my disdain is no longer a question of party.' But what was I to think when I heard him sometimes approve dogmas contrary to those of the Roman Church and show little esteem for all its ceremonies? I would have believed him a disguised Protestant if I had observed him to be less faithful to these very practices by which he seemed to set little store. But knowing that he acquitted himself of his priestly duties as punctiliously when there were no witnesses as in the public eye, I no longer knew how to judge these contradictions. With the exception of the failing which had formerly brought on his disgrace, and of which he was not too well corrected, his life was exemplary, his morals were irreproachable, his speech was decent and judicious. In living with him in the greatest intimacy I learned to respect him more every day; and as so much goodness had entirely won my heart, I was waiting with agitated curiosity for the moment when I would learn the principle on which he founded the uniformity of so singular a life.

"That moment did not come so soon. Before opening himself to his disciple, he made an effort to ensure the germination of the seeds of reason and goodness he was sowing in his disciple's soul. What was most difficult to destroy in me was a proud misanthropy, a certain bitterness against the rich and happy of the world, as though they were such at my expense and their pretended happiness had been usurped from mine. The mad vanity of youth, which revolts against humiliation, gave me only too much of an inclination to that angry humor, and the *amour-propre* my mentor tried to awaken in me, by leading me to pride, rendered men even more vile in my eyes and succeeded only in adding contempt to my hatred for them.

"Without directly combating this pride, the priest prevented it from turning into hardness of soul; and without taking self-esteem from me, he made it less disdainful of my neighbor. In always setting aside vain appearance and showing me the real evils it covers, he taught me to regret the errors of my fellows, to be touched by their miseries, and to pity them more than to envy them. Moved with compassion for human weaknesses by the profound sentiment of his own, he saw men everywhere the victims of their own and others' vices. He saw the poor groaning under the yoke of the rich and the rich under the yoke of prejudice. 'Believe me,' he said, 'our illusions, far from hiding our ills from us, increase them by giving a value to that which has none and by making us sensitive to countless false privations we would not feel without them. Peace of soul consists in contempt for everything which can trouble it. The man who sets the greatest store by life is he who knows least how to enjoy it. And the one who aspires most avidly to happiness is always most miserable.'

" 'Oh, what sad pictures!' I cried out with bitterness. 'If one must turn away from everything, what was the use for us of being born? And if one must despise happiness itself, who knows how to be happy?' 'I do,' answered the priest one day in a tone which struck me. 'You happy! So little fortunate, so poor, exiled, persecuted, you are happy! And what have you done to be so?' 'My child,' he went on, 'I shall be glad to tell you.'

"Thereupon he made me understand that after having received my confessions, he wanted to make me his. 'I shall unbosom all the sentiments of my heart to you,' he said, embracing me. 'You shall see me, if not as I am, at least as I see myself. When you have received my whole profession of faith, when you know well the state of my heart, you will know why I esteem myself happy and, if you think as I do, what you have to do to be so. But what I have to avow is not the business of a moment. Time is required to expound to you all I think about man's fate and the true value of life. Let us pick a time and a place suitable for devoting ourselves peacefully to this conversation.'

"I indicated eagerness to hear him. The appointment was put off till no later than the next morning. It was summer. We got up at daybreak. He took me outside of the city on a high hill beneath which ran the Po, whose course was seen along the fertile banks it washes. In the distance the immense chain of the Alps crowned the landscape. The rays of the rising sun already grazed the plains and, projecting on the fields long shadows of the trees, the vineyards, and the houses, enriched with countless irregularities of light the most beautiful scene which can strike the human eye. One would have said that nature displayed all its magnificence to our eyes in order [41] to present them with the text for our conversation. It was there that after having contemplated these objects in silence for some time, the man of peace spoke to me as follows:

Profession of Faith of the Savoyard Vicar

My child, do not expect either learned speeches or profound reasonings from me. I am not a great philosopher, and I care little to be one. But I sometimes have good sense, and I always love the truth. I do not want to argue with you or even attempt to convince you. It is enough for me to reveal to you what I think in the simplicity of my heart. Consult yours during my speech. This is all I ask of you. If I am mistaken, it is in good faith. That is enough for my error not to be imputed to crime. If you were to be similarly mistaken, there would be little evil in that. Reason is common to us, and we have the same interest in listening to it. If I think well, why would you not think as do I?

I was born poor and a peasant, destined by my station to cultivate the earth. But it was thought to be a finer thing for me to learn to earn my bread in the priest's trade, and the means were found to permit me to study. Certainly neither my parents nor I thought very much of seeking what was good, true, and useful, but rather we thought of what had to be known in order to be ordained. I learned what I was supposed to learn; I said what I was supposed to say. I committed myself as I was supposed to, and I was made a priest. But it was not long before I sensed that in obliging myself not to be a man I had promised more than I could keep.

We are told that conscience is the work of prejudices. Nevertheless I know by my experience that conscience persists in following the order of nature against all the laws of men. We may very well be forbidden this or that, but remorse always reproaches us feebly for what well-ordered nature permits us, and all the more so for what it prescribes to us. Oh, good young man, nature has as yet said nothing to your senses! May you live a long time in the happy state in which its voice is that of innocence. Remember that nature is offended even more when one anticipates it than when one combats it. One must begin by learning how to resist in order to know when one can give in without its being a crime.

From my youth on I have respected marriage as the first and the holiest institution of nature. Having taken away my right to submit myself to it, I resolved not to profane it; for in spite of my classes and studies, I had always led a uniform and simple life, and I had preserved all the clarity of the original understanding in my mind. The maxims of the world had not obscured it, and my poverty removed me from the temptations dictated by the sophisms of vice.

This resolve was precisely what destroyed me. My respect for the bed of others left my faults exposed. The scandal had to be expiated. Arrested, interdicted, driven out, I was far more the victim of my scruples than of my incontinence; and I had occasion to understand, from the reproaches with which my disgrace was accompanied, that often one need only aggravate the fault to escape the punishment.

A few such experiences lead a reflective mind a long way. Seeing the ideas that I had of the just, the decent, and all the duties of man overturned by gloomy observations, I lost each day one of the opinions I had received. Since those opinions that remained were no longer sufficient to constitute together a self-sustaining body, I felt the obviousness of the principles gradually becoming dimmer in my mind. And finally reduced to no longer knowing what to think, I reached the same point where you are, with the difference that my incredulity, the late fruit of a riper age, had been more painfully formed and ought to have been more difficult to destroy.

I was in that frame of mind of uncertainty and doubt that Descartes demands for the quest for truth. This state is hardly made to last. It is disturbing and painful. It is only the self-interest of vice or laziness of soul which leaves us in it. My heart was not sufficiently corrupted to enjoy myself in it, and nothing preserves the habit of reflection better than being more content with oneself than with one's fortune.

I meditated therefore on the sad fate of mortals, floating on this sea of human opinions without rudder or compass and delivered to their stormy passions without any other guide than an inexperienced pilot who is ignorant of his route and knows neither where he is coming from nor where he is going. I said to myself, "I love the truth, I seek it and cannot recognize it. Let it be revealed to me, and I shall remain

[267]

attached to it. Why must it hide itself from the eagerness of a heart made to adore it?"

Although I have often experienced greater evils, I have never led a life so constantly disagreeable as during those times of perplexity and anxiety, when I ceaselessly wandered from doubt to doubt and brought back from my long meditations only uncertainty, obscurity, and contradictions about the cause of my being and the principle of my duties.

How can one systematically and in good faith be a skeptic? I cannot understand it. These skeptic philosophers either do not exist or are the unhappiest of men. Doubt about the things it is important for us to know is too violent a state for the human mind, which does not hold out in this state for long. It decides in spite of itself one way or the other and prefers to be deceived rather than to believe nothing.

What doubled my confusion was that I was born in a church which decides everything and permits no doubt; therefore, the rejection of a single point made me reject all the rest, and the impossibility of accepting so many absurd decisions also detached me from those which were not absurd. By being told "Believe everything," I was prevented from believing anything, and I no longer knew where to stop.

I consulted the philosophers. I leafed through their books. I examined their various opinions. I found them all to be proud, assertive, dogmatic (even in their pretended skepticism), ignorant of nothing, proving nothing, mocking one another; and this last point, which was common to all, appeared to me the only one about which they are all right. Triumphant when they attack, they are without force in defending themselves. If you ponder their reasoning, they turn out to be good only at destructive criticism. If you count votes, each is reduced to his own. They agree only to dispute. Listening to them was not the means of getting out of my uncertainty.

I comprehended that the insufficiency of the human mind is the first cause of this prodigious diversity of sentiments and that pride is the second. We do not have the measurements of this immense machine; we cannot calculate its relations; we know neither its first laws nor its final cause. We do not know ourselves; we know neither our nature nor our active principle. We hardly know if man is a simple or a compound being. Impenetrable mysteries surround us on all sides; they are above the region accessible to the senses. We believe we possess intelligence for piercing these mysteries, but all we have is imagination. Through this imaginary world each blazes a trail he believes to be good. None can know whether his leads to the goal. Nevertheless we want to penetrate everything, to know everything. The only thing we do not know is how to be ignorant of what we cannot know. We would rather decide at random and believe what is not than admit that none of us can see what is. We are a small part of a great whole whose limits escape us and whose Author delivers us to our mad disputes; but we are vain enough to want to decide what this whole is in itself and what we are in relation to it.

If the philosophers were in a position to discover the truth, who among them would take an interest in it? Each knows well that his system is no better founded than the others. But he maintains it because it is his. There is not a single one of them who, if he came to know the true and the false, would not prefer the lie he has found to the truth discovered by another. Where is the philosopher who would not gladly deceive mankind for his own glory? Where is the one who in the secrecy of his heart sets himself any other goal than that of distinguishing himself? Provided that he raises himself above the vulgar, provided that he dims the brilliance of his competitors, what more does he ask? The essential thing is to think differently from others. Among believers he is an atheist; among atheists he would be a believer.

The first fruit I drew from these reflections was to learn to limit my researches to what was immediately related to my interest, to leave myself in a profound ignorance of all the rest, and to worry myself to the point of doubt only about things it was important for me to know.

I understood further that the philosophers, far from delivering me from my useless doubts, would only cause those which tormented me to multiply and would resolve none of them. Therefore, I took another guide, and I said to myself, "Let us consult the inner light; it will lead me astray less than they lead me astray; or at least my error will be my own, and I will deprave myself less in following my own illusions than in yielding to their lies."

Then, going over in my mind the various opinions which had one by one drawn me along since my birth, I saw that although none of them was evident enough to produce conviction immediately, they had various degrees of verisimilitude, and inner assent was given or refused to them in differing measure. On the basis of this first observation, I compared all these different ideas in the silence of the prejudices, and I found that the first and most common was also the simplest and most reasonable, and that the only thing that prevented it from gaining all the votes was that it had not been proposed last. Imagine all your ancient and modern philosophers having first exhausted their bizarre systems of forces, chances, fatality, necessity, atoms, an animate world, living matter, and materialism of every kind; and after them all the illustrious Clarke [42] enlightening the world, proclaiming at last the Being of beings and the Dispenser of things. With what universal admiration, with what unanimous applause would this new system have been received—this new system so great, so consoling, so sublime, so fit to lift up the soul and to give a foundation to virtue, and at the same time so striking, so luminous, so simple, and, it seems to me, presenting fewer incomprehensible things to the human mind than the absurdities it finds in any other system! I said to myself, "Insoluble objections are common to all systems because man's mind is too limited to resolve them. They do not therefore constitute a proof against any one in particular. But what a difference in direct proofs! Must not the only one which explains everything be preferred, if it contains no more difficulties than the others?"

Therefore, taking the love of the truth as my whole philosophy, and as my whole method an easy and simple rule that exempts me from the vain subtlety of arguments, I pick up again on the basis of this rule the examination of the knowledge that interests me. I am resolved to accept as evident all knowledge to which in the sincerity of my heart I cannot refuse my consent; to accept as true all that which appears to me to have a necessary connection with this first knowledge; and to leave all the rest in uncertainty without rejecting it or accepting it and without tormenting myself to clarify it if it leads to nothing useful for practice.

But who am I? What right have I to judge things, and what determines my judgments? If they are swept along, forced by the impressions I receive, I tire myself out in vain with these researches; they will or will not be made on their own without my mixing in to direct them. Thus my glance must first be turned toward myself in order to know the instrument I wish to use and how far I can trust its use.

I exist, and I have senses by which I am affected. This is the first truth that strikes me and to which I am forced to acquiesce. Do I have a particular sentiment of my existence, or do I sense it only through my sensations? This is my first doubt, which it is for the present impossible for me to resolve; for as I am continually affected by sensations, whether immediately or by memory, how can I know whether the sentiment of the I is something outside these same sensations and whether it can be independent of them?

My sensations take place in me, since they make me sense my existence; but their cause is external to me, since they affect me without my having anything to do with it, and I have nothing to do with producing or annihilating them. Therefore, I clearly conceive that my sensation, which is in me, and its cause or its object, which is outside of me, are not the same thing.

Thus, not only do I exist, but there exist other beings—the objects of my sensations; and even if these objects were only ideas, it is still true that these ideas are not me.

Now, all that I sense outside of me and which acts on my senses, I call *matter*; and all the portions of matter which I conceive to be joined together in individual beings, I call *bodies*. Thus all the disputes of idealists and materialists signify nothing to me. Their distinctions concerning the appearance and reality of bodies are chimeras.

Already I am as sure of the universe's existence as of my own. Next, I reflect on the objects of my sensations; and, finding in myself the faculty of comparing them, I sense myself endowed with an active force which I did not before know I had.

To perceive is to sense; to compare is to judge. Judging and sensing are not the same thing. By sensation, objects are presented to me separated, isolated, such as they are in nature. By comparison I move them, I transport them, and, so to speak, I superimpose them on one another in order to pronounce on their difference or their likeness and generally on all their relations. According to me, the distinctive faculty of the active or intelligent being is to be able to give a sense to the word *is*. I seek in vain in the purely sensitive being for this intelligent force which superimposes and which then pronounces; I am not able to see it in its nature. This passive being will sense each object separately, or it will even sense the total object formed by the two; but, having no force to bend them back on one another, it will never compare them, it will not judge them.

To see two objects at once is not to see their relations or to judge their differences. To perceive several objects as separate from one another is not to number them. I can at the same instant have the idea of a large stick and of a small stick without comparing them and without judging that one is smaller than the other, just as I can see my entire hand at once without making the count of my fingers.* These comparative ideas, *larger* and *smaller*, just like the numerical ideas of *one, two,* etc., certainly do not belong to the sensations, although my mind produces them only on the occasion of my sensations.

We are told that the sensitive being distinguishes the sensations from one another by the differences among these very sensations. This requires explication. When the sensations are different, the sensitive being distinguishes them by their differences. When they are similar, it distinguishes them because it senses them as separate from one another. Otherwise, how in a simultaneous sensation would the sensitive being distinguish two equal objects? It would necessarily have to confound these two objects and take them to be the same, especially in a system in which it is claimed that the sensations representing extension are not extended.

When the two sensations to be compared are perceived, their impression is made, each object is sensed, the two are sensed; but, for all that, their relation is not yet sensed. If the judgment of this relation were only a sensation and came to me solely from the object, my judgments would never deceive me, since it is never false that I sense what I sense.

Why is it, then, that I am deceived about the relation of these two sticks, especially if they are not parallel? Why do I say, for example, that the small stick is a third of the large one, whereas it is only a quarter? Why is the image, which is the sensation, not conformable to its model, which is the object? It is because I am active when I judge, because the operation which compares is faulty, and because my understanding, which judges the relations, mixes its errors in with the truth of the sensations, which reveal only the objects.

Add to that a reflection I am sure will strike you when you have thought about it. It is that if we were purely passive in the use of our senses, there would be no communication among them. It would be impossible for us to know that the body we touch and the object we see are the same. Either we would never sense anything outside of us, or there would be five sensible substances for us whose identity we would have no means of perceiving.

Let this or that name be given to this force of my mind which brings together and compares my sensations; let it be called *attention, meditation, reflection,* or whatever one wishes. It is still true that it is in me and not in things, that it is I alone who produce it, although I produce it only on the occasion of the impression made on me by objects.

* The reports of M. de la Condamine tell us of a people who only know how to count to three. Nevertheless the men who composed this people had hands, and thus had often perceived their fingers without knowing how to count to five.[43]

Without being master of sensing or not sensing, I am the master of giving more or less examination to what I sense.

Therefore, I am not simply a sensitive and passive being but an active and intelligent being; and whatever philosophy may say about it, I shall dare to pretend to the honor of thinking. I know only that truth is in things and not in the mind which judges them, and that the less of myself I put in the judgments I make, the more sure I am of approaching the truth. Thus my rule of yielding to sentiment more than to reason is confirmed by reason itself.

Having, so to speak, made certain of myself, I begin to look outside of myself, and I consider myself with a sort of shudder, cast out and lost in this vast universe, as if drowned in the immensity of beings, without knowing anything about what they are either in themselves or in relation to me. I study them, I observe them, and the first object which presents itself to me for comparison with them is myself.

Everything I perceive with the senses is matter; and I deduce all the essential properties of matter from the sensible qualities that make me perceive it and are inseparable from it. I see it now in motion and now at rest,* from which I infer that neither rest nor motion is essential to it. But motion, since it is an action, is the effect of a cause of which rest is only the absence. Therefore, when nothing acts on matter, it does not move; and by the very fact that it is neutral to rest and to motion, its natural state is to be at rest.

I perceive in bodies two sorts of motion—communicated motion and spontaneous or voluntary motion. In the first the cause of motion is external to the body moved; and in the second it is within it. I do not conclude from this that the movement of a watch, for example, is spontaneous; for if nothing external to the spring acted on it, it would not strain to straighten itself out and would not pull the chain. For the same reason neither would I grant spontaneity to fluids or to fire itself, which causes their fluidity.†

You will ask me if the motions of animals are spontaneous. I shall tell you that I know nothing about it, but analogy supports the affirmative. You will ask me again how I know that there are spontaneous motions. I shall tell you that I know it because I sense it. I want to move my arm, and I move it without this movement's having another immediate cause than my will. It would be vain to try to use reason to destroy this sentiment in me. It is stronger than any evidence. One might just as well try to prove to me that I do not exist.

If there were no spontaneity in the actions of men or in anything which takes place on earth, one would only be more at a loss to imagine the first cause of all motion. As for me, I sense myself to be so persuaded that the natural state of matter is to be at rest and that by

---

* This rest is, if you wish, only relative. But since we observe degrees of more and less in motion, we have a very clear conception of one of the two extreme terms, which is rest; and we have such a good conception of it that we are even inclined to take as absolute rest, rest that is only relative. Now, it is not true that motion is of the essence of matter if it can be conceived at rest.

† Chemists regard phlogiston, or the element of fire, as scattered, immobile, and stagnant in the mixtures of which it is part until external causes disengage it, gather it together, set it in motion, and change it into fire.

itself it has no force for acting, that when I see a body in motion, I judge
immediately either that it is an animate body or that this motion has
been communicated to it. My mind rejects all acquiescence to the idea
of unorganized matter moving itself or producing some action.

Meanwhile, this visible universe is matter, scattered and dead matter * which as a whole has nothing in it of the union, the organization,
or the sentiment common to the parts of an animate body, since it is
certain that we do not sense ourselves as parts of a sentient whole. This
same universe is in motion; and in its motion, which is regular, uniform,
and subjected to constant laws, it contains nothing of that liberty appearing in the spontaneous motions of man and the animals. The world
therefore is not a large animal that moves itself. Therefore there is
some cause of its motions external to it, one which I do not perceive.
But inner persuasion makes this cause so evident to my senses that I
cannot see the sun rotate without imagining a force that pushes it; or if
the earth turns, I believe I sense a hand that makes it turn.

If I have to accept general laws whose essential relations with matter I do not perceive, how does that help me? These laws, not being
real beings or substances, must have some other foundation which is
unknown to me. Experience and observation have enabled us to know
the laws of motion; these laws determine the effects without showing the
causes. They do not suffice to explain the system of the world and
the movement of the universe. Descartes formed heaven and earth
with dice, but he was not able to give the first push to these dice or to put
his centrifugal force in action without the aid of a rotary motion.[44]
Newton discovered the law of attraction, but attraction alone would soon
reduce the universe to an immobile mass. To this law he had to add a
projectile [45] force in order to make the celestial bodies describe curves.
Let Descartes tell us what physical law made his vortices turn. Let
Newton show us the hand which launched the planets on the tangent
of their orbits.

The first causes of motion are not in matter. It receives motion and
communicates it, but it does not produce it. The more I observe the
action and the reaction of the forces of nature acting on one another,
the more I find that one must always go back from effects to effects
to some will as first cause; for to suppose an infinite regress of causes
is to suppose no cause at all. In a word, every motion not produced
by another can come only from a spontaneous, voluntary action. Inanimate bodies act only by motion, and there is no true action without
will. This is my first principle. I believe therefore that a will moves the
universe and animates nature. This is my first dogma, or my first article
of faith.

How does a will produce a physical and corporeal action? I do not
know, but I experience within myself that it does so. I want to act,
and I act. I want to move my body, and my body moves. But that an
inanimate body at rest should succeed in moving itself or in producing

---

* I have made every effort to conceive of a living molecule without succeeding.
The idea of matter sensing without having senses appears unintelligible and contradictory to me. To accept or to reject this idea one would have to begin by understanding it, and I admit that I have not been so fortunate.

motion—that is incomprehensible and without example. The will is known to me by its acts, not by its nature. I know this will as a cause of motion; but to conceive of matter as productive of motion is clearly to conceive of an effect without a cause; it is to conceive of absolutely nothing.

It is no more possible for me to conceive of how my will moves my body than it is to conceive of how my sensations affect my soul. I do not even know why one of these mysteries has appeared more explicable than the other. As for me, whether it is when I am passive or when I am active, the means of uniting the two substances appears absolutely incomprehensible. It is quite strange to begin from this very incomprehensibility in order to confound the two substances, as if operations of such different natures were better explained in a single subject than in two.

It is true that the dogma I have just established is obscure, but still it makes sense and contains nothing repugnant to reason or to observation. Can one say as much of materialism? Is it not clear that if motion were essential to matter, it would be inseparable from it and would always be in it in the same degree? Always the same in each portion of matter, it would be incommunicable, it could not increase or decrease, and one could not even conceive of matter at rest. When someone tells me that motion is not essential but necessary to matter, he is trying to lead me astray with words which would be easier to refute if they contained a bit more sense; for either the motion of matter comes to it from itself and is then essential to it, or if it comes to it from an external cause, it is necessary to matter only insofar as the cause of motion acts on it. We are back with the first difficulty.

General and abstract ideas are the source of men's greatest errors. The jargon of metaphysics has never led us to discover a single truth, and it has filled philosophy with absurdities of which one is ashamed as soon as one has stripped them of their big words. Tell me, my friend, whether someone who talks to you about a blind force spread throughout the whole of nature brings any veritable idea to your mind? People believe that they say something with those vague words *universal force* and *necessary motion*, and they say nothing at all. The idea of motion is nothing other than the idea of transport from one place to another. There is no motion without some direction, for an individual being could not move in all directions at once. In what direction, then, does matter necessarily move? Does all the matter in a body have a uniform motion, or does each atom have its own movement? According to the former idea, the whole universe ought to form a solid and indivisible mass. According to the latter, it ought to form only a scattered and incoherent fluid without it ever being possible for two atoms to join. What direction will this common movement of all matter take? Will it be in a straight line, up, down, right, or left? If each molecule of matter has its particular direction, what will be the causes of all these directions and all these differences? If each atom or molecule of matter only turns around its own center, nothing would ever leave its place, and there would not be any communicated motion. Moreover, this circular motion would have to be determined in some direction. To give matter abstract motion is to speak words signifying nothing; and to give it a determinate motion is to suppose a cause determining it. The more I multiply particular forces, the more I have new causes to explain without ever finding any common agent directing them. Far from being able to imagine any order in the fortuitous concurrence of elements, I am not even able to imagine their conflict, and the chaos of the universe is more inconceivable to me than is its harmony. I comprehend that the mechanism of the world may not be intelligible to the human mind, but as soon as a man meddles with explaining it, he ought to say things men understand.

If moved matter shows me a will, matter moved according to certain laws shows me an intelligence. This is my second article of faith. To act, to compare, and to choose are operations of an active and thinking being. Therefore this being exists. "Where do you see him existing?" you are going to say to me. Not only in the heavens which turn, not only in the star which gives us light, not only in myself, but in the ewe which grazes, in the bird which flies, in the stone which falls, in the leaf carried by the wind.

I judge that there is an order in the world although I do not know its end; to judge that there is this order it suffices for me to compare the parts in themselves, to study their concurrences and their relations, to note their harmony. I do not know why the universe exists, but that does not prevent me from seeing how it is modified, or from perceiving the intimate correspondence by which the beings that compose it lend each other mutual assistance. I am like a man who saw a watch opened for the first time and, although he did not know the machine's use and had not seen the dial, was not prevented from admiring the work. "I do not know," he would say, "what the whole is good for, but I do see tht each piece is made for the others; I admire the workman in the details of his work; and I am quite sure that all these wheels are moving in harmony only for a common end which it is impossible for me to perceive."

Let us compare the particular ends, the means, the ordered relations of every kind. Then let us listen to our inner sentiment. What healthy mind can turn aside its testimony; to which unprejudiced eyes does the sensible order not proclaim a supreme intelligence; and how many sophisms must be piled up before it is impossible to recognize the harmony of the beings and the admirable concurrences of each piece in the preservation of the others? They can talk to me all they want about combination and chance. Of what use is it to you to reduce me to silence if you cannot lead me to persuasion, and how will you take away from me the involuntary sentiment that always gives you the lie in spite of myself? If organized bodies were combined fortuitously in countless ways before taking on constant forms, if at the outset there were formed stomachs without mouths, feet without heads, hands without arms, imperfect organs of every kind which have perished for want of being able to preserve themselves, why do none of these unformed attempts strike our glance any longer, why did nature finally prescribe laws to itself to which it was not subjected at the outset? I should not, I agree, be surprised that a thing happens, if it is possible and the difficulty of its occurrence is compensated for by the number of throws of the dice. Nevertheless, if someone were to come to me and say that print thrown around at random had produced the *Aeneid* all in order, I would not deign to take a step to verify the lie. "You forget," I shall be told, "the number of throws." But how many of those throws must I assume in order to make the combination credible? As for me, seeing only a single throw, I can give odds of infinity to one that what it produced is not the result of chance. Consider also that combination and chance will never result in anything but products of the same nature as the elements that are combined; that organization and life will not result from a throw of atoms; and that a chemist combining mixtures will not make them feel and think in his crucible.*

I was surprised, and almost scandalized, at reading Nieuventit.[47] How could that man have wanted to compose a book detailing the wonders of nature that show the wisdom of its Author? His book could be as big as the world without his having exhausted his subject; and as soon as one wishes to enter into the details, the greatest wonder—the harmony and accord of the whole—is overlooked. The generation of living and organized bodies is by itself an abyss for the human mind. The insurmountable barrier that nature set between the various species, so that they would not be confounded, shows its intentions with the utmost clarity. It was not satisfied with establishing order. It took certain measures so that nothing could disturb that order.

There is not a being in the universe that cannot in some respect be regarded as the common center around which all the others are ordered, in such a way that they are all reciprocally ends and means relative to one another. The mind is confused and gets lost in this infinity of relations, not a single one of which is either confused or lost in the crowd. How many absurd suppositions are needed to deduce all this harmony from the blind mechanism of matter moved fortuitously! Those who deny the unity of intention manifested in the relations of all the parts of this great whole can try to cover their nonsense with abstractions, coordinations, general principles, and symbolic terms. Whatever they do, it is impossible for me to conceive of a system of beings so constantly ordered without conceiving of an intelligence which orders it. I do not have it within me to believe that passive and dead matter could have produced living and sensing beings, that a blind fatality could have produced intelligent beings, that what does not think could have produced thinking beings.

I believe therefore that the world is governed by a powerful and wise will. I see it or, rather, I sense it; and that is something important for me to know. But is this same world eternal or created? Is there a single principle of things? Or, are there two or many of them, and what is

---

* Would anyone believe, if he did not have the proof, that human foolishness could have been brought to this point? Amatus Lusitanus affirmed that he had seen a little man an inch long, closed up in a bottle, whom Julius Camillus, like another Prometheus, had made by the science of alchemy. Paracelsus, *De natura rerum*,[46] teaches the way to produce these little men and maintains that the pygmies, the fauns, the satyrs, and the nymphs were engendered by chemistry. Indeed, I do not see that anything further remains to be done to establish the possibility of these facts, other than to advance that organic matter resists the heat of fire and that its molecules can be preserved alive in a reverberatory furnace.

their nature? I know nothing about all this, and what does it matter to me? As soon as this knowledge has something to do with my interests, I shall make an effort to acquire it. Until then I renounce idle questions which may agitate my *amour-propre* but are useless for my conduct and are beyond my reason.

Always remember that I am not teaching my sentiment; I am revealing it. Whether matter is eternal or created, whether there is or is not a passive principle, it is in any event certain that the whole is one and proclaims a single intelligence; for I see nothing which is not ordered according to the same system and does not contribute to the same end —namely, the preservation of the whole in its established order. This Being which wills and is powerful, this Being active in itself, this Being, whatever it may be, which moves the universe and orders all things, I call *God.* I join to this name the ideas of intelligence, power, and will which I have brought together, and that of goodness which is their necessary consequence. But I do not as a result know better the Being to which I have given them; it is hidden equally from my senses and from my understanding. The more I think about it, the more I am confused. I know very certainly that it exists, and that it exists by itself. I know that my existence is subordinated to its existence, and that all things known to me are in absolutely the same situation. I perceive God everywhere in His works. I sense Him in me; I see Him all around me. But as soon as I want to contemplate Him in Himself, as soon as I want to find out where He is, what He is, what His substance is, He escapes me, and my clouded mind no longer perceives anything.

Suffused with the sense of my inadequacy, I shall never reason about the nature of God without being forced to by the sentiment of His relations with me. These reasonings are always rash; a wise man ought to yield to them only with trembling and with certainty that he is not made to plumb their depths; for what is most insulting to the divinity is not thinking not at all about it but thinking badly about it.

After having discovered those attributes of the divinity by which I know its existence, I return to myself and I try to learn what rank I occupy in the order of things that the divinity governs and I can examine: I find myself by my species incontestably in the first rank; for by my will and by the instruments in my power for executing it, I have more force for acting on all the bodies surrounding me, for yielding to or eluding their actions as I please, than any of them has for acting on me against my will by physical impulsion alone; and by my intelligence I am the only one that has a view of the whole. What being here on earth besides man is able to observe all the others, to measure, calculate, and foresee their movements and their effects, and to join, so to speak, the sentiment of common existence to that of its individual existence? What is there so ridiculous about thinking that everything is made for me, if I am the only one who is able to relate everything to himself?

It is true, then, that man is the king of the earth he inhabits; for not only does he tame all the animals, not only does his industry put the elements at his disposition, but he alone on earth knows how to do so, and he also appropriates to himself, by means of contemplation, the very stars he cannot approach. Show me another animal on earth who knows how to make use of fire and who knows how to wonder at the sun. What! I can observe and know the beings and their relations, I can sense what order, beauty, and virtue are, I can contemplate the universe and raise myself up to the hand which governs it, I can love the good and do it, and I would compare myself to the brutes? Abject soul, it is your gloomy philosophy which makes you similar to them. Or, rather, you want in vain to debase yourself. Your genius bears witness against your principles, your beneficent heart gives the lie to your doctrine, and the very abuse of your faculties proves their excellence in spite of you.

As for me—I who have no system to maintain, I, a simple and true man who is carried away by the fury of no party and does not aspire to the honor of being chief of a sect, I who am content with the place in which God has put me, I see nothing, except for Him, that is better than my species. And if I had to choose my place in the order of beings, what more could I choose than to be a man?

The effect of this reflection is less to make me proud than to touch me; for this state is not of my choice, and it was not due to the merit of a being who did not yet exist. Can I see myself thus distinguished without congratulating myself on filling this honorable post and without blessing the hand which placed me in it? From my first return to myself there is born in my heart a sentiment of gratitude and benediction for the Author of my species; and from this sentiment my first homage to the beneficent divinity. I adore the supreme power, and I am moved by its benefactions. I do not need to be taught this worship; it is dictated to me by nature itself. Is it not a natural consequence of self-love to honor what protects us and to love what wishes us well?

But when next I seek to know my individual place in my species, and I consider its various ranks and the men who fill them, what happens to me? What a spectacle! Where is the order I had observed? The picture of nature had presented me with only harmony and proportion; that of mankind presents me with only confusion and disorder! Concert reigns among the elements, and men are in chaos! The animals are happy; their king alone is miserable! O wisdom, where are your laws? O providence, is it thus that you rule the world? Beneficent Being, what has become of your power? I see evil on earth.

Would you believe, my good friend, that from these gloomy reflections and these apparent contradictions there were formed in my mind the sublime ideas of the soul which had not until then resulted from my researches? In meditating on the nature of man, I believed I discovered in it two distinct principles; one of which raised him to the study of eternal truths, to the love of justice and moral beauty, and to the regions of the intellectual world whose contemplation is the wise man's delight; while the other took him basely into himself, subjected him to the empire of the senses and to the passions which are their ministers, and by means of these hindered all that the sentiment of the former inspired in him. In sensing myself carried away and caught up in the combat of these two contrary motions, I said to myself, "No, man is not one. I want and I do not want; I sense myself enslaved and free at the same time. I see the good, I love it, and I do the bad. I am active when I listen to reason, passive when my passions carry me away; and my worst torment, when I succumb, is to sense that I could have resisted."

Young man, listen with confidence; I shall always be of good faith. If conscience is the work of the prejudices, I am doubtless wrong, and there is no demonstrable morality. But if to prefer oneself to everything is an inclination natural to man, and if nevertheless the first sentiment of justice is innate in the human heart, let him who regards man as a simple being overcome these contradictions, and I shall no longer acknowledge more than one substance.

You will note that by this word *substance* I understand in general being that is endowed with some primary quality, abstracting from all particular or secondary modifications. Therefore, if all the primary qualities known to us can be joined in the same being, one ought to admit only one substance; but if some are mutually exclusive, there are as many diverse substances as there are such possible exclusions. You will reflect on that; as for me, whatever Locke says about it,[48] I need only know that matter is extended and divisible in order to be sure that it cannot think. And for all that any philosopher who comes to tell me that trees sense and rocks think * may entangle me in his subtle arguments, I can see in him only a sophist speaking in bad faith who prefers to attribute sentiment to rocks than to grant a soul to man.

Let us suppose a deaf man who denies the existence of sounds because they have never struck his ear. By means of a hidden stringed instrument, I make another stringed instrument that I have placed before his eyes sound in unison with it. The deaf man sees the string vibrate. I say to him, "It is sound which causes that." "Not at all," he answers. "The cause of the string's vibration is in it. It is a quality common to all bodies to vibrate thus." "Then show me," I respond, "this vibration in other bodies or, at least, its cause in this string." "I cannot,"

---

* It seems to me that far from saying that rocks think, modern philosophy has discovered, on the contrary, that men do not think. It no longer recognizes anything but sensitive beings in nature, and the whole difference it finds between a man and a stone is that man is a sensitive being with sensations while a stone is a sensitive being without them. But if it is true that all matter senses, where shall I conceive the sensitive unity or the individual *I* to be? Will it be in each molecule of matter or in the aggregate bodies? Shall I put this unity equally in fluids and solids, in compounds and elements? There are, it is said, only individuals in nature. But what are these individuals? Is this stone an individual or an aggregate of individuals? Is it a single sensitive being, or does it contain in it as many sensitive beings as it does grains of sand? If each elementary atom is a sensitive being, how shall I conceive that intimate communication by means of which one senses itself in another so that their two *I*'s merge into one? Attraction may be a law of nature whose mystery is unknown to us; but we can at least conceive that attraction, acting according to mass, contains nothing incompatible with extension and divisibility. Can you conceive the same thing of sentiment? The sensible parts are extended, but the sensitive being is indivisible and one. It cannot be divided; it is whole, or it is nothing. The sensitive being is therefore not a body. I do not know how our materialists understand it; but it seems to me that the same difficulties that make them reject thought also ought to make them reject sentiment, and I do not see why, having made the first step, they would not also make the other. What more would it cost them; and since they are sure that they do not think, how do they dare to affirm that they sense?

replies the deaf man, "but because I cannot conceive how this string vibrates, why must I go and explain that by your sounds, of which I do not have the slightest idea? That is to explain an obscure fact by a cause still more obscure. Either make your sounds accessible to my senses, or I say that they do not exist."

The more I reflect on thought and on the nature of the human mind, the more I find that the reasoning of materialists resembles that of this deaf man. They are indeed deaf to the inner voice crying out to them in a tone difficult not to recognize. A machine does not think; there is neither motion nor figure which produces reflection. Something in you seeks to break the bonds constraining it. Space is not your measure; the whole universe is not big enough for you. Your sentiments, your desires, your uneasiness, even your pride have another principle than this narrow body in which you sense yourself enchained.

No material being is active by itself, and I am. One may very well argue with me about this; but I sense it, and this sentiment that speaks to me is stronger than the reason combating it. I have a body on which other bodies act and which acts on them. This reciprocal action is not doubtful. But my will is independent of my senses; I consent or I resist; I succumb or I conquer; and I sense perfectly within myself when I do what I wanted to do or when all I am doing is giving way to my passions. I always have the power to will, I do not always have the force to execute. When I abandon myself to temptations, I act according to the impulsion of external objects. When I reproach myself for this weakness, I listen only to my will. I am enslaved because of my vices and free because of my remorse. The sentiment of my freedom is effaced in me only when I become depraved and finally prevent the voice of the soul from being raised against the law of the body.

I know will only by the sentiment of my own will, and understanding is no better known to me. When I am asked what the cause is which determines my will, I ask in turn what the cause is which determines my judgment; for it is clear that these two causes are only one; and if one clearly understands that man is active in his judgments, and that his understanding is only the power of comparing and judging, one will see that his freedom is only a similar power or one derived from the former. One chooses the good as he has judged the true; if he judges wrong, he chooses badly. What, then, is the cause which determines his will? It is his judgment. And what is the cause which determines his judgment? It is his intelligent faculty, it is his power of judging: the determining cause is in himself. Beyond this I understand nothing more.

Doubtless, I am not free not to want my own good; I am not free to want what is bad for me. But it is in this precisely that my freedom consists—my being able to will only what is suitable to me, or what I deem to be such, without anything external to me determining me. Does it follow that I am not my own master, because I am not the master of being somebody else than me?

The principle of every action is in the will of a free being. One cannot go back beyond that. It is not the word *freedom* which means nothing; it is the word *necessity*. To suppose some act, some effect, which does not derive from an active principle is truly to suppose effects without cause; it is to fall into a vicious circle. Either there is no first impulse, or every first impulse has no prior cause; and there is no true will without freedom. Man is therefore free in his actions and as such is animated by an immaterial substance. This is my third article of faith. From these three you will easily deduce all the others without my continuing to count them out.

If man is active and free, he acts on his own. All that he does freely does not enter into the ordered system of providence and cannot be imputed to it. Providence does not will the evil a man does in abusing the freedom it gives him; but it does not prevent him from doing it, whether because this evil, coming from a being so weak, is nothing in its eyes, or because it could not prevent it without hindering his freedom and doing a greater evil by degrading his nature. It has made him free in order that by choice he do not evil but good. It has put him in a position to make this choice by using well the faculties with which it has endowed him. But it has limited his strength to such an extent that the abuse of the freedom it reserves for him cannot disturb the general order. The evil that man does falls back on him without changing anything in the system of the world, without preventing the human species from preserving itself in spite of itself. To complain about God's not preventing man from doing evil is to complain about His having given him an excellent nature, about His having put in man's actions the morality which ennobles them, about His having given him the right to virtue. The supreme enjoyment is in satisfaction with oneself; it is in order to deserve this satisfaction that we are placed on earth and endowed with freedom, that we are tempted by the passions and restrained by conscience. What more could divine power itself do for us? Could it make our nature contradictory and give the reward for having done well to him who did not have the power to do evil? What! To prevent man from being wicked, was it necessary to limit him to instinct and make him a beast? No, God of my soul, I shall never reproach You for having made him in Your image, so that I can be free, good, and happy like You!

It is the abuse of our faculties which makes us unhappy and wicked. Our sorrows, our cares, and our sufferings come to us from ourselves. Moral evil is incontestably our own work, and physical evil would be nothing without our vices, which have made us sense it. Is it not for preserving ourselves that nature makes us sense our needs? Is not the pain of the body a sign that the machine is out of order and a warning to look after it? Death . . . Do not the wicked poison their lives and ours? Who would want to live always? Death is the remedy for the evils you do to yourselves; nature did not want you to suffer forever. How few ills there are to which the man living in primitive simplicity is subject! He lives almost without diseases as well as passions and neither foresees nor senses death. When he senses it, his miseries make it desirable to him; from then on it is no longer an evil for him. If we were satisfied to be what we are, we would not have to lament our fate. But to seek an imaginary well-being, we give ourselves countless real ills. Whoever does not know how to endure a bit of suffering ought to expect to suffer much. When someone has ruined his constitution by a disorderly life, he wants to restore it with remedies. To the evil he senses, he adds the evil he fears. Foresight of death makes it horrible and accelerates it. The more he wants to flee it, the more he senses it, and he dies of terror throughout his whole life, while blaming nature for evils which he has made for himself by offending it.

Man, seek the author of evil no longer. It is yourself. No evil exists other than that which you do or suffer, and both come to you from yourself. General evil can exist only in disorder, and I see in the system of the world an unfailing order. Particular evil exists only in the sentiment of the suffering being, and man did not receive this sentiment from nature: he gave it to himself. Pain has little hold over someone who, having reflected little, possesses neither memory nor foresight. Take away our fatal progress, take away our errors and our vices, take away the work of man, and everything is good.

Where everything is good, nothing is unjust. Justice is inseparable from goodness. Now, goodness is the necessary effect of a power without limit and of the self-love essential to every being aware of itself. The existence of Him who is omnipotent is, so to speak, coextensive with the existence of the beings. To produce and to preserve are the perpetual acts of power. He does not act on what is not. God is not the God of the dead. He could not be destructive and wicked without hurting Himself. He who can do everything can want only what is good.* Therefore, the supremely good Being, because He is supremely powerful, ought also to be supremely just. Otherwise He would contradict Himself; for the love of order which produces order is called *goodness*; and the love of order which preserves order is called *justice*.

God, it is said, owes His creatures nothing. I believe He owes them all He promises them in giving them being. Now, to give them the idea of a good and to make them feel the need of it is to promise it to them. The more I return within myself, and the more I consult myself, the more I see these words written in my soul: *Be just and you will be happy.* That simply is not so, however, considering the present state of things: the wicked man prospers, and the just man remains oppressed. Also, see what indignation is kindled in us when this expectation is frustrated! Conscience is aroused and complains about its Author. It cries out to Him in moaning, "Thou hast deceived me!"

"I have deceived you, rash man! And who told you so? Is your soul annihilated? Have you ceased to exist? O Brutus! O my son! Do not soil your noble life by ending it. Do not leave your hope and your glory with your body on the field of Philippi. Why do you say, 'Virtue is nothing,' when you are going to enjoy the reward for yours? You are going to die, you think. No, you are going to live, and it is then that I shall keep all the promises I have made you."

From the complaints of impatient mortals, one would say that God owes them the recompense before they have deserved it, and that He is obliged to pay their virtue in advance. O, let us be good in the first place, and then we shall be happy. Let us not demand the prize before the

---

* When the ancients called the supreme God *Optimus Maximus*, they spoke very truly. But in saying *Maximus Optimus*, they would have spoken more exactly, since His goodness comes from His power. He is good because He is great.

victory nor the wage before the work. It is not at the starting block, said Plutarch, that the victors in our sacred games are crowned; it is after they have gone around the track.⁴⁹

If the soul is immaterial, it can survive the body; and if it survives the body, providence is justified. If I had no proof of the immateriality of the soul other than the triumph of the wicked and the oppression of the just in this world, that alone would prevent me from doubting it. So shocking a dissonance in the universal harmony would make me seek to resolve it. I would say to myself, "Everything does not end with life for us; everything returns to order at death." There would in truth be the quandary of wondering where man is when everything which can be sensed about him is destroyed. But this question is no longer a difficulty for me as soon as I have acknowledged two substances. It is very simple to see that, since during my corporeal life I perceive nothing except by my senses, what is not subject to them escapes me. When the union of body and soul is broken, I conceive that the former can be dissolved while the latter can be preserved. Why would the destruction of the one entail the destruction of the other? On the contrary, since they are of such different natures, they were in a violent condition during their union; and when this union ceases, they both return to their natural condition. The active and living substance regains all the strength that it used in moving the passive and dead substance. Alas! I sense it only too much by my vices: man lives only halfway during his life, and the life of the soul begins only with the death of the body.

But what is this life, and is the soul immortal by its nature? My limited understanding conceives nothing without limits. All that is called infinite escapes me. What can I deny and affirm, what argument can I make about that which I cannot conceive? I believe that the soul survives the body long enough for the maintenance of order. Who knows whether that is long enough for it to last forever? However, whereas I can conceive how the body wears out and is destroyed by the division of its parts, I cannot conceive of a similar destruction of the thinking being; and, not imagining how it can die, I presume that it does not die. Since this presumption consoles me and contains nothing unreasonable, why would I be afraid of yielding to it?

I sense my soul. I know it by sentiment and by thought. Without knowing what its essence is, I know that it exists. I cannot reason about ideas I do not have. What I know surely is that the identity of the I is prolonged only by memory, and that in order to be actually the same I must remember having been. Now, after my death I could not recall what I was during my life unless I also recalled what I felt, and consequently what I did; and I do not doubt that this memory will one day cause the felicity of the good and the torment of the wicked. Here on earth countless ardent passions absorb the inner sentiment and lead remorse astray. The humiliation and the disgrace attracted by the practice of the virtues prevent all their charms from being felt. But when, after being delivered from the illusions given us by the body and the senses, we will enjoy the contemplation of the Supreme Being and the eternal truths of which He is the source; when the beauty of the order will strike all the powers of our soul; when we are solely occupied with comparing what we have done with what we ought to have done—then the voice of conscience will regain its strength and its empire. It is then that the pure delight born of satisfaction with oneself and the bitter regret at having debased oneself will distinguish by inexhaustible sentiments the fate that each has prepared for himself. Do not ask me, my good friend, whether there will be other sources of happiness and suffering. I do not know; and those I imagine are enough to console me for this life and to make me hope for another. I do not say that the good will be recompensed, for what good can an excellent being attain other than to exist according to its nature? But I do say that they will be happy, because their Author, the Author of all justice, having created them as sensitive beings did not create them to suffer; and since they did not abuse their freedom on earth, they did not fail to attain their destiny due to their own fault. Nevertheless they suffered in this life; therefore they will be compensated in another. This sentiment is founded less on the merit of man than on the notion of goodness which seems to me inseparable from the divine essence. I am only supposing that the laws of order are observed and that God is constant to Himself.*

Do not ask me whether the torments of the wicked will be eternal. I do not know that either and do not have the vain curiosity to clarify useless questions. What difference does it make to me what will become of the wicked? I take little interest in their fate. However, I have difficulty in believing that they are condemned to endless torments. If supreme justice does take vengeance, it does so beginning in this life. O nations, you and your errors are its ministers. Supreme justice employs the evils that you do to yourselves to punish the crimes which brought on those evils. It is in your insatiable hearts, eaten away by envy, avarice, and ambition, that the avenging passions punish your heinous crimes in the bosom of your false prosperity. What need is there to look for hell in the other life? It begins in this one in the hearts of the wicked.

Where our perishable needs end, where our senseless desires cease, our passions and our crimes ought also to cease. To what perversity would pure spirits be susceptible? Needing nothing, why would they be wicked? If they are deprived of our coarse senses, and all their happiness is in the contemplation of the beings, they would be able to will only the good; and can anyone who ceases to be wicked be miserable forever? This is what I am inclined to believe without making an effort to come to a decision about it. O clement and good Being, whatever Your decrees are, I worship them! If You punish the wicked, I annihilate my weak reason before Your justice. But if the remorse of these unfortunates is to be extinguished in time, if their ills are to end, and if the same place awaits us all equally one day, I praise You for it. Is not the wicked man my brother? How many times have I been tempted to be like him? If, when he is delivered from his misery, he also loses

* Not for us, not for us, Lord,
But for Your name, but for Your own honor,
O God, make us live again! [50]

Psalm 115

the malignity accompanying it, let him be happy as I am. Far from arousing my jealousy, his happiness will only add to mine.

In this way, contemplating God in His works and studying Him by those of His attributes which it matters for me to know, I have succeeded in extending and increasing by degrees the initially imperfect and limited idea I had of this immense Being. But if this idea has become nobler and greater, it is also less proportionate to human reason. As my mind approaches the eternal light, its brilliance dazzles and confuses me, and I am forced to abandon all the terrestrial notions which helped me to imagine it. God is no longer corporeal and sensible. The supreme intelligence which rules the world is no longer the world itself. I lift and fatigue my mind in vain to conceive His essence. When I think that it is what gives life and activity to the living and active substance that rules animate bodies, when I hear it said that my soul is spiritual and that God is a spirit, I am indignant about this debasement of the divine essence. As if God and my soul were of the same nature! As if God were not the only absolute being, the only one that is truly active, sensing, thinking, willing by itself, and from which we get thought, sentiment, activity, will, freedom, and being. We are free only because He wants us to be, and His inexplicable substance is to our souls what our souls are to our bodies. I know nothing about whether He created matter, bodies, minds, and the world. The idea of creation confuses me and is out of my reach. I believe it insofar as I can conceive it. But I do know that He formed the universe and all that exists, that He made everything, ordered everything. God is doubtless eternal; but can my mind embrace the idea of eternity? Why fob myself off with words unrelated to an idea? What I do conceive is that He exists before things, that He will exist as long as they subsist, and that He would exist even after that, if all were to end one day. That a being which I cannot conceive of gives existence to other beings is only obscure and incomprehensible; but that being and nothingness turn themselves into one another on their own is a palpable contradiction, a clear absurdity.

God is intelligent, but in what way? Man is intelligent when he reasons, and the supreme intelligence does not need to reason. For it there are neither premises nor conclusions; there are not even propositions. It is purely intuitive; it sees equally everything which is and everything which can be. For it all truths are only a single idea, as all places are a single point, and all times a single moment. Human power acts by means; divine power acts by itself. God can because He wills. His will causes His power. God is good; nothing is more manifest. But goodness in man is the love of his fellows, and the goodness of God is the love of order; for it is by order that He maintains what exists and links each part with the whole. God is just, I am convinced of it; it is a consequence of His goodness. The injustice of men is their work and not His. Moral disorder, which gives witness against providence in the eyes of the philosophers, only serves to demonstrate it in mine. But man's justice is to give each what belongs to him, and God's justice is to ask from each for an accounting of what He gave him.

If I have just discovered successively these attributes of which I have no absolute idea, I have done so by compulsory inferences, by the good use of my reason. But I affirm them without understanding them, and at bottom that is to affirm nothing. I may very well tell myself, "God is thus; I sense it, I prove it to myself." I cannot conceive any the better how God can be thus.

Finally, the more effort I make to contemplate His infinite essence, the less I can conceive it. But it is; that is enough for me. The less I can conceive it, the more I worship it. I humble myself and say to Him, "Being of beings, I am because You are; it is to lift myself up to my source to meditate on You ceaselessly. The worthiest use of my reason is for it to annihilate itself before You. It is my rapture of mind, it is the charm of my weakness to feel myself overwhelmed by Your greatness."

After having thus deduced the principal truths that it mattered for me to know from the impression of sensible objects and from the inner sentiment that leads me to judge of causes according to my natural lights, I still must investigate what manner of conduct I ought to draw from these truths and what rules I ought to prescribe for myself in order to fulfill my destiny on earth according to the intention of Him who put me there. In continuing to follow my method, I do not draw these rules from the principles of a high philosophy, but find them written by nature with ineffaceable characters in the depth of my heart. I have only to consult myself about what I want to do. Everything I sense to be good is good; everything I sense to be bad is bad. The best of all casuists is the conscience; and it is only when one haggles with it that one has recourse to the subtleties of reasoning. The first of all cares is the care for oneself. Nevertheless how many times does the inner voice tell us that, in doing our good at another's expense, we do wrong! We believe we are following the impulse of nature, but we are resisting it. In listening to what it says to our senses, we despise what it says to our hearts; the active being obeys, the passive being commands. Conscience is the voice of the soul; the passions are the voice of the body. Is it surprising that these two languages often are contradictory? And then which should be listened to? Too often reason deceives us. We have acquired only too much right to challenge it. But conscience never deceives; it is man's true guide. It is to the soul what instinct is to the body; * he who follows conscience obeys nature and

* Modern philosophy, accepting only what it explains, is careful not to accept that obscure faculty called instinct, which appears without any acquired knowledge to guide animals toward some end. Instinct, according to one of our wisest philosophers,[51] is, however, only a habit without reflection which is, however, acquired by reflecting; and from the way he explains this development, it ought to be concluded that children reflect more than men, a paradox strange enough to deserve the effort of examination. Without going into this discussion here, I ask what name I ought to give to the ardor with which my dog makes war on moles he does not eat, to the patience with which he sometimes watches for them for whole hours, and to the skill with which he grabs them, throws them out on the earth the moment they push up, and then kills them, only to leave them there, without anyone ever having trained him for this hunt and taught him moles were there? I ask further—and this is more important—why, the first time I threatened this same dog, he lay with his back on the ground, his paws bent back in a supplicant attitude, the one most suited to touch me, a posture he would have certainly not kept if, without letting myself be moved, I had beaten him in this position? What! Had my dog, still very

BOOK IV

does not fear being led astray. This point is important [continued my benefactor, seeing that I was going to interrupt him]. Allow me to tarry a bit to clarify it.

All the morality of our actions is in the judgment we ourselves make of them. If it is true that the good is good, it must be so in the depths of our hearts as it is in our works, and the primary reward for justice is to sense that one practices it. If moral goodness is in conformity with our nature, man could be healthy of spirit or well constituted only to the extent that he is good. If it is not and man is naturally wicked, he cannot cease to be so without being corrupted, and goodness in him is only a vice contrary to nature. If he were made to do harm to his kind, as a wolf is made to slaughter his prey, a humane man would be an animal as depraved as a pitying wolf, and only virtue would leave us with remorse.

Let us return to ourselves, my young friend! Let us examine, all personal interest aside, where our inclinations lead us. Which spectacle gratifies us more—that of others' torments or that of their happiness? Which is sweeter to do and leaves us with a more agreeable impression after having done it—a beneficent act or a wicked act? In whom do you take an interest in your theaters? Is it in heinous crimes that you take pleasure? Is it to their authors when they are punished that you give your tears? It is said that we are indifferent to everything outside of our interest; but, all to the contrary, the sweetness of friendship and of humanity consoles us in our suffering; even in our pleasures we would be too alone, too miserable, if we had no one with whom to share them. If there is nothing moral in the heart of man, what is the source of these transports of admiration for heroic actions, these raptures of love for great souls? What relation does this enthusiasm for virtue have to our private interest? Why would I want to be Cato, who disembowels himself, rather than Caesar triumphant? Take this love of the beautiful from our hearts, and you take all the charm from life. He whose vile passions have stifled these delicious sentiments in his narrow soul, and who, by dint of self-centeredness, succeeds in loving only himself, has no more transports. His icy heart no longer palpitates with joy; a sweet tenderness never moistens his eyes; he has no more joy in anything. This unfortunate man no longer feels, no longer lives. He is already dead.

But however numerous the wicked are on the earth, there are few of these cadaverous souls who have become insensitive, except where their own interest is at stake, to everything which is just and good. Iniquity pleases only to the extent one profits from it; in all the rest one wants the innocent to be protected. One sees some act of violence

---

little and practically just born, already acquired moral ideas? Did he know what clemency and generosity are? On the basis of what acquired understanding did he hope to mollify me by thus abandoning himself to my discretion? Every dog in the world does pretty nearly the same thing in the same situation, and I am saying nothing here that cannot be verified by everyone. Let the philosophers who so disdainfully reject instinct be so good as to explain this fact by the mere action of the sensations and the knowledge they cause us to acquire. Let them explain it in a way satisfying to every man of good sense. Then I shall have nothing more to say, and I shall no longer speak of instinct.

and injustice in the street or on the road. Instantly an emotion of anger and indignation is aroused in the depths of the heart, and it leads us to take up the defense of the oppressed; but a more powerful duty restrains us, and the laws take from us the right of protecting innocence. On the other hand, if some act of clemency or generosity strikes our eyes, what admiration, what love it inspires in us! Who does not say to himself, "I would like to have done the same"? It is surely of very little importance to us that a man was wicked or just two thousand years ago; nevertheless, we take an interest in ancient history just as if it all had taken place in our day. What do Catiline's crimes do to me? Am I afraid of being his victim? Why, then, am I as horrified by him as if he were my contemporary? We do not hate the wicked only because they do us harm, but because they are wicked. Not only do we want to be happy; we also wish for the happiness of others. And when this happiness does not come at the expense of our own, it increases it. Finally, in spite of oneself, one pities the unfortunate; when we are witness to their ills, we suffer from them. The most perverse are unable to lose this inclination entirely. Often it puts them in contradiction with themselves. The robber who plunders passers-by still covers the nakedness of the poor, and the most ferocious killer supports a fainting man.

We speak of the cry of remorse which in secret punishes hidden crimes and so often brings them to light. Alas, who of us has never heard this importunate voice? We speak from experience, and we would like to stifle this tyrannical sentiment that gives us so much torment. Let us obey nature. We shall know with what gentleness it reigns, and what charm one finds, after having hearkened to it, in giving favorable testimony on our own behalf. The wicked man fears and flees himself. He cheers himself up by rushing outside of himself. His restless eyes rove around him and seek an object that is entertaining to him. Without bitter satire, without insulting banter, he would always be sad. The mocking laugh is his only pleasure. By contrast, the serenity of the just man is internal. His is not a malignant laugh but a joyous one; he bears its source in himself. He is as gay alone as in the midst of a circle. He does not draw his contentment from those who come near him; he communicates it to them.

Cast your eyes on all the nations of the world, go through all the histories. Among so many inhuman and bizarre cults, among this prodigious diversity of morals and characters, you will find everywhere the same ideas of justice and decency, everywhere the same notions of good and bad. Ancient paganism gave birth to abominable gods who would have been punished on earth as villains and who presented a picture of supreme happiness consisting only of heinous crimes to commit and passions to satisfy. But vice, armed with a sacred authority, descended in vain from the eternal abode; moral instinct repulsed it from the heart of human beings. While celebrating Jupiter's debauches, they admired Xenocrates' continence. The chaste Lucretia worshiped the lewd Venus. The intrepid Roman sacrificed to fear. He invoked the god who mutilated his father, and he himself died without a murmur at his own father's hand. The most contemptible divinities were served by the greatest men. The holy voice of nature, stronger than that of the gods, made itself respected on earth and seemed to relegate crime, along with the guilty, to heaven.

There is in the depths of souls, then, an innate principle of justice and virtue according to which, in spite of our own maxims, we judge our actions and those of others as good or bad. It is to this principle that I give the name *conscience*.

But at this word I hear the clamor of those who are allegedly wise rising on all sides: errors of childhood, prejudices of education, they all cry in a chorus. Nothing exists in the human mind other than what is introduced by experience, and we judge a thing on no ground other than that of acquired ideas. They go farther. They dare to reject this evident and universal accord of all nations. And in the face of this striking uniformity in men's judgment, they go and look in the shadows for some obscure example known to them alone—as if all the inclinations of nature were annihilated by the depravity of a single people, and the species were no longer anything as soon as there are monsters. But what is the use of the torments to which the skeptic Montaigne subjects himself in order to unearth in some corner of the world a custom opposed to the notions of justice? Of what use is it to him to give to the most suspect travelers the authority he refuses to give to the most celebrated writers? [52] Will some uncertain and bizarre practices, based on local causes unknown to us, destroy the general induction drawn from the concurrence of all peoples, who disagree about everything else and agree on this point alone? O Montaigne, you who pride yourself on frankness and truth, be sincere and true, if a philosopher can be, and tell me whether there is some country on earth where it is a crime to keep one's faith, to be clement, beneficent, and generous, where the good man is contemptible and the perfidious one honored?

It is said that everyone contributes to the public good for his own interest. But what then is the source of the just man's contributing to it to his prejudice? What is going to one's death for one's interest? No doubt, no one acts for anything other than for his good; but if there is not a moral good which must be taken into account, one will never explain by private interest anything but the action of the wicked. It is not even likely that anyone will attempt to go farther. This would be too abominable a philosophy—one which is embarrassed by virtuous actions, which could get around the difficulty only by fabricating base intentions and motives without virtue, which would be forced to vilify Socrates and calumniate Regulus. If ever such doctrines could spring up among us, the voice of nature as well as that of reason would immediately be raised against them and would never leave a single one of their partisans the excuse that he is of good faith.

It is not my design here to enter into metaphysical discussions which are out of my reach and yours, and which, at bottom, lead to nothing. I have already told you that I wanted not to philosophize with you but to help you consult your heart. Were all the philosophers to prove that I am wrong, if you sense that I am right, I do not wish for more.

For that purpose I need only to make you distinguish our acquired ideas from our natural sentiments; for we sense before knowing, and since we do not learn to want what is good for us and to flee what is bad for us but rather get this will from nature, by that very fact love of the good and hatred of the bad are as natural as the love of ourselves. The acts of the conscience are not judgments but sentiments. Although all our ideas come to us from outside, the sentiments evaluating them are within us, and it is by them alone that we know the compatibility or incompatibility between us and the things we ought to seek or flee.

To exist, for us, is to sense; our sensibility is incontestably anterior to our intelligence, and we had sentiments before ideas. Whatever the cause of our being, it has provided for our preservation by giving us sentiments suitable to our nature, and it could not be denied that these, at least, are innate. These sentiments, as far as the individual is concerned, are the love of self, the fear of pain, the horror of death, the desire of well-being. But if, as cannot be doubted, man is by his nature sociable, or at least made to become so, he can be so only by means of other innate sentiments relative to his species; for if we consider only physical need, it ought certainly to disperse men instead of bringing them together. It is from the moral system formed by this double relation to oneself and to one's fellows that the impulse of conscience is born. To know the good is not to love it; man does not have innate knowledge of it, but as soon as his reason makes him know it, his conscience leads him to love it. It is this sentiment which is innate.

Thus I do not believe, my friend, that it is impossible to explain, by the consequences of our nature, the immediate principle of the conscience independently of reason itself. And were that impossible, it would moreover not be necessary; for, those who deny this principle, admitted and recognized by all mankind, do not prove that it does not exist but are satisfied with affirming that it does not; so when we affirm that it does exist, we are just as well founded as they are, and we have in addition the inner witness and the voice of conscience, which testifies on its own behalf. If the first glimmers of judgment dazzle us and at first make a blur of objects in our sight, let us wait for our weak eyes to open up again and steady themselves, and soon we shall see these same objects again in the light of reason as nature first showed them to us. Or, rather, let us be more simple and less vain. Let us limit ourselves to the first sentiments that we find in ourselves, since study always leads us back to them when it has not led us astray.

Conscience, conscience! Divine instinct, immortal and celestial voice, certain guide of a being that is ignorant and limited but intelligent and free; infallible judge of good and bad which makes man like unto God; it is you who make the excellence of his nature and the morality of his actions. Without you I sense nothing in me that raises me above the beasts, other than the sad privilege of leading myself astray from error to error with the aid of an understanding without rule and a reason without principle.

Thank heaven, we are delivered from all that terrifying apparatus of philosophy. We can be men without being scholars. Dispensed from consuming our life in the study of morality, we have at less expense a more certain guide in this immense maze of human opinions. But it is not enough that this guide exists; one must know how to recognize it and to follow it. If it speaks to all hearts, then why are there so few of them who hear it? Well, this is because it speaks to us in nature's language, which everything has made us forget. Conscience is timid; it likes refuge and peace. The world and noise scare it; the prejudices from which they claim it is born are its cruelest enemies. It flees or keeps quiet before them. Their noisy voices stifle its voice and prevent it from making itself heard. Fanaticism dares to counterfeit it and to dictate crime in its name. It finally gives up as a result of being dismissed. It no longer speaks to us. It no longer responds to us. And after such long contempt for it, to recall it costs as much as banishing it did.

How many times in my researches have I grown weary as a result of the coldness I felt within me! How many times have sadness and boredom, spreading their poison over my first meditations, made them unbearable for me! My arid heart provided only a languid and lukewarm zeal to the love of truth. I said to myself, "Why torment myself in seeking what is not? Moral good is only a chimera. There is nothing good but the pleasures of the senses." O, when one has once lost the taste for the pleasures of the soul, how difficult it is to regain it! How much more difficult gaining it is when one has never had it! If there existed a man miserable enough to be unable to recall anything he had done in all his life which made him satisfied with himself and glad to have lived, that man would be incapable of ever knowing himself; and for want of feeling the goodness suitable to his nature, he would necessarily remain wicked and be eternally unhappy. But do you believe there is a single man on the whole earth depraved enough never to have yielded in his heart to the temptation of doing good? This temptation is so natural and so sweet that it is impossible always to resist it, and the memory of the pleasure that it once produced suffices to recall it constantly. Unfortunately it is at first hard to satisfy. One has countless reasons to reject the inclination of one's heart. False prudence confines it within the limits of the human _I_; countless efforts of courage are needed to dare to cross those limits. To enjoy doing good is the reward for having done good, and this reward is obtained only after having deserved it. Nothing is more lovable than virtue, but one must possess it to find it so. Virtue is similar to Proteus in the fable: when one wants to embrace it, it at first takes on countless terrifying forms and finally reveals itself in its own form only to those who did not let go.

Constantly caught up in the combat between my natural sentiments, which spoke for the common interest, and my reason, which related everything to me, I would have drifted all my life in this continual alternation—doing the bad, loving the good, always in contradiction with myself—if new lights had not illuminated my heart, and if the truth, which settled my opinions, had not also made my conduct certain and put me in agreement with myself. For all that one might want to establish virtue by reason alone, what solid base can one give it? Virtue, they say, is the love of order. But can and should this love win out in me over that of my own well-being? Let them give me a clear and sufficient reason for preferring it. At bottom, their alleged principle is a pure play on words; for I say that vice is the love of order, taken in a different sense. There is some moral order wherever there is sentiment and intelligence. The difference is that the good man orders himself in relation to the whole, and the wicked one orders the whole in relation to himself. The latter makes himself the center of all things; the former measures his radius and keeps to the circumference. Then he is ordered in relation to the common center, which is God, and in relation to all the concentric circles, which are the creatures. If the divinity does not exist, it is only the wicked man who reasons, and the good man is nothing but a fool.

O my child! May you one day sense what a weight one is relieved of when, after having exhausted the vanity of human opinions and tasted the bitterness of the passions, one finally finds so near to oneself the road of wisdom, the reward of this life's labors, and the source of the happiness of which one has despaired. All the duties of the natural law, which were almost erased from my heart by the injustice of men, are recalled to it in the name of the eternal justice which imposes them on me and sees me fulfill them. I no longer sense that I am anything but the work and the instrument of the great Being who wants what is good, who does it, and who will do what is good for me through the conjunction of my will and His and through the good use of my liberty. I acquiesce in the order that this Being establishes, sure that one day I myself will enjoy this order and find my felicity in it; for what felicity is sweeter than sensing that one is ordered in a system in which everything is good? Subject to pain, I bear it with patience in thinking that it is fleeting and that it comes from a body that does not belong to me. If I do a good deed without a witness, I know that it is seen, and I make a record for the other life of my conduct in this one. In suffering an injustice, I say to myself, "The just Being who rules everything will certainly know how to compensate me for it." The needs of my body and the miseries of my life make the idea of death more bearable for me. They will be so many fewer bonds to break when it is necessary to leave everything.

Why is my soul subjected to my senses and chained to this body which enslaves it and interferes with it? I know nothing about it. Did I take part in God's decrees? But I can, without temerity, form modest conjectures. I tell myself: "If man's mind had remained free and pure, what merit would he gain from loving and following the order which he saw established and which he would have no interest in troubling? He would be happy, it is true. But his happiness would be lacking the most sublime degree, the glory of virtue and the good witness of oneself. He would be only like the angels, and doubtless the virtuous man will be more than they are. He is united to a mortal body by a bond no less powerful than incomprehensible. The care for this body's preservation incites the soul to relate everything to the body and gives it an interest contrary to the general order, which the soul is nevertheless capable of seeing and loving. It is then that the good use of the soul's liberty becomes both its merit and its recompense, and that it prepares itself an incorruptible happiness in combating its terrestrial passions and maintaining itself in its first will."

If, even in the state of abasement which we are in during this life, all our first inclinations are legitimate, and if all our vices come to us from ourselves, why do we complain of being subjugated by them? Why do we reproach the Author of things for the evils we do to ourselves and the enemies we arm against ourselves? Ah, let us not corrupt man! He will always be good without difficulty and always be happy without remorse! The guilty who say they are forced to crime are as dishonest as they are wicked. How is it they do not see that the weakness of which they complain is their own work; that their first depravity comes from their own will; that by willing to yield to their temptations, they finally yield to them in spite of themselves and make them irresistible? It is doubtless no longer in their power not to be wicked and weak; but not becoming so was in their power. Oh how easily we would remain masters of ourselves and of our passions—even during this life—if when our habits were not yet acquired, when our mind was beginning to open, we knew how to occupy it with the objects that it ought to know in order to evaluate those which it does not know; if we sincerely wanted to enlighten ourselves—not to be conspicuous in others' eyes, but to be good and wise according to our nature, to make ourselves happy in practicing our duties! This study appears boring and painful to us because we think about it only when we are already corrupted by vice, already given over to our passions. We settle our judgments and our esteem before knowing good and bad, and then, in relating everything to this false measure, we give to nothing its just value.

There is an age when the heart is still free, but ardent, restless, avid for the happiness it does not know; it seeks it with a curiosity born of incertitude and, deceived by the senses, finally settles on a vain image of happiness and believes it has found it where it is not. These illusions have lasted too long for me. Alas, I recognized them too late and have been unable to destroy them completely. They will last as long as this mortal body which causes them. At least, although they may very well seduce me, they no longer deceive me. I know them for what they are; in following them, I despise them. Far from seeing them as the object of my happiness, I see them as its obstacle. I aspire to the moment when, after being delivered from the shackles of the body, I shall be *me* without contradiction or division and shall need only myself in order to be happy. While waiting, I am already happy in this life because I take little account of all its ills, because I regard it as almost foreign to my being, and because all the true good that I can get out of it depends on me.

To raise myself beforehand as much as possible to this condition of happiness, strength, and freedom, I practice sublime contemplations. I meditate on the order of the universe, not in order to explain it by vain systems but to admire it constantly, to worship the wise Author who makes himself felt in it. I converse with Him; I fill all my faculties with His divine essence; I am moved by His benefactions; I bless Him for his gifts. But I do not pray to Him. What would I ask of Him? That He change the course of things for me, that He perform miracles in my favor? I who ought to love, above all, the order established by His wisdom and maintained by His providence, would I want this order to be disturbed for me? No, this rash wish would deserve to be punished rather than fulfilled. Nor do I ask Him for the power to do good. Why ask Him for what He has given me? Did He not give me conscience for loving the good, reason for knowing it, and liberty for choosing it? If I do the bad, I have no excuse. I do it because I want to. To ask Him to change my will is to ask Him what He asks of me. It is to want Him to do my work while I collect the wages for it. Not to be contented with my condition is to want no longer to be a man, it is to want something other than what is, it is to want disorder and evil. Source of justice and truth, God, clement and good, in my confidence in You, the supreme wish of my heart is that Your will be done! In joining my will to Yours, I do what you do; I acquiesce in Your goodness; I believe that I share beforehand in the supreme felicity which is its reward.

As I justly distrust myself, the only thing that I ask of Him, or rather that I expect of His justice, is to correct my error if I am led astray and if this error is dangerous to me. The fact that I act in good faith does not mean I believe myself infallible. Those of my opinions which seem truest to me are perhaps so many lies; for what man does not hold on to his opinions, and how many men agree about everything? The illusion deceiving me may very well come from myself; it is He alone who can cure me of it. I have done what I could to attain the truth, but its source is too elevated. If the strength for going farther is lacking to me, of what can I be guilty? It is up to the truth to come nearer.

The good priest had spoken with vehemence. He was moved, and so was I. I believed I was hearing the divine Orpheus sing the first hymns and teaching men the worship of the gods. Nevertheless I saw a multitude of objections to make to him. I did not make any of them, because they were less solid than disconcerting, and persuasiveness was on his side. To the extent that he spoke to me according to his conscience, mine seemed to confirm what he had told me.

The sentiments you have just expounded to me, I said to him, appear more novel in what you admit you do not know than in what you say you believe. I see in them pretty nearly the theism or the natural religion that the Christians pretend to confound with atheism or irreligiousness, which is the directly contrary doctrine. But in the present condition of my faith I have to ascend rather than descend in order to adopt your opinions, and I find it difficult to remain precisely at the point where you are without being as wise as you. In order to be at least as sincere as you, I want to take counsel with myself. Following your example, I ought to be guided by the inner sentiment. You yourself have taught me that, after one has long imposed silence on it, to recall it is not the business of a moment. I will carry your discourse with me in my heart. I must meditate on it. If after taking careful counsel with myself, I remain as convinced of it as you are, you will be my final apostle, and I shall be your proselyte unto death. Continue, however, to instruct me. You have only told me half of what I must know. Speak to me of revelation, of the scriptures, of those obscure dogmas through which I have been wandering since childhood, without being able either to conceive or to believe them and without knowing how I could either accept or reject them.

Yes, my child, he said, embracing me, I shall finish telling you what I think. I do not want to open my heart to you halfway. But the desire you give evidence of was necessary to authorize my having no reserve with you. I have told you nothing up to now which I did not believe could be useful to you and of which I was not profoundly persuaded. The examination which remains to be made is very different. I see in it only perplexity, mystery, and obscurity. I bring to it only uncertainty and distrust. I decide only in trembling, and I tell you my doubts rather than my opinions. If your sentiments were more stable, I would hesitate to expound mine to you. But in your present condition you will profit from thinking as I do.* Moreover, attribute to my discourse only the authority of reason. I do not know whether I am in error. It is difficult in discussion not to adopt an assertive tone sometimes. But remember that all my assertions here are only reasons for doubt. Seek the truth yourself. As for me, I promise you only good faith.

You see in my exposition only natural religion. It is very strange that any other is needed! How shall I know this necessity? What can I be guilty of in serving God according to the understanding He gives to my mind and the sentiments He inspires in my heart? What purity of morality, what dogma useful to man and honorable to his Author can I derive from a positive doctrine which I cannot derive without it from the good use of my faculties? Show me what one can add, for the glory of God, for the good of society, and for my own advantage, to the duties of the natural law, and what virtue you produce from a new form of worship that is not a result of mine? The greatest ideas of the divinity come to us from reason alone. View the spectacle of nature; hear the inner voice. Has God not told everything to our eyes, to our conscience, to our judgment? What more will men tell us? Their revelations have only the effect of degrading God by giving Him human passions. I see that particular dogmas, far from clarifying the notions of the great Being, confuse them; that far from ennobling them, they debase them; that to the inconceivable mysteries surrounding the great Being they add absurd contradictions; that they make man proud, intolerant, and cruel; that, instead of establishing peace on earth, they bring sword and fire to it. I ask myself what good all this does, without knowing what to answer. I see in it only the crimes of men and the miseries of mankind.

I am told that a revelation was needed to teach men the way God wanted to be served. They present as proof the diversity of bizarre forms of worship which have been instituted, and do not see that this very diversity comes from the fancifulness [53] of revelations. As soon as peoples took it into their heads to make God speak, each made Him speak in its own way and made Him say what it wanted. If one had listened only to what God says to the heart of man, there would never have been more than one religion on earth.

---

* This is, I believe, what the good vicar could say to the public at present.

There had to be uniformity of worship. Very well. But was this point so important that the whole apparatus of divine power was needed to establish it? Let us not confuse the ceremony of religion with religion itself. The worship God asks for is that of the heart. And that worship, when it is sincere, is always uniform. One must be possessed of a mad vanity indeed to imagine that God takes so great an interest in the form of the priest's costume, in the order of the words he pronounces, in the gestures he makes at the altar, and in all his genuflexions. Ah, my friend, remain upright! You will always be near enough to the earth. God wants to be revered in spirit and in truth. This is the duty of all religions, all countries, all men. As to the external worship, if it must be uniform for the sake of good order, that is purely a question of public policy; no revelation is needed for that.

I did not begin with all these reflections. I was carried along by the prejudices of education and by that dangerous *amour-propre* which always wants to carry man above his sphere, and, unable to raise my feeble conceptions up to the great Being, I made an effort to lower Him down to my level. I reduced the infinite distance He has put in the relations between His nature and mine. I wanted more immediate communications, more particular instructions; not content with making God like man, I wanted supernatural understanding in order that I myself would be privileged among my fellows, I wanted an exclusive form of worship; I wanted God to have said to me what He had not said to others, or what others had not understood in the same way as I did.

Regarding the point at which I had arrived as the common point from which all believers start in order to arrive at a more enlightened form of worship, I found nothing in natural religion but the elements of every religion. I considered this diversity of sects which reign on earth, and which accuse each other of lying and error. I asked, "Which is the right one?" Each answered, "It is mine." * Each said, "I and my partisans alone think rightly; all the others are in error." "And how do you know that your sect is the right one?" "Because God said so." "And who told you that God said so?" "My pastor, who certainly knows. My pastor told me this is what to believe, and this is what I believe. He assures me that all those who say something other than he does are lying, and I do not listen to them."

What, I thought, is the truth not one, and can what is true for me

---

* A good and wise priest says:

All say that they get it and believe it (and all use this jargon) not from men nor from any creature but from God.

But to tell the truth without any flattery or disguise, there is nothing to it. Religions are, whatever is said, gotten from human hands and by human means. Witness first the way religions were and still are received every day in the world by individuals: nation, country, and place give religion. One belongs to the religion observed in the place where one is born and raised. We are circumcised, baptised, Jews, Mohammedans, Christians before we know that we are men. Religion is not of our choice and election. Witness next how ways of life and morals are in such poor agreement with religion. Witness that on human and very slight occasions one goes counter to the tenor of one's religion. [Charron, *de la Sagesse*, vol. II, chap. 5, p. 257, Bordeaux edition 1601.]

It appears very much as though the sincere profession of faith of the virtuous theolog of Condam would not have been very different from that of the Savoyard Vicar.[54]

be false for you? If the methods of the man who follows the right road and of the man who goes astray are the same, what merit or what fault belongs to one of these men more than the other? Their choice is the effect of chance; to blame them for it is iniquitous. It is to reward or punish them for being born in this or in that country. To dare to say that God judges us in this way is to insult His justice.

Either all religions are good and agreeable to God; or if there is one which He prescribes to men and punishes them for refusing to recognize, He has given it certain and manifest signs so that it is distinguished and known as the only true one. These signs exist in all times and all places, equally to be grasped by all men, great and small, learned and ignorant, Europeans, Indians, Africans, savages. If there were a religion on earth outside of whose worship there was only eternal suffering, and if in some place in the world a single mortal of good faith had not been struck by its obviousness, the God of that religion would be the most iniquitous and cruel of tyrants.

Are we, then, sincerely seeking the truth? Let us grant nothing to the right of birth and to the authority of fathers and pastors, but let us recall for the examination of conscience and reason all that they have taught us from our youth. They may very well cry out, "Subject your reason." He who deceives me can say as much. I need reasons for subjecting my reason.

All the theology that I can acquire on my own from the inspection of the universe and by the good use of my faculties is limited to what I have explained to you previously. To know more one must have recourse to extraordinary means. These means could not be the authority of men; for since no man belongs to a different species from me, all that a man knows naturally I too can know, and another man can be mistaken as well as I. When I believe what he says, it is not because he says it but because he proves it. Therefore the testimony of men is at bottom only that of my own reason and adds nothing to the natural means God gave me for knowing the truth.

Apostle of the truth, what then have you to tell me of which I do not remain the judge? "God Himself has spoken. Hear His revelation." That is something else. God has spoken! That is surely a great statement. To whom has He spoken? "He has spoken to men." Why, then, did I hear nothing about it? "He has directed other men to give you His word." I understand: it is men who are going to tell me what God has said. I should have preferred to have heard God Himself. It would have cost Him nothing more, and I would have been sheltered from seduction. "He gives you a guarantee in making manifest the mission of his messengers." How is that? "By miracles." And where are these miracles? "In books." And who wrote these books? "Men." And who saw these miracles? "Men who attest to them." What! Always human testimony? Always men who report to me what other men have reported! So many men between God and me! Nevertheless let us see, examine, compare, verify. Oh, if God had deigned to relieve me of all this labor, would I have served him any less heartily?

Consider, my friend, in what a horrible discussion I am now engaged, what immense erudition I need to go back to the most remote antiquity

—to examine, weigh, and compare the prophecies, the revelations, the facts, all the monuments of faith put forth in every country of the world, to fix times, places, authors, occasions! What critical precision is necessary for me to distinguish the authentic documents from the forged ones; to compare the objections to the responses, the translations to the originals; to judge of the impartiality of witnesses, of their good sense, of their understanding; to know whether anything has been suppressed, anything added, anything transposed, changed, falsified; to resolve the contradictions which remain; to judge what weight should be given to the silence of adversaries concerning facts alleged against them; whether these allegations were known to them; whether they took them seriously enough to deign to respond; whether books were common enough for ours to reach them; whether we have been of good enough faith to allow their books to circulate among us and to let remain their strongest objections just as they made them.

Once all these monuments are recognized as incontestable, one must next move on to the proofs of their authors' mission. One must have a good knowledge of all of the following: the laws of probability and the likelihood of events, in order to judge which predictions cannot be fulfilled without a miracle; the particular genius of the original languages, in order to distinguish what is prediction in these languages and what is only figure of speech; which facts belong to the order of nature and which other facts do not, so as to be able to say to what extent a skillful man can fascinate the eyes of simple people and can amaze even enlightened ones; how to discern to which species a miracle ought to belong and what authenticity it ought to have—not only for it to be believed, but for it to be a punishable offense to doubt it; how to compare the proof of true and false miracles and how to find certain rules for discerning them; and, finally, how to explain why God chose, for attesting to His word, means which themselves have so great a need of attestation, as though He were playing on men's credulity and intentionally avoiding the true means of persuading them.

Let us suppose that the divine Majesty were to deign to lower itself sufficiently to make a man the organ of its sacred will. Is it reasonable, is it just to demand that all of mankind obey the voice of this minister without making him known to it as such? Is there equity in providing this minister as his only credentials some special signs given to a few obscure people, signs of which all the rest of men will never know anything except by hearsay? In every country in the world, if one were to accept the truth of all the miracles which the people and the simple folk say they have seen, every sect would be the right one; there would be more miracles than natural events, and the greatest of all miracles would be if there were not miracles wherever fanatics are persecuted. It is the unalterable order of nature which best shows the Supreme Being. If many exceptions took place, I would no longer know what to think; and as for me, I believe too much in God to believe in so many miracles that are so little worthy of Him.

Let a man come and use this language with us: "Mortals, I announce the will of the Most High to you. Recognize in my voice Him who sends me. I order the sun to change its course, the stars to form another arrangement, the mountains to become level, the waters to rise up, the earth to change its aspect." At these marvels who will not instantly recognize the Master of nature? It does not obey impostors. Their miracles are worked at crossroads, in deserts, within the confines of a room; it is there that they have an easy time with a small number of spectators already disposed to believe everything. Who will dare to tell me how many eyewitnesses are needed in order to make a miracle worthy of faith? If your miracles, which are performed to prove your doctrine, themselves need to be proved, of what use are they? You might as well perform none.

The most important examination of the proclaimed doctrine remains. For since those who say that God performs miracles on earth also claim that the Devil sometimes imitates them, we are no farther advanced than before, even with the best-attested miracles; and since the magicians of Pharaoh dared, in the very presence of Moses, to produce the same signs he did by God's express order, why would they not in his absence have claimed, with the same credentials, the same authority? Thus, after the doctrine has been proved by the miracle, the miracle has to be proved by the doctrine,* for fear of taking the Demon's work for God's work. What do you think of this vicious circle?

Doctrine coming from God ought to bear the sacred character of the divinity. Not only should it clarify for us the confused ideas which reasoning draws in our mind, but it should also propound a form of worship, a morality, and maxims that are suitable to the attributes with which we conceive His essence on our own. If it taught us only things that are absurd and without reason, if it inspired in us only sentiments of aversion for our fellows and terror for ourselves, if it depicted for us only a god who is angry, jealous, vengeful, partisan, one who hates men, a god of war and battles always ready to destroy and strike down, always speaking of torments and suffering, and boasting of punishing even the innocent, my heart would not be attracted toward this terrible god, and I would take care not to give up the natural religion for this one. For you surely see that one must necessarily choose. Your God is not ours, I would say to its sectarians. He who begins by choosing a single people for Himself and proscribing the rest of mankind is not the common Father of men. He who destines the great majority of His

---

* This is explicit in countless passages of scripture, among others Deuteronomy 13, where it is said that if a prophet proclaiming foreign gods confirms his speeches by miracles and what he predicts comes to pass, far from paying any attention to him, one ought to put this prophet to death. Thus, when pagans put to death apostles proclaiming a foreign god and proving their mission by predictions and miracles, I do not see what solid objection there was to the pagans which they could not instantly turn back against us. Now, what is to be done in such a case? One thing only. Return to reasoning, and leave aside the miracles. It would have been better not to have had recourse to them. This is the simplest good sense, which is obscured only by dint of distinctions that at the very least are quite subtle. Subtleties in Christianity! But was Jesus Christ wrong then, to promise the Kingdom of Heaven to the simple? Was he wrong, then, to begin the most beautiful of his speeches by congratulating the poor in spirit, if so much spirit is needed to understand his doctrine and to learn how to believe in him? When you have proved to me that I ought to submit, all will be quite well. But to prove that to me, put yourself within my reach. Measure your reasonings according to the capacity of a poor spirit, or I no longer recognize in you the true disciple of your master, and it is not his doctrine that you proclaim to me.

creatures to eternal torment is not the clement and good God my reason has shown me.

With respect to dogmas, my reason tells me that they ought to be clear, luminous, and striking by their obviousness. If natural religion is insufficient, this is due to the obscurity in which it leaves the great truths it teaches us. It is for revelation to teach us these truths in a manner evident to man's mind, to put them within his reach, to make him conceive them in order that he may believe them. Faith is given certainty and solidity by the understanding. The best of all religions is infallibly the clearest. He who burdens the worship he teaches me with mysteries and contradictions teaches me thereby to distrust it. The God I worship is not a god of shadows. He did not endow me with an understanding in order to forbid me its use. To tell me to subject my reason is to insult its Author. The minister of the truth does not tyrannize my reason; he enlightens it.

We have set aside all human authority, and without it I cannot see how one man can convince another by preaching an unreasonable doctrine to him. Let us have these two men confront each other for a moment and find out what they can say to one another, using that harshness of language which is usual for the two parties.

THE INSPIRED MAN   Reason teaches you that the whole is greater than its part, but I teach you on behalf of God that it is the part which is greater than the whole.

THE REASONER   And who are you to dare tell me that God contradicts Himself, and whom would I prefer to believe—Him who teaches me eternal truths by reason, or you who proclaim an absurdity on His behalf?

THE INSPIRED MAN   Me, for my instruction is more positive, and I am going to prove invincibly that it is He Who sends me.

THE REASONER   How? You will prove to me that it is God who sends you to testify against Him? And what kind of proof will you use to convince me that it is more certain that God speaks to me by your mouth than by the understanding He gave me?

THE INSPIRED MAN   The understanding He gave you! Small and vain man! As if you were the first impious person led astray by his reason corrupted by sin!

THE REASONER   Nor would you, man of God, be the first imposter who gave his arrogance as proof of his mission.

THE INSPIRED MAN   What! Do philosophers, too, indulge in insults?

THE REASONER   Sometimes, when saints set the example for them.

THE INSPIRED MAN   Oh, I have the right to. I speak on God's behalf.

THE REASONER   It would be well to show me your credentials before making use of your privileges.

THE INSPIRED MAN   My credentials are authentic. The earth and the heavens will testify for me. Follow my reasonings carefully, I beg you.

THE REASONER   Your reasonings! You are not thinking. To teach me that my reason deceives me, is that not to refute what it has said in your favor? Whoever wants to impugn reason should convince others without making use of it. For let us suppose that you have convinced me by reasoning; how will I know whether it is not my reason, corrupted by sin, which makes me acquiesce to what you tell me? Moreover, what proof, what demonstration will you ever be able to use that is more evident than the axiom it is supposed to destroy? It is just as believable that a good syllogism is a lie as it is that the part is greater than the whole.

THE INSPIRED MAN   What a difference! My proofs are irrefutable. They belong to a supernatural order.

THE REASONER   Supernatural! What does that word mean? I do not understand it.

THE INSPIRED MAN   Changes in the order of nature, prophecies, miracles, wonders of every sort.

THE REASONER   Wonders, miracles! I have never seen anything of the kind.

THE INSPIRED MAN   Others have seen it for you. Crowds of witnesses, the testimony of peoples . . .

THE REASONER   Is the testimony of peoples of a supernatural order?

THE INSPIRED MAN   No, but when it is unanimous, it is incontestable.

THE REASONER   There is nothing more incontestable than the principles of reason, and an absurdity cannot be made authoritative by the testimony of men. Once again, let us see supernatural proofs, for the attestation of mankind is not such a proof.

THE INSPIRED MAN   O hardened heart! Grace does not speak to you.

THE REASONER   It is not my fault, for, according to you, one must have already received grace to be able to ask for it. Therefore, begin to speak to me in place of it.

THE INSPIRED MAN   Ah, that is what I am doing, and you do not hear me. But what do you say of prophecies?

THE REASONER   I say, in the first place, that I have no more heard prophecies than I have seen miracles. I say, moreover, that no prophecy could be an authority for me.

THE INSPIRED MAN   Henchman of the Demon! And why are prophecies not an authority for you?

THE REASONER   Because for them to be an authority three things would be required whose coincidence is impossible: that is, that I was witness to the prophecy, that I was witness to the event, and that it was demonstrated to me that this event could not have tallied fortuitously with the prophecy. For even if a prophecy were more precise, more clear, and more luminous than an axiom of geometry, the clarity of a prediction made at random does not make its fulfillment impossible; and therefore when that fulfillment does take place, it is not a strict proof of anything about him who predicted it.

See, then, what your alleged supernatural proofs, your miracles and prophecies come down to: a belief in all this on the faith of others, and a subjection of the authority of God, speaking to my reason, to the authority of men. If the eternal truths which my mind conceives could be impaired, there would no longer be any kind of certainty for me, and far from being sure that you speak to me on behalf of God, I would not even be sure that He exists.

There are many difficulties here, my child, and these are not all. Among so many diverse religions which mutually proscribe and exclude one another, a single one is the right one, if indeed there is a right one. In order to recognize it, it is not sufficient to examine one of them; they must all be examined, and in any matter whatsoever one must not condemn without hearing.* The objections must be compared to the proofs; it must be known what each objects to in the others, and what it responds to their objections against itself. The more a sentiment appears to us to have been demonstrated, the more we ought to try to find out the basis for so many men's not finding it so. One would have to be quite simple to believe that it suffices to hear the learned men of one's own party to inform oneself of the arguments of the opposing party. Where are the theologians who pride themselves on good faith? Where are those who, in order to refute the arguments of their adversaries, do not begin by weakening them? Each shines in his own party; but one who in the midst of his own people is proud of his proofs would cut a very foolish figure with these same proofs among people of another party. Do you want to inform yourself from books? What erudition must be acquired, how many languages must be learned, how many libraries must be gone through, what an immense amount of reading must be done! Who will guide me in the choice? It will be difficult to find in one country the best books of the opposing party, and even more so those of all the parties. If one were to find them, they would soon be refuted. The absent party is always wrong, and poor arguments spoken with assurance easily efface good ones expounded with contempt. Moreover, there is often nothing which is more deceptive than books, and which renders less faithfully the sentiments of those who wrote them. If you had wanted to judge the Catholic faith on the basis of Bossuet's book,[56] you would have discovered that you were wide of the mark after having lived among us. You would have seen that the doctrine used to respond to the Protestants is not the one taught to the people, and that Bossuet's book bears little resemblance to the instructions of the sermon. In order to judge a religion well, it is necessary not to study it in the books of its sectarians, but to go and learn it amongst them. That is very different. Each religion has its traditions, its views, its customs, and its prejudices which constitute the spirit of its belief and must also be considered for it to be judged.

How many great peoples print no books and do not read ours! How can they judge our opinions? How can we judge theirs? We scoff at them, they despise us; and if our travelers ridicule them, they need only travel among us to return the favor. In what country are there

* Plutarch reports that the Stoics maintained, among other bizarre paradoxes, that in an adversary proceeding it was useless to hear the two parties; for, they say, either the first has proved his assertion, or he has not proved it. If he has proved it, there is nothing more to say, and his adversary ought to be condemned. If he has not proved it, he is wrong, and his suit ought to be dismissed. I find that the method of all those who accept an exclusive revelation closely resembles that of these Stoics. As soon as each claims to be the only right one, it is necessary, in order to choose among so many parties, to listen to them all; otherwise, one is being unjust.[55]

not sensible people, people of good faith, decent people, friends of the truth who, in order to profess it, would need only to know it? However, each sees the truth in his own worship and finds absurd the worship of other nations. Therefore, either these foreign forms of worship are not as extravagant as they seem to us, or the reason we find in our own proves nothing.

We have three principal religions in Europe. One accepts a single revelation, the second accepts two, the third accepts three. Each detests and curses the other two, accusing them of being blind, hardhearted, opinionated, and dishonest. What impartial man will dare to judge among them if he has not carefully weighed their proofs, carefully listened to their arguments? The religion which accepts only one revelation is the oldest and appears to be the most certain. The one which accepts three is the most modern and appears to be the most consistent. The one which accepts two and rejects the third may very well be the best, but it certainly has all the prejudices against it. The inconsistency leaps to the eyes.

In the three revelations the sacred books are written in languages unknown to the people who follow them. The Jews no longer understand Hebrew; the Christians understand neither Hebrew nor Greek; neither the Turks nor the Persians understand Arabic, and the modern Arabs themselves no longer speak the language of Mohammed. Is this not a simple way of instructing men—always speaking to them in a language they do not understand? These books are translated, it will be said. A fine answer! Who will assure me that these books are faithfully translated, that it is even possible that they be? And if God has gone so far as to speak to men, why must He need an interpreter?

I shall never be able to conceive that what every man is obliged to know is confined to books, and that someone who does not have access to these books, or to those who understand them, is punished for an ignorance which is involuntary. Always books! What a mania. Because Europe is full of books, Europeans regard them as indispensable, without thinking that in three-quarters of the earth they have never been seen. Were not all books written by men? Why, then, would man need them to know his duties, and what means had he of knowing them before these books were written? Either he will learn these duties by himself, or he is excused from knowing them.

Our Catholics make a great to-do about the authority of the Church; but what do they gain by that, if they need as great an apparatus of proofs to establish this authority as other sects need for establishing their doctrine directly? The Church decides that the Church has the right to decide. Is that not an authority based on good proofs? Step outside of that, and you return to all our discussions.

Do you know many Christians who have taken the effort to examine with care what Judaism alleges against them? If some individuals have seen something of this, it is in the books of Christians. A good way of informing oneself about their adversaries' arguments! But what is there to do? If someone dared to publish among us books in which Judaism were openly favored, we would punish the author, the publisher, the bookseller.* This is a convenient and sure policy for always being right. There is a pleasure in refuting people who do not dare to speak.

Those among us who have access to conversation with Jews are not much farther advanced. These unfortunates feel themselves to be at our mercy. The tyranny practiced against them makes them fearful. They know how little troubled Christian charity is by injustice and cruelty. What will they dare to say without laying themselves open to our accusing them of blasphemy? Greed gives us zeal, and they are too rich not to be wrong. The most learned, the most enlightened among them are always the most circumspect. You will convert some miserable fellow, who is paid to calumniate his sect. You will put words into the mouths of some vile old-clothes dealers, who will yield in order to flatter you. You will triumph over their ignorance or their cowardice, while their learned men will smile in silence at your ineptitude. But do you believe that in places where they feel secure you would win out over them so cheaply? At the Sorbonne it is. as clear as day that the predictions about the Messiah relate to Jesus Christ. Among the Amsterdam rabbis it is just as clear that they do not have the least relation to Jesus. I shall never believe that I have seriously heard the arguments of the Jews until they have a free state, schools, and universities, where they can speak and dispute without risk. Only then will we be able to know what they have to say.

At Constantinople the Turks state their arguments, but we do not dare to state our own. There it is our turn to crawl. If the Turks demand from us the same respect for Mohammed that we demand for Jesus Christ from the Jews, who do not believe in him any more than we believe in Mohammed, are the Turks wrong? Are we right? According to what equitable principle shall we resolve this question?

Two-thirds of mankind are neither Jews nor Mohammedans nor Christians, and how many million men have never heard of Moses, Jesus Christ, or Mohammed? This is denied; it is maintained that our missionaries go everywhere. That is easily said. But do they go into the still unknown heart of Africa, where no European has ever penetrated up to now? Do they go to deepest Tartary, to follow on horseback the wandering hordes who are never approached by a foreigner, and who, far from having heard of the Pope, hardly even know of the Grand Lama? Do they go into the immense continents of America, where whole nations still do not know that peoples from another world have set foot in theirs? Do they go to Japan, from which their maneuvers got them thrown out forever, and where their predecessors are known to the generations now being born only as guileful intriguers who came with a hypocritical zeal to take hold of the empire by stealth? Do they go into the harems of the princes of Asia to proclaim the Gospel to thousands of poor slaves? What have the women of this part of the

* Among countless known facts, here is one which needs no commentary. In the sixteenth century the Catholic theologians had condemned to the fire all the books of the Jews, without exception. The illustrious and learned Reuchlin, consulted about this affair, brought upon himself terrible troubles which almost ruined him merely by expressing the opinion that one could preserve those books which were not anti-Christian and which dealt with matters neutral to religion.[57]

world done to prevent any missionary from preaching the faith to them? Will they all go to hell for having been recluses?

Even if it were true that the Gospel has been proclaimed everywhere on earth, what would be gained by it? Surely on the eve of the day that the first missionary arrived in some country, someone died there who was not able to hear him. Now tell me what we are going to do with that person? If there were only a single man in the whole universe who had never been preached to about Jesus Christ, the objection would be as strong for that single man as for a quarter of mankind.

Even if the ministers of the Gospel have made themselves heard by distant peoples, what have they told them which could reasonably be accepted on their word and which did not demand the most exact verification? You proclaim to me a God born and dead two thousand years ago at the other end of the world in some little town, and you tell me that whoever has not believed in this mystery will be damned. These are very strange things to believe so quickly on the sole authority of a man whom I do not know! Why did your god make these events take place so far from me, if he wanted me to be under an obligation to be informed of them? Is it a crime not to know what takes place at the antipodes? Can I divine that there were a Hebrew people and a city of Jerusalem in another hemisphere? I might as well be obliged to know what is happening on the moon! You say that you come to teach this to me. But why did you not come to teach it to my father, or why do you damn this good old man for never having known anything about it? Ought he to be eternally punished for your laziness, he who was so good and beneficent, and who sought only the truth? Be of good faith; then put yourself in my place. See if I ought to believe on your testimony alone all the unbelievable things you tell me and to reconcile so many injustices with the just God whom you proclaim to me. I beg you, let me go and see this distant country where so many marvels take place that are unheard of in this one. Let me go and find out why the inhabitants of this Jerusalem treated God like a thief. They did not, you say, recognize him as god? What shall I do then, I who have never even heard Him mentioned except by you? You add that they were punished, dispersed, oppressed, enslaved, that none of them comes near that city anymore. Surely they well deserved all that. But what do today's inhabitants say of the deicide committed by their predecessors? They deny it; they, too, do not recognize God as God. The children of the others, then, might as well have been left there.

What! In the very city where God died, neither the old nor the new inhabitants acknowledged him, and you want me to acknowledge him, me who was born two thousand years after and two thousand leagues away? Do you not see that before I put faith in this book which you call sacred, and of which I understand nothing, I must be informed by people other than you when and by whom it was written, how it was preserved, how it was transmitted to you, what arguments are given by those in your country who reject it, although they know as well as you all that you teach me? You are well aware that I must necessarily go to Europe, Asia, and Palestine and examine everything for myself. I would have to be mad to listen to you prior to that time.

Not only does this discourse appear reasonable to me, but I maintain that every man in his senses ought to speak thus in a similar case and dismiss without more ado the missionary who is in a hurry to instruct and baptize him before verification of the proofs. Now, I maintain that there is no revelation against which the same objections do not have as much strength as, or more strength than, against Christianity. From this it follows that if there is only one true religion and every man is obliged to follow it under penalty of damnation, one's life must be spent in studying them all, in going deeper into them, in comparing them, in roaming around the country where each is established. No one is exempt from the first duty of man; no one has a right to rely on the judgment of others. The artisan who lives only by his work, the laborer who does not know how to read, the delicate and timid maiden, the invalid who can hardly leave his bed—all without exception must study, meditate, engage in disputation, travel, roam the world. There will no longer be any stable and settled people; the whole earth will be covered only with pilgrims going at great expense and with continuous hardships to verify, to compare, and to examine for themselves the various forms of worship that people observe. Then it will be goodbye to the trades, the arts, the humane sciences, and all the civil occupations. There can no longer be any other study than that of religion. He who has enjoyed the most robust health, best employed his time, best used his reason, and lived the most years will hardly know what to think in his old age; and it will be a great deal if he learns before his death in what worship he ought to have lived.

Do you want to modify this method and give the least hold to the authority of men? At that moment you surrender everything to it. And if the son of a Christian does well in following his father's religion without a profound and impartial examination, why would the son of a Turk do wrong in similarly following his father's religion? I defy all the intolerant people in the world to answer this question in a manner satisfactory to a sensible man.

Pressed by these arguments, some would prefer to make God unjust and to punish the innocent for their father's sin rather than to renounce their barbarous dogma. Others get out of it by obligingly sending an angel to instruct whoever, despite living in invincible ignorance, has lived morally. What a fine invention that angel is! Not content with subjecting us to their contrivances, they make it necessary for God Himself to use them.

You see, my son, to what absurdity pride and intolerance lead, when each man is so sure of his position and believes he is right to the exclusion of the rest of mankind. All my researches have been sincere—I take as my witness that God of peace Whom I adore and Whom I proclaim to you. But when I saw that these researches were and always would be unsuccessful, and that I was being swallowed up in an ocean without shores, I retraced my steps and restricted my faith to my primary notions. I have never been able to believe that God commanded me, under penalty of going to hell, to be so learned. I therefore closed all the books. There is one open to all eyes: it is the book of nature. It is from this great and sublime book that I learn to serve and worship its divine Author. No one can be excused for not reading it, because it speaks to all men a language that is intelligible to all minds. Let us assume that I was born on a desert island, that I have not seen any man other than myself, that I have never learned what took place in olden times in some corner of the world; nonetheless, if I exercise my reason, if I cultivate it, if I make good use of my God-given faculties which require no intermediary, I would learn of myself to know Him, to love Him, to love His works, to want the good that He wants, and to fulfill all my duties on earth in order to please Him. What more will all the learning of men teach me?

If I were a better reasoner or better educated, perhaps I would sense the truth of revelation, its utility for those who are fortunate enough to acknowledge it. But if I see in its favor proofs I cannot combat, I also see against it objections I cannot resolve. There are so many solid reasons for and against that I do not know what to decide, and I neither accept nor reject it. I reject only the obligation to acknowledge it, because this alleged obligation is incompatible with God's justice and because, far from removing the obstacles to salvation, it would have multiplied them and made them insurmountable for the greater part of mankind. With this exception I remain in respectful doubt about this point. I am not so presumptuous as to believe myself infallible. Other men have been able to achieve certainty about what seems uncertain to me. I reason for myself and not for them. I neither blame them nor imitate them. Their judgment may be better than mine, but it is not my fault that it is not mine.

I also admit that the majesty of the Scriptures amazes me, and that the holiness of the Gospel speaks to my heart. Look at the books of the philosophers with all their pomp. How petty they are next to this one! Can it be that a book at the same time so sublime and so simple is the work of men? Can it be that he whose history it presents is only a man himself? Is his the tone of an enthusiast or an ambitious sectarian? What gentleness, what purity in his morals! What touching grace in his teachings! What elevation in his maxims! What profound wisdom in his speeches! What presence of mind, what finesse, and what exactness in his responses! What a dominion over his passions! Where is the man, where is the sage who knows how to act, to suffer, and to die without weakness and without ostentation? When Plato depicts his imaginary just man,* covered with all the opprobrium of crime and worthy of all the rewards of virtue, he depicts Jesus Christ feature for feature. The resemblance is so striking that all the Fathers have sensed it; it is impossible to be deceived about it. What prejudices, what blindness one must have to dare to compare the son of Sophroniscus to the son of Mary? What a distance from one to the other! Socrates, dying without pain and without ignominy, easily sticks to his character to the end; and if this easy death had not honored his life, one would doubt whether Socrates, for all his intelligence, were anything but a sophist. He invented morality, it is said. Others before him put it into practice; all he did was to say what they had done; all he did

* De Rep, Dial. 2.⁵⁸

was to draw the lesson from their examples. Aristides was just before Socrates said what justice is. Leonidas died for his country before Socrates had made it a duty to love the fatherland. Sparta was sober before Socrates had praised sobriety. Before he had defined virtue, Greece abounded in virtuous men. But where did Jesus find among his own people that elevated and pure morality of which he alone gave the lessons and the example? * From the womb of the most furious fanaticism was heard the highest wisdom, and the simplicity of the most heroic virtues lent honor to the vilest of all peoples. The death of Socrates, philosophizing tranquilly with his friends, is the sweetest one could desire; that of Jesus, expiring in torment, insulted, jeered at, cursed by a whole people, is the most horrible one could fear. Socrates, taking the poisoned cup, blesses the man who gives it to him and who is crying. Jesus, in the midst of a frightful torture, prays for his relentless executioners. Yes, if the life and death of Socrates are those of a wise man, the life and death of Jesus are those of a god. Shall we say that the story of the Gospel was wantonly contrived? My friend, it is not thus that one contrives; the facts about Socrates, which no one doubts, are less well attested than those about Jesus Christ. At bottom, this is to push back the difficulty without doing away with it. It would be more inconceivable that many men in agreement had fabricated this book than that a single one provided its subject. Never would Jewish authors have found either this tone or this morality; and the Gospel has characteristics of truth that are so great, so striking, so perfectly inimitable that its contriver would be more amazing than its hero. With all that, this same Gospel is full of unbelievable things, of things repugnant to reason and impossible for any sensible man to conceive or to accept! What is to be done amidst all these contradictions? One ought always to be modest and cirumspect, my child—to respect in silence what one can neither reject nor understand, and to humble oneself before the great Being who alone knows the truth.

This is the involuntary skepticism in which I have remained. But this skepticism is in no way painful for me, because it does not extend to the points essential to practice and because I am quite decided on the principles of all my duties. I serve God in the simplicity of my heart. I seek to know only what is important for my conduct. As for the dogmas which have an influence neither on actions nor on morality, and about which so many men torment themselves, I do not trouble myself about them at all. I regard all the particular religions as so many salutary institutions which prescribe in each country a uniform manner of honoring God by public worship. These religions can all have their justifications in the climate, the government, the genius of the people, or some other local cause which makes one preferable to another according to the time and place. I believe them all to be right as long as one serves God suitably. The essential worship is that of the heart. God does not reject its homage, if it is sincere, in whatever form it is offered to Him. I have been called—in the form of worship which I profess—to the service of the Church, and I perform with all possible exactness

* See in the Sermon on the Mount the parallel he himself draws between the morality of Moses and his own. *Matth*. C.5. 21 et seq.

the tasks prescribed to me. My conscience would reproach me for voluntarily failing to do so on any point. You know that after a long interdict I obtained, through M. de Mellarède's [59] influence, permission to resume my functions in order to help me to live. Formerly I said the Mass with the lightness with which one eventually treats the most serious things when one does them too often. But since adopting my new principles, I celebrate it with more veneration. I am filled with the majesty of the Supreme Being, with His presence, and with the insufficiency of the human mind, which has so little conception of what relates to its Author. Bearing in mind that I bring to Him the prayers of the people in a prescribed form, I carefully follow all the rites, I recite attentively, I take care never to omit either the least word or the least ceremony. When I approach the moment of the consecration, I collect myself so as to perform it in the frame of mind that the Church and the grandeur of the sacrament demand. I try to annihilate my reason before the supreme intelligence. I say to myself: "Who are you to measure infinite power?" I pronounce the sacramental words with respect, and I put into them all the faith within my power. Whatever may be the case in regard to this inconceivable mystery, I have no fear that I shall be punished on Judgment Day for having profaned it in my heart.

I have been honored with a sacred ministry, although in the lowest rank, and I shall never do or say anything to make myself unworthy of fulfilling its sublime duties. I shall always preach virtue to men; I shall always exhort them to do good; and insofar as I am able, I shall set them a good example. I shall not fail to make religion lovable to them; I shall not fail to strengthen their faith in the truly useful dogmas every man is obliged to believe. But God forbid that I ever preach the cruel dogma of intolerance to them, that I ever bring them to detest their neighbor, to say to other men, "You will be damned." * Were I in a more noticeable rank, this reservation could cause me trouble. But I am too unimportant to have much to fear, and I can hardly fall lower than I now am. Whatever happens, I shall never blaspheme divine justice and shall never lie about the Holy Spirit.

It has long been my ambition to have the honor of being a parish priest. I still have this ambition, but I no longer hope for its fulfillment. My good friend, I find nothing so fine as being a parish priest. A good parish priest is a minister of goodness, just as a good magistrate is a minister of justice. A parish priest never has to do harm. If he cannot always accomplish the good by himself, he is always in a fitting position to encourage it, and he often obtains it if he knows how to make himself respected. O if I could ever serve some poor parish of good people in our mountains, I would be happy, for it seems to me that I would be the cause of my parishioners' happiness. I would not make them rich, but I would share their poverty. I would remove from

---

* The duty to follow and love the religion of one's country does not extend to dogmas contrary to good morals, such as that of intolerance. It is this horrible dogma which arms men against one another and makes them all enemies of mankind. The distinction between civil tolerance and theological tolerance is puerile and vain. These two tolerances are inseparable, and one cannot be accepted without the other. Even angels would not live in peace with men they regarded as enemies of God.

them the stigma and the contempt they suffer, more unbearable than indigence. I would make them love concord and equality, which often banish poverty and always make it bearable. When they saw that I was in no way better off than they and nevertheless lived in contentment, they would learn how to be consoled for their fate and how to live in contentment like me. When instructing them, I would be less attached to the spirit of the Church than to the spirit of the Gospel, in which the dogma is simple and the morality sublime, and in which one sees few religious practices and many works of charity. Before teaching them what must be done, I would always make an effort to practice it, so that they would clearly see that I believe all that I say to them. If I had Protestants in my neighborhood or in my parish, I would not distinguish them at all from my true parishioners in everything connected with Christian charity. I would bring them all to love one another without distinction and to regard one another as brothers, to respect all religions, and to live in peace, with each observing his own. I think that to urge someone to leave the religion in which he was born is to urge him to do evil, and consequently is to do evil oneself. While waiting for greater enlightenment, let us protect public order. In every country let us respect the laws, let us not disturb the worship they prescribe; let us not lead the citizens to disobedience. For we do not know with certainty whether it is a good thing for them to abandon their opinions in exchange for others, and we are very certain that it is an evil thing to disobey the laws.

My young friend, I have just recited to you with my own mouth my profession of faith such as God reads it in my heart. You are the first to whom I have told it. You are perhaps the only one to whom I shall ever tell it. So long as there remains some sound belief among men, one must not disturb peaceful souls or alarm the faith of simple people with difficulties which they cannot resolve and which upset them without enlightening them. But once everything is shaken, one ought to preserve the trunk at the expense of the branches. Consciences which are agitated, uncertain, almost extinguished, and in the condition in which I have seen yours, need to be reinforced and awakened; and in order to put them back on the foundation of eternal truths, it is necessary to complete the job of ripping out the shaky pillars to which they think they are still attached.

You are at the critical age when the mind opens to certitude, when the heart receives its form and its character, and when one's whole life, whether for good or for bad, is determined. Later the substance is hardened, and new impressions no longer leave a mark. Young man, receive the stamp of truth on your still flexible soul. If I were more sure of myself, I would have taken a dogmatic and decisive tone with you. But I am a man; I am ignorant and subject to error. What could I do? I have opened my heart to you without reserve. What I hold to be sure, I have told to you as being sure. I have told you my doubts as doubts, my opinions as opinions. I have told you my reasons for doubting and for believing. Now it is for you to judge. You have taken your time. This caution is wise and makes me think well of you. Begin by putting your conscience in a condition where it wishes to be enlightened. Be sincere with yourself. Make your own those of my sentiments which have persuaded you. Reject the rest. You are not yet depraved enough by vice to be in danger of choosing badly. I would suggest our conferring about it, but as soon as people engage in disputation, they get heated. Vanity and obstinacy get mixed up with it; good faith is no longer present. My friend, never engage in disputation, for one enlightens neither oneself nor others by it. As for me, it is only after many years of meditation that I have made my decision. I am sticking to it; my conscience is tranquil, my heart is contented. If I wanted to start over again with a new examination of my sentiments, I would not bring to it a purer love of the truth, and my mind, which has already become less active, would be less in a condition to know it. I shall stay as I am, lest the taste for contemplation gradually become an idle passion and make me lukewarm about the exercise of my duties, and lest I fall back into my former Pyrrhonism, without recovering the strength to get out of it. More than half of my life is past; I have left only the time I need for turning the rest of it to account and for effacing my errors by my virtues. If I am deceived, it is in spite of myself. He who reads in the depth of my heart well knows that I do not like my blindness. In my powerlessness to escape from it by my own lights, the only means that remains to me for getting out of it is a good life; and if God can bring forth children for Abraham from the very stones, every man has a right to hope for enlightenment when he makes himself worthy of it.

If my reflections lead you to think as I do, if my sentiments are also yours and we have the same profession of faith, here is the advice I give you. No longer expose your life to the temptations of poverty and despair; no longer spend it loitering ignominiously at the mercy of foreigners; and stop eating the vile bread of charity. Go back to your own country, return to the religion of your fathers, follow it in the sincerity of your heart, and never leave it again. It is very simple and very holy. I believe that of all the religions on earth it is the one which has the purest morality and which is most satisfactory to reason. As to the expenses of the trip, don't worry; they will be provided for. And do not fear the shame of a humiliating return. One ought to blush at making a mistake and not at correcting it. You are still at an age when everything can be pardoned, but when one no longer sins with impunity. If you wish to listen to your conscience, countless vain obstacles will disappear at its voice. You will sense that in the uncertainty in which we dwell, it is an inexcusable presumption to profess a religion other than that in which we were born, and a falseness not to practice sincerely the religion which we profess. For if we go astray, we deprive ourselves of a great excuse at the tribunal of the Sovereign Judge. Will He not pardon the error on which we were weaned sooner than the error we dared to choose ourselves?

My son, keep your soul in a condition where it always desires that there be a God, and you shall never doubt it. What is more, whatever decision you may make, bear in mind that the true duties of religion are independent of the institutions of men; that a just heart is the true temple of the divinity; that in every country and in every sect the sum of the law is to love God above everything and one's neighbor as one-self; that no religion is exempt from the duties of morality; that nothing is truly essential other than these duties; that inner worship is the first of these duties; and that without faith no true virtue exists.

Flee those who sow dispiriting doctrines in men's hearts under the pretext of explaining nature. Their apparent skepticism is a hundred times more assertive and more dogmatic than the decided tone of their adversaries. Under the haughty pretext that they alone are enlightened, true, and of good faith, they imperiously subject us to their peremptory decisions and claim to give us as the true principles of things the unintelligible systems they have built in their imaginations. Moreover, by overturning, destroying, and trampling on all that men respect, they deprive the afflicted of the last consolation of their misery, and the powerful and the rich of the only brake on their passions. They tear out from the depths of our hearts remorse for crime and hope of virtue, and yet boast that they are the benefactors of mankind. They say that the truth is never harmful to men. I believe it as much as they do, and in my opinion this is a great proof that what they teach is not the truth.*

* The two parties attack each other reciprocally with so many sophisms that to want to deal with them all would be an immense and rash undertaking. It is already a lot to take note of some of them as they arise. One of the most familiar sophisms of the philosophist party is to contrast a supposed people of good philosophers with a people of bad Christians, as if a people of true philosophers were easier to make than a people of true Christians! I do not know whether one is easier to find than the other among individuals. But I do know that as soon as it is a question of peoples, it is necessary to suppose one which will abuse philosophy without religion, just as our peoples abuse religion without philosophy. And this seems to me to be a very different question.

Bayle has proved very well that fanaticism is more pernicious than atheism, and this is incontestable.[9] But what he did not take care to say, and which is no less true, is that fanaticism, although sanguinary and cruel, is nevertheless a grand and strong passion which elevates the heart of man, makes him despise death, and gives him a prodigious energy that need only be better directed to produce the most sublime virtues. On the other hand, irreligion—and the reasoning and philosophic spirit in general—causes attachment to life, makes souls effeminate and degraded, concentrates all the passions in the baseness of private interest, in the abjectness of the human *I*, and thus quietly saps the true foundations of every society. For what private interests have in common is so slight that it will never outweigh what sets them in opposition.

If atheism does not cause the spilling of men's blood, it is less from love of peace than from indifference to the good. Whatever may be going on is of little importance for the allegedly wise man, provided that he can remain at rest in his study. His principles do not cause men to be killed, but they prevent them from being born by destroying the morals which cause them to multiply, by detaching them from their species, by reducing all their affections to a secret egoism as deadly to population as to virtue. Philosophic indifference resembles the tranquility of the state under depotism. It is the tranquility of death. It is more destructive than war itself.

Thus fanaticism, although more deadly in its immediate effects than what is today called the philosophic spirit, is much less so in its consequences. Moreover, it is easy to put fair maxims on display in books; but the question is whether these maxims really are well connected with the doctrine, whether they flow from it necessarily; and that is what has not appeared clear up to now. It still remains to be known whether philosophy, if it were at its ease and on the throne, would have a good command over vainglory, interest, ambition, and the petty passions of man, and whether it would practice that gentle humanity it lauds to us in its writings.

From the point of view of principles, there is nothing that philosophy can do well that religion does not do still better, and religion does many things that philosophy could not do.

Practice is something else. But further examination is required. It is true that no man follows his religion, when he has one, in every point. It is also true that most

BOOK IV

Good young man, be sincere and true without pride. Know how to be ignorant. You will deceive neither yourself nor others. If ever you have cultivated your talents and they put you in a position to speak to men, never speak to them except according to your conscience, without worrying whether they will applaud you. The abuse of learning produces incredulity. Every learned man disdains the common sentiment; each wants to have his own. Proud philosophy leads to freethinking as blind devoutness leads to fanaticism. Avoid these extremes. Always remain firm in the path of truth (or what in the simplicity of your heart appears to you to be the truth), without ever turning away from it out of vanity or weakness. Dare to acknowledge God among the philosophers; dare to preach humanity to the intolerant. You will perhaps be the only member of your party, but you will have within yourself a witness which will enable you to do without the witness of men. Whether they love you or hate you, whether they read or despise your writings, it does not matter: speak the truth; do the good. What does matter for man is to fulfill his duties on earth, and it is in forgetting oneself that one works for oneself. My child, private interest deceives us. It is only the hope of the just which never deceives.[63]

I have transcribed this writing not as a rule for the sentiments that one ought to follow in religious matters, but as an example of the way one can reason with one's pupil in order not to diverge from the method I have tried to establish. So long as one concedes nothing to the authority of men or to the prejudices of the country in which one was born, the light of reason alone cannot, in the education founded by nature, lead us any farther than natural religion. This is what I limit myself to with

---

men hardly have one and do not follow at all the one they have. Still, some men do have one and follow it at least in part; and it is indubitable that religious motives often prevent them from doing harm and produce virtues and laudable actions which would not have occurred without these motives.

If a monk denies having received something with which he was entrusted, what follows, other than the fact that a fool confided it to him? If Pascal had denied having received such a deposit, that would prove that Pascal was a hypocrite and nothing more. But a monk! . . . Are the people who traffic in religion those who are religious? All the crimes committed among the clergy, as elsewhere, do not prove that religion is useless, but that very few people are religious.

Our modern governments incontestably owe their more solid authority and less frequent revolutions to Christianity. It has made these governments less sanguinary themselves. This is proved by actually comparing them to ancient governments. A better understanding of religion, by dispelling fanaticism, has given more gentleness to Christian morals. This change is not the work of literature, for wherever the latter has flourished humanity has not been any more respected. This is attested by the cruelties of the Athenians, the Roman emperors, and the Chinese. How many works of mercy are the result of the Gospel! Among the Catholics, how many restitutions, how many reparations are caused by the confession! Among us, how many reconciliations and deeds of charity are fostered by the approach of Communion time. How much less greedy usurers were made by the Jubilee of the Hebrews, and how many miseries it prevented![61] The brotherhood promoted by this law united the whole nation, and not a beggar was to be seen among them. Nor are any seen among the Turks, who have innumerable pious institutions. They are hospitable from religious principle, even toward the enemies of their worship.

The Mohammedans say [according to Chardin] that after the examination which will follow the universal resurrection, all the bodies will pass over a bridge called Poul-Serrho which crosses over the eternal fire. This bridge, they say, can be called the third and last examination and the true final judgment,

my Emile. If he must have another religion, I no longer have the right to be his guide in that. It is up to him alone to choose it.

We work in collaboration with nature, and while it forms the physical man, we try to form the moral man. But we do not make the same progress. The body is already robust and strong while the soul is still languorous and weak, and no matter what human art does, temperament always precedes reason. Up to now we have given all our care to restraining the former and arousing the latter, in order that man may as much as possible always be one. In developing his nature, we have sidetracked its nascent sensibility; we have regulated it by cultivating reason. The intellectual objects moderated the impression of the objects of sense. In going back to the principle of things we have protected him from the empire of the senses. It was simple to rise from the study of nature to the quest for its Author.

When we have gotten there, what new holds we have given ourselves over our pupil. How many new means we have for speaking to his heart! It is only then that he finds his true interest in being good, in doing good far from the sight of men and without being forced by the laws, in being just between God and himself, in fulfilling his duty, even at the expense of his life, and in carrying virtue in his heart. He does this not only for the love of order, to which each of us always prefers love of self, but for the love of the Author of his being—a love which is confounded with that same love of self—and, finally, for the enjoyment of that durable happiness which the repose of a good conscience and the contemplation of this Supreme Being promise him in the other life after he has spent this one well. Abandon this, and I no longer see anything but injustice, hypocrisy, and lying among men. Private interest, which in case of conflict necessarily prevails over everything,

---

because it is there that the separation of the good from the wicked will be made . . . etc.

The Persians [continues Chardin] are very much infatuated by this bridge, and when someone suffers an insult for which he cannot in any way or at any time get satisfaction, his final consolation is to say, "Very well, by the living God, you will pay double for it on the final day. You shall not pass over Poul-Serrho without having given me satisfaction beforehand. I shall hold on to the hem of your jacket and throw myself at your legs." I have seen many eminent men, belonging to all sorts of professions, who were apprehensive that someone would thus shout "Haro" at them when they crossed this formidable bridge, and entreated those who complained of them to pardon them. That happened to me a hundred times myself. Men of quality who had badgered me into acting otherwise than I would have wanted, approached me after they thought the irritation had passed and said to me, "I beg you, *halal becon antchisra*," which means, "Make this affair lawful or just for me." Some have even given me gifts and rendered services to me in order that I pardon them and declare that I did so sincerely. The cause of this is nothing other than the belief that one will not cross the bridge of hell without having rendered the last penny to those one has oppressed. [vol. VII, p. 50] [62]

Should I believe that the idea of this bridge, which corrects so many iniquities, never prevents any? If one took this idea away from the Persians by persuading them that there is no Poul-Serrho or any place like it where the oppressed wreak vengeance on their tyrants after death, is it not clear that this would put the latter very much at their ease and would deliver them from the care of placating these unfortunates? It is false, therefore, that this doctrine would not be harmful. Therefore, this doctrine would not be the truth.

Philosopher, your moral laws are very fine, but I beg you to show me their sanction. Stop beating around the bush for a moment, and tell me plainly what you put in the place of Poul-Serrho.

teaches everyone to adorn vice with the mask of virtue. Let all other men do what is good for me at their expense; let everything be related to me alone; let all mankind, if need be, die in suffering and poverty to spare me a moment of pain or hunger. This is the inner language of every unbeliever who reasons. Yes, I shall maintain it all my life. Whoever speaks otherwise although he has said in his heart, "There is no God," is nothing but a liar or a fool.

Reader, I am well aware that no matter what I do, you and I will never see my Emile with the same features. You will always picture him as similar to your young people, always thoughtless, petulant, flighty, wandering from party to party, from entertainment to entertainment, never able to concentrate on anything. You will laugh when you see me make a contemplative, a philosopher, a veritable theologian out of an ardent, lively, intense, and impulsive young man at the most ebullient age of life. You will say, "This dreamer always pursues his chimera. In giving us a pupil of his making, he not only forms him, he creates him, he pulls him out of his brain; and though he believes he is always following nature, he diverges from it at every instant." I, comparing my pupil to yours, hardly find anything that they can have in common. Since they are reared so differently, it would almost be a miracle if Emile resembled yours in anything. Just as he spent his childhood in all the freedom they take as young men, he begins as a young man to take the discipline to which they were subjected as children. This discipline becomes a plague to them. They loathe it; they see in it only the long tyranny of their masters; they believe they leave childhood only in shaking off every kind of yoke; * they compensate themselves then for the long constraint in which they were kept, just as a prisoner freed from chains stretches, shakes, and flexes his limbs.

Emile, on the contrary, considers it an honor to make himself a man and to subject himself to the yoke of nascent reason. His body, already formed, no longer needs the same movements and by itself begins to quiet down, while his mind, half developed, seeks its turn to take flight. Thus, for the others the age of reason is only the age of license; for Emile it becomes the age of reasoning.

Do you want to know whether they or he is thereby closer to the order of nature? Consider the differences in those who are more or less distant from it. Observe young people in the country, and see if they are as petulant as are your young people. "During the childhood of savages," says Le Beau, "they are always active and involved in various games which stir the body; but almost as soon as they reach the age of adolescence, they become tranquil and dreamy, and they no longer engage in any games other than serious ones or games of chance." † Emile, who has been raised with all the freedom of young peasants and young savages, should change and quiet down as they do in growing up. The

---

* There is no one who sees childhood with so much contempt as those who are leaving it, just as there is no country where the distinction of ranks is preserved with more affectation than in those where inequality is not great and where everyone always fears being confounded with his inferior.

† Le Beau, *Aventures du Sieur Le Beau, avocat en Parlement.* Vol. II, p. 70.

whole difference is that instead of acting solely to play or to feed himself, he has learned to think in his labors and games. As he has reached this point by this road, he is all ready for the road on which I am now setting him. The subjects of reflection which I present to him inflame his curiosity because they are in themselves fair, because they are entirely new for him, and because he is in a condition to understand them. On the other hand, how could your young people, who are bored and exasperated by your insipid lessons, your long-winded moralizing, and your eternal catechisms, fail to refuse to apply their minds to what has been made a gloomy business for them—the heavy precepts with which they have constantly been burdened, and the meditations on the Author of their being, Who has been made the enemy of their pleasures? They have conceived only aversion, disgust, and distaste for all that; constraint has repelled them. What means is left to make them devoted to such things when they begin to decide for themselves? They have to have novelty to be pleased; they no longer can stand anything children are told. The same is the case with my pupil. When he becomes a man, I speak to him as to a man and tell him only new things. It is precisely because they bore the others that he ought to find them to his taste.

Consider how I gain time for him doubly by delaying the progress of nature to the advantage of reason. But have I actually delayed this progress? No, I have only prevented imagination from accelerating it. I have counterbalanced the premature lessons the young man receives elsewhere with lessons of another kind. While the torrent of our institutions carries him away, I attract him in the opposite direction by other institutions. This is not to remove him from his place but to keep him in it.

The true moment of nature comes at last. It must come. Since man must die, he must reproduce in order that the species may endure and the order of the world be preserved. When, by the signs of which I have spoken, you have a presentiment of the critical moment, instantly abandon your old tone with him forever. He is still your disciple, but he is no longer your pupil. He is your friend, he is a man. From now on treat him as such.

What! Must I abdicate my authority when it is most necessary to me? Must the adult be left to himself at the moment when he least knows how to conduct himself, and when he makes the greatest slips? Must I renounce my rights when it is most important for him that I make use of them? Your rights! Who is telling you to renounce them? It is only at present that they begin for him. Up to now you got nothing from him except by force or ruse. Authority and the law of duty were unknown to him. He had to be constrained or deceived to make him obey you. But see how many new chains you have put around his heart. Reason, friendship, gratitude, countless affections speak to him in a tone he cannot fail to recognize. Vice has not yet made him deaf to their voice. He is still sensitive only to the passions of nature. The first of all, which is self-love, puts him in your hands. Habit also puts him in your hands. If the transport of a moment tears him away from you, regret immediately brings him back. The sentiment attaching him to you is the only permanent one; all the others pass and blot one another out. Do not let him be corrupted; he will always be docile. He will not begin to be rebellious until he is already depraved.

I readily admit that if you were to clash head on with his nascent desires and foolishly were to treat as crimes the new needs he is feeling, you would not be listened to for long. But as soon as you abandon my method, I no longer guarantee you anything. Always remember that you are the minister of nature, and you will never be its enemy.

But what course should be taken? Here the only choice is between encouraging his inclinations and fighting them, between being his tyrant and being his accomplice; and both alternatives have such dangerous consequences that hesitation about the decision is only too justified.

The first means that presents itself for resolving this difficulty is to marry him off very quickly. This is incontestably the surest and the most natural expedient. I doubt, however, that it is the best or the most useful. I shall tell my reasons later. In the meantime I agree that young people must be married when they reach the age at which they are nubile. But that age comes before its proper time for them; it is we who have induced its early arrival. It ought to be put off until maturity.

If one had only to listen to the inclinations and follow where they lead, the job would soon be done. But there are so many contradictions between the rights of nature and our social laws that one must constantly twist and turn in order to reconcile them. One must use a great deal of art to prevent social man from being totally artificial.

For the reasons previously presented I believe that by the means I have related and other similar ones the ignorance of the desires and the purity of the senses can be extended at least until the age of twenty. This is so true that among the Germans a young man who lost his virginity before that age suffered a permanent loss of reputation. With good reason, writers have attributed the vigorous constitutions of the Germans and the multitude of their children to the continence practiced by these peoples during their youth.

One can even greatly prolong this period of continence; only a few generations ago nothing was more common in France itself. Among other known examples, Montaigne's father, a man who was scrupulous and true as well as strong and well formed, swore that he was married a virgin at the age of thirty-three after long service in the wars of Italy; and one can see in the son's writings what vigor and what gaiety the father preserved when he was over sixty.[64] Certainly the contrary opinion is a result more of our morals and our prejudices than of knowledge of the species in general.

Therefore I can leave aside the example of our young. They prove nothing about those who were not raised like them. Given that nature has in this respect no fixed point that cannot be moved ahead or back, I believe that, without departing from nature's law, I can assume that through my efforts Emile has remained in his first innocence up to now. I see this happy period about to end. Surrounded by ever growing perils, he is going to get away from me no matter what I do. At the first occasion—and this occasion will not be slow in arising—he is going to follow the blind instinct of the senses. The odds are a thousand to one that he is going to be ruined. I have reflected on men's morals too much not to see the invincible influence of this first moment on the rest of his life. If I dissimulate and pretend to see nothing, he takes advantage of my weakness. Believing he deceives me, he despises me, and I am the accomplice of his ruin. If I try to straighten him out, it is too late; he does not listen to me any more. I become inconvenient, odious, and unbearable to him. He will not delay in getting rid of me. Therefore I have only one reasonable course to take—to make him accountable to himself for his actions, to protect him at least from the surprises of error, and to show him openly the perils by which he is surrounded. Up to now I stopped him by his ignorance; now he has to be stopped by his enlightenment.

This new instruction is important, and it is advisable to go back and pick up the thread from a more general point of view. This is the moment to present my accounts to him, so to speak; to show him how his time and mine have been employed; to disclose to him what he is and what I am, what I have done, what he has done, what we owe each other, all his moral relations, all the commitments he has contracted, all those that have been contracted with him, what point he has reached in the progress of his faculties, how much of the road he still has to cover, the difficulties he will find there, the means of getting over these difficulties, what I can still help him with, what he alone must now help himself with, and finally, the critical point at which he stands, the new perils which surround him, and all the solid reasons which ought to oblige him to keep an attentive watch over himself before listening to his nascent desires.

Remember that to guide an adult it is necessary to take another tack than the one taken to guide a child. Do not hesitate to instruct him in these dangerous mysteries which you have so long hidden from him with so much care. Since he must finally know about them, it is important that he learn them neither from another nor from himself but from you alone. Since he is now forced to fight, he must know his enemy, so that he will not be taken by surprise.

Young people who are found to be knowledgeable about these matters and who are unaware how they came to this knowledge have never come to it with impunity. This indiscreet instruction, which can have no decent purpose, at the very least soils the imagination of those who receive it and disposes them to the vices of those who give it. This is not all. Domestics insinuate themselves in this way into a child's mind, gain his confidence, and make him regard his governor as a gloomy, boring fellow; one of the favorite subjects of their secret colloquies with the child is slandering his governor. When the child has reached this point, the master can withdraw; he can do no more good.

But why does the child choose special confidants? Always due to the tyranny of those who govern him. Why would he keep secrets from them, if he were not forced to do so? Why would he complain of them, if he had no subject of complaint? They are naturally his first confidants. From the eagerness with which he comes to tell them what he thinks, it is clear that he believes he has only half thought it until he has told them. You can be sure that if the child fears neither a sermon nor a reprimand on your part, he will always tell you everything; you can also be sure that no one will dare to confide anything to him which he ought to keep secret from you when it is quite certain that there is nothing he will keep secret from you.

What gives me most confidence in my method is that, in following its effects as exactly as I can, I see no situation in the life of my pupil which does not leave me some agreeable image of him. At the very moment when he is carried away by the furies of temperament and, revolting against the hand which restrains him, he struggles and begins to escape me, I still find in his agitation, in his anger, his first simplicity. His heart, as pure as his body, is no more familiar with disguise than with vice. Neither reproaches nor contempt have made him a coward; never has vile fear taught him to disguise himself. He has all the indiscretion of innocence. He is uncalculatingly naïve. He does not yet know what use there is in deceit. Not a single movement takes place in his soul which his mouth or his eyes do not reveal, and often the sentiments he experiences are known to me sooner than to him.

As long as he continues freely to open his soul to me and to tell me with pleasure what he feels, I have nothing to fear. But if he becomes more timid and reserved, if I perceive in his conversation the first embarrassment of shame, instinct is already developing. There is no longer a moment to lose, and if I do not hurry to instruct him, he will soon be instructed in spite of me.

More than one reader, even among those who adopt my ideas, will think that what is needed here is only a conversation held at random, and the job will be done. Oh, that is not the way the human heart is governed! What one says means nothing if one has not prepared the moment for saying it. Before sowing, the earth must be plowed; the seed of virtue sprouts with difficulty, long preparation is required to make it take root. One of the things that makes preaching most useless is that it is done indiscriminately to everyone without distinction or selectivity. How can one think that the same sermon is suitable to so many auditors of such diverse dispositions, so different in mind, humor, age, sex, station, and opinion? There are perhaps not even two auditors for whom what one says to all can be suitable; and all our affections are so inconstant that there are perhaps not even two moments in the life of each man when the same speech would make the same impression on him. Judge whether the time for listening to grave lessons of wisdom is when the inflamed senses derange the understanding and tyrannize the will. Therefore, never talk reason to young people, even when they are at the age of reason, without first putting them in a condition to understand it. Most wasted speeches are wasted due to the fault of masters rather than of disciples. The pedant and the teacher say pretty much the same things, but the former says them on every occasion, while the latter says them only when he is sure of their effect.

As a somnambulist, wandering during his slumber, sleepwalks on the brink of a precipice into which he would fall if he were suddenly awakened, so my Emile, in the slumber of ignorance, escapes perils that he does not perceive. If I awaken him with a start, he is lost. Let us first try to get him away from the precipice; and then we shall awaken him in order to show it to him from farther off.

Reading, solitude, idleness, the soft and sedentary life, and the society of women and young people are dangerous trails to blaze at his age, and they keep him constantly close to the peril. It is by means of other objects of sense that I put his senses off the track; it is by setting another course for his energies that I turn them away from the one they were beginning to take. It is by exercising his body with hard labor that I restrain the activity of imagination that is carrying him away. When the arms work hard, the imagination rests. When the body is tired out, the heart does not become inflamed. The promptest and easiest precaution is to tear him away from the locality of danger. First I take him out of the cities, far from objects capable of tempting him. But this is not enough. In what desert, in what wild abode will he escape the images pursuing him? Removing dangerous objects is nothing, if I do not also remove the memory of them, if I do not find the art of detaching him from everything, if I do not distract him from himself. Otherwise I might as well have left him where he was.

Emile knows a trade, but this trade is not our expedient here. He likes and understands agriculture, but agriculture does not suffice for us. The occupations he knows become a routine; when he devotes himself to them, it is as though he were doing nothing. He thinks about entirely different things; the head and the arms act separately. He must have a new occupation which interests him by its novelty, which keeps him on his toes, which pleases him, which requires application, which makes him exert himself, an occupation for which he has a passion and to which he gives himself completely. Now the only one which appears to me to unite all these qualities is hunting. If hunting is ever an innocent pleasure, if it is ever suitable to man, it is at present that one must have recourse to it. Emile has everything needed to succeed at it. He is robust, adroit, patient, indefatigable. He will infallibly get a taste for this exercise. He will give it all the ardor of his age. He will lose in it—at least for a time—the dangerous inclinations born of softness. The hunt hardens the heart as well as the body. It accustoms one to blood, to cruelty. Diana has been presented as the enemy of love, and the allegory is quite accurate. The languors of love are born only in sweet repose; violent exercise stifles the tender sentiments. In the woods, in rural places, the lover and the hunter are so differently affected that from the same objects they take away entirely different images. The cool shady spots, the groves, the sweet refuges of the former are for the latter only the grazing places of deer, the thickets in which game withdraw, their hiding places when pursued. Where the lover hears only nightingales and warbling, the hunter fancies horns and the yapping of dogs; the lover imagines only dryads and nymphs, the hunter only whippers-in, packs of hounds and horses. Take a walk in the country with these two kinds of men; from the difference in their language you will soon recognize that the earth does not have a similar aspect for them, and the turn of their ideas is as different as the choice of their pleasures.

I understand how these tastes are joined, and how one finally finds time for everything. But the passions of youth are not to be divided in this way. Give it a single occupation which it loves, and all the rest will soon be forgotten. The variety of desires comes from the variety of kinds of knowledge, and the first pleasures a person knows are long the only ones he seeks. I do not want Emile's whole youth to be spent in killing animals, and I do not even pretend to justify in every respect this ferocious passion. It is enough for me that it serves to suspend a more dangerous passion, so that he will listen coolly to me when I speak of it and I will have the time to depict it without exciting it.

There are periods in human life which are made never to be forgotten. The period of the instruction about which I am speaking is such a time for Emile. It ought to influence the rest of his days. Let us try therefore to engrave it in his memory in such a way that it will never be effaced. One of the errors of our age is to use reason in too unadorned a form, as if men were all mind. In neglecting the language of signs that speak to the imagination, the most energetic of languages has been lost. The impression of the word is always weak, and one speaks to the heart far better through the eyes than through the ears. In wanting to turn everything over to reasoning, we have reduced our precepts to words; we have made no use of actions. Reason alone is not active. It sometimes restrains, it arouses rarely, and it has never done anything great. Always to reason is the mania of small minds. Strong souls have quite another language. It is with this language that one persuades and makes others act.

I observe that in the modern age men no longer have a hold on one another except by force or by self-interest; the ancients, by contrast, acted much more by persuasion and by the affections of the soul because they did not neglect the language of signs. All their covenants took place with solemnity in order to make them more inviolable. Before force was established, the gods were the magistrates of mankind. It was in their presence that individuals made their treaties and alliances and uttered their promises. The face of the earth was the book in which their archives were preserved. Stones, trees, heaps of rocks consecrated by these acts and thus made respectable to barbaric men, were the pages of this book, which was constantly open to all eyes. The well of the oath, the well of the living and seeing, the old oak of Mamre, the mound of the witness,[65] these were the crude but august monuments of the sanctity of contracts. None would have dared to attack these monuments with a sacrilegious hand, and the faith of men was more assured by the guarantee of these mute witnesses than it is today by all the vain rigor of the laws.

In regard to government, the august display of royal power impressed the subjects. Marks of dignity—a throne, a scepter, a purple robe, a crown, a diadem—were sacred things for them. These respected signs made the man who was thus adorned venerable to them. Without soldiers, without threats, he was obeyed as soon as he spoke. Now that we make an affectation of abolishing these signs,* what happens as a result of this contempt? Royal majesty is effaced from all hearts, kings no longer make themselves obeyed except by dint of troops; the respect of subjects comes only from the fear of punishment. Kings no longer have the burden of wearing their diadem, and the nobility no longer have the insignia of their rank; but a hundred thousand arms must always be ready in order to get their orders executed. Although this perhaps seems finer to them, it is easy to see that in the long run this exchange will not turn out to have been profitable for them.

What the ancients accomplished with eloquence was prodigious. But that eloquence did not consist solely in fine, well-ordered speeches, and never did it have more effect than when the orator spoke least. What was said most vividly was expressed not by words but by signs. One did not say it, one showed it. The object that is exhibited to the eyes shakes the imagination, arouses curiosity, keeps the mind attentive to what is going to be said. Often this object alone has said everything. Thrasybulus and Tarquin cutting off the tops of the poppies,[67] Alexander placing his seal on his favorite's mouth,[68] Diogenes walking before Zeno [69]—did they not speak better than if they had made long speeches? What series of words would have rendered the same ideas so well? Darius, after he has entered Scythia with his army, receives from the king of the Scythians a bird, a frog, a mouse, and five arrows.[70] The ambassador leaves his present and departs without saying anything. In our days this man would have been regarded as crazy. This terrifying harangue made its point, and Darius hurried to get back to his country in whatever way he could. Substitute a letter for these signs. The more threatening it is, the less it will frighten. It will only be bluster at which Darius would only have laughed.

How great was the attention that the Romans paid to the language of signs! Different clothing according to ages and according to stations —togas, sagums, praetexts, bullas, laticlaves; [71] thrones, lictors, fasces, axes; crowns of gold or of herbs or of leaves; ovations, triumphs. Everything with them was display, show, ceremony, and everything made an impression on the hearts of the citizens. It was important to the state that the people assemble in this place rather than in that other one, that they saw or did not see the Capitol, that they were or were not turned in the direction of the Senate, that they deliberated on this or that day. Accused persons changed costume, and so did candidates; warriors did not vaunt their exploits, they showed their wounds. On the death of Caesar I imagine one of our orators wishing to move the people; he exhausts all the commonplaces of his art to present a pathetic description of Caesar's wounds, his blood, his corpse.

---

* The Roman clergy has very cleverly preserved them, and, following its example, so have some republics, among them that of Venice. Thus the Venetian government, in spite of the collapse of the state, still enjoys all the affection and adoration of the people thanks to the pomp of its antique majesty. Apart from the Pope adorned with his tiara, there can be neither king nor potentate nor man in the world so respected as the Doge of Venice—without power, without authority, but rendered sacred by his pomp and dressed up in a woman's hairdo under his ducal bonnet. The ceremony of the bucentaur, which makes so many fools laugh, would cause the population of Venice to shed all its blood for the maintenance of its tyrannical government.[66]

Antony, although eloquent, does not say all that. He has the body brought in.[72] What rhetoric!

But this digression, like many others, gradually carries me far from my subject, and my wanderings are too frequent to admit of being both long and tolerable. I therefore return to my subject.

Never reason in a dry manner with youth. Clothe reason in a body if you want to make youth able to grasp it. Make the language of the mind pass through the heart, so that it may make itself understood. I repeat, cold arguments can determine our opinions, but not our actions. They make us believe and not act. They demonstrate what must be thought, not what must be done. If that is true for all men, it is a fortiori true for young people, who are still enveloped in their senses and think only insofar as they imagine.

Therefore, even after the preparations of which I have spoken, I shall be very careful not to go all of a sudden to Emile's room and pompously make a long speech to him about the subject in which I want to instruct him. I shall begin by moving his imagination. I shall choose the time, the place, and the objects most favorable to the impression I want to make. I shall, so to speak, call all of nature as a witness to our conversations. I shall bring the Eternal Being, who is the Author of nature, to testify to the truth of my speech; I shall take Him as judge between Emile and me. I shall mark the place where we are—the rocks, the woods, and the mountains surrounding us shall be monuments of his promises and mine. I shall put in my eyes, my accent, and my gestures the enthusiasm and the ardor that I want to inspire in him. Then I shall speak to him, and he will listen to me. I shall be tender, and he will be moved. By concentrating upon the sanctity of my duties, I shall make his duties more respectable to him. I shall heighten the force of my reasoning with images and figurative language. My speeches will not be long and diffuse and filled with cold maxims but will be abundant with overflowing sentiments. My reasoning will be grave and sententious, but my heart will never have said enough. Then, in revealing to him all I have done for him, I shall reveal that I have done it for myself, and he will see in my tender affection the reason for all my care. What surprise, what agitation I am going to cause in him by suddenly changing language! Instead of narrowing his soul by always speaking of his interest, I shall now speak of mine alone, and I shall thereby touch him more. I shall inflame his young heart with all the sentiments of friendship, generosity, and gratitude which I have already aroused and which are so sweet to cultivate. I shall press him to my breast and shed tears of tenderness on him. I shall say to him, "You are my property, my child, my work. It is from your happiness that I expect my own. If you frustrate my hopes, you are robbing me of twenty years of my life, and you are causing the unhappiness of my old age." It is in this way that you get a young man to listen to you and that you engrave the memory of what you say to him in the depths of his heart.

Up to now I have tried to give examples of the way a governor ought to instruct his disciple in difficult situations. I have tried to do the same in this situation. But after many attempts I give up, convinced that the

French language is too precious to express in a book the naïveté of the first lessons on certain subjects.

The French language is said to be the chastest of languages. For my part, I believe it to be the most obscene. For it seems to me that the chasteness of a language consists not in the careful avoidance of indecent meanings but in not having them. In fact, to avoid them, one must think of them, and there is no language in which it is more difficult to speak purely, in every sense, than in French. The reader, always more clever at finding obscene meanings than the author is at keeping them out, is scandalized and shocked by everything. How could what passes through impure ears not be stained by them? A people with good morals, on the other hand, has appropriate terms for all things, and these terms are always decent because they are always used decently. It is impossible to imagine a language more modest than that of the Bible, precisely because there everything is said with naïveté. To render the same things immodest, it suffices to translate them into French. What I am going to say to my Emile will contain nothing that is not decent and chaste to his ear, but to find it such in reading it, one must have a heart as pure as his.

I even think that reflections on the true purity of speech and on the false delicacy of vice could have a useful place in the discussions about morality to which this subject leads us; for in learning the language of decency, Emile must also learn that of seemliness,[73] and it is quite necessary that he learn why these two languages are so different. However that may be, I maintain that if one waits, instead of hammering vain precepts into the ears of the young before the proper time—precepts which they then mock at the age when they would be opportune; if one prepares the moment for making oneself understood; if one then expounds the laws of nature in all their truth; if one shows him the sanction of these same laws in the physical and moral ills that their infraction brings down upon the guilty; if in speaking of this inconceivable mystery of generation, one joins to the idea of the allure given to this act by the Author of nature the idea of the exclusive attachment which makes it delicious, and the idea of the duties of fidelity and of modesty which surround it and redouble its charm in fulfilling its object; if, in depicting marriage to him not only as the sweetest of associations but as the most inviolable and holiest of all contracts, one tells him forcefully all the reasons which make so sacred a bond respectable to all men, and which bring hatred and maledictions to whoever dares to stain its purity; if one presents him with a striking and true picture of the horrors of debauchery, of its foolish degradation, of the gradual decline by which a first disorder leads to them all and finally drags to destruction whoever succumbs to it; if, I say, one shows him clearly how the taste for chastity is connected with health, strength, courage, the virtues, love itself, and all the true goods of man, I maintain that one will then render this chastity desirable and dear to him and that his mind will be amenable to the means he will be given for preserving it; for, so long as chastity is preserved, it is respected; it is despised only after having been lost.

It is not true that the inclination to evil is untamable, and that one is not able to conquer it before having gotten the habit of succumbing to it. Aurelius Victor says that many men in the transports of love voluntarily bought a night with Cleopatra with their lives; and this sacrifice is not impossible for the drunkenness of passion.[74] But let us suppose that the most desperate man—the one least in command of his senses—sees the apparatus of torture and is sure of perishing on it in torments a quarter of an hour later. Not only would this man instantaneously become superior to temptations; it would even cost him little to resist them. The frightful image by which they would be accompanied would soon distract him from them; and, always rebuffed, these temptations would tire of returning. It is only our lukewarm will which causes all of our weakness, and we are always strong enough to do what we strongly wish. *Volenti nihil difficile*.[75] O if we detested vice as much as we love life, we would abstain from a pleasurable crime as easily as from a mortal poison in a delicious dish!

How do we fail to see that if all the lessons given to a young man on this point are without success, it is because they are without reasons suitable to his age, and because it is important at every age to clothe reason in forms which will make it loved. Speak to him gravely when necessary, but let what you say always have an attraction that forces him to listen to you. Do not combat his desires with dryness. Do not stifle his imagination; guide it lest it engender monsters. Speak to him of love, of women, of pleasures. Make him find a charm in your conversations which delights his young heart. Spare nothing to become his confidant. It is only by this title that you will truly be his master. Then no longer fear that your discussions will bore him; he will make you talk more than you want to.

If I have been able, in accordance with these maxims, to take all the necessary precautions and to make speeches to my Emile suitable for the juncture of life that he has reached, I do not doubt for an instant that he will come by himself to the point where I want to lead him, that he will eagerly put himself in my safekeeping, that he will be struck by the dangers with which he sees himself surrounded, and will say to me with all the warmth of his age, "O my friend, my protector, my master! Take back the authority you want to give up at the very moment that it is most important for me that you retain it. You had this authority up to this time only due to my weakness; now you shall have it due to my will, and it shall be all the more sacred to me. Defend me from all the enemies who besiege me, and especially from those whom I carry within myself and who betray me. Watch over your work in order that it remain worthy of you. I want to obey your laws; I want to do so always. This is my steadfast will. If ever I disobey you, it will be in spite of myself. Make me free by protecting me against those of my passions which do violence to me. Prevent me from being their slave; force me to be my own master and to obey not my senses but my reason."

When you have brought your pupil to this point (and if he does not get there, it will be your fault), be careful not to take him too quickly at his word lest, if ever your dominion appear too hard for him, he will believe he has a right to escape it by accusing you of having taken him by surprise. It is at this moment that reserve and gravity have their place, and this tone will impress him so much the more because it will be the first time he will have seen you take it.

Therefore, you will say to him, "Young man, you make difficult commitments lightly. You would have to know what they mean in order to have the right to undertake them. You do not know the fury with which the senses, by the lure of pleasure, drag young men like you into the abyss of the vices. I know that you do not have an abject soul. You will never break faith, but how often you will repent having given it! How often you will curse the one who loves you when he finds himself forced to rend your heart in order to save you from the evils which threaten you! Just as Ulysses, moved by the Sirens' song and seduced by the lure of the pleasures, cried out to his crew to unchain him,[76] so you will want to break the bonds which hinder you. You will importune me with your complaints; you will reproach me for being a tyrant when I am most tenderly concerned with you. In thinking only of making you happy, I shall bring your hate down upon me. O my Emile, I can never bear the pain of being odious to you. Even your happiness is too dear at this price. Good young man, do you not see that in obliging yourself to obey me, you oblige me to guide you, to forget myself in order to devote myself to you, to listen neither to your complaints nor to your grumbling, to combat incessantly your desires and mine? You are imposing a harsher yoke on me than on yourself. Before burdening both of us with it, let us consult our strength. Take your time and give me mine for thinking about it; remember that he who is slowest to make a promise is always most faithful at keeping it."

You also should remember, masters, that the harder you make it to get your assent to the commitment, the easier you make its fulfillment. It is important that the young man be aware that he is promising much, and that you are promising yet more. When the moment has come, and he has, so to speak, signed the contract, then change your language. Make your dominion as gentle as you had indicated it would be severe. You will say to him, "My young friend, you lack experience, but I have fixed things so that you would not lack reason. You are in a position to see the motives of my conduct in all things. To do so, you have only to wait until you are calm. Always begin by obeying, and then ask me for an account of my orders. I shall be ready to give you a reason for them as soon as you are in a position to understand me, and I shall never be afraid of taking you as the judge between you and me. You promise to be docile, and I promise to make use of this docility only to make you the happiest of men. I give as a guarantee of my promise the fate that you have enjoyed up to now. Find anyone else of your age who has passed a life as sweet as yours, and I shall no longer promise you anything."

After establishing my authority, my first care will be to avoid the necessity of using it. I shall spare nothing to establish myself more and more in his confidence, to make myself more and more the confidant of his heart and the arbiter of his pleasures. Far from combating the inclinations of his age, I shall consult them in order to be their master. I shall join in his plans in order to direct them; I shall not seek a distant happiness for him at the expense of the present. I want him to be happy not once but always, if it is possible.

Those who want to guide the young soberly, in order to preserve them from the traps of the senses, make love disgusting to them and would gladly make it a crime for them to think of it at their age, as though love were made for the old. All these deceitful lessons, to which the heart gives the lie, are not persuasive. The young man, guided by a surer instinct, secretly laughs at the gloomy maxims to which he feigns acquiescence, and all he waits for is the occasion to discard them. All this is contrary to nature. By following an opposite route, I shall more surely arrive at the same goal. I shall not be afraid to indulge him in the sweet sentiment for which he has such a thirst. I shall depict it to him as the supreme happiness of life, because in fact it is. In depicting it to him, I want him to yield to it. In making him sense how much charm the union of hearts adds to the attraction of the senses, I shall disgust him with libertinism, and I shall make him moderate by making him fall in love.

How limited one must be to see only an obstacle to the lessons of reason in the nascent desires of a young man! I see in them the true means of making him amenable to these very lessons. One has a hold on the passions only by means of the passions. It is by their empire that their tyranny must be combated; and it is always from nature itself that the proper instruments to regulate nature must be drawn.

Emile is not made to remain always solitary. As a member of society he ought to fulfill its duties. Since he is made to live with men, he ought to know them. He knows man in general; it remains for him to know individuals. He knows what is done in society; it remains for him to see how one lives in it. It is time to show him the exterior of this great stage, all of whose hidden mechanisms he already knows. He will bring to it no longer the stupid admiration of a giddy young man, but the discernment of a sound and exact mind. His passions will doubtless be able to lead him astray. When do they not lead astray those who yield to them? But at least he will not be deceived by the passions of others. If he sees them, it will be with the eyes of the wise man, and he will not be carried away by the example of others or seduced by their prejudices.

Just as there is a proper age for the study of the sciences, there is a proper age for getting a good grasp of social practices. Whoever learns these practices too young follows them throughout his whole life without selectivity, without reflection, and—despite his competence— without ever having clear knowledge of what he does. But he who learns these practices and sees the reasons for them follows them with more discernment and, consequently, with more exactness and grace. Give me a child of twelve who knows nothing at all; I should return him at fifteen to you as knowledgeable as the child you have instructed from the earliest age—but with the difference that your child's knowledge will be only in his memory, while mine's will be in his judgment. Similarly, introduce a young man of twenty into society; if he is well guided, in a year he will be more amiable and more judiciously polite than a young man who has been reared in society from childhood; for the former, capable of sensing the reasons for all the forms of conduct related to a given age, station, and sex—which constitute social custom —can reduce them to principles and extend them to unforeseen cases; whereas the latter, having nothing but his routine as a guiding rule, is in trouble as soon as he departs from it.

Young French ladies are all raised in convents until they are married off. Does anyone perceive that they have any difficulty in adopting these manners which are so new to them? And will anyone accuse the women of Paris of having a gauche and awkward bearing or of being ignorant of the ways of society because they have not been sent into it from childhood? This prejudice comes from society people themselves, who know nothing more important than this little science and hence falsely imagine that one cannot begin learning it too soon.

It is true that one ought not to wait too long either. Whoever has spent his whole youth far from polite society brings to it for the rest of his life an awkward and constrained bearing, conversation that is always off key, and clumsy and maladroit manners which the habit of living in society can no longer undo and which are only made doubly ridiculous by an effort to improve them. Each sort of instruction has its proper time, which must be known, and its dangers, which must be avoided. It is above all in learning the ways of society that the dangers multiply, but I do not expose my pupil to them without precautions to protect him.

When my method deals satisfactorily with all aspects of a single problem and, in avoiding one difficulty, prevents another, then I judge that my method is good and that I am on the right path. This is what I believe I see in the expedient it suggests to me here. If I wish to be austere and dry with my pupil, I shall lose his confidence, and soon he will hide himself from me. If I wish to be agreeable and pliant or to close my eyes, what is the use of his being under my protection? I only authorize his disorder and relieve his conscience at the expense of mine. If I introduce him to society with the sole aim of instructing him, he will instruct himself more than I want. If I keep him away from society to the end, what will he have learned from me? Everything perhaps, except the most necessary art for a man and a citizen, which is knowing how to live with his fellows. If I attribute to his efforts a utility which is too far off, it will be as nothing for him. He cares only about the present. If I am satisfied with providing entertainment for him, what good am I doing him? He becomes enervated and gets no instruction.

None of that for Emile. My expedient by itself provides for everything. "Your heart," I say to the young man, "needs a companion. Let us go seek her who suits you. We shall not easily find her perhaps. True merit is always rare. But let us neither be in a hurry nor become disheartened. Doubtless there is such a woman and in the end we shall find her, or at least the one who is most like her." With a project that is so appealing to him, I introduce him into society. What need have I to say more? Do you not see that I have done everything?

Imagine whether I shall know how to get his ear when I depict the beloved whom I destine for him. Imagine whether I shall know how to make agreeable and dear to him the qualities he ought to love, whether I shall know how to make all his sentiments properly disposed with respect to what he ought to seek or to flee? I would have to be the clumsiest of men not to be able to make him passionate in advance of his knowing about whom. It is unimportant whether the object I depict for him is imaginary; it suffices that it make him disgusted with those that could tempt him; it suffices that he everywhere find comparisons which make him prefer his chimera to the real objects that strike his eye. And what is true love itself if it is not chimera, lie, and illusion? We love the image we make for ourselves far more than we love the object to which we apply it. If we saw what we love exactly as it is, there would be no more love on earth. When we stop loving, the person we loved remains the same as before, but we no longer see her in the same way. The magic veil drops, and love disappears. But, by providing the imaginary object, I am the master of comparisons, and I easily prevent my young man from having illusions about real objects.

For all that, I do not want to deceive a young man by depicting for him a model of perfection which cannot exist. But I shall choose such defects in his beloved as to suit him, as to please him, and to serve to correct his own. Nor do I want to lie to him by falsely affirming that the object depicted for him exists. But if he takes pleasure in the image, he will soon hope that it has an original. From the hope to the supposition, the path is easy; it is a matter of some skillful descriptions which clothe this imaginary object with features he can grasp with his senses and give it a greater air of truth. I would go so far as to give her a name. I would say, laughing, "Let us call your future beloved Sophie. The name Sophie augurs well. If the girl whom you choose does not bear it, she will at least be worthy of bearing it. We can do her the honor in advance." If, after giving all these details, you neither affirm nor deny her existence but slip out of it by evasions, his suspicions will turn into certainty. He will believe that you are keeping a secret about the spouse who is intended for him and that he will see her when the time has come. Once he is at that point, and if you have chosen well the features he should be showed, all the rest is easy. He can be exposed to society almost without risk. Defend him only against his senses; his heart is safe.

But whether or not he believes the model I have succeeded in making lovable to him is a real person, this model, if well made, will nonetheless attach him to everything resembling it and will estrange him from everything not resembling it, just as if his passion had a real object. What an advantage this is for preserving his heart from the dangers to which his person must be exposed; for repressing his senses by his imagination; and especially for tearing him away from those ladies who give an education that is purchased so dearly and who teach a young man good manners only by taking all decency from him! Sophie is so modest! How will he view their advances? Sophie has so much simplicity! How will he like their airs? Too great a distance separates his ideas from his observations for the latter ever to be dangerous to him.

All those who speak of the governance of children adhere to the same prejudices and the same maxims, because they observe badly and reflect still worse. It is due to neither temperament nor the senses that the wildness of youth begins; it is due to opinion. If boys raised in colleges and girls raised in convents were at issue here, I would make it plain that this is true even with respect to them; for the first lessons that both get—the only ones which bear fruit—are those of vice; and it is not nature which corrupts them, it is example. But let us abandon the students living in colleges and convents to their bad morals, which will always be irremediable. I am speaking here only of domestic education. Take a young man soberly raised in his father's home in the country, and examine him at the moment he arrives in Paris or enters society. You will find that he is right-thinking about decent things and even that his will is as healthy as his reason. You will find in him contempt for vice and horror of debauchery. At the very mention of a prostitute you will see scandalized innocence in his eyes. I maintain that there is not one such young man who can resolve to enter by himself the gloomy abodes of these unfortunate women, even if he were to know their use and to feel the need of them.

Consider the same young man again six months later. You will no longer recognize him. The easy talk, the fashionable maxims, the jaunty bearing would cause him to be taken for a different man, if his jokes about his former simplicity, and his shame when it is recalled to him, did not show that he is the same man and that this fact makes him blush. O how much he has been educated in so short a time! Whence comes so great and so sudden a change? From the progress of temperament? Would his temperament not have made the same progress in his paternal home? And there, surely, he would have acquired neither this style nor these maxims. From the first pleasures of the senses? On the contrary. When one begins to yield to these pleasures, one is fearful and uneasy; one flees broad daylight and gossip. The first delights are always mysterious. Modesty seasons them and hides them. His first mistress makes a man not brazen but timid. Totally absorbed in a condition so new for him, the young man withdraws into himself to enjoy it and constantly dreads losing it. If he is loud, he is neither voluptuous nor tender. So long as he boasts, he has not enjoyed.

New ways of thinking have by themselves produced these differences. His heart is still the same, but his opinions have changed. His sentiments, slower to alter, will eventually be spoiled by these opinions, and it is only then that he will be truly corrupted. He has hardly entered society when he receives there a second education completely opposed to his first, an education from which he learns to despise what he esteemed and to esteem what he despised. He is made to regard the lessons of his parents and his masters as a pedantic jargon and the duties they have preached to him as a puerile morality that ought to be disdained when one has grown up. He believes himself honor-bound to change his conduct. He becomes a seducer without desires and a fop out of fear of ridicule. He mocks good morals before having gotten the taste for bad ones and prides himself on debauchery without knowing how to be debauched. I shall never forget the admission of a young officer in the Swiss Guards who was greatly bored by the brazen pleasures of his comrades but did not dare to abstain for fear of being ridiculed. "I am getting practice at that," he said, "as I am at taking tobacco in spite of my repugnance. The taste will come from habit. One must not remain a child forever."

Thus, a young man entering society must be preserved less from sensuality than from vanity. He yields more to the inclinations of others than to his own, and *amour-propre* produces more libertines than love does.

Therefore I ask whether there is a young man on the entire earth who is better armed than Emile against everything that can attack his morals, his sentiments, or his principles? Whether there is one better prepared to resist the torrent? For against what seduction is he not on guard? If his desires lead him to women, he does not find what he is looking for, and his preoccupied heart holds him back. If his senses agitate and impel him, where will he find the means of satisfying them? His horror of adultery and debauchery keeps him away from both prostitutes and married women, and it is always with one of these two classes of women that the disorders of youth begin. A marriageable girl may be coquettish, but she will not be brazen; she will not throw herself at a young man who might marry her if he believes her to be chaste. Besides, she will have someone looking after her. Nor will Emile be left completely to himself. Both will at least be guarded by fear and shame, which are inseparable from our first desires. They will not immediately proceed to extreme familiarities, and they will not have the time to get to them by degrees without hindrance. To go about it otherwise, Emile would have to have already taken lessons from his comrades, to have learned from them to regard his restraint as ridiculous, and to have become insolent in imitation of them. But who in the world is less of an imitator than Emile? Who is less governed by ridicule than the man who has no prejudices and does not know how to concede anything to those of others? I have worked for twenty years to arm Emile against mockers. They will need more than a day to make him their dupe; for in his eyes ridicule is only the argument of fools, and nothing makes one more insensitive to mockery than being above opinion. Instead of jokes, he has to have reasons; and so long as that is the case, I am not afraid that wild young men are going to take him from me. I have conscience and truth on my side. If prejudice has to be mixed in, an attachment of twenty years is also something. Emile will never be made to believe that I bored him with vain lessons; and in an honest and sensitive heart, the voice of a faithful and true friend can surely drown out the cries of twenty seducers. Since it then becomes only a question of showing him that they deceive him and that, in feigning to treat him as a man, they really treat him as a child, I shall always use arguments that are simple but grave and clear, so that he will sense that it is I who treat him like a man. I shall say to him, "You see that your interest alone, which is also mine, dictates my speeches; I can have no other interest. But why do these young people want to persuade you? It is because they want to seduce you. They do not love you. They take no interest in you. Their whole motive is a secret spite at seeing that you are better than they are. They want to bring you down to their low level, and they reproach you for letting yourself be governed only in order to govern you themselves. Can you believe that there would be any profit for you in this change? Is their wisdom, then, so superior, and is their brief attachment to you stronger than mine? To give some weight to their ridicule, one would have to be able to give some weight to their authority; but what experience do they have that would make their maxims superior to ours? All they have done is to imitate other giddy fellows, just as they want to be imitated in their turn. To set themselves above the alleged prejudices of their fathers, they enslave themselves to those of their comrades. I do not see what they gain by that, but I do see that they surely lose two great advantages: paternal affection, which provides tender and sincere advice; and experience, which allows one to judge what one knows; for fathers have been children, and children have not been fathers.

"But do you believe that they are at least sincere in their rash maxims? Not even that, dear Emile. They deceive themselves in order to deceive you. They are not in harmony with themselves. Their hearts constantly give them the lie, and their mouths often contradict them. One man derides everything decent but would be in despair if his wife thought as he does. Another will extend his indifference about morals to those of the wife he does not yet have or—the crown of infamy—to those of the wife he already has. But go farther; speak to him of his mother, and see if he will gladly be looked upon as a child of adultery and the son of a woman of easy virtue, as one who has wrongfully assumed a family name, as a thief of the natural heir's patrimony; finally, see if he will patiently allow himself to be called a bastard! Who among them will want to have his own daughter dishonored as he dishonors the daughter of another? There is not one of them who would not make an attempt upon your very life if in practice you adopted toward him all the principles he makes an effort to teach you. It is thus that they finally disclose their inconsistency and that one senses that none of them believes what he says. These are my arguments, dear Emile. Weigh them against theirs, if they have any, and compare them. If I wanted to use contempt and ridicule as they do, you would see that they leave themselves open to ridicule as much as and perhaps more than I do. But I am not afraid of a serious examination. The triumph of mockers does not last long. Truth remains, and their foolish laughter vanishes."

You cannot image how Emile can be docile at twenty? How differently we think! I cannot conceive how he could have been docile at ten, for what hold did I have on him at that age? It has taken fifteen years of care to contrive this hold for myself. I did not educate him then; I prepared him to be educated. He is now sufficiently prepared to be docile. He recognizes the voice of friendship, and he knows how to obey reason. It is true that I leave him the appearance of independence, but he was never better subjected to me; for now he is subjected because he wants to be. As long as I was unable to make myself master of his will, I remained master of his person; I was never a step away from him. Now I sometimes leave him to himself, because I govern him always. In leaving him, I embrace him, and I say to him in a confident manner, "Emile, I entrust you to my friend; I deliver you to his decent heart. It will answer to me for you!"

It is not the business of a moment to corrupt healthy affections that have suffered no previous impairment and to blot out principles immediately derived from the first lights of reason. If some change takes place during my absence, that absence will never be long enough, and he will never know how to hide himself from me well enough for me not to perceive the danger before the disease and not be in time to remedy it. Just as one does not suddenly become depraved, one does not suddenly learn to dissimulate; and if ever a man was maladroit at this art, it is Emile, who has not had a single occasion to use it in his life.

By these measures and other similar ones I believe he will be so well protected against external objects and vulgar maxims that I would rather see him in the midst of the worst society of Paris than alone in his room or in a park, given over to all the restlessness of his age. No matter what one does, the most dangerous of all the enemies that can attack a young man, and the only one that cannot be put out of the way, is himself. This enemy, however, is dangerous only through our own fault; for as I have said countless times, the senses are awakened by the imagination alone. Their need is not properly a physical need. It is not true that it is a true need. If no lewd object had ever struck our eyes, if no indecent idea had ever entered our minds, perhaps this alleged need would never have made itself felt to us, and we would have remained chaste without temptation, without effort, and without merit. We do not know what mute fermentation certain situations and certain spectacles arouse in the blood of the young without their being able to discern for themselves the cause of this first disturbance, a disturbance not easily calmed nor slow to recur. As for me, the more I reflect on this important crisis and its near or distant causes, the more I am persuaded that a solitary man raised in a desert, without books, without instruction, and without women, would die there a virgin at whatever age he had reached.

But we are not talking here about a savage of this kind. In raising a man among his fellows for a life in society, it is impossible, it is even counter to my intention, to keep him always in this salutary ignorance; and the worst situation for chastity is to be halfway knowledgeable. The memory of objects that have made an impression upon us, the ideas that we have acquired follow us in our retreat and people it in spite of ourselves with images more seductive than the objects themselves; they make solitude as fatal to the man who carries these images to his retreat as it is useful to the man who has always remained there alone.

Therefore watch the young man carefully. He can protect himself from everything else, but it is up to you to protect him from himself. Do not leave him alone, day or night. At the very least, sleep in his room.[77] Distrust instinct as soon as you no longer limit yourself to it. It is good as long as it acts by itself; it is suspect from the moment it operates within man-made institutions. It must not be destroyed, but it must be regulated, and that is perhaps more difficult than annihilating it. It would be very dangerous if instinct taught your pupil to trick his senses and to find a substitute for the opportunity of satisfying them. Once he knows this dangerous supplement, he is lost. From then on he will always have an enervated body and heart. He will suffer until his death the sad effects of this habit, the most fatal to which a man can be subjected. Surely, rather than that . . . If the furies of an ardent temperament become invincible, my dear Emile, I pity you; but I shall not hesitate for a moment, I shall not allow nature's goal to be eluded. If a tyrant must subjugate you, I prefer to yield you to one from whom I can deliver you. Whatever happens, I shall tear you away more easily from women than from yourself.

The body grows until the age of twenty, and it needs all its substance. Continence then is in accordance with the order of nature, and one can scarcely deviate from it except at the expense of one's constitution. After the age of twenty continence is a duty of morality; it is important to learn to rule oneself, to remain the master of one's appetites. But moral duties have their modifications, their exceptions, their rules. When human weakness makes a choice inevitable, let us prefer the lesser of two evils. In any event, it is better to commit an offense than to contract a vice.

Remember that I am no longer speaking of my pupil here, but of yours. Do his passions, which you have allowed to ferment, subjugate you? Then yield to them openly, without disguising his victory from him. If you know how to reveal his victory to him in its true light, he will be less proud than ashamed of it, and you will keep the right of guiding him when he strays, so that you can at least make him avoid the precipices. It is important that the pupil not do anything that the master does not know about and does not want him to do—even if it is evil; and it is a hundred times better that the governor approve an offense and deceive himself than that he be deceived by his pupil and that the offense take place without his knowing anything about it. He who believes he ought to close his eyes to something soon finds himself forced to close them to everything; the first abuse that is tolerated leads to another, and this chain ends only with the overturning of all order and contempt for all law.

Another error which I have already combated, but which small minds will never abandon, is that of always affecting magisterial dignity and wanting to pass for a perfect man in the mind of one's disciple. This method is misconceived. How can such masters fail to see that in wanting to strengthen their authority, they destroy it; to make yourself heard, you must put yourself in the place of those you are addressing, and you must be a man in order to know how to speak to the human heart? All those perfect people are neither touching nor persuasive. One always tells oneself that it is quite easy for them to combat passions they do not feel. Show your weaknesses to your pupil if you want to cure his own. Let him see that you undergo the same struggles which he experiences. Let him learn to conquer himself by your example. And do not let him say as other pupils do: "These old men are spiteful because they are no longer young; they want to treat young people like old men; and because all their desires are extinguished, they treat ours as a crime."

Montaigne says that one day he asked Seigneur de Langey how many times during his negotiations with Germany he had gotten drunk in the king's service.[78] I would gladly ask the governor of some young man how often he went to a house of ill fame in his pupil's service. How many times? I am mistaken. If the first time does not forever destroy the pupil's desire to return, if he does not bring away repentance and shame, if he does not shed torrents of tears on your bosom, abandon him immediately. He is nothing but a monster, or you are nothing but an imbecile. You will never be of any use to him. But let us pass over these extreme expedients which are as sad as they are dangerous and have no relation to our education.

How many precautions must be taken with a well-born young man before exposing him to the scandalous morals of our age! These precautions are difficult, but they are indispensable. It is negligence on this point which dooms all our young people; it is due to the disorder of their early life that men degenerate and that one sees them become what they are today. Vile and cowardly even in their vices, they have only small souls because their worn-out bodies were corrupted early. There hardly remains enough life in them to move. Their subtle thoughts are signs of minds without substance. They do not know how to feel anything great and noble; they have neither simplicity nor vigor. Abject in all things and basely wicked, they are only vain, rascally, and false; they do not even have enough courage to be illustrious criminals. Such are the contemptible men who form the scum of our youth. If there were a single man among them who knew how to be temperate and sober and who knew how in their midst to preserve his heart, his blood, and his morals from the contagion of their example, at the age of thirty he would crush all these insects and become their master with less effort than he had exerted in remaining his own master!

No matter how little birth and fortune had done for Emile, he would be that man if he wanted to be. But he would despise these young men too much to deign to enslave them. Let us see him now in their midst, entering society not in order to excel in it, but to know it and to find there a companion worthy of him.

In whatever rank he may have been born, into whatever society he begins to enter, his debut will be simple and without brilliance. God forbid that he be unfortunate enough to shine. The qualities which strike people at first glance are not his. He neither has them nor wants to have them. He values men's judgments too little to value their prejudices, and he does not care to be esteemed before being known. His way of presenting himself is neither modest nor vain; it is natural and true. He knows neither embarrassment nor disguise, and in the midst of a group he is the same as he is when he is alone and without any witnesses. Will he therefore be coarse, disdainful, heedless of everyone? On the contrary. When he is alone, he does not think that other men count for nothing. Why would he think that they count for nothing when he lives among them? He does not prefer other men to himself in his manners because he does not prefer them to himself in his heart.

But neither does he display to them an indifference which he is very far from having. If he does not use polite formulas, he does have humane concerns. He does not like to see anyone suffer. He will not offer his place to someone else out of affectation, but he will gladly yield it out of goodness if he sees that someone else is forgotten and judges that the man is mortified by this neglect. For it will cost my young man less to remain standing voluntarily than to see the other person forced to remain standing.

Although in general Emile does not esteem men, he will not show contempt for them, because he pities them and is touched by them. Unable to give them the taste for things that are really good, he leaves them with the things that are good according to popular opinion, with which they are contented. Otherwise, by taking these things from them to no avail, he will make them unhappier than before. Therefore, he is not disputatious or contradictory; neither is he accommodating and flattering. He gives his opinion without combating anyone else's, because he loves freedom above everything and frankness is one of the finest of rights.

He speaks little because he hardly cares whether any attention is paid to him. For the same reason he says only useful things; otherwise, who would engage him in conversation? Emile is too well informed ever to be talkative. Babbling inevitably comes either from pretentions to cleverness—about which I shall speak hereafter—or from the value we give to bagatelles which we foolishly believe others care about as much as we do. He who knows enough about things to assign them all their true value never speaks too much, for he also knows how to evaluate the attention paid to him and the interest that can be taken in his conversation. Generally people who know little speak a great deal, and people who know a great deal speak little. It is easy for an ignoramus to find everything he knows important and to tell it to everyone. But a well-informed man does not easily open up his repertoire. He would have too much to say, and he sees yet more to be said after he has spoken. He keeps quiet.

Far from shocking others, Emile is quite willing to conform to their ways—not to appear knowledgeable about social practice or to affect the airs of an elegant man; but, on the contrary, he does so for fear of being singled out, in order to avoid being noticed. And he is never more at ease than when no attention is paid to him.

Although he is absolutely ignorant of the ways of the world when he enters it, this does not make him timid and fearful. If he conceals himself, it is not due to embarrassment; it is because in order to see well one must not be seen. What people think of him hardly bothers him, and ridicule does not frighten him in the least. The result is that he is always serene and cool and never troubled by shame. Whether he is observed or not, he always does his best; and since he is always entirely self-possessed in order to observe others well, he grasps their practices with a facility that the slaves of opinion cannot match. It may be said that he more readily adopts the practices of society precisely because he cares so little about them.

Do not deceive yourself about his comportment, however, and do not try to compare it to that of your young charmers. He is firm and not conceited. His manners are free and not disdainful. An insolent air belongs only to slaves; independence has nothing affected about it. I have never seen a man who has pride in his soul display it in his bearing. This affectation is far more fitting for vile and vain souls who can make an impression only in that way. I read in a book that when a foreigner presented himself one day at the studio of the famous Marcel,[79] the latter asked him what country he came from. "I am English," responded the foreigner. "You, English?" replied the dancer. "You are from that island where the citizens take part in public administration and have a portion of the sovereign power? * No, sir, this hanging head, this timid glance, this uncertain bearing proclaim to me only the titled slave of a German Elector."

I do not know whether this judgment reveals a great knowledge of the true relation which exists between a man's character and his exterior. As for me, since I do not have the honor of being a dancing master, I would have thought exactly the opposite. I would have said, "This Englishman is not a courtier. I have never heard it said that courtiers have hanging heads or an uncertain bearing. A man who is timid at a dancer's studio might very well not be timid in the House of Commons." Certainly, this M. Marcel must take his compatriots for nothing but Romans.

When one loves, one wants to be loved. Emile loves men; therefore he wants to please them. A fortiori, he wants to please women. His age, his morals, and his project all unite to foster this desire. I say his morals, for they have a great deal to do with it. Men who have morals are the true worshipers of women. They do not have that mocking jargon of gallantry as the others do, but they have a truer and more tender eagerness which comes from the heart. In the presence of a young woman, I could pick out a man who has morals and is in command of his nature from a hundred thousand debauchés. Judge what Emile must be like, with a wholly fresh temperament and so many reasons for resisting it! I believe he will sometimes be timid and embarrassed in the company of women. But surely this will not be displeasing to them, and even the least roguish women will only too often possess the art of taking advantage of his embarrassment and increasing it. Moreover, his eagerness will noticeably change its form according to a woman's status. He will be more modest and more respectful toward married women, and livelier and more tender with marriageable girls. He does not lose sight of the object of his search, and he always pays the most attention to what reminds him of that search.

No one will be more exact than Emile in observing all the signs of respect that are founded on the order of nature and even on the good order of society; but he will always prefer the former to the latter, and

* As if there were citizens who were not members of the city, and who did not as such have a part of the sovereign authority! But the French, having judged it suitable to usurp the respectable name of citizens—a name formerly merited by the members of the Gallic cities—have denatured the idea of citizenship to the point where one no longer has any conception of it. A man who just wrote me a pack of stupidities against *La Nouvelle Héloïse* adorned his signature with the title "Citizen of Paimboeuf" and believed he had made an excellent joke at my expense.[80]

he will respect a private man older than himself more than a magistrate of his own age. Since he will ordinarily be one of the youngest members of the society in which he finds himself, he will always be one of the most modest—not out of a desire to appear humble founded upon vanity, but out of a sentiment that is both natural and founded on reason. He will not have the impertinent *savoir-vivre* of a young fop who, in order to amuse the company, speaks louder than the wise and interrupts the old. He will not justify the response given to Louis XV by an old gentleman who was asked by the king whether he preferred his own time or the present: "Sire, I spent my youth respecting the old, and I have to spend my old age respecting children."

Emile possesses a tender and sensitive soul, but he values nothing according to the price set by opinion; thus, although he likes to please others, he will care little about being esteemed by them. From this it follows that he will be more affectionate than polite, that he will never put on airs or make a display, and that he will be more touched by a caress than by a thousand praises. For the same reasons he will neglect neither his manners nor his bearing. He may even take some care with his dress, not in order to appear to be a man of taste but to make his looks more agreeable. He will not resort to the gilded frame, and his clothing will never be stained by the mark of riches.

It can be seen that all this does not require a display of precepts from me and is only an effect of his first education. The practices of society are made out to be a great mystery, as though at the age when these practices are acquired one did not take to them naturally and as though their first laws were not to be found in a decent heart! True politeness consists in showing benevolence to men. It reveals itself without difficulty when one possesses it. It is only for the man who does not possess true politeness that one is forced to make an art of its outward forms.

> The most unfortunate effect of formal politeness is to teach the art of getting along without the virtues it imitates. Let humanity and beneficence be inspired in us by education, and we shall have politeness, or we shall no longer need it.
>
> If we do not possess the politeness heralded by the graces, we shall have that politeness which heralds the decent man and the citizen; we shall not need to resort to falseness.
>
> Instead of being artificial in order to please, it will suffice to be good. Instead of being false in order to flatter the weaknesses of others, it will suffice to be indulgent.
>
> Those whom one treats in such a way will neither have their pride flattered nor be corrupted. They will only be grateful and will be made better.*

It seems to me that if any education ought to produce the kind of politeness which M. Duclos calls for here, it is the one I have outlined up to now.

I agree, however, that with maxims so different from theirs, Emile

* *Considerations sur les moeurs de ce siècle* by M. Duclos, p. 65.

will not be like everyone else, and God preserve him from ever being so. But he will be neither troublesome nor ridiculous in his difference from others. This difference will be noticeable without being offensive. Emile will be, you might say, a likable foreigner. At first they will pardon him his singularities by saying, "He will develop." Later they will be completely accustomed to his ways, and since they see that he does not change, they will pardon him again by saying, "That's the way he is."

He will not be celebrated as a likable man, but they will like him without knowing why. No one will vaunt Emile's intelligence, but he will be gladly taken as a judge among intelligent men. His intelligence will be sharp and limited. He will have solid sense and healthy judgment. As he never runs after new ideas, he could not pride himself on his cleverness. I have made him feel that all the ideas which are salutary and truly useful to men were the first to be known; that in all times they constitute the only true bonds of society; and that the only way transcendent minds can now distinguish themselves is by means of ideas that are pernicious and destructive for mankind.

This way of becoming admired does not appeal to him very much. He knows where he ought to find the happiness of his life and how he can contribute to the happiness of others. The sphere of his knowledge does not extend farther than what is profitable. His route is narrow and well marked. He is not tempted to leave it, and so he remains indistinguishable from those who follow it. He wants neither to stray from his path nor to shine. Emile is a man of good sense, and he does not want to be anything else. One may very well try to insult him by this title; he will stick to it and always feel honored by it.

Although his desire to please does not leave him absolutely indifferent to the opinion of others, he will concern himself with their opinion only insofar as it relates immediately to his person, and he will not worry about arbitrary evaluations whose only law is fashion or prejudice. He will have the pride to want to do everything he does well, even to do it better than another. He will want to be the swiftest at running, the strongest at wrestling, the most competent at working, the most adroit at games of skill. But he will hardly seek advantages which are not clear in themselves and which need to be established by another's judgment, such as being more intelligent than someone else, talking better, being more learned, etc.; still less will he seek those advantages which are not at all connected with one's person, such as being of nobler birth, being esteemed richer, more influential, or more respected, or making an impression by greater pomp.

He loves men because they are his fellows, but he will especially love those who resemble him most because he will feel that he is good; and since he judges this resemblance by agreement in moral taste, he will be quite gratified to be approved in everything connected with good character. He will not precisely say to himself, "I rejoice because they approve of me," but rather, "I rejoice because they approve of what I have done that is good. I rejoice that the people who honor me do themselves honor. So long as they judge so soundly, it will be a fine thing to obtain their esteem."

While studying men's morals in society, as he previously studied their passions in history, he will often have occasion to reflect on what delights or offends the human heart. Now he is philosophizing about the principles of taste, and this is the study which suits him during this period.

The farther afield one goes in seeking definitions of taste, the more one loses one's way. Taste is only the faculty of judging what pleases or displeases the greatest number. Abandon that, and you no longer know what taste is. It does not follow that there are more people who have taste than others who lack it; for although the majority judge each object soundly, there are few men who judge as the majority do about everything. And although the conjunction of the most general tastes constitutes good taste, there are few people who have taste—just as there are few beautiful persons despite the fact that the union of the most common features constitutes beauty.

It should be noted that we are not dealing here with what we love because it is useful to us nor with what we hate because it harms us. Taste is exercised only in regard to things which are neutral or which are at most of interest as entertainment, and not in regard to those things connected with our needs. To judge the latter, taste is not necessary. Appetite alone suffices. This is what makes pure decisions of taste so difficult and, it seems, so arbitrary; for, apart from the instinct which determines it, one no longer sees the reason for these decisions. One must also distinguish between its laws in moral things and its laws in physical things. In regard to the latter the principles of taste seem absolutely inexplicable. But it is important to observe that something moral enters into everything connected with imitation.* In this way one can explain beauties which appear physical and which really are not. I shall add that taste has local rules which in countless things make it depend on climates, morals, government, institutions; that it has other rules connected with age, sex, character; and that it is in this sense that tastes should not be disputed.

Taste is natural to all men, but they do not all have it to the same degree; it does not develop in all men to the same degree; and in all it is subject to corruption due to diverse causes. The level of taste a man may reach depends on the sensitivity with which he has been endowed. The cultivation of taste and its form depend on the societies in which one has lived. First, one must live in societies with many members in order to make many comparisons. Second, one needs societies dedicated to entertainment and idleness; for societies dedicated to business are ruled not by pleasure but by interest. In the third place, one needs societies where inequality is not too great, where the tyranny of opinion is limited and where voluptuousness reigns more than vanity does; for in the opposite case, fashion stifles taste, and people no longer seek what pleases them but seek rather what distinguishes them.

In this latter case, it is no longer true that good taste is that of the greatest number. Why is that? Because the object of taste changes. Then

* This is proved in an essay on the *Principles of Melody* which will be found in the collection of my writings.[81]

the multitude no longer has judgment of its own. It now judges only according to the views of those whom it believes more enlightened than itself. It approves not what is good but what they have approved. In all times, see to it that each man has his own sentiments, and the plurality of votes will always go to what is most agreeable in itself.

In their works men make nothing beautiful except by imitation. All the true models of taste are in nature. The farther we move from this master, the more our paintings are disfigured. It is then that we draw our models from the objects we love; and beauty which has its source in whim is subject to caprice and authority and is no longer anything other than what pleases those who lead us.

Those who lead us are the artists, the nobles, and the rich, and what leads them is their interest or their vanity. The rich, in order to display their wealth, and the artists, in order to take advantage of that wealth, vie in the quest for new means of expense. This is the basis on which great luxury establishes its empire and leads people to love what is difficult and costly. Then what is claimed to be beautiful, far from imitating nature, is beautiful only by dint of thwarting it. This is how luxury and bad taste become inseparable. Wherever taste is expensive, it is false.

It is especially in the relations between the two sexes that taste, good or bad, gets its form. Its cultivation is a necessary effect of the aim of these relations. But when the ease of enjoyment cools the desire to please, taste must degenerate; and this, it seems to me, is another very evident reason why good taste depends on good morals.

Consult the taste of women in physical things connected with the judgment of the senses, but consult the taste of men in moral things that depend more on the understanding. When women are what they ought to be, they will limit themselves to things within their competence and will always judge well. But since they have established themselves as the arbiters of literature, since they have set about judging books and relentlessly producing them, they no longer know anything. Authors who consult the learned ladies about their works are always sure of being badly counseled. The gallants who consult them about their dress are always ridiculously attired. I shall soon have occasion to speak of the true talents of this sex, of the way to cultivate them, and of the things about which its decisions ought then to be heard.

These are the elementary considerations that I shall set down as principles in reasoning with my Emile about a matter which is far from indifferent to him in his present circumstances—and in the quest that occupies him. And to whom should it be indifferent? Knowledge of what can be agreeable or disagreeable to men is necessary not only to someone who needs men but also to someone who wishes to be useful to them. It is even important to please them in order to serve them, and the art of writing is far from an idle study when one uses it to make the truth heard.

If, in order to cultivate my disciple's taste, I had to choose between taking him to countries where there has not yet been any cultivation of taste and to others where taste has already degenerated, I would proceed in reverse order. That is, I would begin his tour with the latter countries and end with the former. This reason for this choice is that taste is corrupted by an excessive delicacy which creates a sensitivity to things that the bulk of men do not perceive. This delicacy leads to a spirit of discussion, for the more subtle one is about things, the more they multiply. This subtlety makes feelings more delicate and less uniform. Then as many tastes are formed as there are individuals. In the disputes about preference, philosophy and enlightenment are extended, and it is in this way that one learns to think. Fine observations can hardly be made except by people who get around a lot, given that those observations strike us only after all the others and that people unaccustomed to large societies exhaust their attention on the gross features of things. At the present time there is perhaps not a civilized place on earth where the general taste is worse than in Paris. Nevertheless it is in this capital that good taste is cultivated, and there appear few books esteemed in Europe whose author has not been in Paris for the purpose of forming himself. Those who think that it suffices to read the books produced there are mistaken. One learns much more in conversation with authors than in their books, and the authors themselves are not those from whom one learns the most. It is the spirit of societies which develops a thoughtful mind and extends our vision as far as it can go. If you have a spark of genius, go and spend a year in Paris. Soon you will be all that you can be, or you will never be anything.

One can learn to think in places where bad taste reigns; but one must not think as do those who have this bad taste—and it is quite difficult for this not to happen when one stays among them too long. With their assistance one must perfect the instrument which judges, while avoiding using it as they do. I shall be careful not to polish Emile's judgment so much as to spoil it, and when his feelings are refined enough to sense and compare men's diverse tastes, I shall bring him back to simpler objects to establish his own taste.

I shall go further still to preserve in him a pure and healthy taste. Amidst the tumult of dissipation I shall know how to arrange useful discussions with him; and by always directing these discussions toward objects which please him, I shall take care to make them as enjoyable to him as they are instructive. This is the time for reading, for reading enjoyable books. This is the time to teach him how to analyze speech, to make him sensitive to all the beauties of eloquence and diction. It is trivial to learn languages for their own sake; their use is not as important as people believe. But the study of languages leads to that of grammar. Latin has to be learned in order to know French. Both must be studied and compared in order to understand the rules of the art of speaking.

There is, moreover, a certain simplicity of taste that speaks straight to the heart and is found only in the writings of the ancients. In eloquence, in poetry, in every kind of literature Emile will again find the ancients—as he found them in history—rich in facts and sparing in judgments. Our authors, by contrast, say little and make many pronouncements. Constantly to give us their judgment as the law is not the way to form our judgment. The difference between the two tastes makes itself felt in all monuments, even including tombs. Our tomb-stones are covered with praise; on those of the ancients one read facts.

Sta viator, Heroem calcas [82]

Even if I had found this epitaph on an ancient monument, I would have immediately guessed that it was modern; for nothing is so ordinary among us heroes, but among the ancients they were rare. Instead of saying that a man was a hero, they would have said what he had done to become one. To the epitaph of this hero compare that of the effeminate Sardanapalus:

I built Tarsus and Anchialus in a day
and now I am dead.[83]

Which says more in your opinion? Our bombastic lapidary style is good only for inflating dwarfs. The ancients showed men as they are naturally, and one saw that they were men. Xenophon, honoring the memory of some warriors who were treacherously killed during the retreat of the ten thousand, says, "They died irreproachable in war and in friendship." [84] That is all. But consider what must have filled the author's heart in writing this short and simple eulogy. Woe unto him who does not find that entrancing!

One read these words carved in marble at Thermopylae:

Passer-by, tell them at Sparta that we died here to obey
her holy laws.[85]

It is quite obvious that it was not the Academy of Inscriptions which wrote that.

I am mistaken if my pupil, who sets so little store by words, does not immediately turn his attention to these differences, and if they do not influence his choice of reading. Drawn by the masculine eloquence of Demosthenes, he will say, "This is an orator." But in reading Cicero, he will say, "This is a lawyer."

In general, Emile will get more of a taste for the books of the ancients than for ours, for the sole reason that the ancients, since they came first, are closest to nature and their genius is more their own. Whatever La Motte and the Abbé Terrasson may have said, there is no true progress of reason in the human species, because all that is gained on one side is lost on the other: all minds always start from the same point, and since the time used in finding out what others have thought is wasted for learning to think for ourselves, we have acquired more enlightenment and less vigor of mind. We exercise our minds, like our arms, by having them do everything with tools and nothing by themselves. Fontenelle said that this whole dispute about ancients and moderns comes down to knowing whether the trees in the past were bigger than those today.[86] If agriculture had changed, it would not be impertinent to ask this question.

After having thus helped Emile ascend to the sources of pure literature, I also show him its sewers in the reservoirs of modern compilers, newspapers, translations, and dictionaries. He casts a glance at all this, then leaves it never to return. In order to amuse him, I have him listen to the chatter of the academies; I see to it that he notices that the individuals who compose the academies are always worth more alone than as part of the group. He will draw for himself the implication about the utility of all these fine establishments.

I take him to the theater to study not morals but taste, for it is here that taste reveals itself to those who know how to reflect. "Leave aside precepts and morality," I would say to him, "it is not here that they are to be learned." The theater is not made for the truth. It is made to delight, to entertain men. There is no school in which one learns so well the art of pleasing men and of interesting the human heart. The study of the theater leads to that of poetry. They have exactly the same aim. If he has a spark of taste for it, with what pleasure he will cultivate the languages of the poets—Greek, Latin, and Italian! These studies will be entertainments without constraint for him, and thus he will profit all the more from them. They will be delicious to him at an age and in circumstances when his interest is aroused by the great charm of all the sorts of beauty capable of touching the heart. Picture my Emile, on the one hand, and a young college scamp, on the other, reading the fourth book of the *Aeneid*, or Tibullus, or Plato's *Banquet*. What a difference! How much the heart of the one is stirred by what does not even affect the other. O good young man, stop, suspend your reading. I see that you are too moved. I certainly want the language of love to please you, but I do not want it to lead you astray. Be a sensitive man, but also a wise one. If you are only one of the two, you are nothing. Moreover, I care little whether he succeeds or not at the dead languages, at letters, at poetry. He will be worth no less if he knows none of all that, and it is not with all these trifles that his education is concerned.

My principle aim in teaching him to feel and to love the beautiful of all sorts is to fix his affections and tastes on it, to prevent his natural appetites from becoming corrupted, and to see to it that he does not one day seek in his riches the means for being happy—means that he ought to find nearer to him. I have said elsewhere that taste is only the art of knowing all about petty things, and that is very true. But since the agreeableness of life depends on a tissue of petty things, such concerns are far from being matters of indifference. It is through such concerns that we learn to fill life with the good things within our reach in all the truth they can have for us. I am talking here not about the moral goods which depend on the good disposition of the soul, but only about what is connected with sensuality and with real voluptuousness, apart from prejudices and opinion.

Permit me for a moment, in order to develop my idea better, to leave aside Emile, whose pure and healthy heart can no longer serve as a rule for anyone, and to seek in myself an example that is more evident and closer to the morals of the reader.

There are situations which seem to change our nature and to recast, for better or worse, the men who fill them. A poltroon becomes brave upon entering the regiment of Navarre. It is not only in the military that one gets esprit de corps, and its effects are not always to the good. I have a hundred times thought with terror that if I had the misfortune today of filling a particular position in a certain country, tomorrow I would almost inevitably be a tyrant, an extortionist, a destroyer of the people, and a source of harm to the prince; due to my situation I would be an enemy of all humanity, of all equity, of every sort of virtue.

Similarly, if I were rich, I would have done everything necessary to become so. I would therefore be insolent and low, sensitive and delicate toward myself alone, pitiless and hard toward everyone else, a disdainful spectactor of the miseries of the rabble—for I would no longer give any other name to the indigent, in order to make people forget that I once belonged to their class. Finally, I would make my fortune the instrument of my pleasures, with which I would be wholly occupied. Up to this point I would be like all other rich men.

But I believe I would differ from them very much by being sensual and voluptuous rather than proud and vain and by devoting myself to indolent luxury far more than to ostentatious luxury. I would even be somewhat ashamed to display my riches too much; I would always believe I saw the envious man whom I had overwhelmed with my pomp saying into his neighbor's ear, "Here is a rascal who is very much afraid of being known for what he is!"

From this immense profusion of goods which cover the earth I would seek what is most agreeable to me and what I could best make use of. To that end, the first use of my riches would be to purchase leisure and freedom, to which I would add health, if it were for sale. But since it is purchased only with temperance and since there is no true pleasure in life without health, I would be temperate out of sensuality.

I would always stay as close as possible to nature, in order to indulge the senses I received from nature—quite certain that the more nature contributed to my enjoyments, the more reality I would find in them. In choosing objects for imitation, I would always take nature as my model; in my appetites I would always give it preference; in my tastes I would always consult it; in foods I would always want those which are best prepared by nature and pass through the fewest hands before reaching our tables. I would prevent myself from becoming the victim of fraudulent adulterations by going out after pleasure myself. My foolish and coarse gluttony would not enrich an innkeeper. He would not sell me terribly expensive poison in the guise of fish. My table would not be covered with a display of magnificent garbage and exotic carrion. I would lavish my own efforts on the satisfaction of my sensuality, since then those efforts are themselves a pleasure and thus add to the pleasure one expects from them. If I wanted to taste a dish from the end of the earth, I would, like Apicius,[87] go and seek it out rather than have it brought to me. For the most exquisite dishes always lack a seasoning that does not travel with them and no cook can give them: the air of the climate which produced them.

For the same reason I would not imitate those who are never contented with where they are and thus always put the seasons in contradiction with one another and the climate in contradiction with the season. These are the people who seek summer in winter and winter in summer, who go to Italy when it is cold and to the north when it is warm, unaware that in intending to escape the rigor of the seasons they encounter it in places where men have not learned to protect themselves from it. I would remain where I was, or I would take exactly the opposite course. I would want to extract from each season all that is agreeable in it and from each climate all that is peculiar to it. I would have a diversity of pleasures and habits which would not resemble one another and which would always be part of nature. I would go to spend the summer at Naples and the winter at Petersburg—now inhaling a gentle breeze while reclining in the cool grottoes of Tarentum, now enjoying the illuminations of an ice palace, out of breath and exhausted by the pleasures of the ball.

In the setting of my table and the decorating of my dwelling, I would want to imitate the variety of the seasons with very simple ornaments and to extract all its delights from each season without anticipating the ones that will follow it. It takes effort—and not taste—to disturb the order of nature, to wring from it involuntary produce which it gives reluctantly and with its curse. Such produce has neither quality nor savor; it can neither nourish the stomach nor delight the palate. Nothing is more insipid than early fruits and vegetables. It is only at great expense that the rich man of Paris succeeds, with his stoves and hothouses, in having bad vegetables and bad fruits on his table the whole year round. If I could have cherries when it is freezing and amber-colored melons in the heart of winter, what pleasure would I take in them when my palate needs neither moistening nor cooling? Would the heavy chestnut be very agreeable to me during the broiling dog days of summer? Would I prefer it—straight from the oven—to currants, strawberries, and other refreshing fruits that the earth offers me without so much trouble? To cover the mantel of one's fireplace in the month of January with forced vegetation, with pale and odorless flowers, is less to embellish winter than to spoil spring; it is to take away the pleasure of going into the woods to seek the first violet, spy out the first bud, and shout in a fit of joy, "Mortals, you have not been abandoned; nature still lives."

In order to be well served, I would have few domestics. This has already been said, and it is well to say it yet again. A bourgeois gets more true service from his only lackey than a duke gets from the ten gentlemen surrounding him. I have a hundred times thought that, with my glass beside me at the table, I drink at the instant I please; whereas if I dined in grand style, twenty voices would have to repeat "Drink" before I could quench my thirst. Try as you will, all that is done by means of other people is done badly. I would not send someone to shop for me, I would go myself. I would go in order to prevent my servants from making deals with the shopkeepers and to choose more surely and pay less dearly. I would go in order to take some agreeable exercise, to see a bit of what goes on outside of the house—it is entertaining, and sometimes it is instructive. Finally I would go in order to go—that is always something. Boredom begins with too sedentary a life.

When one goes out a great deal, one rarely gets bored. A porter and some lackeys are poor interpreters. I would not want to have these people always between me and the rest of the world, nor would I want always to move accompanied by the roar of a carriage, as though I were afraid of being approached. The horses of a man who uses his legs are always ready. If his horses are tired or sick, he knows it before anyone, and he is not afraid of being obliged to give this excuse for staying at home when his coachman decides to take off on a lark. On the road countless delays do not make him fidget impatiently or stand still at the moment when he would want to hurry ahead. In sum, if no one ever serves us so well as ourselves—even if we were more powerful than Alexander or richer than Croesus—we ought to receive from others only the services that we cannot get from ourselves.

I would not want to have a palace for a dwelling, for in that palace I would inhabit only one room. Every common room belongs to no one, and the room of each of my servants would be as foreign to me as that of my neighbor. The Orientals, although quite voluptuous, have simple houses and furniture. They regard life as a journey, and their home as a way station. This argument has little effect on us rich people who are arranging to live forever; but I have a different one which would produce the same effect. It would seem to me that to set myself up with so much gear in one place would be to banish myself from all others and to imprison myself, so to speak, in my palace. The world itself is a fine enough palace. Does not everything belong to the rich man when he wants to enjoy himself? *Ubi bene, ibi patria* [88] is his motto; his lares are the places where money can buy anything; his country is wherever his strongbox can go, just as Philip possessed every fortress where a mule bearing money could enter.[89] Why then be circumscribed by walls and by gates as though one were never to leave? Does an epidemic, a war, a revolt drive me out of some place? I go to another and find my mansion has gotten there before me. Why bother building mansions for myself, when others do it for me throughout the universe? Since I am in such a hurry to live, why prepare so far in advance enjoyments that are available to me right now? No one could make an agreeable lot for himself if he were constantly living in contradiction with himself. It is thus that Empedocles reproached the Agrigentines for cramming in pleasures as though they had only a day to live and building as though they were never going to die.[90]

Moreover, what is the use of so vast a lodging to me, since I have so little with which to people it and less with which to fill it? My furnishings would be as simple as my tastes. I would have neither gallery nor library, especially if I liked reading and knew something about paintings. I would then know that such collections are never complete and that the absence of what is lacking causes more chagrin than having nothing at all. In this, abundance makes poverty; there is not a single collector who has not experienced it. When someone has knowledge of such things, he ought not to make collections. A man has no study to show to others when he knows how to use it for himself.

Gambling is not a rich man's entertainment; it is the resource of the unemployed; and my pleasures would give me too much activity to leave me much time to fill so poorly. Since I am solitary and poor, I do not gamble at all, except sometimes at chess, and even that is too much. If I were rich, I would gamble still less and only for very small stakes, in order not to see any malcontents and not to be one. Since the opulent man lacks a motive for gambling, his interest in it can never turn into a rage, except if he has an ill-constituted mind. The profits that a rich man can make at gambling are always less perceptible to him than his losses. And since gambling for moderate stakes—where the winnings are played away in the long run—in general winds up producing more losses than gains, anyone who reasons well cannot be very fond of an entertainment in which the risks of every sort are against him. Whoever feeds his vanity on the preferences of fortune can seek them in much more piquant objects, and these preferences are no more marked in the smallest game than in the biggest. The taste for gambling is the fruit of avarice and boredom, and it takes hold only in an empty mind and heart; it seems to me that I would have enough sentiment and knowledge to do without such a supplement. One rarely sees thinkers enjoying themselves much in gambling, which interrupts the habit of thinking or turns it to arid combinations of elements. Thus one of the good things, and perhaps the only one, which the taste for the sciences has produced is to deaden this sordid passion a bit; people would rather exert themselves to prove the utility of gambling than to indulge in it. I would combat gambling among gamblers, and I would get more pleasure out of ridiculing them when they lose than out of winning their money.

I would be the same in my private life and in my social relations. I would want my fortune to provide ease everywhere and never to create a feeling of inequality. Garishness of dress is inconvenient in countless respects. In order to retain all possible liberty, when I am among other men, I would want to be dressed in such a way that in every rank I appeared to be in my place, and that I did not stand out in any—so that without affectation and without changing my appearance I could be one of the people at the *guinguette* and good company at the Palais-Royal.[91] In this way I would be more the master of my conduct, and I would put the pleasures of all stations always within my reach. It is said that there are women who close their doors on embroidered cuffs and receive no one who does not wear lace. I would go and spend my day elsewhere. But if these women were young and pretty, I could sometimes put on lace in order to spend—at the very most—the night there.

The only bond of my associations would be mutual attachment, agreement of tastes, suitableness of characters. I would give myself over to them as a man and not as one of the rich. I would never permit their charms to be poisoned by interest. If my opulence had left me some humanity, I would extend my services and my benefactions at a distance, but I would want to have a society around me, not a court; friends, and not protegés. I would not be the patron of my guests; I would be their host. This independence and equality would permit my relationships to have all the candor of benevolence; and where neither duty nor interest entered in any way, pleasure and friendship would alone make the law.

Neither a friend nor a mistress can be bought. It is easy to have women with money, but that way one is never the lover of any of them. Far from being for sale, love is infallibly killed by money. Whoever pays for it—even if he is the most lovable of men—by that fact alone cannot be loved for long. Soon he will be paying for another man, or, rather, that other man will be paid with his money. And in this double liaison—formed by interest and debauchery, without love, without honor, without true pleasure—the greedy, unfaithful, and miserable woman is treated by the vile man who takes her money as she treats the foolish man who gives it to her, and thus she breaks even between the two. It would be sweet to be liberal toward the person one loves, if this did not constitute a purchase. I know only one way of satisfying this inclination toward one's mistress without poisoning love. It is to give her everything and then to be supported by her. It remains to be known where there is a woman with whom this procedure would not be a folly.

He who said, "I possess Laïs without her possessing me," [92] uttered a witless phrase. Possession which is not reciprocal is nothing. It is at most possession of the sexual organ, not of the individual. Now, where the moral aspect of love is not present, why make so great a business of the rest? Nothing is so easy to find. A mule driver is in that respect closer to happiness than is a millionaire.

Oh, if one could sufficiently unfold the inconsistencies of vice, how wide of its mark one would find it, precisely when it gets what it wanted! Why this barbarous avidity to corrupt innocence, to make a victim of a young person who ought to have been protected, and who by this first step is inevitably dragged into an abyss of miseries from which she will emerge only at death? Brutality, vanity, folly, error, and nothing more. The pleasure itself does not come from nature; it comes from opinion, and from the vilest opinion, since it is connected with self-contempt. He who feels himself to be the basest of men fears comparison with all others and wants to be the first to get there in order to be less odious. Consider whether those most avid for this imaginary dish are ever lovable young people, worthy of winning favor, who would be more excusable for being hard to please? No, someone who has looks, merit, and sentiments has little to fear from an experienced mistress. With justified confidence, such a man says to her, "You know the pleasures. It makes no difference. My heart promises you pleasures you have never known."

But an old satyr—worn out by debauchery, without charm, without respect, without consideration, without any kind of decency, incapable and unworthy of pleasing any woman who knows anything about lovable people—believes he can make up for all that with a young innocent by taking advantage of her inexperience and stirring her senses for the first time. His last hope is to be attractive by means of novelty. That is incontestably the secret motive of this whim. But he is mistaken. The disgust he causes comes from nature as much as do the desires he would like to arouse. He is also mistaken in his foolish expectations; this same nature is careful to claim its rights: any girl who sells herself has already given herself to someone else and, having given herself to the man of her choice, she has made the comparison the old satyr fears. He therefore buys an imaginary pleasure and is nonetheless abhorred.

As for me, for all that I may change when I am rich, there is one point on which I shall never change. If neither morals nor virtue remain to me, at least there will remain some taste, some sense, some delicacy. This will protect me from being the dupe of my fortune, from using it to run after chimeras, from exhausting my purse and my life in getting myself betrayed and ridiculed by children. If I were young, I would seek the pleasures of youth; and wanting them in all their voluptuousness, I would not seek them as a rich man. If I remained as I am now, that would be another matter. I would prudently limit myself to the pleasures of my age. I would indulge the tastes that I could enjoy, and I would stifle those which would no longer be anything but my torture. I would not expose my gray beard to the mocking disdain of young girls. I could not bear to see my disgusting caresses make them sick to the stomach, to provide them with the most ridiculous stories at my expense, or to imagine them describing the dirty pleasures of the old ape in such a way as to avenge themselves for having endured them. And if unconquered habits had turned my old desires into needs, I would perhaps satisfy them, but I would blush with shame. I would remove the passion from the need; I would find as good a match as was possible for me, and I would leave it at that. I would not make an occupation of my weakness; and, above all, I would not want to have more than a single witness to it. Human life has other pleasures when these are lacking; by vainly running after those that flee, we also deprive ourselves of those that are left to us. Let us change tastes with the years; let us not displace ages any more than seasons. One must be oneself at all times and not battle against nature. Such vain efforts use up life and prevent us from making good use of it.

The people hardly ever get bored. Their life is active. If their entertainments are not varied, they are rare. Many days of fatigue make them taste a few days of festival with delight. An alternation of long periods of labor and short periods of leisure takes the place of seasoning in the pleasures of the people. For the rich, boredom is their great plague. Amongst so many entertainments assembled at great expense, in the midst of so many people joining together to please them, boredom consumes them and kills them. They pass their lives in fleeing it and in being overtaken by it. They are overwhelmed by its unbearable weight. Women who no longer know how to occupy or entertain themselves are especially devoured by it, under the name of vapors. For them boredom is transformed into a horrible illness which sometimes deprives them of their reason and finally their lives. As for me, I know of no fate more frightful than that of a pretty woman of Paris—except for that of the agreeable little fellow who attaches himself to her and is also turned into an idle woman, thus becoming doubly removed from

BOOK IV

his station. The vanity of being a lady's man enables him to bear the length of the gloomiest days that any human creature has ever spent.

The propriety, the fashions, and the customs which derive from luxury and high style confine the course of life to the dullest uniformity. The pleasure one wants to enjoy in others' eyes is lost for everyone; it is enjoyed neither by them nor by oneself.* Ridicule, which opinion dreads above all else, is always at its side to tyrannize it and to punish it. A person is never ridiculous except when he follows fixed practices. He who knows how to vary his situations and his pleasures effaces today the impression he made the day before. He is nothing in men's minds, but he enjoys himself, for he devotes himself entirely to each hour and to each thing he does. This would be my only constant practice. In each situation I would be occupied with no other, and I would take each day by itself as though it were independent of the day before and the day after. Just as I would be one of the people when I am among the people, I would be a rustic when I am in the country. And when I spoke of agriculture, the peasants would not make fun of me. I would not build myself a city in the country and set up the Tuileries at my doorstep deep in the provinces. I would have a little rustic house—a white house with green shutters—on the slope of some agreeable, well-shaded hill. Although a thatch roof would be the best in every season, I would grandly prefer not gloomy slate but tile, because it makes a cleaner and gayer impression than thatch and because that is how the houses are roofed in my country—it would remind me a little of the happy time of my youth. Instead of a courtyard, I would have a farmyard, and instead of a stable, a shed full of cows, so that I would have the dairy products I like so much. For my garden I would have a vegetable patch, and for my park, a pretty orchard similar to the one which will be spoken about hereafter. The fruits would be freely available to strollers and would neither be counted nor gathered by my gardener; my avaricious magnificence would not display to the eyes stately espaliers which one would hardly dare to touch. This petty prodigality would not be very costly, because I would have chosen my haven in some distant province where one sees little money and many commodities, and where abundance and poverty reign.

There I would gather a society that was select rather than large, composed of friends who love pleasure and know something about it, and of women who are able to leave their easy chairs and take part in pastoral games—women who will sometimes take up, instead of the shuttle and cards, fishing lines, bird snares, the haymaker's rake, and the harvester's basket. There all the fashions of the city would be forgotten; and, becoming villagers in the village, we would surrender ourselves to throngs of diverse entertainments; our only difficulty each evening would be which entertainment to choose for the next day.

* Two women of the world, in order to give the impression of enjoying themselves very much, make it a law for themselves never to go to bed before five in the morning. Amidst the rigor of winter their servants spend the night in the street waiting for them, at a loss about how to prevent themselves from freezing. One evening or, to put it better, one morning, someone enters the apartment where these two persons who have such a good time let the hours flow by without counting them. He finds them entirely alone, each asleep in her easy chair.

Exercise and the active life would provide us with new digestions and new tastes. All our meals would be feasts where abundance would please more than delicacy. Gaiety, rustic labors, and frolicsome games are the premier chefs of the world, and delicate ragouts are quite ridiculous to people who have been breathless since sunrise. The serving would be neither orderly nor elegant. The dining room would be everywhere—in the garden, in a boat, under a tree, or sometimes near a distant spring, on the cool, green grass, beneath clumps of elder and hazel. A long procession of merry guests would sing while carrying the preparations for the feast. We would have the lawn for our table and chairs; the ledges of the fountain would serve as our buffet table; and the dessert would hang from the trees. The dishes would be served without order; appetite would dispense with ceremony. Each of us, openly preferring himself to everyone else, would find it good that all the others similarly preferred themselves to him. From this cordial and moderate familiarity there would arise—without coarseness, without falseness, and without constraint—a playful conflict a hundred times more charming than politeness and more likely to bind together our hearts. There would be no importunate lackeys spying on our conversation, whispering criticisms of our demeanor, counting our helpings with a greedy eye, or enjoying themselves by making us wait for our drinks and muttering about our taking too long at dinner. We would be our own valets in order to be our own masters; each of us would be served by all the others; the time would pass without being measured. The repast would be our repose and would last as long as the heat of the day. If some peasant returning to work with his tools on his shoulder passed near us, I would gladden his heart with some good talk and a drink of good wine, which would make him bear his poverty more gaily; and I would also have the pleasure of feeling deep in my vitals an emotion of sympathy, secretly saying to myself, "I am still a man."

If some country celebration brought the inhabitants of the place together, my companions and I would be among the first ones there. If some country marriages—more blessed by heaven than city ones—took place in my neighborhood, it would be known that I like joy, and I would be invited. I would bring these good people some gifts as simple as they are, which would contribute to the celebration, and I would find in exchange goods of an inestimable value, goods so little known to my equals—frankness and true pleasure. I would sup gaily at the end of their long table. I would join in the refrain of an old rustic song, and I would dance in their barn more gladly than at the opera ball.

"Up to this point everything is marvelous," I will be told, "but what about the hunt? Is one really in the country if one does not hunt?" I understand. I only wanted a little farm, and I was wrong. I assume that I am rich; therefore I must have exclusive pleasures, destructive pleasures. This is an entirely different affair. I need lands, woods, guards, rents, seignorial honors, and, above all, incense and holy water.

Very well. But this land will have neighbors jealous of their rights and desirous of usurping those of others. Our guards will squabble, and so perhaps will their masters. Now there are altercations, quarrels,

hatreds, lawsuits, at the very least. Already things are no longer very agreeable. My vassals will not take pleasure in seeing their wheat ripped up by my hares and their beans ripped up by my boars. Not daring to kill the enemy who destroys his work, each will at least want to drive him from his field. After having spent the day cultivating their lands, they will have to spend the night guarding them. They will have watchdogs, drums, cornets, bells. With all this racket they will disturb my sleep. In spite of myself, I shall think of the misery of these poor people and will not be able to refrain from reproaching myself for it. If I had the honor of being a prince, all this would hardly touch me. But as I would be a parvenu who had recently become rich, I would still have a trace of a plebeian heart.

That is not all. The abundance of the game will tempt hunters. There will soon be poachers whom I shall have to punish. I shall need prisons, jailers, armed guards, galleys. All this appears rather cruel to me. The wives of these unfortunate men will come to besiege my doors and to importune me with their cries, or they will have to be driven away and maltreated. Those among the poor who have not poached and whose harvest has been foraged by my game will also come to complain. The former group will be punished for having killed the game, and the latter ruined for having spared it. What a sad choice! I shall see only examples of misery on all sides; I shall hear only groans. It seems to me that this ought greatly to disturb the pleasure of massacring at one's ease—practically under one's feet—throngs of partridges and hares.

Do you wish to disengage the pleasures from their pains? Then remove exclusiveness from the pleasures. The more you leave them to men in common, the more you will always taste them pure. Therefore I shall not do all that I just said; but, without changing tastes, I shall at less expense pursue the taste I am here supposing is mine. I shall establish my country abode in a spot where the hunt is open to everyone, and where I can have the entertainment without the bother. The game will be rarer, but there will be more skill in seeking it and more pleasure in shooting it. I remember the heartthrobs that my father experienced at the flight of the first partridge, and the transports of joy with which he found the hare he had sought all day. Yes, I maintain that my father, alone with his dog and burdened with his rifle, his game bag, his kit, and his little prey, returned in the evening—exhausted and ripped by brambles—more satisfied by his day than all your ladies' men passing as hunters who, riding a good horse and followed by twenty loaded rifles, do nothing but change rifles, shoot, and kill things around them without art, without glory, and almost without exercise. The pleasure is not any less, then, and the inconvenience is removed when one has neither land to guard nor poachers to punish nor unfortunate people to torment. Here, then, is a solid reason for preference. No matter what the situation, one does not torment men endlessly without also receiving some discomfort from it; and the continued maledictions of the people sooner or later make the game bitter.

Yet another point. Exclusive pleasures are the death of pleasure. True entertainments are those one shares with the people. Those one wants to have for oneself alone, one no longer has at all. If the walls I raise around my park make it a gloomy cloister for me, I have at great expense done nothing but deprive myself of the pleasure of walking. Now I am forced to go far away to seek it. The demon of property infects everything it touches. A rich man wants to be the master everywhere and is only well off where he is not the master; he is always forced to flee from himself. As for me, when I am rich, I shall act in this respect just as I did when I was poor. I am richer now with the property of others than I shall ever be with my own—I lay hold of all that suits me in my vicinity. There is no conqueror more determined than I am. I usurp even from princes. I make myself at home on any open pieces of land that please me. I give them names. I make one my park, another my terrace, and so I am their master. From then on, I walk about on them with impunity. I return often to maintain possession. By dint of walking on them, I use their soil as much as I want; and I shall never be persuaded that the man who holds the title to the property I appropriate draws more use from the money it yields for him than I draw from his land. And if they come to vex me with ditches and hedges, it matters little to me. I take my park on my shoulders, and I go to set it down elsewhere. Sites are not lacking in the vicinity, and I shall be pillaging my neighbors for a long time before I lack a haven.

This is a kind of essay on true taste in the choice of agreeable leisure. This is the spirit in which a person enjoys himself. All the rest is only illusion, chimera, foolish vanity. Whoever deviates from these rules, however rich he may be, will find that his gold will buy him nothing but manure and will never know the value of life.

Someone will doubtless object that such entertainments are within the reach of all men and that one does not need to be rich to enjoy them. This is precisely what I wanted to get at. One has pleasure when one wants to have it. It is only opinion that makes everything difficult and drives happiness away from us. It is a hundred times easier to be happy than to appear to be happy. The man who has taste and is truly voluptuous has nothing to do with riches. It suffices for him to be free and master of himself. Whoever enjoys health and does not lack the necessities is rich enough if he roots the goods of opinion out of his heart. It is Horace's *aurea mediocritas*.[93] So, you men with strongboxes, seek some other use for your opulence, since it is good for nothing so far as pleasure is concerned. Emile will not know all this better than I do, but since he has a purer and healthier heart, he will feel it even more keenly, and all his observations in society will only confirm it for him.

While thus passing the time, we are still in search of Sophie, and we do not find her. It was important that she not be found so quickly, and we have looked for her where I was quite sure she was not to be found.*

Finally, the moment has come. It is time to seek her in earnest, lest he find someone on his own whom he takes for her and not learn

* *Mulierum fortem quis inveniet? Procul, et de ultimis finibus pretium eius.* Proverbs 31:10.[94]

his error until it is too late. Adieu, then, Paris, celebrated city, city of noise, smoke, and mud, where the women no longer believe in honor and the men no longer believe in virtue. Adieu, Paris. We are seeking love, happiness, innocence. We shall never be far enough away from you.

End of the Fourth Book

BOOK
V

NOW we have come to the last act in the drama of youth, but we are not yet at the dénouement. It is not good for man to be alone.[1] Emile is a man. We have promised him a companion. She has to be given to him. That companion is _Sophie_. In what place is her abode? Where shall we find her? To find her, it is necessary to know her. Let us first learn what she is; then we shall better judge what places she inhabits. And even when we have found her, everything will still not have been done. "Since our young gentleman," says Locke, "is ready to marry, it is time to leave him to his beloved."[2] And with that he finishes his work. But as I do not have the honor of raising a gentleman, I shall take care not to imitate Locke on this point.

Sophie

OR THE WOMAN

Sophie ought to be a woman as Emile is a man—that is to say, she ought to have everything which suits the constitution of her species and her sex in order to fill her place in the physical and moral order. Let us begin, then, by examining the similarities and the differences of her sex and ours.

In everything not connected with sex, woman is man. She has the same organs, the same needs, the same faculties. The machine is constructed in the same way; its parts are the same; the one functions as does the other; the form is similar; and in whatever respect one considers them, the difference between them is only one of more or less.

In everything connected with sex, woman and man are in every respect related and in every respect different. The difficulty of comparing them comes from the difficulty of determining what in their constitutions is due to sex and what is not. On the basis of comparative anatomy

[357]

Is Rousseau turning around here?

and even just by inspection, one finds general differences between them that do not appear connected with sex. They are, nevertheless, connected with sex, but by relations which we are not in a position to perceive. We do not know the extent of these relations. The only thing we know with certainty is that everything man and woman have in common belongs to the species, and that everything which distinguishes them belongs to the sex. From this double perspective, we find them related in so many ways and opposed in so many other ways that it is perhaps one of the marvels of nature to have been able to construct two such similar beings who are constituted so differently.

These relations and these differences must have a moral influence. This conclusion is evident to the senses; it is in agreement with our experience; and it shows how vain are the disputes as to whether one of the two sexes is superior or whether they are equal—as though each, in fulfilling nature's ends according to its own particular purpose, were thereby less perfect than if it resembled the other more! In what they have in common, they are equal. Where they differ, they are not comparable. A perfect woman and a perfect man ought not to resemble each other in mind any more than in looks, and perfection is not susceptible of more or less.

In the union of the sexes each contributes equally to the common aim, but not in the same way. From this diversity arises the first assignable difference in the moral relations of the two sexes. One ought to be active and strong, the other passive and weak. One must necessarily will and be able; it suffices that the other put up little resistance.

Once this principle is established, it follows that woman is made specially to please man. If man ought to please her in turn, it is due to a less direct necessity. His merit is in his power; he pleases by the sole fact of his strength. This is not the law of love, I agree. But it is that of nature, prior to love itself.

If woman is made to please and to be subjugated, she ought to make herself agreeable to man instead of arousing him. Her own violence is in her charms. It is by these that she ought to constrain him to find his strength and make use of it. The surest art for animating that strength is to make it necessary by resistance. Then *amour-propre* unites with desire, and the one triumphs in the victory that the other has made him win. From this there arises attack and defense, the audacity of one sex and the timidity of the other, and finally the modesty and the shame with which nature armed the weak in order to enslave the strong.

Who could think that nature has indiscriminately prescribed the same advances to both men and women, and that the first to form desires should also be the first to show them? What a strange depravity of judgment! Since the undertaking has such different consequences for the two sexes, is it natural that they should have the same audacity in abandoning themselves to it? With so great an inequality in what each risks in the union, how can one fail to see that if reserve did not impose on one sex the moderation which nature imposes on the other, the result would soon be the ruin of both, and mankind would perish by the means established for preserving it? If there were some unfortunate region on earth where philosophy had introduced this practice —especially in hot countries, where more women are born than men— men would be tyrannized by women. For, given the ease with which women arouse men's senses and reawaken in the depths of their hearts the remains of ardors which are almost extinguished, men would finally be their victims and would see themselves dragged to death without ever being able to defend themselves.

If females among the animals do not have the same shame, what follows from that? Do they have, as women do, the unlimited desires to which this shame serves as a brake? For them, desires comes only with need. When the need is satisfied, the desire ceases. They no longer feign to repulse the male * but really do so. They do exactly the opposite of Augustus' daughter; they accept no more passengers when the ship has its cargo.[3] Even when they are free, their times of good will are short and quickly pass. Instinct impels them, and instinct stops them. What will be the substitute for this negative instinct when you have deprived women of modesty? To wait until they no longer care for men is equivalent to waiting until they are no longer good for anything.

The Supreme Being wanted to do honor to the human species in everything. While giving man inclinations without limit, He gives him at the same time the law which regulates them, in order that he may be free and in command of himself. While abandoning man to immoderate passions, He joins reason to these passions in order to govern them. While abandoning woman to unlimited desires, He joins modesty to these desires in order to constrain them. In addition, He adds yet another real recompense for the good use of one's faculties—the taste we acquire for decent things when we make them the rule of our actions. All this, it seems to me, is worth more than the instinct of beasts.

Whether the human female shares man's desires or not and wants to satisfy them or not, she repulses him and always defends herself— but not always with the same force or, consequently, with the same success. For the attacker to be victorious, the one who is attacked must permit or arrange it; for does she not have adroit means to force the aggressor to use force? The freest and sweetest of all acts does not admit of real violence. Nature and reason oppose it: nature, in that it has provided the weaker with as much strength as is needed to resist when it pleases her; reason, in that real rape is not only the most brutal of all acts but the one most contrary to its end—either because the man thus declares war on his companion and authorizes her to defend her person and her liberty even at the expense of the agressor's life, or because the woman alone is the judge of the condition she is in, and a child would have no father if every man could usurp the father's rights.

Here, then, is a third conclusion drawn from the constitution of the

---

* I have already noticed that affected and provocative refusals are common to almost all females, even among animals, even when they are most disposed to give themselves. One has to have never observed their wiles not to agree with this.

sexes—that <u>the stronger appears to be master but actually depends on the weaker.</u> This is due not to a frivolous practice of gallantry or to the proud generosity of a protector, but to an invariable law of nature which gives woman more facility to excite the desires than man to satisfy them. This causes the latter, whether he likes it or not, to depend on the former's wish and constrains him to seek to please her in turn, so that she will consent to let him be the stronger. Then what is sweetest for man in his victory is the doubt whether it is weakness which yields to strength or the will which surrenders. And the woman's usual ruse is always to leave this doubt between her and him. In this the spirit of women corresponds perfectly to their constitution. Far from blushing at their weakness, they make it their glory. Their tender muscles are without resistance. They pretend to be unable to lift the lightest burdens. They would be ashamed to be strong. Why is that? It is not only to appear delicate; it is due to a shrewder precaution. They prepare in advance excuses and the right to be weak in case of need.

The progress of the enlightenment acquired as a result of our vices has greatly changed the old opinions on this point among us. Rapes are hardly ever spoken of anymore, since they are so little necessary and men no longer believe in them.* By contrast, they are very common in early Greek and Jewish antiquity, because those old opinions belong to the simplicity of nature, and only the experience of libertinism has been able to uproot them. If fewer acts of rape are cited in our day, this is surely not because men are more temperate but because they are less credulous, and such a complaint, which previously would have persuaded simple peoples, in our days would succeed only in attracting the laughter of mockers. It is more advantageous to keep quiet. In Deuteronomy there is a law by which a girl who had been abused was punished along with her seducer if the offense had been committed in the city. But if it had been committed in the country or in an isolated place, the man alone was punished: "For," the law says, "the girl cried out and was not heard." [4] This benign interpretation taught the girls not to let themselves be surprised in well-frequented places.

The effect of these differences of opinion about morals is evident. Modern gallantry is their work. Finding that their pleasures depended more on the will of the fair sex than they had believed, men have captivated that will by attentions for which the fair sex has amply compensated them.

Observe how the physical leads us unawares to the moral, and how the sweetest laws of love are born little by little from the coarse union of the sexes. Women possess their empire not because men wanted it that way, but because nature wants it that way. It belonged to women before they appeared to have it. The same Hercules who believed he raped the fifty daughters of Thespitius was nevertheless constrained

---

* There can be such a disproportion of age and strength that real rape takes place; but treating here the relation between the sexes according to the order of nature, I take them both as they ordinarily are in that relation.

to weave while he was with Omphale; and the strong Samson was not so strong as Delilah.[5] This empire belongs to women and cannot be taken from them, even when they abuse it. If they could ever lose it, they would have done so long ago.

There is no parity between the two sexes in regard to the consequences of sex. The male is male only at certain moments. The female is female her whole life or at least during her whole youth. Everything constantly recalls her sex to her; and, to fulfill its functions well, she needs a constitution which corresponds to it. She needs care during her pregnancy; she needs rest at the time of childbirth; she needs a soft and sedentary life to suckle her children; she needs patience and gentleness, a zeal and an affection that nothing can rebuff in order to raise her children. She serves as the link between them and their father; she alone makes him love them and gives him the confidence to call them his own. How much tenderness and care is required to maintain the union of the whole family! And, finally, all this must come not from virtues but from tastes, or else the human species would soon be extinguished.

The strictness of the relative duties of the two sexes is not and cannot be the same. When woman complains on this score about unjust man-made inequality, she is wrong. This inequality is not a human institution—or, at least, it is the work not of prejudice but of reason. It is up to the sex that nature has charged with the bearing of children to be responsible for them to the other sex. Doubtless it is not permitted to anyone to violate his faith, and every unfaithful husband who deprives his wife of the only reward of the austere duties of her sex is an unjust and barbarous man. But the unfaithful woman does more; she dissolves the family and breaks all the bonds of nature. In giving the man children which are not his, she betrays both. She joins perfidy to infidelity. I have difficulty seeing what disorders and what crimes do not flow from this one. If there is a frightful condition in the world, it is that of an unhappy father who, lacking confidence in his wife, does not dare to yield to the sweetest sentiments of his heart, who wonders, in embracing his child, whether he is embracing another's, the token of his dishonor, the plunderer of his own children's property. What does the family become in such a situation if not a society of secret enemies whom a guilty woman arms against one another in forcing them to feign mutual love?

It is important, then, not only that a woman be faithful, but that she be judged to be faithful by her husband, by those near her, by everyone. It is important that she be modest, attentive, reserved, and that she give evidence of her virtue to the eyes of others as well as to her own conscience. If it is important that a father love his children, it is important that he esteem their mother. These are the reasons which put even appearances among the duties of women, and make honor and reputation no less indispensable to them than chastity. There follows from these principles, along with the moral difference of the sexes, a new motive of duty and propriety which prescribes especially to women the most scrupulous attention to their conduct, their manners, and their bearing. To maintain vaguely that the two sexes are equal and that their duties are the same, is to lose oneself in vain declaiming; it is to say nothing so long as one does not respond to these considerations.

Is it not a sound way of reasoning to present exceptions in response to such well-grounded general laws? Women, you say, do not always produce children? No, but their proper purpose is to produce them. What! Because there are a hundred big cities in the universe where women living in license produce few children, you claim that it is proper to woman's status to produce few children! And what would become of your cities if women living more simply and more chastely far away in the country did not make up for the sterility of the city ladies? In how many provinces are women who have only produced four or five children taken to be infecund! * Finally, what does it matter that this or that woman produces few children? Is woman's status any less that of motherhood, and is it not by general laws that nature and morals ought to provide for this status?

Even if there were intervals as long as one supposes between pregnancies, will a woman abruptly and regularly change her way of life without peril and risk? Will she be nurse today and warrior tomorrow? Will she change temperament and tastes as a chameleon does colors? Will she suddenly go from shade, enclosure, and domestic cares to the harshness of the open air, the labors, the fatigues, and the perils of war? Will she be fearful † at one moment and brave at another, delicate at one moment and robust at another? If young people raised in Paris have difficulty enduring the profession of arms, will women, who have never endured the sun and hardly know how to walk, endure it after fifty years of softness? Will they take up this harsh profession at the age when men leave it?

There are countries where women give birth almost without pain and nurse their children almost without effort. I admit it. But in these same countries the men go half naked at all times, vanquish ferocious beasts, carry a canoe like a knapsack, pursue the hunt for up to seven or eight hundred leagues, sleep in the open air on the ground, bear unbelievable fatigues, and go several days without eating. When women become robust, men become still more so. When men get soft, women get even softer. When the two change equally, the difference remains the same.

In his *Republic*, Plato gives women the same exercises as men.[6] I can well believe it! Having removed private families from his regime and no longer knowing what to do with women, he found himself forced to make them men. That noble genius had planned everything, foreseen everything. He was forestalling an objection that perhaps no one would have thought of making to him, but he provided a poor solution to the one which is made to him. I am not speaking of that alleged

* Without that, the species would necessarily fade away. In order for it to be preserved, every woman must, everything considered, produce nearly four children; for nearly half of the children who are born die before they can have others, and the two remaining ones are needed to represent the father and the mother. See if the cities will provide you with this population.

† The timidity of women is another instinct of nature against the double risk they run during their pregnancy.

Rousseau would, of course, recalculate this based on current mortality/population rates

Plato had no family effections. Purpose is different

community of women; the often repeated reproach on this point proves that those who make it against him have never read him. I am speaking of that civil promiscuity which throughout confounds the two sexes in the same employments and in the same labors and which cannot fail to engender the most intolerable abuses. I speak of that subversion of the sweetest sentiments of nature, sacrificed to an artificial sentiment which can only be maintained by them—as though there were no need for a natural base on which to form conventional ties; as though the love of one's nearest were not the principle of the love one owes the state; as though it were not by means of the small fatherland which is the family that the heart attaches itself to the large one; as though it were not the good son, the good husband, and the good father who make the good citizen!

Once it is demonstrated that man and woman are not and ought not to be constituted in the same way in either character or temperament, it follows that they ought not to have the same education. In following nature's directions, man and woman ought to act in concert, but they ought not to do the same things. The goal of their labors is common, but their labors themselves are different, and consequently so are the tastes directing them. After having tried to form the natural man, let us also see how the woman who suits this man ought to be formed so that our work will not be left imperfect.

Do you wish always to be well guided? Then always follow nature's indications. Everything that characterizes the fair sex ought to be respected as established by nature. You constantly say, "Women have this or that failing which we do not have." Your pride deceives you. They would be failings for you; they are their good qualities. Everything would go less well if they did not have these qualities. Prevent these alleged failings from degenerating, but take care not to destroy them.

For their part, women do not cease to proclaim that we raise them to be vain and coquettish, that we constantly entertain them with puerilities in order to remain more easily their masters. They blame on us the failings for which we reproach them. What folly! And since when is it that men get involved in the education of girls? Who prevents their mothers from raising them as they please? They have no colleges. What a great misfortune! Would God that there were none for boys; they would be more sensibly and decently raised! Are your daughters forced to waste their time in silliness? Are they made in spite of themselves to spend half their lives getting dressed up, following the example you set them? Are you prevented from instructing them and having them instructed as you please? Is it our fault that they please us when they are pretty, that their mincing ways seduce us, that the art which they learn from you attracts us and pleases us, that we like to see them tastefully dressed, that we let them sharpen at their leisure the weapons with which they subjugate us? So, decide to raise them like men. The men will gladly consent to it! The more women want to resemble them, the less women will govern them, and then men will truly be the masters.

All the faculties common to the two sexes are not equally distributed between them; but taken together, they balance out. Woman is worth more as woman and less as man. Wherever she makes use of her rights, she has the advantage. Wherever she wants to usurp ours, she remains beneath us. One can respond to this general truth only with exceptions, the constant mode of argument of the gallant partisans of the fair sex.

To cultivate man's qualities in women and to neglect those which are proper to them is obviously to work to their detriment. Crafty women see this too well to be duped by it. In trying to usurp our advantages, they do not abandon theirs. But it turns out that they are unable to manage both well—because the two are incompatible—and they remain beneath their own level without getting up to ours, thus losing half their value. Believe me, judicious mother, do not make a decent man of your daughter, as though you would give nature the lie.[7] Make a decent woman of her, and be sure that as a result she will be worth more for herself and for us.

Does it follow that she ought to be raised in ignorance of everything and limited to the housekeeping functions alone? Will man turn his companion into his servant? Will he deprive himself of the greatest charm of society with her? In order to make her more subject, will he prevent her from feeling anything, from knowing anything? Will he make her into a veritable automaton? Surely not. It is not thus that nature has spoken in giving women such agreeable and nimble minds. On the contrary, nature wants them to think, to judge, to love, to know, to cultivate their minds as well as their looks. These are the weapons nature gives them to take the place of the strength they lack and to direct ours. They ought to learn many things but only those that are suitable for them to know.

Whether I consider the particular purpose of the fair sex, whether I observe its inclinations, whether I consider its duties, all join equally in indicating to me the form of education that suits it. Woman and man are made for one another, but their mutual dependence is not equal. Men depend on women because of their desires; women depend on men because of both their desires and their needs. We would survive more easily without them than they would without us. For them to have what is necessary to their station, they depend on us to give it to them, to want to give it to them, to esteem them worthy of it. They depend on our sentiments, on the value we set on their merit, on the importance we attach to their charms and their virtues. By the very law of nature women are at the mercy of men's judgments, as much for their own sake as for that of their children. It is not enough that they be estimable; they must be esteemed. It is not enough for them to be pretty; they must please. It is not enough for them to be temperate; they must be recognized as such. Their honor is not only in their conduct but in their reputation; and it is not possible that a woman who consents to be regarded as disreputable can ever be decent. When a man acts well, he depends only on himself and can brave public judgment; but when a woman acts well, she has accomplished only half of her task, and what is thought of her is no less important to her than what she actually is. From this it follows that the system of woman's education ought to be contrary in this respect to the system of our education. Opinion is the grave of virtue among men and its throne among women.

The good constitution of children initially depends on that of their mothers. The first education of men depends on the care of women. Men's morals, their passions, their tastes, their pleasures, their very happiness also depend on women. Thus the whole education of women ought to relate to men. To please men, to be useful to them, to make herself loved and honored by them, to raise them when young, to care for them when grown, to counsel them, to console them, to make their lives agreeable and sweet—these are the duties of women at all times, and they ought to be taught from childhood. So long as one does not return to this principle, one will deviate from the goal, and all the precepts taught to women will be of no use for their happiness or for ours.

But although every woman wants to please men and should want to, there is quite a difference between wanting to please the man of merit, the truly lovable man, and wanting to please those little flatterers who dishonor both their own sex and the one they imitate. Neither nature nor reason can bring a woman to love in men what resembles herself; nor is it by adopting their ways that she ought to seek to make herself loved.

When women leave the modest and composed tone of their sex and adopt the airs of these giddy fellows, far from following their own vocation, they renounce it and divest themselves of the rights they think they are usurping. "If we acted differently," they say, "we would not please men." They lie. One has to be foolish to love fools. The desire to attract these people reveals the taste of the woman who indulges it. If there were no frivolous men, she would be eager to produce some; and she is much more responsible for their frivolities than they are for hers. The woman who loves true men and who wants to please them employs means appropriate to her intention. To be a woman means to be coquettish, but her coquetry changes its form and its object according to her views. Let us regulate her views according to those of nature, and woman will have the education which suits her.

Little girls love adornment almost from birth. Not satisfied with being pretty, they want people to think that they are pretty. One sees in their little airs that this concern preoccupies them already; and when they are hardly in a condition to understand what is said to them, they can already be governed by speaking to them of what will be thought of them. When the same motive is—very inappropriately— suggested to little boys, it by no means has a similar empire over them. Provided that they are independent and that they have pleasure, they care little what might be thought of them. It is only by dint of time and effort that they are subjected to the same law.

From whatever source this first lesson comes to girls, it is a very good one. Since the body is born, so to speak, before the soul, the body ought to be cultivated first. This order is common to the two sexes, but the aim of this cultivation is different. For man this aim is the development of strength; for woman it is the development of attractiveness. Not that these qualities ought to exclude one another; their rank order is merely reversed in each sex: women need enough strength to do everything they do with grace; men need enough adroitness to do everything they do with facility.

Extreme softness on the part of women leads to softness in men. Women ought not to be robust *like* men, but they should be robust *for* men, so that the men born from them will be robust too. In this respect convents, where the boarders have coarse food but many sports, races, and games outdoors in gardens, are to be preferred to the paternal household, where a girl—delicately fed, always pampered or scolded, always seated within range of her mother's eyes, shut up in a room— does not dare stand up, walk, speak, or breathe, and does not have a moment of freedom to play, jump, run, shout, or indulge in the petulance natural to her age. It is always a case of either dangerous slackness or ill-conceived severity—never anything according to reason. This is how the body and the heart of youth are ruined.

The girls of Sparta exercised in military games like the boys—not to go to war but one day to bear children capable of withstanding war's fatigues.[8] That is not what I recommend. It is not necessary for mothers to have carried the musket and done the Prussian drill in order for them to provide soldiers to the state. But I do find that in general this part of Greek education was very well conceived. The young girls appeared often in public, not mixed in with the boys but gathered together among themselves. There was hardly a festival, a sacrifice, or a ceremony where groups of daughters of the first citizens were not seen crowned with flowers, chanting hymns, forming dancing companies, bearing baskets, vases, and offerings, and presenting to the depraved senses of the Greeks a charming spectacle fit to counterbalance the bad effect of their indecent gymnastic. Whatever impression this practice made on men's hearts, it was still an excellent way of giving the fair sex a good constitution in youth by means of agreeable, moderate, and salutary exercises. It sharpened and formed the girls' taste by means of the continual desire to please and did so without ever endangering their morals.

As soon as these young persons were married, they were no longer seen in public. Shut up in their houses, they limited all their cares to their households and their families. Such is the way of life that nature and reason prescribe for the fair sex. From these mothers were born the healthiest, the most robust, the most well-built men in the world. And in spite of the ill repute of some islands, it is an unchanging fact that of all the peoples of the world—without excepting even the Romans— none is cited where the women were both purer and more lovable, and where they better combined morals with beauty than in ancient Greece.

It is known that comfortable clothing which did not hinder the body contributed a great deal to leaving both sexes among the Greeks with those beautiful proportions seen in their statues—statues which still serve as models for art today, when disfigured nature has ceased furnishing art with models among us. They had not a single one of all these gothic shackles, these multitudes of ligatures which squeeze our bodies on all sides. Their women were ignorant of the use of these whalebone corsets with which our women counterfeit their waists rather than display them. I cannot believe that this abuse, pushed to an inconceivable extent in England, will not finally cause the species to degenerate, and I even maintain that the attraction that it offers is in bad taste. It is not attractive to see a woman cut in half like a wasp. That is shocking to the sight, and it makes the imagination suffer. The narrowness of the waist has, like everything else, its proportions, its limit, beyond which it is certainly a defect. This defect would even be an assault on the eye when seen naked. Why should it be a beautiful thing under clothing?

I dare not pursue the reasons why women are obstinate about thus putting themselves in armor: a drooping bosom, a fat stomach, etc. This is most displeasing, I agree, in a twenty-year-old, but it is no longer shocking at thirty. And since we must, in spite of ourselves, at all times be what nature pleases, and since man's eye is not deceived, these defects are less displeasing at all ages than the foolish affectation of a little girl of forty.

Everything that hinders and constrains nature is in bad taste. This is as true of the adornments of the body as it is of the ornaments of the mind. Life, health, reason, and well-being ought to go ahead of everything. Grace does not exist without comfort. Delicacy is not sickliness, and it is not requisite to be unhealthy in order to please. One arouses pity when one suffers, but pleasure and desire seek the freshness of health.

The children of both sexes have many common entertainments, and that ought to be so. Is this not also the case when they are grown up? They also have particular tastes which distinguish them. Boys seek movement and noise: drums, boots, little carriages. Girls prefer what presents itself to sight and is useful for ornamentation: mirrors, jewels, dresses, particularly dolls. The doll is the special entertainment of this sex. This is evidently its taste, determined by its purpose. The physical part of the art of pleasing lies in adornment. This is the only part of that art that children can cultivate.

Observe a little girl spending the day around her doll, constantly changing its clothes, dressing and undressing it hundreds and hundreds of times, continuously seeking new combinations of ornaments—well- or ill-matched, it makes no difference. Her fingers lack adroitness, her taste is not yet formed, but already the inclination reveals itself. In this eternal occupation time flows without her thinking of it; the hours pass, and she knows nothing of it. She even forgets meals. She is hungrier for adornment than for food. But, you will say, she adorns her doll and not her person. Doubtless. She sees her doll and does not see herself. She can do nothing for herself. She is not yet formed; she has neither talent nor strength; she is still nothing. She is entirely in her doll, and she puts all her coquetry into it. She will not always leave it there. She awaits the moment when she will be her own doll.

This is a very definite primary taste. You have only to follow and regulate it. It is certain that the little girl would want with all her heart to know how to adorn her doll, to make its bracelets, its scarf, its flounce, its lace. For all of this she is put in such a harsh dependence on the good will of others that it would be far more convenient for her to owe everything to her own industry. In this way there emerges the reason for the first lessons she is given. They are not tasks prescribed to her, they are kindnesses done for her. In fact, almost all little girls learn to read and write with repugnance. But as for holding a needle, that they always learn gladly. They imagine themselves to be grown up and think with pleasure that these talents will one day be useful for adorning themselves.

Once this first path is opened, it is easy to follow. Sewing, embroidery, and lacemaking come by themselves. Tapestry is not so much to their taste. Furniture is too far from them: it is not connected to the person; it is connected with other sets of opinions. Tapestry is the entertainment of women; young girls will never take a very great pleasure in it.

This voluntary progress is easily extended to drawing, for this art is not without importance for the art of dressing oneself up tastefully. But I would not want them to apply themselves to landscapes, still less to figures. Leaves, fruits, flowers, draperies, everything which is useful for giving an elegant turn to clothing and for making an embroidery pattern for oneself when one does not find any to one's taste—that is enough for them. In general, if it is important for men to limit their studies to useful knowledge, it is even more important for women, because the latter's lives, although less laborious, are—or ought to be—more attached to their cares and more interrupted by various cares. Thus their lives do not permit them to indulge themselves in any preferred talent to the prejudice of their duties.

Whatever humorists may say, good sense belongs equally to the two sexes. Girls are generally more docile than boys, and one should even use more authority with them, as I shall say a little later. But it does not follow that anything ought to be demanded from them whose utility they cannot see. The art of mothers is to show them the utility of everything they prescribe to them, and that is all the easier since intelligence is more precocious in girls than in boys. This rule banishes —for their sex as well as for ours—not only idle studies which lead to no good and do not even make those who have pursued them more attractive to others, but even those which are not useful at their age and whose usefulness for a more advanced age the child cannot foresee. If I do not want to push a boy to learn to read, a fortiori I do not want to force girls to before making them well aware of what the use of reading is. In the way this utility is ordinarily showed to them, we follow our own idea far more than theirs. After all, where is the necessity for a girl to know how to read and write so early? Will she so soon have a household to govern? There are very few girls who do not abuse this fatal science more than they make good use of it. And all of them have too much curiosity not to learn it—without our forcing them to do so—when they have the leisure and the occasion. Perhaps they ought to learn to do arithmetic before anything, for nothing presents a more palpable utility at all times, requires longer practice, and is so exposed to error as calculation. If the little girl were to get cherries for her snack only by doing an arithmetical operation, I assure you that she would soon know how to calculate.

BOOK V

I know a young person who learned to write before learning to read, and who began to write with the needle before writing with the quill. Of all the letters, she first wanted only to make O's. She incessantly made big and little O's, O's of all sizes, O's inside one another, and always drawn backward. Unfortunately, one day when she was busy with this useful exercise, she saw herself in a mirror; and finding that this constrained attitude was not graceful for her, like another Minerva [9] she threw away the pen and no longer wanted to make O's. Her brother did not like to write any more than she did, but what irritated him was the discomfort and not the appearance it gave him. Another tack was taken to bring her back to writing. The little girl was refined and vain. She did not stand for her linen being used by her sisters. Others marked it for her; they no longer wanted to mark it. She had to learn how to mark it herself. The rest of her progress can easily be conceived.

Always justify the cares that you impose on young girls, but always impose cares on them. Idleness and disobedience are the two most dangerous defects for them and the ones least easily cured once contracted. Girls ought to be vigilant and industrious. That is not all. They ought to be constrained very early. This misfortune, if it is one for them, is inseparable from their sex, and they are never delivered from it without suffering far more cruel misfortunes. All their lives they will be enslaved to the most continual and most severe of constraints—that of the proprieties. They must first be exercised in constraint, so that it never costs them anything to tame all their caprices in order to submit them to the wills of others. If they always wanted to work, one would sometimes have to force them to do nothing. Dissipation, frivolity, and inconstancy are defects that easily arise from the corruption and continued indulgence of their first tastes. To prevent this abuse, teach them above all to conquer themselves. Amidst our senseless arrangements a decent woman's life is a perpetual combat against herself. It is just that this sex share the pain of the evils it has caused us.

Prevent girls from being bored by their work and enthusiastic about their entertainment, as is always the case in vulgar educations where, as Fénelon says, all the boredom is put on one side and all the pleasure on the other. [10] If one follows the preceding rules, the first of these two difficulties will arise only when the persons with them are displeasing to them. A little girl who loves her mother or her lady friend will work at her side all day without boredom. Chatter alone will compensate her for all her constraint. But if she finds the woman who governs her unbearable, she will develop the same distaste for everything she does under that woman's eyes. It is very difficult for girls who do not enjoy themselves more with their mothers than with anyone else in the world to turn out well one day. But to judge their true sentiments, one must study them and not trust what they say, for they are flatterers and dissimulators, and they quickly learn to disguise themselves. Neither ought one to prescribe that they love their mother. Affection does not come from duty, and constraint is of no use here. Attachment, care, and mere habit make the mother loved by her daughter, if she does nothing to make herself hated. Even the constraint in which she keeps her daughter, if it is well directed, will, far from weakening this attachment, only increase it; for dependence is a condition natural to women, and thus girls feel themselves made to obey.

For the same reason that they have—or ought to have—little freedom, they tend to excess in the freedom that is left to them. Extreme in everything, they indulge themselves in their games with even more intensity than boys do. This is the second difficulty of which I was just speaking. This intensity ought to be moderated, for it is the cause of several vices peculiar to women, such as, among others, the capriciousness and infatuation which cause a woman to be in transports today for some object she will not look at tomorrow. Inconstancy of tastes is as deadly for them as is excess, and both come from the same source. Do not deprive them of gaiety, laughter, noise, and frolicsome games, but prevent them from getting their fill of one in order to run to another; do not allow for a single instant in their lives that they no longer know any restraint. Accustom them to being interrupted in the midst of their games and brought back to other cares without grumbling. Habit alone suffices in this as well, because it does nothing other than to reinforce nature.

From this habitual constraint comes a docility which women need all their lives, since they never cease to be subjected either to a man or to the judgments of men and they are never permitted to put themselves above these judgments. The first and most important quality of a woman is gentleness. As she is made to obey a being who is so imperfect, often so full of vices, and always so full of defects as man, she ought to learn early to endure even injustice and to bear a husband's wrongs without complaining. It is not for his sake, it is for her own, that she ought to be gentle. The bitterness and the stubbornness of women never do anything but increase their ills and the bad behavior of their husbands. Men feel that it is not with these weapons that women ought to conquer them. Heaven did not make women ingratiating and persuasive in order that they become shrewish. It did not make them weak in order that they be imperious. It did not give them so gentle a voice in order that they utter insults. It did not give them such delicate features to be disfigured by anger. When they get upset, they forget themselves. They are often right to complain, but they are always wrong to scold. Each sex ought to keep to its own tone. A husband who is too gentle can make a woman impertinent; but unless a man is a monster, the gentleness of a woman brings him around and triumphs over him sooner or later.

Let girls always be subjected, but let mothers not always be inexorable. To make a young person docile, one must not make her unhappy; to make her modest, one must not brutalize her. On the contrary, I would not be upset if she were allowed to use a little cleverness, not to elude punishment for disobedience but to get herself exempted from obeying. It is not a question of making her dependence painful for her; it suffices to make her feel it. Guile is a natural talent with the fair sex, and since I am persuaded that all the natural inclinations are good and right in themselves, I am of the opinion that this one should be cultivated like the others. The only issue is preventing its abuse.

BOOK V

As to the truth of this remark, I rely on every observer of good faith. I do not want women themselves to be examined on this point. Our constraining institutions may have forced them to sharpen their wits. I want girls to be examined—little girls who are, so to speak, just born—and I want them to be compared with little boys of the same age; and if the latter do not appear heavy, giddy, and stupid next to the girls, I shall be incontestably wrong. Permit me a single example taken in all its puerile naïveté.

It is very common to forbid children to ask for anything at meals; for it is believed that their education is never more successful than when it is overburdened with useless precepts—as though a morsel of this or that could not be speedily granted or refused * without making a poor child constantly die of covetousness whetted by hope. Everybody knows the skill of a young boy subjected to this law who had been forgotten at a meal and took it into his head to ask for salt, etc. I shall not say that one could quibble with him for having directly asked for salt and indirectly for meat. The omission was so cruel that, if he had openly infringed the law and straightforwardly said that he was hungry, I cannot believe that he would have been punished for it. But here is how a six-year-old girl went about solving such a problem in my presence. The case was much more difficult. Not only was she strictly forbidden ever to ask for anything either directly or indirectly, but since she had eaten some of all the dishes—except one which they had forgotten to give her and which she coveted very much—disobedience would not have been pardonable.

Now, in order to obtain redress for this oversight without anyone being able to accuse her of disobedience, she stuck out her finger and passed all the dishes in review, saying aloud as she pointed to them, "I have eaten some of that one; I have eaten some of that one." But she made so visible a display of silently passing over the one of which she had not eaten that someone noticed it and said to her, "Didn't you eat some of that one?" "Oh, no," replied the little glutton, sweetly lowering her eyes. I shall add nothing. Compare. This trick is the ruse of a girl; the other is the ruse of a boy.

What is, is good, and no general law is bad. This peculiar cleverness given to the fair sex is a very equitable compensation for their lesser share of strength, a compensation without which women would be not man's companion but his slave. It is by means of this superiority in talent that she keeps herself his equal and that she governs him while obeying him. Woman has everything against her—our defects, her timidity, and her weakness. She has in her favor only her art and her beauty. Is it not just that she cultivate both? But beauty is not general; it is destroyed by countless accidents; it passes with the years; habit destroys its effect. Wit alone is the true resource of the fair sex—not that stupid wit which the social world values so highly and which is of no use for making women's lives happy, but the wit which suits their position and consists in an art of exploiting man's position and putting

* A child becomes importunate when he finds that it is to his advantage to be so. But he will never ask for the same thing twice if the first response is always irrevocable.

our peculiar advantages to their use. We do not recognize how useful
this feminine cleverness is to us, how much charm it adds to the society
of the two sexes, how much it serves to repress the petulance of children,
how many brutal husbands it restrains, how many good households it
maintains which would be troubled by discord without it. I know that
crafty and wicked women abuse it. But what does vice not abuse?
Let us not destroy the instruments of happiness because the wicked
sometimes use them to do harm.

One can shine by means of adornment, but one can please only by
means of one's person. We are not our clothes. Often they detract from
us by their elaborateness. The clothes that make the woman who wears
them most noticed are often those that are least noticed in themselves.
On this point the education of young girls is completely mistaken. They
are promised ornaments as a reward and are taught to like elaborate
finery. "How beautiful she is!" we say to them when they are heavily
adorned. We ought, on the contrary, to make them understand that so
much clothing is put on only to hide some defects and that the true
triumph of beauty is to shine by itself. The love of fashions is in bad
taste because our visages do not change with them; and since one's
looks stay the same, what suits them once, suits them always.

If I saw the young girl strutting in her finery, I would appear anxious
about her looks being disguised in this way and about what someone
might think about it. I would say, "All these ornaments adorn her too
much. That's too bad. Do you believe that she could get by with simpler ones? Is she beautiful enough to do without this one or that one?"
Perhaps she will then be the first to beg that this ornament be taken
from her, and that she then be judged. This is the case in which she
should be applauded, if there are grounds for it. I would never praise
her so much as when she is most simply dressed. When she regards
adornment only as a supplement to the graces of her person and as a
tacit avowal that she needs help in order to please, she will not be
proud of her clothes, she will be humble about them. And if, when she
is more adorned than usual, she hears someone say, "How beautiful she
is!" she will blush with chagrin.

Moreover, some people have looks that need adornment, but none
requires rich finery. Costly adornments come from the vanity of rank
and not from vanity about one's person; they depend solely on prejudice.
True coquetry is sometimes elaborate, but it is never showy; and Juno
dressed herself up more superbly than Venus did.[11] "Unable to make
her beautiful, you made her rich," said Appelles to a bad painter who
painted Helen heavily loaded with finery.[12] I have also noticed that
the most sumptuous adornment usually marks ugly women. There could
not be a more maladroit kind of vanity. Give some ribbons, gauze,
muslin, and flowers to a tasteful young girl who despises fashion. Without diamonds, tassels, or lace * she is going to produce for herself an

* Women who have skin white enough to do without lace would cause a great
deal of chagrin to the others if they were not to wear it. It is almost always ugly
persons who lead the fashions to which the beautiful ones are so stupid as to
subject themselves.

outfit that will make her a hundred times more charming than all the brilliant rags of La Duchapt would.[13]

Since what is good is always good, and one must always do the best one can, women who know something about styles choose good ones and stick to them; and since they are not changing them every day, they are less involved with them than are those who do not know what to choose. True care for adornment requires little time at the dressing table. Young misses rarely indulge in the ceremony of the dressing table; [14] work and lessons fill their day. Nevertheless they are in general made up—with the exception of rouge—with as much care as fashionable ladies, and often in better taste. The abuse of the dressing table is not what one thinks; it comes far more from boredom than from vanity. A woman who spends six hours at her dressing table is not unaware that she does not go out better made up than a woman who only spends half an hour at it, but those hours are subtracted from the tedious march of time; and it is better to be entertained with oneself than to be bored with everything. Without the dressing table what could one do with life from noon to nine o'clock? By gathering around themselves other women to irritate, they can entertain themselves. That is already something. They avoid being alone with a husband whom they see only at this hour. That is much more. And then come the merchants, the salesmen, the fops, the scribblers, the poems, the songs, the pamphlets. Without the dressing table all this could not be so conveniently assembled. The only real profit connected with the thing is the pretext that it gives them for showing off a bit more of themselves than when they are dressed. But this profit is perhaps not as great as is thought, and women at their dressing table do not gain by it as much as they would like to say. Do not scruple to give women a woman's education; see to it that they like the cares of their sex, that they are modest, that they know how to watch over their households and busy themselves in their homes. The dressing table ceremonial will disappear by itself, and they will consequently be dressed in better taste.

The first thing that young persons notice in growing up is that all these external attractions are not sufficient for them if they have none of their own. A girl can never give herself beauty, and she is not all that soon in a condition to acquire the art of coquetry. But she can already seek to give an attractive turn to her gestures and a flattering accent to her voice, to gain composure in her bearing, to walk lightly, to assume gracious attitudes, and to choose situations where she looks her best. The voice's range increases, it gets stronger and gains timbre; the arms develop; the step becomes sure; and she perceives that, however she is dressed, there is an art of getting looked at. From then on, needlework and household tasks are no longer her only concerns. New talents present themselves and already make their utility felt.

I know that severe teachers want neither song nor dance nor any of the pleasing arts to be taught to young girls. That seems amusing to me! And to whom do they want them to be taught? To boys? To whom, men or women, do these talents specially belong? "To no one," they will respond. "Profane songs are nothing but crimes. Dance is an invention of the Demon. A young girl ought to have only her work and prayer as entertainment." Strange entertainments for a ten-year-old child. As for me, I am very much afraid that these little saints who are forced to spend their childhood in praying to God will spend their youth in something entirely different and when married do their best to make up for the time they think they wasted as girls. I consider it necessary to take account of what is suitable to age as well as to sex—that a young girl ought not to live like her grandmother, that she ought to be lively, playful, and frolicsome, to sing and dance as much as she pleases, and to taste all the innocent pleasures of her age. The time to be composed and to adopt a more serious bearing will come only too soon.

But is there a genuine necessity even for this change in behavior? Is it not perhaps also a fruit of our prejudices? By enslaving decent women only to gloomy duties, we have banished from marriage everything which could make it attractive to men. Ought we to be surprised if the taciturnity they see reigning at home drives them from it or if they are scarcely tempted to embrace so unpleasant a condition? By exaggerating all duties, Christianity makes them impractable and vain. By forbidding women song, dance, and all the entertainments of the world, it makes them sullen, shrewish, and unbearable in their homes. There is no other religion in which marriage is subjected to such severe duties and none in which so holy an obligation is so despised. So much has been done to prevent women from being lovable that husbands have become indifferent. I understand quite well that this ought not to be. But I say that it had to be, since, after all, Christians are men. As for me, I would want a young Englishwoman to cultivate pleasing talents that will entertain her future husband with as much care as a young Albanian cultivates them for the harem of Ispahan. It will be said that husbands do not care too much for all these talents. Indeed, I believe it, when these talents, far from being employed to please them, are used only as bait for attracting to their homes impudent young men who dishonor them. But do you think that a lovable and pure woman who possessed such talents and consecrated them to the entertainment of her husband would not add to the happiness of his life and would not prevent him, when he left his office exhausted, from going to look for recreation outside his home? Has no one seen happy families assembled where each member knows how to provide something of his own for the common entertainments? Let him say whether the confidence and familiarity which are combined there and whether the innocence and the gentleness of the pleasures which are tasted there do not amply compensate for the greater boisterousness of public pleasures.

The pleasing talents have been too much reduced into arts. People have generalized too much about them. Everything has been made into maxims and precepts, and what ought to be only entertainment and frolicsome games for young people has been made quite boring to them. I can imagine nothing more ridiculous than the sight of a dancing or singing master with a scowling aspect approaching young persons eager to laugh and adopting with them a more pedantic and more magisterial tone in order to teach them his frivolous science than if the subject were their catechism. Does the art of singing, for example, depend on written music? Cannot someone make his voice flexible and true, learn to sing with taste, and even to accompany himself, without knowing a single note? Does the same kind of music suit all voices? Does the same method suit all minds? No one will ever make me believe that the same attitudes, the same steps, the same movements, the same gestures, and the same dances suit a lively and piquant little brunette and a big, beautiful blonde with languid eyes. Therefore, when I see a master giving both exactly the same lessons, I say, "This man follows his routine, but he understands nothing of his art."

It is asked whether girls ought to have male or female masters. I do not know. I would much prefer that they needed neither the one nor the other, that they learned freely what they have so strong an inclination to want to learn, and that so many glittering mountebanks were not constantly seen wandering about our cities. I have some difficulty in believing that relations with these people are not more harmful to young girls than their lessons are useful. Their jargon, their tone, and their airs give the first taste for the frivolities that are so important for them to their pupils; and the pupils will be quick, following their masters' example, to make these their sole occupation.

In the arts which aim only at being pleasing, everything can serve as a master for young people—their fathers, their mothers, their brothers, their sisters, their friends, their governesses, their mirrors, and above all their own taste. They should not be offered lessons; they should be the ones to ask for them. A reward ought not to be made into a chore; and it is especially in this sort of study that the first step toward success is to want to succeed. Finally, if regular lessons are absolutely required, I shall not decide about the sex of those who ought to give them. I do not know whether a dancing master should take a young pupil by her delicate white hand, make her raise her skirt, lift her eyes, spread her arms, and thrust out her palpitating breast; but I know that I would not want to be that master for anything in the world.

Taste is formed by means of industriousness and talents. By means of taste the mind is imperceptibly opened to ideas of the beautiful of every sort and, finally, to the moral notions related to them. This is perhaps one of the reasons why the sentiment of seemliness and decency is to be found sooner in girls than in boys; for to believe that this precocious sentiment is the work of governesses, one would have to be ill informed about the bent of girls' studies and the development of the human mind. Talent at speaking holds first place in the art of pleasing; it is by means of this talent alone that new charms can be added to those to which the senses grow accustomed with habit. It is the mind which not only gives life to the body but in a way renews it. It is by the succession of sentiments and ideas that the mind animates and varies the face; and it is by speech that the mind inspires sustained attention and keeps it focused with the same interest on the same objects for a long time. It is for all these reasons, I believe, that young girls learn to chatter attractively so quickly, that they put expression into their remarks even before having the sentiments that go with them, and that men are entertained by listening to those remarks at so early an age, even before the girls themselves are able to understand them. The men are spying out the first moment of this intelligence in order to enter into the first moment of sentiment.

Women have flexible tongues; they talk sooner, more easily, and more attractively than men. They are also accused of talking more. This ought to be so, and I would gladly turn this reproach into praise. The mouth and the eyes are both very active among women, and for the same reason. Man says what he knows; woman says what pleases. He needs knowledge to speak; she needs taste. Useful things ought to be his principal object and pleasing things ought to be hers. The truth ought to be the only element common to their discourse.

Therefore, one should not restrain the chatter of girls, like that of boys, with this harsh question: "What is it good for?" but one should put another question, whose response is no easier: "What effect will it have?" At this early age, when they are still unable to discern good and bad and are no one's judges, they ought to impose a law on themselves to say only what is pleasing to those to whom they speak. And what makes the practice of this rule more difficult is that it always remains subordinate to the first law, which is never to lie.

I see many more difficulties as well, but they belong to a more advanced age. For the present, being truthful can cost young girls only the effort of being so without coarseness, and since this coarseness is naturally repugnant to them, education easily teaches them to avoid it. In social relations I note that generally the politeness of men is more obliging and that of women more caressing. This difference does not come from education; it is natural. Man appears to make more of an effort to serve you, and woman to please you. It follows from this that, whatever the character of women may be, their politeness is less false than ours; it only extends their first instinct. But when a man feigns to prefer my interest to his own, no matter what protestations he may make to cover this lie, I am quite sure that he is telling one. It does not, then, cost women much to be polite; nor consequently does it cost girls much to learn to become so. The first lesson comes from nature; art does no more than follow nature and determine in what form politeness ought to be manifested according to our usages. The politeness of women with one another is an entirely different matter. They give it such an air of constraint and their attentions are so cold that, in making one another mutually uncomfortable, they take little care to hide their own discomfort; thus they seem sincere in their lie by scarcely seeking to disguise it. Nevertheless young girls sometimes make genuine and franker friendships. At their age gaiety takes the place of good nature; and since they are satisfied with themselves, they are satisfied with everyone. They also invariably kiss one another more readily and caress one another with more grace in the presence of men; for they take pride in sharpening men's lust by the image of those favors they know how to make men desire.

If one ought not to permit young boys to ask prying questions, one ought a fortiori to forbid them to young girls. The satisfaction of their curiosity—or the clumsy evasion of it—is of much greater significance given their keen sense of—and skill at discovering—the mysteries

BOOK V

one hides from them. But without permitting them to make interroga-tions, I would wish that they be interrogated a good deal themselves, that care be taken to make them chat, and that they be stirred up in order to make them speak easily, to make them lively at retort, to loosen their minds and their tongues while it can be done without dan-ger. These conversations, which should always be marked by gaiety but also artfully arranged and well directed, would make a charming entertainment at that age and could bring to the innocent hearts of these young persons the first and perhaps the most useful moral lessons they will receive in their lives. While enticing them through pleasure and vanity, these conversations would teach them which qualities men truly esteem and what constitutes the glory and happiness of a decent woman.

One can easily understand that if male children are not in a position to form for themselves any true idea of religion, a fortiori the same idea is beyond the conception of girls. It is for that very reason that I would wish to speak to them about it earlier, for if one had to wait for girls to be in a position to discuss these profound questions methodically, one would run the risk of never speaking to them about it at all. Women's reason is practical and makes them very skillful at finding means for getting to a known end, but not at finding that end itself. The social relationship of the sexes is an admirable thing. This partnership produces a moral person of which the woman is the eye and the man is the arm, but they have such a dependence on one another that the woman learns from the man what must be seen and the man learns from the woman what must be done. If woman could ascend to general principles as well as man can, and if man had as good a mind for details as woman does, they would always be independent of one an-other, they would live in eternal discord, and their partnership could not exist. But in the harmony which reigns between them, everything tends to the common end; they do not know who contributes more. Each follows the prompting of the other; each obeys, and both are masters.

Due to the very fact that in her conduct woman is enslaved by public opinion, in her belief she is enslaved by authority. Every girl ought to have her mother's religion, and every woman her husband's. If this religion is false, the docility which subjects mother and daughter to the order of nature erases from God's sight the sin of this error. Since women are not in a position to be judges themselves, they ought to re-ceive the decision of fathers and husbands like that of the Church.

Unable to draw the rule of their faith from themselves alone, women cannot set limits of certainty and reason to their faith; they let them-selves be carried away by countless external influences, and thus they are always beneath or beyond the true. Always extreme, they are all libertines or fanatics; there are none who know how to join wisdom with piety. The source of this evil is not only in the extravagant charac-ter of their sex but in the ill-regulated authority of ours: our libertinism of morals makes piety despised; the terrors of repentance render piety tyrannical; and that is how we always do too much or too little with respect to piety.

Since authority ought to rule the religion of women, the issue is not so much one of explaining to them the reasons there are for believing as of explaining distinctly what we believe; for faith that is given to obscure ideas is the first source of fanaticism, and faith that one is required to give to absurd things leads to madness or disbelief. I do not know which our catechisms lead to most—impiety or fanaticism— but I certainly know that they necessarily lead to one or the other.

If you are teaching religion to young girls, in the first place never make it an object of gloom and constraint for them, and never make it a task or a duty. Consequently, never make them learn anything relating to it by heart, not even prayers. Be content to say yours in their presence without forcing them to be there. Make your prayers short, according to the teaching of Jesus Christ.[15] Always say them with suitable meditation and respect. Consider that, when we ask the Supreme Being for His attention, it is certainly incumbent upon us to give our attention to what we are going to say to Him.

It is less important that young girls know their religion early than that they know it well and, above all, that they love it. When you make it onerous for them, when you always depict God as being angry with them, when you impose on them in His name countless irksome duties that they never see you fulfilling, what can they think, other than that to know one's catechism and to pray to God are the duties of little girls; thus they desire to be grown-up in order to be exempted like you from all this subjection. Set an example! Otherwise one never succeeds at anything with children.

When you expound articles of faith to them, do it in the form of direct teaching and not by question and answer. They ought to respond only with what they think and never with what has been dictated to them. All the answers of the catechism are misconceived. It is the pupil who teaches the master. In the mouths of children these answers are really lies, since the children expound what they do not understand and affirm what they are not in a position to believe. Even among the most intelligent men, show me those who do not lie in saying their catechism.

The first question I see in our catechism is the following: "Who created you and put you in the world?" To this the little girl, really believing that it is her mother, nevertheless says without hesitation that it is God. The only thing she sees here is that in reply to a question she hardly understands, she gives an answer she does not understand at all.

I wish that a man who knows the development of children's minds would be willing to make a catechism for them. This would perhaps be the most useful book ever written, and in my opinion it would not be the one which would do the least honor to his Author. What is quite certain is that, if this book were good, it would hardly resemble our catechisms.

Such a catechism will be good only if the child, when he is asked the questions, gives the answers on his own without having to learn them. Of course, the child will sometimes be ready to ask questions in turn. To make what I mean understood a sort of model would be needed, and I certainly sense what I lack for outlining it. I shall attempt at least to give some slight idea of it.

BOOK V

I imagine, then, that to get to the first question of our catechism, it would have to begin pretty much as follows:

NURSE Do you remember the time when your mother was a girl?
LITTLE GIRL No, nurse.
NURSE Why not, since you have so good a memory?
LITTLE GIRL Because I was not yet in the world.
NURSE Then you have not always been alive?
LITTLE GIRL No.
NURSE Will you always be alive?
LITTLE GIRL Yes.
NURSE Are you young or old?
LITTLE GIRL I am young.
NURSE And is your grandmother young or old?
LITTLE GIRL She is old.
NURSE Was she once young?
LITTLE GIRL Yes.
NURSE Why isn't she young anymore?
LITTLE GIRL Because she got old.
NURSE Will you get old like her?
LITTLE GIRL I don't know.*
NURSE Where are your last year's dresses?
LITTLE GIRL They have been torn up.
NURSE And why were they torn up?
LITTLE GIRL Because they were too small for me.
NURSE And why were they too small for you?
LITTLE GIRL Because I have grown.
NURSE Will you still grow?
LITTLE GIRL Oh, yes.
NURSE And what do big girls become?
LITTLE GIRL They become women.
NURSE And what do women become?
LITTLE GIRL They become mothers.
NURSE And what do mothers become?
LITTLE GIRL They become old.
NURSE Will you, then, become old?
LITTLE GIRL When I am a mother.
NURSE And what do old people become?
LITTLE GIRL I don't know.
NURSE What became of your grandfather?
LITTLE GIRL He died.†
NURSE And why did he die?
LITTLE GIRL Because he was old.

* If at any point where I have put, "I don't know," the little girl answers otherwise, her answer must be distrusted, and she must be made to explain it carefully.
† The little girl will say this because she has heard it said, but it must be verified whether she has some accurate idea of death; for this idea is not so simple or so much within the reach of children as is thought. One can see in the little poem "Abel" an example of the way in which it ought to be imparted to them. This charming work breathes a delicious simplicity which one cannot draw upon too much for one's conversations with children.[16]

NURSE   What, then, becomes of old people?

LITTLE GIRL   They die.

NURSE   And you, when you are old, what . . .

LITTLE GIRL   (*interrupting her*)   O, nurse, I don't want to die.

NURSE   My child, no one wants to die, but everyone dies.

LITTLE GIRL   What? Will mama die, too?

NURSE   Like everyone else. Women get old just as men do, and old age leads to death.

LITTLE GIRL   What must be done to grow old very late?

NURSE   Be good when one is young.

LITTLE GIRL   Nurse, I shall always be good.

NURSE   So much the better for you. But, still, do you believe you will live forever?

LITTLE GIRL   When I am very old, very old . . .

NURSE   Well, then?

LITTLE GIRL   Finally, when one is so old, you say that one has to die.

NURSE   Will you, then, die sometime?

LITTLE GIRL   Alas, yes.

NURSE   Who was alive before you?

LITTLE GIRL   My father and my mother.

NURSE   Who was alive before them?

LITTLE GIRL   Their father and their mother.

NURSE   Who will be alive after you?

LITTLE GIRL   My children.

NURSE   Who will be alive after them?

LITTLE GIRL   Their children, etc.

In following this route one finds, by easily sensed inductions, a beginning and an end for the human race as for all things—that is to say, a father and a mother who had neither father nor mother and children who will have no children.* It is only after a long series of such questions that the way is sufficiently paved for the first question of the catechism. Then only can one ask it, and the child understand it. But from there to the second answer—which is, so to speak, the definition of the divine essence—what an immense leap! When will this gap be filled? God is a spirit! And what is a spirit? Will I launch the mind of a child into this obscure metaphysics from which men have such trouble extricating themselves? It is not for a little girl to resolve these questions. At most, she can pose them. Then I would simply answer her, "You ask me what God is? It is not easy to say. God can neither be heard nor seen, nor touched. He is known only by His works. To judge what He is, wait until you know what He has done."

If our dogmas are all of equal truth, they are not for that reason all of equal importance. It is quite unimportant for the glory of God that it be known to us in all things; but it is important for human society and for each of its members that every man know and fulfill the duties toward his neighbor and toward himself which the law of God imposes on him. This is what we ought to teach one another constantly, and

---

* The mind will not consent to apply the idea of eternity to human generations. Actually going through any numerical succession is incompatible with this idea.

it is above all about this that fathers and mothers are obliged to instruct their children. Whether a virgin is the mother of her Creator, whether she gave birth to God or only to a man with whom God joined Himself, whether the substance of the Father and the Son are the same or only similar, whether the Spirit proceeds from one of these two who are the same or from both conjointly—I do not see that the decision about these apparently essential questions is more important to the human species than knowing on what day of the moon one ought to celebrate Easter, whether one ought to tell one's beads, fast, abstain from meat, speak Latin or French in church, adorn the walls with images, say or hear Mass, and not have a wife of one's own. Let each person think about these things as he pleases. I do not know in what way it can interest others; it does not interest me at all. But what interests me and all my fellow men is that each person know that an arbiter of the fate of human beings exists and that we are all His children; that He prescribes that we all be just, love one another, be beneficent and merciful, and keep our promises to everyone—even to our enemies and His; that the apparent happiness of this life is nothing; that there is another life after it in which this Supreme Being will be the rewarder of the good and the judge of the wicked. These and similar dogmas are the ones it is important to teach the youth and to persuade all the citizens to accept. Whoever combats them doubtless deserves punishment. He is the disturber of order and the enemy of society. Whoever goes beyond them and wants to enslave us to his private opinions gets to the same point by the opposite route. To establish order in his way, he disturbs the peace; in his reckless pride he makes himself the interpreter of the divinity. He demands in its name the homage and the respect of men. He makes himself God and tries, insofar as he can, to take His place. He ought to be punished for being sacrilegious, if he were not punished for being intolerant.

Therefore, neglect all these mysterious dogmas which are only words without ideas for us—all these bizarre doctrines whose vain study takes the place of virtues in those who indulge in it and serves to make them mad rather than good. Always keep your children within the narrow circle of the dogmas connected with morality. Persuade them that there is nothing useful for us to know except that which teaches us to do good. Do not make your daughters theologians and reasoners; teach them regarding heaven only those things that serve human wisdom. Accustom them always to feel themselves under the eyes of God; to have Him as witness of their actions, their thoughts, their virtue, and their pleasures; to do good without ostentation because He loves it; to suffer evil without a murmur because He will compensate them for it; finally, to be all the days of their lives as they will be glad to have been when they appear before Him. This is the true religion; this is the only one which is susceptible of neither abuse nor impiety nor fanaticism. Let them preach more sublime religions as much as they want; I recognize none other than this.

Moreover, it is well to observe that up to the age when reason is enlightened, and when nascent sentiment makes the conscience speak, what is good or bad for young girls is what the people around them have decided it to be. What is commanded them is good; what is forbidden them is bad. They ought not to know more. From this one can see how important—even more so for them than for boys—is the choice of the persons who are going to be near them and have some authority over them. Finally, the moment comes when they begin to judge things by themselves, and then it is time to change the plan of their education.

Perhaps I have said too much about it up to now. To what will we reduce women if we give them as their law only public prejudices? Let us not bring down so low the sex that governs us and honors us when we have not abased it. A rule prior to opinion exists for the whole human species. It is to the inflexible direction of this rule that all the others ought to be related. This rule judges prejudice itself, and only insofar as the esteem of men accords with it ought this esteem to be authoritative for us.

This rule is the inner sentiment. I shall not repeat what has been said about it above. It suffices for me to remark that if these two rules do not cooperate in the education of women, that education will always be defective. Sentiment without opinion will not give them that delicacy of soul which adorns good morals with worldly honor; and opinion without sentiment will only make them false and dishonest women who put appearance in the place of virtue.

It is important, therefore, that they cultivate a faculty that serves as arbiter between the two guides, which does not let the conscience go astray, and which corrects the errors of prejudice. That faculty is reason. But how many questions are raised by this word! Are women capable of solid reasoning? Is it important that they cultivate it? Will they succeed in cultivating it? Is its cultivation useful for the functions which are imposed on them? Is it compatible with the simplicity that suits them?

The various ways of envisaging and resolving these questions result in opposite extremes: those on one side limit woman to sewing and weaving in her household with her servants and thus make her only the master's first servant; those on the other side, not content with ensuring her rights, make her also usurp ours. For to leave her above us in the qualities proper to her sex and to make her our equal in all the rest is to transfer to the wife the primacy that nature gives to the husband.

The use of reason that leads man to the knowledge of his duties is not very complex. The use of reason that leads woman to the knowledge of hers is even simpler. The obedience and the fidelity she owes to her husband and the tenderness and the care she owes to her children are consequences of her position so natural and easily sensed that she cannot without bad faith refuse her consent to the inner sentiment that guides her, nor fail to recognize her duty if her inclinations are still uncorrupted.

I would not indiscriminately object to a woman's being limited to the labors of her sex alone and left in profound ignorance of all the rest. But that would require very simple and very healthy public morals or a very retired way of life. In big cities and among corrupt men such a woman would be too easy to seduce. Often her virtue would depend only on the occasion; in this philosophic age she needs a virtue that can be put to the test. She needs to know beforehand what might be said to her and what she ought to think about it.

Moreover, since she is subject to the judgment of men, she ought to merit their esteem. She ought, above all, to obtain the esteem of her spouse. She ought to make him not only love her person but also approve her conduct. She ought to justify the choice he has made before the public and make her husband honored through the honor given to his wife. How will she go about all this if she is ignorant of our institutions, if she knows nothing of our practices and our proprieties, if she knows neither the source of human judgments nor the passions determining them? As soon as she depends on both her own conscience and the opinions of others, she has to learn to compare these two rules, to reconcile them, and to prefer the former only when the two are in contradiction. She becomes the judge of her judges; she decides when she ought to subject herself to them and when she ought to take exception to them. Before rejecting or accepting their prejudices, she weighs them. She learns to go back to their source, to anticipate them, to use them to her advantage. She is careful never to attract blame to herself when her duty permits her to avoid it. None of this can be done well without cultivating her mind and her reason.

I always return to my principle, and it provides me with the solution to all my difficulties. I study what is, I seek its cause, and I finally find that what is, is good. I go to parties at which master and mistress jointly do the honors. Both have had the same education; both are equally polite, equally endowed with taste and wit, and animated by the same desire to receive their guests well and to send each away satisfied with them. The husband omits no care in order to be attentive to all. He goes; he comes; he makes his rounds and puts himself out in countless ways; he would like to be all attentiveness. The woman stays put; a little circle forms around her and seems to hide the rest of the gathering from her. However, nothing takes place that she does not notice; no one leaves to whom she has not spoken; she has omitted nothing that could interest everyone; she has said nothing to anyone that was not agreeable to him; and without in any way upsetting the order, the least important person among her company is no more forgotten than the most important. Dinner is served. All go to the table. The man, knowledgeable about who gets along with whom, will seat them on the basis of what he knows. The woman, without knowing anything, will make no mistakes about it. She will have already read, in their eyes and in their bearing, everything about who belongs with whom, and each guest will find himself placed where he wants to be. I do not say that when the food is served, no one is forgotten. But even though the master of the house may have forgotten no one when he passed around the food, his wife goes further and divines what you look at with pleasure and offers you some. In speaking to her neighbor, she has her eye on the end of the table; she distinguishes between the guest who does not eat because he is not hungry, and the one who does not dare to help himself or to ask because he is awkward or timid. On leaving the table each guest believes that she has thought only of him. All think that she has not had time to eat a single bite. But the truth is that she has eaten more than anyone.

When everyone has left, they talk about what has happened. The man reports what was said to him, what those with whom he conversed said and did. It is not always here that the woman is most accurate, but she has seen what was whispered at the other end of the room. She knows what this person thought, to what this remark or that gesture related. Hardly a meaningful gesture was made for which she does not have a ready interpretation, and one almost always in conformity with the truth.

The same turn of mind that makes a woman of the world excel in the art of being a hostess makes a coquette excel in the art of entertaining several suitors. The skills of coquetry require a discernment even more refined than those of politeness; for provided that a woman be polite toward everyone, she has always done well enough; but the coquette would soon lose her empire by this maladroit uniformity. By dint of wanting to oblige all her lovers, she would repel them all. In society, the manners a woman adopts with all men do not fail to please each. Provided that a man is well treated, he does not look too closely for preferences. But in love, the favors which are not exclusive are an insult. A sensitive man would prefer a hundred times over to be the only one ill treated than to be caressed with all the others, and the worst thing that can happen to him is not to be singled out. Therefore, a woman who wants to preserve several lovers has to persuade each of them that she prefers him, and she has to persuade him of it under the eyes of all the others—whom she is persuading of the same thing under his eyes.

Do you want to see an embarrassed person? Put a man between two women with whom he has secret relations, and then observe what a foolish figure he cuts. Put a woman in the same situation between two men (and surely the example will be no rarer); you will be amazed at the skill with which she will put both off the scent and act so that each will laugh at the other. Now if this woman gave witness of the same confiding behavior to both and adopted the same familiarity with both, how would they be her dupes for an instant? By treating them equally, would she not show that they have the same rights over her? Oh, how much better than that she goes about it! Far from treating them in the same way, she affects to establish an inequality between them. She does so well that the one she flatters believes it is out of tenderness, and the one she maltreats believes that it is out of spite. Thus each is content with his share and always believes she is concerned with him, while actually she is concerned with herself alone.

Coquetry suggests similar means to the general desire to please; capriciousness would only repel if it were not prudently managed, and it is by dispensing it artfully that she makes the strongest chains for her slaves.

Usa ogn' arte la donna, onde sia colto
Nella sua rete alcun novello amante;
Ne con tutti, ne sempre un stesso volto
Serba, ma cangia a tempo atto e sembiante.[17]

On what does this whole art depend if not on sharp and continuous observations which make her see what is going on in men's hearts at every instant, and which dispose her to bring to each secret movement that she notices the force needed to suspend or accelerate it? Now, is this art learned? No, it is born with women. They all possess it, and men never have it to the same degree. This is one of the distinctive characteristics of the fair sex. Presence of mind, incisiveness, and subtle observations are the science of women; cleverness at taking advantage of them is their talent.

This is what is, and it has been seen why it ought to be. We are told that women are false. They become so. Their particular gift is skill and not falseness. According to the true inclinations of their sex, even when they are lying they are not false. Why do you consult their mouth when it is not the mouth which ought to speak? Consult their eyes, their color, their breathing, their fearful manner, their soft resistance. This is the language nature gives them for answering you. The mouth always says no and ought to say so. But the accent it adds to this answer is not always the same, and this accent does not know how to lie. Does not woman have the same needs as man without having the same right to express them? Her fate would be too cruel if, even in the case of legitimate desires, she did not have a language equivalent to the one she dare not use. Must her modesty make her unhappy? Must she not have an art of communicating her inclinations without laying them bare? What skill she needs to get stolen from her what she is burning to give! How important it is for her to learn to touch the heart of man without appearing to think of him! Is not Galatea's apple and her maladroit flight a charming speech? [18] What will she need to add to that? Will she go and tell the shepherd who follows her among the willows that she flees there only with the design of attracting him? She would be lying, so to speak, for then she would no longer attract him. The more reserve a woman has, the more art she must have, even with her husband. Yes, I maintain that in keeping coquetry within its limits, one makes it modest and true; one makes it a law of decency.

Virtue is one, as one of my adversaries has very well said.[19] One cannot split virtue up to accept one part and reject another. When someone loves it, he loves it in all its wholeness; and he closes his heart when he can—and always closes his mouth—to sentiments he ought not to have. Moral truth is not what is, but what is good. What is bad ought not to be and ought not to be admitted, especially when this admission gives it an effect it would not otherwise have had. If I were tempted to steal and by saying so I tempted another to be my accomplice, would not declaring my temptation to him be to succumb to it? Why do you say that modesty makes women false? Are those who lose it most completely also truer than the others? Far from it. They

[385]

are a thousand times more false. One gets to that point of depravity only by dint of vices all of which one keeps and which reign only under the cover of intrigues and lies.* On the contrary, those who still have shame, who do not take pride in their faults, who know how to hide their desires from the very persons who inspire them, and whose avowals are the hardest to extract are also the truest, the most sincere, and the most constant in all their engagements and those on whose faith one can generally most rely.

I know of no one other than Mademoiselle de l'Enclos who can be cited as a known exception to these remarks. And Mademoiselle de l'Enclos passed for a marvel. In her contempt for the virtues of her sex, she had, it is said, preserved those of ours. People praise her frankness, her rectitude, the security one had in associating with her, her fidelity in friendship. Finally, to complete the picture of her glory, it is said that she had made herself a man. Wonderful. But with all her great reputation, I would have no more wanted that man for my friend than for my mistress.[21]

All this is not so much off the subject as it appears to be. I see where the maxims of modern philosophy lead in ridiculing the modesty of the fair sex and its alleged falseness, and I see that the most certain effect of this philosophy will be to take from the women of our age the bit of honor remaining to them.

On the basis of these considerations I believe that one can determine in general what kind of cultivation suits the minds of women and toward what objects their reflections ought to be turned from their youth.

I have already said that the duties of their sex are easier to see than to fulfill. The first thing that they ought to learn is to love their duties out of regard for their advantages. This is the only way to make their duties easy for them. Each station and each age has its duties. We soon know our own, provided we love them. Honor woman's station, and in whatever rank heaven puts you, you will always be a good woman. The essential thing is to be what nature made us. A woman is always only too much what men want her to be.

The quest for abstract and speculative truths, principles, and axioms in the sciences, for everything that tends to generalize ideas, is not within the competence of women. All their studies ought to be related to practice. It is for them to apply the principles man has found, and to make the observations which lead man to the establishment of principles. Regarding what is not immediately connected with their duties, all the reflections of women ought to be directed to the study of men or to the pleasing kinds of knowledge that have only taste as their aim; for, as regards works of genius, they are out of the reach of women.

---

* I know that women who have openly taken a position on a certain question claim that they make the most of this frankness, and swear that, with only this exception, there is nothing estimable which is not to be found in them. But I do know that they never persuaded anyone but a fool of that. With the greatest curb on their sex removed, what remains to restrain them, and what part of honor will they take seriously when they have renounced that which belongs to them? Once having put their passions at ease, they no longer have any interest in resisting: *nec femina amissa pudicitia alia abnuerit.*[20] Did an author ever know the human heart in the two sexes better than the one who said that?

BOOK V

Nor do women have sufficient precision and attention to succeed at the exact sciences. And as for the physical sciences, they are for the sex which is more active, gets around more, and sees more objects, the sex which has more strength and uses it more to judge the relations of sensible beings and the laws of nature. <u>Woman, who is weak and who sees nothing outside the house, estimates and judges the forces she can put to work to make up for her weakness, and those forces are men's passions.</u> Her science of mechanics is more powerful than ours; all her levers unsettle the human heart. She must have the art to make us want to do everything which her sex cannot do by itself and which is necessary or agreeable to it. She must, therefore, make a profound study of the mind of man—not an abstraction of the mind of man in general, but the minds of the men around her, the minds of the men to whom she is subjected by either law or opinion. She must learn to penetrate their sentiments by their words, their actions, their looks, their gestures. She must know how to communicate to them—by her words, her actions, her looks, her gestures—the sentiments that she wishes to communicate without appearing even to dream of it. Men will philosophize about the human heart better than she does; but she will read in men's hearts better than they do. It is for women to discover experimental morality, so to speak, and for us to reduce it to a system. Woman has more wit, man more genius; woman observes, and man reasons. From this conjunction results the clearest insight and the most complete science regarding itself that the human mind can acquire—in a word, the surest knowledge of oneself and others available to our species. And this is how art can constantly tend to the perfection of the instrument given by nature.

The world is the book of women. When they do a bad job of reading it, it is their fault, or else some passion blinds them. Nevertheless, the true mother of a family is hardly less of a recluse in her home than a nun is in her cloister. Thus it is necessary to do for young persons who are about to be married what is done or ought to be done for those who are put in convents—to show them the pleasures they abandon before letting them renounce them, lest the false image of those pleasures which are unknown to them come one day to lead their hearts astray and disturb the happiness of their retreat. In France girls live in convents and women frequent society. With the ancients it was exactly the opposite. Girls, as I have said, had many games and public festivals. Women led retired lives. This practice was more reasonable and maintained morals better. A sort of coquetry is permitted to marriageable girls; enjoying themselves is their chief business. Women have other concerns at home and no longer have husbands to seek; but they would not find this reform to their advantage, and unfortunately they set the tone. Mothers, at least make your daughters your companions. Give them good sense and a decent soul; then hide nothing from them which a chaste eye can look at. Balls, feasts, games, even the theater—everything which, seen in the wrong way, constitutes the charm of an imprudent youth—can be offered without risk to healthy eyes. The better they see these boisterous pleasures, the sooner they will be disgusted by them.

[387]

I hear the clamor raised against me. What girl resists such dangerous examples? They have hardly seen society before all their heads are turned. Not one of them wants to leave it. That may be so. But before presenting this deceptive picture to them, did you prepare them to see it without emotion? Have you made the objects it represents quite clear to them? Have you carefully depicted these objects as they are? Did you arm these girls well against the illusions of vanity? Did you impart to their young hearts a taste for the true pleasures which are not found amidst this tumult? What precautions, what measures have you taken to preserve them from the false taste that leads them astray? Far from opposing in any way the empire of public prejudices over their minds, you have fed these prejudices! You have made these girls love every frivolous entertainment before they experienced it. You make them love these entertainments even more when they indulge in them. Young persons entering society have no governess other than their mother, who is often more foolish than they are and who cannot show them objects other than as she herself sees them. Her example, which is stronger than reason itself, justifies them in their own eyes, and the mother's authority is an unanswerable excuse for the daughter. When I say that I want a mother to introduce her daughter into society, I make the supposition that she will make her daughter see it as it is.

The evil begins even earlier. Convents are veritable schools of coquetry—not of that decent coquetry about which I spoke, but of a coquetry which leads to all the perversities of women and produces the most extravagant ladies of high fashion. When young women make the abrupt transition from the convent to wild company, they immediately feel they belong. They have been raised to live there. Should one be surprised that they are content there? I do not advance what I am going to say without fear of taking a prejudice for an observation, but it seems to me that in Protestant countries there is generally more attachment to family and there are worthier wives and tenderer mothers than in Catholic countries; and if this is the case, one cannot doubt that this difference is in part due to convent education.

In order to love the peaceful and domestic life, we must know it. We must have sensed its sweetness from childhood. It is only in the paternal home that one gets the taste for one's own home, and any woman whose mother has not raised her will not like raising her own children. Unfortunately there is no longer private education in the big cities. Society there is so general and so mixed that there is no longer a refuge to which to retire, and a person is in public even in his own home. By dint of living with everyone, he no longer has a family, and he hardly knows his own parents. They are viewed as strangers, and the simplicity of domestic morals is extinguished along with the sweet familiarity which constituted their charm. It is thus that we suck with our mother's milk a taste for the pleasures of the age and its reigning maxims.

An apparent constraint is imposed on girls for the sake of finding the dupes who marry them on the strength of their bearing. But study these young persons for a moment. The lust that devours them is poorly disguised under a constrained air, and one already reads in their eyes the ardent desire to imitate their mothers. What they covet is not a husband but the license of marriage. What need is there of a husband with so many resources for doing without one? But a husband is needed as a screen for the use of these resources.* Modesty is on their faces, and libertinism is in the depths of their hearts. This feigned modesty itself is a sign of libertinism. They affect modesty only to be able to get rid of it sooner. Women of Paris and London, pardon me, I beg you. No locale excludes miracles, but I do not know of any; and if a single one of you has a truly decent soul, I understand nothing of our institutions.

All these diverse educations equally deliver young persons over to a taste for the pleasures of high society and to the passions soon born of this taste. In big cities depravity begins with life, and in little cities it begins with reasoning. Young provincial women, taught to despise the happy simplicity of their morals, hurry to Paris to share the corruption of ours. The vices, adorned with the fair name of talents, are the sole object of their trip. When they arrive, they are ashamed to find themselves so far behind the noble license of the local women, and they do not delay in becoming worthy to live in the capital. Where does the evil begin, in your opinion? In the places where the project is formed, or in those where it is accomplished?

I do not want a sensible mother to take her daughter from the provinces to Paris to show her these scenes which are so pernicious for others. But I say that even if she did this, unless her daughter is badly raised, these scenes will hold little danger for her. If one has taste, sense, and a love of decent things, one does not find them so attractive as they are for those who let themselves be charmed by them. In Paris one notices young scatterbrains who hurry to adopt the local tone and make themselves fashionable for six months, only to be hooted for the rest of their lives. But who notices those who are repelled by all this uproar and go back to their provinces, content with their fate after having compared it to the one others envy? How many young women I have seen who were brought to the capital by obliging husbands able to take up residence there, and who then persuaded them not to remain, who left more gladly than they came, and who said with emotion on the eve of their departure, "Ah, let us return to our cottage! One lives more happily there than in the palaces here." One does not know, moreover, how many good folk there are who have never bent their knees before the idol and despise its senseless worship. Only foolish women are boisterous; wise women do not make a sensation.

If in spite of the general corruption, in spite of universal prejudices, and in spite of the bad education of girls, some still preserve a judgment that withstands the test, what will it be when this judgment has been nourished by suitable instruction—or, to put it better, when it has not been corrupted by vicious instruction, for everything always consists in preserving or in restoring the natural sentiments? The object is not to bore young girls with your long sermons or to recite your

---

* The way of man in his youth was one of the four things the wise man could not understand. The fifth was the impudence of the adulterous woman, *quae comedit, et tergens os suum dicit: non sum operata malum* (Proverbs 30:20).[22]

dry moralisms to them. Moralizing is, for both sexes, the death of all good education. Gloomy lessons are good only for producing hatred of those who give them and everything they say. In speaking to young persons, the aim is not to make them afraid of their duties nor to aggravate the yoke imposed on them by nature. In expounding these duties to them, be precise and simple; do not let them believe that a girl is afflicted when she fulfills these duties—no aggrieved bearing, no pomposity. Everything that is to reach the heart must come from it. Their moral catechism ought to be as short and as clear as their religious catechism, but it ought not to be as grave. Show them in their very duties the source of their pleasures and the foundation of their rights. Is it so hard to love in order to be loved, to make oneself lovable in order to be happy, to make oneself estimable in order to be obeyed, to honor oneself in order to be honored? How fine these rights are! How respectable they are! How dear they are to the heart of man when woman knows how to turn them to account! To enjoy them, she does not have to await the passage of the years or the coming of old age. Her empire begins with her virtues. Although her attractions have hardly developed, she already reigns by the sweetness of her character and makes her modesty imposing. What insensitive and barbarous man does not soften his pride and adopt more attentive manners near a sixteen-year-old girl who is lovable and pure, who speaks little, who listens, whose bearing is seemly and whose conversation is decent, whose beauty does not make her forget either her sex or her youth, who knows how to inspire interest by her very timidity and to gain for herself the respect she gives to everyone?

Although external, these testimonials are not frivolous. They are not founded solely on the attraction of the senses. They come from the intimate sentiment we all have that women are the natural judges of men's merit. Who wants to be despised by women? No one in the world, not even a man who no longer wishes to love them. And I who tell them such harsh truths, do you believe that their judgments are indifferent to me? No, their approval is dearer to me than yours, readers—you who are often more womanish than they are. In despising their morals, I still wish to honor their justice. It is of little importance to me that they hate me if I force them to esteem me.

How many great things could be done by means of this motive if one knew how to set it in motion! Woe to the age in which women lose their ascendancy and in which their judgments no longer have an effect on men! This is the last degree of depravity. All peoples who have had morals have respected women. Look at Sparta; look at the ancient Germans; look at Rome—Rome, home of glory and of virtue if ever they had one on earth. It is there that women honored the exploits of great generals, that they wept publicly for the fathers of the fatherland, that their vows or their mourning were consecrated as the most solemn judgment of the republic. All the great revolutions there came from women. Due to a woman Rome acquired liberty; due to a woman the plebeians obtained the consulate; due to a woman the tyranny of the Decemvirs was ended; due to women Rome, when besieged, was saved from the hands of an outlaw. Gallant Frenchman, what would you have said when you saw this procession, so ridiculous to your mocking eyes, passing by? You would have accompanied it with your jeers. How we see the same objects with a different eye! And perhaps all of us are right. Form this cortege of fair French ladies; I know nothing more indecent. But compose it of Roman women, and you will have the eyes of all the Volsci and the heart of Coriolanus.[23]

I shall say more, and I maintain that virtue is no less favorable to love than to the other rights of nature, and that the authority of the beloved gains no less from virtue than does the authority of wives and mothers. There is no true love without enthusiasm, and no enthusiasm without an object of perfection, real or chimerical, but always existing in the imagination. What will enflame lovers for whom this perfection no longer exists and who see in what they love only the object of sensual pleasure? No, it is not thus that the soul is warmed and delivered to those sublime transports which constitute the delirium of lovers and the charm of their passion. In love everything is only illusion, I admit it. But what is real are the sentiments for the truly *sublime* beautiful with which love animates us and which it makes us love. This beauty is not in the object one loves; it is the work of our errors. So, what of it? Does the lover any the less sacrifice all of his low sentiments to this imaginary model? Does he any the less suffuse his heart with the virtues he attributes to what he holds dear? Does he detach himself any the less from the baseness of the human *I*? Where is the true lover who is not ready to immolate himself for his beloved, and where is the sensual and coarse passion in a man who is willing to die? We make fun of the paladins.[24] That is because they knew love, and we no longer know anything but debauchery. When these romantic maxims began to become ridiculous, the change was less the work of reason than of bad morals.

Throughout the ages the natural relations do not change, and the standards of what is or is not suitable that result from them remain the same. Prejudices parading under the vain name of reason change nothing but the appearance of these standards. It will always be a grand and beautiful thing to be in command of oneself, even in order to obey fantastic opinions; and the true motives of honor will always speak to the heart of every woman of judgment who knows how to seek life's happiness in her position. Chastity must be a delicious virtue for a beautiful woman who has an elevated soul. While she sees the whole earth at her feet, she triumphs over all and over herself. She raises in her own heart a throne to which all come to render homage. The tender or jealous but always respectful feelings of both sexes toward her, the universal esteem she enjoys, and her own self-esteem constantly reward her with a tribute of glory for a few momentary struggles. The privations are fleeting, but the reward for them is permanent. What a joy for a noble soul when the pride of virtue is joined to beauty! Bring the heroine of a romantic novel into reality. She will taste delights more exquisite than the Laïses [25] or the Cleopatras tasted. And when her beauty is no more, her glory and her pleasure will still remain. She alone will know how to enjoy the past.

The more our duties are great and difficult, the more they ought to be founded on both strong and easily sensed reasons. There is a certain pious language about the gravest subjects which is drummed into the ears of young girls without persuading them. This language, which is all out of proportion with their ideas and to which they secretly attach little importance, promotes in them a facility at yielding to their inclinations, inasmuch as they lack reasons for resistance founded on things themselves. A girl who is soberly and piously raised doubtless has powerful arms against temptations; but one whose heart—or, rather, whose ears —is fed solely with a mystical jargon infallibly becomes the prey of the first adroit seducer who goes after her. A young and beautiful girl will never despise her body, she will never in good faith grieve for the great sins her beauty causes to be committed, she will never sincerely shed tears before God for being a coveted object, and she will never be able to believe within herself that the sweetest sentiment of the heart is an invention of Satan. Give her other reasons that she can believe within and for herself, for these will never get through to her. It will be worse yet if, as is almost always the case, one gives her contradictory ideas, and after having humiliated her by disparaging her body and its charms as the dirtiness of sin, one then makes her respect as the temple of Jesus Christ the very body which has been made so contemptible to her. Ideas that are too sublime and ideas that are too base are equally insufficient and cannot be combined. A reason within the reach of her sex and her age is needed. Considerations of duty have real force only to the extent that motives which lead us to fulfill that duty are joined to it.

Quae quia non liceat non facit, illa facit [26]

One would not suspect that it is Ovid who passes so severe a judgment.

Do you want, then, to inspire young girls with the love of good morals? Without constantly saying to them "Be pure," give them a great interest in being pure. Make them feel all the value of purity, and you will make them love it. It does not suffice to place this interest in the distant future. Show it to them in the present moment, in the relationships of their own age, in the character of their lovers. Depict for them the good man, the man of merit; teach them to recognize him, to love him, and to love him for themselves; prove to them that this man alone can make the women to whom he is attached—wives or beloveds —happy.[27] Lead them to virtue by means of reason. Make them feel that the empire of their sex and all its advantages depend not only on the good conduct and the morals of women but also on those of men, that they have little hold over vile and base souls, and that a man will serve his mistress no better than he serves virtue. You can then be sure that in depicting to them the morals of our own days, you will inspire in them a sincere disgust. In showing them fashionable people, you will make them despise them; you will only be keeping them at a distance from their maxims and giving them an aversion for their sentiments and a disdain for their vain gallantry. You will cause a nobler ambition to be born in them—that of reigning over great and strong

BOOK V

souls, the ambition of the women of Sparta, which was to command men.[28] A bold, brazen, scheming woman who knows how to attract her lovers only by coquetry and to keep them only by favors makes them obey her like valets in servile and common things; however, in important and weighty things she is without authority over them. But the woman who is at once decent, lovable, and self-controlled, who forces those about her to respect her, who has reserve and modesty, who, in a word, sustains love by means of esteem, sends her lovers with a nod to the end of the world, to combat, to glory, to death, to anything she pleases. This seems to me to be a noble empire, and one well worth the price of its purchase.*

This is the spirit in which Sophie has been raised—with more care than effort, and more by following her taste than by hindering it. Let us now say a word about her person in accordance with the portrait I made of her for Emile, on the basis of which he himself imagines the wife who can make him happy.

I shall never repeat often enough that I am leaving prodigies aside. Emile is no prodigy, and Sophie is not one either. Emile is a man and Sophie is a woman; therein consists all their glory. In the confounding of the sexes that reigns among us, someone is almost a prodigy for belonging to his own sex.

Sophie is well born; she has a good nature; she has a very sensitive heart, and this extreme sensitivity sometimes makes her imagination so active that it is difficult to moderate. Her mind is less exact than penetrating; her disposition is easy but nevertheless uneven; her face is ordinary but agreeable; her expression gives promise of a soul and does not lie. One can approach her with indifference but not leave her without emotion. Some have good qualities that are lacking to her; others have a greater measure of those good qualities she does possess; but none has a better combination of qualities for making a favorable character. She knows how to take advantage even of her defects, and if she were more perfect, she would be much less pleasing.

Sophie is not beautiful, but in her company men forget beautiful women, and beautiful women are dissatisfied with themselves. She is hardly pretty at first sight, but the more one sees her, the better she looks; she gains where so many others lose, and what she gains, she never loses again. Someone else may have more beautiful eyes, a more beautiful mouth, a more impressive face; but no one could have a better figure, a more beautiful complexion, a whiter hand, a daintier foot, a gentler glance, or a more touching expression. Without dazzling, she inspires interest, she charms, and one cannot say why.

Sophie loves adornment and is an expert at it. She is her mother's

---

* Brantôme says that in the time of François I a young girl who had a talkative lover imposed an absolute and unlimited silence on him, which he kept so faithfully for two whole years that it was believed he had become mute as a result of illness. One day in the midst of company, his beloved—who, in those times when love was practiced with mystery, was not known to be such—boasted that she would cure him on the spot and did so with the single word "Speak." Is there not something grand and heroic in that love? What more could the philosophy of Pythagoras—for all its ostentation—have accomplished? What woman today could count on a similar silence for one day, even if she were to reward it with the greatest prize she can offer? [29]

only lady's maid. She has considerable taste in dressing herself up to advantage, but she hates rich apparel; in her clothes one always sees simplicity joined with elegance. She likes not like what is brilliant but what is suitable. She is ignorant of what colors are fashionable, but she knows marvelously which look well on her. There is no young girl who appears to be dressed with less study and whose outfit is more studied; not a single piece of her clothing is chosen at random, and yet art is apparent nowhere. Her adornment is very modest in appearance and very coquettish in fact. She does not display her charms; she covers them, but, in covering them, she knows how to make them imagined. When someone sees her, he says, "Here is a modest, temperate girl." But so long as he stays near her, his eyes and his heart roam over her whole person without his being able to take them away; and one would say that all this very simple attire was put on only to be taken off piece by piece by the imagination.

Sophie has natural talents. She is aware of them and has not neglected them. But not having been in a position to devote much art to their cultivation, she was content to train her pretty voice to sing tunefully and tastefully, her little feet to walk lightly, easily, and gracefully and to curtsey in all sorts of situations without difficulty and without awkwardness. Furthermore, she has had no singing master other than her father and no dancing master other than her mother. An organist in the neighborhood gave her some lessons in accompaniment on the harpsichord which she has since cultivated alone. At first, she thought only of making her hands appear to advantage on its black keys. Then she found that the harsh, dry sound of the harpsichord made the sound of her voice sweeter. Little by little she became sensitive to harmony. Finally, as she was growing up, she began to feel the charms of expression and to love music for itself. But it is a taste rather than a talent. She does not know how to read the notes of a tune.

What Sophie knows best and has been most carefully made to learn are the labors of her own sex, even those that are not usually considered, like cutting and sewing her dresses. There is no needlework which she does not know how to do and which she does not do with pleasure. But the work she prefers to every other is lacework, because there is none which results in a more agreeable pose and in which the fingers are put to use more gracefully and lightly. She has also devoted herself to all the details of the household. She understands the kitchen and the pantry. She knows the price of foodstuffs and their qualities; she knows very well how to keep the accounts; she serves her mother as butler. Destined to be mother of a family herself one day, she learns to govern her own household by governing her parents'. She can substitute for the domestics in the performance of their functions, and she always does so gladly. One can never command well except when one knows how to do the job oneself. That is her mother's reason for keeping her busy in this way. Sophie herself does not think so far ahead. Her first duty is that of a girl, and it is now the only one she thinks of fulfilling. The only thing she has in view is serving her mother and relieving her of a part of her cares. It is nevertheless true that she does not undertake them all with equal pleasure. For example, although she is a glutton, she does not like the kitchen. There is something that disgusts her in its details; she never finds it clean enough. In this regard she has an extreme delicacy, and its excessiveness has become one of her failings. She would rather let her whole dinner be thrown into the fire than get a spot on her cuff. She has never wanted to oversee the garden for the same reason. The earth seems unclean to her. As soon as she sees manure, she believes she smells its odor.

She owes this defect to her mother's lessons. According to the latter, cleanliness is one of the first duties of women—a special duty, indispensable, imposed by nature. Nothing in the world is more disgusting than an unclean woman, and the husband who is disgusted by her is never wrong. Sophie's mother has so often preached this duty to her daughter since childhood, has so often demanded cleanliness in Sophie's person, her things, her room, her work, her grooming, that all these attentions, which have turned into a habit, take a rather large part of her time and also preside over the rest of it. The result is that to do what she does well is only the second of her cares. The first is always to do it cleanly.

However, all this has not degenerated into vain affectation or softness. The refinements of luxury play no part in it. In her rooms there was never anything but simple water. She knows no perfume other than that of flowers; and her husband will never smell anything sweeter than her breath. Finally, the attention she gives to her exterior does not make her forget that she owes her life and her time to nobler cares. She is ignorant of or disdains that excessive cleanliness of body which soils the soul. Sophie is much more than clean. She is pure.

I said that Sophie was a glutton. She was naturally so. But she became moderate through habit, and now she is so through virtue. The case is not the same for girls as for boys, whom one can govern by gluttony up to a certain point. This inclination is not inconsequential for the fair sex. It is too dangerous to be left unchecked. When little Sophie went into her mother's cupboard as a child, she did not always come back empty-handed, and her fidelity was not above every temptation so far as sugarplums and bonbons were concerned. Her mother surprised her, scolded her, punished her, and compelled her to fast. She finally succeeded in persuading Sophie that bonbons spoil the teeth and that eating too much fattens the figure. Thus Sophie mended her ways. In growing up, she acquired other tastes which diverted her from this base sensuality. In women as in men, as soon as the heart becomes animated, gluttony is no longer a dominant vice. Sophie has preserved the taste proper to her sex. She loves dairy products and sugared things. She loves pastry and sweets but has very little taste for meat. She has never tasted either wine or hard liquor. Moreover, she eats very moderate amounts of everything. Her sex, which is less laborious than ours, has less need of restoratives. In all things she loves what is good and knows how to appreciate it. She also knows how to accommodate herself to what is not good without this privation being painful to her.

Sophie has a mind that is agreeable without being brilliant, and solid without being profound—a mind about which people do not say anything, because they never find in it either more or less than what they find in their own minds. She has a mind which always pleases people who speak with her, although it is not ornamented according to the idea we have of the cultivation of women's minds; for hers is formed not by reading but only by the conversations of her father and mother, by her own reflections, and by the observations she has made in the little bit of the world she has seen. Gaiety is natural to Sophie; she was even frolicsome in her childhood, but her mother took care to repress her dizzy moods little by little, lest too sudden a change would give her instruction in the circumstance which made the repression necessary. She has therefore become modest and reserved even before the time to be so; and now that this time has come, it is easier for her to maintain the tone she has acquired than it would be for her to adopt it without an indication of the reason for this change. It is amusing to see her, due to a remnant of habit, abandon herself sometimes to childhood vivacities, and then suddenly come back to herself, become silent, lower her eyes, and blush. The intermediate stage between the two ages has to partake a bit of both.

Sophie's sensitivity is too great for her to preserve a perfect stability of disposition, but she is too gentle for that sensitivity to importune others very much; she harms only herself. Let one word which wounds her be spoken—she does not pout, but her heart swells. She tries to get away to cry. In the midst of her tears, let her father or her mother recall her and say one word, and she comes immediately to play and laugh while adroitly drying her tears and trying to stifle her sobs.

Nor is she entirely exempt from caprice. Her disposition, which is a bit too intense, degenerates into refractoriness, and then she is likely to forget herself. But leave her time to come back to herself, and her way of blotting out her wrong will almost make a merit of it. If she is punished, she is docile and submissive, and one sees that her shame comes not so much from the punishment as from the offense. If nothing is ever said to her, she will not fail to make amends for her offense herself, and so frankly and with such good grace that it is impossible to bear a grudge against her. She would kiss the ground before the lowliest domestic without this abasement causing her the least discomfort; and as soon as she is pardoned, her joy and her caresses show what a weight has been removed from her good heart. In a word, she suffers the wrongs of others with patience and makes amends for her own with pleasure. Such is the lovable nature of her sex before we have spoiled it. Woman is made to yield to man and to endure even his injustice. You will never reduce young boys to the same point. The inner sentiment in them rises and revolts against injustice. Nature did not constitute them to tolerate it.

gravem
Pelidae stomachum cedere nescii.[30]

Sophie is religious, but her religion is reasonable and simple, with little dogma and less in the way of devout practices—or, rather, she knows no essential practice other than morality, and she devotes her

BOOK V

entire life to serving God by doing good. In all the instructions her parents have given her on this subject, they have accustomed her to a respectful submission by always saying to her, "My daughter, this knowledge is not for your age. Your husband will instruct you in it when the time comes." For the rest, instead of long speeches about piety, they are content to preach piety to her by their example, and that example is engraved on her heart.

Sophie loves virtue. This love has become her dominant passion. She loves it because there is nothing so fine as virtue. She loves it because virtue constitutes woman's glory and because to her a virtuous woman appears almost equal to the angels. She loves it as the only route of true happiness and because she sees only misery, abandonment, unhappiness, and ignominy in the life of a shameless woman. She loves it, finally, as a thing that is dear to her respectable father and to her tender and worthy mother. They are not content with being happy because of their own virtue; they also want to be happy because of hers, and her chief happiness for herself is the hope of causing theirs. All these sentiments inspire in her an enthusiasm which lifts her soul and keeps all her petty inclinations subjected to so noble a passion. Sophie will be chaste and decent until her last breath. She has sworn it in the depth of her soul, and she has sworn it at a time when she already senses all that it costs to keep such an oath. She has sworn it at a time when she would have had to revoke the commitment if her senses were made to reign over her.

Sophie does not have the good fortune to be an amiable French woman, cold by temperament and coquettish by vanity, who wants to shine more than to please, and who seeks entertainment and not pleasure. The need to love by itself devours her. It comes to distract her and trouble her heart at festivals. She has lost her former gaiety; frolicsome games no longer suit her. Far from fearing the boredom of solitude, she seeks it. She thinks of him who is going to make solitude sweet for her. All men to whom she is indifferent importune her; she wants not a courtship but a lover. She would rather please a single decent man—and please him forever—than gain the acclaim of the fashionable which lasts one day and then changes into jeers the next.

Women's judgment is formed earlier than men's. Since almost from infancy women are on the defensive and entrusted with a treasure that is difficult to protect, good and evil are necessarily known to them sooner. Sophie, who is precocious in everything because her temperament inclines her to be so, also has had her judgment formed sooner than other girls her age. There is nothing very extraordinary about that. Maturity is not everywhere the same at the same time.

Sophie is knowledgeable about the duties and rights of her sex and of ours. She knows the failings of men and the vices of women. She also knows the corresponding good qualities and virtues and has engraved them all in the depths of her heart. No one could have a higher idea of the decent woman than the idea she has conceived. And this idea does not dismay her; rather, she thinks with more satisfaction of the decent man, the man of merit; she feels that she is made for that man, that she is worthy of him, that she can return to him the happiness she will receive from him. She feels that she will surely know how to recognize him. The only problem is finding him.

Women are the natural judges of men's merit as men are of women's merit. That is their reciprocal right, and neither men nor women are ignorant of it. Sophie knows she has this right and makes use of it, but with the modesty suitable to her youth, her inexperience, and her position. She judges only things within her reach, and she judges only when it serves to develop some useful maxim. She speaks of those who are absent only with the greatest circumspection, especially if they are women. She thinks that what makes women slanderous and satirical is to speak of their own sex. So long as they limit themselves to speaking of ours, they are only equitable. Sophie, therefore, limits herself to that. As for women, she never speaks about them except to say the good things about them which she knows. It is an honor she believes she owes to her own sex. And as for those about whom she knows nothing good to say, she says nothing at all—and what that means is clear.

Sophie has little experience of the practices of society, but she is obliging and attentive, and she puts grace in everything she does. A happy nature serves her better than would a great deal of art. She has a certain politeness of her own which does not depend on formulas. This politeness is not enslaved to fashions nor does it change with them; it does nothing on the basis of custom but comes from a true desire to please—and it does please. She is not acquainted with the trivial compliments, and she invents none that are more studied. She does not say that she is very obliged, that one does her great honor, that one should not take the trouble, etc. Still less does she take it into her head to turn phrases. She responds to an attention or to an act of routine politeness with a curtsey or a simple "thank you," but from her mouth that expression is well worth any other. In response to a true service, she lets her heart speak, and it is not a compliment that it finds. She has never allowed French customs to enslave her to the yoke of affectations —such as, when passing from one room to the next, placing her hand on the arm of a sexagenarian whom she would very much like to support. When an affected gallant offers her this impertinent service, she announces that she is not crippled and, leaving the officious fellow, bounds up the stairs and into the room with two leaps. In fact, although she is not tall, she has never wanted high heels. She has feet small enough to do without them.

She is quiet and respectful not only with women, but even with men married or men much older than she is. She will never accept a place above them except out of obedience, and she will resume her own below them as soon as she can. For she knows that the rights of age go before those of sex, since they have in their favor the prejudice of wisdom, which ought to be honored before everything else.

With young people of her own age, it is another matter. She needs a different tone to command respect from them, and she knows how to adopt it without abandoning the modest manner suitable to her. If they are modest and reserved themselves, she will gladly maintain with them the amiable familiarity of youth. Their conversations, full of innocence, will be bantering but decent. If they become serious, she wants them to be useful. If they degenerate into insipidity, she will soon make them stop, for she especially despises the petty jargon of gallantry, which she regards as very offensive to her sex. She knows that the man she seeks does not use that jargon, and she never willingly tolerates from another man anything that does not suit the one whose character is imprinted in the depth of her heart. The high opinion she has of the rights of her sex, the pride of soul which the purity of her sentiments gives her, that energy of virtue which she feels in herself and which makes her respectable in her own eyes—all cause her to hear with indignation the sugary remarks intended for her entertainment. She receives them not with an evident anger but with a disconcerting, ironical approval or an unexpectedly cold tone. Let a fair Phoebus [31] retail his kindnesses to her, cleverly praise her for her cleverness, for her beauty, for her graces, for the reward of happiness that comes from pleasing her; she is the girl to interrupt him politely and say, "Monsieur, I am very much afraid I know all those things better than you do. If we have nothing less banal to say, I believe we can terminate the conversation here." To accompany these words with a full curtsey and then be twenty steps from him is the matter of only an instant. Ask your pleasing little fellows if it is easy to display their chitchat to a mind as prickly as this one.

It is not the case that she lacks a strong love of praise, provided that it is the real thing and she can believe that the good which is said of her is actually thought. To appear touched by her merit, it is necessary to begin by showing that one has some oneself. A homage founded on esteem can flatter her haughty heart, but all gallant persiflage is always rebuffed. Sophie is not constituted to give exercise to the small talents of a clown.

Possessing so great a maturity of judgment and full-grown in all respects like a girl of twenty, Sophie at fifteen will not be treated as a child by her parents. As soon as they perceive the first restlessness of youth in her, they will hasten to provide against it before it develops any further. They will make tender and sensible speeches to her. Tender and sensible speeches are suitable to her age and her character. If that character is such as I imagine it, why would her father not speak to her pretty much as follows:

"Sophie, you are a big girl now, and it is not for the purpose of remaining a big girl forever that you have become one. We want you to be happy. It is for our sake that we want it, because our happiness depends on yours. The happiness of a decent girl lies in causing the happiness of a decent man. You must therefore think about getting married. You must think about it early, for the destiny of life depends on marriage, and there is never too much time to think about it.

"Nothing is more difficult than the choice of a good husband, unless it is perhaps the choice of a good wife. Sophie, you will be that rare woman, you will be the glory of our life and the happiness of our old age. But no matter how much merit you possess, the earth is not lacking in men who have still greater merit than you do. There is no man who ought not to be honored to get you; there are many who would honor you even more. The issue is to find among this number one who suits you, to know him, and to make yourself known to him.

"The greatest happiness of marriage depends on so many kinds of suitability that it is folly to want to obtain all of them together. It is necessary first to secure the most important ones. If the others happen to be there, one takes advantage of them; if they are lacking, one does without them. Perfect happiness is not of this earth, but the greatest unhappiness, and the one that can always be avoided, is being unhappy due to one's own fault.

"Some kinds of suitability are natural, others come from convention, and some depend only on opinion. Parents are the judges of the two latter kinds. Children alone are the judges of the former. Marriages made by the authority of fathers are guided uniquely by the suitability of convention and by that of opinion. It is not persons who are married; it is positions and wealth. But those things can change. The persons alone always remain, wherever the couple may go. In spite of fortune, it is only as a result of personal relations that a marriage can be happy or unhappy.

"Your mother had position. I was rich. These were the only considerations which led our parents to unite us. I lost my wealth. She lost her name and was forgotten by her family. Of what use is it to her today to have been born a lady? In our disasters the union of our hearts consoled us for everything. The similarity of our tastes caused us to choose this retreat. We live here happily in poverty. We take the place of everything else for each other. Sophie is our common treasure. We bless heaven for having given us this and taken away all the rest. See, my child, where providence has led us! The kinds of suitability which caused us to be married have vanished. We are happy due only to those that were counted for nothing.

"It is up to the spouses to match themselves. Mutual inclination ought to be their first bond. Their eyes and their hearts ought to be their first guides. Their first duty once they are united is to love each other; and since loving or not loving is not within our control, this duty necessarily involves another, which is to begin by loving each other before being united. This is the right of nature, which nothing can abrogate. Those who have hindered it by so many civil laws have paid more attention to the appearance of order than to the happiness of marriage and the morals of citizens. You see, my Sophie, that we are not preaching a difficult morality to you. It leads only to making you your own mistress and having us rely on you for the choice of your husband.

"After having told you our reasons for leaving you entirely at liberty, it is just that we also speak to you about the reasons why you should use this liberty wisely. My daughter, you are good and reasonable, you have rectitude and piety. you have talents which suit decent women, and you are not unendowed with attractions. But you are poor. You have the most estimable goods, and you lack only those which are most esteemed. Therefore, aspire only to what you can get, and guide your ambition not by your judgments nor by ours, but by the opinion of men. If it were only a question of an equality of merit, I do not know any limit that I ought to put on your hopes. But do not raise them above your fortune, and do not forget that it is of the lowest rank. Although a man worthy of you would not count this inequality as an obstacle, you ought to do what he will not do. Sophie ought to imitate her mother, and enter only into a family which considers itself honored by her. You did not see our opulence; you were born during our poverty. You make that poverty sweet for us, and you share it without difficulty. Believe me, Sophie, do not seek goods that we bless heaven for having delivered us from. We have tasted happiness only after having lost our riches.

"You are too lovable to please no one, and your poverty is not so great that a decent man would be embarrassed by you. You will be sought after, possibly by people who are not worthy of you. If they revealed themselves to you as they are, you would esteem them for what they are worth; all their pomp would not impress you for long. But although you have good judgment and you know what merit is, you lack experience and you are ignorant of the extent to which men can counterfeit themselves. A skillful faker can study your tastes in order to seduce you and feign virtues in your presence which he does not have. He would ruin you before you were aware of it, Sophie, and when you recognized your error, you would only be able to weep for it. The most dangerous of all traps, and the only one reason cannot avoid, is that of the senses. If you ever have the misfortune of falling into this trap, you will no longer see anything but illusions and chimeras; your eyes will be fascinated, your judgment clouded, your will corrupted. Your very error will be dear to you, and even if you were in a condition to recognize it, you would not want to recover from it. My daughter, it is to Sophie's reason that I entrust you; I do not entrust you to the inclination of her heart. So long as your blood is cool, remain your own judge. But as soon as you are in love, return yourself to your mother's care.

"I propose an agreement which is a mark of our esteem for you and re-establishes the natural order among us. Parents choose the husband of their daughter and consult her only for the sake of form. Such is the usual practice. We shall do exactly the opposite. You will choose, and we will be consulted. Use your right, Sophie; use it freely and wisely. The husband who suits you ought to be of your choice and not of ours. But it is for us to judge whether you are mistaken concerning this suitability and whether, without knowing it, you do something other than what you want. Birth, wealth, rank, and opinion will in no way enter in our decision. Take a decent man whose person pleases you and whose character suits you; whatever else he is, we will accept him as our son-in-law. His wealth will always be great enough if he can use his arms to work and if he has morals and loves his family. His rank will always be illustrious enough if he ennobles it by virtue. If the whole world should blame us, what difference does it make? We do not seek public approval. Your happiness is enough for us."

Readers, I do not know what effect a similar speech would have on girls raised in your way. As for Sophie, it is possible she will not respond with words. Shame and tenderness would not easily let her express herself. But I am quite sure that such a speech will remain engraved on her heart for the rest of her life, and that if one can count on any human resolution, it is on her heartfelt resolution to be worthy of her parents' esteem.

Let us take the worst case and give her an ardent temperament which makes a long wait painful for her. I say that her judgment, her knowledge, her taste, her delicacy, and especially the sentiments on which her heart has been fed in her childhood will oppose to the impetuosity of her senses a counterweight sufficient to vanquish them or at least to resist them for a long time. She would rather die a martyr to her condition than afflict her parents, wed a man without merit, and expose herself to the unhappiness of an ill-matched marriage. The very liberty she has received has the effect only of giving her a new elevation of soul and making her harder to please in the choice of her master. Possessing the temperament of an Italian woman and the sensitivity of an Englishwoman, Sophie combines with them—in order to control her heart and her senses—the pride of a Spanish woman, who, even when she is seeking a lover, does not easily find one she esteems worthy of her.

It does not belong to everyone to feel what a source of energy the love of decent things can give the soul and what force one can find within oneself when one wants to be sincerely virtuous. There are people to whom everything great appears chimerical, and who in their base and vile reasoning will never know what effect even a mania for virtue can have upon the human passions. To these people one must speak only with examples; so much the worse for them if they persist in denying these examples. If I said to them that Sophie is not an imaginary being, that her name alone is of my invention, that her education, her morals, her character, and even her looks have really existed, and that her memory still brings tears to every member of a decent family, they undoubtedly would believe nothing of it. Nonetheless, what would I risk in straightforwardly completing the history of a girl so similar to Sophie that her story could be Sophie's without occasioning any surprise? Whether it is believed to be true or not, it makes little difference. I shall, if you please, have told fictions, but I shall still have explicated my method, and I shall still be pursuing my ends.

The young person with the temperament I have just given to Sophie also resembled her in all the ways which could make her merit the name, and I shall continue to call her by it. After the conversation I have reported, her father and her mother, judging that eligible men would not come to offer themselves in the hamlet where they lived, sent her to spend a winter in the city at the home of an aunt, who was secretly informed of the purpose of this trip. For the haughty Sophie carried in the depth of her heart a noble pride in knowing how to triumph over herself; and whatever need she had of a husband, she would die a maiden rather than resolve to look for one.

To fulfill the intentions of Sophie's parents, her aunt presented her in homes, took her out to groups and parties, and made her see society

BOOK V

—or rather made society see her, for Sophie cared little for all this bustle. It was noted, however, that she did not flee young people with agreeable appearances who appeared decent and modest. In her very reserve, she had a certain art of attracting them which rather resembled coquetry. But after having conversed with them two or three times, she gave up. She soon substituted for that air of authority which seems to accept homages a more humble bearing and a more forbidding politeness. Always attentive to herself, she no longer gave them the occasion to do her the least service. This was an adequate way of saying she did not want to be their beloved.

Sensitive hearts never like boisterous pleasures, the vain and sterile happiness of people who feel nothing and who believe that to numb one's life is to enjoy it. Sophie had not found what she was seeking and, despairing of finding it in this way, she became bored by the city. She loved her parents tenderly; nothing compensated her for their absence, nothing was able to make her forget them. She went back to join them long before the date fixed for her return.

She had hardly resumed her functions in her parents' household before it was observed that, although she maintained the same conduct, her disposition had changed. She had moments of distraction and impatience; she was sad and dreamy; she hid herself in order to cry. At first they believed she was in love and was ashamed of it. They spoke to her about it; she denied it. She protested that she had seen no one who could touch her heart, and Sophie did not lie.

However, her languor constantly increased, and her health began to deteriorate. Her mother, upset by this change, finally resolved to find out its cause. She took Sophie aside and set to work on her with that winning language and those invincible caresses that only maternal tenderness knows how to employ. "My daughter, you whom I carried in my womb and whom I unceasingly carry in my heart, pour out the secrets of your heart on your mother's bosom. What are these secrets that a mother cannot know? Who pities your troubles? Who shares them? Who wants to relieve them, if not your father and mother? Ah, my child, do you want me to die of your pain without knowing what it is?"

Far from hiding her chagrins from her mother, the young girl asked for nothing better than to have her as a consoler and confidant. But shame prevented Sophie from speaking, and her modesty found no language to describe a condition so little worthy of her as the emotion which was disturbing her senses in spite of herself. Finally, her very shame served her mother as an indication, and she drew out these humiliating admissions from her daughter. Far from afflicting Sophie with unjust reprimands, her mother consoled her, pitied her, cried for her. She was too wise to make a crime out of an ill that Sophie's virtue alone made so cruel. But why endure without necessity an ill for which the remedy was so easy and so legitimate? Why did she not make use of the freedom she had been given? Why did she not accept a husband, why did she not choose one? Did she not know that her fate depended on herself alone, and that, whomever she chose, he would be approved, since she could not choose a man who was not decent? She had been sent to the city. She had not wanted to remain. Several eligible men had presented themselves; she had rebuffed them all. What was she waiting for, then? What did she want? What an inexplicable contradiction!

The answer was simple. If she had only to find someone to help satisfy youthful needs, the choice would soon be made. But a master for the whole of life is not so easy to choose. And since these two choices cannot be separated, a girl must simply wait, and often lose her youth before finding the man with whom she wants to spend all the days of her life. Such was Sophie's case. She needed a lover, but that lover had to be a husband; and given the heart needed to match hers, the former was almost as difficult to find as the latter. All these glamorous young people were suitable to her only from the point of view of age; they always failed to suit her in all other ways. Their superficial minds, their vanity, their jargon, their unruly morals, and their frivolous imitations disgusted her. She sought a man and found only monkeys; she sought a soul and found none.

"How unhappy I am!" she said to her mother. "I need to love, and I see nothing pleasing to me. My heart rejects all those who attract my senses. I see not one who does not excite my desires, and not one who does not repel my desires. An attraction that is not accompanied by esteem cannot endure. Ah, that is not the man for your Sophie! The charming model of the man for her is imprinted too deeply on her soul. She can love only him; she can make only him happy; she can be happy with him alone. She prefers to pine away and do constant battle; she prefers to die unhappy and free rather than in despair with a man she does not love and whom she would make unhappy. It is better no longer to exist than to exist only to suffer."

Struck by this singular discourse, her mother found it too bizarre not to suspect some mystery. Sophie was neither affected nor silly. How had this extravagant delicacy been able to take root in her—she who had been taught from her childhood nothing so much as to adjust herself to the people with whom she had to live and to make a virtue of necessity? This model of the lovable man with which she was so enchanted and which returned so often in all her conversations caused her mother to conjecture that this caprice had some other foundation of which she was still ignorant, and that Sophie had not told all. The unfortunate girl, oppressed by her secret pain, sought only to unburden herself. Her mother pressed. Sophie hesitated; she finally yielded, and, going out without saying anything, returned a moment later with a book in her hand. "Pity your unhappy daughter. Her sadness is without remedy. Her tears will never dry up. You want to know the cause. Well, here it is," she said, throwing the book on the table. The mother took the book and opened it. It was *The Adventures of Telemachus*.[32] At first she understood nothing of this enigma. But by dint of questions and obscure answers, she finally saw, with a surprise that is easy to conceive, that her daughter was the rival of Eucharis.[33]

Sophie loved Telemachus and loved him with a passion of which nothing could cure her. As soon as her father and her mother knew of her mania, they laughed about it and believed they would bring her around by reason. They were mistaken. Reason was not entirely on their side. Sophie also had her own reason and knew how to turn it to account. How many times she reduced them to silence by using their own reasoning again them, by showing them that they had done all the harm themselves: that they had not formed her for a man of her times; that she would necessarily have to adopt her husband's ways of thinking or convert him to her own; that they had made the first means impossible by the way they had raised her, and that the other was precisely what she was seeking. "Give me," she said, "a man imbued with my maxims or one whom I can bring around to them, and I shall marry him. But until then, why do you scold me? Pity me. I am unhappy, not mad. Does the heart depend on the will? Didn't my father say so himself? Is it my fault if I love what does not exist? I am not a visionary. I do not want a prince. I do not seek Telemachus. I know that he is only a fiction. I seek someone who resembles him. And why cannot this someone exist, since I exist—I who feel within myself a heart so similar to his? No, let us not thus dishonor humanity. Let us not think that a lovable and virtuous man is only a chimera. He exists; he lives; perhaps he is seeking me. He seeks a soul that knows how to love him. But what sort of man is he? Where is he? I do not know. He is none of those I have seen. Doubtless he is none of those I shall see. O my mother, why have you made virtue too lovable for me? If I can love nothing but virtue, the fault is less mine than yours."

Shall I bring this sad narrative to its catastrophic end? Shall I tell of the long disputes which preceded the catastrophe? Shall I portray an exasperated mother exchanging her earlier caresses for harshness? Shall I show an irritated father forgetting his earlier agreements and treating the most virtuous of daughters like a madwoman? Shall I, finally, depict the unfortunate girl—even more attached to her chimera as a result of the persecution she has suffered for it—going with slow steps toward death and descending into the grave at the moment when they believe they are leading her to the altar? No, I put aside these dreadful objects. I need not go so far to show by what seems to me a sufficiently striking example that, in spite of the prejudices born of the morals of our age, enthusiasm for the decent and the fine is no more foreign to women than to men, and that there is nothing that cannot be obtained under nature's direction from women as well as from men.

Here someone will stop me and ask whether it is nature which prescribes our expending so much effort for the repression of immoderate desires? My answer is no, but it also is not nature which gives us so many immoderate desires. Now, everything that is not nature is against nature. I have proved that countless times.

Let us render his Sophie to our Emile. Let us resuscitate this lovable girl to give her a less lively imagination and a happier destiny. I wanted to depict an ordinary woman, and by dint of elevating her soul I have disturbed her reason. I went astray myself. Let us retrace our steps. Sophie has only a good nature in a common soul. Every advantage she has over other women is the effect of her education.

<----------------------->

I proposed to say in this book all that can be done and to leave to the reader the choice—among the good things I may have said—of those that are within his reach. I had thought at the beginning that I would form Emile's companion at the outset and raise them for and with each other. But on reflection I found that all these arrangements were too premature and ill conceived, and that it was absurd to destine two children to be united before being able to know whether this union was in the order of nature and whether they had between them the compatibilities suitable for forming it. One must not confound what is natural in the savage state with what is natural in the civil state. In the former state all women are suitable for all men because both still have only the primitive and common form. In the latter, since each character is developed by social institutions and each mind has received its peculiar and determinate form not from education alone but from the well-ordered or ill-ordered conjunction of nature and education, men and women can no longer be matched except by presenting them to one another in order to see whether they suit one another in all respects—or at least in order to determine the choice resulting in the greatest degree of suitability.

The trouble is that as the social state develops characters, it distinguishes ranks, and since the order based on character is different from the order based on rank, the more one distinguishes among classes, the more one blurs the distinctions among characters. The consequences are ill-matched marriages and all the disorders deriving from them. From this one sees, by an evident inference, that the farther we are removed from equality, the more our natural sentiments are corrupted; the more the gap between noble and commoner widens, the more the conjugal bond is relaxed; and the more there are rich and poor, the less there are fathers and husbands. Neither master nor slave any longer has a family; each of the two sees only his status.

Do you wish to prevent such abuses and to promote happy marriages? Stifle prejudices, forget human institutions, and consult nature. Do not unite people who suit each other only in a given condition and who will no longer suit one another if this condition happens to change; instead, unite people who will suit one another in whatever situation they find themselves, in whatever country they inhabit, in whatever rank they may wind up. I do not say that compatibilities based on convention are immaterial in marriage, but I do say that the influence of natural compatibilities is so much more important that it alone is decisive for the fate of married life. There is a suitability of tastes, dispositions, sentiments, and characters which ought to engage a wise father—were he a prince or a monarch—to give to his son without hesitation the girl who would suit him in all these respects, were she born of a dishonorable family, were she the daughter of the hangman. Yes, I maintain that even if all the misfortunes imaginable were to fall upon a well-united couple, they would enjoy a truer happiness in weeping together than they would have if their enjoyment of all the good fortune in the world were poisoned by the disunion of their hearts.

Instead of determining a wife for my Emile from childhood, I have therefore waited to know the one who will suit him. It is not I who make this determination; it is nature. My job is to find out the choice that nature has made. I say my job and not that of Emile's father, for in confiding his son to me he yields his place to me, and he substitutes my right for his. I am Emile's true father; I made him a man. I would have refused to raise him if I had not been the master of marrying him to the woman of his choice—that is, of my choice. Only the pleasure of making a happy man can pay for what it costs to put him in a position to become happy.

Nor should you believe that I waited until I gave Emile the responsibility of looking for a wife before I found her. This feigned search is only a pretext for making him learn about women, so that he will sense the value of the one who suits him. For a long time Sophie has been found. Perhaps Emile has already seen her. But he will recognize her only when it is time.

Although equality of status is not necessary to marriage, when this equality is joined to the other kinds of suitability, it gives them a new value. It is not weighed against any of them, but it tips the scale when all else is equal.

Unless he is a monarch, a man cannot seek a woman in every class, for the prejudices he himself does not have he will find in others, and a certain girl who would perhaps suit him might nonetheless be unattainable for him. Thus there are maxims of prudence that ought to limit the search of a judicious father. He should not want to establish his pupil above his rank, for that is not within the father's control. Even if he could, he still should not want to, for what difference does rank make to a young man—at least my young man? Moreover, by climbing in rank he exposes himself to countless real ills which he will sense for his whole life. I even say that he should not want to trade off goods of different natures, like nobility and money, for what is gained by each is less than what it loses in the exchange. Furthermore, there is never agreement between the two parties about the value of what each has contributed. Finally, the preference each gives to his own contribution prepares the way for discord between the two families, and often between the two spouses.

It also makes a great difference for the good order of the marriage whether the man makes an alliance above or below himself. The former case is entirely contrary to reason; the latter is more conformable to it. Since the family is connected with society only by its head, the position of the head determines that of the entire family. When he makes an alliance in a lower rank, he does not descend, he raises up his wife. On the other hand, by taking a woman above him, he lowers her without raising himself. Thus, in the first case there is good without bad, and in the second bad without good. Moreover, it is part of the order of nature that the woman obey the man. Therefore, when he takes her from a lower rank, the natural and the civil order agree, and everything goes well. The contrary is the case when the man allies himself with a woman above him and thereby faces the alternative of curbing either his rights or his gratitude and of being either ungrateful or despised. Then the woman, pretending to authority, acts as a tyrant toward the head of the house, and the master becomes a slave and finds himself the most ridiculous and most miserable of creatures. Such are those unfortunate favorites whom the Asian kings honor and torment by marrying them to their daughters, and who are said to dare to approach only from the foot of the bed in order to sleep with their wives.

I expect that many readers, remembering that I ascribe to woman a natural talent for governing man, will accuse me of a contradiction here. They will, however, be mistaken. There is quite a difference between arrogating to oneself the right to command and governing him who commands. Woman's empire is an empire of gentleness, skill, and obligingness; her orders are caresses, her threats are tears. She ought to reign in the home as a minister does in a state—by getting herself commanded to do what she wants to do. In this sense, the best households are invariably those where the woman has the most authority. But when she fails to recognize the voice of the head of the house, when she wants to usurp his rights and be in command herself, the result of this disorder is never anything but misery, scandal, and dishonor.

There remains the choice between one's equals and one's inferiors; and I believe that some restriction must be placed upon the latter, for it is difficult to find among the dregs of the people a wife capable of making a gentleman happy. It is not that they are more vicious in the lowest rank than in the highest, but that they have few ideas of what is beautiful and decent, and that the injustice of the other estates makes the lowest see justice in its very vices.

By nature man hardly thinks. To think is an art he learns like all the others and with even more difficulty. In regard to relations between the two sexes, I know of only two classes which are separated by a real distinction—one composed of people who think, the other of people who do not think; and this difference comes almost entirely from education. A man from the first of these two classes ought not to make an alliance in the other, for the greatest charm of society is lacking to him when, despite having a wife, he is reduced to thinking alone. People who literally spend their whole lives working in order to live have no idea other than that of their work or their self-interest, and their whole mind seems to be at the end of their arms. This ignorance harms neither probity nor morals. Often it even serves them. Often one compromises in regard to one's duties by dint of reflecting on them and ends up replacing real things with abstract talk. Conscience is the most enlightened of philosophers. One does not need to know Cicero's *Offices* to be a good man, and the most decent woman in the world perhaps has the least knowledge of what decency is. But it is no less true that only a cultivated mind makes association agreeable, and it is a sad thing for a father of a family who enjoys himself in his home to be forced to close himself up and not be able to make himself understood by anyone.

Besides, how will a woman who has no habit of reflecting raise her children? How will she discern what suits them? How will she incline them toward virtues she does not know, toward merit of which she has no idea? She will know only how to flatter or threaten them, to make them insolent or fearful. She will make mannered monkeys or giddy rascals of them, never good minds or lovable children.

Therefore, it is not suitable for a man with education to take a wife who has none, or, consequently, to take a wife from a rank in which she could not have an education. But I would still like a simple and coarsely raised girl a hundred times better than a learned and brilliant one who would come to establish in my house a tribunal of literature over which she would preside. A brilliant wife is a plague to her husband, her children, her friends, her valets, everyone. From the sublime elevation of her fair genius she disdains all her woman's duties and always begins by making herself into a man after the fashion of Mademoiselle de l'Enclos. Outside her home she is always ridiculous and very justly criticized; this is the inevitable result as soon as one leaves one's station and is not fit for the station one wants to adopt. All these women of great talent never impress anyone but fools. It is always known who the artist or the friend is who holds the pen or the brush when they work. It is known who the discreet man of letters is who secretly dictates their oracles to them. All this charlatanry is unworthy of a decent woman. Even if she had some true talents, her pretensions would debase them. Her dignity consists in her being ignored. Her glory is in her husband's esteem. Her pleasures are in the happiness of her family. Readers, I leave it to you. Answer in good faith. What gives you a better opinion of a woman on entering her room, what makes you approach her with more respect—to see her occupied with the labors of her sex and the cares of her household, encompassed by her children's things, or to find her at her dressing table writing verses, surrounded by all sorts of pamphlets and letters written on tinted paper? Every literary maiden would remain a maiden for her whole life if there were only sensible men in this world:

Quaeris cur nolim te ducere, Galla? diserta es.[34]

After these considerations comes that of looks. It is the first consideration which strikes one and the last to which one ought to pay attention, but still it should count for something. Great beauty appears to me to be avoided rather than sought in marriage. Beauty promptly wears out in possession. After six weeks it is nothing more for the possessor, but its dangers last as long as it does. Unless a beautiful woman is an angel, her husband is the unhappiest of men; and even if she were an angel, how will she prevent his being ceaselessly surrounded by enemies? If extreme ugliness were not disgusting, I would prefer it to extreme beauty; for in a short time both are nothing for the husband, and thus beauty becomes a drawback and ugliness an advantage. But ugliness which produces disgust is the greatest of misfortunes. This sentiment, far from fading away, increases constantly and turns into hatred. Such a marriage is a hell. It would be better to be dead than to be thus united.

Desire mediocrity in everything, without excepting even beauty. An attractive and prepossessing face that inspires not love but benevolence is what one ought to prefer. It is not prejudicial to the husband, and its advantages contribute to the profit of both. Graces do not wear out like beauty. They have life, they are constantly renewed, and at the end of thirty years of marriage a decent woman with graces pleases her husband as she did on the first day.

Such are the reflections which have determined me on the choice of Sophie. She is a pupil of nature just as Emile is, and she, more than any other, is made for him. She will be the woman of the man. She is his equal in birth and merit, his inferior in fortune. She does not enchant at first glance, but she pleases more each day. Her greatest charm acts only by degrees. It unfolds only in the intimacy of association, and her husband will sense it more than anyone in the world. Her education is neither brilliant nor neglected. She has taste without study, talents without art, judgment without knowledge. Her mind does not know, but it is cultivated for learning; it is a well-prepared soil that only awaits seed in order to bear fruit. She has read no other books than Barrême [35] and *Telemachus*, which fell into her hands by chance. But does a girl capable of becoming impassioned about Telemachus have a heart without sentiment and a mind without delicacy? O what lovable ignorance! Happy is he who is destined to instruct her. She will be not her husband's teacher but his pupil. Far from wanting to subject him to her tastes, she will adopt his. She is better for him as she is than if she were learned: he will have the pleasure of teaching her everything. It is finally time that they see each other. Let us work to bring them together.

We are sad and dreamy as we leave Paris. This city of chatter is not the place for us. Emile turns a disdainful eye toward this great city and says resentfully, "How many days lost in vain searches! Ah, the wife of my heart is not there. My friend, you knew it well. But my time scarcely costs you anything, and my ills cause you little suffering." I give him a fixed look and say, without getting aroused, "Do you believe what you are saying?" At once, very much embarrassed, he embraces me and hugs me in his arms without answering. This is always his answer when he is wrong.

Here we are in the country like true knights-errant, although not seeking adventures as they do; on the contrary, we flee adventures in leaving Paris. But we imitate the pace of those knights in our wandering, sometimes proceeding at full tilt and sometimes meandering. By dint of following my practice, one will have finally grasped its spirit, and I cannot imagine a reader still so prejudiced by custom as to suppose us both asleep in a good, well-closed post-chaise, progressing without seeing or observing anything, making worthless for ourselves the interval between departure and arrival, and by the speed of our progress wasting time in order to save it.

Men say that life is short, and I see that they exert themselves to make it so. Not knowing how to employ it, they complain of the rapidity of time, and I see that it flows too slowly for their taste. Always occupied with the goal toward which they are straining, they regard with regret the interval separating them from that goal. One man wants it to be tomorrow, another next month, another ten years from now. None wants to live today. None is content with the present hour; all find it too slow in passing. When they complain that time flows too fast, they lie. They would gladly pay for the power to accelerate it. They would gladly use their fortune to consume their whole lives; and there is perhaps not a single one who would not have reduced his years to very few hours if he had been the master of eliminating, at the prompting of his boredom, those hours which were burdensome to him, and, at the prompting of his impatience, those hours which separated him from the desired moment. A man spends half his life going from Paris to Versailles, from Versailles to Paris, from the city to the country, from the country to the city, and from one part of town to the next, and he would be very much at a loss about what to do with his hours if he did not know the secret of wasting them in this way; he purposely goes far away from his business in order to keep busy going back to it. He believes he gains the extra time he spends in this way, for otherwise he would not know how to fill it. Or, on the contrary, he hurries in order to hurry and comes with post-horses for no other reason than to return in the same way. Mortals, will you never cease to calumniate nature? Why do you complain that life is short, since it is still not short enough for your taste? If there is a single one among you who knows how to temper his desires so that he never wishes for time to pass, he will not regard life as too short. To live and to enjoy will be the same thing for him, and even if he were to die young, he would die full with days.

Even if there were only this advantage to my method, it alone would make it preferable to any other. I have not raised my Emile to desire or to wait but to enjoy; and when he extends his desires beyond the present, his ardor is not so impetuous that he is bothered by the slowness of time. He will enjoy not only the pleasure of desiring but that of going to the object he desires, and his passions are so moderate that he is always more where he is than where he will be.

Therefore, we travel not like messengers but like travelers. We do not think only about the departure and the arrival but also about the interval separating them. The trip itself is a pleasure for us. We do not make it seated sadly, like prisoners, in a small, closed-up cage. We do not travel in softness and repose, as women do. We do not deprive ourselves of the fresh air, or the sight of the objects surrounding us, or the ease of contemplating them at our will when it pleases us. Emile never enters a post-chaise and does not travel about on post-horses unless he is in a hurry. But why would Emile ever be in a hurry? For one reason alone—to enjoy life. Shall I add another—to do good when he can? No, for that itself is to enjoy life.

I can conceive of only one way of traveling that is more agreeable than going by horse. That is going by foot. The traveler leaves at his own good time; he stops at will; he takes as much or as little exercise as he wants. He observes the whole country; he turns aside to the right or the left; he examines all that appeals to him; he stops to see all the views. Do I notice a river? I walk along it. A thick wood? I go beneath its shade. A grotto? I visit it. A quarry? I examine the minerals. Everywhere I enjoy myself, I stay. The moment I get bored, I go. I depend on neither horse nor coachman. I do not need to choose ready-made paths, comfortable roads; I pass wherever a man can pass. I see all that a man can see; and, depending only on myself, I enjoy all the liberty a man can enjoy. If bad weather stops me and boredom overtakes me, then I take horses. If I am weary . . . but Emile hardly gets weary. He is robust, and why should he get weary? He is not in a hurry. If he stops, how can he get bored? He carries everywhere the means of enjoying himself. He enters a master's establishment and works. He exercises his arms to rest his feet.

To travel on foot is to travel like Thales, Plato, and Pythagoras.[36] It is hard for me to understand how a philosopher can resolve to travel any other way and tear himself away from the examination of the riches which he tramples underfoot and which the earth lavishly offers to his sight. Who that has some liking for agriculture does not want to know the products peculiar to the climate of the places he passes through and the way in which they are cultivated? Who that has some taste for natural history can resolve to pass by a piece of land without examining it, a boulder without chipping it, mountains without herborizing, stones without looking for fossils? Your city philosophers learn natural history in museums; they have gadgets; they know names and have no idea of nature. But Emile's museum is richer than those of kings; it is the whole earth. Each thing is in its place. The naturalist in charge has put the whole in very beautiful order; d'Aubenton [37] could not do better.

How many different pleasures are brought together by this agreeable way of traveling, without counting strengthened health and brightened humor! I have always observed that those who traveled in good, smooth-riding vehicles were dreamy, sad, scolding, or ailing, while pedestrians were gay, easygoing, and content with everything. How the heart laughs when one approaches lodgings! How savory a coarse meal appears! With what pleasure one rests at the table! What a good sleep one has in a bad bed! When one wants only to arrive, one can hurry in a post-chaise. But when one wants to travel, one has to go on foot.

If Sophie is not forgotten before we have gone fifty leagues in the way I imagine, either I must not be very skillful or Emile must not be very curious; for since Emile possesses so many kinds of elementary knowledge, it is difficult for him not to be tempted to go farther in them. One is curious only to the extent that one is informed. He knows exactly enough to want to learn.

Meanwhile one object attracts us to another, and we always go forward. I have set a distant goal for our first trip. The pretext for doing so is easy: one has to go a long way from Paris to look for a wife.

One day, after having strayed more than usual in valleys and mountains where no path can be perceived, we can no longer find our way again. It makes little difference to us. All paths are good, provided one arrives. But, still, one has to arrive somewhere when one is hungry. Happily we find a peasant who takes us to his cottage. We eat his meager dinner with great appetite. On seeing us so tired and famished, he says to us, "If the good Lord had led you to the other side of the hill, you would have been better received . . . you would have found a house of peace . . . such charitable people . . . such good people . . . They are not better-hearted than I am, but they are richer, although it is said that they were previously much more so . . . they are not suffering, thank God, and the whole countryside feels the effects of what remains to them."

At this mention of good people, the good Emile's heart gladdens. "My friend," he says, looking at me, "let us go to that house whose masters are blessed in the neighborhood. I would be glad to see them. Perhaps they will be glad to receive us, too. I am sure they will receive us well. If they are of our kind, we shall be of theirs."

Having received good directions to the house, we leave and wander through the woods. On the way heavy rain surprises us. It slows us up without stopping us. Finally we find our way, and in the evening we arrive at the designated house. In the hamlet which surrounds it, this house alone, although simple, stands out. We present ourselves. We ask for hospitality. We are taken to speak to the master. He questions us, but politely. Without telling him the subject of our trip, we tell him the reason for our detour. From his former opulence he has retained a facility for recognizing the station of people by their manners. Whoever has lived in high society is rarely mistaken about that. On the basis of this passport we are admitted.

We are shown to a very little, but clean and comfortable apartment. A fire is made. We find linen, garments, everything we need. "What!" says Emile. "It is as though we were expected! Oh how right the peasant was! What attention, what goodness, what foresight! And for unknowns! I believe I am living in Homer's time." "Be sensitive to all this," I say to him, "but don't be surprised. Wherever strangers are rare, they are welcome. Nothing makes one more hospitable than seldom needing to be. It is the abundance of guests which destroys hospitality. In the time of Homer people hardly traveled, and travelers were well received everywhere. We are perhaps the only transients who have been seen here during the whole year." "It makes no difference," he replies. "That itself is praise—to know how to get along without guests and always to receive them well."

After we have dried ourselves and straightened up, we go to rejoin the master of the house. He presents his wife to us. She receives us not only politely but with kindness. The honor of her glances belongs to Emile. A mother in her situation rarely sees a man of that age enter her home without uneasiness or at least curiosity.

For our sake they have supper served early. On entering the dining room, we see five settings. We are seated, but an empty place remains. A girl enters, curtseys deeply, and sits down modestly without speaking. Emile, busy with his hunger or his answers, greets her and continues to speak and eat. The principle object of his trip is as distant from his thoughts as he believes himself to be still distant from its goal. The discussion turns to the travelers' losing their way. "Sir," the master of the house says to him, "you appear to me to be a likable and wise young man, and that makes me think that you and your governor have arrived here tired and wet like Telemachus and Mentor on Calypso's island." "It is true," Emile answers, "that we find here the hospitality of Calypso." His Mentor adds, "And the charms of Eucharis." [38] But although Emile knows the *Odyssey*, he has not read *Telemachus*. He does not know who Eucharis is. As for the girl, I see her blush up to her eyes, lower them toward her plate, and not dare to murmur. Her mother, who notices her embarrassment, gives a sign to her father, and he changes the subject. In speaking of his solitude, he gradually gets involved in the story of the events which confined him to it: the misfortunes of his life, the constancy of his wife, the consolations they have found in their union, the sweet and peaceful life they lead in their retreat—and still without saying a word about the girl. All this forms an agreeable and touching story which cannot be heard without interest. Emile, moved and filled with tenderness, stops eating in order to listen. Finally, at the part where the most decent of men enlarges with great pleasure on the attachment of the worthiest of women, the young traveler is beside himself; with one hand he grips the husband's hand, and with the other he takes the wife's hand and leans toward it rapturously, sprinkling it with tears. The young man's naïve vivacity enchants everyone, but the girl, more sensitive than anyone to this mark of his good heart, believes she sees Telemachus affected by Philoctetes' [39] misfortunes. She furtively turns her eyes toward him in order to examine his face better. She finds nothing there which denies the comparison. His easy bearing is free without being arrogant. His manners are lively without being giddy. His sensitivity makes his glance gentler, his expression more touching. The girl, seeing him cry, is ready to mingle her tears with his. But even with so fair a pretext, a secret shame restrains her. She already reproaches herself for the tears about to escape her eyes, as though it were bad to shed them for her family.

Her mother, who from the beginning of the supper has not stopped watching her, sees her constraint and delivers her from it by sending her on an errand. A minute later the young girl returns, but she is so little recovered that her disorder is visible to all eyes. Her mother gently says to her, "Sophie, pull yourself together. Will you never stop crying over the misfortunes of your parents? You, who console them for their misfortunes, must not be more sensitive to them than they are themselves."

At the name Sophie, you would have seen Emile shiver. Struck by so dear a name, he is wakened with a start and casts an avid glance at the girl who dares to bear it. "Sophie, O Sophie! Is it you whom my heart seeks? Is it you whom my heart loves?" He observes her and contemplates her with a sort of fear and distrust. He does not see exactly the face that he had depicted to himself. He does not know whether the one he sees is better or worse. He studies each feature; he spies on each movement, each gesture. In all he finds countless confused interpretations. He would give half his life for her to be willing to speak a single word. Uneasy and troubled, he looks at me. His eyes put a hundred questions to me and make a hundred reproaches all at once. He seems to say to me with each look, "Guide me while there is time. If my heart yields and is mistaken, I shall never recover in all my days."

Emile is worse at disguising his feelings than any man in the world. How would he disguise them in the greatest disturbance of his life, in the presence of four spectators who examine him and of whom the most distracted in appearance is actually the most attentive? His disorder does not escape Sophie's penetrating eyes. Moreover, his eyes teach her that she is the cause of his disorder. She sees that this apprehensiveness is not yet love. But what difference does it make? He is involved with her, and that is enough. She will be most unlucky if he becomes involved with her with impunity.

Mothers have eyes just as their daughters do, and they have experience to boot. Sophie's mother smiles at the success of our projects. She reads the hearts of the two young people. She sees that it is time to captivate the heart of the new Telemachus. She gets her daughter to speak. Her daughter responds with her natural gentleness in a timid voice which makes its effect all the better. At the first sound of this voice Emile surrenders. It is Sophie. He no longer doubts it. If it were not she, it would be too late for him to turn back.

It is then that the charms of this enchanting girl flow in torrents into his heart, and he begins to swallow with deep draughts the poison with which she intoxicates him. He no longer speaks, he no longer responds; he sees only Sophie, he hears only Sophie. If she says a word, he opens his mouth; if she lowers her eyes, he lowers his; if he sees her breathe, he sighs. It is Sophie's soul which appears to animate him. How his own soul has changed in a few instants! It is no longer Sophie's turn to tremble; it is Emile's. Farewell freedom, naïveté, frankness! Confused, embarrassed, fearful, he no longer dares to look around him for fear of seeing that he is being looked at. Ashamed to let the others see through him, he would like to make himself invisible to everyone in order to sate himself with contemplating her without being observed. Sophie, on the contrary, is reassured by Emile's fear. She sees her triumph. She enjoys it:

Nol mostra già, ben che in suo cor ne rida.[40]

Her countenance has not changed. But in spite of this modest air and these lowered eyes, her tender heart palpitates with joy and tells her that Telemachus has been found.

If I enter here into the perhaps too naïve and too simple history of their innocent love, people will regard these details as a frivolous game, but they will be wrong. They do not sufficiently consider the influence which a man's first liaison with a woman ought to have on the course of both their lives. They do not see that a first impression as lively as that of love, or the inclination which takes its place, has distant effects whose links are not perceived in the progress of the years but do not cease to act until death. We are given treatises on education consisting of useless, pedantic, bloated verbiage about the chimerical duties of children, and we are not told a word about the most important and most difficult part of the whole of education—the crisis

EMILE

that serves as a passage from childhood to man's estate. If I have been
able to make these essays useful in some respect, it is especially by
having expanded at great length on this essential part, omitted by all
others, and by not letting myself be rebuffed in this enterprise by false
delicacies or frightened by difficulties of language. If I have said what
must be done, I have said what I ought to have said. It makes very little
difference to me if I have written a romance.[41] A fair romance it is
indeed, the romance of human nature. If it is to be found only in this
writing, is that my fault? This ought to be the history of my species.[42]
You who deprave it, it is you who make a romance of my book.

Another consideration which strengthens the first is that I am dealing here not with a young man given over from childhood to fear,
covetousness, envy, pride, and all the passions that serve as instruments
for common educations, but with a young man for whom this is not
only his first love but his first passion of any kind. On this passion,
perhaps the only one he will feel intensely in his whole life, depends
the final form his character is going to take. Once fixed by a durable
passion, his way of thinking, his sentiments, and his tastes are going to
acquire a consistency which will no longer permit them to deteriorate.

One can conceive that for Emile and me the night following such an
evening is not spent entirely in sleeping. What? Ought the mere agreement of a name to have so much power over a wise man? Is there only
one Sophie in the world? Do they all resemble one another in soul as
they do in name? Are all the Sophies he will see his? Is he mad, getting
passionate in this way about an unknown girl to whom he has never
spoken? Wait, young man. Examine. Observe. You do not even know
yet whose house you are in, and to hear you one would believe you are
already in your own home.

This is not the time for lessons, and such lessons are not going to be
heard. They only have the effect of giving the young man a new
interest in Sophie out of the desire to justify his inclination. This
resemblance of names, this meeting (which he believes is fortuitous),
and my very reserve have only the effect of exciting his vivacity. Already Sophie appears too estimable for him not to be sure of making
me love her.

I suspect that the next morning Emile will try to dress himself up
more carefully in his sorry traveling outfit. He does not fail to do so.
But I laugh at his eagerness to make use of the household linen. I see
through his thought. I realize with pleasure that, by seeing to it that
there are things to be returned or exchanged, he seeks to establish for
himself a sort of connection which gives him the right to send things
back here and come back himself.

I had also expected to find Sophie a bit more dressed up. I was mistaken. This vulgar coquetry is good for those whom one only wants to
please. The coquetry of true love is more refined; it has very different
pretensions. Sophie is dressed up even more simply and casually than
the day before, although still with scrupulous cleanliness. I see coquetry
in this casualness only because I see affectation in it. Sophie knows
that more studied adornment is a declaration, but she does not know
that more casual adornment is also a declaration. She shows that she

BOOK V

is not content to please by her dress, that she also wants to please by her person. What difference does it make to her lover how she is dressed provided that he sees that she is concerned with him? Already sure of her empire, Sophie does not content herself with appealing to Emile's eyes with her charms; his heart must seek them out. It is no longer enough for her that he see her charms; she wants him to suppose them. Has he not seen enough of them to be obliged to guess the rest?

It may be believed that, during the time of our discussions that night, Sophie and her mother also did not remain silent. There were confessions extracted, instructions given. The next day's gathering has been well prepared. It is not yet twelve hours since our young people saw each other for the first time. They have not yet said a single word to each other, and already one sees that they have reached an understanding. Their manner is not familiar; it is embarrassed and timid; they do not speak to each other. Their eyes are lowered and seem to avoid each other; that is itself a sign of communication; they avoid each other, but by agreement. They already sense the need of mystery before having said anything to each other. As we leave, we ask permission to come back ourselves to return what we are taking away with us. Emile's mouth asks this permission from the father and the mother, while his apprehensive eyes, turned to the daughter, ask it from her much more insistently. Sophie says nothing, makes no sign, appears to see nothing and hear nothing. But she blushes, and this blush is a still clearer answer than her parents'.

We are permitted to return without being invited to stay over. This conduct is suitable. Board is given to passers-by who are at a loss for lodging, but it is not seemly for a lover to sleep in his beloved's home.

We hardly are out of this dear house before Emile thinks of establishing ourselves in the neighborhood. Even the nearest cottage seems too distant. He would like to sleep in the ditches of the manor. "Giddy young man!" I say to him in a tone of pity. "What, does passion already blind you? Do you already no longer see either propriety or reason? Unfortunate one! You believe you are in love, and you want to dishonor your beloved! What will be said when it is known that a young man who leaves her home sleeps in the vicinity? You love her, you say! Will you then ruin her reputation? Is that the payment for the hospitality her parents have granted you? Will you cause the disgrace of the girl from whom you expect your happiness?" "Well," he answers, "what difference do the vain talk of men and their unjust suspicions make? Haven't you yourself taught me to take no notice of it? Who knows better than I how much I honor Sophie, how much I want to respect her? My attachment will not cause her shame; it will cause her glory; it will be worthy of her. If my heart and my attentions everywhere render her the homage she deserves, how can I insult her?" "Dear Emile," I respond, embracing him, "you reason for yourself. Learn to reason for her. Do not compare the honor of one sex to that of the other. They have entirely different principles. These principles are equally solid and reasonable because they derive equally from nature; and the same virtue which makes you despise men's talk for yourself obliges you to respect it for your beloved. Your honor is in you alone, and hers depends on others. To neglect it would be to wound your own honor; and you do not render yourself what you owe yourself if you are the cause of her not being rendered what is owed her."

Then I explain the reasons for these differences to him, making him sense what an injustice it would be to take no account of these differences. Who has told him that he will be the husband of Sophie, whose sentiments he is ignorant of, whose heart (or whose parents) has perhaps made prior commitments, whom he does not know, and who perhaps suits him in none of the ways which can make for a happy marriage? Does he not know that for a girl every scandal is an indelible stain, which even her marriage to the man who caused it does not remove? What sensitive man wants to ruin the girl he loves? What decent man wants to make an unfortunate girl weep forever for the misfortune of having pleased him?

The young man, who is always extreme in his ideas, is frightened by the consequences I make him envisage, and he now believes he is never far enough away from Sophie's dwelling. He doubles his pace to flee more quickly. He looks around to see whether we are overheard. He would sacrifice his happiness a thousand times for the honor of the one he loves. He would rather not see her again in his life than cause her any displeasure. This is the first fruit of the cares I took in his youth to form in him a heart that knows how to love.

We have to find, then, an abode that is distant but within range. We seek, and we make inquiries; we learn that two leagues away there is a town. We go to find lodging there rather than in nearer villages, where our stay would become suspect. The new lover finally arrives there full of love, hope, joy, and, especially, good sentiments. And this is how, by directing his nascent passion little by little toward what is good and decent, without his being aware of it I dispose all of his inclinations to take the same bent.

I approach the end of my career. I already see it in the distance. All the great difficulties are overcome. All the great obstacles are surmounted. Nothing difficult is left for me to do, except not to spoil my work by hurrying to consummate it. In the uncertainty of human life, let us avoid above all the false prudence of sacrificing the present for the future; this is often to sacrifice what is for what will not be. Let us make man happy at all ages lest, after many cares, he die before having been happy. Now, if there is a time to enjoy life, it is surely the end of adolescence when the faculties of body and soul have acquired their greatest vigor. Man is then in the middle of his course, and he sees from the greatest distance the two end points which make him feel its brevity. If imprudent youth makes mistakes, it is not because it wants enjoyment; it is because it seeks enjoyment where it is not, and because, while preparing a miserable future for itself, it does not even know how to use the present moment.

Consider my Emile—now past twenty, well formed, well constituted in mind and body, strong, healthy, fit, skillful, robust, full of sense, reason, goodness, and humanity, a man with morals and taste, loving the beautiful, doing the good, free from the empire of cruel passions, exempt from the yoke of opinion, but subject to the law of wisdom and submissive to the voice of friendship, possessing all the useful talents and some of the agreeable ones, caring little for riches, with his means of support in his arms, and not afraid of lacking bread whatever happens. Now he is intoxicated by a nascent passion. His heart opens itself to the first fires of love. Its sweet illusions make him a new universe of delight and enjoyment. He loves a lovable object who is even more lovable for her character than for her person. He hopes for, he expects a return that he feels is his due. It is from the similarity of their hearts, from the conjunction of decent sentiments that their first inclination was formed. This inclination ought to be durable. He yields confidently, even reasonably, to the most charming delirium, without fear, without regret, without remorse, without any other worry than that which is inseparable from the sentiment of happiness. What is lacking to his happiness? Look, consider, imagine what he still needs that can accord with what he has. He enjoys together all the goods that can be obtained at once. None can be added except at the expense of another. He is as happy as a man can be. Shall I at this moment shorten so sweet a destiny? Shall I trouble so pure a delight? Ah, the whole value of life is in the felicity he tastes! What could I give him which was worth what I had taken away from him? Even in putting the crown on his happiness, I would destroy its greatest charm. This supreme happiness is a hundred times sweeter to hope for than to obtain. One enjoys it better when one looks forward to it than when one tastes it. O good Emile, love and be loved! Enjoy a long time before possessing. Enjoy love and innocence at the same time. Make your paradise on earth while awaiting the other one. I shall not shorten this happy time of your life. I shall spin out its enchantment for you. I shall prolong it as much as possible. Alas, it has to end, and end soon. But I shall at least make it last forever in your memory and make you never repent having tasted it.

Emile does not forget that we have things to return. As soon as they are ready, we take horses and set out at full speed; this one time, Emile would like to have arrived as soon as we leave. When the heart is opened to the passions, it is opened to life's boredom. If I have not wasted my time, his whole life will not pass in this way.

Unhappily there is a severe break in the road and the countryside proves heavy going. We get lost. He notices it first, and without impatience and without complaint he gives all his attention to finding his way again. He wanders for a long time before knowing where he is, always with the same coolness. This means nothing to you but a great deal to me, since I know his hot nature. I see the fruit of the care I have taken since his childhood to harden him against the blows of necessity.

Finally we arrive. The reception given us is far more simple and more obliging than the first time. We are already old acquaintances. Emile and Sophie greet each other with a bit of embarrassment and still do not speak to each other. What would they say to each other in our presence? The conversation they require has no need of witnesses. We take a walk in the garden. It has as its parterre a very well-arranged kitchen garden; as its park it has an orchard covered with large, beautiful fruit trees of every kind, interspersed with pretty streams and beds full of flowers. "What a beautiful place," cries out Emile, full of his Homer and always enthusiastic. "I believe I see the garden of Alcinous." The daughter would like to know who Alcinous is, and the mother asks. "Alcinous," I tell them, "was a king of Corcyra whose garden, described by Homer, is criticized by people of taste for being too simple and without enough adornment.* This Alcinous had a lovable daughter who dreamed, on the eve of a stranger's receiving hospitality from her father, that she would soon have a husband." [44] Sophie is taken aback and blushes, lowers her eyes, bites her tongue. One cannot imagine such embarrassment. Her father, who takes pleasure in increasing it, joins in and says that the young princess herself went to wash the linen in the river. "Do you believe," he continues, "that she would have disdained to touch the dirty napkins, saying that they smelled of burnt fat?" Sophie, against whom the blow is directed, forgets her natural timidity and excuses herself with vivacity: her papa knows very well that all the small linen would have no other laundress than her if she had been allowed to do it,† and that she would have done more of it with pleasure if she had been so directed. While speaking these words, she looks at me on the sly with an apprehensiveness which I cannot help laughing at, reading in her ingenuous heart the alarm which makes her speak. Her father is cruel enough to pick up this bit of giddiness by asking her in a mocking tone what occasion she has for speaking on her own behalf here, and what she has in common with Alcinous' daughter? Ashamed and trembling, she no longer dares to breathe a word or look at anyone. Charming girl, the time for feigning is past. You have now made your declaration in spite of yourself.

Soon this little scene is forgotten, or appears to be. Very happily for Sophie, Emile is the only one who has understood nothing of it. The walk continues, and our young people, who at first were at our sides, have difficulty adjusting themselves to the slowness of our pace. Imperceptibly they move ahead of us, approach each other, and finally meet, and we see them rather far in front of us. Sophie seems attentive and composed. Emile speaks and gesticulates with fire. Their discussion does not appear to bore them. At the end of a solid hour we turn back;

---

* On leaving the palace one finds a vast garden of four acres, hedged in all around, planted with great flowering trees, producing pears, pomegranates, and others of the fairest species, fig trees with sweet fruit and verdant olive trees. Never during the whole year are these beautiful trees without fruit; winter and summer the west wind's gentle breeze both fecundates some and ripens others. One sees the pear and the apple grow old and dry on their trees, the fig on the fig tree and the clusters of grapes on the vine stock. The inexhaustible vine does not stop bearing new grapes; some are cooked and preserved in the sun on a threshing floor, while others are used to make wine, leaving on the plant those still blossoming, fermenting, or beginning to turn dark. At one of its ends two well-cultivated patches covered with flowers are each adorned by a fountain, of which one waters the whole garden, and the other, after having passed through the house, is piped to a tall building in the city to provide water for the citizens.

Such is the description of Alcinous' royal garden in the seventh book of the *Odyssey*, where, to the shame of that old dreamer Homer and the princes of his time, one sees neither trellises nor statues nor waterfalls nor bowling greens. [43]

† I admit that I am rather grateful to Sophie's mother for not having let her spoil with soap hands as soft as hers, hands which Emile will so often kiss.

we call them, and they return, but now they are the slow ones, and we see that they use the time profitably. Finally their conversation suddenly stops before we are within range of hearing them, and they speed up in order to rejoin us. Emile approaches us with an open and caressing air. His eyes sparkle with joy; however, he turns them with a bit of apprehensiveness toward Sophie's mother to see the reception she will give him. Sophie is far from having so relaxed a bearing; as she approaches, she seems quite embarrassed to be seen in a tête-à-tête with a young man—she who has so often been with other young men without being bothered by it and without its ever having been treated as wrong. Hurrying to reach her mother, she is a bit out of breath; she says a few words which do not mean a great deal, as if to give the impression of having been there for a long time.

From the serenity visible on the faces of these lovable children one sees that this conversation has relieved their young hearts of a great weight. They are no less reserved with one another, but it is a less embarrassed reserve. It now comes only from Emile's respect, Sophie's modesty, and the decency of both. Emile dares to address a few words to her; sometimes she dares to respond, but never does she open her mouth for that purpose without casting her eyes toward her mother's. She changes most palpably in her behavior toward me. She gives evidence of a more eager regard for me. She looks at me with interest; she speaks to me affectionately. She is attentive to what might please me. I see that she honors me with her esteem, and that she is not indifferent to obtaining mine. I understand that Emile has spoken to her about me. One would say that they have already plotted to win me over. Nothing of the kind has happened, however, and Sophie herself is not won so quickly. He will perhaps need my favor with her more than hers with me. Charming couple! . . . In thinking that my young friend's sensitive heart has given me a great part in his first discussion with his beloved, I enjoy the reward for my effort. His friendship has repaid everything.

The visits are repeated. The conversations between our young people become more frequent. Intoxicated by love, Emile believes he has already attained his happiness. However, he does not get Sophie's formal consent. She listens to him and says nothing to him. Emile knows the extent of her modesty. He is not very surprised by so much restraint. He senses that he does not stand badly with her. He knows that it is fathers who marry off children. He supposes that Sophie is waiting for an order from her parents. He asks her permission to solicit it. She does not oppose his doing so. He speaks to me about it; I speak for him in his own presence. What a surprise for him to learn that it is up to Sophie alone, and that to make him happy she has only to want to do so. He begins no longer to understand anything about her conduct. His confidence diminishes. He is alarmed; he sees that he has not gotten as far as he thought he had. And it is then that his tenderest love employs its most touching language to sway her.

Emile is not the kind of man who can guess what is hindering him. If he is not told, he will never find out, and Sophie is too proud to tell him. The difficulties which are holding her back would only make another girl more eager. She has not forgotten her parents' lessons. She is poor, and Emile is rich; she knows it. He has a great deal to do in order to gain her esteem! What merit must he possess in order to wipe away this inequality? But how could he dream of these obstacles? Does Emile know he is rich? Does he even deign to inquire about it? Thank heaven he has no need to be rich. He knows how to be beneficent without riches. The good he does is drawn from his heart and not from his purse. He gives his time, his care, his affections, and his person to the unhappy; and in estimating his benefactions, he hardly dares to count the money he scatters among the indigent.

Not knowing what to blame for his disgrace, he attributes it to his own fault: for who would dare to accuse the object of his adoration of caprice? The humiliation of his *amour-propre* increases his regret that his love has been spurned. He no longer approaches Sophie with that lovable confidence of a heart which feels it is worthy of hers. He is fearful and trembling before her. He no longer hopes to touch her by tenderness. He seeks to sway her by pity. Sometimes his patience wearies, and vexation is ready to take its place. Sophie seems to foresee these storms, and glances at him. This glance alone disarms and intimidates him. He is more thoroughly subjected than before.

Troubled by this obstinate resistance and this invincible silence, he opens his heart to his friend. He confides to him the pain of a heart broken by sadness. He implores his assistance and his counsel. "What an impenetrable mystery! She is interested in my fate; I cannot doubt it. Far from avoiding me, she enjoys being with me. When I arrive, she gives signs of joy, and when I leave, of regret. She receives my attentions kindly. My services appear to please her. She deigns to give me advice, sometimes even orders. Nevertheless, she rejects my entreaties and my prayers. When I dare to speak of union, she imperiously imposes silence on me; and if I add another word, she leaves me on the spot. For what strange reason does she want me to be hers without wanting to hear a word about her being mine? You whom she honors, you whom she loves and whom she will not dare to silence, speak, make her speak. Serve your friend. Crown your work. Do not make all your care fatal to your pupil. Ah, what he has gotten from you will cause his misery if you do not complete his happiness!"

I speak to Sophie, and with little effort I extract from her a secret I knew before she told it to me. I have more difficulty in obtaining permission to inform Emile. Finally, I do obtain it and make use of it. This explanation sends him into a state of astonishment from which he cannot recover. He understands nothing of this delicacy. He cannot imagine what effect a few *écus* more or less have on character and merit. When I make him understand what they do to prejudices, he starts laughing, and, transported with joy, he wants to leave on the spot to go and tear up everything, throw out everything, renounce everything in order to have the honor of being as poor as Sophie and to return worthy of being her husband.

"What!" I say, stopping him and laughing in turn at his impetuosity. "Will this young mind never become mature; and after having philosophized your whole life, will you never learn to reason? How can you not see that, in following your insane project, you are going to make your situation worse and Sophie more intractable? It is a small advantage to have a bit more property than she does, but it would be a very big advantage to have sacrificed it all for her; and if her pride cannot resolve to accept the former obligation to you, how will it resolve to accept the latter? If she cannot endure that a husband be able to reproach her for having enriched her, will she endure that he be able to reproach her with having impoverished himself for her? O unhappy fellow, tremble lest she suspect you of having had this project! Instead, become economical and careful for love of her, lest she accuse you of wanting to win her by trickery and of voluntarily sacrificing to her what you lose by neglect.

"Do you believe that at bottom great property frightens her and that it is precisely wealth that is the source of her opposition? No, dear Emile, it has a more solid and weightier cause—namely, the effect that wealth has on the soul of the possessor. She knows that fortune's goods are always preferred over everything else by those who have them. The rich all count gold before merit. In regard to the family resources constituted by the contribution of money and services, they always find that the latter never compensate for the former; they think that someone is still in their debt when he has spent his life serving them while eating their bread. What is there for you to do, Emile, to reassure her about her fears? Make yourself well known to her. That is not the business of a day. Show her treasures in your noble soul that are sufficient to redeem those with which you have the misfortune to be endowed. By dint of constancy and time surmount her resistance. By dint of great and generous sentiments force her to forget your riches. Love her, serve her, serve her respectable parents. Prove to her that these efforts are the effect not of a mad and fleeting passion but of ineffaceable principles engraved in the depths of your heart. Give proper honor to merit that has been insulted by fortune. This is the only means of reconciling her to merit favored by fortune."

One may conceive what transports of joy this speech gives to the young man, how much confidence and hope it gives him. His decent heart is delighted that in order to please Sophie he has to do exactly what he would do on his own if Sophie did not exist or if he were not in love with her. However little one has understood his character, who will not be able to imagine his conduct on this occasion?

Now I am the confidant of my two good young people and the mediator of their loves! A fine employment for a governor! So fine that never in my life have I done anything which raised me so much in my own eyes and made me so satisfied with myself. Moreover, this employment does not fail to have its agreeable aspects. I am not unwelcome in the house. I am entrusted with the care of keeping the lovers in order. Emile, who is constantly trembling for fear of displeasing me, was never so docile. The little girl overwhelms me with friendliness by which I am not deceived, and I take for myself only what is intended for me. It is thus that she compensates herself indirectly for the respect she imposes on Emile. Through me she gives him countless tender caresses which she would rather die than give to him directly. And Emile, who knows that I do not want to harm his interests, is charmed that I am on good terms with her. When she refuses his arm in walking, he consoles himself with the fact that it is to prefer mine to his. He leaves without complaint, grasping my hand, and saying softly to me with his eyes as well as his voice, "Friend, speak for me." His eyes follow us with interest. He tries to read our sentiments in our faces and to interpret our speeches by our gestures. He knows that nothing of what is said between us is inconsequential for him. Good Sophie, how your sincere heart is at ease when, without being heard by Telemachus, you can converse with his Mentor! With what lovable frankness you let him read everything going on in your tender heart! With what pleasure you show him all your esteem for his pupil! With what touching ingenuousness you let him discern even sweeter sentiments! With what feigned anger you send the importunate Emile away when impatience forces him to interrupt you! With what charming vexation you reproach him for his tactlesness when he comes and prevents you from speaking well of him, from hearing good things about him, and from always drawing some new reason for loving him from my responses!

Having thus gotten himself tolerated as a suitor, Emile takes advantage of all the rights of that position. He speaks, he urges, he entreats, he importunes. If he is spoken to harshly or if he is mistreated, it makes little difference to him provided that he make himself heard. Finally, though not without effort, he induces Sophie to be kind enough to assume openly a beloved's authority over him—to prescribe to him what he must do, to order instead of to ask, to accept instead of to thank, to regulate the number and the time of his visits, to forbid him to come until this day or to stay past that hour. All this is not done as a game but very seriously. Although it was an effort to get her to accept these rights, she makes use of them with a rigor that often reduces poor Emile to regret that he has given them to her. But whatever she commands, he does not reply, and often, when leaving to obey her, he looks at me with eyes full of joy telling me: "You see that she has taken possession of me." Meanwhile, the proud girl observes him stealthily and smiles secretly at her slave's pride.

Albani [45] and Raphael, loan me the brush with which to paint sensuous delight. Divine Milton, teach my coarse pen to describe the pleasures of love and innocence. But, no, hide your lying arts before the holy truth of nature. You need only have sensitive hearts and decent souls; then let your imagination wander without constraint in contemplating the transports of two young lovers who—under the eyes of their parents and their guides—are untroubled as they yield themselves to the sweet illusion delighting them; in the intoxication of their desires they advance slowly toward their goal, weaving flowers and garlands around the happy bond which is going to unite them until the grave. So many charming images intoxicate me that I bring them together without order and without coherence; the delirium they cause prevents me from connecting them. Oh, who has a heart and does not know how to depict for himself the delicious scenes of the father, the mother, the daughter, the governor, and the pupil in their various situations and their respective contributions to the union of the most charming couple that can be made happy by love and virtue?

Having become truly eager to please, Emile now begins to sense the value of the agreeable talents with which he has provided himself. Sophie loves to sing. He sings with her. He does more; he teaches her music. She is lively and light, and she likes to jump. He dances with her; he turns her jumps into steps; he trains her. These lessons are charming. Rollicking gaiety animates them, and it mitigates the timid respect of love. A lover is permitted to give these lessons voluptuously. He is permitted to be his mistress's master.

They have an old harpsichord that is in very bad shape. Emile fixes it and tunes it. He is a maker of keyboard and stringed instruments as well as a carpenter. His maxim was always to learn to do without the help of others in regard to everything he could do himself. The house is in a picturesque setting. He draws different views of it—to which Sophie sometimes puts her hand—and she ornaments her father's study with them. Their frames are not gilded and do not need to be. By watching Emile sketch and imitating him, she becomes more skillful from following his example. She cultivates all the talents, and her charm embellishes them all. Her father and mother recall their former opulence in seeing the fine arts, which alone made opulence dear to them, flourishing around them again. Love has adorned their entire home. Without expense and without effort, love alone establishes there the reign of the same pleasures which they previously assembled only by dint of money and boredom.

As the idolator enriches the object of his worship with treasures that he esteems and adorns on the altar the God he adores, so the lover—although he may very well see his mistress as perfect—constantly wants to add new ornaments to her. She does not need them in order to please him, but he needs to adorn her. It is a new homage he believes he is doing her and a new interest he adds to the pleasure of contemplating her. It seems to him that nothing beautiful is in its place when it is not ornamenting the supreme beauty. It is both a touching and a laughable spectacle to see Emile eager to teach Sophie all he knows, without considering whether what he wants to teach her is to her taste or is suitable for her. He tells her about everything, he explains everything to her with a puerile eagerness. He believes he has only to speak and she will understand on the spot. He fancies beforehand the pleasure he will have in reasoning and in philosophizing with her. He regards as useless all the attainments he cannot display to her eyes. He almost blushes at knowing something she does not know.

Therefore, he gives her lessons in philosophy, physics, mathematics, history—in a word, in everything. Sophie lends herself with pleasure to his zeal and tries to profit from it. When he can obtain permission to give his lessons on his knees before her, how content Emile is! He believes he sees the heavens opened. However this position, more constricting for the student than for the master, is not the most favorable for instruction. On such occasions she does not know exactly what to do with her eyes to avoid those that are pursuing them; and when they meet, the lesson does not gain by it.

The art of thinking is not foreign to women, but they ought only to skim the sciences of reasoning. Sophie gets a conception of everything and does not remember very much. Her greatest progress is in ethics and in matters of taste. As for physics, she remembers only some idea of its general laws and of the cosmic system. Sometimes on their walks, as they contemplate nature's marvels, their innocent and pure hearts dare to lift themselves up to its Author. They do not fear His presence. They open their hearts jointly before Him.

"What, two lovers in the flower of age use their tête-à-tête to speak of religion? They spend their time saying their catechism?" Why must you debase something sublime? Yes, no doubt they do say it, under the influence of the illusion which charms them. They see each other as perfect; they love one another; they converse with each other enthusiastically about what gives virtue its reward. The sacrifices they make to virtue render it dear to them. In the midst of transports that they must vanquish, they sometimes shed tears together purer than heaven's dew, and these sweet tears constitute the enchantment of their life. They are in the most charming delirium that human souls have ever experienced. Their very privations add to their happiness and do them honor in their own eyes for their sacrifices. Sensual men, bodies without souls, one day they will know your pleasures, and for their whole lives they will regret the happy time during which they denied them to themselves.

Despite their being on such good terms, they do not fail to have some disagreements, even some quarrels. The mistress is not without caprice nor the lover without anger. But these little storms pass rapidly and only have the effect of strengthening their union. Experience even teaches Emile not to fear them so much; the reconciliations are always more advantageous to him than the spats are harmful. The fruit of their first spat made him hope for as much from the others. He was wrong. But, in the end, if he does not always take away so palpable a profit, he always gains from these spats by seeing Sophie confirm her sincere interest in his heart. People will want to know what this profit is. I will gladly consent to tell them, for this example gives me the occasion to expound a most useful maxim and to combat a most baneful one.

Emile loves. Therefore, he is not bold. And it can even more readily be conceived that the imperious Sophie is not the girl to overlook his familiarities. Since moderation has its limits in all things, she could be charged with too much harshness rather than too much indulgence; and her father himself sometimes fears that her extreme pride will degenerate into haughtiness. In their most secret tête-à-têtes Emile would not dare to solicit the least favor nor even to appear to aspire to one. When she is so kind as to take his arm during a walk—a favor she does not allow to be turned into a right—he hardly dares occasionally to sigh and press this arm against his breast. Nevertheless, after long constraint he furtively ventures to kiss her dress, and several times he is lucky enough for Sophie to be so kind as not to notice it. One day when he wants to take the same liberty a bit more openly, she decides to take it amiss. He persists. She gets irritated. Vexation dictates a few stinging words. Emile does not endure them without reply. The rest of the day is passed in pouting, and they separate very discontented.

Sophie is ill at ease. Her mother is her confidant. How could she hide her chagrin from her? It is her first spat, and a spat that lasts an hour is so great a business! She repents her mistake. Her mother permits her to make amends. Her father orders her to do so.

The next day Emile is apprehensive and returns earlier than usual. Sophie is in her mother's dressing room. Her father is also there. Emile enters respectfully but with a sad air. Sophie's father and mother have hardly greeted him when Sophie turns around and, extending her hand, asks him in a caressing tone how he is. It is clear that this pretty hand has been extended only in order to be kissed. He takes it and does not kiss it. Sophie is a bit ashamed, and she withdraws her hand with as good grace as is possible for her. Emile, who is not experienced in women's ways and does not know the purpose of their caprices, does not forget easily and is not so quickly appeased. Sophie's father, seeing her embarrassment, succeeds in disconcerting her by mockery. The poor girl is confused and humiliated; she no longer knows what she is doing and would give anything in the world to dare to cry. The more she constrains herself, the more her heart swells. A tear finally escapes her in spite of her efforts. Emile sees this tear, rushes to her knees, takes her hand, and kisses it several times, entranced. "Really, you are too good," says her father, bursting out laughing. "I would have less indulgence for all these mad girls, and I would punish the mouth that offended me." Emboldened by this speech, Emile turns a suppliant eye toward Sophie's mother and, believing he sees a sign of consent, tremblingly approaches Sophie's face. She turns her head away and, in order to save her mouth, exposes a rosy cheek. The tactless boy is not satisfied. She resists feebly. What a kiss, if it were not stolen under a mother's eyes! Severe Sophie, take care. He will often ask you for permission to kiss your dress, provided that you sometimes refuse it.

After this exemplary punishment Sophie's father leaves to attend to some business; her mother sends Sophie away under some pretext, and then she addresses Emile and says to him in quite a serious tone: "Monsieur, I believe that a young man as well born and as well raised as you, who has sentiments and morals, would not want to repay the friendship a family has showed him by dishonoring it. I am neither unsociable nor a prude. I know what must be overlooked in the wildness of youth, and what I have tolerated under my eyes sufficiently proves it to you. Consult your friend about your duties. He will tell you what a difference there is between the games authorized by the presence of a father and mother and the liberties taken far away from them, liberties which abuse their confidence and turn into traps the same favors which are innocent under their eyes. He will tell you, sir, that my daughter has done you no other wrong than that of not noticing at the outset a practice she ought never to have tolerated. He will tell you that everything taken to be a favor becomes one, and that it is unworthy of a man of honor to abuse a young girl's simplicity to usurp in secret the same liberties that she can permit before everyone. One knows what propriety can permit in public; but no one knows where the man who sets himself up as the sole judge of his whims will stop himself in the shadows of secrecy."

After this just reprimand, addressed much more to me than to my pupil, this wise mother departs and leaves me admiring her rare prudence, which takes little account of one's kissing her daughter's mouth in front of her but is frightened of someone's daring to kiss her daughter's dress in private. Reflecting on the folly of our maxims, which always sacrifice true decency to propriety, I understand why language is more chaste as hearts become more corrupted and why rules of conduct are more exact as those subject to them become more dishonest.

In using this occasion to fill Emile's heart with the duties I ought to have dictated to him earlier, I am struck by a new reflection which perhaps honors Sophie the most and which I am nevertheless very careful not to communicate to her lover. It is clear that this pretended pride for which others reproach her is only a very wise precaution to protect her from herself. Since she has the misfortune to sense a combustible temperament within herself, she dreads the first spark and keeps it at a distance with all her power. It is not from pride that she is severe; it is from humility. She assumes an empire over Emile which she fears she does not have over Sophie. She uses the one to fight the other. If she were more confident, she would be much less proud. Apart from this one point, what girl in the world is more yielding and sweeter? Who endures an offense more patiently? Who is more fearful of committing one against others? Who makes fewer claims of every kind, except for the claim of virtue? Furthermore, it is not her virtue of which she is proud; she is proud only in order to preserve it. And when she can yield to the inclination of her heart without risk, she caresses even her lover. But her discreet mother does not relate all these details even to her father. Men ought not to know everything.

Far from seeming to have become proud as a result of her conquest, Sophie has become still more affable and less demanding with everyone—except perhaps with him who is the cause of this change. The sentiment of independence no longer swells her noble heart. She triumphs with modesty, winning a victory which costs her her freedom. Her bearing is less free and her speech is more timid now that she no longer hears the word *lover* without blushing. But contentment pierces through her embarrassment, and this very shame is not a disagreeable sentiment. It is especially with other young men that the difference in her conduct is most easily sensed. Since she no longer fears them, the extreme reserve that she used to have with them has been much relaxed. Now that she has made her choice, she has no qualms about acting graciously toward those to whom she is indifferent. Since she no longer takes any interest in them, she is less demanding about their merits, and she finds them always likable enough for people who will never mean anything to her.

If true love could make use of coquetry, I would even believe that I see some traces of it in the way Sophie behaves with these young men in the presence of her lover. One would say that, not content with the ardent passion which she kindles in him by means of an exquisite mixture of reserve and endearment, she is not sorry if she excites this passion still more by means of a bit of anxiety. One would say that by purposely making her young guests merry, she intends to torment Emile with the charms of a playfulness she does not dare to indulge in with him. But Sophie is too attentive, too good, and too judicious actually to torment him. Love and decency take the place of prudence for her in tempering this dangerous stimulant. She knows how to alarm him and to reassure him precisely when it is necessary. And if she sometimes makes him anxious, she never makes him sad. Let us pardon the concern she causes the man she loves by attributing it to her fear that he is never bound to her closely enough.

But what effect will this little trick have on Emile? Will he or won't he be jealous? This is what must be examined, for such digressions also enter into the aim of my book and stray very little from my subject.[46]

I have previously showed how this passion is introduced into man's heart in regard to things which depend only on opinion. But in regard to love the case is different. Jealousy then appears to depend so closely on nature that it is hard to believe that it does not come from it. And the example of the animals, several of whom are jealous to the point of fury, seems unanswerably to establish that it does come from nature. Is it men's opinion which teaches cocks to tear one another apart and bulls to fight to the death?

The aversion against everything which disturbs and combats our pleasures is a natural emotion; that is incontestable. Up to a certain point the case is still the same with the desire for exclusive possession of what pleases us. But when this desire becomes a passion and transforms itself into a fury or a suspicious and gloomy whim called jealousy, then the case is different. This passion may or may not be natural. A distinction must be made.

The example drawn from the animals has been heretofore examined in the *Discourse on Inequality*; and now that I reflect on it anew, this examination appears to me solid enough to dare to refer readers to it.[47] I shall add to the distinctions I have made in that writing only that the jealousy coming from nature depends very much on sexual potency. When this potency is or appears to be unlimited, this jealousy is at its peak; for then the male measures his rights according to his needs and can never see another male as anything but an intrusive competitor. In these same species the females, who always obey the first male that arrives, belong to the males only by right of conquest and cause eternal fights among them.

By contrast, in species in which one male is united with one female, in which mating produces a sort of moral bond—a sort of marriage—the female belongs by her own choice to the male to whom she has given herself, and commonly resists all others. And the male, who has this affection founded on preference as a guarantee of her fidelity, is thus less anxious at the sight of other males and lives more peacefully with them. In these species the male shares the care of the little ones, and by one of those laws of nature that one does not observe without being touched, it seems that the female repays the father for the attachment he has for his children.

Now, if we consider the human species in its primitive simplicity, it is easy to see from the male's limited potency and the moderation of his desires that he is destined by nature to be content with one female. This is confirmed by the numerical equality of the individuals of the two sexes, at least in our climates—an equality which by no means exists in species in which the greater strength of males causes several females to be united with a single male. And although it is the case that a man does not sit on the eggs like a pigeon, nor does he have breasts for giving milk and therefore in that respect belongs to the class of the quadrupeds, nevertheless the children crawl and are weak for so long that they and the mother would have difficulty doing without the attachment of the father and the care which results from it.

All these observations concur to prove that the jealous fury of the males in some species of animals is not at all conclusive for man, and the very exception of the southern climates where polygamy is established only confirms the principle. For the husbands' tyrannical precautions come from the plurality of women, and the sentiment of his own weakness leads the man to have recourse to coercion in order to elude the laws of nature.

Among us, where these same laws are less eluded in this way, but are eluded in an opposite and more odious manner, jealousy has its motive in the social passions more than in primitive instinct. In most liaisons of gallantry the lover hates his rivals far more than he loves his mistress. If he fears that he is not the only object of her attentions, it is the effect of that *amour-propre* whose origin I have showed, and he suffers far more out of vanity than out of love. Moreover, our maladroit institutions have made women so dissembling * and have so strongly inflamed their appetites that one can hardly count on their most proved attachment and that they can no longer demonstrate preferences which reassure a man against the fear of competitors.

As regards true love, the case is different. I have showed in the writing already cited that this sentiment is not as natural as is thought. There is a great difference between the sweet habit which makes a man affectionate toward his companion and that unbridled ardor which intoxicates him with the chimerical attractions of an object which he no longer sees as it really is. This passion longs only for exclusions and preferences, and it differs from vanity only in that the latter, which demands everything and grants nothing, is always iniquitous, whereas love, which gives as much as it demands, is in itself a sentiment filled with equity. Moreover, the more love is demanding, the more it is credulous. The same illusion which causes it makes it easy to persuade. If love is anxious, esteem is confident; and love without esteem

* The species of dissimulation I mean here is the opposite of that which suits them and which they get from nature. The one consists in disguising the sentiments they have, and the other in feigning those they do not have. All society women spend their lives priding themselves on their pretended sensitivity and never love anything but themselves.

BOOK V

never existed in a decent heart because it is only the qualities he values that anyone loves in his beloved.

With all of this well clarified, one can specify with certainty the sort of jealousy Emile will be capable of; since this passion hardly has any seeds in the human heart, its form is determined exclusively by education. When he is in love and jealous, Emile will be not quick to anger, suspicious, and distrustful but delicate, sensitive, and timid. He will be more alarmed than irritated; he will pay far more attention to winning his mistress than to threatening his rival. If he can, he will get rid of him as an obstacle, without hating him as an enemy. If he hates his rival, it will not be for the audacity of contending with him for a heart to which he has laid a claim, but for making him run the real danger of losing her. His unjust pride will not be stupidly offended by someone's daring to enter into competition with him. Understanding that the right of preference is founded solely on merit and that honor is to be found in sucess, he will redouble his efforts to make himself lovable, and he will probably succeed. The generous Sophie, in exciting his love by giving him some moments of alarm, will know how to regulate them well and to compensate him for them; and it will not be long before the competitors, who were tolerated only to put Emile to the test, will be dismissed.

But where do I sense myself imperceptibly being led? O Emile, what have you become? Can I recognize my pupil in you? How far you seem to have fallen! Where is the young man brought up with such hardness, the young man who braved the rigors of the seasons, who gave his body to the harshest labors and his soul only to the laws of wisdom, who was inaccessible to prejudices and to the passions, who loved only truth, who yielded only to reason and depended on nothing except himself? Now, softened by an idle life, he lets himself be governed by women. Their amusements are his occupations, their wills are his laws; a young girl is the arbiter of his destiny, and he crawls and bends before her. The grave Emile is a child's plaything!

This is how the scenes of life change. Each age has its own springs that make it move, but man is always the same. At ten he is led by cakes, at twenty by a mistress, at thirty by the pleasures, at forty by ambition, at fifty by avarice. When does he run after wisdom? Happy is the man who is led to it in spite of himself! What difference does it make what guide is used, provided that it leads to the goal? Heroes and wise men themselves have paid this tribute to human weakness; and the man who put his clumsy fingers to the spindle was no less a great man because of that.[48]

Do you want to extend the effect of a successful education throughout a whole life? Prolong the good habits of childhood during youth; and when your pupil is what he ought to be, fix it so that he will be the same at all times. This is the final perfection that you still must give to your work. It is for this above all that it is important to leave a governor with young men, for it is hardly to be feared that they will not know how to make love without him. What misleads teachers and especially fathers is their belief that one way of life excludes another and that, as soon as someone is grown up, he ought to renounce everything he did when he was young. If that were so, what would be the use of devoting so much care to childhood, since the good or the bad use made of childhood would disappear along with it and, when someone adopted an absolutely different way of life, he would necessarily adopt other fashions of thinking?

Just as it is only great illnesses that interrupt the continuity of memory, it is generally only great passions that interrupt the continuity of morals. Although our tastes and our inclinations change, this change, which is sometimes rather brusque, is moderated by our habits. In the sequence of our inclinations, as in a good gradation of colors, the skillful artist ought to make the transitions imperceptible, confounding and mixing the tints and, in order that none clashes, extending several throughout his whole work. This rule is confirmed by experience. Immoderate people change their affections, tastes, and sentiments every day, and they are constant only in the habit of change. But the steady man always returns to his old practices and even in his old age does not lose his taste for the pleasures he loved as a child.

If you see to it that in passing into a new age young people do not develop a contempt for the preceding one; that in contracting new habits they do not abandon their old ones; and that they always love to do what is good without regard to the time when they began doing it—only then will you have preserved your work, and you will be sure of these young people unto the end of their days. For the revolution most to be feared belongs to the age over which you are now keeping watch. Since one always yearns to return to this age, later it is difficult to destroy any childhood tastes that were preserved during it; whereas when such tastes are interrupted at this age, they are never resumed in one's whole life.

Most of the habits you believe you give to children and young people are not true habits. Because children only adopt such habits by force and stick to them grudgingly, they are only waiting for the occasion to be rid of them. One does not get the taste for being in prison by dint of staying there. Far from diminishing the aversion, the habit then increases it. It is not thus with Emile, who in his childhood did everything voluntarily and with pleasure. In continuing to act the same way as a man, he therefore only adds the empire of habit to the sweetness of freedom. The active life, work with his hands, exercise, and movement have become so necessary to him that he could not give them up without suffering. To reduce him all of a sudden to a soft and sedentary life would be to imprison him, to enchain him, to keep him in a violent and constrained state. I do not doubt that his disposition and his health would be equally corrupted. He can hardly breathe at his ease in a well-closed room. He needs fresh air, movement, toil. Even when he is at Sophie's knee, he cannot prevent himself from sometimes looking at the countryside out of the corner of his eye and desiring to roam it with her. Nevertheless, he stays when he has to stay, but he is restless and agitated; he seems to struggle with himself; he stays because he is in irons. You are going to say that these are needs to which I have submitted him, subjections that I have given him, and all that is true. I have subjected him to man's estate.

Emile loves Sophie. But what are the chief charms which have attached him to her? Sensitivity, virtue, love of decent things. While loving this love in his mistress, will he have lost it in himself? For what price did Sophie in turn give herself? She was won by all the sentiments natural to her lover's heart: esteem of true goods, frugality, simplicity, generous disinterestedness, contempt for show and riches. Emile had these virtues before love imposed them on him. How, then, has Emile truly changed? He has new reasons to be himself. This is the single point where he differs from what he was.

I do not imagine that anyone reading this book with some attention could believe that all the circumstances of the situation in which Emile finds himself have been gathered around him by chance. Is it by chance that, although the cities furnish so many lovable girls, the one who pleases him is to be found only in the depths of a distant retreat? Is it by chance that he meets her? Is it by chance that they suit one another? Is it by chance that they cannot lodge in the same place? Is it by chance that he finds a dwelling so far from her? Is it by chance that he sees her so rarely and that he is forced to purchase the pleasure of seeing her once in a while with so much exertion? He is becoming effeminated, you say? On the contrary, he is hardening himself. He has to be as robust as I have made him to withstand the exertion Sophie makes him endure.

He lodges two leagues away from her. This distance is the bellows of the forge. By means of it I temper the arrows of love. If they lived next door to each other, or if he could go to see her seated in softness in a good carriage, he would love her at his ease as a Parisian loves. Would Leander have wanted to die for Hero if the sea had not separated him from her? [49] Reader, spare me words. If you are made for understanding me, you will be quite able to follow my rules in my detailed examples.

The first times that we went to see Sophie, we had traveled on horseback in order to go more quickly. We find this expedient convenient, and the fifth time we are still traveling on horseback. We are expected. At more than half a league from the house we perceive people on the path. Emile observes them, his heart throbs, he approaches; he recognizes Sophie, leaps from his horse, dashes off, and is quickly at the feet of the lovable family. Emile loves fine horses. His own horse is lively; when it becomes aware that it is free, it takes off through the fields. I follow it, catch it with some effort, and bring it back. Unhappily Sophie is afraid of horses; I do not dare to approach her. Emile sees nothing. But Sophie informs him in a whisper of the effort he has let his friend make. Quite ashamed, Emile runs up to take the horses and stays back. It is just for each to have his turn. He leaves first in order to get rid of our mounts. On leaving Sophie behind him in this way, he no longer finds the horse so convenient a vehicle. He returns out of breath and meets us halfway.

On our next trip Emile no longer wants to use horses. "Why?" I say to him. "We have only to take a lackey to care for them." "Ah," he says, "are we to burden Sophie's respectable family in this way? You see that they want to feed everyone, both men and horses." "It is true," I respond, "that they have the noble hospitality of indigence. The rich, who are miserly amidst their ostentation, lodge only their friends, but the poor also lodge their friends' horses." "Let us go on foot," he says. "Don't you have the courage, you who so goodheartedly share your child's fatiguing pleasures?" "Very gladly," I respond at once. "Moreover, it seems to me that love prefers to go about its business without so much stir."

On approaching, we find mother and daughter still farther out on the path than the first time. We have traveled like a thunderbolt. Emile is all in a sweat. A dear hand deigns to wipe his cheeks with a handkerchief. There would have to be a lot of horses in the world before we would be tempted to make use of them again.

However, it is quite cruel for Emile and Sophie never to be able to spend the evening together. Summer advances. The days begin to get shorter. No matter what we say, we are never permitted to wait until nightfall before going home; and if we do not come early in the morning, we have to leave practically as soon as we have arrived. As a result of pitying us and being anxious about us, Sophie's mother concludes that although in truth they could not properly lodge us in their house, a bed in which to sleep could sometimes be found for us in the village. At these words Emile claps his hands and shivers with joy. And Sophie, without being aware of it, kisses her mother a little more often on the day she comes up with this expedient.

Little by little the sweetness of friendship and the familiarity of innocence are established and strengthened between us. On the days prescribed by Sophie or by her mother I usually come with my friend; sometimes I let him go alone. Confidence elevates the soul, and one ought no longer to treat a man as a child. And what progress would I have made if my pupil did not merit my esteem? I, too, occasionally go without him. Then he is sad but does not grumble. What would be the use of grumbling? Besides, he knows that I am not going to hurt his interests. Finally, whether we go together or separately, no weather stops us, and we are quite proud to arrive in a pitiable state. Unfortunately Sophie prohibits us this honor and forbids us to come in bad weather. It is the only time I find her rebellious against the rules which I dictate to her in secret.

One day when Emile has gone alone, and I am not expecting him until the next day, I see him arrive that same evening. Embracing him, I say, "What, dear Emile, you return to your friend!" But, instead of responding to my caresses, he says to me, with a bit of bile, "Don't believe that I come back so soon of my own will. I come in spite of myself. She wanted me to come. I come for her and not for you." Touched by this naïveté, I embrace him once again and say to him, "Frank soul, sincere friend, do not deprive me of what is mine. If you come for her, it is for me that you say so. Your return is her work, but your frankness is mine. Always retain that noble candor of beautiful souls. People who do not matter can be allowed to think what they want, but it is a crime to let a friend give us credit for something we did not do for him."

I carefully avoid debasing the value of his admission in his eyes. This would be the result if I were to find more love and generosity in it and say to him that he wants less to deprive himself of the credit of this return than to give it to Sophie. But this is how he discloses the depths of his heart to me without being aware of it: if he comes at a leisurely pace, dreaming of his love, Emile is only Sophie's lover. But if he arrives with great strides and is heated up, although in a bit of a grumbling mood, Emile is his Mentor's friend.

From the arrangements I have made, one sees that my young man is far from spending his life near Sophie and seeing her as much as he would want. A trip or two a week are all that he receives permission to make, and his visits, which are often limited to a single half day, are rarely extended to the next day. He employs far more time in hoping to see Sophie or in congratulating himself on having seen her than in actually seeing her. And of the time devoted to his trips he spends less of it with her than in getting there or going back. His pleasures, which are true, pure, and delicious but less real than imaginary, exacerbate his love without effeminating his heart.

On the days when he does not see her, he is not idle and sedentary. On those days he is Emile again. He has not been transformed at all. Most often he roams through the surrounding countryside. He pursues his natural history; he observes and examines the earth, its products, and its cultivation; he compares the way of farming he sees to the ones he knows; he seeks the reasons for the differences. When he judges other methods preferable to the local ones, he gives them to the farmers. If he proposes a better form of plow, he has it made according to his designs. If he finds a marl quarry, he teaches them its use which is unknown in these parts. Often he puts his hand to the work himself. The farmers are all surprised to see him handle their tools more easily than they do themselves, dig furrows deeper and straighter than theirs, sow more evenly, and lay out embankments with more intelligence. They do not make fun of him as a fine talker about agriculture. They see that he actually knows about it. In a word, he extends his zeal and his care to everything which is of primary and general utility. He does not even limit himself to that. He visits the peasants' houses, inquires about their condition, their families, the number of their children, the quantity of their lands, the nature of their produce, their market, their means, their expenses, their debts, etc. He does not give them much money, knowing that they usually employ it badly; but he directs its employment himself and makes it useful to them in spite of themselves. He provides them with workers and often pays them wages themselves to do the work they need. He gets one farmer to rebuild or roof his cottage which is half in ruins; he gets another to clear his land which has been abandoned for want of means; he provides a third with a cow, a horse, and livestock of all kinds to replace those he has lost. Two neighbors are ready to enter into litigation; he wins them over and reconciles them. A peasant falls ill; he has him cared for; he cares for him himself.* Another is harassed by a powerful neighbor; he protects and advises him. Two poor young people want to be united; he helps them to get married. A good woman has lost her dear child; he goes to see her and consoles her; he does not leave as soon as he has gone in. He does not disdain the indigent, and he is not in a hurry to get away from the unhappy. He often takes his meal with the peasants he assists. He also accepts a meal from those who do not need him. In becoming the benefactor of some and the friend of the others, he does not cease to be their equal. Finally, he always does as much good with his person as with his money.

Sometimes he takes his walks in the direction of the happy dwelling. He could hope to see Sophie on the sly, to see her taking her walk without himself being seen. But Emile's conduct is never devious; he does not know how to be evasive and does not want to be. He has that amiable delicacy which flatters and feeds *amour-propre* with the good witness of oneself. He rigorously sticks to his banishment and never approaches near enough to get from chance what he wants to owe only to Sophie. On the other hand, he wanders with pleasure in her neighborhood, seeking for traces of his beloved's steps, touched by the efforts she has taken and the errands she has been kind enough to run for the sake of obliging him. On the eve of the days when he is going to see her, he will go to some neighboring farm to order a snack for the next day. Their walk is directed toward this place without appearing to be. They enter as though by chance; they find fruits, cakes, and custard. The dainty Sophie is not insensitive to these attentions and gladly gives us credit for our foresight; for I always get a share of the compliment, although I had no share in the effort that elicits it. This is the evasion used by a little girl to feel less embarrassed in giving thanks. Her father and I eat cakes and drink wine. But Emile is part of the women's crowd, and he is always on the lookout to steal some dish of custard into which Sophie has dipped her spoon.

Apropos of cakes, I speak to Emile of his former races. The others want to know what these races were. I explain, and they laugh. They ask him whether he still knows how to run. "Better than ever," he answers. "I would be very upset if I were to forget." One of the company would like very much to see him run but does not dare to say so. Someone else takes responsibility for making the request. He accepts. Two or three young people from the neighborhood are gathered together. A prize is established and, in order better to imitate Emile's former games, a cake is placed on the goal. All are ready. Sophie's papa gives the signal by striking his hands. The agile Emile cleaves the air and arrives at the end of the course almost before my three bumpkins have started. Emile receives the prize from Sophie's hands, and, no less generous than Aeneas, he gives presents to all the vanquished.[50]

* To care for a sick peasant, do not purge him, give him drugs, or send him a surgeon. These poor people need none of those things in their illnesses. They need better and more plentiful food. You others should fast when you have a fever. But when your peasants have one, give them meat and wine. Almost all their illnesses come from poverty and exhaustion. Their best herb tea is in your cellar; their only apothecary ought to be your butcher.

BOOK V

Amidst the brilliance of Emile's triumph Sophie dares to defy the conqueror and boasts that she runs as well as he. He does not refuse to enter the lists with her. While she prepares her entry on the course —trussing up her dress on both sides and, more concerned to display a slender leg to Emile's eyes than to vanquish him in this combat, seeing whether her skirt is short enough—he says a word in her mother's ear. The mother smiles and gives a sign of approval. Emile then comes and places himself beside his competitor, and no sooner is the signal given than she is seen to take off and fly like a bird.

Women are not made to run. When they flee, it is in order to be caught. Racing is not the only thing they do maladroitly, but it is the only thing they do gracelessly; their elbows, drawn back and glued to their bodies, give them a ridiculous aspect, and the high heels on which they are perched make them appear like grasshoppers who want to run without jumping.

Imagining that Sophie runs no better than any other woman, Emile does not deign to leave his place and watches her depart with a mocking smile. But Sophie is light and wears low heels. She needs no artifice to appear to have a small foot. She takes the lead with such rapidity that Emile has just enough time to catch this new Atalanta [51] when he perceives her so far ahead of him. He therefore departs in turn, like an eagle swooping down on its prey. He pursues her, follows close on her heels, and finally catches up with Sophie who is all out of breath. Gently putting his left arm around her, he lifts her like a feather and, pressing this sweet burden to his heart, completes the course. He makes her touch the goal first and then, shouting, "Sophie is the winner," puts his knee on the ground before her and admits that he is conquered.

To these various occupations is added the trade we have learned. At least one day a week and on all those days when bad weather does not permit us to stay out in the countryside, Emile and I go to work at a master's. We work there not for form's sake, as men above this station, but as true workers. Once when Sophie's father comes to see us, he finds us at work and does not fail to report with admiration to his wife and his daughters what he has seen. "Go and see this young man in the workshop," he says, "and you will see whether he despises the condition of the poor!" One can imagine whether Sophie is glad to hear this speech! They talk about it again; they would like to surprise him at work. They question me without giving any indication of what they are about, and after making sure about one of our workdays, mother and daughter take a calèche and come to the city on that day.

On entering the shop, Sophie perceives at the far end a young man in a jacket who has his hair carelessly bound up and is so busy with what he is doing that he does not see her. She stops and gives her mother a sign. Emile, with a chisel in one hand and the mallet in the other, is completing a mortise. Then he saws a plank and fixes one piece in the vise to polish it. This sight does not make Sophie laugh. It touches her; it is respectable. Woman, honor the head of your house. It is he who works for you, who wins your bread, who feeds you. This is man.

While they are attentively observing Emile, I notice them and tug on Emile's sleeve. He turns around, sees them, drops his tools, and darts toward them with a shout of joy. After having yielded to his initial transports, he makes them sit down and picks up his work again. But Sophie cannot stay seated. She gets up with vivacity, roams the shop, examines the tools, touches the polished surfaces of the planks, gathers shavings from the floor, looks at our hands, and then says that she likes this trade because it is clean. The silly girl even tries to imitate Emile. With her frail white hand she pushes a plane along the plank. The plane slides and does not bite. I believe I see Love in the air laughing and beating his wings. I believe I hear him let out shouts of gladness and say, "Hercules is avenged." [52]

Meanwhile her mother questions the master. "Sir, how much do you pay these fellows?" "Madame, I give them each twenty sous a day, and I feed them. But if this young man wished, he could earn a lot more, for he is the best worker hereabouts." "Twenty sous a day, and you feed them!" says Sophie's mother looking at us with emotion. "Madame, that's the way it is," responds the master. At these words she runs to Emile, embraces him, presses him to her bosom while shedding tears on him, unable to say anything other than to repeat several times, "My son! O my son!"

After having spent some time chatting with us but without distracting us, the mother says to her daughter, "Let us go; it is late, and we must not keep people waiting." Then, approaching Emile, she gives him a little pat on the cheek and says to him, "Well, good worker, don't you want to come with us?" He answers in a very sad tone, "I am committed. Ask the master." The master is asked if he would be kind enough to do without us. He answers that he cannot. "I have pressing work which must be delivered the day after tomorrow," he says. "Counting on these gentlemen, I have turned away other workers who showed up. If these two fail me, I do not know where to find others, and I will not be able to deliver the work on the promised day." The mother makes no reply. She expects Emile to speak. Emile lowers his head and keeps quiet. "Sir," she says, a bit surprised by this silence, "have you nothing to say to this?" Emile looks tenderly at her daughter and answers with only these words, "You see that I have to stay." At that the ladies depart and leave us. Emile accompanies them to the door, follows them with his eyes as far as he can, sighs, returns without speaking, and sets to work.

Sophie's mother is piqued, and on the way she speaks to her daughter about the strangeness of this behavior. "What?" she says. "Was it so difficult to satisfy the master without being obliged to stay? Doesn't this young man, who is so prodigal and who pours out money without necessity, any longer know how to find money on suitable occasions?" "O mother," Sophie answers, "God forbid that Emile put so much emphasis on money that he use it to break a personal commitment, to violate his word with impunity, and to cause someone else's word to be violated! I know that he could easily compensate the worker for the slight harm his absence would cause him. But meanwhile he would enslave his soul to riches; he would accustom himself to putting his riches in the place of his duties and to believing that one is excused from everything provided one pays. Emile has other ways of thinking, and I hope not to be the cause of his changing them. Do you believe it cost him nothing to stay? Mama, don't deceive yourself. It is for me that he stays. I saw it in his eyes."

It is not that Sophie is easygoing in regard to the true attentions of love. On the contrary, she is imperious and exacting. She would rather not be loved than be loved moderately. She has that noble pride based on merit which is conscious of itself, esteems itself, and wants to be honored as it honors itself. She would disdain a heart which did not feel the full value of her heart, which did not love her for her virtues as much as, and more than, for her charms, and which did not prefer its own duty to her and her to everything else. She did not want a lover who knew no law other than hers. She wants to reign over a man whom she has not disfigured. It is thus that Circe, having debased Ulysses' companions, disdains them and gives herself only to him whom she was unable to change.[53]

But apart from this inviolable and sacred right, Sophie is excessively jealous of all her rights and watches to see how scrupulously Emile respects them, how zealously he accomplishes her will, how skillfully he guesses it, and how vigilant he is to arrive at the prescribed moment. She wants him to be neither late nor early. She wants him to be on time. To be early is to prefer himself to her; to be late is to neglect her. Neglect Sophie! That would not happen twice. The unjust suspicion that it happened once came close to ruining everything. But Sophie is equitable, and she knows how to make amends for her wrongs.

One evening we are awaited. Emile has received the order. They come out to meet us. We do not arrive. "What became of them? What misfortune has befallen them? Why haven't they sent anyone?" The evening is spent waiting for us. Poor Sophie believes us dead. She is desolate; she torments herself; she spends the night crying. In the evening they had sent a messenger to inquire after us and report news of us the next morning. The messenger returns accompanied by another messenger from us who makes our excuses orally and says that we are well. A moment later we ourselves appear. Then the scene changes. Sophie dries her tears; or if she sheds any, they are tears of rage. Her haughty heart has not profited from being reassured about our lives. Emile lives and has kept her waiting needlessly.

At our arrival she wants to closet herself. She is asked to stay. She has to stay. But, making her decision on the spot, she affects a tranquil and contented air intended to make an impression on others. Her father comes out to meet us and says, "You have kept your friends in a state of distress. There are people here who will not easily pardon you." "Who is that, papa?" says Sophie, affecting the most gracious smile she can. "What difference does it make to you," her father answers, "provided it is not you?" Sophie does not reply and lowers her eyes to her work. Her mother receives us with a cold and composed air. Emile is embarrassed and does not dare approach Sophie. She speaks to him first, asks him how he is, invites him to sit down, and counterfeits so well that the poor young man, who still understands nothing of the language of the violent passions, is taken in by this coolness and as a result is about to get piqued himself.

To disabuse him, I go and take Sophie's hand. I want to bring it to my lips as I sometimes do. She withdraws it briskly, saying the word "Monsieur!" in such a singular manner that this involuntary movement at once opens Emile's eyes.

Seeing that she has betrayed herself, Sophie is less constrained. Her apparent coolness changes into an ironical contempt. She responds to everything said to her in monosyllables pronounced in a slow and unsure voice, as though she is afraid to let the accent of indignation pierce through too much. Emile, who is half-dead with fright, looks at her sorrowfully and tries to get her to cast her eyes on his so that he can better read her true sentiments. Sophie is further irritated by his confidence and casts a glance at him which takes away his desire to solicit a second one. Taken aback and trembling, Emile no longer dares—very fortunately for him—to speak to her or look at her; for even were he not guilty, she would never have pardoned him if he had been able to bear her anger.

Seeing that it is my turn and that it is time to explain ourselves, I return to Sophie. I take her hand which she no longer withdraws, for she is about to faint. I tell her gently, "Dear Sophie, we are luckless fellows, but you are reasonable and just, and you will not judge us without hearing us. Listen to us." She does not answer, and I speak as follows:

"We left yesterday at four o'clock. We were told to arrive at seven o'clock, and we always set aside more time than we need so that we can rest before approaching here. We had already come three-quarters of the way when we heard pained laments. They came from a gorge between the hills at some distance from us. We ran toward the cries. We found an unfortunate peasant who had been a bit drunk as he rode back from the city and had fallen off his horse so heavily that he broke his leg. We shouted for help. No one answered. We tried to put the injured man back on his horse, but did not succeed; at the slightest movement the luckless fellow suffered horrible pain. We decided to tie up his horse out of the way in the woods. Then, making a stretcher of our arms, we set the injured man on it and carried him as gently as possible, following his directions about the route to be taken in order to get to his home. The way was long. We had to rest several times. We finally arrived, completely worn out. We found with bitter surprise that we already knew the house, and that this poor fellow whom we were carrying back with such effort was the same man who had received us so cordially the day of our first arrival here. In our mutual distress we had not recognized each other until that moment.

"He had only two little children. His wife, who was about to give him a third, was so overwhelmed at the sight of him that she felt sharp pains and gave birth a few hours later. What was to be done in this situation in an isolated cottage where one could not hope for any help? Emile decided to go and get the horse that we had left in the woods, to mount it and to ride at full gallop to look for a surgeon in the city. He gave the horse to the surgeon. As he was not able to find a nurse quickly enough, he returned on foot with a domestic after having sent you a messenger. Meanwhile in the house I was at a loss, as you can believe, between a man with a broken leg and a woman in labor;

but I readied everything which I could foresee might be necessary to help them both.

"I shall not give you the rest of the details. That is not now the question. It was two hours past midnight before either of us had a moment's respite. Finally, we returned before dawn to our rooms near here, where we awaited the hour of your rising in order to give you an account of our accident."

I stop speaking without adding anything. But before anyone speaks, Emile approaches his beloved, raises his voice, and says to her with more firmness than I would have expected, "Sophie, you are the arbiter of my fate. You know it well. You can make me die of pain. But do not hope to make me forget the rights of humanity. They are more sacred to me than yours. I will never give them up for you."

At these words Sophie, instead of responding, rises, puts an arm around his neck, and gives him a kiss on the cheek. Then, extending her hand with inimitable grace, she says to him, "Emile, take this hand. It is yours. Be my husband and master when you wish. I will try to merit this honor."

Hardly has she embraced him, before her delighted father claps his hands, shouting, "Encore, encore!" Without having to be urged, Sophie immediately gives him two kisses on the other cheek. But almost at the same instant, frightened by all she has done, she escapes into her mother's arms and hides her face, afire with shame, in that maternal bosom.

I will not describe the common joy. Everyone ought to sense it. After dinner Sophie asks whether those poor sick people are too far away for us to go to see them. Sophie desires it, and it is a good deed. We go. We find them in two separate beds. Emile had had a second bed brought in. We find them surrounded by people who are there to help them. Emile had provided for that. But both husband and wife are lying in such disorder that they suffer as much from discomfort as from their conditions. Sophie gets one of the good woman's aprons and goes to settle the wife in her bed. Next she does the same for the man. Her gentle and light hand knows how to get at everything that hurts them and to place their sore limbs in a more relaxed position. They feel relieved at her very approach. One would say that she guesses everything which hurts them. This extremely delicate girl is rebuffed neither by the dirtiness nor the bad smell and knows how to make both disappear without ordering anyone about and without the sick being tormented. She who always seems so modest and sometimes so disdainful, she who would not for anything in the world have touched a man's bed with the tip of her finger, turns the injured man over and changes him without any scruple, and puts him in a position in which he can stay more comfortably for a long time. The zeal of charity outweighs modesty. What she does, she does so lightly and with so much skill that he feels relieved almost without having noticed that he has been touched. Wife and husband together bless the lovable girl who serves them, who pities them, who consoles them. It is an angel from heaven that God sends them. She has the appearance and the grace, as well as the gentleness and the goodness of an angel. Emile is moved and contemplates her in silence. Man, love your companion. God gives her to you to console you in your pains, to relieve you in your ills. This is woman.

The newborn child is baptized. The two lovers present it, yearning in the depths of their hearts to give others an occasion to perform the same task. They long for the desired moment. They believe they have reached it. All of Sophie's scruples have been removed, but mine are aroused. They are not yet where they think they are. Each must have his turn.

One morning, when they have not seen each other for two days, I enter Emile's room with a letter in my hand; staring fixedly at him, I say, "What would you do if you were informed that Sophie is dead?" He lets out a great cry, gets up, striking his hands together, and looks wild-eyed at me without saying a single word. "Respond then," I continue with the same tranquility. Then, irritated by my coolness, Emile approaches, his eyes inflamed with anger, and stops in an almost threatening posture: "What would I do . . . I don't know. But what I do know is that I would never again in my life see the man who had informed me." "Reassure yourself," I respond, smiling. "She is alive. She is well. She thinks of you, and we are expected this evening. But let us go and take a stroll, and we will chat."

The passion with which he is preoccupied no longer permits him to give himself to purely reasoned conversations as he had before. I have to interest him by this very passion to make him attentive to my lessons. This is what I have done by this terrible preamble. I am now quite sure that he will listen to me.

"You must be happy, dear Emile. That is the goal of every being which senses. That is the first desire which nature has impressed on us, and the only one which never leaves us. But where is happiness? Who knows it? All seek it, and none finds it. One man uses up life in pursuing it, and another dies without having attained it. My young friend, when I took you in my arms at your birth and, calling the Supreme Being to be witness of the commitment I dared to contract, dedicated my days to the happiness of yours, did I myself know what I was committing myself to? No, I only knew that in making you happy, I was sure to be. In making this useful quest for you, I was making it for both of us in common.

"So long as we do not know what we ought to do, wisdom consists in remaining inactive. Of all the maxims, this is the one of which man has the greatest need, and the one which he least knows how to follow. To seek happiness without knowing where it is, is to expose oneself to the danger of fleeing it and to run as many risks of finding the opposite of happiness as there are roads on which to go astray. But it is not everyone who knows how to refrain from acting. In the anxiety in which the ardor for well-being keeps us, we would rather make a mistake in pursuing it than do nothing to seek it; and once we have left the place where we can know it, we no longer know how to get back to it.

"Although afflicted with the same ignorance, I have tried to avoid the same mistake. In taking care of you, I resolved not to take a useless step and to prevent you from taking one. I kept to the road of nature while waiting for it to show me the road of happiness. It turned out that they were the same and that, by not thinking about it, I had followed the road of happiness.

"Be my witness and my judge. I shall never impugn you. Your first years were not sacrificed to those which were to follow. You have enjoyed all the goods nature gave you. Of the ills to which it subjects you and from which I could protect you, you have felt only those which could harden you against other ills. You have never suffered any of them except to avoid greater ones. You have known neither hatred nor slavery. Free and contented, you have stayed just and good; for pain and vice are inseparable, and man never becomes wicked except when he is unhappy. May the memory of your childhood be prolonged until your old age. I am not afraid that your good heart will ever recall your childhood without giving some thanks to the hand which governed it.

"When you entered the age of reason, I protected you from men's opinions. When your heart became sensitive, I preserved you from the empire of the passions. If I had been able to prolong this inner calm to the end of your life, I would have secured my work, and you would always be as happy as man can be. But, dear Emile, it is in vain that I have dipped your soul in the Styx; I was not able to make it everywhere invulnerable. A new enemy is arising which you have not learned to conquer and from which I can no longer save you. This enemy is yourself. Nature and fortune had left you free. You could endure poverty; you could tolerate the pains of the body; those of the soul were unknown to you. You were bound to nothing other than the human condition, and now your are bound to all the attachments you have given to yourself. In learning to desire, you have made yourself the slave of your desires. Without anything changing in you, without anything offending you, without anything touching your being, how many pains can now attack your soul! How many ills you can feel without being sick! How many deaths you can suffer without dying! A lie, a mistake, or a doubt can put you in despair.

"In the theater, you saw heroes, overcome by extreme pains, make the stage reverberate with their senseless cries, grieving like women, crying like children, and thus meriting public applause. Do you remember how scandalized you were by these lamentations, cries, and complaints on the part of men from whom one ought to expect only acts of constancy and firmness? 'What?' you said very indignantly. 'Are these the examples we are given to follow, the models we are offered for imitation! Are they afraid that man is not small enough, unhappy enough, and weak enough without someone extolling his weakness under the false image of virtue?' My young friend, be more indulgent with the stage henceforward. Now you have become one of its heroes.[54]

"You know how to suffer and die. You know how to endure the law of necessity in physical ills, but you have not yet imposed laws on the appetites of your heart, and the disorder of our lives arises from our affections far more than from our needs. Our desires are extended; our strength is almost nil. By his wishes man depends on countless things, and by himself he depends on nothing, not even his own life. The more he increases his attachments, the more he multiplies his pains. Everything on earth is only transitory. All that we love will escape us sooner or later, and we hold on to it as if it were going to last eternally. What a fright you had at the mere suspicion of Sophie's death! Did you, then, count on her living forever? Does no one die at her age? She is going to die, my child, and perhaps before you. Who knows if she is living at this very instant? Nature had enslaved you only to a single death. You are enslaving yourself to a second. Now you are in the position of dying twice.

"How pitiable you are going to be, thus subjected to your unruly passions! There will always be privations, losses, and alarms. You will not even enjoy what is left to you. The fear of losing everything will prevent you from possessing anything. As a result of having wanted to follow only your passions, you will never be able to satisfy them. You will always seek repose, but it will always flee before you. You will be miserable, and you will become wicked. How could you not be, since you have only your unbridled desires as a law? If you cannot tolerate involuntary privations, how will you impose any on yourself voluntarily? How will you know how to sacrifice inclination to duty and to hold out against your heart in order to listen to your reason? You who already wish never again to see the man who will inform you of your mistress's death, how would you see the man who would want to take her from you while she is still living—the one who would dare to say to you, 'She is dead to you. Virtue separates you from her'? If you have to live with her no matter what, it makes no difference whether Sophie is married or not, whether you are free or not, whether she loves you or hates you, whether she is given you or refused you; you want her, and you have to possess her whatever the price. Inform me, then, at what crime a man stops when he has only the wishes of his heart for laws and knows how to resist nothing that he desires?

"My child, there is no happiness without courage nor virtue without struggle. The word *virtue* comes from *strength*. Strength is the foundation of all virtue. Virtue belongs only to a being that is weak by nature and strong by will. It is in this that the merit of the just man consists; and although we call God good, we do not call Him virtuous, because it requires no effort for Him to do good. I have waited for you to be in a position to understand me before explaining this much profaned word to you. So long as virtue costs nothing to practice, there is little need to know it. This need comes when the passions are awakened. It has already come for you. Raising you in all the simplicity of nature, I have not preached painful duties to you but instead have protected you from the vices that make these duties painful. I have made lying more useless than odious to you; I have taught you not so much to give unto each what belongs to him as to care only for what is yours. I have made you good rather than virtuous. But he who is only good remains so only as long as he takes pleasure in being so. Goodness is broken and perishes under the impact of the human passions. The man who is only good is good only for himself.

"Who, then, is the virtuous man? It is he who knows how to conquer his affections; for then he follows his reason and his conscience;

he does his duty; he keeps himself in order, and nothing can make him deviate from it. Up to now you were only apparently free. You had only the precarious freedom of a slave to whom nothing has been commanded. Now be really free. Learn to become your own master. Command your heart, Emile, and you will be virtuous.

"Here, then, is another apprenticeship, and this apprenticeship is more painful than the first; for nature delivers us from the ills it imposes on us, or it teaches us to bear them. But nature says nothing to us about those which come from ourselves. It abandons us to ourselves. It lets us, as victims of our own passions, succumb to our vain sorrows and then glorify ourselves for the tears at which we should have blushed.

"You now have your first passion. It is perhaps the only one worthy of you. If you know how to rule it like a man, it will be the last. You will subject all the others, and you will obey only the passion for virtue.

"This passion is not criminal, as I well know. It is as pure as the souls which feel it. Decency formed it, and innocence nourished it. Happy lovers! For you the charms of virtue only add to those of love, and the gentle bond that awaits you is as much the reward of your moderation as it is of your attachment. But, tell me, sincere man, has this passion, which is so pure, any the less subjected you? Did you any the less make yourself its slave; and if tomorrow Sophie ceased being innocent, would you stifle it beginning tomorrow? Now is the moment to try your strength. There is no longer time to do so when that strength has to be employed. These dangerous trials ought to be made far from peril. A man does not exercise for battle in the face of the enemy but prepares himself for it before the war. He presents himself at the battle already fully prepared.

"It is an error to distinguish permitted passions from forbidden ones in order to yield to the former and deny oneself the latter. All passions are good when one remains their master; all are bad when one lets oneself be subjected to them. What is forbidden to us by nature is to extend our attachments further than our strength; what is forbidden to us by reason is to want what we cannot obtain; what is forbidden to us by conscience is not temptations but rather letting ourselves be conquered by temptations. It is not within our control to have or not to have passions. But it is within our control to reign over them. All the sentiments we dominate are legitimate; all those which dominate us are criminal. A man is not guilty for loving another's wife if he keep this unhappy passion enslaved to the law of duty. He is guilty for loving his own wife to the point of sacrificing everything to that love.

"Do not expect lengthy precepts of morality from me. I have only one precept to give you, and it comprehends all the others. Be a man. Restrain your heart within the limits of your condition. Study and know these limits. However narrow they may be, a man is not unhappy as long as he closes himself up within them. He is unhappy only when he wants to go out beyond them. He is unhappy only when, in his senseless desires, he puts in the rank of the possible what is not possible. He is unhappy when he forgets his human estate in order

to forge for himself imaginary estates from which he always falls back into his own. The only goods that it is costly to be deprived of are those one believes one has a right to. The evident impossibility of obtaining them detaches one from them. Wishes without hope do not torment us. A beggar is not tormented by the desire to be a king. A king wants to be God only when he believes he is no longer a man.

"The illusions of pride are the source of our greatest ills. But the contemplation of human misery makes the wise man always moderate. He stays in his place: he does not stir himself to leave it; he does not uselessly wear out his strength in order to enjoy what he cannot keep; and since he employs all his strength to get secure possession of what he has, he is actually more powerful and richer than we are to the extent that he desires less than we do. As a mortal and perishable being, should I go and form eternal ties on this earth where everything changes, where everything passes away, and from which I shall disappear tomorrow? O Emile, o my son, if I lost you, what would remain of me? And nevertheless I must learn to lose you, for who knows when you will be taken from me?

"Do you want, then, to live happily and wisely? Attach your heart only to imperishable beauty. Let your condition limit your desires; let your duties come before your inclinations; extend the law of necessity to moral things. Learn to lose what can be taken from you; learn to abandon everything when virtue decrees it, to put yourself above events and to detach your heart lest it be lacerated by them; to be courageous in adversity, so as never to be miserable; to be firm in your duty, so as never to be criminal. Then you will be happy in spite of fortune and wise in spite of the passions. Then you will find in the possession even of fragile goods a voluptuousness that nothing will be able to disturb. You will possess them without their possessing you; and you will feel that man, who can keep nothing, enjoys only what he knows how to lose. You will not, it is true, have the illusion of imaginary pleasures, but you will also not have the pains which are their fruit. You will gain much in this exchange, for these pains are frequent and real, and these pleasures are rare and vain. As the conqueror of so many deceptive opinions, you will also be the conqueror of the opinion that places so great a value on life. You will pass your life without disturbance and terminate it without fright. You will detach yourself from it as from all things. How many others are horror-stricken because they think that, in departing from life, they cease to be? Since you are informed about life's nothingness, you will believe that it is then that you begin to be. Death is the end of the wicked man's life and the beginning of the just man's."

Emile hears me with an attention that is mixed with anxiety. He fears some sinister conclusion to this preamble. He has a presentiment that, in showing him the necessity for exercising strength of soul, I want to subject him to this hard exercise. Like a wounded man who shudders on seeing the surgeon approach, he believes that he already feels on his wound the painful but salutary hand which prevents it from becoming infected.

Uncertain, troubled, and eager to know what I am getting at, Emile

fearfully questions me instead of answering. "What must be done?" he asks me, almost trembling and without daring to raise his eyes. "That which must be done!" I answer in a firm tone: "You must leave Sophie." "What are you saying?" he shouts with anger. "Leave Sophie! Leave her, deceive her, be a traitor, a cheat, a perjuror . . . !" "What!" I respond, interrupting him. "Is it from me that Emile is afraid of learning to merit such names?" "No," he continues with the same impetuosity. "Not from you nor from another. In spite of you, I shall know how to preserve your work. I shall know how not to merit those names."

I had expected this initial fury. I let it pass without getting upset. A fine preacher of moderation I would make if I did not possess what I am preaching to him! Emile knows me too well to believe me capable of demanding from him anything which is bad, and he knows that it would be bad to leave Sophie in the sense he is giving to that word. Therefore, he waits for me finally to explain myself. Then I return to my discourse.

"Do you believe, dear Emile, that a man, in whatever situation he finds himself, can be happier than you have been for these past three months? If you believe it, disabuse yourself. Before tasting the pleasures of life, you have exhausted its happiness. There is nothing beyond what you have felt. The felicity of the senses is fleeting. It always loses its flavor when it is the heart's habitual state. You have enjoyed more from hope than you will ever enjoy in reality. Imagination adorns what one desires but abandons it when it is in one's possession. Except for the single Being existing by itself, there is nothing beautiful except that which is not. If your present state could have lasted forever, you would have found supreme happiness. But everything connected with man feels the effects of his transitoriness. Everything is finite and everything is fleeting in human life; and if the state which makes us happy lasted endlessly, the habit of enjoying it would take away our taste for it. If nothing changes from without, the heart changes. Happiness leaves us, or we leave it.

"Time, which you did not measure, was flowing during your delirium. The summer is ending; winter approaches. Even if we could continue our visits during so hard a season, they would never tolerate it. In spite of ourselves, we must change our way of life; this one can no longer last. I see in your impatient eyes that this difficulty does not bother you. Sophie's confession and your own desires suggest to you an easy means for avoiding the snow and no longer having to make a trip in order to go and see her. The expedient is doubtless convenient. But when spring has come, the snow melts, and the marriage remains. You must think about a marriage for all seasons.

"You want to marry Sophie, and yet you have known her for less than five months! You want to marry her not because she suits you but because she pleases you—as though love were never mistaken about what is suitable, and as though those who begin by loving each other never end by hating each other. She is virtuous, I know. But is that enough? Is being decent sufficient for people to be suitable for each other? It is not her virtue I am putting in doubt; it is her character. Does a woman's character reveal itself in a day? Do you know in how many situations you must have seen her in order to get a deep knowledge of her disposition? Do four months of attachment give you assurance for a whole life? Perhaps two months of absence will make her forget you. Perhaps someone else is only waiting for your withdrawal in order to efface you from her heart. Perhaps on your return you will find her as indifferent as up to now you have found her responsive. The sentiments do not depend on principles. She may remain very decent and yet cease to love you. She will be constant and faithful. I tend to believe it. But who is answerable to you for her, and who is answerable to her for you so long as you have not put one another to the test? Will you wait to make this test until it becomes useless for you? Will you wait to know each other until you can no longer separate?

"Sophie is not yet eighteen; you are just twenty-two. This is the age of love, but not that of marriage. What a father and mother of a family! To know how to raise children, at least wait until you cease being children! Do you know how many young persons there are who have had their constitutions weakened, their health ruined, and their lives shortened by enduring the fatigues of pregnancy before the proper age? Do you know how many children have remained sickly and weak for want of having been nourished in a body that was sufficiently formed? When mother and child grow at the same time and the substance necessary to the growth of each of them is divided, neither has what nature destined for it. How is it possible that both should not suffer from it? Either I have a very poor knowledge of Emile, or he would rather have a robust wife and robust children than satisfy his impatience at the expense of their life and their health.

"Let us speak about you. In aspiring to the status of husband and father, have you meditated enough upon its duties? When you become the head of a family, you are going to become a member of the state, and do you know what it is to be a member of the state? Do you know what government, laws, and fatherland are? Do you know what the price is of your being permitted to live and for whom you ought to die? You believe you have learned everything, and you still know nothing. Before taking a place in the civil order, learn to know it and to know what rank in it suits you.

"Emile, you must leave Sophie. I do not say abandon her. If you were capable of it, she would be only too fortunate not to have married you. You must leave in order to return worthy of her. Do not be so vain as to believe that you already merit her. Oh, how much there remains for you to do! Come and fulfill this noble task. Come and learn to bear her absence. Come and win the prize of fidelity, so that on your return you can lay claim to some honor from her and ask for her hand not as an act of grace but as a recompense."

Not yet practiced at struggling against himself and not yet accustomed to desire one thing and to will another, the young man does not give in. He resists; he argues. Why should he deny himself the happiness awaiting him? Would delaying to accept the hand which is offered him not be to disdain it? What need is there to go away from her in order to inform himself about what he ought to know? And even if that were necessary, why should he not leave her the assured pledge of his return in the form of indissoluble bonds? Let him be her husband, and he will be ready to follow me. Let them be united, and he will leave her without fear . . . "To be united in order to be separated. Dear Emile, what a contradiction! It is a fine thing for a lover to be able to live without his beloved, but a husband ought never to leave his wife except in case of necessity. To cure your scruples, I see that your delay ought to be involuntary. You must be able to tell Sophie that you are leaving her in spite of yourself. Very well, be content; and since you do not obey reason, recognize another master. You have not forgotten the promise you made to me. Emile, you have to leave Sophie. I wish it."

After this statement he lowers his head, keeps quiet, and dreams for a moment; then, looking at me with assurance, he asks, "When do we leave?" "In a week," I answer. "Sophie must be prepared for this departure. Women are weaker. One owes them special consideration; and since this absence is not a duty for her as it is for you, it is permissible for her to bear it less courageously."

I am only too tempted to prolong the journal of my two young people's love up to their separation, but I have for a long time abused the indulgence of my readers. Let us be brief in order to finish once and for all.

Will Emile dare to act at his beloved's feet with the same assurance he has just shown to his friend? As for me, I believe he will. He ought to draw this assurance from the very truth of his love. He would be more uncomfortable before her if it cost him less to leave her. He would leave as the guilty party, and this role is always embarrassing for a decent heart. But the more the sacrifice costs him, the more he can lay a claim to honor in the eyes of her who makes it so difficult for him. He is not afraid that she will be misled about the motive which determines him. He seems to say to her with each glance, "O Sophie, read my heart and be faithful! You do not have a lover without virtue."

The proud Sophie, for her part, tries to bear with dignity the unforeseen blow which strikes her. She makes an effort to appear insensitive to it. But since she, unlike Emile, does not have the honor of combat and victory, her firmness holds up less well. She cries and groans in spite of herself, and the fear of being forgotten embitters the pain of separation. She does not cry before her lover; it is not to him that she shows her fears. She would choke rather than let a sigh escape her in his presence. It is I who receive her complaints, who see her tears, whom she affects to take as her confidant. Women are skillful and know how to disguise themselves. The more she grumbles in secret against my tyranny, the more attentive she is in flattering me. She senses that her fate is in my hands.

I console her. I reassure her. I make myself answerable for her lover, or rather her husband. Let her be as faithful to him as he will be to her, and I swear that in two years he will be her husband. She esteems me enough to believe that I do not want to deceive her. I am the guarantor of each for the other. Their hearts, their virtue, my probity, their parents' confidence—everything reassures them. But what good does reason do against weakness? They separate as if they were never to see each other again.

It is then that Sophie recalls the regrets of Eucharis [55] and really believes she is in her place. Let us not allow these fantastic loves to awaken during Emile's absence. "Sophie," I say to her one day, "make an exchange of books with Emile. Give him your *Telemachus* in order that he learn to resemble him, and let Emile give you *The Spectator*,[56] which you like to read. Study in it the duties of decent women, and recall that in two years these duties will be yours." This exchange pleases both and gives them confidence. Finally the sad day comes. They must separate.

Sophie's worthy father, with whom I have arranged everything, embraces me on receiving my farewell. Then, taking me aside, he says the following words to me in a grave tone and with a somewhat emphatic accent: "I have done everything to be obliging to you. I knew that I was dealing with a man of honor. There remains only one word to say to you. Remember that your pupil has signed his marriage contract on my daughter's lips."

What a difference there is in the bearing of the two lovers! Emile is impetuous, ardent, agitated, beside himself; he lets out cries, sheds torrents of tears on the hands of the father, the mother, the daughter; he sobs as he embraces all the domestics and repeats the same things a thousand times in a disorder that would cause laugher on any other occasion. Sophie is gloomy and pale, with expressionless eyes and a somber glance; she keeps quiet, says nothing, does not cry, and sees no one, not even Emile. It is in vain that he takes her hands and holds her in his arms; she remains immobile, insensitive to his tears, to his caresses, to everything he does. For her, he is already gone. How much more touching her behavior is than her lover's importunate complaints and noisy regrets! He sees it, he feels it, he is grieved by it. I drag him away with difficulty. If I leave him another moment, he will no longer be willing to part. I am charmed by the fact that he takes this sad image with him. If he is ever tempted to forget what he owes to Sophie, I shall recall her to him as he saw her at the moment of his departure. His heart would have to have changed very much for me not to be able to return it to her.

On Travel

It is asked whether it is good for young people to travel, and there is much dispute about it. If the question were put differently and it were asked whether it is good that men have traveled, perhaps there would not be so much dispute.

The abuse of books kills science. Believing that we know what we have read, we believe that we can dispense with learning it. Too much reading only serves to produce presumptuous ignoramuses. Among all literary ages there has been none in which men read so much as in this one, and none in which men are less knowledgeable. Among all the countries of Europe there is none in which so many histories and accounts of voyages are printed as in France, and none in which so little is known about the genius and the morals of other nations. So great a number of books makes us neglect the book of the world; or if we still read in it, each sticks to his own page. If the phrase "Can one be Persian?" [57] were unknown to me, I would guess on hearing it that it comes from the country where national prejudices are most prevalent and from the sex which most propagates them.

A Parisian believes he knows men, and he knows only the French. In his city, which is always full of foreigners, he regards each foreigner as an extraordinary phenomenon which has no equal in the rest of the universe. One has to have seen the bourgeoisie of this great city close up and to have lived with them to believe that people with so much cleverness can be so stupid. The bizarre thing is that each of them has read perhaps ten times the description of a country and yet to him one of its inhabitants will be an object of wonder.

It is too much to have to pierce through both the authors' prejudices and our own in order to get to the truth. I have spent my life reading accounts of travels, and I have never found two which have given me the same idea of the same people. In comparing the little that I could observe myself with what I have read, I have ended by dropping the travelers and regretting the time that I gave to informing myself by reading them. I am quite convinced that in matters of observation of every kind one must not read, one must see. This would be true even if all the travelers were sincere, said only what they have seen or what they believe, and disguised the truth only with the false colors it takes on in their own eyes. What is the situation when one has, in addition, to discern the truth through their lies and their bad faith!

Let us then leave the vaunted resource of books to those who are so constituted as to be satisfied by books. Like Raymond Lulle's art, they are good for learning to babble about what one does not know. They are good for training fifteen-year-old Platos to philosophize in polite society and for informing a gathering about the practices of Egypt and India on the testimony of Paul Lucas or Tavernier. [58]

I hold it to be an incontestable maxim that whoever has seen only one people does not know men; he knows only the people with whom he has lived. Hence there is another way of putting the same question about travel: does it suffice for a well-educated man to know only his compatriots, or is it important for him to know men in general? Here there no longer remains either dispute or doubt. Observe how much the solution of a difficult question sometimes depends on the way of posing it!

But if one wants to study men, is it necessary to roam the entire earth? Is it necessary to go to Japan to observe Europeans? Is it necessary to know all the individuals to know the species? No. There are men who have such a strong resemblance to one another that it is not worth the effort to study them separately. Whoever has seen ten Frenchmen has seen them all. Although one cannot say as much of the English and some other peoples, it is nonetheless certain that each nation has its own specific character which can be inferred from the observation not of a single member but of several. Whoever has compared ten peoples knows men, just as whoever has seen ten Frenchmen knows the French.

To become informed, it is not sufficient to roam through various countries. It is necessary to know how to travel. To observe, it is necessary to have eyes and to turn them toward the object one wants to know. There are many persons who are informed still less by travel than by books, because they are ignorant of the art of thinking; because when they read, their minds are at least guided by the author; and because when they travel, they do not know how to see anything on their own. Others do not become informed because they do not want to be informed. Their aim in traveling is so different that this one hardly occurs to them. It is very much an accident if one sees with exactitude what one does not care to look at. Of all the peoples of the world, it is the French who travel most; but they are so full of the practices of their own country that they confound everything which does not resemble those practices. There are Frenchmen in every corner of the world. There is no country in which one finds more persons who have traveled than in France. Yet in spite of that, of all the peoples of Europe, the one which sees other countries most knows them least. The Englishman travels too, but in another way. These two peoples have to be opposites in everything. The English nobility travels, the French nobility does not. The French people travel, the English people do not. This difference appears to me to do honor to the latter. The French almost always have some self-interest in view in their travels. But the English do not go fortune hunting in other nations, unless it is by means of commerce, and they go with their hands full. When they travel, it is to spend their money, not to work for a living. They are too proud to go away from home and crawl. As a result, they inform themselves better abroad than the French, who always have an entirely different aim in mind. Nevertheless, the English also have their national prejudices. Indeed, they have more of them than anyone, but these prejudices come less from ignorance than from passion. The Englishman has the prejudices of pride, and the Frenchman has those of vanity.

Just as the least cultured peoples are generally the wisest, so those who travel least are the ones who travel best. Since they are less advanced than we are in our frivolous researches and less occupied by the objects of our vain curiosity, they give all their attention to what is truly useful. I know none but the Spanish who travel in this way. While a Frenchman runs to the artists of a country, an Englishman has a sketch made of some antique, and a German carries his notebook around to all the learned men, the Spaniard quietly studies the country's government, morals, and public order, and he is the only one of the four who brings home with him some observation useful to his country.

The ancients traveled little, read little, and wrote few books, and yet one sees in those of their books which remain to us that they observed one another better than we observe our contemporaries. I will not go back to the writings of Homer, the only poet who transports us to the country he describes. But one cannot deny Herodotus the honor of having depicted manners and morals in his history—even though he does so more in his narratives than in his reflections—and of having depicted them better than all our historians, who burden their books with portraits and characteristics. Tacitus has described the Germans of his times better than any writer has described the Germans of today. Those who are conversant with ancient history incontestably know the Greeks, the Carthaginians, the Romans, the Gauls, and the Persians better than any people of our day knows its neighbors.

It must also be admitted that as the original character of a people fades from day to day, it becomes proportionately more difficult to grasp. To the extent that races are mixed and peoples confounded, one sees the gradual disappearance of those national differences which previously struck the observer at first glance. Formerly each nation remained more closed in upon itself. There was less communication, less travel, fewer common or contrary interests, and fewer political and civil relations among peoples; there were not so many of those royal annoyances called negotiations, and no regular or resident ambassadors; great voyages were rare; there was little far-flung commerce, and what little there was was done by the prince himself who used foreigners for it, or by despised men who set the tone for no one and did not bring the nations together. There is now a hundred times more contact between Europe and Asia than there formerly was between Gaul and Spain. Europe alone used to be more diverse than the whole world is today.

Moreover, the ancient peoples, who for the most part regarded themselves as autochthonous or native to their own country, occupied their homeland long enough to have lost the memory of the distant ages when their ancestors had established themselves there and long enough to have given the climate time to make durable impressions on them. Among us, by contrast, the recent emigrations of the barbarians after the invasions of the Romans have mixed up and confounded everything. Today's Frenchmen are no longer those great blond-haired and white-skinned bodies of the past; the Greeks are no longer those beautiful men made to serve as the models for art. The appearance of the Romans themselves has changed character, just as their nature has. The Persians, who are natives of Tartary, lose their former ugliness every day through the admixture of Circassian blood. The Europeans are no longer Gauls, Germans, Iberians, and Allobroges. They are nothing but Scythians who have degenerated in various ways in their looks and still more in their morals.

This is why the ancient distinctions of races and the qualities of air and soil distinguished the temperaments, looks, morals, and characters of different peoples more strongly than all these things can be distinguished in our day. For today, European inconstancy does not leave any natural cause enough time to make its impressions; and with the forests leveled, the marshes dried up, and the land more uniformly—although worse—cultivated, there is no longer even the same physical difference from land to land and from country to country.

Perhaps on the basis of such reflections we would be in less of a hurry to subject Herodotus, Ctesias, and Pliny to ridicule for having represented the inhabitants of diverse countries with original features and distinct differences which we no longer see in them. It would be necessary to rediscover the same men in order to recognize the same looks. It would be necessary for nothing to have changed them in order for them to have stayed the same. If we could at one time consider all the men who have ever lived, can it be doubted that we would find that they varied more from age to age than they do today from nation to nation?

At the same time that observations of other peoples become more difficult, they are made more negligently and less well. This is another reason for the slight success of our researches into the natural history of mankind. The instruction that one extracts from travel is related to the aim that causes travel to be undertaken. When this aim is a system of philosophy, the traveler never sees anything but what he wants to see. When this aim is profit, it absorbs all the attention of those who devote themselves to it. Commerce and the arts, which mingle and confound peoples, also prevent them from studying one another. When they know the profit they can make from one another, what more do they have to know?

It is useful for man to know all the places where he can live so that he then may choose where he can live most comfortably. If each man were self-sufficient, the only important thing for him to know would be the land capable of providing him with subsistence. The savage, who needs no one and covets nothing in the world, knows and seeks to know no lands other than his own. If he is forced to wander in order to subsist, he flees the places inhabited by men. He has designs only on beasts and has need only of them to feed himself. But for us to whom civil life is necessary and who can no longer get along without devouring men, our interest is to frequent the countries where the most men are found. This is why all flock to Rome, Paris, and London. It is always in the capitals that human blood is sold most cheaply. Thus one knows only the large nations, and the large nations all resemble one another.

It is said that we have learned men who travel to inform themselves. This is an error. The learned travel for profit like the others. The Platos and the Pythagorases are no longer to be found; or if they do exist, it is quite far away from us. Our learned men travel only by order of the court. They are dispatched, subsidized, and paid to observe such and such an object, which is very surely not a moral object. They owe all their time to this single object. They are too decent to steal their money. If in some country there happen to be men who are curious and travel at their own expense, it is never to study men but rather to instruct them. It is not science they need but ostentation. How would they learn to shake off the yoke of opinion in their travels? They only undertake them for the sake of opinion.

There is a big difference between traveling to see lands and traveling to see peoples. The former is always the object of the curious; the latter is only subsidiary for them. It ought to be exactly the opposite for someone who wants to philosophize. The child observes things while waiting to be able to observe men. The man ought to begin by observing his kind and then observe things if he has the time.

Therefore, it is bad reasoning to conclude from the fact that we travel badly that travel is useless. But once the utility of travel is recognized, does it follow that it is suitable for everyone? Far from it. On the contrary, it is suitable for only very few people. It is suitable only for men sure enough about themselves to hear the lessons of error without letting themselves be seduced and to see the example of vice without letting themselves be carried away. Travel pushes a man toward his natural bent and completes the job of making him good or bad. Whoever returns from roaming the world is, upon his return, what he will be for his whole life. More men come back wicked than good, because more leave inclined to evil than to good. In their travels ill-raised and ill-guided young people contract all the vices of the peoples they frequent and none of the virtues with which these vices are mixed. But all those who are happily born, whose good nature has been well cultivated, and who travel with the true intention of informing themselves, return better and wiser than they left. It is in this way that my Emile will travel. Thus traveled that young man, worthy of a better age, whose merit an astonished Europe admired; although he deserved to live, he died for his country in the flower of his years, and his grave, adorned by his virtues alone, was not honored until a foreign hand covered it with flowers.[59]

Everything that is done by reason ought to have its rules. Travel— taken as a part of education—ought to have its rules. To travel for the sake of traveling is to wander, to be a vagabond. To travel to inform oneself is still to have too vague an aim. Instruction which has no determined goal is nothing. I would want to give the young man a palpable interest in informing himself, and if this interest were well chosen, it would then determine the nature of the instruction. This is only a continuation of the method I have tried to put into practice all along.

Now that Emile has considered himself in his physical relations with other beings and in his moral relations with other men, it remains for him to consider himself in his civil relations with his fellow citizens. To do that, he must begin by studying the nature of government in general, the diverse forms of government, and finally the particular government under which he was born, so that he may find out whether it suits him to live there. For by a right nothing can abrogate, when each man attains his majority and becomes his own master, he also becomes master of renouncing the contract that connects him with the community by leaving the country in which that community is established. It is only by staying there after attaining the age of reason that he is considered to have tacitly confirmed the commitment his ancestors made. He acquires the right of renouncing his fatherland just as he acquires the right of renouncing his father's estate. Furthermore, since place of birth is a gift of nature, one yields one's own place of birth in making this renunciation. According to rigorous standards of right, each man remains free at his own risk in whatever place he is born unless he voluntarily subjects himself to the laws in order to acquire the right to be protected by them.

Therefore, I might say to him: "Up to now you have lived under my direction. You were not in a condition to govern yourself. But now you are approaching the age when the laws put your property at your disposition and thus make you the master of your own person. You are going to find yourself alone in society, dependent on everything, even on your patrimony. You plan to settle down. This plan is laudable; it is one of man's duties. But, before marrying, you must know what kind of man you want to be, what you want to spend your life doing, and what measures you want to take to assure yourself and your family of bread. Although one ought not to make such a care his principal business, one must nonetheless think about it once. Do you want to commit yourself to dependence on men whom you despise? Do you want to establish your fortune and determine your status by means of civil relations which will put you constantly at the discretion of others and force you to become a rascal yourself in order to escape from the clutches of other rascals?"

Then I shall describe to him all the possible means of taking advantage of his property, whether in commerce or public office or finance, and I shall show him that every one of them will leave him risks to run, put him in a precarious and dependent state, and force him to adjust his morals, his sentiments, and his conduct to the example and the prejudices of others.

"There is," I shall say to him, "another means of employing one's time and person. That is to join the service—that is to say, to hire yourself out very cheaply to go and kill people who have done us no harm. This trade is in high esteem among men, and they make an extraordinary fuss about those who are good only for this. Furthermore, this trade, far from allowing you to dispense with other resources, only makes them more necessary to you. For one aspect of the honor of the military estate is the impoverishment of those who devote themselves to it. It is true that they are not all impoverished by it. It is even gradually becoming fashionable to enrich oneself in this trade as in the others. But when I explain to you how those who succeed in doing so go about it, I doubt that I will make you eager to imitate them.

"You will also find out that even in this trade the main point is no longer courage or valor, except perhaps with women. On the contrary, the most groveling, the basest, and the most servile is always the most honored. If you take it into your head to really want to perform your trade, you will be despised, hated, and perhaps driven out; at best, you will be overwhelmed by improper treatment and supplanted by all your comrades for having done your service in the trenches while they did theirs in ladies' dressing rooms."

One strongly suspects that all these diverse employments will not be very much to Emile's taste. "What?" he will say to me. "Have I forgotten the games of my childhood? Have I lost my hands? Is my strength exhausted? Do I no longer know how to work? Of what importance to me are all your fine employments and all men's silly opinions? I know no other glory than being beneficent and just. I know no other happiness than living in independence with the one I love, earning my appetite and my health every day by my work. All these complications you tell me about hardly touch me. I want as all my property only a little farm in some corner of the world. I shall use all my avarice to improve it, and I shall live without worrying. Give me Sophie and my field—and I shall be rich."

"Yes, my friend, a woman and a field that belong to him are enough for the wise man's happiness. But although these treasures are modest, they are not as common as you think. You have found the rarer one. Let us now speak of the other.

"A field which is yours, dear Emile! And in what place will you choose it? In what corner of the earth will you be able to say, 'Here I am master of myself and of the land which belongs to me?' One knows where it is easy to get rich, but who knows where one can get along without being rich? Who knows where one can live independent and free, without needing to harm anyone and without fear of being harmed? Do you believe that it is so easy to find the country where one is always permitted to be a decent man? I agree that if there is any legitimate and sure means of subsisting without intrigue, without involvements, and without dependence, it is to live by cultivating one's own land with the labor of one's own hands. But where is the state where a man can say to himself, 'The land I tread is mine'? Before choosing this happy land, be well assured that you will find there the peace you seek. Be careful that a violent government, a persecuting religion, or perverse morals do not come to disturb you there. Shelter yourself from boundless taxes that would devour the fruit of your efforts and from endless litigation that would consume your estate. Arrange it so that, in living justly, you do not have to pay court to administrators, their deputies, judges, priests, powerful neighbors, and rascals of every kind, who are always ready to torment you if you neglect them. Above all, shelter yourself from vexation by the noble and the rich. Keep in mind that everywhere their lands can border on Naboth's vineyard.[60] If you are unlucky enough to have a man of position buy or build a house near your cottage, can you be sure that he will not find the means, under some pretext, to invade your inheritance in order to round off his own, or that you will not see—perhaps tomorrow—all your resources absorbed into a large highway? And if you preserve influence in order to fend off all these problems, you might as well also preserve your riches, for they are no costlier to keep. Wealth and influence mutually prop each other up. The one is always poorly maintained without the other.

"I have more experience than you, dear Emile. I see the difficulty of your project better. Nevertheless it is a fine and decent one which would really make you happy. Let us make an effort to execute it. I have a proposition to make to you. Let us consecrate the two years until your return to choosing an abode in Europe where you can live happily with your family, sheltered from all the dangers of which I have just spoken to you. If we succeed, you will have found the true happiness vainly sought by so many others, and you will not regret the time you have spent. If we do not succeed, you will be cured of a chimera. You will console yourself for an inevitable unhappiness, and you will submit yourself to the law of necessity."

I do not know whether all my readers will perceive where this proposed research is going to lead us. But I do know that if Emile, at the conclusion of his travels begun and continued with this intention, does not come back versed in all matter of government, in public morals, and in maxims of state of every kind, either he or I must be quite poorly endowed—he with intelligence and I with judgment.

The science of political right is yet to be born, and it is to be presumed that it never will be born. Grotius, the master of all our learned men in this matter, is only a child and, what is worse, a child of bad faith. When I hear Grotius praised to the skies and Hobbes covered with execration, I see how few sensible men read or understand these two authors. The truth is that their principles are exactly alike. They differ only in their manner of expression. They also differ in method. Hobbes bases himself on sophisms, and Grotius on poets. They have everything else in common.

The only modern in a position to create this great and useless science was the illustrious Montesquieu. But he was careful not to discuss the principles of political right. He was content to discuss the positive right of established governments, and nothing in the world is more different than these two studies.

Nevertheless, whoever wants to make healthy judgments about existing governments is obliged to unite the two. It is necessary to know what ought to be in order to judge soundly about what is. The greatest difficulty in clarifying these important matters is to interest an individual in discussing them by answering these two questions: What importance does it have for me? and, What can I do about it? We have put our Emile in a position to answer both questions for himself.

The second difficulty comes from the prejudices of childhood, from the maxims on which one has been raised, and above all from the partiality of authors who always speak of the truth—which they scarcely care about—but think only of their interest, which they are silent about. Now, the people do not give chairs or pensions or places in academies. You may judge how the peoples' rights are likely to be protected by these men! I have done things in such a way that this is not yet a difficulty for Emile. He hardly knows what government is. The only thing important to him is to find the best one. His aim is not to write books, and if he ever does, it will be not in order to pay court to the powers that be but to establish the rights of humanity.

There remains a third difficulty which is more specious than solid and which I want neither to resolve nor to pose. It is enough for me that it does not daunt my zeal, since I am certain that in researches of this kind great talents are less necessary than a sincere love of justice and a true respect for the truth. If matters of government can be equitably treated, then I believe that the occasion for it is now or never.

Before observing, one must make some rules for one's observations. One must construct a standard to which measurements one makes can be related. Our principles of political right are that standard. Our measurements are the political laws of each country.

BOOK V

Our elements are clear, simple, and taken immediately from the nature of things. They will be formed from questions discussed between us, and we shall convert them into principles only when they are sufficiently resolved.[61]

For example, by first going back to the state of nature, we shall examine whether men are born enslaved or free, associated with one another or independent. Whether they join together voluntarily or by force. Whether the force which joins them can form a permanent right by which this prior force remains obligatory, even when it is surmounted by another. If so, ever since the force of King Nimrod[62] who is said to have subjected the first peoples, all the other forces which have destroyed Nimrod's have been iniquitous and usurpatory, and there are no longer any legitimate kings other than the descendants of Nimrod or his assignees. Or whether, once this force has expired, the force which succeeds it becomes obligatory in turn and destroys the obligation of the other, in such a way that one is only obliged to obey as long as one is forced to do so and is dispensed from it as soon as one can offer resistance—a right which, it seems, would not add very much to force and would hardly be anything but a play on words.

We shall examine whether one cannot say that every illness comes from God, and whether it follows from this that it is a crime to call the doctor.

We shall further examine whether conscience obliges one to give one's purse to a bandit who demands it on the highway, even if one could hide it from him. For, after all, the pistol he holds is also a power.

Whether the word *power* on this occasion means anything other than a legitimate power, one that consequently is subject to the laws from which it gets its being.

Assuming that one rejects this right of force and accepts the right of nature, or paternal authority, as the principle of societies, we shall investigate the extent of that authority, how it is founded in nature, and whether it has any other ground than the utility of the child, his weakness, and the natural love the father has for him. Whether when the child's weaknesses comes to an end and his reason matures, he does not therefore become the sole natural judge of what is suitable for his preservation, and consequently his own master, as well as become independent of every other man, even of his father. For it is even more certain that the son loves himself than it is that the father loves his son.

Whether when the father dies, the children are obliged to obey the eldest among them or someone else who will not have a father's natural attachment for them; and whether there will always be a single chief in each clan whom the whole family is obliged to obey. In which case we would investigate how the authority could ever be divided, and by what right there would be more than one chief on the whole earth governing mankind.

Assuming that peoples were formed by choice, we shall then distinguish right from fact; since men have thus subjected themselves to their brothers, uncles, or parents not because they were obliged to but because they wanted to, we shall ask whether this sort of society is not always simply a case of free and voluntary association.

Moving next to the right of slavery, we shall examine whether a man can legitimately alienate himself to another without restriction, without reserve, without any kind of condition: that is to say, whether he can renounce his person, his life, his reason, his *I*, and all morality in his actions—in a word, whether he can cease to exist before his death in spite of nature, which gives him immediate responsibility for his own preservation, and in spite of his conscience and his reason, which prescribe to him what he ought to do and what he ought to abstain from doing.

And if there is some reserve or restriction in the transaction of enslavement, we shall discuss whether this transaction does not then become a true contract in which each of the parties, having no common superior in this capacity,* remains his own judge as to the conditions of the contract; and whether each consequently remains free in this respect and master of breaking the contract as soon as he considers himself injured.

If a slave, then, cannot alienate himself without reserve to his master, how can a people alienate itself without reserve to its chief? And if the slave remains judge of whether his master observes their contract, will the people not remain judge of whether their chiefs observe their contract?

Forced to retrace our steps in this way, and examining the sense of the collective word *people,* we shall investigate whether the establishment of a people does not require at least a tacit contract prior to the one we are supposing.

Since the people is a people before electing a king, what made it such if not the social contract? Therefore the social contract is the basis of every civil society, and the nature of the society it forms must be sought in the nature of this transaction.

We shall investigate what the tenor of this contract is and whether it can be summed up in this formula: *Each of us puts his goods, his person, his life, and all his power in common under the supreme direction of the general will, and we as a body accept each member as a part indivisible from the whole.*

Assuming this, we shall note, in order to define the terms we need, that this act of association produces—in place of the particular person of each contracting party—a moral and collective body composed of as many members as the assembly has voices. This public person, understood generally, takes the name *body politic*; its members call it *state* when it is passive, *sovereign* when it is active, and *power* when it is compared with other bodies politic. Speaking of the members collectively they take the name *people*; individually they are called both *citizens*, as members of the city or participants in the sovereign authority, and *subjects*, as subject to the same authority.

We shall note that this act of association contains a reciprocal commitment of the public and the individuals, and that each individual,

---

* If they had one, this common superior would be none other than the sovereign; and then the right of slavery would be founded on the right of sovereignty and would not be its source.

who is, so to speak, contracting with himself, is committed in two respects—as a member of the sovereign, to the individuals; as a member of the state, to the sovereign.

We shall further note that since no one is held to commitments made only with himself, public deliberation—which can obligate all the subjects with respect to the sovereign because of the two different relations in which each of them is envisaged—cannot obligate the state to itself. From which one can see that there neither is nor can be any other fundamental law properly speaking than the social pact alone. This does not mean that the body politic cannot in certain respects commit itself to another; for with respect to foreigners, it becomes a simple being, an individual.

Since the two contracting parties—that is, each individual and the public—have no common superior who can judge their differences, we shall examine whether each party remains the master of breaking the contract when it pleases him—that is to say, of renouncing it as soon as he believes himself injured.

In order to clarify this question, we shall observe that according to the social pact the sovereign is able to act only by common and general wills and that therefore its acts ought similarly to have only general and common objects. From this it follows that an individual could not be directly injured by the sovereign without everyone's being injured; but this cannot be, since it would be to want to harm oneself. Thus the social contract never has need of any guarantee other than the public force, because the injury can come only from individuals; and in that case they are not thereby free from their commitment but are punished for having violated it.

In order to decide all such questions, we shall be careful always to remind ourselves that the social pact is of a particular and unique nature, in that the people contracts only with itself—that is to say, the people as sovereign body contracts with the individuals as subjects. This condition constitutes the whole artifice of the political machine and sets it in motion. It alone renders legitimate, reasonable, and free from danger commitments that otherwise would be absurd, tyrannical, and subject to the most enormous abuses.

Inasmuch as the individuals have subjected themselves only to the sovereign, and the sovereign authority is nothing other than the general will, we shall see how each man who obeys the sovereign obeys only himself, and how one is more free under the social pact than in the state of nature.

After having compared natural liberty to civil liberty with respect to persons, we shall, with respect to possessions, compare the right of property with the right of sovereignty, individual domain with eminent domain. If the sovereign authority is founded on the right of property, this right is the one it ought to respect most. The right of property is inviolable and sacred for the sovereign authority as long as it remains a particular and individual right. But as soon as it is considered as common to all the citizens, it is subject to the general will, and this will can suppress it. Thus the sovereign has no right to touch the possessions of one or more individuals. But it can legitimately seize the possessions of all, as was done at Sparta in the time of Lycurgus; the abolition of debts by Solon, on the other hand, was an illegitimate act.[63]

Since nothing obligates the subjects except the general will, we shall investigate how this will is manifested, by what signs one is sure of recognizing it, what a law is, and what the true characteristics of law are. This subject is entirely new: the definition of law remains to be made.

The moment the people considers one or more of its members individually, the people is divided. A relation is formed between the whole and its part which makes them into two separate beings: the part is one, and the whole, less this part, is the other. But the whole less a part is not the whole. Therefore, as long as this relation subsists, there is no longer a whole but two unequal parts.

By contrast, when the whole people makes a statute applying to the whole people, it considers only itself; and if a relation is formed, it is between the whole object seen from one point of view and the whole object seen from another point of view, without any division of the whole. Then the object applying to which the statute is made is general, and the will which makes the statute is also general. We shall examine whether there is any other kind of act that can bear the name of law.

If the sovereign can speak only by laws, and if the law can never have anything but a general object—one that relates equally to all the members of the state—it follows that the sovereign never has the power to make any statute applying to a particular object. But since it is important for the preservation of the state that particular things also be decided, we shall investigate how that can be done.

The acts of the sovereign can only be acts of general will—that is, laws. There must next be determining acts—acts of force or of government—for the execution of these same laws, and these acts can have only particular objects. Thus the act by which the sovereign decrees that a chief will be elected is a law, and the act by which that chief is elected in execution of the law is only an act of government.

Here, then, is a third relation in which the assembled people can be considered—as magistrate or executor of the law that it has declared in its capacity as sovereign.*

We shall examine whether it is possible for the people to divest itself of its right of sovereignty in order to vest that right in one or more men. For, since the act of election is not a law, and in this act the people itself is not sovereign, it is hard to see how it can transfer a right it does not have.

Inasmuch as the essence of sovereignty consists in the general will, it is also hard to see how one can be certain that a particular will always will agree with this general will. One ought rather to presume that the particular will will often be contrary to the general will, for private interest always tends to preferences, and the public interest

* Most of these questions and propositions are extracts from the treatise *The Social Contract,* itself an extract from a larger work that was undertaken without consulting my strength and has long since been abandoned. The little treatise I have detached from it—of which this is the summary—will be published separately.

always tends to equality. And even if such agreement were possible but not necessary and indestructible, that would suffice for making it impossible for sovereign right to result from it.

We shall investigate whether the chiefs of the people, under whatever name they may be elected, can ever, without violating the social pact, be anything but officers of the people whom the people direct to execute the laws; and whether these chiefs owe the people an account of their administration and are themselves subject to the laws whose observance they are charged with ensuring.

If the people cannot alienate its supreme right, can it entrust that right to others for a time? If it cannot give itself a master, can it give itself representatives? This question is important and merits discussion.

If the people can have neither a sovereign nor representatives, we shall examine how it can declare its laws by itself; whether it ought to have many laws, whether it ought to change them often, and whether it is easy for a large populace to be its own legislator.

Whether the Roman populace was not a large populace.

Whether it is good to have large populaces.

It follows from the preceding considerations that within the state there is an intermediate body between the subjects and the sovereign. This intermediate body, which is formed of one or more members, is in charge of public administration, the execution of the laws, and the maintenance of civil and political liberty.

The members of this body are called *magistrates* or *kings*—that is, governors. The whole body is called *prince* when considered with regard to the men who compose it, and *government* when considered with regard to its action.

If we consider the action of the whole body acting upon itself—that is, the relation of the whole to the whole or of the sovereign to the state —we can compare this relation to that of the extremes of a continuous proportion which has the government as its middle term. The magistrate receives from the sovereign the orders he gives to the people; and when everything is calculated, his product or power is of the same magnitude as the product or power of the citizens, who are on the one hand subjects and on the other sovereigns.[64] None of the three terms could be altered without immediately breaking the proportion. If the sovereign wants to govern, or if the prince wants to give laws, or if the subject refuses to obey, disorder replaces order, and the state is dissolved, falling into despotism or anarchy.

Let us suppose the state to be composed of ten thousand citizens. The sovereign can be considered only collectively and as a body. But each individual, as a subject, has a personal and independent existence. Thus the sovereign is to the subject as ten thousand is to one. That is, each member of the state has only a ten-thousandth part of the sovereign authority as his share, although he is totally subjected to that authority. If the people is composed of one hundred thousand men, the condition of the subjects does not change, and each always endures the whole empire of the laws, but his suffrage, which is reduced to a one-hundred-thousandth share, has ten times less influence in drawing up the laws. Thus, while the subject always remains one, the ratio of the sovereign to the subject increases in proportion to the number of citizens. From this it follows that the more the state expands, the more liberty diminishes.

Now, the less the particular wills correspond to the general will—that is, the less morals correspond to laws—the more the repressing force ought to increase. From another point of view, a larger state gives the depositories of public authority greater temptations and more means for abusing them; therefore the more force the government has in order to contain the people, the more force the sovereign ought to have in order to contain the government.

It follows from this double relation that the continuous proportion among the sovereign, the prince, and the people is not an arbitrary idea but a consequence of the nature of the state. Further, it follows that since one of the extremes—that is, the people—is fixed, every time the doubled ratio increases or decreases, the simple ratio increases or decreases in turn, which cannot happen without the mean term changing the same number of times.[65] From this we can draw the conclusion that there is not a single and absolute constitution of government, but that there ought to be as many governments differing in nature as there are states differing in size.

If it is the case that the more numerous the people are, the less morals correspond to the laws, we shall examine whether, by an evident enough analogy, it can also be said that the more numerous the magistrates are, the weaker the government is.

In order to clarify this maxim, we shall distinguish three essentially different wills in the person of each magistrate. First, there is the personal will of the individual, which is directed only to his own particular advantage. Second, there is the common will of the magistrates, which relates solely to the profit of the prince; this will can be called the "will de corps," [66] which is general in relation to the government and particular in relation to the state of which the government is a part. In the third place, there is the will of the people or the sovereign will, which is general both in relation to the state considered as the whole and in relation to the government considered as part of the whole. Where there is perfect legislation, the particular and individual will ought to be almost nonexistent, and the will de corps belonging to the government ought to be very subordinate; consequently the general and sovereign will is the standard for all the others. However, according to the natural order, these different wills become more active to the extent that they are concentrated. The general will is always the weakest, the will de corps has the second rank, and the particular will is preferred over all others. The result is that each man is first of all himself, and then a magistrate, and then a citizen—a gradation directly opposed to that which the social order demands.

Once this has been granted, we shall suppose the government in the hands of a single man. Here the particular will and the will de corps are perfectly united, and consequently the latter has the highest degree of intensity it can have. Now, since the use of force depends on this degree of intensity, and since the absolute force of the government

—which is always that of the people—does not vary, it follows that the most active government is that of a single man.

Alternatively, let us unite the government to the supreme authority, making the sovereign into the prince and the citizens into so many magistrates. Then the will *de corps,* which is perfectly confounded with the general will, will not be more active than the general will and will leave the particular will with all its force. Thus the government, although it always possesses the same absolute force, will be at its *minimum* level of activity.

These rules are incontestable, and other considerations serve to confirm them. For example, one sees that the magistrates are more active in the body of magistrates than the citizen is in the citizen body. Consequently the particular will has much more influence in the body of magistrates, for each magistrate is almost always in charge of some particular function of government, while each citizen, taken separately, has no particular function of sovereignty. Furthermore, the more the state expands, the more its real force increases, although it does not increase in proportion to its extent. But when the state remains the same, it is vain to multiply the number of magistrates; the government does not thereby acquire a greater real force, because it is the depository of the state's force which we are supposing is still the same. Thus, as a result of the greater number of magistrates, the government's activity decreases without its force being able to increase.

After having found that the government slackens to the extent that the magistrates multiply, and that the more people there are the more the repressive force of the government ought to increase, we shall conclude that the ratio of magistrates to government ought to be inverse to that of subjects to sovereign. In other words, the more the state expands, the more the government ought to contract, so that the number of chiefs decreases in proportion to the increase in the size of the people.

Next, in order to fix this diversity of forms under more precise denominations, we first shall note that the sovereign can entrust the government to the whole people or to the greater part of the people, so that there are more citizens who are magistrates than citizens who are simple individuals. The name *democracy* is given to this form of government.

Or it can confine the government in the hands of a lesser number, so that there are more simple citizens than magistrates. This form bears the name *aristocracy.*

Finally, it can concentrate the whole government in the hands of a single magistrate. This third form is the most common and is called *monarchy* or *royal government.*

We shall note that all these forms—or at least the first two—are susceptible to degrees of more and less, and even have a rather great latitude in this respect. Democracy can embrace the whole people or can be confined to as little as half of it. Aristocracy, in turn, can be confined to any number from half the people down to the smallest group. Even royalty someimes admits of division, whether between father and son or beween two brothers, or otherwise. There were always two kings in

Sparta, and up to eight emperors were seen at the same time in the Roman Empire without its being possible to say that the empire was divided.[67] There is a point where each form of government is confounded with the next one; and under these three specific denominations government is really capable of as many forms as the state has citizens.

What is more, since each of these governments can be subdivided in certain respects into diverse parts—with one administered in one way and another in another way—the combinations of these three forms can give rise to a multitude of mixed forms, each of which is multipliable by all the simple forms.

There has always been much dispute about the best form of government, without its being considered that each is best in certain cases and worst in certain others. But if the number of magistrates * in the different states ought to be inverse to the number of citizens, we shall conclude that generally democratic government is suitable for small states, aristocratic government for medium-sized states, and monarchic government for large states.

By following the thread of these researches, we shall come to know what the duties and the rights of citizens are, and whether the former can be separated from the latter. We shall also learn what the fatherland is, precisely what it consists in, and how each person can know whether or not he has a fatherland.

Once we have thus considered each species of civil society in itself, we shall compare them in order to observe their diverse relations: some large, others small; some strong, others weak; attacking, resisting, and destroying one another, and in this continual action and reaction, responsible for more misery and loss of life than if men had all kept their initial freedom. We shall examine whether the establishment of society accomplished too much or too little; whether individuals—who are subject to laws and to men, while societies among themselves maintain the independence of nature—remain exposed to the ills of both conditions without having their advantages; and whether it would be better to have no civil society in the world than to have many. Is it not this mixed condition which participates in both and secures neither *per quem neutrum licet, nec tanquan in bello paratum esse, nec tanquam in pace securum?* [68] Is it not this partial and imperfect association which produces tyranny and war; and are not tyranny and war the greatest plagues of humanity?

Finally, we shall examine the kind of remedies for these disadvantages provided by leagues and confederations, which leave each state its own master within but arm it against every unjust aggressor from without. We shall investigate how a good federative association can be established, what can make it durable, and how far the right of confederation can be extended without jeopardizing that of sovereignty.

The Abbé de Saint-Pierre proposed an association of all the states of Europe in order to maintain perpetual peace among them. Was this association feasible? And if it had been established, can it be presumed that

* It will be remembered that I mean to speak here only of supreme magistrates or chiefs of the nation; the others are only their substitutes in this or that function.

it would have lasted? * These investigations lead us directly to all the questions of public right which can complete the clarification of the questions of political right.

Finally, we shall lay down the true principles of the right of war, and we shall examine why Grotius and the others presented only false ones.

I would not be surprised if my young man, who has good sense, were to interrupt me in the middle of all our reasoning and say, "Someone might say that we are building our edifice with wood and not with men, so exactly do we align each piece with the ruler!" "It is true, my friend, but keep in mind that right is not bent by men's passions, and that our first concern was to establish the true principles of political right. Now that our foundations are laid, come and examine what men have built on them; and you will see some fine things!"

Then I make him read *Telemachus* while proceeding on his journey. We seek the happy Salente and the good Idomeneus, made wise by dint of misfortunes. On our way we find many Protesilauses, and no Philocles. Adrastus, king of the Dorians, is also not impossible to find.[70] But let us leave the readers to imagine our travels—or to make them in our stead with *Telemachus* in hand; and let us not suggest to them invidious comparisons that the author himself dismisses or makes in spite of himself.

Besides, since Emile is not a king and I am not a god, we do not fret about not being able to imitate Telemachus and Mentor in the good that they did for men. No one knows better than we do how to keep in our place, and no one has less desire to leave it. We know that the same task is given to all, and that whoever loves the good with all his heart and does it with all his power has fulfilled his task. We know that Telemachus and Mentor are chimeras. Emile does not travel as an idle man, and he does more good than if he were a prince. If we were kings, we would no longer be beneficent. If we were kings and were beneficent, we would do countless real evils without knowing it for the sake of an apparent good that we believed we were doing. If we were kings and were wise, the first good thing that we would want to do for ourselves and others would be to abdicate our royal position and become again what we are.

I have said why travel is not fruitful for everyone. What makes it still more unfruitful for young people is the way they are made to do it. Governors, who are more interested in their own entertainment than in their pupils' instruction, lead them from city to city, from palace to palace, from social circle to social circle; or, if the governors are learned and men of letters, they make their pupils spend their time roaming libraries, visiting antique shops, going through old monuments, and transcribing old inscriptions. In each country the pupils are involved with another century. It is as if they were involved with another country. The result is that, after having roamed Europe at great expense, abandoned to frivolities or boredom, they return without hav-

---

* Since I wrote this, the arguments *for* have been expounded in the extract from the Abbé's project; the arguments *against*—at least those which appeared solid to me—are to be found in the collection of my writings that follows this extract.[69]

ing seen anything which can interest them or learned anything which can be useful to them.

All capitals resemble one another. All peoples are mixed together in them, and all morals are confounded. It is not to capitals that one must go to study nations. Paris and London are but the same city in my eyes. Their inhabitants have some different prejudices, but an equal share of them, and all their practical maxims are the same. One knows what kinds of men must gather in courts and what morals must everywhere be produced by the crowding together of the people and the inequality of fortunes. As soon as I am told of a city of two hundred thousand souls, I know beforehand how people live there. Whatever else I would find out on the spot is not worth the effort of going to learn.

One must go to the remote provinces—where there is less movement and commerce, where foreigners travel less, where the inhabitants move around less and change fortune and status less—in order to study the genius and the morals of a nation. See the capital in passing, but go far away from it to observe the country. The French are not in Paris, they are in Touraine. The English are more English in Mercia than in London, and the Spanish are more Spanish in Galicia than in Madrid. It is at these great distances from the capital that a people reveals its character and shows itself as it is without admixture. There the good and bad effects of the government are more strongly felt, just as the measurement of arcs is more exact at the end of a longer radius.

The necessary relations between morals and government have been so well expounded in the book *The Spirit of the Laws* that one can do no better than have recourse to this work to study these relations. But in general, there are two easy and simple rules for judging the relative goodness of governments. One is population. In every country which is becoming depopulated the state is tending toward its ruin; and the country which has the highest rate of population growth, even if it is the poorest, is infallibly the best governed.[71]

But for this to be the case, it is necessary that the size of a country's population be a natural effect of its government and morals. For if population growth is accomplished by bringing in colonists or by other accidental and temporary means, they would prove the disease by the need for the remedy. When Augustus proclaimed laws against celibacy, these laws already showed the decline of the Roman Empire.[72] It is necessary that the goodness of the government incline the citizens to marry rather than that the law constrain them to do so. One should not examine what is done by force; for the law which combats the constitution is evaded and becomes vain. Instead, one should examine what is accomplished by the influence of morals and by the natural bent of the government, for these means alone have a constant effect. It was the policy of the good Abbé de Saint-Pierre always to seek a small remedy for each individual ill instead of going back to a common source and seeing that all the ills can only be cured together. It is a matter not of treating separately each ulcer that appears on a sick man's body but of purging the bulk of the blood that produces all the ulcers. It is said that in England there are prizes for agriculture. I need no more evidence. That alone proves to me that agriculture will not flourish there for long.

BOOK V

The second sign of the relative goodness of government and laws is also drawn from population, but in another way—namely, from its distribution, and not from its quantity. Two states equal in size and in the number of men can be very unequal in strength; and the most powerful of the two is always the one whose inhabitants are most evenly distributed over its territory. The one which does not have such big cities, and which is consequently less brilliant, will always defeat the other. It is big cities which exhaust a state and cause its weakness. The wealth they produce is only apparent and illusory—a lot of money that has little effect. It is said that the city of Paris is worth a province to the king of France. I believe that it costs him several, that Paris is fed by the provinces in more than one respect, and that most of their revenues are paid out in this city and stay there without ever returning to the people or the king. It is inconceivable that in this age of calculators there is none who can perceive that France would be much more powerful if Paris were annihilated. The uneven distribution of the people is not only disadvantageous to the state, it is even more ruinous than depopulation itself; for depopulation results only in a product which is nonexistent, whereas badly arranged consumption results in a negative product. When I hear a Frenchman and an Englishman, very proud of the size of their capitals, disputing between them whether Paris or London contains the most inhabitants, it seems to me as though they were disputing together about which of the two peoples has the honor of being the worst governed.

Study a people outside of its cities; it is only in this way that you will know it. You gain nothing by seeing the apparent form of a government disguised by the machinery of administration and the jargon of administrators if you do not also study its nature by the effects it produces on the people and throughout all the levels of administration. Since the difference between form and substance is distributed throughout all the levels, it is only by embracing them all that this difference is known. In one country you begin to sense the spirit of the ministry by the maneuvers of the subdelegates. In another you have to see the members of parliament elected in order to judge whether it is true that the nation is free. In no land whatever is it possible for someone who has seen only the cities to know the government, given that its spirit is never the same in the city and the country. Now, it is the country which constitutes the land, and it is the people of the country who constitute the nation.

This study of diverse peoples in their remote provinces and in the simplicity of their original genius results in a general observation quite favorable to my epigraph [73] and quite consoling to the human heart. It is that all nations appear much better when they are observed in this way. The closer they are to nature, the more their character is dominated by goodness. It is only by closing themselves up in cities and corrupting themselves by means of culture that they become depraved and exchange a few defects that are more coarse than harmful for appealing and pernicious vices.

From this observation there results a new advantage for the way of traveling I propose. By sojourning less in big cities where a horrible corruption reigns, young people are less exposed to being corrupted themselves. Among simpler men and in smaller societies they preserve a surer judgment, a healthier taste, and more decent morals. But in any event, this contagion is hardly to be feared for my Emile. He has all that is needed to guarantee him against it. Among all the precautions I have taken in this respect I give great weight to the attachment he bears in his heart.

People no longer know what true love is capable of doing to the inclinations of young people because those who govern them, understanding true love no better than their pupils do, turn them away from it. Nevertheless, a young man must either love or be debauched. It is easy to deceive by appearances. Countless young people will be cited who are said to live very chastely without love. But let someone name to me a grown man who is truly a man and who says in good faith that he has spent his youth this way. In regard to all the virtues and all our duties only the appearance is sought. I seek the reality, and I am mistaken if there are other means of getting at it than those I give.

The idea of getting Emile to fall in love before making him travel is not my invention. Here is the incident which suggested it to me.

I was in Venice visiting the governor of a young Englishman. It was winter, and we were sitting around the fire. The governor received his letters from the post. He read them and then reread one letter aloud to his pupil. It was in English, and I understood none of it. But during the reading I saw the young man tear off the very fine lace cuffs he was wearing and throw them one after the other into the fire. He did this as gently as he could so as not to be noticed. Surprised by this caprice, I looked him in the face and believed I saw some emotion there. But the external signs of the passions, which are quite similar in all men, nonetheless have national differences about which it is easy to be mistaken. Peoples have diverse languages on their faces as well as in their mouths. I awaited the end of the reading; then I showed the governor his pupil's naked wrists—which the young man nevertheless did his best to hide—and I said, "Is it possible for me to know what this means?"

The governor, seeing what had happened, started laughing and embraced his pupil with an air of satisfaction. After having obtained the latter's consent, he gave me the explanation I wished.

"The cuffs which Monsieur John has just torn off," he said to me, "are a present given to him by a lady of this city not long ago. Now you should know that Monsieur John is promised to a young lady in his country whom he loves very much and who deserves his love even more. This letter is from his beloved's mother, and I am going to translate for you the passage which caused the damage you witnessed.

"'Lucy does not cease working on Lord John's cuffs. Miss Betty Roldham came yesterday to spend the afternoon with her and insisted on joining in her work. Knowing that Lucy had risen earlier today than usual, I wanted to see what she was doing, and I found her busy undoing all that Miss Betty had done yesterday. She does not want a single stitch in her gift to be done by a hand other than her own.'"

Monsieur John went out a moment later to put on other cuffs, and

BOOK V

I said to his governor, "You have a pupil with an excellent nature. But tell me the truth, wasn't the letter from Miss Lucy's mother arranged? Is it not an expedient you devised against the lady of the cuffs?" "No," he answered, "the thing is real. I have not put so much art in my efforts. I have made them with simplicity and zeal, and God has blessed my work."

The incident involving this young man did not leave my memory. It was not apt to produce nothing in the head of a dreamer like me.

It is time to finish. Let us take Lord John back to Miss Lucy—that is to say, Emile back to Sophie. With a heart no less tender than it was before his departure, Emile brings back to her a more enlightened mind, and he brings back to his country the advantage of having known governments by all their vices and peoples by all their virtues. I have even seen to it that in each nation he is connected with some man of merit by a treaty of hospitality, after the fashion of the ancients. I would not be vexed if he were to cultivate these acquaintances by an exchange of letters. Not only is it sometimes useful and always agreeable to carry on correspondences with distant countries, but it is also an excellent precaution against the empire of national prejudices which attack us throughout life and sooner or later get some hold on us. Nothing is more likely to deprive such prejudices of their hold than disinterested interchange with sensible people whom one esteems. Since they do not have our prejudices and combat them with their own, they give us the means to pit one set of prejudices unceasingly against the other and thus to guarantee ourselves from them all. It is not the same thing to associate with foreigners in our country as it is in theirs. In the former case they always have a certain discretion about the country where they are living which makes them disguise what they think of it or which makes them think favorably of it while they are there. When they get back home, they reconsider and are merely just. I would be quite glad if the foreigner whom I consult had seen my country, but I will only ask him his opinion of it in his own country.

After having employed almost two years in roaming some of the great states of Europe and more of the small ones, after having learned Europe's two or three principal languages, and after having seen what is truly worthy of curiosity—whether in natural history, or in government, or in arts, or in men—Emile is devoured by impatience and warns me that the end is approaching. Then I say to him, "Well, my friend, you remember the principal object of our travels. You have seen and observed. What is the final result of your observations? What course have you chosen?" Either I am mistaken in my method, or he will answer me pretty nearly as follows:

"What course have I chosen! To remain what you have made me and voluntarily to add no other chain to the one with which nature and the laws burden me. The more I examine the work of men in their institutions, the more I see that they make themselves slaves by dint of wanting to be independent and that they use up their freedom in vain efforts to ensure it. In order not to yield to the torrent of things, they involve themselves in countless attachments. Then as soon as they want to take a step, they cannot and are surprised at depending on everything. It seems to me that in order to make oneself free, one has to do nothing. It suffices that one not want to stop being free. It is you, my master, who have made me free in teaching me to yield to necessity. Let it come when it pleases. I let myself be carried along without constraint, and since I do not wish to fight it, I do not attach myself to anything to hold me back. In our travels I have sought to find some piece of land where I could be absolutely on my own. But in what place among men does one not depend on their passions? All things considered, I have found that my very wish was contradictory; for, were I dependent on nothing else, I would at least depend on the land where I had settled. My life would be attached to this land like that of dryads was to their trees. I have found that dominion and liberty are two incompatible words; therefore, I could be master of a cottage only in ceasing to be master of myself.

Hoc erat in votis modus agri non ita magnus.[74]

"I remember that my property was the cause of our investigations. You proved very solidly that I could not keep my wealth and my freedom at the same time. But when you wanted me to be free and without needs at the same time, you wanted two incompatible things, for I could withdraw myself from dependence on man only by returning to dependence on nature. What will I do then with the fortune my parents left me? I shall begin by not depending on it. I shall loosen all the bonds which attach me to it. If it is left with me, it will stay with with me. If it is taken from me, I shall not be carried along with it. I shall not worry about holding on to it, but I shall remain firmly in my place. Rich or poor, I shall be free. I shall not be free in this or that land, in this or that region; I shall be free everywhere on earth. All the chains of opinion are broken for me; I know only those of necessity. I learned to bear these chains from my birth, and I shall bear them until my death, for I am a man. And why would I not know how to bear them as a free man since, if I were a slave, I would still have to bear them and those of slavery to boot?

"What difference does it make to me what my position on earth is? What difference does it make to me where I am? Wherever there are men, I am at the home of my brothers; wherever there are no men, I am in my own home. As long as I can remain independent and rich, I have property to live on, and I shall live. When my property subjects me, I shall abandon it without effort. I have arms for working, and I shall live. When my arms fail me, I shall live if I am fed, and I shall die if I am abandoned. I shall also die even if I am not abandoned. For death is not a punishment for poverty but a law of nature. At whatever time death comes, I defy it. It will never surprise me while I am making preparations to live. It will never prevent me from having lived.

"This, my father, is my chosen course. If I were without passions, I would, in my condition as a man, be independent like God himself; for I would want only what is and therefore would never have to struggle against destiny. At least I have no more than one chain. It is the only one

I shall ever bear, and I can glory in it. Come, then, give me Sophie, and I am free."

"Dear Emile, I am very glad to hear a man's speeches come from your mouth and to see a man's sentiments in your heart. This extravagant disinterestedness does not displease me at your age. It will decrease when you have children, and you will then be precisely what a good father of a family and a wise man ought to be. Before your travels I knew what their effect would be. I knew that when you looked at our institutions from close up, you would hardly gain a confidence in them which they do not merit. One aspires in vain to liberty under the safeguard of the laws. Laws! Where are there laws, and where are they respected? Everywhere you have seen only individual interest and men's passions reigning under this name. But the eternal laws of nature and order do exist. For the wise man, they take the place of positive law. They are written in the depth of his heart by conscience and reason. It is to these that he ought to enslave himself in order to be free. The only slave is the man who does evil, for he always does it in spite of himself. Freedom is found in no form of government; it is in the heart of the free man. He takes it with him everywhere. The vile man takes his servitude everywhere. The latter would be a slave in Geneva, the former a free man in Paris.

"If I were speaking to you of the duties of the citizen, you would perhaps ask me where the fatherland is, and you would believe you had confounded me. But you would be mistaken, dear Emile, for he who does not have a fatherland at least has a country. In any event, he has lived tranquilly under a government and the simulacra of laws. What difference does it make that the social contract has not been observed, if individual interest protected him as the general will would have done, if public violence guaranteed him against individual violence, if the evil he saw done made him love what is good, and if our institutions themselves have made him know and hate their own iniquities? O Emile, where is the good man who owes nothing to his country? Whatever country it is, he owes it what is most precious to man —the morality of his actions and the love of virtue. If he had been born in the heart of the woods, he would have lived happier and freer. But he would have had nothing to combat in order to follow his inclinations, and thus he would have been good without merit; he would not have been virtuous; and now he knows how to be so in spite of his passions. The mere appearance of order brings him to know order and to love it. The public good, which serves others only as a pretext, is a real motive for him alone. He learns to struggle with himself, to conquer himself, to sacrifice his interest to the common interest. It is not true that he draws no profit from the laws. They give him the courage to be just even among wicked men. It is not true that they have not made him free. They have taught him to reign over himself.

"Do not ask then, 'What difference does it make to me where I am?' It makes a difference to you that you are where you can fulfill all your duties, and one of those duties is an attachment to the place of your birth. Your compatriots protected you as a child; you ought to love them as a man. You ought to live amidst them, or at least in a place where you can be useful to them insofar as you can, and where they know where to get you if they ever have need of you. There are circumstances in which a man can be more useful to his fellow citizens outside of his fatherland than if he were living in its bosom. Then he ought to listen only to his zeal and to endure his exile without grumbling. This exile itself is one of his duties. But you, good Emile, on whom nothing imposes these painful sacrifices, you who have not taken on the sad job of telling the truth to men, go and live in their midst, cultivate their friendship in sweet association, be their benefactor and their model. Your example will serve them better than all our books, and the good they see you do will touch them more than all our vain speeches.

"I do not exhort you to go to live in the big cities for this purpose. On the contrary, one of the examples good men ought to give others is that of the patriarchal and rustic life, man's first life, which is the most peaceful, the most natural, and the sweetest life for anyone who does not have a corrupt heart. Happy is the country, my young friend, where one does not need to seek peace in a desert! But where is this country? A beneficent man can hardly satisfy his inclination in the midst of cities. There he finds he can exercise his zeal almost only on behalf of schemers or rascals. The greeting that cities give to the idlers who come there to hunt their fortunes succeeds only in completing the devastation of the country which instead ought to be repopulated at the expense of the cities. All men who withdraw from the hub of society are useful precisely because they withdraw from it, since all its vices come from its being overpopulated. They are even more useful when they can bring life, cultivation, and the love of their first state to forsaken places. I am moved by contemplating how many benefactions Emile and Sophie can spread around them from their simple retreat, and how much they can vivify the country and reanimate the extinguished zeal of the unfortunate village folk. I believe I see the people multiplying, the fields being fertilized, the earth taking on a new adornment. The crowd and the abundance transform work into festivals, and cries of joy and benedictions arise from the midst of the games which center on the lovable couple who brought them back to life. The golden age is treated as a chimera, and it will always be one for anyone whose heart and taste have been spoiled. It is not even true that people regret the golden age, since those regrets are always hollow. What, then, would be required to give it a new birth? One single but impossible thing: to love it.

"It seems to be already reborn around Sophie's dwelling. You will do no more than complete together what her worthy parents have begun. But, dear Emile, do not let so sweet a life make you regard painful duties with disgust, if such duties are ever imposed on you. Remember that the Romans went from the plow to the consulate. If the prince or the state calls you to the service of the fatherland, leave everything to go to fulfill the honorable function of citizen in the post assigned to you. If this function is onerous to you, there is a decent and sure means to free yourself from it—to fulfill it with enough integrity so that it will not be left to you for long. Besides, you need have little fear of being burdened with such a responsibility. As long as there are men who belong to the present age, you are not the man who will be sought out to serve the state."

Why am I not permitted to paint Emile's return to Sophie and the conclusion of their love or rather the beginning of the conjugal love which unites them—love founded on esteem which lasts as long as life, on virtues which do not fade with beauty, on suitability of character which makes association pleasant and prolongs the charm of the first union into old age? But all these details might be pleasing without being useful, and up to now I have permitted myself only those agreeable details which I believed were of some utility. Shall I abandon this rule at the end of my task? No; I also feel that my pen is weary. I am too weak for works requiring so much endurance and would abandon this one if it were less advanced. In order not to leave it imperfect, it is time for me to finish.

Finally I see dawning the most charming of Emile's days and the happiest of mine. I see my attentions consummated, and I begin to taste their fruit. An indissoluble chain unites the worthy couple. Their mouths pronounce and their hearts confirm vows which will not be vain. They are wed. In returning from the temple, they let themselves be led. They do not know where they are, where they are going, or what is done around them. They do not hear; they respond only with confused words; their clouded eyes no longer see anything. O delirium! O human weakness! The sentiment of happiness crushes man. He is not strong enough to bear it.

There are very few people who know how to adopt a suitable tone with newly-weds on their wedding day. The gloomy propriety of some and the light remarks of others seem equally out of place to me. I would prefer to let these young hearts turn in on themselves and yield to an agitation that is not without charm rather than to cruelly distract them in order to make them gloomy by a false seemliness or embarrass them by tasteless jokes. For even if such jokes were to please at all other times, they would very surely be importunate on such a day.

In the sweet languor which excites them, my two young people seem to hear none of the speeches made to them. Would I, who want every day of life to be enjoyed, let them lose such a precious one? No, I want them to taste it, to savor it, and to enjoy its delight by themselves. I tear them away from the tactless crowd harassing them and take them for a walk. I bring them back to themselves by speaking to them about themselves. I wish to speak not only to their ears but to their hearts. I am not ignorant of the sole subject which can occupy them on this day.

Taking them both by the hand, I say to them, "My children, three years ago I saw the birth of this lively and pure flame which causes your happiness today. It has grown constantly. I see in your eyes that it is at its highest degree of intensity. It can only become weaker." Readers, do you not see Emile's transports, his fury, his vows; do you not see the disdainful air with which Sophie disengages her hand from mine and the tender protestations they make to each other with their eyes that they will adore each other until their last breath? I let them go on, and then I continue.

"I have often thought that if one could prolong the happiness of love in marriage, one would have paradise on earth. Up to now, that has never been seen. But if the thing is not utterly impossible, you both are quite worthy of setting an example that you will not have been given by anyone and that few couples will know how to imitate. Do you want me to tell you, my children, a means which I imagine can achieve that, a means which I believe to be the only possible one?"

They look at each other, smiling and making fun of my simplicity. Emile thanks me curtly for my recipe, saying he believes Sophie has a better one, and that so far as he is concerned, that one is enough for him. Sophie approves his response and appears just as confident. However, beneath her mocking manner I believe I detect a bit of curiosity. I examine Emile. His ardent eyes devour the charms of his wife. This is the only thing he is curious about, and all my remarks do not upset him at all. I smile in turn, saying to myself, "I shall soon be able to make you attentive."

The almost imperceptible difference between these secret emotions is the sign of a most characteristic difference between the two sexes, one quite contrary to the received prejudices. It is that men generally are less constant than women and grow weary of happy love sooner than they do. The woman has a presentiment of the man's inconstancy and is uneasy about it. This is also what makes her more jealous. When he begins to become lukewarm, she is forced, in order to keep him, to give him all the attentions he formerly gave to her; she cries and she humiliates herself in her turn, but rarely with the same success. Attachment and attentions win hearts, but they rarely regain them. I return to my recipe against the cooling off of love in marriage.

"The means is simple and easy," I continue. "It is to go on being lovers when one is married." "Quite so," Emile says, laughing secretly. "It won't be hard for us."

"It will be harder for you who are doing the talking than you may think. I beg you, give me the time to explain myself.

"Knots that one wants to tighten too much will burst. This is what happens to the marriage knot when one wants to give it more strength than it ought to have. The fidelity it imposes on the two spouses is the holiest of all rights, but the power it gives to each of the two over the other is too great. Constraint and love go ill together, and pleasure is not be to be commanded. Do not blush, Sophie, and do not think of fleeing. God forbid that I should want to offend your modesty. But the destiny of your life is at issue. For so great a matter, tolerate speech between a husband and a father that you would not tolerate elsewhere.

"It is not so much possession as subjection which satiates, and a man stays attached to a kept woman far longer than to a wife. How could a duty be made of the tenderest caresses and a right be made of the sweetest proofs of love? It is mutual desire which constitutes the right. Nature knows no other. Law can restrict this right, but it cannot extend it. Voluptuousness is so sweet in itself! Should it receive from painful constraint the strength it could not draw from its own attractions? No, my children, hearts are bound in marriage, but bodies are not enslaved. You owe each other fidelity, not compliance. Each of you ought to belong only to the other. But neither of you ought to be the other's more than he pleases.

"If it is true, then, dear Emile, that you want. to be your wife's lover, let her always be your mistress and her own. Be a fulfilled but respectful lover. Obtain everything from love without demanding anything from duty, and always regard Sophie's least favors not as your right but as acts of grace. I know that modesty flees formal confessions and asks to be conquered. But does the lover who has delicacy and true love make mistakes about his beloved's secret will? Is he unaware when her heart and her eyes accord what her mouth feigns to refuse? Let each of you always remain master of his own person and his caresses and have the right to dispense them to the other only at his own will. Always remember that even in marriage pleasure is legitimate only when desire is shared. Do not fear, my children, that this law will keep you at a distance. On the contrary, it will make both of you more attentive to pleasing each other, and it will prevent satiety. Since you are limited solely to each other, nature and love will bring you sufficiently close together."

Upon hearing these remarks and others of the kind, Emile becomes irritated and protests. Sophie is ashamed; she holds her fan over her eyes and says nothing. The most discontented of the two is perhaps not the one who complains the most. I insist pitilessly. I make Emile blush at his lack of delicacy. I stand as guarantor for Sophie's accepting the treaty on her side. I provoke her to speak. One can easily guess that she does not dare to give me the lie. Emile uneasily consults the eyes of his young wife. He sees that beneath their embarrassment they are full of a voluptuous agitation which reassures him about the risk he takes in trusting her. He throws himself at her feet, ecstatically kisses the hand she extends to him, and swears that, with the exception of the promised fidelity, he renounces every other right over her. "Dear wife," he says to her, "be the arbiter of my pleasures as you are of my life and my destiny. Were your cruelty to cost me my life, I would nonetheless give to you my dearest rights. I want to owe nothing to your compliance. I want to get everything from your heart."

Good Emile, reassure yourself: Sophie is too generous herself to let you die a victim of your generosity.

That evening, when I am ready to leave them, I say to them in the gravest tone possible for me, "Remember, both of you, that you are free, and that the question here is not one of marital duties. Believe me, let there be no false deference. Emile, do you want to come with me? Sophie gives you permission." Emile is in a fury and would like to hit me. "And you, Sophie, what do you say about it? Should I take him away?" The liar, blushing, says yes. How charming and sweet a lie, worth more than the truth!

The next day . . . The image of felicity no longer attracts men. The corruption of vice has depraved their taste as much as it has depraved their hearts. They no longer know how to sense what is touching nor how to see what is lovable. You who wish to paint voluptuousness and can only imagine satisfied lovers swimming in the bosom of delights, how imperfect your paintings still are! You have captured only the coarsest half of it. The sweetest attractions of voluptuousness are not there. O who among you has never seen a young couple, united under happy auspices, leaving the nuptial bed? Their languid and chaste glances express all at once the intoxication of the sweet pleasures they have just tasted, the lovable assurance of innocence, and the certitude— then so charming—of spending the rest of their days together. This is the most ravishing object which can be presented to man's heart. This is the true painting of voluptuousness! You have seen it a hundred times without recognizing it. Your hardened hearts are no longer capable of loving it. Sophie is happy and peaceful, and she passes the day in the arms of her tender mother. This is a very sweet rest to take after having passed the night in the arms of a husband.

On the day after that, I already perceive some change of scene. Emile wants to appear a bit discontented. But beneath this affectation I note such tender eagerness and even such submissiveness that I augur nothing very distressing. As for Sophie, she is gayer than the day before. I see satisfaction gleaming in her eyes. She is charming with Emile. She is almost flirtatious with him, which only vexes him more.

These changes are hardly noticeable, but they do not escape me. I am uneasy about them. I question Emile in private. I learn that, to his great regret and in spite of all his appeals, he had had to sleep in a separate bed the previous night. The imperious girl had hastened to make use of her right. Explanations are given. Emile complains bitterly, and Sophie responds with jests. But finally, seeing him about to get really angry, she gives him a glance full of sweetness and love; and, squeezing my hand, she utters only these two words, but in a tone which goes straight to the soul: "The ingrate!" Emile is so dumb that he understands none of this. I understand it. I send Emile away, and now I speak to Sophie in private.

"I see the reason for this caprice," I say to her. "One could not have greater delicacy nor make a more inappropriate use of it. Dear Sophie, reassure yourself. I have given you a man. Do not fear to take him for a man. You have had the first fruits of his youth. He has not squandered it on anyone. He will preserve it for you for a long time.

"My dear child, I must explain to you what my intentions were in the conversation all three of us had the day before yesterday. You perhaps perceived in my advice only an art of managing your pleasures in order to make them durable. O Sophie, it had another object more worthy of my efforts. In becoming your husband, Emile has become the head of the house. It is for you to obey, just as nature wanted it. However, when the woman resembles Sophie, it is good that the man be guided by her. This is yet another law of nature. And it is in order to give you as much authority over his heart as his sex gives him over your person that I have made you the arbiter of his pleasures. It will cost you some painful privations, but you will reign over him if you know how to reign over yourself; what has happened already shows me that this difficult art is not beyond your courage. You will reign by means of love for a long time if you make your favors rare and precious, if you know how to make them valued. Do you want to see your husband constantly at your feet? Then keep him always at some distance from your person. But put modesty, and not capriciousness, in your severity. Let him view you as reserved, not whimsical. Take care that in managing his love you do not make him doubt your own. Make yourself cherished by your favors and respected by your refusals. Let him honor his wife's chastity without having to complain of her coldness.

"It is by this means, my child, that he will give you his confidence, listen to your opinions, consult you about his business, and decide nothing without deliberating with you about it. It is by this means that you can bring him back to wisdom when he goes astray; lead him by a gentle persuasion; make yourself lovable in order to make yourself useful; and use coquetry in the interests of virtue and love to the benefit of reason.

"Nevertheless, do not believe that even this art can serve you forever. Whatever precautions anyone may take, enjoyment wears out pleasures, and love is worn out before all others. But when love has lasted a long time, a sweet habit fills the void it leaves behind, and the attraction of mutual confidence succeeds the transports of passion. Children form a relationship between those who have given them life that is no less sweet and is often stronger than love itself. When you stop being Emile's beloved, you will be his wife and his friend. You will be the mother of his children. Then, in place of your former reserve, establish between yourselves the greatest intimacy. No more separate beds, no more refusals, no more caprices. Become his other half to such an extent that he can no longer do without you, and that as soon as he leaves you, he feels he is far from himself. You were so good at making the charms of domestic life reign in your paternal household; now make them reign in your own. Every man who is pleased in his home loves his wife. Remember that if your husband lives happily at home, you will be a happy woman.

"As for the present, do not be so severe with your lover. He has merited more obligingness. He would be offended by your fears. No longer be so careful about his health at the expense of his happiness, and enjoy your own happiness. You must not expect disgust, nor rebuff desire. You must refuse not for refusing's sake but to give value to what is granted."

Then I reunite them, and I say to her young husband in her presence: "It is necessary to bear the yoke which you have imposed on yourself. Try to merit having it made light for you. Above all, sacrifice to the graces, and do not imagine that you make yourself more lovable by pouting." It is not difficult to make peace between them, and everyone can easily figure out the terms. The treaty is signed with a kiss. Then I say to my pupil, "Dear Emile, a man needs advice and guidance throughout his life. Up to now I have done my best to fulfill this duty toward you. Here my long task ends, and another's begins. Today I abdicate the authority you confided to me, and Sophie is your governor from now on."

Little by little the first delirium subsides and allows them to taste the charms of their new condition in peace. Happy lovers! Worthy couple! To honor their virtues and to paint their felicity, one would have to tell the history of their lives. How many times, as I contemplate my work in them, I feel myself seized by a rapture that makes my heart palpitate! How many times I join their hands in mine while blessing providence and sighing ardently! How many kisses I give to these two hands which clasp each other! How many times have these hands felt the tears I shed on them! The young couple share my raptures, and they too are moved. Their respectable parents once again enjoy their youth in that of their children. They begin, so to speak, to live again in them—or rather they come to know the value of life for the first time. They curse their former wealth which prevented them from tasting so charming a fate at the same age. If there is happiness on earth, it must be sought in the abode where we live.

A few months later Emile enters my room one morning, embraces me, and says, "My master, congratulate your child. He hopes soon to have the honor of being a father. Oh, what efforts are going to be imposed on our zeal, and how we are going to need you! God forbid that I let you also raise the son after having raised the father. God forbid that so holy and so sweet a duty should ever be fulfilled by anyone but myself, even if I were to make as good a choice for my son as was made for me. But remain the master of the young masters. Advise us and govern us. We shall be docile. As long as I live, I shall need you. I need you more than ever now that my functions as a man begin. You have fulfilled yours. Guide me so that I can imitate you. And take your rest. It is time."

End

Notes

References to Rousseau's other works which are not readily available in translation and are not divided into small chapters will be to the French edition, *Oeuvres Complètes de Jean-Jacques Rousseau*, ed. Bernard Gagnebin and Marcel Raymond, 4 vols. (Paris: Gallimard, 1959–1969, Bibliothèque de la Pléiade). It will be cited as *O.C.* References to the two *Discourses* and the *Confessions* will be to both French and English editions.

PREFACE

1. Whether there is any particular significance to the name chosen by Rousseau is unclear. A possible source is Plutarch's *Life of Aemilius Paulus*. Aemilius was descended from either the philosopher Pythagoras or the legislator Numa. He was devoted to education, and his life was particularly characterized by contemplation and independence of fortune, which are perhaps the central goals of Emile's education. La Bruyère used the name Aemile, after Aemilius Paulus, for his portrait of the Prince de Condé (*Characters* II. 32).

2. "We are sick with evils that can be cured; and nature, having brought us forth sound, itself helps us if we wish to be improved." The work from which this quotation is drawn, *On Anger*, is significant for Rousseau's intention. Anger is *the* passion which must be overcome, and his analysis of human psychology gives it a central place. It has pervasive and protean effects. His correction of education consists essentially in extirpating the roots of anger.

3. For Rousseau's own presentation of the background and the intention of the *Emile*, see *Confessions* IX, especially *O.C.* I, p. 409 or *Confessions*, 2 vols. (New York and London: Everyman's Library, Dent, 1931; hereafter referred to as Everyman's), II, p. 60, and *Letters from the Mountain* V, *O.C.* III, p. 783. For his judgment of it cf. *Confessions*, *O.C.* I, pp. 386, 573 or Everyman's II, pp. 37, 213–214.

4. *Some Thoughts Concerning Education*, 1690, in *Locke's Educational Writings*, ed. James L. Axtell (Cambridge: Cambridge University Press, 1968). This book is of capital importance for Rousseau's project, not only because he adopts much of it, but especially because it represents the other great modern alternative. Rousseau defines much of his position as over against that of Locke. A deep understanding of *Emile* presupposes a knowledge of Locke's teaching.

5. See Book I, note 19.

6. These explanations are Rousseau's, who planned and commissioned the engravings. He considered them an integral part of the text. I am grateful to the Thomas Fisher Rare Book Library of the University of Toronto for providing the photographs made from the illustrations, in a copy of the first edition in its collection.

7. The first edition consisted of four volumes.

BOOK I

1. For a different statement about the true addressees of *Emile* cf. Introduction, p. 28 and note 28.

2. Rousseau omitted the following note, which was in his manuscript, from the first edition but apparently intended to restore it in later ones. His reasons for doing so were evidently prudential and reflect the rhetorical problems posed by the political and religious conditions prevailing: "Thus the wars of republics are crueller than those of monarchies. But if the war of kings is moderate, it is their peace which is terrible. It is better to be their enemy than their subject."

3. Livy *Roman History*, Summary of XVIII; Cicero *Offices* III 26–27; Horace *Odes* III 5.

4. Plutarch *Lycurgus* XXV; *Sayings of Spartans* 231B, *Sayings of Kings* 191F.

5. Plutarch *Agesilaus* XXIX; *Sayings of Spartan Women* 241C.

6. Rousseau is the first writer to use the word *bourgeois* in the modern sense popularized by Marx. It is defined in opposition to *citizen*, and the understanding connected with the term is central to all later political thought. Cf. *Social Contract* I 6 note. However, Rousseau does frequently use it in its more ordinary meaning of *middle-class* as opposed to *peasant, poor,* or *noble.* Of course, these two senses are closely related.

7. Rousseau bases himself particularly on Plutarch's *Lycurgus.*

8. Cf. *Social Contract* IV 8.

9. Public schools, almost exclusively under clerical supervision and with clerics as teachers. Rousseau's first draft of the note was somewhat different; in particular "forced to follow the established practice . . ." was originally "forced to follow rules which they did not make . . ." This change indicates the problem and clarifies the last sentence of the preceding paragraph. Rousseau's book contains the new rules intended to take the place of the old ones which are the true source of the modern corruption. The first of these new rules is that man is naturally good.

10. Cicero *Tusculan Disputations* V ix 27, cf. Montaigne *Essays* II 2. "I have caught you, Fortune, and blocked all your means of access, so that you could not get near me." Metrodorus, an Epicurean, is the source of the saying, and the two contexts cited are of interest for the theme of *Emile.*

11. "The midwife delivers, the nurse feeds, the pedagogue instructs, the master teaches." A definition of Varro quoted by Nonius Marcellus *De compendiosa doctrina* V 447.

12. For a discussion of the sentiment of existence, a central notion in Rousseau's thought, see *Dreams of a Solitary Walker* V.

13. *Histoire Naturelle* by Georges Louis Leclerc de Buffon (1707–1788) was a great source for Rousseau's understanding of nature. It was published in forty-four volumes between 1749 and 1804.

14. Achilles plays in *Emile,* as in the *Republic,* a great role. The frontispiece of Book I represents Thetis plunging Achilles in the Styx, and the first education is intended to fulfill the pedagogic intention of that symbolic act. Even the inevitable vulnerable heel is given central significance in Rousseau's interpretation. Cf. V., p. 443.

15. Plutarch *Cato the Elder* XX; Suetonius *Augustus* 64. Rousseau apparently took these examples from Locke. Cf. Axtell, *Locke's Educational Writings,* p. 164, note 4.

16. Cf. *Confessions,* O.C. I, pp. 344–345, p. 594; Everyman's I, pp. 315–316, II, p. 234.

17. Cf. *Social Contract* II 7. The comparison to the legislator is illuminating in many ways, particularly with respect to Rousseau's own role and motivation as thinker and writer.

18. Cf. *Confessions,* O.C. I, pp. 267–270; Everyman's I, pp. 245–248.

19. In traditional logic a maxim was the major premise of a practical syllogism and hence both the beginning point of reasoning about action and the end or goal of action. For example, "Men should seek to preserve themselves" is a maxim. Rousseau uses the term frequently. The establishment in Emile's soul of the true maxims of the good life is the purpose of his education. Simply, a maxim is a principle of conduct.

20. Xenophon *Education of Cyrus* I ii 2–14. The passage is mentioned by Montaigne *Essays* I 20.

21. *Confessions* is the description of the education of a genius.

22. Cf. Plato *Phaedo* 64A; Montaigne *Essays* I 20.

23. Locke, *Some Thoughts,* in Axtell, ed., *Locke's Educational Writings,* paragraphs 29–30.

24. Antonio Celestina Cocchi, *Del vitto pitagorico per uso della medicina,* Florence, 1743. Giovanni Bianchi, *Se il vitto pitagorico di soli vegetabilis sia giovevole per conservare la sanita e per la cura d'alcune malatie,* Venice, 1752.

Although much of this passage on diet is based on an antiquated nutritional science, it is easy to recognize that the kernel of Rousseau's thesis can be maintained and is recognizable in currently fashionable positions. Rousseau does not commit himself to any particular set of facts or interpretations. All of this is derivative, and he uses what fits his intention which seems to support vegetarianism, a position further elaborated in p. 153–155 (but cf. pp. 320–321, 353, 435). However, vegetarianism is only a superficial expression of a deeper intention, and neither Rousseau nor Emile seems in fact to be a vegetarian. Vegetarianism is connected with a certain view of the harmoniousness of nature and man's peaceful relation to it and the other species as opposed to the state of war. This section belongs properly with the one preceding on medicine, in which nature is given primacy over art. The deepest strand is indicated by this diet's being called Pythagorean and thus connected with a particular philosophic way of life.

25. Simon de La Loubère, *Du royaume de Siam,* Amsterdam, 1691, I, p. 80; Claude

NOTES

Le Beau, *Aventures du Sr. C. Le Beau, avocat en Parlement*, Amsterdam, 1738, II, p. 66.

26. Homer *Iliad* VI 466–475. The whole context should be examined.

27. Hermann Boerhaave (1668–1738) was a Dutch professor of medicine among whose works is a *Treatise on Children's Diseases* which Rousseau studied in preparation for writing *Emile*. Rousseau, however, quickly gives a moral explanation of the phenomenon he is describing, and Boerhaave is used only to give physiological support. This is characteristic of his procedure in all the passages which appear merely technical.

28. For the Abbé de St. Pierre and Rousseau's relation to him see *Confessions* IX, O.C. I, pp. 407–408; Everyman's II, pp. 57–58. Rousseau edited and published some of his works. The opinion here cited is not to be found in the works edited by Rousseau but is repeated in the passage in *Confessions* referred to above. Cf. pp. 466–467 below and note 69.

29. *De Cive*, Preface. The context should be examined.

30. Pp. 257–313 below.

31. The French word is *fantaisie*. It is closely allied to *imagination*, a most important word for *Emile*. It will always be translated by *whim*. Cf. p. 48.

32. Cf. Plato *Laws* VII 791E–792D.

33. Replacing the letter *r* with a guttural trill.

34. "He lives and is unconscious of his own life." Ovid in the previous sentence says that, struck by his banishment, he was "no less stupid than a man struck by Jove's thunderbolts."

BOOK II

1. Valerius Maximus *Memorable Sayings and Deeds* I vi 5. The French *enfant* means both infant and child.

2. The success of medicine, particularly in the last forty years and with respect to infant mortality, is the change since Rousseau wrote which would seem most to undermine his arguments. (Cf. p. 362, note.) But it should be observed that he uses this statistic to support a point which could be argued without it. Here Rousseau makes use of the high death rate among children to lend rhetorical support to the deeper argument against the teleologies of the afterlife and of adulthood. That argument in turn goes to the heart of his teaching concerning the tension between nature and society and the connection of the aforementioned teleologies with society.

3. Quoted in Aulus Gellius *Attic Nights* IX 8: "It is not possible for the man who needs fifteen thousand coats to need less than that number; thus when I need more than I have, I subtract from what I have and am content with what I have."

4. Rousseau added the following note for the later edition: "It is understood that I speak here of men who reflect, and not of all men."

5. Cf. p. 442 below.

6. Plutarch *Themistocles* XVIII 5.

7. I, note 31 above.

8. For the state of nature, cf. *Discourse on the Origins of Inequality* in R. Masters, ed., *The Discourses* (New York: St. Martin's 1964), or O.C. III. Of all Rousseau's works it is probably the one that is most important for *Emile*.

9. This is the second title of the *Social Contract*. See note 10 below.

10. For the general and particular wills, cf. *Social Contract* I 6–8.

11. Cf. pp. 67–68 above.

12. *Leviathan* XIV; *de Cive* X.

13. Herodotus *Histories* VII 35; Plutarch *On the Control of Anger* 455D–E. Cf. Homer *Iliad* XXI 130–132, 212–226, 322ff.; Plato *Republic* III 391A–B.

14. Rousseau implies that monarchy is the political version of perverse infancy. Hobbes in *de Cive* X, just referred to by Rousseau (cf. note 12 above), defends monarchy in spite of the possibility of infant rulers. This point in the education is a fundamental response to Hobbes' political thought.

15. Locke, *Some Thoughts*, in Axtell, ed., *Locke's Educational Writings*, end of paragraph 80, and paragraph 81.

16. In the original sense of *learned* men.

17. This is the first discussion of *amour-propre* in *Emile*. It is the central term in

Rousseau's psychology and will remain untranslated throughout. Ordinarily, in its non-"extended sense," it would be translated by vanity or pride, but it is a word too full of nuance and too important for *Emile* not to be defined contextually and revealed in its full subtlety. It is usually opposed to *amour de soi.* Both expressions mean *self-love.* Rousseau, instead of opposing love of self to love of others, opposes two kinds of self-love, a good and bad form. Thus without abandoning the view of modern political philosophy that man is primarily concerned with himself—particularly his own preservation—he is enabled to avoid Hobbes' conclusion that men, as a result of their selfishness, are necessarily in competition with one another. His earliest statement on this issue—the foundation of his argument that man is naturally good—is *Discourse on the Origins of Inequality*, note XV: "*Amour-propre* and *amour de soi,* two passions very different in their nature and their effects, must not be confused. Love of oneself is a natural sentiment which inclines every animal to watch over its own preservation, and which directed in man by reason and modified by pity, produces humanity and virtue. *Amour-propre* is only a relative sentiment, artificial, and born in society, which inclines each individual to have a greater esteem for himself than for anyone else, inspires in all the harm they do to one another, and is the true source of honor." In this passage of *Emile* Rousseau is emphasizing the original unity of self-love which is lost in relations with other men.

18. It should be remembered that paradox means *apparent* contradiction, or contradiction of *common opinion*, not self-contradiction. Rousseau, who is reputed as the philosopher of paradox, actually only follows Socrates in this. Cf. Plato *Republic* V.

19. The pervasiveness of the theme of anger should cause one to think back on the book from which Rousseau drew the epigraph for *Emile*, Seneca's *On Anger.* Cf. Plutarch *On the Control of Anger* 455E–456F.

20. This reproduces the teaching of modern natural right as first formulated by Hobbes (*Leviathan* XIV). Rights precede duties, the latter are derivative from the former, and the primary natural right is to seek the means of preservation.

21. This is simply Locke's account of the origin of property (*Second Treatise on Civil Government* V, paragraphs 25–27).

22. This is the language of criminal investigation.

23. An old tennis term "for the odds which one player gives the other in allowing him to score one point once during the 'set' at any time he may elect" (*Oxford English Dictionary*, s. v. "bisque").

24. Locke, *Some Thoughts* in Axtell, ed., *Locke's Educational Writings*, paragraph 110.

25. Diderot, Preface to *Fils Naturel.* Rousseau had just withdrawn to a solitary existence and took the phrase to be directed against him. Cf. *Confessions, O.C.* I, pp. 455–456; Everyman's II, p. 102; *Dialogues* II *O.C.* I, pp. 788–789; Plato *Republic* I 332A–B, 335B–E.

26. Pierre Bayle, *Pensées diverses sur la comète* XVIII.

27. The residue after liquors have been distilled from fruit. The child's mind is compared to a still, and the tutor to a distiller.

28. Plutarch *Cato the Younger* I–III.

29. Condillac, Rousseau's contemporary, whose works, particularly *Essai sur l'origine des connaissances humaines* and *Traité des sensations,* are important sources for *Emile.* He is derivative from the tradition which has its source in Locke's *Essay on Human Understanding.* This very passage and the ones immediately following are within the domain of his researches.

30. This refers to Plato *Laws* VII, which is altogether the most capital part of the *Laws* for *Emile*, and after the *Republic* as a whole, the most important Platonic source for it. For this particular reference see 793E, where play is linked with punishment by Plato, and 796E–805C. At 803D–E the Athenian stranger says: "We must go through life playing certain games—sacrificing, singing and dancing." The stranger treats sacrifice as a form of play. Rousseau characteristically drops the religious context. Cf. Book I, note 32; Montaigne *Essays* I xxvi, where the same passage is referred to.

31. Seneca *Letters to Lucilius* LXXXVIII 19; Cf. Montaigne *Essays* II 21. This letter is about liberal education and was obviously carefully read by Rousseau.

32. Plutarch *Alexander* XIX.

33. Montaigne (*Essays* I 24) regards Alexander's act as a sign of firmness.

34. This modern heir of Aesop, in the Preface to his *Fables*, compares himself to Socrates who put Aesop's tales into verse at the end of his life. Rousseau's rejection of La Fontaine's tales is also the rejection of Socrates' argument about the teaching of tales to children (*Republic* II–III).

35. A synonym for fable. La Fontaine says in his Preface, as does Littré's dictionary, that the parables of Jesus are species of the genus apologue. He suggests that all apologues are god-sent. Thus Rousseau's rejection of fables aims beyond La Fontaine or even Socrates.

NOTES

36. Cf. Plato *Republic* II 378D–E. Rousseau draws a more extreme conclusion from Socrates' observation.

37. Here Rousseau uses La Fontaine's own language in his Preface against him. Locke uses the same expression in rejecting teaching the Bible to children, although he favors reading Aesop's *Fables* (*Some Thoughts* in Axtell, ed., *Locke's Educational Writings*, paragraph 158).

38. It is actually second, as Rousseau intended to mention in future editions. The first is the *Cicada and the Ant*. Rousseau in his manuscript, at the end of the previous paragraph, first wrote, "I am not afraid to attack La Fontaine in his strength," and "I shall begin with the best, as is my method." Similarly, in *Letter to d'Alembert* he criticizes Molière's masterpiece *The Misanthrope*. The serious critic chooses only the greatest opponents and only their greatest works.

39. *Master*, joined to a name, usually applies to someone possessing a skill, to a master workman. It is also a title of lawyers.

40. Prior to the French Revolution *Monsieur* was a form of address reserved for members of certain classes of society.

41. This would mean that he is of noble family.

42. La Fontaine wrote *pretty*.

43. Cf. note 38 above. It is actually the first. The cicada comes in the winter to ask the ant for food. The ant asks what he did all summer. The cicada replies, "I sang," to which the ant says: "Now you can dance."

44. In the first instance Rousseau refers especially to *Fables* I vi, *The Heifer, the Nanny-goat and the Ewe in Society with the Lion*. The lion divides up a stag in four parts and lays claim to all four, the first because he is called lion, the second by right of the stronger, the third because he is the most valiant, the fourth because he will strangle any of the others who touch it. The second is II ix, *The Lion and the Gnat*, in which a gnat, at whom the lion cannot get, defeats the lion with his stings—only to be eaten by a spider.

45. *Fables* I v, *The Wolf and the Dog*. A hungry wolf who is offered luxury by a dog turns down the offer when he sees that the dog's neck is rubbed bare by his collar. The wolf prefers freedom if the price of luxury is chains.

46. La Fontaine also wrote a collection of tales of a licentious character, partially inspired by Boccaccio. This sentence is Voltaire's, who intended it as praise.

47. Locke's discussion of learning how to read (*Some Thoughts*, in Axtell, ed., *Locke's Educational Writings*, paragraph 148–155) is altogether a good point from which to see the confrontation between Locke and Rousseau on education. The description of the dice is contained in that passage. The desks of the previous sentence were elaborate devices like printer's tables, with pigeonholes containing cards instead of print. The cards had letters, syllables, and sounds written out on them; the child stood before the desk and, using the cards, laid out words and sentences.

48. "Above all it is proper to watch out that he not hate studies which he is not yet able to love and, the bitterness once perceived, still shun them after the ignorant years are past."

49. There is no other source in Rousseau's writings for this story as true history, but it can be related to *Confessions*, O.C. I, pp. 292–293; Everyman's I, p. 266. Mme. Dupin's son was much older than the child of whom Rousseau speaks here.

50. By Molière. Sbrigani (a name meaning *rascal*) is akin to the fox who plays on the vanity of the crow in the fable. He sets up a comedy within the comedy, as does Rousseau here to accomplish his ends.

51. "There is no root here."

52. Montaigne *Essays* I 26; Locke, *Some Thoughts*, in Axtell, ed., *Locke's Educational Writings*, paragraphs 205–206. The other three were authors of treatises on education at the end of the seventeenth and the beginning of the eighteenth centuries. Rousseau's opinion of each is expressed in the adjective he attaches to his name. None is very significant for Rousseau's thought.

53. Modeled after the uniforms of Hussars (light cavalry troops): a narrow jacket with a row of buttons on the left side fastened with braided loops running across the chest; pants large in the thighs, but tight around the calves and the ankles.

54. "In open air."

55. *Politics and the Arts, Letter to M. d'Alembert*, ed. A. Bloom (Ithaca: Cornell University Press, 1968), p. 101. Herodotus *Histories* III 12. Chardin, a Frenchman who settled in England and died there in 1713 as Sir John Chardin, was the author of *The Travels of Sir John Chardin into Persia and the East Indies etc.*, which was a great source of information for eighteenth-century thinkers. Rousseau refers to vol. II, p. 51.

56. This remark is fraught with political meaning. Cf. p. 52 above. Rousseau, following Montesquieu, holds that "liberty is not the fruit of all climates" (*Social Contract* III 8) and that Europe is the natural seat of liberty and Asia that of despotism.

57. Locke, *Some Thoughts,* in Axtell, ed., *Locke's Educational Writings,* paragraphs 5–7. There he cites "the Scythian philosopher who gave a very significant answer to the Athenian who wondered how he could go naked in frost and snow. 'How,' said the Scythian, 'can you endure your face exposed to the sharp winter air?' 'My face is used to it,' said the Athenian. 'Think me all face,' replied the Scythian."

58. Montaigne *Essays* I 20.

59. Montaigne *Essays* II 21.

60. Inoculation was new and still controversial. There was strong opposition to it on religious grounds in France. Voltaire had championed it (*Lettres philosophiques* XI). Rousseau, who clearly has no doubts about its effectiveness, finds himself equally distant from both its enlightened proponents and its pious opponents, and the nuanced presentation of this issue indicates the difficulty as well as the importance of his alternative view of it.

61. Locke, *Some Thoughts,* in Axtell, ed., *Locke's Educational Writings,* paragraph 138. The context in Locke is helpful for understanding Rousseau's intention here.

62. An important use of this important word for Rousseau. It is almost equivalent to the Greek *dēmos.* The people is opposed either to the noble or the educated.

63. "Passion is not caused by habitual things."

64. This period in Rousseau's life is described in *Confessions* I, *O.C.* I, pp. 12–24; Everyman's I, pp. 8–16.

65. I Samuel 26; *Iliad* X 465–525.

66. In 1602 the Duke of Savoy attacked Geneva—using ladders to scale the walls, hence the attack was later called the *Escalade*—with the intention of reimposing Catholicism on Calvin's city. The citizens of Geneva won a great victory which has been celebrated ever since.

67. Plato *Republic* X 596E–598B.

68. Considered the greatest painter of antiquity. He worked particularly at the court of Alexander the Great and made famous paintings of him.

69. This note did not appear in the first edition and was intended for the later edition. The boy was Mozart, who played in Paris in 1763.

70. The use of letters for the fixed notes and of sol-fa syllables for the relative degrees of the scale is in fact the practice of the English, Italian, and German nations. The French still use the method criticized by Rousseau despite the disadvantages he points out.

Rousseau was an accomplished musician, a composer of some fame, the inventor of a system of musical notation, and a controversialist in the quarrel between French and Italian music. He earned a living as a musical copyist. Among his works are an extensive musical dictionary and many essays on music.

71. *Arcadia* I 5–6. Pelasgus taught men to eat acorns. His son Lycaon (II 3–4) used human sacrifice.

72. "Born to consume the produce of the earth." Horace *Epistles* I ii 27.

73. The Banians are Brahman merchants in India; the Gaures are the same as the Guebres or Parsees, adherents of the Zoroastrian religion.

74. This is an error, although butchers could not be jurors. Rousseau wrote a note to this effect to be added to the later edition.

75. Homer *Odyssey* IX 82–566.

76. Homer *Odyssey* XII 395–396. This is an adaptation by Rousseau, who took it seriously enough to look at the Greek original, which he copied in the margin of the manuscript. The translation of the first two lines is almost literal, and a literal translation of the last two would read, "both roasted and raw, and there was a voice as of kine." These were, according to Homer, god-sent portents of doom for eating the kine of Helios, forbidden flesh, and they occur prior to the eating. Plutarch immediately after the quote—where Rousseau says, "This is what he must have imagined and felt"—says, "This is a fabrication and a myth, but the meal is truly portentous."

77. The passage is from Plutarch *On the Eating of Flesh* 993B–995B, liberally adapted with many omissions and additions.

78. Herodotus *Histories* I 94.

79. In French it meant "born in," "coming from a certain place" as opposed to "given by nature." In English, of course, it has both senses.

80. Plutarch *Alexander* VI–VIII. According to Plutarch, Alexander tamed Bucephalus before Aristotle became his teacher.

BOOK III

1. Emile learns Ptolemaic astronomy because it is the observation of common sense. Copernican astronomy will follow when he himself makes the observations which lead to it.

2. "A skeleton celestial globe or sphere, consisting merely of metal rings or hoops

representing the equator, ecliptic, tropics, arctic and antarctic circles, and colures, revolving on an axis within a wooden horizon" (*Oxford English Dictionary*, s. v. "armillary"). Rousseau evidently had used ones made of cardboard, not metal.

3. ". . . two great circles which intersect each other at right angles at the poles, and divide the equinoctial and the ecliptic into four equal parts. One passes through the equinoctial points, the other through the solstitial points of the ecliptic" (*Oxford English Dictionary*, s. v. "colures").

4. The distinction between the analytic and synthetic ("resolutive" and "compositive") methods, found in Galileo and Hobbes, was given its best-known formulation by Descartes (*Meditations, Second Responses*, final four pages). It is closely related to the distinction between induction and deduction familiar to more recent discussion of scientific method, although Rousseau avoids using these latter terms.

According to Aristotle (*Nic. Ethics* 1095a 31ff), it was Plato who taught us to distinguish between beginning with what is first to us and ascending ("analytically") to first principles, and beginning with first principles and descending ("synthetically"). This difference is mirrored in Descartes' distinction between beginning with parts (or what is "better known to us"—e.g. the ego cogitans) and beginning with wholes. Here it is found in the movement from the child's home to the cosmic system (analysis), and the movement from the cosmic system to the child's home (synthesis).

Descartes argues for the superiority of the analytic method on both pedagogic and philosophic grounds. For him it is the way of instruction and the way of discovery (although Rousseau here identifies synthesis with the method of instruction), and therefore only it contents the philosophic student. The synthetic ("Euclidean," syllogistic) procedure, on the other hand, is best able to convince or silence the inattentive or hostile student. Yet a simple disjunction between the analytic and synthetic mode is untenable. Beginning with the part, or what is first or most knowable to us, is impossible without some concept of the whole, at least the whole of human knowledge accessible to us. And this is evident from the actual philosophic procedures of a Descartes or a Plato, or from the empiricism of Locke and Condillac known to Rousseau.

He therefore judiciously mixes the modes without making explicit to his pupil his varying procedure. The child who was taught solid geometry by cakes would be a good example of this. In the end his systematic knowledge of the science would indicate that a certain solid would contain more cake, and his experience, or his stomach, would confirm this fact. And the experience would lead to the discovery of the principle. These are the reciprocal proofs of which Rousseau speaks. He tries to combine the philosopher's method with the child's of p. 172 below. The combination of the two methods, and their meeting point, is further used in the discovery of the compass immediately following and in Emile's discovery of the use of astronomy for getting his lunch. Finally, the entire education is a model of this union: the production of a man who can move by sound reasoning from his experience and needs to their place in the whole, and who, knowing the whole, finds his place within it, like the insect in his web. (cf. p. 80–81 above).

In this Rousseau differs from the new science's single-minded concentration on discovery and returns to reflection on the "bottomless sea" of which he speaks on this page. (I am grateful to Richard Kennington for his help with this note.)

5. A meridian here is simply a north-south line. In the northern hemisphere, the sun is due south at high noon, so that a shadow cast by a stake points due north. Shadows of equal length are cast by a stake in the morning and evening at times equally distant from noon; and the north-south line (as also the shadow at noon) bisects the angle formed by any such pair of shadows. There are several ways of obtaining this bisector; what Rousseau has in mind here is the construction of a rhombus where one morning shadow and two evening shadows of the same length as the first form the sides. The fourth side can be easily supplied. The diagonal at right angles to the course of the sun is the meridian.

6. Rousseau added a note for the next edition in response to a man who had written an *Anti-Emile*. "I could not keep from laughing in reading a subtle critique of this little tale by M. de Formey. 'This magician,' he says, 'who prides himself on his emulation with a child and gravely sermonizes his teacher is an individual of the world of Emiles.' The clever M. de Formey was unable to suppose that this little scene was arranged and that the magician had been instructed about the role he had to play; for, indeed, I did not say so. But on the other hand, how many times have I declared that I did not write for people who have to be told everything?"

7. Cf. p. 111.

8. Cf. Plato *Phaedrus* 274C–275D. The god Theuth there mentioned was identified with Hermes.

9. In the manuscript Rousseau had originally continued, "for although this state is not that of social man, it is by it that he ought in truth to evaluate all the objects of his esteem."

10. "I want only those good things which are envied by the people." Petronius *Satyricon* 100. The context concerns love.

11. The identity of this person is unknown.

12. Parisian jewelers.

13. *Discourse on the Origins of Inequality*, as Rousseau himself indicated in a later note. Cf. particularly, O.C. III, p. 164, 173–178; R. Masters, ed., *The Discourses*, pp. 141–142, 154–160. See also *Discourse on Political Economy* and Plato *Republic* 369B–373E.

14. These two examples are drawn from Plutarch's lives of *Timoleon* and *Aemilius Paulus*, a parallel pair. Dionysius the younger, Plato's pupil, is described in *Timoleon* 14–16. Aemilius Paulus, whose namesake Emile possibly is (see Preface, note 1 above), conquered Perseus, king of Macedon, and his son ended as Rousseau says (*Aemilius Paulus* 37). The entire context beginning with 27 should be considered as well as the comparison between Timoleon and Aemilius. Plutarch judges that Aemilius is the more perfect because he was unbroken by bad fortune in the loss of his children.

15. This obscure Vonones was, on the request of the Parthian people, installed as king by Augustus around 8 A.D. They soon rejected him. His story is to be found in Tacitus *Annals* II 1–4, 58, 68. I do not find a source for his father's being called a "king of kings." The manuscript indicates that Rousseau intended to mention the Stuart pretender living in France, but he decided against it, evidently on prudential grounds.

16. Cf. *Dreams of a Solitary Walker* VI, end, where Rousseau speaks of himself as a useless member of society.

17. Swiss were frequently used in France in domestic service and became synonymous with it.

18. Locke too believed that a trade should be learned, but the spirit of his instruction is very different as is the style of his presentation. *Some Thoughts*, in Axtell, ed., *Locke's Educational Writings*, paragraphs 201–210.

19. The Abbé de Saint Pierre, cf. I, note 28 above.

20. "Few women wrestle, few eat the athlete's food; you spin wool, and when the work is finished, you carry it in baskets."

21. The trade of Spinoza, whose example might well be contemplated for this whole segment.

22. The Ottoman court at Constantinople.

23. Rousseau combines the stories of Midas' golden touch and his ass's ears, given him by Apollo when Midas, as judge, chose Marsyas over Apollo in their musical contest.

24. A dupe in the famous French farce, Maître Patelin. This is another *Crow and Fox* story. M. Guillaume is a cloth manufacturer who is done out of some cloth by Patelin. According to L. J. Courtois (*Annales J. J. Rousseau*, vol. XXII, 242–243), Rousseau is referring to a version of the story by the Abbé D. A. de Brueys, *L'Avocat Patelin*, in which Patelin, flattering Guillaume, says, "M. Guillaume, I bet you thought up that color." To which the latter responds, "Oh yes, I and my dyer."

25. The political power of the guilds at Zurich was such that it was difficult to become a member of the city council without being a master craftsman from one of them. Rousseau indicates that the system had been corrupted and that the status of master now came from holding the office rather than practicing the art.

26. In a note for the next edition Rousseau wrote: "I have since found the opposite by a more exact experiment. Refraction acts circularly, and the end of the stick in the water appears larger than the other end. But that changes nothing of the force of the reasoning, and the conclusion is no less exact."

27. Compare Plato *Republic* X 602B–E for the same example. The liberation from the illusion is the intention of both authors but the means are radically different. Rousseau believed that the senses could correct the senses and hence that Platonic transcendence can be avoided along with the illusion of the senses. He indicated in a first draft of this passage that he followed, although improved upon, the Epicureans in their respect for the senses.

28. Montaigne *Essays* II 27.

BOOK IV

1. Homer *Odyssey* X 19–75.

2. The following lines were written in the earliest draft of *Emile* and then crossed out: "If I am asked how it is possible for the morality of human life to emerge from a purely physical revolution, I will answer that I do not know. I base myself throughout on experience and do not seek the reasons for the facts. I do not know what connection there may be between the seminal spirits and the soul's affects,

between sexual development and the sentiment of good and evil. I see that these connections exist. I reason not to explain them but to draw out their consequences."

3. In both the manuscript and in the corrections for a future edition Rousseau wrote, "if there are any."

4. In an early draft Rousseau had written, and then crossed out, in the place of the preceding sentence the following one: "One takes an interest in him, one helps him in his misfortunes because one hopes that they will end and then one will be recompensed."

5. "Not ignorant of ills, I learn to assist the needy." Virgil *Aeneid* I 630.

6. Rousseau probably refers to the *Thousand and One Nights*.

7. This passage is an important commentary on the apparent Stoicism to be found elsewhere in *Emile*, particularly at the beginning of Book II.

8. The French word translated by *face* is *physionomie*, and Rousseau here tries to give a serious explanation of the phenomena treated by the pseudoscience of physiognomy.

9. The public square in Paris where executions took place and where men out of work gathered.

10. Military recruiters tricked men by giving them money which was later alleged to be a bonus for enlistment. Cf. Voltaire *Candide* II.

11. Cf. Plato *Republic* I 338D–339A. The investigation proposed here by Rousseau is identical to that undertaken in the *Republic*.

12. Cicero *Tusculan Disputations* V 3; Montaigne *Essays* I 26.

13. Historical novels by La Calprenède.

14. Montaigne *Essays* II 10. Montaigne wrote "what *comes from* within" and not *takes place*.

15. Charles Duclos, who wrote a history of Louis XI, *Considerations sur les moeurs de ce siècle* and *Memoires pour servir a l'histoire du XVIIIe siècle*, was one of Rousseau's earliest literary friends and one of the last with whom he broke.

16. Plutarch *Fabius Maximus* XV.

17. Plutarch *Agesilaus* XXV.

18. Plutarch *Caesar* XI.

19. Cf. pp. 110–111 and note 32 above.

20. Plutarch *Aristides* VII.

21. Plutarch *Philopoemen* II.

22. Andrew Ramsey (1686–1743), a Scotsman, became French in the service of the Stuart pretenders to the British throne; he was a disciple of Fénelon. He wrote a biography of Turenne.

23. Turenne was the second son of the Duc de Bouillon, sovereign prince of Sedan. The son of his older brother succeeded to the dukedom.

24. Plutarch *Pyrrhus* XIV.

25. Ibid. XXXIV.

26. Suetonius *Augustus* XXIII.

27. Ibid. LXV; Tacitus *Annals* I 3–6.

28. Plutarch *Gaius Marius* XXIII.

29. "The Venetian character in Italian comedy represented as a lean and foolish old man, wearing spectacles, pantaloons, and slippers. Hence in modern harlequinade or pantomime, a character represented as a foolish and vicious old man, the butt of the clown's [harlequin's] jokes, and his abettor in his pranks and tricks" (*Oxford English Dictionary*, s. v. "pantaloon").

30. *Fables* I iii:

> The world is full of people who are no wiser;
> Every bourgeois wants to build like great lords;
> Every little prince has ambassadors;
> Every marquis wants to have pages.

31. In a slightly different formulation of this paragraph in the earlier manuscripts, the preceding sentence is replaced by the following revealing one: "All this is to his advantage in any event, for you must consider that I am making him beneficent here not for the advantage of others but for his own instruction."

32. *Some Thoughts*, in Axtell, ed., *Locke's Educational Writings*, paragraphs 190–192; cf. paragraphs 136–139; and pp. 134–137 above.

33. Genesis 31:19, 32.

34. The Algonquin Indians.

35. In the earliest draft of *Emile* Rousseau formulates this tentative assertion of the existence of two substances even more tentatively. He leaves the irreducibility of spirit to matter as a question. *O.C.* IV, pp. 218–219.

36. Plutarch *Dialogue on Love* 756B.

37. Plutarch *On Superstition* 169F–170A; Bayle *Pensées diverses sur la comète* CXV.

38. Horace *Odes* II i 7–8. "I walk on fires covered by deceitful cinders." Horace wrote *you*. The context is a lament for the destruction of the republic, the bloodshed

of the civil wars, and the establishment of universal tyranny. The "you" refers to Asinius Pollion, who wrote a history of the civil wars and who, according to Horace, defended accused men. This is the role Rousseau adopts.

39. *Vitam impendere vero,* "Dedicate life to truth," Juvenal *Satires* IV 91. Rousseau uses this quote as the epigraph of *Letters from the Mountain.* His typical use of it can be seen in *Letter to d'Alembert* (A. Bloom, ed. and trans. [Ithaca, N.Y.: Cornell University Press, 1968]), p. 132. He discusses the problem of living according to this motto in *Dreams of a Solitary Walker* IV. The original context of the quote should be considered.

40. The autobiographical elements of the following section can be compared to *Confessions,* O.C. I, pp. 60–70, 90–92, 118–119; Everyman's I, pp. 52–61, 80–83, 106–107.

41. In the earlier manuscripts Rousseau wrote ". . . in order to set aside low thoughts in our souls and lift us up to sublime contemplations."

42. Samuel Clarke (1675–1729), English theologian, admirer of the teachings of Descartes, friend of Newton, and famous for his correspondence with Leibniz, published a work called *A Discourse concerning the Being and Attributes of God, the Obligations of Natural Religion, and the Truth and Certainty of the Christian Revelation, in opposition to Hobbes, Spinoza, the author of the Oracles of Reason, and other Deniers of Natural and Revealed Religion.*

43. Charles-Marie de la Condamine, *Relation abregé d'un voyage fait dans l'interieur de l'Amerique meridionale,* Paris 1745, pp. 66–67.

44. Descartes *Principles of Philosophy* III 43–47.

45. I.e., centrifugal.

46. Amatus Lusitanus and Paracelsus were famous doctors of the sixteenth century.

47. Bernard Nieuwentyt, a Dutch doctor (1654–1718), wrote a book entitled *The Existence of God Demonstrated by the Wonders of Nature.*

48. *Essay on Human Understanding* IV 3–6.

49. Plutarch *Epicurus actualy makes a pleasant life impossible* 1105C.

50. The third line is not in the psalm, and there is nothing in it as a whole which has to do with afterlife. Rather it relates entirely to God's role on earth and to living men.

51. Condillac *Traité des animaux* II 5. However cf. p. 62 above and *Discourse on the Origins of Inequality,* O.C. III, p. 135; R. Masters, ed., *The Discourses,* pp. 105–106.

52. For example, in *Essays* I 23.

53. The word is *fantaisie,* which has elsewhere been translated by *whim.*

54. Pierre Charron (1541–1603), a friend of Montaigne and strongly influenced by the *Essays.* His motto was the "I don't know" adopted by Jean-Jaques and Emile (p. 206). A theologal is a canon attached to a diocesan cathedral whose function is to teach theology.

55. Plutarch *On Stoic Self-contradictions,* 1034E–F.

56. *Exposition de la doctrine de l'Eglise Catholique sur les matières de controverse.*

57. Johann Reuchlin (1455–1522), German, Greek, and Hebrew scholar. He tried to preserve almost all the books of the Jews and vigorously defended himself against his antagonists who thought the Jews would be converted if they no longer had their books. He proposed that there be two chairs of Hebrew at every German university. Jewish worship was licensed by Papal and Imperial law at the time, and ultimately the books were not burned. Reuchlin was in continual controversy around the issue for seven years (1510–1517) and was charged before the Inquisition.

58. *Republic* II 361B–362A.

59. He was a real person, a minister of the king of Sardinia. Cf. *Confessions,* O.C. I, p. 90; Everyman's I, p. 80.

60. Bayle, *Pensées sur la comète* CXIV, CXXXIII, and CLXII. Cf. p. 259 and note 37 above.

61. Cf. Leviticus 25.

62. Cf. II, note 55 above. Where Rousseau writes "etc." at the end of the previous paragraph, Chardin wrote that the bridge ". . . narrower than a stretched hair and sharper than a razor's edge, is impossible to walk on without being supported by God's all-powerful hand. The unbelievers and the wicked will stumble at the first step and fall into the *Gehenne* of the eternal fire. But for the believers God will steady their feet on this narrow path. By God's mercy they will pass over this bridge more quickly than a bird cleaves the air and will enter eternal Paradise."

Rousseau leaves out the direct intervention of God and the emphasis on belief or faith and concentrates on justice among human beings.

63. *The Profession of Faith of a Savoyard Vicar* had fatal consequences for Rousseau. It was condemned by the Catholics in France and the Protestants in Geneva. He thereby fell afoul of the authorities and became that outcast so familiar from *Confessions* and *Dreams of a Solitary Walker.* He explicitly elaborated

NOTES

the discussion of religion in his *Lettre à Beaumont* and *Lettres écrites de la Montaigne,* although the theme pervades all his works. The theological-political situation was such that he, no more than Charron (cf. p. 296 above), could say directly all he thought on the question, and his own views can only be elaborated on the basis of all his works. The teaching of the Vicar should be compared to Rousseau's statement on civil religion, *Social Contract* IV 8.

64. *Essays* II 2.

65. Genesis 26:32–33; 16:14; 18:1; 21:46–48.

66. Bucentaur was the name of the state galley. Every year—from the eleventh through the eighteenth centuries—on Ascension Day the Doge was wed to the Adriatic on its deck.

67. Herodotus *Histories* V 92. Thrasybulus, tyrant of Miletus in the seventh century b.c., received an ambassador sent by Periander of Corinth who asked for general advice. Thrasybulus replied nothing but silently walked through the cornfields cutting off the tops of the highest stalks. This was taken by Periander to mean that he must do away with all outstanding men in his city. Essentially the same story is told by Livy (*Roman History* I 54) with Lucius Tarquinius Superbus, the last of the kings, taking the place of Thrasybulus and his son Sextus that of Periander. In Livy it is poppies which are leveled.

68. Plutarch *Alexander* 39. Alexander thus commanded Hephaestion not to reveal what he had read in a letter to Alexander from his mother.

69. Diogenes Laertius *Lives of the Philosophers* VI 39. Zeno in his paradoxes denied the existence of motion. Diogenes' refutation, which Dr. Johnson imitated in his refutation of Berkeley (although Johnson had the bad taste to enunciate his conclusion), was not performed in the presence of Zeno but of some unnamed man who made the assertion. Diogenes Laertius does not mention Zeno who lived more than a century before Diogenes.

70. Herodotus *Histories* IV 132. As interpreted by Gobryas (Darius at first interpreted it otherwise) the message was, "Unless you Persians become birds and fly up in the sky, or mice and hide yourselves in the earth, or frogs and leap into the lakes, you will never return home again, having been struck by these arrows."

71. "Toga: the outer garment of a citizen. Sagum: the military cloak. Praetext: the youth's first outer clothing, worn until he assumed the man's toga. Bulla: a golden amulet worn by patrician youths until they assumed the man's toga. Laticlave: a badge consisting of two broad purple stripes on the edge of the tunic, worn by senators and other persons of high rank" (*Oxford English Dictionary,* s. v. "toga," "sagum," "praetext," "bulla," and "laticlave").

72. Plutarch *Antony* XIV.

73. The French *honnête* has been uniformly translated as decent. Here the word translated *seemliness* is *décence* which in this context to do with the kind of conduct dictated by social propriety, particularly in relation to women, and the world of gallantry. It is the refinement of the surface, the knowledge of the exquisite rules of the game. Rousseau, in an earlier manuscript, added after *seemliness,* "invented by the false delicacy of vice."

74. Aurelius Victor *De viribus illustribus Romae* 86.

75. "Nothing is difficult for him who wills."

76. Homer *Odyssey* XII 39–55, 192–200.

77. In the corrections for the later edition Rousseau strengthens his advice with the phrase: "he must go to bed only when ready to drop and get out of it the moment he wakes up." Cf. *Confessions, O.C.* I, pp. 16–17, 108–109; Everyman's I, pp. 11–13, 96–98.

78. Montaigne *Essays* I 26.

79. For Marcel cf. p. 139 above. Marcel takes the Englishman for a German noble from one of the states ruled by an elector. The book where Rousseau read the story is *De l'Esprit* (II 1) by Helvetius. It was the commonplace source of much of the philosophic thought criticized by the Savoyard Vicar.

80. Cf. p. 39 and n. 6 above and *Social Contract* I 6. Rousseau, out of republican pride, eschewed all titles of honor, civil or academic, and signed himself *Citizen of Geneva.* Paimboeuf is a town on the Loire.

81. For the later edition, Rousseau changed the title to *Essay on the Origin of Languages.* In that work he deals with this subject in chapters XIII–XIX.

82. "Stop, passerby, you are trampling on a hero." This was the epitaph of François de Mercy, defeated at the battle of Nordlingen in 1645 by Condé (with whom Emile's name may have some connection, cf. Preface, note 1). Cf. Voltaire *The Age of Louis XIV* III.

83. Strabo *Geography* XIV v 9.

84. Xenophon *Anabasis* II vi 30. "No one ever laughed at them as cowards in war or blamed them in friendship" is the exact text.

85. Herodotus *Histories* VII 228. "Passerby, tell the Lacedaemonians that here we lie obedient to their word" is the exact text.

86. This is the first sentence of Fontenelle's *Digression sur les Anciens et les Modernes* (1686). La Motte and Terrasson, in *Discours sur Homère* and *Dissertation Critique sur l'Iliade d'Homère* (1715) respectively, had joined in asserting the superiority of modern poetry over ancient. This was a minor skirmish in the "Battle of the Books," the "Quarrel between the Ancients and Moderns," a now forgotten struggle which pitted the totality of ancient philosophy, science, art, literature, politics, and morals against their modern counterparts. No issue is more important in the history of thought, and Rousseau emphatically takes the side of the ancients here, at least so far as literature and morals are concerned. No study of Rousseau can be serious which does not take seriously "The Quarrel."

87. Athenaeus *Banquet of the Sophists* I 12.

88. "Where there is something good, there is my fatherland."

89. Plutarch *Sayings of Kings* 178A–B.

90. Diogenes Laertius *Lives of the Philosophers* VIII 63; Montaigne *Essays* II 1.

91. "Name given to the taverns or roadhouses in the vicinity of Paris and other cities where the people go to drink and enjoy themselves on holidays" (translation of the Littré dictionary definition s. v. "guingette"). The gardens and the arcades of the Palais-Royal in Paris were the meeting-place of fashionable and corrupt Paris society. Cf. p. 141 above.

92. The remark is attributed to Aristippus by Diogenes Laertius and Athenaeus. Laïs was a celebrated courtesan of the fourth century B.C. who associated with the likes of Diogenes and Demosthenes as well as Aristippus. She is rumored to have been Alcibiades' daughter and she is mentioned in an epigram attributed to Plato. Cf. Diogenes Laertius II 75; Athenaeus XII 544, 535, XIII 588. Plato *Epigr.* Diehl 15. Rousseau mentions her again on p. 391 below.

93. "Golden mean." Horace *Odes* II x 5.

94. "Who can find a strong woman? She is far; brought from the ends of the earth, she is precious." This proverb introduces the last section of Proverbs which is devoted to the good wife.

BOOK V

1. Cf. Genesis 2:18.

2. *Some Thoughts*, in Axtell, ed., *Locke's Educational Writings,* paragraph 215.

3. Julia, who would only commit adultery when pregnant so that her infidelities would remain undiscovered. Brantôme, *La Vie des dames galantes* (Paris: Garnier, 1960), p. 105.

4. Deuteronomy 22:23–27.

5. Thespitius, king of Athens, contrived for Hercules to sleep with his fifty daughters in order that they have children by such a great hero. According to one version, he did so in one night (sparing one who was a priestess); or, according to another version, he took fifty nights (Diodorus Siculus *Biblioteca Historica* IV 29; Apollodorus *Biblioteca* II 10). It is doubtful whether Hercules understood these to be rapes. For the murder of Iphitus he was commanded to serve Queen Omphale of Lydia who dressed him in woman's clothes and made him do woman's work. Nevertheless she had children by him (Diodorus Siculus IV 31). For Samson and Delilah, cf. Judges 16.

6. Plato *Republic* V 451D–452B, 457A.

7. Cf. note 21 below.

8. Plutarch *Lycurgus* XIV.

9. Minerva threw away the flute because it distorted her face. Ovid *Fasti* VI 703.

10. Fénelon, *Education des Filles,* chap. 5. Fénelon's book is the parallel in the girl's education to Locke's in the boy's education. Fénelon's didactic novel, *Telemachus,* is Sophie's *Robinson Crusoe;* cf. note 32 below.

11. Rousseau probably refers to *Iliad* XIV 153–223.

12. Clement of Alexandria *Pedagogue* II xii 125.

13. A famous Parisian dressmaker.

14. In French *toilette.* Great ladies in the last reigns of the French monarchy made a ceremony out of dressing—akin to the king's levée—and received callers, particularly gentlemen, while performing it. The *toilette* was an integral part of the elaborate conventions governing coquetry in the *ancien régime.*

15. Matthew 6:7. This is the part of the Sermon on the Mount introducing the Lord's Prayer.

16. Solomon Gessner, *The Death of Abel,* published in German in 1758. Gessner was a German Swiss much admired by men such as Lessing and Goethe as well as by Rousseau. The poem is an epic, not unlike *Paradise Lost* in character, and presents a very gentle reading of the biblical account of the first death.

17. Tasso *Jerusalem Delivered* IV 87: "Woman uses every art in order to catch

NOTES

a new lover in her web. Neither with all men nor always with each one does she keep the same aspect, but she changes attitudes and visage according to the time."

18. Virgil *Eclogues* III 64–72.

19. Cf. *Dernière Response, O.C.* III, pp. 93–94.

20. "When a woman has given up her chastity, she refuses nothing else." Tacitus *Annals* IV 3.

21. Ninon de Lenclos (1615–1705) was a leading lady of Parisian society, loose in love and frank and generous in friendships. Saint-Évremond called her an *honnête homme*, a decent man, a gentleman. She tried to liberate herself from the constraints of her condition. Involved with many of the great literary and political figures of her time, she protected the young Voltaire and was championed by him.

22. "Who eats and wipes her mouth and says: 'I have not done evil.' "

23. Rousseau refers particularly to Plutarch's *Lycurgus* XIV–XV for Sparta and Tacitus *Germania* 7–8, 18 for Germany. The Roman stories can be found in Livy *Roman History*: the rape of Lucretia and consequent fall of the Tarquin monarchy, I 58–60; the suggestion of Licinius' wife that led to his agitation for plebeian admission to consular rank, VI 34; the lust of Appius Claudius for Virginia and his downfall, III 44–48; the embassy of Veturia and Volumnia to the rebel Coriolanus, II 40.

24. Paladins are the twelve peers or famous warriors of Charlemagne's court, of whom the Count Palatine was foremost. By extension, any hero of a medieval romance is a paladin.

25. Cf. p. 349 and note 92 above.

26. "She who does not do something because it is forbidden, does it." Ovid *Amores* III iv 4; cf. Montaigne *Essays* II 16.

27. In an earlier draft Rousseau had added this sentence here: "Show them the qualities that he ought to honor in them, for what reasons they can deserve his esteem and solidify his attachment. Lead them to virtue by means of *amour-propre*."

28. Plutarch *Lycurgus* XIV.

29. I cannot find this story in Brantôme (cf. note 3 above). Matteo Bandello (1480–1562) tells, in his *Novelle* (III 17), the story of Madonna Zilia who made a similar demand on a lover. Given the enormous popularity of Bandello and the number of writers who used his stories (e.g., Shakespeare for *Romeo and Juliet*), the tale Rousseau tells here probably goes back in one way or another to Bandello.

30. "The terrible anger of the son of Peleus who does not know how to yield." Horace *Odes* I vi 5–6.

31. This epithet of the beautiful, seductive Apollo was used proverbially in French to describe a clever, fast talker.

32. Cf. note 10 above. This modern epic should be consulted in any careful reading of Book V. Telemachus is the hero with whom Sophie is in love and with whom she identifies Emile. She, unlike Emile, is given a literary basis for her taste. Telemachus has a tutor, Mentor, who is the parallel to Jean-Jacques. Just as *Telemachus* is Sophie's guide in love, it becomes Emile's guidebook in his travels, hence in politics. Fénelon wrote *Telemachus* for the instruction of Louis XIV's grandson and heir-apparent, the Duc de Bourgogne, whose tutor Fénelon was.

33. *Telemachus*, Book VI.

34. "You ask Galla, why I do not want to marry you? You are eloquent." Martial *Epigrams* XI 19.

35. François Barrême (1638–1703) was a French arithmetician who published a series of accounting handbooks.

36. Cf. *Discourse on the Origins of Inequality*, note x.

37. Daubenton (1716–1800) was a collaborator of Buffon in the preparation of his treatise on natural history.

38. Fénelon *Telemachus* VI; cf. p. 404 and note 33 above.

39. Fénelon *Telemachus* XV–XVI.

40. "She does not show it, although she rejoices in her heart." Tasso *Jerusalem Delivered* IV 33.

41. The French word is *roman*, most ordinarily translated by novel. Rousseau's *La Nouvelle Héloise* is a *roman*. The first novels were stories of love and chivalry, hence the identity of *romance* and *novel*.

42. Cf. *Discourse on the Origins of Inequality, O.C.* III, p. 133; Masters, ed., *The Discourses*, pp. 103–104.

43. Homer *Odyssey* VII 114–132.

44. *Odyssey* VI, beginning, esp. 273–289.

45. Francesco Albani (1578–1660), a Bolognese painter noted for his painting of mythological subjects and called "the painter of the Graces."

46. In the place of this paragraph Rousseau originally wrote: "The imaginary history of my young lovers ought not to make me forget the aim of my book. Let me be permitted a short digression on jealousy which will not take me far from them."

47. *O.C.* III, pp. 157–160, 168–169; Masters, ed., *The Discourses*, pp. 134–137, 146–147. Cf. Lucretius *On the Nature of Things* IV 1030–1287.

48. Cf. note 5 above.

49. Hero and Leander were lovers famous in antiquity, best known to us by the poem of Musaeus (sixth century A.D.). Leander of Abydos was in love with Hero, a priestess of Aphrodite at Sestos, whose parents were opposed to the marriage. Every night he swam the Hellespont to meet her clandestinely—following a light she set out by the shore. One night the wind blew out the lamp and Leander drowned. When Hero found his body, she drowned herself.

50. Vergil *Aeneid* V 286–361.

51. Atalanta would only marry a man who could vanquish her in running. Melanion won her hand by trickery in a race. She killed all suitors who failed in such contests. Ovid *Metamorphoses* X 568.

52. Cf. p. 360–361 and note 5 above.

53. Homer *Odyssey* X 274–399. This story is the theme of the frontispiece of Book V and also of the text.

54. Cf. Plato *Republic* III 387, and X 603 ff.

55. Cf. p. 404 and note 33 and p. 431 above.

56. *The Spectator* was a periodical, written by Joseph Addison and Richard Steele during 1711 and 1712, devoted to commentary on the life and literature of the times. It was enormously influential, and the entire collection has been available continuously in book form. There was already a French translation in 1714, and it was one of the young Rousseau's favorite books.

57. Montesquieu *Persian Letters* 30.

58. Raymond Lull, a Spaniard (1235–1315), wrote a treatise on logic entitled *Ars Magna* (The Great Art) which claimed to reduce all the learning of all the sciences to a few basic formulae. He hoped to convert the infidels with his art. Descartes said "... the art of Lull [is better fitted] for speaking about the things one does not know than for learning them" (*Discourse on Method* II). Paul Lucas (1664–1737) and Jean-Baptiste Tavernier (1605–1689) were travelers who wrote accounts of their voyages.

59. Rousseau, in response to Mme. de la Tour who asked to whom he referred here, on September 27, 1762, wrote that, "I meant M. de Gisors, of course. I did not believe it possible to mistake my reference. We do not have the good fortune to live in an age when this kind of praise can be given to many young people" (M. R. A. Leigh, ed., *Correspondence complete de J. J. Rousseau* [Geneva: Publications de l'Institut et Musée Voltaire, 1971] vol. XIII, p. 122). The Comte de Gisors (1732–1758) was an exceptionally virtuous youth and intrepid soldier who commanded a regiment at seventeen and died at twenty-six, leading his troops during the Seven Years War. Gisors is probably the lad referred to in the last two paragraphs of Book II. Rousseau, the foreigner, makes up for the neglect Gisors suffers in France.

60. I Kings 21:1–16.

61. For the following passage the *Social Contract* should be consulted. The account of politics given to Emile closely follows that of the *Social Contract* with some notable omissions (particularly the legislator and the civil religion, *Social Contract* II 7 and IV 8).

62. Genesis 10:8–9.

63. Solon abolished debts prior to giving his laws; whereas Lycurgus, as part of the establishment of a new polity, took over all the property of all the Spartans and redistributed it equally to all. Solon's decree discriminated against the rich; Lycurgus' measure was general. Cf. Plutarch *Lycurgus* VII–X and *Solon* XV–XVI.

64. "Continuous proportion" is a French mathematical expression for a proportion in which the consequent of the first ratio is the same as the antecedent of the second, as in $A:B = B:C$. In this case the proportion would be So (sovereign): g (government) $= g: Su$ (subject). The equation formulated in the second sentence is, since $So/g = g/Su$, then $g^2 = So \times Su$.

65. The mathematical formulation here is obscure. What Rousseau means by simple and doubled ratios is difficult to determine and to relate to usage in French mathematical language. The example of a "doubled ratio" seems to be $So\,Su/g^2$ which is derived from the equation $g^2 = So \times Su$ established on the preceding page. It in turn was derived by cross multiplying $So/g = g/Su$, which apparently are simple ratios. This doubled ratio expresses the relation between government and citizens considered under their double aspect of members of the sovereign and subjects. Since Su (the people, considered as the individual subject and hence always as unity) is fixed, an increase or decrease in $So\,Su$ is necessarily an increase or decrease in So, and hence in the value of the simple ratio So/g. But $So/g = g/Su$, so when the simple ratio varies, the value of g must vary accordingly. In this way Rousseau constructs his demonstration that government must vary as the sovereign varies. The sequel shows that an increase in the sovereign (an increase in the

NOTES

number of citizens) necessitating an increase in the government (an increase in its intensity or force) actually means a decrease in the number of magistrates.

66. By analogy to *ésprit de corps*, which is difficult to translate but easy to understand.

67. In 307–308 A.D. there were six Roman emperors at the same time. Cf. Gibbon *Decline and Fall of the Roman Empire* XIV.

68. "In which it is neither permitted to be prepared in war nor to be secure in peace." Seneca *De tranquillitate animi* I 1.

69. Rousseau edited the Abbé de Saint Pierre's *Extrait du Projet de Paix Perpetuelle* (published in 1761) and wrote a critique of it (*Jugement sur le Projet de Paix Perpetuelle*) which appeared posthumously. For Rousseau's opinions on the Abbé's thought cf. *Confessions, O.C.* I, IX, pp. 422–424; Everyman's II, pp. 72–75. This project provided the inspiration for Kant's *Perpetual Peace*. Cf. p. 67 and note 28 above.

70. The misfortunes of Idomeneus (his sacrifice of his son, and his expulsion from Crete) are recounted in *Telemachus*, Book V. Salente is the new city over which Idomeneus rules after his expulsion from Crete. Telemachus arrives there in Book IX. The loyalty of Philocles, a true friend of Idomeneus, and the perfidy of Protesilaus, a false friend, are recounted in Books XIII–XIV. The attack of Adrastus upon the allied forces whom Telemachus aids is described in XVI–XVII, XX. Rousseau says in *Confessions* XII, *O.C.* I, p. 593; Everyman's II, p. 233, that he intended that Frederick II of Prussia be recognized under his description of Adrastus. He thereby makes clear that *Telemachus* is indeed intended to make the "invidious comparisons" he mentions in the next sentence.

71. The early manuscripts had the following notes: "I know only one exception to this rule. It is China. The author of the Spirit of the Laws excepted it too." Cf. Montesquieu *Spirit of the Laws* VIII 21.

72. Cf. Montesquieu *Spirit of the Laws* XXIII 21.

73. Cf. p. 31 and Preface, note 2.

74. "These are my wishes: a piece of land of moderate size." Horace *Satires* II 6. This line is also the epigraph of Book VI of the *Confessions*.

Index

Editorial note: *n* indicates a note of Rousseau's; *n* followed by a number indicates a note of the translator's.

INDEX

INDEX

```
  148
   83
 ─────
2 31
   83
 ─────
3 14
   83
 ─────
3 97
   83
 ─────
4 80
```

```
480
148
───
33 2
     SS
Th.f
   83
4 ⟌33
   3   2
```